Philosophy and Medicine

Founding Editors
H. Tristram Engelhardt
Stuart F. Spicker

Volume 142

Series Editors
Søren Holm, The University of Manchester, Manchester, UK
Lisa M. Rasmussen, UNC Charlotte, Charlotte, USA

Editorial Board
George Agich, National University of Singapore, Singapore, Singapore
Bob Baker, Union College, Schenectady, NY, USA
Jeffrey Bishop, Saint Louis University, St. Louis, USA
Ana Borovecki, University of Zagreb, Zagreb, Croatia
Ruiping Fan, City University of Hong Kong, Kowloon, Hong Kong
Volnei Garrafa, International Center for Bioethics and Humanities,
University of Brasília, Brasília, Brazil
D. Micah Hester, University of Arkansas for Medical Sciences, Little Rock, AR, USA
Bjørn Hofmann, Norwegian University of Science and
Technology, Gjøvik, Norway
Ana Iltis, Wake Forest University, Winston-Salem, NC, USA
John Lantos, Childrens' Mercy, Kansas City, MO, USA
Chris Tollefsen, University of South Carolina, Columbia, USA
Dr Teck Chuan Voo, Centre for Biomedical Ethics, Yong Loo Lin School
of Medicine, National University of Singapore, Singapore, Singapore

The Philosophy and Medicine series is dedicated to publishing monographs and collections of essays that contribute importantly to scholarship in bioethics and the philosophy of medicine. The series addresses the full scope of issues in bioethics and philosophy of medicine, from euthanasia to justice and solidarity in health care, and from the concept of disease to the phenomenology of illness. The Philosophy and Medicine series places the scholarship of bioethics within studies of basic problems in the epistemology, ethics, and metaphysics of medicine. The series seeks to publish the best of philosophical work from around the world and from all philosophical traditions directed to health care and the biomedical sciences. Since its appearance in 1975, the series has created an intellectual and scholarly focal point that frames the field of the philosophy of medicine and bioethics. From its inception, the series has recognized the breadth of philosophical concerns made salient by the biomedical sciences and the health care professions. With over one hundred and twenty five volumes in print, no other series offers as substantial and significant a resource for philosophical scholarship regarding issues raised by medicine and the biomedical sciences.

More information about this series at https://link.springer.com/bookseries/6414

Laurence B. McCullough

Thomas Percival's Medical Ethics and the Invention of Medical Professionalism

With Three Key Percival Texts, Two Concordances, and a Chronology

Springer

Laurence B. McCullough
Center for Medical Ethics & Health Policy
Baylor College of Medicine
Houston, TX, USA

ISSN 0376-7418   ISSN 2215-0080 (electronic)
Philosophy and Medicine
ISBN 978-3-030-86038-7   ISBN 978-3-030-86036-3 (eBook)
https://doi.org/10.1007/978-3-030-86036-3

© The Editor(s) (if applicable) and The Author(s), under exclusive license to Springer Nature Switzerland AG 2022

This work is subject to copyright. All rights are solely and exclusively licensed by the Publisher, whether the whole or part of the material is concerned, specifically the rights of translation, reprinting, reuse of illustrations, recitation, broadcasting, reproduction on microfilms or in any other physical way, and transmission or information storage and retrieval, electronic adaptation, computer software, or by similar or dissimilar methodology now known or hereafter developed.

The use of general descriptive names, registered names, trademarks, service marks, etc. in this publication does not imply, even in the absence of a specific statement, that such names are exempt from the relevant protective laws and regulations and therefore free for general use.

The publisher, the authors and the editors are safe to assume that the advice and information in this book are believed to be true and accurate at the date of publication. Neither the publisher nor the authors or the editors give a warranty, expressed or implied, with respect to the material contained herein or for any errors or omissions that may have been made. The publisher remains neutral with regard to jurisdictional claims in published maps and institutional affiliations.

This Springer imprint is published by the registered company Springer Nature Switzerland AG
The registered company address is: Gewerbestrasse 11, 6330 Cham, Switzerland

*The living are the custodians of the souls
of the dead, those stealthy migrants.
Love bequeaths this responsibility.*

> Roger Cohen, *The New York Times*,
> April 7, 2014

IN MEMORIAM
Irwin C. Lieb
Ignazio Angelelli
H. Tristram Engelhardt, Jr.
Baruch A. Brody

Preface

The English physician-ethicist Thomas Percival (1740–1804) wrote the first book with the title, *Medical Ethics*, in the global history of medical ethics. Its full title is: *Medical Ethics, or, a Code of Institutes and Precepts Adapted to the Professional Conduct of Physicians and Surgeons: I. In Hospital Practice. II. In Private, or General Practice. III. In Relation to Apothecaries. IV. In Cases Which May Require a Knowledge of Law. To which is added An Appendix: containing A Discourse on Hospital Duties; and Notes and Illustrations by Thomas Percival, M.D., F.R.S. and A.S. Lond. F.R.S. and R.M.S. Edinb. &c. &c.*, published in 1803 in Manchester, England (Percival 1803, [1803] 1807, [1803] 2022). Percival had previously completed a privately published and circulated text, *Medical Jurisprudence; or A Code of Ethics, and Institutes, Adapted to the Professions of Physic And Surgery*, published in 1794 (Percival 1794, [1794] 2022) and later revised and expanded to become *Medical Ethics*.

In Part I, I provide the first comprehensive, historically based, philosophical interpretations of these two texts of Percival's professional ethics in medicine set in the context of his intellectual biography and the work of his predecessor in professional ethics in medicine, John Gregory (1724–1773). I engage in historically based, philosophical interpretation of texts influenced by Percival's medical ethics in the subsequent history of professional ethics in medicine, especially in the United States via *Extracts from the Medical Ethics of Dr. Percival* of the Secret Kappa Lambda Society (Kappa Lambda Society 1823; Percival 1823), a significant bridge from *Medical Ethics* to the *Code of Ethics* of 1847 of the fledgling American Medical Association (AMA) (American Medical Association [1847] 1999; Baker 2013).

In the four chapters of Part I, I will advance two main claims. The first is that Percival was a Baconian moral scientist committed to Baconian deism and Dissent. As a matter of conscience, Dissenters would not accept the intellectual authority of the Church of England. Conscience was properly formed on the basis of the "truth of things" put there by the Creator god of deism. Chapter 2 provides a fuller account of the meaning of "dissenting" and "deist." Baconian science should be based only on the results of carefully made, precisely recorded, and reliably analyzed and reported results of observation and experiment, the two components of what Francis Bacon (1561–1626) called "experience." Like a good Baconian, for Percival the science of nature includes the science of man and, in turn, moral science, as it also did for Gregory and, before them, David Hume (1711–1776). *Medical Jurisprudence* and, especially, *Medical Ethics* should be understood as texts in a distinctive genre in the global history of medical ethics, Baconian moral scientific professional ethics in medicine.

The second claim is that Percival built on and made significant contributions to the invention of the ethical concept of medicine as a profession and thereby of the profession of medicine by his predecessor, the Scottish physician-ethicist John Gregory. Gregory invented the genre of Baconian moral scientific professional ethics in medicine. Gregory wrote the first modern text on professional ethics in medicine in the English – and perhaps any other – language, first anonymously (Gregory 1770, [1770] 1998) and then under his own name (Gregory 1772, [1772] 1998) (McCullough 1998). Percival inherits Gregory's work, making Chap. 1 a necessary introduction to Percival's professional ethics in medicine.

Percival's original contributions – the first treatment of physicians, surgeons, and apothecaries as "branches" of a *single* profession of medicine, the professional virtues of condescension and authority that he added to Gregory's professional virtues of tenderness and steadiness to guide physician's use of power in the hospital setting, the first ethics of cooperation for hospital practice at the Manchester Infirmary, the first account of an organizational culture of professionalism, the first account of the responsible management of drugs and wines in the formulary of the Infirmary, the first proposal that the professional ethics of hospital practice should become the basis of the ethics of private practice, the first articulation of the profession of medicine as a "public trust," and in his "political ethics" the first account of the limited autonomy of the profession of medicine and professional ethics in medicine from the state (Percival 1803) – complement those of Gregory, resulting in a robust and influential professional ethics in medicine. Gregory and Percival should be regarded as the co-inventors of the ethical concept of medicine as a profession and thereby the profession of medicine.

To make good on these claims, I situate interpretation of the two texts of Percival's professional ethics in medicine, especially *Medical Ethics*, in the context of Gregory's professional ethics in medicine, described in Chap. 1, and Percival's intellectual biography, to which I devote Chap. 2. Drawing on the results of Chaps. 1 and 2, Chap. 3 provides an historically based, philosophical interpretation of Percival's Baconian professional ethics in medicine. In Chap. 4, I complete four tasks. I explain why we should consider Gregory and Percival to be the co-inventors of professional ethics in the global history of medical ethics. I explore the reception of Percival's *Medical Ethics* in the subsequent history of medical ethics in England and the United States. I provide an historically based, philosophical interpretation of the historical influence of *Medical Ethics* on the subsequent history of medical ethics, culminating in the AMA 1847 *Code of Ethics*, which explicitly expresses its intellectual debts to both Percival and Gregory. I close with a reflection on Gregory's and Percival's legacy for contemporary professional ethics in medicine.

Part II comprises the three key texts for which Part I provides historically based, philosophical analysis, two concordances to the three key texts, and the first chronology of Percival's life and works.

The first key text is *Medical Jurisprudence or A Code of Ethics And Institutes, Adapted To The Professions Of Physic And Surgery*. Percival has this volume privately published in 1794 and circulated it for comments from many of his contemporaries (Percival 1794).

The second key text is *Medical Ethics, or, a Code of Institutes and Precepts adapted to the Professional Conduct of Physicians and Surgeons: I. In Hospital Practice. II. In private, or general Practice. III. In relation to Apothecaries. IV. In Cases which may require a knowledge of Law. To which is added An Appendix: containing A Discourse on Hospital Duties; and Notes and Illustrations by Thomas Percival, M.D., F.R.S. and A.S. Lond. F.R.S. and R.M.S. Edinb. &c. &c.*, completed in 1803 and published that same year in Manchester, England, where he had lived since 1767 (Percival 1803).

The third text is *Extracts from the Medical Ethics of Dr. Percival*, published by the Kappa Lambda Society in Philadelphia in 1823 (Kappa Lambda Society 1823). *Medical Ethics* became an acknowledged source for the writers of the first national code of medical ethics in the history of medical ethics in the United States (Baker 2013), the American Medical Association's *Code of Ethics* of 1847 (American Medical Association [1847] 1999). The little-known pamphlet, *Extracts from the Medical Ethics of Dr. Percival* (Kappa Lambda Society 1823; Percival 1823), served as an important bridge between *Medical Ethics* and a *Code of Ethics* (Baker 2013).

There are contemporary facsimile editions of *Medical Ethics* (Percival [1803] 1985; [1807] 2010; [1807] 2014). However, there are no contemporary editions of *Medical Jurisprudence* or *Extracts*. Part II of this volume is the first to bring together these two rare texts with *Medical Ethics* in their entirety. Scholars, teachers, and students of professional ethics in medicine, the history of medical ethics, bioethics, the history of medicine, intellectual history, and of the English enlightenment now have the first, single source in which they can follow for themselves the development and influence of Percival's professional ethics in medicine and read these three essential texts closely and comparatively.

Percival included in *Medical Jurisprudence* and *Medical Ethics* a "Discourse … on … Hospital Duties," by his son Thomas Bassnett Percival. I do the same here. This is repetitious, to be sure, but I did so to remain faithful to Percival's texts as he prepared and presented them and allow citation to the different paginations of the "Discourse" as it appears in the two texts.

The three texts are presented unchanged from the original editions of 1794 (*Medical Jurisprudence*), 1803 (*Medical Ethics*), and 1823 (*Extracts*). Spellings and punctuations are original and typical of publications of the later eighteenth century in Britain. Capitalization and italics used for emphasis in the original texts have been retained. Page numbers are included in brackets [nnn] to mark the end of each page in the original. Footnotes are indicated by [Bottom of page nnn] with the original footnote following.

To prepare the text of *Medical Jurisprudence*, I worked from the microfilm of the text in the National Library Medicine in Bethesda, Maryland. To prepare the text of *Medical Ethics*, I worked from my personal copy. I worked from the National Library of Medicine online PDF file of the 1823 *Extracts* to prepare its text for inclusion.

Part II includes two aids to close, comparative reading of the three key texts. The first is a Concordance of *Medical Jurisprudence* with *Medical Ethics*. The second is a Concordance of *Medical Ethics* with the *Extracts*.

Part II concludes with the first Chronology of Thomas Percival's Life and Work. The Chronology starts with the arrival Percival's grandfather, Peter Percival (d. 1701), seeking a better life, what then was called "his fortune," in Warrington, a town midway between Manchester and Liverpool in Lancashire, England. The Chronology ends with the publication of this volume. The Chronology records events in Percival's life from his birth in 1740 in Warrington to his death in 1804 in Manchester. The dates for his works are provided and, for context, the works of Gregory that Percival cites. The sequence of events at Manchester Infirmary, starting in 1788, that led to the writing of *Medical Jurisprudence* and then *Medical Ethics* is included.

The reader will encounter, in quoted passages from the sources upon which I have relied in Part I and in the three texts in Part II, archaic spellings and grammar (e.g., the use of commas, colons, and semi-colons), and the use of italics and capitalization for emphasis. I have presented the texts in their original form. I have left italicized and capitalized words unchanged from the original texts. Given the frequent occurrence of the use of italics and capitalization for emphasis in the texts from which quoted passages are taken, I have not included in Part I "emphasis original" in the call-outs to references, to reduce the burden on the reader. To avoid confusion, I have not added emphasis to any of the quoted passages. Translations from Latin original texts are my own, unless a source is provided in the call-out, for example, to the translation from a text from Cicero that appears on the verso of the title page of *Medical Ethics*.

This book originates in my more than four decades of teaching as a philosopher-medical educator. I have taught professional ethics in medicine to my students, residents, fellows, scientific and clinical colleagues, and ethics colleagues at Texas A&M University College of Medicine (1976–1979), Georgetown University School of Medicine and Kennedy Institute of Ethics (1979–1988), Baylor College of Medicine (1988–2016), Weill Cornell Medical College (1987–2018), and Zucker School of Medicine at Hofstra/Northwell (2019–2021). As adjunct Professor of Philosophy I taught the history of medical ethics to premedical students at Rice University in the aughts of our century. I made sure to teach Gregory and Percival, not as antiquarian figures in the history of medicine, but as living presences in the contemporary profession of medicine. This book contains everything that I have learned about Gregory and, especially, Percival from my learners, as we now call them in contemporary medical education.

In the early 1990s, Robert Baker, then Professor of Philosophy at Union College in Schenectady, New York, and later the William D. Williams Professor of

Philosophy there, invited me to teach in the summer Proseminar on bioethics for undergraduate students in Liberal Arts in Medicine (LIM) component of the joint BA-MD degree program of Union with Albany Medical College. Bob later co-founded master's-degree-level The Bioethics Program with our colleague, the philosopher-medical educator at Mount Sinai Medical School in New York City, Rosamond Rhodes. Graduate students joined the Union pre-medical students in a distinctive blend. In the ensuing more than 25 years, I had the sustained opportunity to learn from Bob's students, and Bob too, as we worked through Gregory's and Percival's texts and their importance for contemporary professional ethics in medicine and bioethics. (The two should never be conflated.) I have, I believe, been successful in finding a place in this book for everything that we learned together. The reader will discover in Chap. 1 how much the method of historically based, philosophical analysis of texts deployed in this book owes to an excellent question posed to me one summer by a LIM student in the Proseminar.

Since the early 1990s I have had the unmatched opportunity to teach physician leaders in the Physician-in-Management Seminar and in the Ethical Challenges of Physician Executives course, in person and online, for the American College of Physician Executives, now the American Association for Physician Leadership. I learned from this teaching, especially from my colleague and co-teacher, Richard Stubbs, M.D., about the concept of an organizational culture of professionalism in healthcare. I have had the sustained pleasure of teaching these accomplished physician colleagues that Percival invented this concept. I learned from their responses to what was, for them, a revelation, just as it had been for me when I first came to understand what Percival was setting out in Section I of *Medical Jurisprudence* and Chapter I of *Medical Ethics*.

Every scholar of the history of medical ethics depends on the generosity of those individuals, institutions, and governments that established and continue to support rare book and manuscript depositories and, even more, on the professional librarians who preside over their precious collections. In undertaking research for this book, I have been the grateful beneficiary of a number of such research centers and their able – and very helpful – professional library staffs, in Scotland at the Universities of Aberdeen and Edinburgh and in England at John Rylands Library of the University of Manchester and Harris Manchester College of the University of Oxford. I also read materials in Scotland in the libraries of the Royal College of Surgeons of Edinburgh, the Royal College of Physicians of Edinburgh, the Royal College of Physicians and Surgeons in Glasgow, and in England in the Chetham's Library in Manchester and the Wellcome and Dr. Williams libraries in London.

In June, as every Texan knows, it should be getting warm. What we call hot comes later – by our standards. When my wife and I arrived in Edinburgh in June of 1991, to continue what became an enormously productive journey of scholarly work, it was snowing. A week later, in the Rylands Library, we had to warm our hands under the exposed bulbs of the green-glass-shaded reading lamps. I had learned by then about steadiness from Gregory and Percival. In the cold of Edinburgh in June, one masters steadiness by downing a bowl of barley soup at the nearest pub. In Manchester cold in June, one masters steadiness by downing a pot of black

English tea from India in a restaurant occupying a former bank in a great, black-marble-columned nineteenth-century monument to the Industrial Revolution.

I read materials related to Warrington Academy and English Dissenters at the Tate Library at Harris Manchester College of the University of Oxford, with its Library of Protestant Dissent. Tate Library stands in the long and proud tradition of the extraordinary Oxford libraries, with its wood-vault ceiling and stained-glass windows. Susan Killoran, Fellow Librarian, was enormously helpful and hosted me for lunch in college (as I learned to say in English English). A white, marble statue of James Martineau (1805–1900), Professor of Mental and Moral Philosophy and Political Economy for 45 years and Principal for 16 years at Harris Manchester's predecessor and Warrington Academy's successor, Manchester New College, presides over the reading room. I would occasionally look at the ceiling and windows as a break from reading old manuscripts and books. Martineau had a fixed – and somewhat fierce – gaze, as he, seated and having seen me, leaned ever so slightly forward and chided me back to work.

Dr. Williams Library, The Library of Protestant Dissent in London, fronts onto the magnificent Gordon Square – in at once ancient and modern city of magnificent squares – in which I would take breaks to think through the texts of Protestant Dissent I had been reading and copying longhand into my research papers. That was in 2015, in November, when it is supposed to be cold in London – but not by Londoners' standards. I would end each day with a pot of English breakfast tea in the lobby of the Montague on the Gardens, around the corner from the extraordinary and now vexed monument to the British Empire, the British Museum. The waitstaff carefully instructed me to obey the brewing time, kept by an hourglass-shaped five-minute-glass with tea-black sand, and then closely observed, from a very British discreet distance, to make sure that I did. Biscuits (English English again) got me through the brewing process.

The only shortcoming that I could identify about the magnificent Wellcome Library and Museum in its new building on busy Euston Road in London is that it is not in Texas. Every scholar of the history of medicine and of the history of medical ethics longs to read old books and manuscripts at the Wellcome. I have had that opportunity, three times.

Four men prepared me for and supported me in the scholarly and philosophical work of this book. Irwin C. Lieb (1925–1992) was Chairman of the Department of Philosophy at the University of Texas at Austin in the early 1970s and was instrumental in my being admitted to its graduate program. In his metaphysics seminar and in all my many conversations with him for years afterward, Chet, as he invited me to call him after he hooded me at graduation on the Main Mall in May of 1976, modeled the life of the mind that a philosopher should cultivate. He once told me that he wanted intellectual variety among the graduate students and, this aim in mind, admitted me and others in my class who had majored in a discipline other than philosophy, in my case art history at Williams College, taking a chance on us. My thank you appears in the closing section of Chap. 4. Ignazio Angelelli (1933–2019) taught me to be a scholar of the history of philosophy and became my Doktorvater at the University, teaching me close and loving reading of old books.

Ignazio encouraged me to combine my training in the history of philosophy with my academic work of being a medical educator, which resulted in an academic adventure in the history of medical ethics that started more than four decades ago and continues in this book. As his research assistant in the Institute for the Medical Humanities at The University of Texas Medical Branch at Galveston in the mid-1970s, the physician-philosopher, baccalaureate and doctoral graduate of the University, H. Tristram Engelhardt, Jr., (1941–2018) taught me the history of medical ethics and how to become a medical educator who incorporates the history of medical ethics into classroom and clinical teaching. He also taught me Texas history. As everyone who knew and loved him will tell you, everything that Tris said about Texas history, continuing the grand tradition of Texican storytellers, was true. In 1988, in the fifth of his 30 years as Leon Jaworski Professor of Biomedical Ethics and the Director of the Center for Medical Ethics and Health at the Baylor College of Medicine in Houston, Texas, the philosopher Baruch Brody (1943–2018) brought my wife, Linda Quintanilla, our Texas dogs, and me back to Texas, back home. He became for me and his colleagues in our Center an exemplar nonpareil of the master teacher who loves his students and an academic leader at once supportive and fiercely protective of his faculty and staff. He gave his support, and Center resources, unstintingly for my work on Gregory and Percival without which this book would not exist.

These four men set me on the path to this book, and so much more in my academic and personal lives. All four became splendid friends. Their names appear on the dedication page of this book, under the familiar Latin inscription *In Memoriam*. Often mistaken for the ablative of place, *"In"* in this phrase is the accusative form of the preposition *in*, translated as "into," the action or motion of going into something. *In Memoriam* means that one takes the deceased *into* memory, as lifelong work and welcome obligation, which I am privileged and honored to do each day. To continue the work bequeathed to me, I gratefully dedicate this book to their memory.

Austin, TX, USA Laurence B. McCullough
May 2021

Acknowledgments

Portions of Chap. 1 in Part I, on Gregory's life, his philosophy of medicine, and his professional ethics in medicine, are based on Laurence B. McCullough, 1998. *John Gregory and the Invention of Professional Medical Ethics and the Profession of Medicine*. Dordrecht, The Netherlands: Kluwer Academic Publishers (now Springer), Chaps. 2 and 3. I have also included quoted passages from primary and secondary sources that appear in these two chapters.

Portions of the final section of Chap. 4 of Part I, Gregory's and Percival's Legacy for Contemporary Professional Ethics in Medicine, have been adapted, with permission, from McCullough, Laurence B., Coverdale, John H., and Frank A, Chervenak. 2020. *Professional Ethics in Obstetrics and Gynecology*. Cambridge and New York: Cambridge University Press, pages 19–21.

Contents

Part I Thomas Percival's *Medical Ethics* and the Invention of Medical Professionalism

1 What Percival Inherits: John Gregory's Moral Revolution Against the Long Tradition of Entrepreneurial Medicine in the History of Western Medicine............................. 3
   1.1 Origins of Thomas Percival's Professional Ethics in Medicine in John Gregory's Professional Ethics in Medicine.. 3
   1.2 A Methodologic Note: Historically Based, Philosophical Interpretation of Texts....................... 5
      1.2.1 The Discovery of Ethical Concepts................. 5
      1.2.2 The Invention of Ethical Concepts.................. 7
      1.2.3 The Quest for Certainty and the Quest for Reliability............................. 9
   1.3 The Long Tradition of Entrepreneurial Medicine in the History of Western Medicine............................ 9
      1.3.1 Hippocratic Entrepreneurialism.................... 11
      1.3.2 The Royal Colleges: Guild Entrepreneurialism........ 14
      1.3.3 *De Cautelis Medici*: Cautious Entrepreneurialism...... 15
      1.3.4 *Medicus Politicus*: Politic Entrepreneurialism......... 16
   1.4 Anomalies for the Paradigm of Entrepreneurial Medical Practice: Unaccountable Power and Distrust........... 20
   1.5 John Gregory's Revolutionary Invention of Professional Ethics in Medicine........................... 22
      1.5.1 Gregory's Invention of the First Commitment of the Ethical Concept of Medicine as a Profession........ 23
          1.5.1.1 Biographical Sketch 23
          1.5.1.2 Intellectual Authority in Bacon's Philosophy of Science and Medicine 25

		1.5.1.3	Intellectual Authority in Gregory's Philosophy of Medicine	28
		1.5.1.4	Gregory's First Paradigm Shift	33
	1.5.2	Gregory's Invention of the Second Commitment of the Ethical Concept of Medicine as a Profession		35
		1.5.2.1	Men of "Interest"	35
		1.5.2.2	Gregory on the Physiologic Principle of Sympathy	36
		1.5.2.3	David Hume's Baconian Moral Science on the Principle of Sympathy	36
		1.5.2.4	John Gregory's Baconian Moral Science of Sympathy and Its Professional Virtues of Tenderness and Steadiness	40
		1.5.2.5	Gregory's Second Paradigm Shift.	46
	1.5.3	Gregory's Invention of the Third Commitment of the Ethical Concept of Medicine as a Profession		46
		1.5.3.1	The "Corporation Spirit" and Guild Self-Interests	47
		1.5.3.2	Gregory's Third Paradigm Shift	48
1.6	Gregory's Invention of the Ethical Concept of Medicine and Professional Ethics in Medicine			49
1.7	Gregory's Professional Ethics of Clinical Research			50
1.8	Conclusion: Gregory's Moral Revolution Against Entrepreneurial Medicine.			52

2 An Intellectual Biography of Thomas Percival 55
  2.1 A Methodological Note 55
  2.2 Thomas Percival of Warrington and Manchester. 56

	2.2.1	The Percival Family in Warrington	56
	2.2.2	Percival's First Seventeen Years.	57
	2.2.3	Percival: The First Student at Warrington Academy	58
	2.2.4	Edinburgh, London, Leyden, and a Tour of the Netherlands and France	59
	2.2.5	Warrington and Marriage to Elizabeth Bassnett of London	63
	2.2.6	Manchester: The English Enlightenment Commitment to Improvement Using Baconian Science.	64

  2.3 Percival's Intellectual and Moral Formation 67

	2.3.1	The English National Enlightenment.	67
	2.3.2	Warrington Academy	69
		2.3.2.1 The Dissenting Academies and the Curriculum of the Warrington Academy.	69
		2.3.2.2 Percival's Teachers at the Warrington Academy	71
		2.3.2.3 "Subjects Which Have a Connection … Explained in a Regular System"	78

		2.3.2.4	Condescension of Gentlemen of the Higher Social Classes to the Poor	79
		2.3.2.5	"You Do Constantly, Carefully, Impartially, and Conscientiously Attend to Evidence"	81
2.4	Percival's Writings		82
	2.4.1	*Dissertatio Medica Inauguralis De Frigore* (1765)		83
		2.4.1.1	Percival's Adoption of the First Commitment of the Ethical Concept of Medicine as a Profession	86
	2.4.2	Essays Medical, Philosophical, and Experimental		86
		2.4.2.1	Essays Medical, Philosophical, and Experimental: Part I	87
		2.4.2.2	Essays Medical, Philosophical, and Experimental: Part II	95
		2.4.2.3	Essays Medical, Philosophical, and Experimental: Part III	101
		2.4.2.4	Essays Medical, Philosophical, and Experimental: Part IV	110
	2.4.3	Writings on Political Philosophy: Baconian Polity		114
	2.4.4	Biographical Memoirs		116
2.5	The Moral Formation and Development of Children		119
	2.5.1	A Father's Instructions		119
		2.5.1.1	The Genre of Paternal Advice	120
		2.5.1.2	Percival's Three Goals	121
		2.5.1.3	Genres Included	122
		2.5.1.4	Sympathy for Animals and the Ethics of Animal Experimentation	123
		2.5.1.5	The Regulatory Virtues of Tenderness and Steadiness	124
		2.5.1.6	Percival's Adoption of the Second Commitment of the Ethical Concept of Medicine as a Profession	124
		2.5.1.7	Condescension and Authority	124
		2.5.1.8	Opposition to Enslavement of Persons	126
		2.5.1.9	Baconian Philosophy of Religion	128
		2.5.1.10	Percival's Adoption of the Third Commitment of the Ethical Concept of Medicine as a Profession	129
		2.5.1.11	Theodicy	129
		2.5.1.12	A Persistent Theme: Stoicism	130
		2.5.1.13	Appetites	131
		2.5.1.14	Whimsy	132
	2.5.2	Moral and Literary Dissertations; Chiefly Intended as a Sequel to *A Father's Instructions* (1788)		133
		2.5.2.1	On the Influence of Habit and Association	139

		2.5.2.2	On Inconsistency of Expectations in Literary Pursuits	140
		2.5.2.3	On the Beauties of Nature and on a General Taste for the Fine Arts	141
		2.5.2.4	Of the Intellectual and Moral Conduct of Experimental Pursuits	142
	2.6	Conclusion: Percival: Life-Long Committed Baconian Scientist		143
		2.6.1	Dissenter and Deist	143
		2.6.2	Baconian Philosophy of Religion and Its Implications for Baconian Philosophy of Medicine	144
		2.6.3	Improvement of Medicine and Healthcare Institutions	145
		2.6.4	Discourse of Peace	146
		2.6.5	Inventing New Words and Changing the Meaning of Existing Words	146
		2.6.6	Hospital Polity	147
		2.6.7	A Way of Life	148
3	**Thomas Percival Joins Gregory's Moral Revolution Against the Long Tradition of Entrepreneurial Medicine in the History of Western Medicine**			149
	3.1	How Events at Manchester Infirmary Resulted in Percival Writing *Medical Jurisprudence* and Then *Medical Ethics*		149
	3.2	Medical Jurisprudence		153
		3.2.1	A "Code"	154
			3.2.1.1 Three Models	154
	3.3	Delay in Completing *Medical Ethics*		160
	3.4	Medical Ethics, or a Code of Institutes and Precepts, Adapted to the Professional Conduct of Physicians and Surgeons		162
		3.4.1	Title Change	162
		3.4.2	Format: Four Chapters, "On Hospital Duties," and Notes and Illustrations	165
		3.4.3	Dedications to Sir George Baker and to Edward Cropper Percival	165
		3.4.4	Preface	167
		3.4.5	The Text of Medical Ethics: Chapter I: Of Professional Conduct, Relative to Hospitals, or Other Medical Charities	171
		3.4.6	The Text of Medical Ethics: Chapter II: Of Professional Conduct in Private, or General Practice	192

		3.4.7	The Text of *Medical Ethics*: Chapter III: Of the Conduct of Physicians Towards Apothecaries	213
		3.4.8	The Text of *Medical Ethics*: Chapter IV: Of Professional Duties, in Certain Cases Which Require a Knowledge of Law......................	219
			3.4.8.1 Political Ethics	222
			3.4.8.2 Baconian Testimony	226
			3.4.8.3 The Autonomy of Professional Ethics in Medicine from State Power	228
	3.5	A Discourse, Addressed to the Gentlemen of the Faculty, the Officers, the Clergy, and the Trustees of the Infirmary at Liverpool, on Their Respective Hospital Duties. By The Rev. Thomas Bassnett Percival, Ll. B.		229
	3.6	Conclusion...		232
		3.6.1	Professional Ethics in Medicine: Three Commitments...................................	232
		3.6.2	Baconian Moral Scientific Professional Ethics in Medicine......................................	233
		3.6.3	"Institutes" and "Precepts" of Professional Ethics in Medicine	234
		3.6.4	Deism and Dissent in Percival's Professional Ethics in Medicine	235
			3.6.4.1 Deism: Medicine and Religion.............	235
			3.6.4.2 Dissent: Medicine and Society	235
		3.7 A Professional Colleague's Instructions		236
4	**The Place of Percival's *Medical Ethics* in the History of Medical Ethics**...			**239**
	4.1	Achievement: *Medical Ethics* and the Invention of Medical Professionalism		239
	4.2	Reception...		246
		4.2.1	Reception in England............................	246
		4.2.2	Reception in the United States.....................	249
	4.3	Influence...		256
	4.4	Gregory's and Percival's Legacy for Contemporary Professional Ethics in Medicine.........................		259
	4.5	Painters Before and After Cimabue		264

Bibliography	267
Bibliographical Note...	267
Privately and Publicly Published Works of Thomas Percival.......	267
Manuscript and Unpublished Sources	272
Online Sources	273
Other Published Primary and Secondary Sources	274

Part II Three Key Texts – *Medical Ethics***,** *Medical Jurisprudence***, and** *Extracts* **– Two Concordances, and a Chronology**

5 Three Key Texts – *Medical Ethics***,** *Medical Jurisprudence***, and** *Extracts* 291
  1794 Medical Jurisprudence or A Code of Ethics and Institutes, Adapted to the Professions of Physic and Surgery 291
  1803 Medical Ethics or, A Code of Institutes and Precepts, Adapted to the Professional Conduct of Physicians and Surgeons 336
  1823 Extracts from the Medical Ethics of Dr. Percival 435

6 Two Concordances 445

7 Chronology 451

Index 459

Part I
Thomas Percival's *Medical Ethics* and the Invention of Medical Professionalism

Chapter 1
What Percival Inherits: John Gregory's Moral Revolution Against the Long Tradition of Entrepreneurial Medicine in the History of Western Medicine

1.1 Origins of Thomas Percival's Professional Ethics in Medicine in John Gregory's Professional Ethics in Medicine

In this book I will use historically based, philosophical interpretation of primary-source and secondary-source texts to explain how the English physician-ethicist, Thomas Percival (1740–1804), having self-consciously joined the Scottish physician-ethicist, John Gregory (1724–1773), co-invented professional ethics in medicine in a moral revolution against the long tradition of entrepreneurial medicine in the history of Western medicine. To create his professional ethics in medicine Percival drew on: Baconian scientific medicine and its insistence on evidence-based reasoning; the Baconian moral science taught by his teachers at the Warrington Academy, as well as their distinctive Baconian and secular commitments as Dissenting Unitarians (one of the several groups of "rational dissenters," a misnomer, as we shall see in Chap. 2; they were Baconian dissenters); David Hume's moral science of sympathy; and Percival's own, extensive scientific, medical, and moral writings – among the latter his very successful *A Father's Instructions* that joined a literature to which genre Gregory had contributed (Gregory 1774). Percival also drew deeply on Gregory's professional ethics in medicine and its discourse of the principle of sympathy and its professional regulatory virtues of tenderness and steadiness. This book therefore starts in this chapter with an account of Gregory's professional ethics in medicine, which Percival inherits and to which he adds in original and important ways, as the reader will discover in Chap. 3.

Gregory mounted a self-conscious moral revolution against the long tradition of entrepreneurialism in the history of Western medicine. Robert Baker's pathbreaking scholarship on moral revolutions, *The Structure of Moral Revolutions* (Baker 2019), has become indispensable for understanding the co-invention of professional ethics in medicine by Gregory and Percival. The reader is alerted by the title of Baker's book of his considerable debt to the philosophy of science of Thomas Kuhn (1922–1996) (Kuhn 1962, 2012). From Kuhn Baker takes the concept of paradigms, or "ways of conceiving" or "seeing as" (Baker 2019, 10). Moral paradigms comprise "… the framework of communal standards for character and conduct that a community's members internalize …" (Baker 2019, 17) Moral paradigms can change by what Baker calls "moral drift" that occurs when "external forces, acting without any conscious intention to effect a change, have altered the community's sense of morality" (Baker 2019, 21). "Moral reform" occurs when dissidents from the community's morality "intend simply to alter the impact of some interpretations of moral norms or the laws enforcing them, without changing underlying moral paradigms" (Baker 2019, 21). "Moral revolutions," by contrast, occur when dissidents have the "intent … to alter underlying moral paradigms" (Baker 2019, 21), resulting in a moral paradigm shift. Baker means for the analogy to Kuhn on scientific revolutions to be direct: When a moral paradigm encounters challenges to which it is inadequate, the paradigm confronts an anomaly (Baker 2019, 42). The moral revolutionary invents an alternative paradigm that can successfully address that anomaly. A moral counterrevolution occurs when dissidents aim to alter a current, dominant moral paradigm by invoking an existing, less dominant paradigm as the replacement. This is a re-invention of an existing paradigm that can appear to have been discovered.

This chapter will describe the paradigm shift made in John Gregory's medical ethics: from the long tradition of entrepreneurialism in the history of Western medical ethics to professional ethics in medicine, based on the ethical concept of medicine as a profession. As a necessary preliminary, the next section of this chapter provides an account of the scholarly method of historically based, philosophical interpretation of texts deployed in the balance of this chapter and in subsequent chapters. The third section provides an historically based, philosophical interpretation of the history of Western medical ethics before Gregory's invention of professional ethics in medicine. The fourth section provides an historically based, philosophical interpretation of Gregory's invention that Percival inherits. Accomplishing these tasks will set the stage for the intellectual biography of Percival in Chap. 2.

1.2 A Methodologic Note: Historically Based, Philosophical Interpretation of Texts

A student in the week-long Proseminar of The Bioethics Program (Union Graduate College, Clarkson University, Icahn School of Medicine at Mount Sinai) in which I taught each July once asked me: Where do philosophical concepts come from? In the history of philosophy, there have been two answers. The first and most frequent answer has been that philosophical concepts are discovered; the second that philosophical concepts are invented.

1.2.1 The Discovery of Ethical Concepts

One of the most famous philosophical texts about the discovery of concepts in the history of Western philosophy is Plato's (429–327 BCE) *Euthyphro* (Plato 1924; Vérsenyi 1963). Plato has Socrates stop the character of Euthyphro on the steps of the courthouse and ask him why is there. Euthyphro responds that he has lodged a charge against his father for allowing an enslaved man to die from injuries sustained from a fall into a pit. Socrates expressed wonder that a son would have someone prosecuted for negligence of a slave and why a son would have his father thusly prosecuted. Euthyphro explains that the gods require his action, which prompts a dialogue on the nature of piety. Socrates wants to know what the concept of piety is in itself, without reference to any other concept. The goal is for Euthyphro to uncover the concept of piety in all its timeless purity. This is the logic of discovery of timeless ethical concepts.

A vivid demonstration of the discovery of concepts also occurs in *Meno* (Plato 2010). In this dialogue Plato has Socrates engage an enslaved boy – meant to be an exemplar of utter ignorance – in the derivation of the Pythagorean Theorem (the square of the diagonal of a right triangle is equal to the sum of the squares of its sides) *a priori*. The enslaved boy is able to do so because Reason has the capacity to discover timeless concepts in geometry. Perhaps Plato is also telling his reader that enslavement cannot change Reason or, more generally, human nature, a theme to which we will return when we consider in Chap. 2 Percival on enslavement of persons.

Timeless concepts transcend individual experience and the collective experience of cultures and societies. Timeless concepts never change. Timeless concepts are thus available to everyone everywhere. Inasmuch as timeless concepts can be more precisely discovered and therefore their implications made clearer, or, better, new implications identified, progress in philosophy is possible.

Timeless moral concepts *eo ipso* inoculate moral reasoning against moral relativism. This phrase names the view that the standards by which we make moral judgments about character (using concepts of virtues such as integrity or compassion) and behavior (using action guides or ethical principles such as the ethical principles of beneficence and respect for patient autonomy) are idiosyncratic matters of individual preference or cultures that have no application to other individuals (a radical form of moral relativism) or other cultures (cultural moral relativism). As universal and therefore universalizable, timeless moral concepts guide judgments for all individuals in all cultural settings in all times. In bioethics this is known as the common morality (Beauchamp and Childress 2019).

Philosophers such as P.F. Strawson (1919–2006) have taken the view that "our conceptual structure" is unchanging and thus common to us all (Strawson 1959). This echoes the commitment of the German Enlightenment philosopher Immanuel Kant (1724–1804) to Transcendental Reason with its unchanging categories of Pure Reason (Kant 1998). Kant's descendant in bioethics, by way of Georg Wilhelm Friedrich Hegel (1770–1831), H. Tristram Engelhardt, Jr. (1941–2018), deployed the methods of transcendental reasoning to discovery the necessary conditions for a peaceable society and thus the foundations of bioethics (Engelhardt 1985, 1996).

Moral and political philosophy in the Anglophone world has deployed two prominent methods for the discovery of timeless concepts. The first comprises thought experiments that, like scientific experiments, aim at discovery. In political philosophy the Harvard philosopher John Rawls (1921–2002) deployed a thought experiment he called the "original position," a hypothetical circumstance in which individuals reason together about the individually necessary and jointly sufficient conditions for a just society while not knowing their station in society (thus constraining the biases inevitably originating in self-interest) (Rawls 1971). In medical ethics, Edmund Pellegrino (1920–2003) described a thought experiment aimed at discovery of the timeless concepts of "fact of illness" and the "act of profession" in response to the vulnerability that illness creates (Pellegrino 2006). The results of this thought experiment became for Pellegrino the basis of a comprehensive account of professional ethics in medicine. Rosamond Rhodes deploys "the hypothetico-deductive method" in thought experiments also aimed at discovery of the timeless concept of medicine as a profession (Rhodes 2019).

The second method deploys compelling examples in response to which moral intuitions are expressed, typically in the familiar locution, "our intuitions." These are then tested in rigorous philosophical reflection with the goal of expressing as clearly as possible the timeless concepts that are discovered in the course of this reflection. James Rachels (1941–2003), in one of the classical and widely influential articles in bioethics, implicitly appealed to moral intuitions as the basis for an argument that the distinction between killing and letting does not withstand close philosophical scrutiny (Rachels 1975). The Trolley example has generated a considerable literature testing the adequacy of moral intuitions and the concepts in which they are expressed (Foot 2002). Robert Audi has recently pointed out that the word 'intuition' lacks a fixed meaning (Audi 2015). This means that any method of moral reasoning that invokes intuitions must specify clearly the meaning of 'intuition', to prevent equivocation on terms, which is not permitted in philosophical reasoning.

1.2.2 The Invention of Ethical Concepts

Historically based philosophical interpretation of texts rejects the assumption that concepts are timeless and thereby transcultural. Historical scholarship calls this assumption essentialism (Pernick 2015; Baker 2019). For example, the ethical concept of being a patient, an individual to whose health and life a physician or other healthcare professional has made a commitment to protect, is not a timeless concept. Textual evidence for this claim appeals to the absence of any word in the ancient Greek and subsequent Latin texts in the history of Western medical ethics that can be translated as 'patient'. Instead, the word '*aegrotus*' is used, or the sick individual. To use 'patient' to refer to sick individuals before Gregory and Percival revolutionized the use of this word in their professional ethics in medicine is an error of essentialism, no less an error for its common occurrence in the literature on the history of medical ethics.

In ancient Greece, a sick individual usually self-diagnosed and self-treated. Sick individuals with the means to do so retained the services of one or more of the many types of practitioners who offered their services in the highly competitive market to those few who could afford their fees. There were almost as many concepts of disease and regimens for them as there were practitioners. The sick therefore understood all too well that practitioners were entrepreneurs, in whom it was risky to place one's trust that any practitioner knew what he was talking about or doing. Similarly, 'profession' meant one's line or work as reported to tax collectors. Pellegrino's (2006) concept of the professional physician as responding to the vulnerabilities of the sick is not to be found in the ethics texts of the Hippocratic Corpus. Finally, the concept of autonomy, which includes "*liberty* (independence from controlling influences) and *agency* (capacity for intentional action)" (Beauchamp and Childress 2019, 99, emphasis original), cannot be found anywhere in the ethical texts of the Hippocratic corpus.

Historically based philosophical interpretation of texts also rejects the assumption that people in the past understood themselves to be engaged with ethical problems that concern us now. This is known in historical scholarship as the error of presentism (Pernick 2009; Baker 2019). Robert Baker, in his masterful case study of the moral revolution about abortion shows that what the jurist John T. Noonan (1926–2017) took without question to be the core concept of the morality of abortion – the "humanity" of the fetus or its moral status as a gestational life form of our species – has no counterpart in the morality of abortion in ancient Greece. For the ancient Greeks the fetus has no moral status – nor did a newborn child that had not been accepted into the family of its birth (Baker 2019).

The prohibition against abortion in the *Hippocratic Oath* had nothing to do with the moral status of the fetus and everything to do with not inserting a "destructive pessary" to cause uterine contractions with the aim of expelling the contents of a gravid uterus. 'Destructive' refers to the life of the pregnant woman, not the life of the fetus. The concern of the Hippocratic *Oath* was to minimize maternal morality to protect the self-interest of the Hippocratic physician in not gaining a reputation for killing his pregnant customers (in an entrepreneurial relation 'customer' is the precisely correct word choice). Indeed, 'reputation' appears in the *Oath* and the physician has a self-interest in a reputation for not killing pregnant customers.

To support the claim that physicians in the past were committed to medical paternalism (interference with the autonomy of a patient based on a clinical judgment that such interference will protect and promote the health-related interests of the patient, i.e., beneficence-based interference), the Hippocratic text, *Decorum*, that the physician should not reveal the ingredients in compound medications, ointments, or potions is cited.

> Perform this calmly and adroitly, concealing most things from the patient while you are attending to him (Hippocrates 1923, 297).

'Patient' and 'autonomy' cannot be found in the Hippocratic texts. More to the point, in an era many, many centuries before the invention of patent law and of state regulation of pharmaceuticals and controlled substances, anyone could buy in the local market the ingredients that the physician was combining according to his recipe. The sick at that time self-diagnosed and self-treated (they still do), using perhaps all or some of the same ingredients used by practitioners. To protect his market share, the entrepreneurial practitioner needed to protect his recipes, which we now call trade secrets protected by intellectual property and patent law. There was no patent law in ancient Greece. The practitioner who prepared his therapeutic recipes in secret therefore did so out of self-interest, indeed, rational self-interest given the harsh and unforgiving realities of an unregulated, highly competitive marketplace. Protecting patients, for their own good, by interfering with their autonomy is a presentist reading of the text, the weight of which the text cannot bear.

Timeless ideas and concepts are transcultural by their very nature or "universalizable" in the discourse of Anglophone moral philosophy (Jollimore 2020). They can be deployed from the "moral point of view" that requires each individual to count for one and no individual to count for more than one (Rawls 1971; Jollimore 2020).

Invented ideas and concepts start out in a cultural and historical context. Some invented concepts never leave their cultural origins while others have influence beyond their origins. The latter can become transcultural, transnational, and transreligious concepts. Invented concepts that gain this standing can appear timeless. Chapter 3 will explain how Percival built on Gregory's professional ethics in medicine to co-invent the ethical concept of medicine as a profession in late eighteenth-century England in the context described in Chap. 2. Chapter 4 will explain how Gregory and Percival's invention contained the basis for it to move beyond its historical and cultural origins.

The rejection of both essentialism and presentism commits the historically based philosophical interpreter of texts to the view that concepts are invented. The set of discovered concepts is empty. The first task becomes that of identifying texts in which we have good reason to believe that the invention occurred: there appears to be no previous text containing the invention. Before Gregory and Percival there appears to have been no text containing the ethical concept of medicine as a profession.

Philosophical methods committed to timeless concepts and their discovery treat the history of philosophy and the history of ideas generally as either of only antiquarian value or as a catalogue of errors that, in their pride of progress, contemporary philosophers have corrected. That this approach to philosophical analysis of concepts commits its adherents to the errors of essentialism and presentism does not even register with them. In sharp contrast, historically based philosophical textual interpretation takes historical scholarship to be essential, because only historically based philosophical scholarship has the tools to identify and then clearly express invented concepts in historical texts (Baker 2019). This is the approach to textual interpretation that will be taken in this book.

1.2.3 The Quest for Certainty and the Quest for Reliability

Diego Gracia (2010) has distinguished between the quest for certainty and the quest for reliability in the history of Western moral philosophy. The quest for certainty is fulfilled by using the methods described just above to discover concepts that are independent of human thought and judgment and thus intellectually and morally authoritative for everyone (Gracia 2010). The quest for reliability in our moral judgments differs. Reliable moral judgments permit one to forms one's character (cultivate virtues, avoid vices) and to engage in behavior with confidence that one has good reason for doing so and requires the commitment that one should always be open to improvement of one's moral judgments (Gracia 2010). The quest for certainty requires methods of discovery of moral concepts. The quest for reliability requires methods of inventing moral concepts. As we shall see later in this chapter, Gregory was engaged in the quest for reliability in his work of inventing the ethical concept of medicine as a profession. Chapter 3 will explain how Percival was committed to the quest for reliability in his additions to the ethical concept of medicine as a profession.

1.3 The Long Tradition of Entrepreneurial Medicine in the History of Western Medicine

Percival's *Medical Ethics* became the first book in the global history of medical ethics to bear this title (Percival 1803, [1803] 1807, [1803] 2022). But it was not the first book on medical ethics, the critical study of medical morality or the actual beliefs and judgments of physicians about how they and the sick (only much later patients) ought to conduct themselves in clinical care and in clinical research (Baker and McCullough 2009b). It is also the case that *Medical Ethics* was not the first book on professional ethics in medicine. *Medical Ethics* was the second book on professional ethics in medicine in the global history of medical ethics, coming after Gregory's 1772 *Lectures on the Duties and Qualifications of a Physician* (Gregory 1772, [1772] 1998; McCullough 1998). These are bold claims. I turn now to making the case for them and thereby setting the stage for the intellectual biography of Percival that follows in Chap. 2.

The claim that there is a long tradition of entrepreneurial medicine in the history of Western medicine cuts against the grain, perhaps unacceptably to many readers. There is a good reason for this resistance: It is commonly believed that professional ethics in medicine has deep historical roots in ancient Greece. The globally influential "Physician Charter" expresses a commitment to this belief: "The medical profession everywhere is embedded in diverse cultures and national traditions, but its members share the role of healer, which has roots extending back to Hippocrates" (Project of the ABIM Foundation 2002, 244). The American Medical Association's *Code of Medical Ethics* takes the same view:

> Since its adoption at the AMA's founding meeting in 1847, the AMA *Code of Medical Ethics* has articulated the values to which physicians commit themselves as members of the medical profession. The *Code* is rooted in an understanding of the goals of medicine as a profession that dates back to the 5th century B.C. and the Greek physician Hippocrates: to relieve suffering and promote well-being in a relationship of fidelity with the patient (American Medical Association n.d.).

Pellegrino ranks Percival's *Medical Ethics* and the Hippocratic ethical texts as of equal importance in the history of medical ethics: "Percival's *Medical Ethics*, with the Oath and Deontological books of the Hippocratic Corpus, remains the most influential document in Anglo-American Medical Ethics" (Pellegrino 1985, 1). Robert Baker calls this the "Hippocratic Footnote" approach (Baker 1993b, 852), referencing the claim of Alfred North Whitehead (1861–1947) that all of Western philosophy is but a footnote to Plato (428/427 or 424/423–348/347 BCE) and Aristotle (385–323 BCE) (Whitehead [1929] 1978).

Steven Miles is more cautious, noting that determining "what the *Oath* might say for medical ethics of our time … is a difficult endeavor" (Miles 2004, 8). The problems of essentialism and presentism must be avoided:

> First, we may find that the *Oath* said something to the medical ethics of its day that still has value of our time. To justify such a finding, it must be demonstrated that the terms, principles, issues and context that the *Oath* addressed in its time sufficiently resemble those in ours to support applying its words to similar issues today (Miles 2004, 8).

The ethical writings comprise the *Oath, The Art, Epidemics*, and other texts from the Hippocratic Corpus, the body of works written during more than a century and therefore by multiple authors. The *Oath* and other ethical texts of the Hippocratic Corpus are taken to be founding documents of a "long tradition" (Jonsen 2000, ix–xi), as Albert Jonsen characterized 'tradition': "the literature about medical ethics does seem to circle around certain common themes, recognizable even under different guises" (Jonsen 2000, ix). Entrepreneurialism was indeed a long tradition in this circumspect sense of 'tradition', with its distinctive ethics literature. And this long

1.3 The Long Tradition of Entrepreneurial Medicine in the History of Western Medicine 11

tradition began with the *Oath* and the Hippocratic entrepreneurialism that its authors invented and continued through guild entrepreneurialism, cautious entrepreneurialism, and politic entrepreneurialism until the latter third of the eighteenth century in Scotland, where Gregory started a moral revolution against it that Percival completed in crucial ways, as we will see in Chaps. 3 and 4. We now turn our attention now to the invention of the long tradition of entrepreneurialism by the writers of the Hippocratic *Oath*.

1.3.1 Hippocratic Entrepreneurialism

Jacques Jouanna in his masterful biography of Hippocrates describes the context in which the *Oath* was invented (Jouanna 2001). At the time the *Oath* may have been set down, the physicians of the Coan school encountered a shortage of sons. In a family-based association the loyalty of sons could be safely assumed. When this was no longer the case, it became necessary to invent a broader association, by demanding expressed and documented loyalty to the masters of the association and its prescriptions and proscriptions. These tenets forged a new, shared interest that would differentiate the resulting group in the competitive, unforgiving medical marketplace of the time.

Oaths have solemnized a promise of loyalty for millennia. Oaths still do, e.g., the oath of loyalty to the United States Constitution by elected and appointed officials, civilian employees of the federal government, and – especially important – members of the armed services. The *Hippocratic Oath* in its very first section solemnized averred loyalty in a "written covenant" between initiates to the Coan school and its master physicians (von Staden 1996). This requirement betrays an understandable deficit of confidence that the Coan school could expand successfully.

1. i. I swear
ii. by Apollo the Physician and by Asclepius and by Health and Panacea and by all the gods as well as goddesses, making them judges [witnesses],
iii. to bring the following oath and written covenant to fulfillment, in accordance with my power and my judgment;
2. i. to regard him who has taught me this techne as equal to my parents, and
ii. to share, in partnership, my livelihood with him and to give him a share when he is in need of necessities, and
iii. to judge the offspring [coming] from him equal to [my] male siblings, and
iv. to teach them this techne, should they desire to learn [it], without fee and written covenant, and to give a share both of rules and of lectures, and of all the rest of learning, to my sons and to the [sons]of him who has taught me and to the pupils who have both make a written contract and sworn by a medical convention but by no other (von Staden 1996)

A covenant is among the most solemn of promises. Entering a covenant is to enter into a close relationship that is exceeded only by blood kinship relationships. The initiate promises to protect *techné* and reputation, the two core concepts deployed in the *Oath* (von Staden 1996).

[8]i. a. If I render this oath fulfilled, and if I do not blur and confound it [making it to no effect]
b. may it be [granted] to me to enjoy the benefits both of life and of techne,
c. being held in good repute among all human beings for time eternal.
ii. a. If, however, I transgress and perjure myself,
b. the opposite of these (von Staden 1996).

Techné has usually been translated as "art" and then misunderstood. *Techné* names the unchanging and unchangeable doctrine of the four humors, interactions among which explain disease. *Techné* also names the clinical approach based on this doctrine: closely observing the course of disease, deploying therapeutic minimalism in non-violent regimens, determining when the prognosis is death, and withdrawing promptly so that incurable disease and not the modest ministrations of the practitioner will be understood by the sick individual's family and others as the cause of death. Change in unchangeable doctrine is anathema, which is why the initiate swears to remain "pure" in *techné*. The initiate also promises to protect "reputation" or the positive estimations of potential customers of Coan School physicians, which estimations are essential for gaining and retaining market share.

The balance of the *Oath* comprises proscriptions and prescriptions. While there are other ethical writings in the Hippocratic Corpus, no references to them appear in the *Oath*. The *Oath* thus becomes its own heuristic context when it refers to itself as a "written covenant." As von Staden points out, the concepts of *techné* and reputation play a central role (von Staden 1996). But these concepts are the basis of the written covenant, the content of which are the association's rules, the prescriptions and proscriptions that follow the opening section. The initiate promises adherence to these rules in the solemnly sworn covenant.

This reading differs from Miles'. Miles claims that the "lack of content for the *Oath* greatly complicates any effort to understand its meaning" (Miles 2004, 3). As we have just seen, the plain text of the *Oath* provides it context. Miles describes the core content of the *Oath* as follows: "The medical ethics of the *Oath* are centered on two principles, beneficence and justice, that are anchored in and lived through the integrity of the physician" (Miles 2004, 180). 'Beneficence' appears nowhere in the text of the *Oath*. 'Integrity' cannot be found in the text of the *Oath*. Miles draws on other works to support this important claim but these other works may not have been written by the author(s) of the *Oath*. Drawing on the heuristic context of the *Oath*'s text itself is more reliable scholarship.

Like *techné*, the admonitions in the *Oath* are not open for discussion and change; they must be maintained, i.e., kept pure from corruption by practicing differently, especially the different ways of competitors. Maintaining the rules means that a practitioner will have a good reputation *within the association*. The public dimension of reputation will be one's low mortality rate and being known for such important practices as keeping secrets, not sexually abusing the sick, and not giving poisons (i.e., hiring out as an assassin who uses drugs that mimic natural death and

1.3 The Long Tradition of Entrepreneurial Medicine in the History of Western Medicine 13

leave no detectable signs of homicide). Failure to maintain the rules will result in the opposite of reputation and, it would seem to follow, expulsion from the association. The resulting damage to a physician's reputation in the community would be ruinous in the crowded, harshly competitive market for medical services. This non-essentialist and non-presentist interpretation of the *Oath* reads it as responding to and reinforcing the individual and group self-interest of the Coanian practitioners that are essential for their entrepreneurial success.

As noted above, the word for 'patient' does not appear in the *Oath*. *Aegrotus* or the sick individual does. The relationship is that of practitioner and his customer; the physician-patient relationship does not exist until the invention of professional ethics in medicine by Gregory and Percival more than two thousand years later.

Grant, for the sake of argument only, that the reading of the Hippocratic *Oath* just presented is mistaken. The claim that current professional ethics in medicine has roots in this ancient text requires that the *Oath* comes down to us in an unbroken, traceable tradition (Pellegrino 1985). The problem for this component of the Hippocratic footnote is that there was no millennia-long tradition of swearing the Hippocratic *Oath* by physicians or trainees. Scribonius Largus (c.1–c.50) refers to the *Oath* but not Galen (born c. 129) (Jonsen 2000). Vivian Nutton has shown that the practice of taking the Hippocratic *Oath* died out in the early centuries of the Common Era (Nutton 2009) Oaths were taken in the medical schools of medieval and Renaissance Europe, usually loyalty oaths to one's professors. Taking the *Oath* was revived in the early decades of the twentieth century in the United States, during a period in which medicine was a socially and economically fragile social institution. Nutton points out that the purpose of doing so was to invoke the revered historical figure of Hippocrates to shore up this weak social standing, The revered figure of Hippocrates has frequently been invoked to give value to ideas and practices with which the Hippocratic physicians would be unfamiliar (Galvão-Sobrinho 1996). The revivers of the *Oath* in American medical schools a century ago did exactly that. The Hippocratic authors were committed to *techné*. Medical educators two millennia later were committed to scientific medicine. The Hippocratic writers would not recognize the emergence of scientific medicine as a form of medicine, because the science of medicine changes while *techné* cannot change, ever. *Techné* is incorruptible.

There are good reasons in our time to be deeply suspect of the *Oath* and the other ethical texts of the Hippocratic Corpus to serve as exemplars of professional ethics in medicine more than two millennia later. Only men were permitted to become initiates. The *Oath* could therefore not be taken by women. The *Oath* is not based on science, which is changing and changeable by its very nature, because *techné* cannot be understood to be science. The *Oath* is not based on a constitutive trait of character like professional integrity, contra Miles (2004). It therefore is a mistake to interpret it as the origin of professional ethics in medicine. Those who subscribe to the "Hippocratic footnote" reading of the history of medical ethics commit the error of essentialism and, as a consequence, read into the *Oath* and other ethical writings a professional ethics in medicine that is not present in the texts. The ethical texts of the Hippocratic Corpus should be understood as texts in medical ethics but not texts in professional ethics in medicine.

1.3.2 The Royal Colleges: Guild Entrepreneurialism

An important variant of Hippocratic entrepreneurial medical practice originated in the *Oath* being an association oath without the formal structure of a merchant guild. A merchant guild is an organization of providers of goods or services created to secure economic, social, and political advantage of its members that has social sanction, usually by leave or charter of the ruling power. When a guild has been successfully formed, it makes possible the attempt to gain monopoly control of the market. A monopoly exists when one (ideally) or only a few guilds control the provision of goods or services in a market.

The Royal College of Physicians of London was chartered by King Henry VIII (Royal College of Physicians n.d.). The Royal College of Surgeons of London has its origins in the mid-sixteenth-century organization of the Company of Barber-Surgeons. In 1745 the surgeons separated themselves to form the Company of Surgeons. They were granted a royal charter in 1800 and became the Royal College of Surgeons of London (Science Museum Group Collection n.d.). Before the Act of Union of 1707 Scotland was an independent nation, requiring its own medical and surgical guilds, inasmuch as English guilds were not competent to represent the interests of Scots, as every good Scot knew then and knows to this day. What is now the Royal College of Physicians of Edinburgh was chartered in 1681 (Royal College of Physicians of Edinburgh n.d.). In 1505 the craft guild, as it was then known, was incorporated by the Town Council of Edinburgh, as the Barber Surgeons of Edinburgh. In 1778 this guild was granted a royal charter by King George III and became The Royal College of Surgeons of the City of Edinburgh (The Royal College of Surgeons of Edinburgh n.d.). In 1599 the Royal College of Physicians and Surgeons of Glasgow was royally chartered (Beaton 2000).

These corporations invented strict rules for membership, one goal of which was to limit through licensure the scope of those who could call themselves a physician or a barber-surgeon or (later) a surgeon. These rules reflected and reinforced group self-interest in gaining monopoly control of the medical and surgical marketplaces. For example, the *Statuta Moralia Collegii Regalis Medicorum Londinensium* (Moral Statutes of the Royal College of Physicians of London) reflect consistent concern for the protection and promotion of the group self-interest of members (Clark 1964, Vol. I, 393–417). The self-interest in reputation has unacknowledged roots in the Hippocratic *Oath*, as this text evidences: "No colleague will accuse by name another either of ignorance, malpractice, wickedness or an ignominious crime; not heap public abuse …" (Clark 1964, Vol. I, 414). Members who violated the *Statuta Moralia* put themselves at risk of expulsion with loss of licensure or even prison. The Royal College of Physicians of Edinburgh "[r]esolved to prosecute, as their Patent authorizes and directs them to do, all such who practice without their

Licence …" (Craig 1976, 221). The attempt to gain monopoly share through licensure and threat of its loss enjoyed varying success (Risse 1986). The "corporation spirit" of the Royal College that Gregory attacks was the spirit of guild self-interest of would-be monopolists. The *Statuta Moralia* should not be read as a text in professional ethics in medicine.

1.3.3 De Cautelis Medici: *Cautious Entrepreneurialism*

Medicine as health-related entrepreneurship dominated Western medicine for many subsequent centuries. One exception were the monk-practitioners in the infirmaries of the monastic foundations of Roman Catholic Europe, who cared for their sick brethren and lay persons who sought their help. These monk-practitioners made the spiritual wellbeing of the sick the primary goal, with the wellbeing of the body a secondary consideration.

Put in economic terms, medicine and surgery were practiced in a marketplace model. There was no established pathway into clinical practice such as a uniform medical curriculum. Moreover, one could become a practitioner by apprenticeship. Licensure, when it existed, was not uniform and often ineffective in limiting access to the marketplace of unlicensed practitioners. Practitioners offered their services in an unforgivingly competitive marketplace that was unregulated, with the exception of principalities and municipalities that sought to impose regulation. There was essentially no regulation of medications and devices. This was a real, robust marketplace model of medicine in which *caveat emptor* became an imperative, with one's life and health in the hands of practitioners whom one could not trust to know what they were doing and to put one's health and life, rather than self-interest in fortune and fame. Contemporary calls to base medical practice on a marketplace model are not serious because their idea of a market is tepid and therefore would be unrecognizable to practitioners of eighteenth-century Britain, and earlier, who experienced a real marketplace, in which failure could plunge a physician into poverty. *Caveat vendor* becomes the watch-phrase for practitioners in a truly entrepreneurial market.

Physicians and surgeons charged fees for their services but the sick, especially the rich and powerful sick, often did not pay these fees. In the absence of independent means, this economic reality was harsh. As a consequence, practitioners did not have power over the sick, making a commitment to medical paternalism impossible. Just as there was no Hippocratic tradition, there was no tradition of medical paternalism. *Caveat emptor.*

One response to the challenges of rational protection of individual entrepreneurial practice took the form of an invention: Latin texts on "cautions" to practitioners the titles of which included the distinctive *de cautelis*. For example, Gabriel Zerbi (1445–1505) published rules for conduct aimed at protection of self-interest in such matters as reputation. The discourse *de cautelis* echoes the self-interested proscriptions of the Hippocratic *Oath*. The *de Cautelis* literature should not be read as professional ethics in medicine.

1.3.4 Medicus Politicus: *Politic Entrepreneurialism*

The economic vulnerability and resultant insecurity became more acute for physicians and surgeons who became part of a new form of clinical practice that was introduced in the fifteenth and sixteenth centuries in European principalities and city-states: court or municipal physician. Some increase of economic security occurred, but only as long as one remained employed. Princes and magistrates could and did hire and fire at will. Physicians became subordinate to state power, resulting in a relationship of unequals. To chronic economic vulnerability was added chronic political vulnerability against which practitioners had no recourse. Not being paid in one's private practice with the well-to-do sick might remain private. Being dismissed from court or municipal service would become public, with potentially ruinous consequences to a practitioner's reputation and therefore socioeconomic status.

There existed no ethics to guide physicians in the management of this unequal power relationship of practitioners to payers, whose power was inherently predatory in an era before employment law provided some measure of protection. The discourse of *medicus politicus* was invented by physician-ethicists to provide needed guidance.

The Latin phrase, *medicus politicus*, invites the unwary to translate it as the "political physician." This is an error. The accurate translation is the "politic physician." Jonsen reads 'politic' to mean that medical ethics "looks beyond the individual to the community within which individuals live their lives" (Jonsen 2000, x). This is not the meaning of *'politicus'*. 'Politic' describes a set of attitudes and skills designed to protect self-interest, especially self-interest in survival, when one is subject to state power or the power of the wealthy, especially state power that is unaccountable and can therefore turn predatory without warning.

An early contributor to the discourse of *medicus politicus* was the Portuguese Jewish physician, Rodrigo de Castro (c. 1546–1627). De Castro urged physicians to provide services irrespective of the religion of the sick individual. The title of his book is *The Politic Physician; or, a treatise concerning the duties of the politic physician, distinguished in four books: in which are not only the morals and virtues of good physicians expressed, but also the frauds and impostures of truly bad physicians detected* … (Castro 1662). The latter continues the *de cautelis* tradition. The former focuses on virtues, especially the virtue of prudence.

For de Castro medicine is "the art of using reason and experience in order to conserve health" and has four components: "inspection of nature, knowledge of causes, affirmation of signs, and indications of cure" (Castro 1662, 3) Clinical practice should be based on the virtue of prudence: "It ought to be said that the physician is a good and prudent man" (Castro 1662, 5) He cites as his authorities Hippocrates (d. 370 BCE, approximately age 90), Aristotle (384–322 BCE), and Avicenna (980–1037).

De Castro's goal is to explore how "a physician ought to be and ought to be said to be a good and prudent man" (Castro 1662, 5), which latter includes reputation, an echo of the Hippocratic *Oath*. The virtues of the physician include: "prudence,

1.3 The Long Tradition of Entrepreneurial Medicine in the History of Western Medicine

circumspection, providence, caution, perspicacity, whence also self-control, sobriety, mildness, modesty or moderation, pleasing costume … taciturnity, gravity, magnanimity, liberality, and honesty." He cites in support of this list of virtues Plato, Aristotle, Plutarch (d. 119 CE, approximately age 70), and Seneca (c.1–65 CE) (Castro 1662, 121) He continues:

> … there are two parts of general prudence. The first concerns one who lives alone prudently, which we call Eremitic prudence. The second concerns one who exercises prudence concerning others, which we call military or economic prudence. We differ little with others about the reasons for how the physician should comport himself with the sick and should be assisted by other physicians, which requires becoming steeped in solitary prudence, by which one makes oneself a good man. For it is shameful to work and to practice for many long years as if one were a good physician, as if one could turn out to be a good physician without undertaking the work required to do so (Castro 1662, 110).

De Castro is correct that becoming a prudent physician requires "work." This work is the self-discipline of prudence: identifying one's legitimate self-interests and then acting effectively to protect and promote them in an effort sustained over a lifetime. In other words, this is the work of stoic character formation and maintenance "for many long years."

The German physician and highly influential medical educator Friedrich Hoffmann (1660–1742) went beyond de Castro's stoic prudence and contributed to the discourse of *medicus politicus* in a distinctive way. Hoffmann was professor of medicine at the University of Halle, in southern modern-day Germany and also a physician at a number of royal courts. He therefore had direct experience with the new forms of medical practice as court and municipal physicians that were becoming available to his medical students.

Hoffmann's response was to deploy the concept of *medicus politicus"* (Hoffmann 1749; Chervenak et al. 2006). Princes could hire and fire court physicians at will, as could the nobility that governed the city-states of that time. Economic security, to which physicians in the United States and other high-income countries have become accustomed since the end of World War II, did not exist. The task was to survive. Survival is guided by the virtue of prudence, which schools one in the discipline of identifying and then acting to protect one's legitimate interest. Hoffmann wrote *Medicus Politicus* as a guide for his medical students, *Medicus Politicus, sive Regulae Prudentiae secundum quas Medicus Juvenis Studia sua et Vitae Rationem Digere Debet* (The Politic Physician, or Rule of Prudence According to which the Young Physician Should Arrange his Studies and the Course of Life) (Hoffmann 1749).

Like his predecessors in the *medicus politicus* literature, Hoffmann based his medical ethics on the virtue of prudence, but prudence based on enlightened self-interest. The concept of enlightened self-interest counts as Hoffmann' distinctive contribution to the history of entrepreneurial medical ethics and marks a significant differentiation from Hippocratic entrepreneurial medical ethics.

The entrepreneurial physician selling his services directly to a sick individual was governed by the logic of market exchanges: the mutual pursuit of self-interest. An interest should be understood to exist when an individual has a stake – something to gain or lose – in the future (Feinberg 1984). The sick individual has a stake in current and future health and life and therefore an interest in the restoration of health and, in cases of grave illness, prevention of death. The practitioner had an interest in these same goals and also in remuneration, reputation (like de Castro and a key legacy of Hippocratic ethics), and some measure of economic security. If the offer of services was met with refusal, the practitioner risked injury to these interests.

A municipal or court physician would also be at risk for the capricious exercise of political power, far more consequential than the loss of a sale. Hoffmann's insight was that prudential the self-interests of the rational entrepreneur in making sales and maintaining and growing market share provided perilously inadequate guidance. The concept of enlightened self-interest, by contrast, promised more reliable moral guidance.

Enlightened self-interest takes into account the interests of those who have power over one. It is "politic" to do so. When interests of the customer and the practitioner overlap in matters of health, they become enlightened self-interest. Aligning one's self-interests with the interests of those with power over one results in an expanded concept prudence as enlightened self-interest. The physician's protection of the sick individual's health-related interests, however, is not a matter of obligation.

For example, the principalities of the time derived their authority from Christianity and its doctrine of the divine right to rule. Hoffmann therefore begins his *Medicus Politicus* with the injunction that the "physician should be a Christian" (*Medicus sit Christianus*) (Hoffmann 1749, Regulae I). The verb "to be" (*sum, esse*) here is in the hortatory subjunctive mood, indicating encouragement. That is, the politic physician should publicly embrace the religion of the royal court, out of prudent self-interest, not as a matter of obligation. Privately, the physician may believe otherwise. This was the strategy of the Marranos in medieval Spain, Jews who publicly converted to Christianity and submitted publicly to Christian morality and law but kept their Jewish faith alive in the privacy of their homes. The Marrano Jews were politic by wedding self-interest to the interests of the Roman Catholic Church.

Hoffmann prescribes a set of rules, designed with the goal of surviving court power in mind. For example, the physician should comport himself as a man worthy of a good reputation:

> Based on the virtues from moral philosophy, the physician ought to accomplish his work with diligence. And so he should be merciful, mild, and humane. Just as from the plague, he should flee from a dissolute life, evil words, drunkenness, and all illicit games and everything else that would lose the trust of the sick (Hoffmann 1749, First Part, Rule I).

De Castro would agree but Hoffmann has changed the discourse of virtues into the discourse of enlightened self-interest. For de Castro "military or economic" prudence concerns the reality that the actions of others can directly impact one's legitimate and other self-interests. For Hoffmann, enlightened self-interest means that the *concepts* of prudence, diligence, humility, discretion, and taciturnity (the word 'taciturn' was used to mean that the physician should keep quiet, i.e., not divulge information, especially secrets, of the sick to anyone else) include in their scope the alignment of the physician's self-interest with the overlapping interests of the sick.

Consider Hoffmann on obstetrics: "Chapter 3 of this part: On the duties of the physician in obstetrics and the care of women" (Hoffmann 1749, Second Part, Chapter 3): "The midwife above all should be pious, chaste, sober, not timid, taciturn, and experienced" (Hoffmann 1749, Second Part, Chapter 3, Rule 1.) He then takes up gynecologic ethics: "On the prudence of the physician regarding sick women" (Hoffmann 1749, Second Part, Chapter 5):

> The physician should be chaste. The physician should be chaste in word and deed, when he is obliged to visit sick women; for this ought not to be the occasion for exciting the lust of the physician, especially concerning unchaste women, unless he wishes to violate the laws of conscience (Hoffmann 1749, Second Part, Chapter 5, Rule 1).

In this treatment of the physician's role in the care of the gravely ill sick, Hoffmann starts with prudential self-regard *simpliciter* and then transitions to enlightened prudence.

> Before all things, the physician ought to defend himself from the contagion of the malignantly ill (Hoffmann 1749, Second Part, Chapter 9, Rule 1).
> Not wisely does the physician persist over time in assisting the sick when their death is near (Hoffmann 1749, Second Part, Chapter 9, Rule 2).
> In cases of malignant disease, the physician should use heroic medications always most cautiously (Hoffmann 1749, Second Part, Chapter 9, Rule 4).
> The physician should form wary prognoses in cases of malignant and acute disease. Hippocrates said it best. Uncertain are all predictions concerning the hope for health in acute illness. The physician therefore should speak circumspectly and neither prostitute himself nor discern immediately and absolutely that death is inevitable. He should not be evasive but always restrictively and with conditions admit danger could be near ... Meditation on death [by the gravely ill] should not be neglected. Indeed, on the basis of Christian hope it is required for the health of the sick person that he should be prepared for dying (Hoffmann 1749, Second Part, Chapter 9, Rule 5).

Notice that Hoffmann does *not* endorse keeping their clinical reality from gravely ill sick individuals. "Restrictively and with conditions" means that the physician should prevent unnecessarily adding to the psychological response of the sick individual to learning that he or she is dying. In other words, prudence as enlightened self-interest creates an ethical obligation to be forthcoming and, simultaneously, to attend to the manner and timing of conveying distressing information, at a time when early death from infectious diseases, cancers, other disorders, and injuries and death in childbirth were far more common than they are now. In addition, the physician should support the spiritual preparation of the sick person for his or her death, an implication of the injunction that the physician should be a Christian, with which *Medicus Politicus* began. In this context, this injunction means that the physician should ally himself with the spiritual needs of the sick individual. By implication, the physician should ally himself with the cleric chosen by the family to minister to the sick individual's spiritual needs.

Hoffmann's account of prudence, based on enlightened self-interest, has contemporary relevance. Prudence as enlightened self-interest becomes the basis for the concept of the physician's legitimate self-interests: self-interest aligned with the health-related interests of patients as understood in deliberative (evidence-based, rigorous, transparent, and accountable) clinical ethical judgment (McCullough et al. 2020). The legitimate self-interests of a physician align with the health-related interests of the sick individual. For example, Hoffmann enjoins physicians to be "chaste" when treating female patients (Hoffmann 1749, Second Part, Chapter 5, Rule 1). Chastity is a virtue that blunts sexual attraction. The result is to protect the female patient from sexual predation and, at the same time, the reputation of the physician as trustworthy by the female patient and – crucially – her husband – or father, or brothers. Improving one's fund of knowledge and clinical skills benefits patients clinically, making the time and expense of doing so a legitimate self-interest of every physician. Aligning oneself with the interests of insurance companies in providing evidence-based clinical management of one's patients protects and promotes the health of one's patients and also protects the business model of one's clinical practice.

Both de Castro and Hoffmann use the Latin '*aegrotus*' or 'the sick'. For medical ethics based on "military prudence" or prudence the scope of which includes the interests of others in the logic of enlightened self-interest, the relationship remains entrepreneurial but with a significant change: the physician needs to be cautious, an echo of the Zerbi and the *de cautelis* literature. The physician must be cautious that the far greater power of the prince or magistrate could turn predatory and dangerous without warning. Neither the discourse of *de cautelis* nor the discourse of *medicus politicus* can support the concept of being a patient – being presented to a physician and there exist forms of clinical management that in deliberative clinical judgment are predicted to result in net clinical benefit (See Chap. 3). A patient is under the protection of the professional physician. The sick individual is under the protection of the prince or magistrate; the prudent physician is under no one's protection. Failure to appreciate this social and political reality and to take appropriate measures to protect oneself would be reckless disregard which both de Castro's and Hoffmann's concepts of the virtue of prudence prohibit.

1.4 Anomalies for the Paradigm of Entrepreneurial Medical Practice: Unaccountable Power and Distrust

There was no Hippocratic tradition of medical paternalism, the *bête noir* of bioethics, and no Hippocratic tradition of professional ethics in medicine assumed by the Physician Charter the AMA Principles of Medical Ethics. There was the paradigm of entrepreneurialism, the lens through which (Baker 2019) physicians viewed their relationships with the sick and with those who paid their fees or salaries. This paradigm was first expressed in the Hippocratic texts and then displayed variation: the guild entrepreneurialism of the Royal Colleges; the cautious entrepreneurialism of the *de cautelis* literature; and the politic entrepreneurialism of the *medicus politicus* literature. The original of the entrepreneurial paradigm and its three variants responded to the perils for the individual entrepreneur of an unforgiving market; the medical and surgical guilds attempting to create monopoly control to cope with an unforgiving market; the prudential, cautious modifications of entrepreneurial practice designed to enhance marketability; and the prudence-as-enlightened self-interest modifications of entrepreneurial practice to cope with unequal and unaccountable power.

Hoffmann's politic physician addressed circumstances in which the sick individual and government payers had power over the physician. Gregory's invention of professional ethics in medicine responded to a different problem: the unaccountable power that physicians came to have over the sick with the invention of the Royal Infirmaries in Great Britain, which still bear this name proudly, and that served as the forerunners of voluntary, not-for-profit hospitals in the English colonies of North America and then the United States. For example, the first American hospital, Pennsylvania Hospital in Philadelphia, was chartered in 1751 by the colonial Legislature and the New York Hospital in New York City was chartered in 1771 by King George III. They continue to care for patients to this day. Physicians also had limited, but consequential, power over their private patients when it came to maintaining confidentiality, especially the consequences of not doing so for female patients and indeed the sexual abuse of women by practitioners, about which Gregory was very concerned.

> A physician, by the nature of his profession, has many opportunities of knowing the private characters and concerns of the families in which he is employed. Besides what he may learn from his own observation, he is often admitted to the confidence of those, who perhaps think they owe their life to his care. He sees people in the most disadvantageous circumstances, very different from those in which the world views them;- oppressed with pain, sickness, and low spirits. In these humiliating situations, instead of wonted chearfulness, evenness of temper, and vigour of mind, he meets with peevishness, impatience, and timidity. Hence appears how much the characters of individuals, and the credit of families, may sometimes depend on the discretion, secrecy, and honour of a physician. Secrecy is particularly requisite where women are concerned. Independent of the peculiar tenderness with which a woman's character should be treated, there are certain circumstances of health, which, though in no respect connected with her reputation, every woman, from the natural delicacy of her sex, is anxious to conceal; and, in some cases, the concealment of these circumstances may be of consequence to her health, her interest, and to her happiness (1772, Gregory [1772] 1998, 26–27).

The "credit of families" refers to the landed aristocracy borrowing against their crops or livestock, loans that could be called in without notice if there was suspicion the debtor was ill. The last sentence is an oblique reference to the practice of some man-midwives or forerunners of modern obstetricians, who had assisted at the infanticide of an unwanted child, especially a bastard child, using forceps. If, later, this physician was threatened with dismissal from service to the household, he might threaten blackmail (McCullough 1998). The discovery of a bastard child would have had severe personal, social, and financial consequences for the woman. This adds new meaning to the watchword of the sick in entrepreneurial medicine, *caveat emptor*. Finally, as Dorothy and Roy Porter (1989) have persuasively documented, in Britain distrust, by the sick who could afford to pay and those who could not, of practitioners of all kinds was common. They were not trusted to know what they were doing. They were not trusted to put the health-related and pecuniary interests of the sick first but rather practitioners' self-interest in income, market share, and reputation.

The entrepreneurial model or moral paradigm, to use Baker's phrase (2019), of medical practice was inadequate to the ethical challenges created by the power over the sick that the hierarchical structure of the Royal Infirmaries created, the abuse of the sick by practitioners, and endemic distrust. The entrepreneurial paradigm was also inadequate to distrust in private practice. This paradigm's tool was pursuit of self-interest, more of which would only exacerbate the imbalance of power and distrust.

When an accepted, longstanding moral paradigm – entrepreneurial, marketplace medicine (and surgery and midwifery) – is not adequate to a challenge, that challenge becomes an anomaly for that paradigm. Baker shows that when this is the case, moral revolutions – the replacement of an existing, inadequate paradigm, with another, adequate paradigm – become possible.

The anomaly of systemic distrust for entrepreneurial medicine had become acute in late eighteenth-century Britain. Power over the sick in the Infirmaries was being abused and had no effective checks. For example, ambitious young physicians who declared patients incurable – not to abandon them, as the norm inherited from the Hippocratic corpus and Hoffmann endorsed, but to perform experiments on them. Public concern about this practice is evidenced in the popular, reviled character of "Dr. MacFloggem" of the Royal Infirmary in stage plays (McCullough 1998). Power over the sick in the private setting was being abused, including abuse of confidentiality and sexual abuse of women, and had no effective checks at a time when anonymous reporting had not yet been invented.

There was also no effective remedy in the entrepreneurial paradigm for distrust. Practitioners responded to distrust by attempting to deflect it onto other practitioners. This was undertaken in the common practice of "flyting," printing and distributing handbills that attacked one's competitors, who, of course, were free to respond in kind (Baker 1993a, 2013). To morally protect the sick and practitioners alike and make medicine worth practicing, a moral revolution was necessary to address these anomalies in entrepreneurial medicine.

1.5 John Gregory's Revolutionary Invention of Professional Ethics in Medicine

Through the lens Baker has provided historians of medical ethics, Gregory can be read as having undertaken a moral revolution, a concept explained at the beginning of this chapter (Baker 2019), against entrepreneurial medicine practiced by men of "interest" and the guilds with their "corporation spirit," a reference to the Royal Colleges. As the basis of professional ethics in medicine, Gregory invented the ethical concept of medicine as a profession. This concept ethically requires three commitments of physicians, in order both to be and to be considered professionals: to becoming and remaining scientifically and clinically competent; to protecting and promoting the health-related interests of each patient as the physician's primary concern and motivation, keeping *individual* self-interest systematically secondary; and to protecting and promoting the health-related interests of each patient as the physician's primary concern and motivation, keeping (Hippocratic association) *group* or (Royal Colleges) *guild* self-interest systematically secondary (McCullough 1998, 2006). (We will see in Chaps. 2 and 3 that Percival adds the concept of "party-interest.") In professional ethics in medicine, the sick individual becomes a patient, a human being presented to a professional physician and there exist forms of clinical management that in Baconian clinical judgment are reliably predicted to result in net clinical benefit. The entrepreneurial the sick-practitioner relationship has been replaced by the physician-patient relationship.

Gregory invented the ethical concept of medicine by invoking Bacon's revolutionary, "experience"-based philosophy of medicine as the basis for the first commitment and its professional virtue of candor. Gregory then invoked David Hume's (1711–1776) account of the principle (a causal process of neurophysiology and therefore of moral physiology) of sympathy from his revolutionary Baconian science of man or moral science as the basis of the second and third commitments and their professional virtues of tenderness and steadiness.

1.5.1 Gregory's Invention of the First Commitment of the Ethical Concept of Medicine as a Profession

1.5.1.1 Biographical Sketch

Gregory was born in Aberdeen, Scotland, June 3, 1724, into a family of distinguished academics (Stewart 1901; McCullough 1998). His grandmother, Janet Gregorie, was an accomplished mathematician, despite not having had the opportunity for a formal education, which was then not available to women. Her son, James Gregory (1638–1675), invented a type of reflecting telescope. Gregory's father, James Gregorie (1674–1733), became a physician, the first in a line of Gregory physicians that include John, his brother James (d. 1755), and his son James (1753–1821). Gregory was a student at the Aberdeen Grammar School and then matriculated at King's College, now a constituent college of the University of Aberdeen. In 1742 Gregory removed himself to Edinburgh to start his medical studies at the University of Edinburgh.

At the University of Leiden Herman Boerhaave (1668–1738) had invented and taught the modern science of human physiology. This helped to mark a major transition in medicine from the static model of anatomy to a dynamic model of organs and organ system functions. "Boerhaave's men," as they were known, populated the faculty at Edinburgh, included Alexander Monro, *primus* (1697–1767) and John

Rutherford (1695–1779). Rutherford was one of the first medical educators to take students onto hospital wards, at the Royal Infirmary of Edinburgh. In 1745, following a pathway common at the time, Gregory attended medical lectures at the University Leiden, where, less than a decade after his death, Boerhaave's influence remained very strong. King's College in Aberdeen, where his brother was the "mediciner" and that had no students, granted Gregory an unearned M.D. March 11, 1746. That June, Gregory returned to King's as the elected Professor of Philosophy. In 1752 he married Elisabeth Forbes, to whom he was deeply devoted. She died in childbirth nine years later.

In 1754 Gregory, unable to enter medical practice in the then-small-town of Aberdeen because of the presence of his physician-brother, James, moved his family to London. He was made a Fellow of the Royal Society in that same year. He was a regular attendee at the intellectual salons hosted by the wealthy widow, Elizabeth Montagu (1718–1800), known as the Queen of the Bluestocking Circle (Meyers 1990). At social gatherings in Mrs. Montagu's home in Portman Square, Gregory met and engaged in serious conversation with the male literati of the day, such as Samuel Johnson (1709–1784) the lexicographer. More important he also met with women intellectuals and writers such as Hester Chapone (1727–1801). His wife, Mrs. Montagu, the writer Hester Chapone (1727–1801), and other women of the Bluestocking Circle became his examples of women of "learning and virtue" and the basis for Gregory's feminine professional ethics in medicine (about which, more below).

When his brother James died in 1755, the opportunity to return to King's in Aberdeen as Professor of Physic was offered to Gregory the next year and he accepted. There still being no medical students, this academic position would today be described as a research professorship, of which Gregory took full advantage. One way he did so was to co-found, with his cousin Thomas Reid (1710–1796), the Aberdeen Philosophical Society (Carter and Pittock 1987).

In Edinburgh and Leiden Gregory had become steeped in and fully committed to the scientific method and philosophy of medicine of Francis Bacon (1561–1626) (Bacon 1875a, b, c, d, e). His formation as a Baconian scientist and physician continued in the sessions of the Aberdeen Philosophical Society, at which members presented their scientific works in progress. The Society also read and debated *A Treatise of Human Nature* by David Hume. Appearing in 1739 the *Treatise* announced itself on its title page to be "an attempt to introduce the experimental method of reasoning into moral subjects" (Hume [1739–1740] 2000). The "experimental method" was Bacon's and Hume deployed it in what his contemporaries, Gregory included (and Percival, as we shall see in Chaps. 2 and 3), knew variously as the "science or man," "science of morals," and "moral science."

1.5.1.2 Intellectual Authority in Bacon's Philosophy of Science and Medicine

Bacon was a scientific revolutionary. He set out self-consciously to reform science by setting his face against unquestioning acceptance of authorities. This acceptance can become unyielding when one becomes unwilling to reconsider the views of authorities when confronted with observation and experiment incompatible with the authoritative views. In Kuhnian terms, dogmatists could not see these anomalies, so powerful was the paradigm or way of seeing the natural world that the authorities had created. Dogmatism in metaphysics took the form of the products of Reason detached from observation and experiment. The Cartesian method of stripping thought of experience and turning to *a priori* inspection of ideas to identify which were clear and distinct and thus the source of the truth (Descartes [1641] 2017) epitomizes Reason doing its exquisite (and very beautiful) work. This was not a rejection of all of metaphysics, just that based on Reason alone, which Bacon dismissed as "speculative" metaphysics. Bacon also attacked the abstract classification systems of disease as merely *nominal*, i.e., a compendium of classifications that named, not disease entities, but concepts untethered from the natural world.

Bacon's antidote was to insist that science, and therefore medicine, should be based on what he called "experience." By this he emphatically did *not* mean personal experience, what Bacon called "simple experience" (Bacon 1875b, 81). By 'experience' Bacon did mean what he called "observation" and "experiment." Observation was the examination, analysis, and reporting of processes in nature, e.g., the course of a disease. Observation required that the observer rid himself or herself of various "idols" that can distort examination, analysis, and reporting of naturally occurring processes. Experiments were what we know as controlled experiments. For example, a compound medication could be reduced to its separate elements and each tested singly for its effects. If the observed effects of one or more of the elements are those claimed for the compound, physicians should cease administration of the compound and alter practice by simplifying it. If none of the elements have the effects claimed for the compound, then combinations of elements should be tried in experiments. The reliability of medications – and other forms of clinical management such as surgery – is no longer a function of the authority who created and uses them but becomes a function of experience-based investigation. This, of course, is a nascent form of evidence-based medicine and its tools of critical appraisal of the literature (Guyatt et al. 2000). Bacon would remind us that, for all the progress in medical science of the past four centuries, modern medicine remains at risk for dogmatism for which evidence-based reasoning – Bacon's experience-based reasoning – is the antidote.

Dogmatism commits the physician to the quest for certainty. Baconian scientific method commits the scientist to the quest for reliability. Baconian method rejects gathering a "few examples" and then proceeding immediately to "the most general conclusions" (Bacon 1875b, 111). Instead, the scientist proceeds diligently, carefully recording observations that constitute a "natural and experimental history" (Bacon 1875b, 127). This history comprises a complete sequence of observations, "as if every particular were stated upon oath" (Bacon 1875e, 261). Interpretation proceeds by induction to hypothesis formation, invented concepts positing patterns in the sequence of observations. "Principles" or real, constitutive causal processes in things are then posited to explain the origin of the carefully observed and reported patterns. This hypothesis is then explored in subsequent observations (e.g., the natural history of a disease posited as the cause of the pattern of signs and symptoms) or in an experiment (e.g., testing the elements of a compound medication, as described above).

The constancy of the observed patterns can vary, as every observational scientist knows all too well and as every physician who misses the atypical presentation of a disease or injury has learned to his or her regret. The results of investigation establish "progressive stages of certainty" (Bacon 1875b, 40). The reader of Bacon's texts must exercise considerable caution to avoid essentialism in the interpretation of 'certainty'. Bacon did not mean by 'certainty' the deliverances of Reason, the denial of which commits one to contradiction. Bacon did mean to deploy a scale of reliability.

The highest level on this scale is what Bacon calls "certainly true" (Bacon 1875e, 260), i.e., no contravening evidence has been reported in multiple observations or experiments. Evolution enjoys this status in contemporary biology The use of 'certainly true' signals to the scientist that a hypothesis is so well established that it can serve with very high confidence as the basis for future investigation. Bacon would, in my reading of his texts, accept the traditional "p value" of 0.5 to establish such confidence in a well-tested hypothesis. The next step on the scale is "doubtful whether true or not" and finally "certainly not true" (Bacon 1875e, 260).

Baconian science is therefore a quest for reliability in its various degrees and not certainty. Baconian metaphysics is also a quest for reliability, leading Baconians such as Hume and Gregory to reject a metaphysics of necessary first principles, such as Descartes' "Cogito, sum," an immediate intuition of Reason as a non-mediated, direct taking up of reality by Reason that must be true. In *Meditations on First Philosophy* Descartes is on the quest for certainty, the outcome of which will be the indubitable foundations of true metaphysics (Descartes [1641] 2017). Kant, too, was on the quest for certainty, in the form of the *a priori* structures of Pure Reason (Reason unadulterated by Baconian observation) and their deliverances in the form of synthetic *a priori* propositions (Kant [1781] 1998). For Baconian metaphysics the quest for *a priori* certainty, what the Baconians (including Hume) called "speculative" metaphysics, is doomed to failure.

Boerhaave's influence on Gregory was profound, even though Boerhaave had died before Gregory studied at Edinburgh and Leiden. Boerhaave's students were fully committed to Baconian physiology. Boerhaave rejected "wholly conjectural" physic, or medicine (Boerhaave 1751a, 48). Wholly conjectural anatomy and physiology, especially the latter, is a "false" view (Boerhaave 1751a, 48). To be sure, Boerhaave held to a mechanistic view of the human body, i.e., the view that impersonal principles explained organ function.

To summarize, Baconian science and scientific medicine embraced seven tenets. First, the Baconian scientist brings a critical attitude toward all propositions of fact.

1.5 John Gregory's Revolutionary Invention of Professional Ethics in Medicine

In particular, unquestioned acceptance of the claims of authorities is impermissible. Authorities included the august Hippocrates or Galen, as well as one's teachers and colleagues. Second, all hypothesis offered to provide causal explanations of carefully observed and reported patterns must be tested against Baconian "experience," as explained above. Third, Baconian method is open to the use of anyone willing to submit to its intellectual discipline. Science is therefore public and transcultural and transnational. It is also secular: no appeal to sources of religious explanation of disease and its management is required. Science is thus transreligious. Fourth, failure to follow rigorous Baconian method ought to result in disrepute owing to a failure of intellectual integrity. We are now at a very far remove from the concept of reputation that shaped the Hippocratic *Oath*. Fifth, Baconian science and therefore scientific medicine is realist: the principles hypothesized to cause observed patterns of organ function in the science of physiology are understood to be real, constitutive, functional components of the physiology of the human body. Sixth, impersonal principles also shaped brain physiology. The physiology of mind became a legitimate area for scientific investigation, paving the way for the invention of psychology by the likes of Hume and of psychiatry by Gregory's teacher at Edinburgh, Robert Whytt (1714–1766). Finally, prominent Baconian scientists held that science was compatible with deism, the view that there is a creator God that is the source of the order observed in nature using Baconian observational method. This is *not* the claim that theism, views of God or gods and their relationship to human beings and to nature based on revelation, sacred texts, and other divine sources, is compatible with science.

Norman Gevitz succinctly describes the intellectual world of Baconian science:

> … there was a growing effort to eschew theory arrived at by deduction [reason unaided and therefore uncorrectable by Baconian experience], and instead to ground medicine upon the direct observation and measurement of phenomena, to conduct experiments and to correlate facts (Gevitz 1991, 605).

Baconian science and medicine form the antidote to bias, what Bacon called "idols" of various sorts. Some biased beliefs derived from deduction, the worthless creatures of Reason and its gossamer systems. Other biased beliefs derived from enthusiasm, beliefs about the world that lacked an evidence base. These were untested hypotheses and therefore at unknown, but assumed high, risk of being false. Experience-based beliefs, tested hypotheses, came in varying degrees of probability and, therefore, reliability. Experienced-based beliefs had intellectual authority: their adherent could reliably claim to know what he or she was talking about and doing. The strength of the claim to intellectual authority was a direct function of the place of the belief among the "progressive stages of certainty."

1.5.1.3 Intellectual Authority in Gregory's Philosophy of Medicine

Bacon's philosophy of science and medicine had been eagerly embraced by scientists and physicians at the medical school of the University of Edinburg. Gregory did the same, as is evidenced in a manuscript from his student days, "Proposall for a Medicall Society, Written in 1743" (AUL 2206/45 1743). Gregory notes progress in the sciences resulting from adoption of Bacon's scientific medicine but is impatient with the incomplete results: "The whole plan laid down by L[ord] Bacon for prosecuting enquirys into nature has been applied in some measure to many branches of natural philosophy [the old phrase to name the natural sciences], tho not with that accuracy and fidelity proposed by its great Author" (AUL 2206/45 1743, 1) Observational and experimental science should be undertaken and the results reported on the scale of "certainty" or probability that Bacon prescribed.

Medicine should be directed to "The Four Capitall Enquirys" or goals: "1. The Preservation of Health. 2. The Retardation of Old Age. 3. The Cure of Diseases. 4. The Improvement of our Nature" (AUL 2206/45 1743, 6). Here Gregory has adapted Bacon's "three offices" of medicine: "the first whereof is the Preservation of Health, the second the Cure of Diseases, and the third the Prolongation of Life" (Bacon 1875b, 383). Preservation of health means what we now know as preventive medicine and had a wide scope, e.g., improving agriculture to prevent and ameliorate the periodic famines that Scots endured. 'Cure' meant any improvement in the signs and symptoms of disease, not the elimination of pathology. Gregory and his contemporaries were committed to the Baconian view that there were real, constitutive, causal, physiological processes of disease but they were all too aware that the then-current state of clinical science did not permit their direct detection. However, the relief of the burden of disease on individuals could be improved by using Baconian methods (AUL 2206/45 1743, 2–3). The prolongation of life, for Bacon, or the retardation of old age for Gregory, meant reducing mortality (which approached 60% for people in the teens and twenties in Scotland at the time) so that more people could live into their old age. 'Prolongation of life' also meant improving medical care for the infirmities of advanced age, a nascent form of the specialty we now know as geriatrics. The improvement of nature meant the improvement of basic bodily functions. Gregory adhered to the view that the Creator god of deism had suited us to Nature, a condition that could be improved. Improvement of all aspects of life became a defining feature, perhaps *the* defining feature, of both the Scottish and English Enlightenments (Porter 2000). Plainly, improvement had this status for Gregory. As we shall see in Chaps. 2 and 3 the same was true for Percival.

I want to emphasize that these "offices," or role-related ethical obligations, were not absolute for either Bacon or Gregory. Taken nonetheless to be absolute these offices become a guide to controlling nature, e.g., defeating death. There is no textual evidence that either was committed to what has come to be known as the "Baconian project" or attempts to alter Nature without limit (Jonas 1966). To think otherwise is to engage in presentism (Pernick 2009), reading into history a concern that many bioethicists had in the early decades (1970s and 1980s) of the field: physicians thought that they had the professional responsibility to prolong life at all costs.

1.5 John Gregory's Revolutionary Invention of Professional Ethics in Medicine

This is also a misreading of the history of critical care, the goal of which has been from its origins in the 1950s progressive reduction of the risk of mortality and, since the 1980s, survival with at least some interactive capacity (McCullough, Coverdale, Chervenak 2020).

Gregory opens his *Lectures on the Duties and Qualifications of a Physician* with three of his four "Capitall Enquirys;"

> The design of the professorship which I have the honour to hold in this university, is to explain the *practice of medicine*, by which I understand, the art of preserving health, of prolonging life, and of curing diseases. This is an art of great extent and importance; and for this all your former medical studies were intended to qualify you (Gregory 1772, [1772] 1998, 1).

"The Retardation of Old Age" has become "prolonging life." His debt to Bacon is plain from the first words of this first text on professional ethics in medicine in the history of medical ethics. It bears repetition to state that the text does not state that three components of clinical practice are absolute or unlimited. There is therefore no textual evidence that Gregory committed himself to the Baconian project, which should be renamed the "Baconian project imaginary" and dismissed as a textually ungrounded critique of Bacon on the offices of medicine and of those who, like Gregory, adopted Bacon's account. Instead, Gregory was committed to Bacon's conception of science and medicine directed to the "relief of man's estate" (Daiches 1986, 5), as a necessary first step toward improvement. The practice and improvement of medicine sought moderate and steady reduction of the then-high mortality rates and the burdens of disease and injury. Gregory set his face against enthusiasm, clinical beliefs and practice without an experience or evidence base that fostered the false belief that there was no limit to what medicine could do to improve the human condition. Respect for the limits of medicine required that physicians always attend to the "cautions" of medical progress (Gregory 2206/45 1743), an echo of the *de cautelis* literature.

Bacon is cited by name twelve times in *Lectures*. In one, Gregory cites *De Augmentis Scientiarum* (Bacon 1875c) and unequivocally endorses Bacon's scientific method and philosophy of medicine:

> The impatience of men to reduce all knowledge, and to refer all events to certain general laws, makes them unwilling to submit to a slow, but sure, method of investigation. They attempt a shorter way of discovering those laws, in which they are misled, either by a false reasoning from imaginary analogies, or by supposing the laws of Nature to be fewer and simpler than they really are. The consequences of which are, the hasty reduction of the sciences into imperfect and erroneous systems (Gregory 1772, [1772] 1998, 120–121).

The fifth of the six lectures provides a detailed account of the accomplishments and advantages of Bacon and Baconian experiential observational and experimental method. This lecture concludes:

> Let me take this opportunity of recommending to your serious study the writings of Lord Bacon, who of all men possessed, perhaps, the most enlarged and penetrating genius. He has explained the method of acquiring knowledge, and promoting science, with incomparable judgment and perspicuity. He has likewise left us some beautiful specimens of true philosophical induction, particularly in his History of the Winds. This, and some other of

his essays in natural history, are to be considered in no other light, than as specimens of his method of carrying on enquiries into nature (Gregory 1772, [1772] 1998, 193).

There is therefore abundant textual evidence, from his writings as a medical student through to the publication of *Lectures* in what turned out to be the penultimate year of Gregory's short life, that he embraced the view that a professional physician earns that moniker by committing to becoming and remaining scientifically and clinically competent in the Baconian meaning of such competence.

Gregory adds to Baconian method and philosophy of medicine two new ideas. The first new idea is the professional virtue of candor.

> I may reckon among the moral duties incumbent on a physician, that candor, which makes him open to conviction, and ready to acknowledge and rectify his mistakes. An obstinate adherence to an unsuccessful method of treating a disease, must be owing to a high degree of self-conceit, and a belief of the infallibility of a system. This error is the more difficult to cure, as it generally proceeds from ignorance. True knowledge and clear discernment may lead one into the extreme of diffidence and humility; but are inconsistent with self-conceit. It sometimes happens too, that this obstinacy proceeds from a defect in the heart. Such physicians see that they are wrong; but are too proud to acknowledge their error, especially if it be pointed out to them by one of the profession. To this species of pride, a pride incompatible with true dignity and elevation of mind, have the lives of thousands been sacrificed (Gregory 1772, [1772] 1998, 28–29).

To be "open to conviction" means that the Baconian physician is open to new hypotheses and, when they are supported, to changing his thinking without resistance. The force of the intellectual virtue of candor – what we now know as the intellectual virtue of integrity – is a function of the probability of an experienced-tested hypothesis. Candor promotes humility, the ready willingness to acknowledge the limits, including errors, of clinical judgment and practice. Candor also promotes diffidence, the habit of stepping back from one's beliefs and practices, especially one's most cherished beliefs and practices, so that critical self-appraisal becomes possible and critical appraisal by others is not taken personally and thus disabled at the outset by powerful, unacknowledged and therefore unmitigated bias. Candor promotes the "true dignity" of accountability and the commitment to improve one's fund of knowledge and skillset. Gregory uses some his strongest language in *Lectures* to describe attitudes antithetical to candor, i.e., the vices of non-scientific physicians: 'ignorance', 'obstinate adherence', 'ignorance', 'defect of the heart', and 'pride'. Put into clinical practice, these vices kill patients. Gregory's contemporaries would have regarded such words as "warm," by which they meant the discourse of righteous anger.

Gregory applies the professional virtue of candor to how the physician should respond if a patient, or another close to the patient, should suggest a course of treatment. In response to illness, the sick first self-diagnosed and self-treated, which was known as "self-physicking." Guides to self-physicking for the layperson became popular, for example, William Buchan's *Domestic Medicine* (Buchan 1769). Physicians knew well the practice of self-physicking.

The sick often did not believe that medical practitioners knew what they were doing and distrusted physicians, surgeons, and other practitioners (Porter and Porter

1.5 John Gregory's Revolutionary Invention of Professional Ethics in Medicine

1989). There were almost as many theories of disease and remedies as there were physicians. Physicians offered "nostrums" to their patients, compound medications the contents of which practitioners who made and sold these remedies kept secret and which practitioners did not produce under conditions of quality control. These nostrums often contained opium, which induced euphoria and increased sales. In addition to this intellectual distrust, the sick experienced moral distrust. The sick could not be confident that the recommendations of medical practitioners were motivated more by their self-interest in income and reputation than by a sustained commitment to the well-being of the sick. Hoffmann's concept of prudence as enlightened self-interest, it would appear, did not take hold in Britain. Gregory goes beyond enlightened self-interest to offer a candor-based approach to self-physicking.

> I have already taken notice of the principal duties a physician owes to his patients, of the propriety of his attending to their tempers and constitutions, and allowing them every indulgence consistent with their safety. Sometimes a patient himself, sometimes one of his friends, will propose to the physician a remedy, which, they believe, may do him service. Their proposal may be a good one; it may even suggest to the ablest physician, what, perhaps, till then, might not have occurred to him. It is undoubtedly, therefore, his duty to adopt it. Yet there are some of the faculty, who, from a pretended regard to the dignity of the profession, but in reality from mean and selfish views, refuse to apply any remedy proposed in this manner, without regard to its merit. But this behaviour can never be vindicated. Every man has a right to speak where his life or his health is concerned, and every man may suggest what he thinks may tend to save the life of his friend. It becomes them to interpose with politeness, and a deference to the judgment of the physician; it becomes him to hear what they have to say with attention, and to examine it with candour; If he really approves, he should frankly own it, and act accordingly; if he disapproves, he should declare his disapprobation in such a manner, as shews it proceeds from conviction, and not from pique or obstinacy. If a patient is determined to try an improper or dangerous medicine, a physician should refuse his sanction, but he has no right to complain of his advice not being followed (Gregory 1772, [1772] 1998, 32–34).

Candor requires the professional physician to be open to information from wherever it arises. Patients and their friends, who are self-physicking, are no exception. In a candor-based assessment the patient receives what we would now call a critical appraisal of his or her proposal: respectfully subjecting the proposal to analysis in evidence-based, beneficence-based clinical judgment and then explaining in a non-judgmental way that judgment and its justification. The physician should be rigorous in this process, role-modeling intellectual rigor for the patient. The physician makes his or her clinical judgment accountable to the patient and, in the process of doing so, invites the patient to become accountable to the physician. Gregory thus invents the deliberative model of the physician-patient relationship more than two centuries before Ezekiel and Linda Emanuel described it (Emanuel and Emanuel 1992).

This text is also important because it is perhaps the earliest use of the discourse of rights. The reader should resist essentialism and attribute the origins of this usage to the ethical principle of respect for autonomy. There are no textual traces of this ethical principle in *Lectures* of any other of Gregory's writings. It appears to be a right the recognition of which is essential for the professional virtue of candor to function in and thus regulate the physician-patient relationship. This makes plausible the reading that Gregory's introduction of the discourse of rights is candor-based.

The second new idea Gregory added to Baconian method and philosophy of medicine he called "laying medicine open." Gregory's call for laying medicine open replicates the professional virtue of candor this process at the societal level. Evidence-based and rigorous science of medicine should become accountable and transparent to sophisticated lay persons. Gregory thus anticipates by more than two centuries the contemporary concept of patient safety and quality, a crucial component of which is physicians and other healthcare professions becoming accountable to sophisticated laypersons – epidemiologists, philosopher-ethicists, cost analysts, and organizational leaders.

Gregory defends laying medicine open as he ends *Lectures*.

> I have thus endeavoured to shew that, by laying medicine open, and encouraging men of science and abilities, who do not belong to the profession, to study it, the interests of humanity would be promoted, the science would be advanced, its dignity more effectually supported, and success more certainly secured to every individual, in proportion to his real merit (Gregory 1772, [1772] 1998, 236).

The combination of candor and laying medicine results in another concept, deliberative clinical judgment. Deliberative clinical judgment is Baconian in that it is experience-based (evidence-based), insistent on following the discipline of scientific reasoning, especially to rooting out of biases (rigorous), explained to patients (transparent), and open to critical appraisal by sophisticated laypersons (accountable). 'Deliberative clinical judgment' means clinical judgment that is evidence-based, rigorous, transparent, and accountable (McCullough et al. 2020).

The intellectual authority of Baconian, deliberative clinical judgment originates in candor and laying medicine open. Gregory uses 'authority' nineteen times in *Lectures*. Most occurrences refer to authorities, accepted leaders in medicine, including historical figures. In the absence of critical appraisal based on candor and laying medicine open authorities have no intellectual authority. The burden of creating and acting on intellectual authority becomes a key component of clinical practice.

> There we have no established authority to which we can refer in doubtful cases. Every physician must rest on his own judgment, which appeals for its rectitude to nature and experience alone. Among the infinite variety of facts and theories with which his memory has been filled in the course of a liberal education, it is his business to make a judicious separation between those founded in nature and experience, and those which owe their birth to ignorance, fraud, or the capricious systems of a heated and deluded imagination. He will likewise find it necessary to distinguish between important facts, and such as, though they may be founded in truth, are notwithstanding trivial, or utterly useless to the main ends of his profession. Supposing all these difficulties surmounted, he will find it no easy matter to apply his knowledge to practice (Gregory 1772, [1772] 1998, 14–15).

Gregory uses the word 'profession' one hundred times in *Lectures*. Physicians in his day had been using 'professional' to mean that they had attended medical school. This was, on its face, a dubious claim inasmuch as there was no standard curriculum, medical students could take a few courses and call themselves physicians, and impecunious medical schools sold unearned M.D. degrees. By insisting that medicine become scientific in the meaningful sense of 'scientific', i.e., by rigorously following Baconian method, submitting to the intellectual virtue of candor, and laying medicine open, Gregory created the basis for the intellectual authority that defines a true professional: he or she can claim reliably to know what he or she is saying and doing. The first commitment of the ethical concept of medicine changed the meaning of 'profession'. To use Baker's (2019) nomenclature, Gregory's texts contain the "linguistic traces" of Gregory's moral revolution, the invention of the ethical concept of medicine as a profession.

It is worth noting that Gregory launched his moral revolution at a time when medicine was not, as historians put it, "socially successful." There was no effective licensure, no regulation of drugs and devices, no accrediting of medical schools, no national examinations of physicians, and no specialty societies with concomitant board certification. There were no third-party payers such as private insurance companies. Court and municipal physicians were salaried but could be dismissed without warning and without cause. The marketplace for services was over-crowded with practitioners, including physicians, surgeons, "man-midwives" or physicians who had taken an obstetrics course in medical school, apothecaries, midwives, and many "irregulars" less cordially known as "quacks." In his first lecture, after defining medicine by invoking his own "Capitall Enquirys" and Bacon's "offices," Gregory appears to acknowledge the socially, politically, and economic insecurity of physicians.

> On this occasion I think it needless to dwell on the utility and dignity of the medical art. Its utility was never seriously called in question; every man who suffers pain or sickness will very gratefully acknowledge the usefulness of an art which gives him relief. People may dispute, whether physic, on the whole, does more good or harm to mankind; just as they may dispute, whether the faculty of reason, considering how it is often perverted, really contributes to make human life more or less happy; whether a vigorous constitution and an independent fortune are blessings or curses to those who possess them; whether the arts and sciences in general have proved beneficial or detrimental to mankind.– Such questions afford opportunities for the display of eloquence, and for saying plausible and ingenious things; but still nobody doubts of the real and substantial advantages attending those acquisitions, if applied to their natural and proper uses. Much wit has, indeed, in all ages, been exerted upon our profession; but after all, we shall find that this ridicule has rather been employed against physicians than physick (Gregory 1772, [1772] 1998, 2–4).

1.5.1.4 Gregory's First Paradigm Shift

Baker identifies key stages of the philosophical component of a moral revolution. The distrust of the sick that practitioners knew what they were doing can be seen as an anomaly of the four variants of the entrepreneurial paradigm for practice then available: the Hippocratic physician, the guild physician, the cautious physician, and the politic physician. *Caveat emptor*, let the buyer beware, in the relationship between a sick individual and a practitioner, including the cautious physician trying to avoid errors and the politic physician practicing on the basis of enlightened self-interest, remains very much in place with respect to any claims of intellectual authority of these practitioners.

Gregory's response was to draw on what he inherited from his teachers and that he had absorbed completely in the spirit of the medical school at Edinburgh: Baconian scientific method and philosophies of science and medicine. He then formulated the professional virtue of candor and wed it to the concept of laying medicine open. Submitting to the intellectual discipline of candor and laying medicine open defines the first commitment of the ethical concept of medicine as a profession: becoming and remaining scientifically and clinically competent. Mastery of deliberative clinical judgment and basing patient care exclusively on it put this first commitment of the ethical concept of medicine as a profession into clinical practice.

The result was to create a new paradigm, a new way of looking at clinical practice. The old paradigm was the entrepreneurial, distrustful, transactional relationship between the sick individual and a practitioner, in which the sick individual must be diligently on guard to protect himself or herself from the practitioner. As a matter of prudence, the sick individual should see every practitioner as a potential predator who deceives the sick with false claims to intellectual authority. All such claims were idiosyncratic. They relied solely on the persuasive skills of the practitioner. The reliability of these claims therefore extended no further than the practitioner who offered theories and remedies, the latter often eponymously named.

Gregory replaced this paradigm with the professional relationship, the physician-patient relationship. 'Patient' was in use before Gregory's professional ethics in medicine, e.g., in Hume's *Treatise*. Gregory changed the meaning of 'patient'. The patient is an individual who has been presented to a professional physician whose claim to have available clinically beneficial remedies and regimens has intellectual authority about human anatomy and physiology and their responsible clinical management. Patients can have intellectual trust in the deliberative clinical judgment and practice of a Baconian physician. As a function of the commitment to experienced-based medicine created by submitting to the discipline of candor and laying medicine open, the claim to intellectual authority of the Baconian physician became scientific. The claim to intellectual authority became intellectually trustworthy. Pet theories of disease and eponymous medicine became idiosyncratic and consigned to the dustbin of incompetence. As a self-conscious actor in the Scottish enlightenment commitment to improve medicine, Gregory fomented a paradigm shift to the professional physician claiming warranted and therefore reliable intellectual authority about health and disease and their clinical management who protects patients and is not a potential predator on them.

1.5.2 Gregory's Invention of the Second Commitment of the Ethical Concept of Medicine as a Profession

The Porters (1989), in their masterful *Patients' Progress*, document the rampant distrust of the sick directed toward practitioners of all kinds. The sick often, and with good reason as just described, lacked confidence that practitioners knew what they were doing. This was intellectual distrust. The sick also questioned whether the real motivation of practitioners was to line their pockets with the money of the sick and to advance their reputations at the expense of the sick. This was moral distrust. Intellectual and moral distrust, when synergistic, become corrosive. The challenges of sickness, injury, and conditions such as pregnancy became compounded with distrust, especially when the self-physicking proved no avail and it became necessary, often out of desperation, to seek medical help.

1.5.2.1 Men of "Interest"

Gregory continues his moral revolution against the entrepreneurial paradigm because, by definition, it is the mutual pursuit of self-interest. In this paradigm, physicians become what Gregory called men of "interest," whom he addresses at length at the beginning of the first lecture of *Lectures*. Just after text quoted just above, Gregory continues:

> There are some reasons for this sufficiently obvious. Physicians, considered as a body of men, who live by medicine as a profession, have an interest separate and distinct from the honour of the science. In pursuit of this interest, some have acted with candour, with honour, with the ingenuous and liberal manners of gentlemen. Conscious of their own worth, they disdained every artifice, and depended for success on their real merit. But such men are not the most numerous in any profession. Some impelled by necessity, some stimulated by vanity, and others anxious to conceal ignorance, have had recourse to various mean and unworthy arts, to raise their importance among the ignorant, who are always the most numerous part of mankind. Some of these arts have been an affectation of mystery in all their writings and conversations relating to their profession; an affectation of knowledge, inscrutable to all, except the adepts in the science; an air of perfect confidence in their own skill and abilities; and a demeanour solemn, contemptuous, and highly expressive of self-sufficiency. These arts, however well they might succeed with the rest of mankind, could not escape the censure of the more judicious, nor elude the ridicule of men of wit and humour (Gregory 1772, [1772] 1998, 4–5).

Men of interest put individual self-interest first, without exception. Commerce, Gregory believed, was predatory on sympathy, causing hard-heartedness in the predator and distrust in his prey (McCullough 1998). The sick risked experiencing clinical management from an incompetent, hard-hearted practitioner resulting in intellectual and moral distrust that only worsened the already stressful experience of illness serious enough to warrant a physician's attention. The entrepreneurial paradigm can offer only more self-interest and more hard-heartedness and therefore more, and more corrosive, intellectual and moral distrust. Gregory has an antidote to this anomaly at the ready, the principle of moral physiology known as "sympathy," described in Hume's moral science.

1.5.2.2 Gregory on the Physiologic Principle of Sympathy

Gregory became acquainted with the physiologic principle of sympathy as early as 1743 while studying medicine at the University of Edinburgh. His notes from that time indicate exposure to the concept of sympathy as "such things as operate on the body at a distance" (AUL 2206/45 1743, 703). He was also acquainted with the work of a former Edinburgh professor, James Crawford (d. 1732) in which he characterized sympathy as "the influence of each part on the other" of the body (EUL E.B. 6104 ED 1 1744, 480). Sympathy is a hypothesized principle, a constitutive causal process in the body, to explain external influences on the body and the interaction of organs in the body. It was thought that there could be sympathy between a fetus and the pregnant woman carrying it, based on the "harmonious consonance" of atoms in the two bodies (Digby 1969, 184). Sympathy explained mind-body interaction: "The sympathy on the body and mind is … such that particular affections of the mind will bring on disorders of the body, and disorders of the body will in turn affect the mind" (Rather 1965, 182).

1.5.2.3 David Hume's Baconian Moral Science on the Principle of Sympathy

Gregory's embrace of the physiologic principle of sympathy created fertile ground for his subsequent embrace of the principle of sympathy in Hume's moral science, the moral physiologic principle of sympathy. The stage was thus very well set for Gregory to learn Hume's account of sympathy in his science of man or moral science when Gregory and other members of the Aberdeen Philosophical Society (1758–1773) read Hume's *Treatise* (McCullough 1998).

Hume did not understand himself to be engaged in moral philosophy as it has, until recently, been understood: an ethical inquiry autonomous from the empirical sciences. Hume understood himself to be doing observational moral science, using Baconian scientific method. The *Treatise* reads like other scientific texts of the time in Scotland: precise descriptive reports on the results of direct observation of the causal processes or principles that constituted the moral physiology of the human species. In a manner that defines the Scottish nation enlightenment (Porter and Teich 1981), in the "Introduction" to the *Treatise* Hume rejects the use of 'principle' in "systems of the most eminent philosophers" that are divorced from experience or evidence (Hume [1739–1740] 2000, 3). These systems "have drawn disgrace upon philosophy itself" (Hume [1739–1740] 2000, 3). Hume thus rejects non-experience-based principles and the metaphysics in which they are expressed. Principles must be founded on the "authority" of "experience" (Hume [1739–1740] 2000, 6). Hume thus does not reject the discourse of principles altogether. No does he reject

1.5 John Gregory's Revolutionary Invention of Professional Ethics in Medicine

metaphysics altogether. He only rejects speculative principles and speculative metaphysics and accepts metaphysics based on the results of moral science or the science of man put on a "new footing" by "Lord Bacon" (Hume [1739–1740] 2000, 5).

Hume regards affections or the passions as the origin and motive force of morality. Reason is but a calculating machine, matching means to the ends of human endeavor that are established by the passions, not reason. The national enlightenments in European countries differed sharply (Porter and Teich 1981). In these Continental enlightenments, the passions were typically understood to be roiling cauldrons that led one astray from the truth, to which only Reason was the guide. Hume would consider this speculative philosophy, far removed from moral science, and therefore utterly unreliable.

Hume's scientific accomplishment, reported in the *Treatise*, was to move from a hypothesized principle of sympathy to direct observation of it as mental and moral physiology. Hume reports from his Baconian observational investigations that there are two types of perceptions, the grist of mental physiology, impressions and ideas.

> All the perceptions of the human mind resolve themselves into two distinct kinds, which I shall call IMPRESSIONS and IDEAS. The difference betwixt these consists in the degree of force and liveliness, with which they strike upon the mind, and make their way into our thought or consciousness. These perceptions, which enter with most force and violence, we may name *impressions*; and under this name I comprehend all our sensations, passions, and emotions, as they make their first appearance in the soul. By *ideas* I mean the faint images of these in thinking and reasoning; such as, for instance, are all the perceptions excited by the present discourse, excepting only, those which arise from the sight and touch, and excepting the immediate pleasure or uneasiness it may occasion. I believe it will not be very necessary to employ many words in explaining this distinction. Everyone of himself will readily perceive the difference betwixt feeling and thinking. The common degrees of these are easily distinguish'd; tho' it is not impossible but in particular instances they may very nearly approach to each other. Thus in sleep, in a fever, in madness, or in any other very violent emotions of soul, our ideas may approach to our impressions: As on the other hand it sometimes happens, that our impressions are so faint and low, that we cannot distinguish them from our ideas. But notwithstanding this near resemblance in a few instances, they are in general so very different, that no one can make a scruple to rank them under different heads, and assign each a peculiar name to mark the difference (Hume [1739–1740] 2000, 7).

Hume here describes the observed effects of causal processes that remained inaccessible to the science of his day. Some mechanism in the external world physically presses against the senses, creating thereby an *im*pression. Impressions then cause images of themselves in thought. Consciousness is understood as a process of having ideas originating in impressions. These can be direct impressions, to which consciousness is passive. These can indirect, the product of combining ideas with origins in diverse impressions. For example, consciousness could combine the idea of a horse with the idea of a single horn of the head of another animal and generate the idea of a unicorn. This process is called imagination, in which consciousness is active. Imagination is always speculative and serves an important role in Baconian science, the generation of hypotheses about possible causal connections between distinct ideas, e.g., of coronary artery disease and infection. Imagination, however, cannot provide an experience base against which to test hypotheses.

The next stage of Hume's observational report on sympathy is to characterize it as an "active principle," like all principles. Morality has to do with judgment (classifying things into conceptually coherent categories) and action, with judgment motivating action. Morality therefore requires an "active principle" (Hume [1739–1740] 2000, 294). An active principle moves us to moral judgment and then moves us to act on that judgment. This is more than motivation, i.e., having reasons to act that are detached from affective responses. Motivation, therefore, cannot serve as an active principle in our moral lives.

This causal, constitutive process of human nature that incites us to judgment and action based on it cannot originate in reason: "Reason is wholly inactive, and can never be the source of so active a principle as conscience, or a sense of morals" (Hume [1739–1740] 2000, 295). He calls this inciting force "sympathy," by which "we enter so deep into the opinions and affectations of others, whenever we discover them" (Hume [1739–1740] 2000, 208). Hume explains further that sympathy accounts for emotive action at distance, then a topic of great interest in both science and the arts. For example, moral scientists of the time remarked on the ability of actors to communicate emotions from the stage that audience members experience, e.g., Lady Macbeth's ambition to murder King Duncan and make her husband king even while he resists her bloodthirsty drive for horrible murder. The principle of sympathy explains this communication:

> No quality of human nature is more remarkable, both in itself and in its consequences, than the propensity we have to sympathize with others, and to receive by communication their inclinations and sentiments, however different from, or even contrary to their own (Hume [1739–1740] 2000, 206).

Hume wrote his moral science before Darwin and his revolutionary concept of variation of traits. For Hume, therefore, sympathy is the same principle with the same force to move or incite us to act morally and to be affected by the moral behavior of others:

> We may begin with consider anew the nature and force of *sympathy*. The minds of all men are similar in their feelings and operations; nor can one be actuated by any affection, of which all others are not, in some degree susceptible. As in strings generally wound up, the motion of one communicates itself to the rest; so all the affections pass from one person to another, and beget correspondent movements in every other human creature (Hume [1739–1740] 2000, 368).

Hume had formed and observationally tested an hypothesis to explain the motive force of morality, the double-relation of impressions and ideas or sympathy. The third step of his observational report is to describe the moral physiology of sympathy, the steps of it being an active principle. He reports the result in a discourse that one can find in texts on physiology of Hume and Gregory's day:

> When I see the *effects* of passion in the voice and gesture of any person, my mind immediately passes from these effects to their causes, and forms such a lively idea of the passion, as is presently converted into the passion itself. In like manner, when I perceive the *causes* of any emotion, my mind is covey'd to the effects and is actuated with a like emotion (Hume [1739–1740] 2000, 368).

1.5 John Gregory's Revolutionary Invention of Professional Ethics in Medicine

The causal sequence of sympathy that Hume described begins with an experience, the impression on one senses of hearing and sight, of the speech and gestures of an individual that originate in the emotional state or felt experience of that individual. We automatically detect that emotional state or felt experience. We have an affective *impression*. This impression produces an *idea* of the emotional state or felt experience of that individual that is "lively," it possesses the force to generate another *idea*, namely, of the observer being in the individual's emotion state or felt experience. This idea is itself "lively" enough to produce a replica of the other individual's emotional state or felt experience. This *impression* moves or "incites" one to respond to the other individual appropriately.

Hume provides a vivid example from surgery, in an era more than a century before the invention of general anesthesia. He appears to have in mind amputation for gangrene or mutilating mastectomy to treat breast cancer using knives, saws, and cautery.

> Were I present at any of the more terrible operations of surgery, 'tis certain, that even before it begun, the preparation of the instruments, the laying of the bandages in order, the heating of the irons, with all the signs of anxiety and concern in the patient and assistants, wou'd have a great effect upon my mind, and excite the strongest sentiments of pity and terror. No passion of another discovers itself immediately to the mind. We are sensible only of its causes or effects. From *these* we infer the passion: And consequently *these* give rise to our sympathy (Hume [1739–1740] 2000, 368).

In additional to moral sensibility, sympathy generates our "sense of beauty" (Hume 2000, 368) and "moral taste … certain sentiments of pleasure or disgust" (Hume 2000, 371), known in the bioethics literature, but with less precision, as the "yuck" factor (Kass 1997).

Sympathy works in all instances to create what was then called "fellow feeling." 'Humanity' was also used interchangeably with 'sympathy'. When there are cultural, socioeconomic, linguistic, religious, customary deportment and other differences between two individuals, the force of sympathy may be less intense than it is with others like us, as Hume also explained (Hume 1987). However, sympathy is always working and therefore always has some force. One result is that the fellow feeling of sympathy prevents others from becoming strangers into whose emotional and felt experience another cannot enter. In other words, to use H. Tristram Engelhardt, Jr.'s (1941–2018) compelling phrase, there are no "moral strangers" (Engelhardt 1996). Thomas Reid (1710–1796), Gregory's cousin, captures a crucial implication for sympathy-generated fellow feeling when, following the Roman African playwright, Terrence (185 BCE – 159 BCE), Reid declared "*Homo sum & nihil humanum a me alienum puto*" (I am human and think nothing human alien to me) (Reid 1990, 315 n. 5).

Sympathy also had an important political dimension. After the Act of Union of 1707 Scotland was no longer a state. But Scots thought of themselves as a nation. Indeed, Hume makes it a point to note that the national character of Scots differs from the national character of the English (Hume 1987), a distinction that did not altogether disappear in the years that intervened until Brexit, when the distinction has come to enjoy recrudescence. Fellow feeling, put to political use, becomes what was then called the "social principle" (Hume 1987; McCullough 1998, 24). Scots share a national character, as Hume had explained, and so have a strong fellow feeling for each other independent of the state of the United Kingdom. While there was no Scottish state, there was therefore a Scottish nation. In this context, the concept of a social principle can be read as an invention born of powerful social and political needs and commitments.

1.5.2.4 John Gregory's Baconian Moral Science of Sympathy and Its Professional Virtues of Tenderness and Steadiness

As noted above, Gregory was concerned about the predation on the sick of men of "interest." Distrust had become survival-positive for the sick. Sympathy puts the physician in the place of the sick individual who has reached the limits of self-physicking and turns to the physician or surgeon as a last resort. The stakes were high, a stressor compounded by the justified fear that the physician or surgeon was incompetent and more interested in his income and reputation than the health or even life of the sick individual. This approaches the terror of the patient about to undergo high-risk surgery in Hume's compelling example above. Sympathy causes the physician to experience the patient's distrust-based fear of the physician. Moral judgment is swift: this needs to change. None of the four variants of the paradigm of entrepreneurial medical practice that eighteenth-century British medicine inherited was adequate even to see that there was a problem. Moral distrust of the sick had become an anomaly for the entrepreneurial paradigm.

Gregory was also concerned that in the new secular charitable hospitals, known as Royal Infirmaries, physicians, surgeons, and apothecaries gained power over the sick that exceeded the limited power over the sick in private practice in the homes of the well-to-do. In the latter setting, physicians were subordinate to the power of wealthy, because he who pays the piper calls the tune. Today, physicians are still subordinate to the power of payers, especially as the insurance market consolidates into ever-larger companies with growing monopsony power. Medicare exerts growing influence over hospital practice in the United States.

The Infirmaries were established by the aristocracy and owners of factories, coal fields, and shipyards, and other industries of the nascent industrial revolution, to provide free medical and surgical care to their employees, the working sick poor (Risse 1986; McCullough 1998). In infirmaries physicians and surgeons for the first time gained power over the sick that derived from an organization upon which the sick poor depended for care paid for by their employers, who valued a healthy workforce, and the aristocracy as an act of charity (McCullough 1998).

Gregory wanted to create a professional ethics of medicine to guide that power so that it was used primarily for the benefit of patients and not primarily for individual self-interest and not primarily for group self-interest as the competition among physicians, surgeons, and apothecaries that was already intense in the private sphere became even more intense in the institutional setting. Finally, Gregory was teaching clinical medicine and ethics to students of remarkable diversity.

Because they would not subscribe to the articles of faith of the Church of England, English Dissenters came north, attracted by the culture of *Lehrnfreiheit* or freedom to teach (perhaps the first expression of academic freedom) for which the University of Edinburgh was increasingly well known. Students of different faiths also came from the England, the North American British colonies, and the Continent. Some of the American colonists were revolutionaries, notably Benjamin Rush (1746–1813), a signer of the Declaration of Independence for Pennsylvania in 1776 and later Surgeon General of the ultimately victorious Continental Army (McCullough 1998). Entrepreneurial medical ethics would only encourage competition, including religious conflict, from which Scotland was working toward peace; a professional ethics of medicine was required that would transcend potential divisive differences of religion and also of culture and nationality.

The first commitment of the ethical concept of medicine as a profession for Gregory appeals to Baconian science that transcends these differences because the experience-based observational and experimental science is open to anyone willing to submit to its intellectual discipline. The resulting intellectual authority is independent of religions, culture, and nationality. To secure the second and third commitments Gregory makes an appeal to Hume's account of sympathy, a principle of moral science that exists in all human beings. Sympathy therefore transcends cultural, religious, and national difference. Its moral authority is independent of religions, cultures, and nations.

Gregory took more seriously, perhaps, than Hume that sympathy is a "force" that "beget[s] correspondent movements in every other human creature" (Hume 2000, 368). The potentially volatile process of the double relation of impressions and ideas requires regulation. Consider Hume's vivid example of the "more terrible operations of surgery" (Hume 2000, 368) when a the patent patient's terror is communicated to the surgeon, who must cut as quickly as possible, to shorten the time of searing pain, and get the procedure right, to prevent death and (serious) disability. Gregory proposes that the required regulation comes from adopting the virtues of tenderness and steadiness that self-discipline the force of sympathy. Gregory invents these virtues to regulate sympathy in the clinical setting.

Gregory argues that medicine creates "a very ample field for the exertion of genius" (Gregory 1772, [1772] 1998, 8). 'Genius' means the developed, sophisticated capacity to discern possible connections between heretofore unconnected observations. This is an essential skill in developing reliable accounts of the signs and symptoms that are unique to a disease, i.e., to making reliable diagnoses. It is also an essential skill in clinical investigation of hypotheses that genius generates. Percival will use 'analogy' to capture the capacity for genius in clinical judgment and reasoning.

Using 'humanity' as a synonym for 'sympathy', perhaps under the influence of the nomenclature of his cousin Reid (Haakonssen 1997), Gregory argues that "medicine presents a no less extensive field for the exercise of humanity" (Gregory 1772, [1772] 1998, 8).

> A physician has numberless opportunities of giving that relief to distress, ['which is' added in errata] not to be purchased by the wealth of India. This, to a benevolent mind, must be one of the greatest pleasures. But, besides the good which a physician has it often in his power to do, in consequence of skill in his profession, there are many occasions that call for his assistance as a man, as a man who feels for the misfortunes of his fellow-creatures. In this respect he has many opportunities of displaying patience, good-nature, generosity, compassion, and all the gentler virtues that do honour to human nature (Gregory 1772, [1772] 1998, 8–9).

Clinical practice comes with a challenge in the clinical context of the day. The pathology of diseases was poorly understood. 'Cure' was a modest concept, meaning any degree of symptom relief. Mortality rates were high, often from malnourishment secondary to famine that affected almost everyone and poverty that affected most. It is difficult to remain compassionate – to be moved by sympathy to prevent and manage the pain, distress, and suffering of patients – when losses of health and life were far more common than they are in high-income countries like Scotland now. Referring to both physicians and surgeons as the 'faculty', Gregory writes.

> The faculty has often been reproached with hardness of heart, occasioned, as is supposed, but their being so much conversant with human misery. I hope and believe the charge is unjust; for habit may beget a command of temper, and a seeming composure, which is often mistaken for absolute insensibility. But, by the way, I must observe, that, when this insensibility is real, it is an misfortune to a physician, as it deprives him of one of the most natural and powerful incitements to exert himself for the relief of his patient (Gregory 1772, [1772] 1998, 9).

Overreaction was also a hazard of humanity-based care of patients.

> On the other hand, a physician of too much sensibility may be rendered incapable of doing his duty from anxiety, and excess of sympathy, which cloud his understanding, depress his spirit, and prevent him from acting with that steadiness and vigour, upon which perhaps the life of his patient in a great measure depends (Gregory 1772, [1772] 1998, 9).

Gregory was well acquainted with the loss of health and life of his patients. He also experienced loss personally: his beloved wife died after only nine years of marriage and several of his children died young. Sympathy requires regulation, self-discipline, if it is to reliably guide moral judgment and clinical action based on it. This is the work of virtues, as Hume explained in the *Treatise*. Before identifying the regulatory virtues of tenderness and steadiness, Gregory sets out an account of sympathy that Hume would have endorsed.

> I come now to mention the moral qualities peculiarly required in the character of a physician. The chief of these is humanity; that sensibility of heart which makes us feel for the distresses of our fellow-creatures, and which, of consequence, incites us in the most powerful manner to relieve them. Sympathy produces an anxious attention to a thousand little circumstances that may tend to relieve the patient; an attention which money can never purchase: hence the inexpressible comfort of having a friend for a physician. Sympathy naturally engages the affection and confidence of a patient, which, in many cases, is of the utmost consequence to his recovery. If the physician possesses gentleness of manners, and a compassionate heart, and what Shakespeare so emphatically calls "the milk of human kindness," the patient feels his approach like that of a guardian angel ministering to his relief: while every visit of a physician who is unfeeling, and rough in his manners, makes his heart sink within him, as at the presence of one, who comes to pronounce his doom.

1.5 John Gregory's Revolutionary Invention of Professional Ethics in Medicine

> Men of the most compassionate tempers, by being daily conversant with scenes of distress, acquire in process of time that composure and firmness of mind so necessary in the practice of physick. They can feel whatever is amiable in pity, without suffering it to enervate or unman them. Such physicians as are callous to sentiments of humanity, treat this sympathy with ridicule, and represent it either as hypocrisy, or as the indication of a feeble mind. That sympathy is often affected, I am afraid is true. But this affectation may be easily seen through. Real sympathy is never ostentatious; on the contrary, it rather strives to conceal itself. But, what most effectually detects this hypocrisy, is a physician's different manner of behaving to people in high and people in low life; to those who reward him handsomely, and those who have not the means to do it. A generous and elevated mind is even more shy in expressing sympathy with those of high rank, than with those in humbler life; being jealous of the unworthy construction so usually annexed to it.- The insinuation that a compassionate and feeling heart is commonly accompanied with a weak understanding and a feeble mind, is malignant and false. Experience demonstrates, that a gentle and humane temper, so far from being inconsistent with vigour of mind, is its usual attendant; and that rough and blustering manners generally accompany a weak understanding and a mean soul, and are indeed frequently affected by men void of magnanimity and personal courage, ['in order' added in errata] to conceal their natural defects (Gregory 1772, [1772] 1998, 19–21).

The moral physiology of sympathy opens the heart to the plight of others via the double relation of impressions and ideas that Hume observed and reported, as explained above. This was warmth of heart in eighteenth-century Scottish enlightenment discourse (McCullough 1998). This discourse may be the source of the use of 'warm-hearted' to characterize the admirable character trait of attention to the needs of others and meeting them without bias or discrimination.

Sympathy "incites" an unhesitating response to patients' clinical needs. 'Incites' is a cognate of Hume's 'excite', to characterize the force of sympathy to move us to moral judgment and action based on it. The resulting direct engagement with the felt experience of the patient promotes trust. Sympathy becomes a powerful antidote to distrust and a powerful constraint on the physician's power over Infirmary patients.

Sympathy results in the same care for the high-born and low-born. Sympathy closes the socioeconomic gap that opens wide when the physician pursues money and reputation to the risk of patients, especially the working sick poor in the Royal Infirmary.

Gregory then adds to Hume two professional virtues of the physician, because sympathy needs regulation in the clinical setting. Gregory invents two regulatory virtues, tenderness and steadiness. Tenderness regulates the sympathy-based direct engagement with the felt experience of the patient. This virtue is especially required, Gregory adds, with patients with "[d]isorders of the imagination" (Gregory 1772, [1772] 1998, 24) or mental illnesses and disorders and female patients (Gregory 1772, [1772] 1998, 26). 'Steadiness' (Gregory 1772, [1772] 1998, 18) names the sustained effort to prevent the Scylla of insensibility of the heart, hard-heartedness, and the Charybdis of loss of emotional control. Both extremes activate self-interest and therefore undermine enlightened self-interest and the primary focus on the patient's health and life.

A virtue-based professional ethics of medicine, like all virtue-based accounts in ethics, requires exemplars. Without exemplars we will not know how to form our character in the ways a virtue requires. Gregory's exemplars were what he called "women of learning and virtue," epitomized especially by his wife and Elizabeth Montague (McCullough 1998). Rosemary Tong (1993) characterizes this approach to moral reasoning as "feminine ethics." Tong distinguishes feminine ethics from "feminist ethics" that asserts rights against oppressive patriarchy. Gregory was publicly known, and encountered resistance for, his feminine ethics (McCullough 1998).

There is textual evidence of this in the passage above, when Gregory defends sympathy-based ethics from the charge that it is the creature of a "feeble," i.e., female mind. This sort of chauvinistic slur prompted the feminist ethics of Mary Wollstonecraft (1759–1797) (McCullough 1998). Gregory's students should not fear that "feel[ing] whatever is amiable in pity," a positive manifestation of sympathy without fear that being a sympathetic physician will "unman or enervate" them, i.e., sever the nerve supply to their genitals. In the final sentence of this passage Gregory uses some of the strongest language in *Lectures* to turn the tables on his critics and immunize his students against them with the discourse of Baconian moral science.

> Experience demonstrates, that a gentle and humane temper, so far from being inconsistent with vigour of mind, is its usual attendant; and that rough and blustering manners generally accompany a weak understanding and a mean soul, and are indeed frequently affected by men void of magnanimity and personal courage, ['in order' added in errata] to conceal their natural defects (Gregory 1772, [1772] 1998, 21).

Gregory deploys sympathy and its invented regulatory virtues of tenderness and steadiness to address a comprehensive problem list: conflicts of interest (Gregory 1772, [1772] 1998, 3–5); the "government" of the patient or limited power over patients (Gregory 1772, [1772] 1998, 20–22); patients with "nervous ailments," which we would now classify as the worried well and patients with anxiety disorders (Gregory 1772, [1772] 1998, 22–25); the risk of callous disregard for patients, or, far worse becoming "rapacious" or a sexual predator on female patients (Gregory 1772, [1772] 1998, 24–25); confidentiality, especially regarding their interest in such matters as concealing bastardy from husbands (Gregory [1772, [1772] 1998, 25–27); "temperance," a practical matter given the custom of taking "cordials" throughout the work-day in patients' homes, at a time when potable water was not available (Gregory 1772, [1772] 1998, 27–28); the intellectual virtue of candor, as described earlier (Gregory 1772, [1772] 1998, 28–29); decorum or what Chauncey Leake called "etiquette" and dismissed as ethically irrelevant (Leake 1927), a view common in the bioethics literature but which Gregory would reject for manners that are founded in "nature" and thus "immutable," i.e., transcultural (Gregory 1772, [1772] 1998, 32) (more on Leake on Percival in Chap. 4); the right of patients to speak up and have their health beliefs taken seriously and critically appraised, as explained above (Gregory 1772, [1772] 1998, 32–33); the "necessary duty" or ethical obligation to be honest with patients about their condition, even though this is "most disagreeable" to the physician; the manner of disclosure eases the burden for the patient (Gregory [1772, 1772] 1998, 34–36); "unhappy jealousies and animosities among those of the profession" that must never occur in the presence of patients to prevent clinically unnecessary burden to the already significant burden of disease or injury (Gregory 1772, [1772] 1998, 36–38), a consideration altogether absent from the *Statuta Moralia* of the Royal College of Physicians, as we saw earlier (Gregory 1772, [1772] 1998, 38–40); the respect that younger physicians should show their seniors, so that the former can learn from the latter (Gregory 1772, [1772] 1998, 40–41); preventing bias of relying on favorite texts rather than those with a solid experience-base, or what we now call critical appraisal (Gregory 1772, [1772] 1998, 41–43); the disputed boundary between medicine and surgery (Gregory 1772, [1772] 1998, 43–49), about which more below; not mistaking credentials for scientific and clinical competence, which did not have the intellectual and moral authority of a medical degree, licensure, of board certification, for scientific and clinical competence (Gregory 1772, [1772] 1998, 49–51); avoiding "formality in dress, and a particular gravity in his behaviour," dress and comportment chosen to mislead patients about one's qualifications and trustworthiness (Gregory 1772, [1772] 1998, 51–53); adopting dress and deportment intended to prevent fear of children when attending to them, an ethical obligation now taken for granted by pediatricians and other pediatric healthcare professionals (Gregory 1772, [1772] 1998, 53–54); not adopting idiosyncratic, self-regarding manners (Gregory 1772, [1772] 1998, 53–56); avoiding false "delicacy," the self-serving belief that the physician is above having to perform basic care functions for patients, including the functions of nursing in the Royal Infirmary (Gregory [1772, 1772] 1998, 56–57); basing scheduled attendance on the response of disease or injury to treatment and not on self-interested pecuniary considerations (Gregory 1772, [1772] 1998, 57–58); "servility of manners towards people of rank and fortune," or special treatment for patients of great wealth or political power or, more generally, basing clinical practice on the source of payment (Gregory [1772, 1772] 1998, 58–59); self-produced medications, usually carrying one's name and a source, potentially, of considerable revenue, what were then known as "secrets and nostrums" (Gregory 1772, [1772] 1998, 59–61); and preserving an air of "mystery" about medications, because experience shows that this promotes compliance (Gregory 1772, [1772] 1998, 61–63), a sharp difference with contemporary bioethics and creating an historical perspective from which the informed consent process appears strange and requiring justification.

Gregory concludes the second lecture with a lengthy response to "a charge of a heinous nature, which has been often urged against our profession; I mean that of infidelity, and contempt of religion" (Gregory 1772, [1772] 1998, 63–70). This charge hit close to home for Gregory, because William Cullen (1710–1790), the brilliant diagnostician and clinical teacher with whom Gregory shared the professorship in medicine at Edinburgh, was under attack for this atheism. In an era before the invention of tenure and in which the Town Council of Edinburgh made faculty appointments, Cullen was in a politically vulnerable position. Gregory's defense against the charge of infidelity can be read as a way to protect Cullen by creating an insurmountable burden of proof for Cullen's rivals and political opponents.

Gregory's consistent point is that medicine is indeed based on Baconian science but that Baconian science supports Deism, the view that there is a creator god that is not the god of any specific religion. The hallmark of Deism is the argument from design: there is an evident, complex order of Nature that could not have originated in Nature and must therefore originate in some transcendent Creator. Gregory explicitly embraces the argument from design, as did Percival, as we will see in Chaps. 2 and 3. This means that medicine is secular in the sense that it does not require reference to sacred of divine sources in written or oral traditions. Medicine is also secular in that there is no inherent hostility on its part toward religious faith, because Baconian science requires deism. Indeed, "I think the charge ill-founded; and will venture to say, that the most eminent of our faculty have been distinguished for real piety. I shall only mention, as examples, Harvey, Sydenham, Arbuthnot, Boerhaave, Stahl, and Hoffman" (Gregory 1772, [1772] 1998, 64). As secular, professional ethics in medicine and therefore the profession of medicine have no religious test. As a consequence, they are transreligious. Gregory's students came from many faith communities and some, no doubt, were agnostics or atheists. None of these stances create an obstacle to sympathy-based clinical practice.

1.5.2.5 Gregory's Second Paradigm Shift

Feminine sympathy and its regulatory virtues of tenderness and steadiness directly and with self-discipline engage the physician in the patient's felt experience of disease, injury, pain, distress, and suffering. Sympathy "incites" the physician to focus primarily on protecting and promoting the patient's health and life. Self-interest becomes systematically secondary. Cautions and enlightened self-interest become unnecessary.

The second commitment of the ethical concept of medicine thus becomes synergistic with the first commitment by at least minimizing, if not eliminating, biases arising from individual self-interest that can infect clinical judgment, undermining its deliberative character, and infect medical science, undermining its experience base. Tenderness and steadiness at least minimize and, better, eliminate biases that might arise from self-interest. These feminine virtues also minimize and, better, eliminate biases that might arise from socioeconomic, religious, national, and other social differences between patients.

1.5.3 Gregory's Invention of the Third Commitment of the Ethical Concept of Medicine as a Profession

The boundary between medicine and surgery had been fraught for centuries, epitomized in the rejection of surgical management of bladder stones by Hippocratic physicians. To be sure, the admonition against surgery in the Hippocratic *Oath* is an association rule designed to prevent gaining a reputation for causing high rates of mortality among the sick, i.e., a very bad reputation that would surely have an adverse effect on one's market share and therefore income and economic security (such as it was). Nonetheless, the boundary was firmly and clearly drawn.

Gregory draws on a more recent example:

> There have arisen at different periods, and particularly in France, about twenty years ago, great disputes about the boundary of physic and surgery, and the proper subordination of surgery to medicine. A dispute hurtful to mankind, and which has been often conducted in a manner unworthy of scholars and gentlemen (Gregory 1772, [1772] 1998, 43).

The dispute was hurtful because it originated in guild self-interest that, in Britain, feeds this dispute.

> The separation of physic from surgery in modern times, has been productive of the worst consequences. The physicians and surgeons, formed into separate societies, had separate interests to support, which, in many cases, clashed with each other. The surgeons claimed not only the exclusive privilege of performing all operations, but likewise the management of most external diseases, and some internal ones, where operations were supposed to be often necessary; by which means the method of cure in many diseases was sometimes left to the direction of ignorant as well as illiterate men (Gregory 1772, [1772] 1998, 44–45).

Gregory proposes a Baconian rebuttal of the guild mentality.

> But it must be apparent to every sensible and ingenuous observer, that the diseases of the human body are so intimately connected, that it is impossible to understand some of them perfectly, and be entirely ignorant of all the rest; and hardly possible to understand any of them, without some knowledge of Anatomy, and of the Animal œconomy [physiology], both in its sound and morbid state. It must at the same time be owned, that a practitioner, well-grounded in such general knowledge, may have considerable advantages; and more readily make improvements, by attaching himself to the study of one or two particular diseases (Gregory 1772, [1772] 1998, 45–46).

The separation of medicine from surgery has engendered the false belief that they are directed to separate diseases. This belief is false because there is no observational-experience-base for the separation. The separation, as we have just seen results in the outcomes "hurtful to mankind" (Gregory 1772, [1772] 1998, 43), which sympathy-based medicine prohibits. The separation is self-serving and harmful to the health and lives of patients and must therefore end.

1.5.3.1 The "Corporation Spirit" and Guild Self-Interests

Gregory's proposal to end the separation is to lay medicine "open to the world" (Gregory 1772, [1772] 1998, 230). The guilds, the royal colleges, became his target because their rules were designed to protect their practices and privileges of its members. To achieve this goal, the Royal Colleges, chartered by the King, attempted to control licensure and thereby enforce orthodoxy. That they were not uniformly successful (McCullough 1998) does not diminish the force of Gregory's attack on the orthodoxy of anti-Baconian "systems" and the failure of group-self-interest serving Colleges to cultivate the intellectual virtue of candor. Rejection of laying medicine open to the world by the Colleges constitutes an egregious violation of the virtue of candor. Gregory therefore attacked what he called the "corporation spirit," the antiscientific protection of group self-interest from competitors, even and especially when those competitors were Baconian, and therefore scientifically and clinically superior, physicians and surgeons. The Colleges epitomized the guild self-interest that so patently expressed in the Hippocratic *Oath*.

Once again, Gregory uses some of the strongest language in *Lectures* to attack the "corporation spirit" or guild self-interest as unacceptable:

> It is a physician's duty to do every thing in his power that is not criminal, to save the life of his patient, and to search for remedies from every source, and from every hand, however mean and contemptible. This, it may be said, is sacrificing the dignity and interests of the faculty. But, I am not here speaking of the private police of a corporation, or the little arts of craft. I am treating of the duties of a liberal profession, whose object is the life and health of the human species, a profession to be exercised by gentlemen of honour and ingenuous manners; the dignity of which can never be supported by means that are inconsistent with its ultimate object, and that only tend to increase the pride and fill the pockets of a few individuals (Gregory 1772, [1772] 1998. 39–40).

Gregory's solution to the boundary dispute was to put physicians in charge of diagnosis and then divide responsibility for the patient based on the skillset called for by the diagnosis:

> Every distemper, external as well as internal, falls under the cognizance of the physician, and it is a reflection on him to be ignorant of any of them; neither is it possible to fix any such precise boundaries between external and internal diseases, as to render the distinction in any degree useful, or applicable in practice. Suppose a person to break his leg, and a fever and gangrene to ensue; the question occurs, whether the limb should be immediately amputated, or to ['whether we should' substituted for 'to' in errata] wait for some time till the effects of certain medicines, given with a view to stop the progress of the mortification, are known. It is evidently the business of a physician, in this case, to judge from the symptoms, from the habit of body, and from other circumstances, whether the delay is prudent or not.– As to the performance of the operation itself, that is a different question. The genius and education requisite to make a good physician, are not necessary to make a good operator.– What is peculiarly necessary to make a good operator, is a resolute, collected mind, a good eye, and a steady hand. These talents may be united with those of an able physician; but they may also be separated from them (Gregory 1772, [1772] 1998, 46–47).

Gregory points toward an ethics of cooperation, which Percival is the first to make an explicit component of professional ethics in medicine, as we shall see in Chap. 3.

1.5.3.2 Gregory's Third Paradigm Shift

Feminine sympathy and its regulatory virtues of tenderness and steadiness directly and with self-discipline engage the physician in the patient's felt experience of disease, injury, pain, distress, and suffering. Virtues-regulated sympathy "incites" the physician to focus primarily on protecting and promoting the patient's health and life. Guild-interest becomes systematically secondary.

Like the second commitment of the ethical concept of medicine as a profession, the third commitment becomes synergistic with the first commitment by eliminating biases arising from guild-interest that can infect clinical judgment, undermining its deliberative character, and infect medical science, undermining its experience base. The paradigm of guild-interest is replaced with the revolutionary paradigm of the primary commitment to protect and promote the health and life of the patient, which requires that guild-interest become systematically secondary.

1.6 Gregory's Invention of the Ethical Concept of Medicine and Professional Ethics in Medicine

Gregory sets out three, synergistic commitments – the first intellectual and the second and third moral – that constitute the ethical concept of medicine as a profession. The professional physician, 'physician' now taking on a new, revolutionary true meaning, commits to becoming and remaining scientifically and clinically competent, to protecting and promoting the health-related interests of each patient as the physician's primary concern and motivation, keeping *individual* self-interest systematically secondary, and to protecting and promoting the health-related interests of each patient as the physician's primary concern and motivation, keeping (Hippocratic association) *group-* or (Royal College) *guild*-interest systematically secondary.

The resulting professional ethics in medicine was disseminated in translations into French (Gregory 1797), German (Gregory 1778), Italian (Gregory 1789), and Spanish (Gregory 1803; Gracia 2009). *Lectures* also appeared in later editions in Britain (Gregory 1788, 1805, 1820) and the United States (1817). Gregory's student, Benjamin Rush, brought *Lectures* to the Province of Pennsylvania about to become the Commonwealth of Pennsylvania in the United States of America (Rush [1789] 1805). As we will see in Chaps. 3 and 4, Gregory's professional ethics in medicine set the stage for and deeply influenced Percival's professional ethics in medicine.

In addition to dissemination, Baker identifies linguistic success as part of a successful moral revolution. The success of Gregory's moral revolution can be seen in the discourse now used in the websites of the Royal Colleges in London (Royal College of Physicians of London n.d.; Royal College of Surgeons of England n.d.), Edinburgh (Royal College of Physicians of Edinburgh; Royal College of Surgeons of Edinburgh n.d.), and Glasgow (Royal College of Physicians and Surgeons of Glasgow n.d.). There are no linguistic traces of their origins as self-interested, monopoly-seeking guilds. Instead, these are the websites of professional associations of physicians, evidencing the linguistic traces of 'patient', 'science' and other terms of the discourse of Gregory's professional ethics in medicine. In Baker's taxonomy Gregory's professional ethics in medicine has been disseminated, globally, and gained new adherents and new rules/laws to support and regulate professional behavior. In this respect it is worth noting that state medical practice acts (in the American federal system the states and not the federal government, including such agencies as the Food and Drug Administration, regulate medical practice) state that national and specialty association codes and statements on ethics establish ethical norms enforceable by professional liability litigation.

1.7 Gregory's Professional Ethics of Clinical Research

In the Royal Infirmary of Edinburgh, young physicians, ambitious to advance their reputations as offering the new and best treatments would early in the course of treatment declare a patient "incurable." This word had been used by physicians in the four pre-Gregorian variants of the entrepreneurial paradigm of medical practice to identify sick individuals who were expected to die even with treatment and then withdraw promptly, so that the disease and not the physician would be seen to be the cause of these individuals' deaths. This was a practice deeply rooted in individual-interest and guild-interest in protecting reputation. Gregory also called for physicians to stay with and care for gravely ill and dying patients (Gregory 1772, [1772] 1998, 35–36). These ambitious young physicians prematurely declared patients incurable to secure a different kind of reputation, for being what we now call "cutting-edge" physicians.

Gregory sets out his professional ethics of clinical research in his lectures on clinical practice, of which student notes survive. In this context, 'incurable' takes on a distinctive meaning"

> A physician who has been educated upon this plan, whose mind has never been enslaved by systems, because he has been a daily witness of their insufficiency, instead of being assuming and dogmatical, becomes modest and diffident. When his patient dies, he secretly laments his own ignorance of the proper means of having saved him, and is little apt to ascribe his death to his disease being incurable. There are indeed so few diseases which can be pronounced in their own nature, desperate, that I should wish you to annex no other idea to the word, but that of a disease which you do not know how to cure. How many patients have been dismissed from hospitals as incurables, who have afterwards recovered, sometimes by the efforts of unassisted nature, sometimes by very simple remedies, and now and then by the random prescriptions of ignorant quacks? To pronounce diseases incurable,* [*"Bacon" at bottom p. 209] is to establish indolence and inattention, as it were, by law, and to skreen ignorance from reproach. This diffidence of our own knowledge, and just sense of the present imperfect state of our art, ought to incite us to improve it, not only from a love of the art itself, but from a principle of humanity (Gregory 1772, [1772] 1998, 209–210).

The improvement of medicine requires clinical investigations, of which Gregory was well aware. He therefore created a professional ethics of clinical research, which would be performed on the patients at the Royal Infirmary. These patients came from the social class of the working sick poor. They needed to be protected from the use of 'incurable' by the ambitious young physicians and surgeons who were violating the "principle of humanity" (Gregory 1772, [1772] 1998, 210) or sympathy.

Implicit in the misuse of 'incurable' by his ambitious, young colleagues is the view that desperate cases justify desperate measures. Incurable cases, especially in

1.7 Gregory's Professional Ethics of Clinical Research

life-threatening conditions, belong in the category of desperate cases. Gregory rejects the view that desperate cases *simpliciter* justify desperate cases.

> Desperate remedies should be used in some cases, where every other method has been provided ineffectual. In such circumstances we should have recourse to medicines which under more favourable circumstances might be thought dangerous (RCPE, Gregory J, 1766, 13).

In Gregory's revolutionary professional ethics in clinical research 'incurable' now means a condition for which all accepted forms of clinical management have been tried and failed to alter the course of the disease or injury. As he puts is, "the Common practice must always have a fair trial" (RCSE C36, 1771, 10). This is the necessary and sufficient condition for the clinical application of the concept of an incurable condition as "a disease which you do not know how to cure" (Gregory 1772, [1772] 1998, 209). Gregory is also asserting the experience-based prerogative of the physician-investigator to determine when a medicine is acceptably dangerous, i.e., to determine the risk-benefit ratio. This judgment requires clinical expertise that a patient who is a potential research subject does not have.

Having made 'incurable' conditions properly understood and with an acceptable risk/benefit ratio, Gregory sets out the remaining elements of his professional ethics of clinical research, which is to be understood in the context of the professional ethics of clinical care:

> In treating Patients under my care I am only to give you my Common Practice, & only to prescribe such Medicines as I have had experience of their good effects in similar cases. I know very well that it is a common practice with many young Gentlemen, that the Physician who attends an Hospital should always try Experiments on the Patients; this I think contrary to both Justice and Humanity: I shall therefore give you my common Practice & not sport with the lives of poor people: I would not give any Person a Medicine that I would not scruple to take myself. I shall always have in my Eye the moral precept, "Do as you would be done by" (RCSE C36 1771, 9).

Justice requires a fair trial of clinical management that is accepted because it has an experience base. Humanity requires tender and steady regard for the felt experience of a patient with an incurable disease, now correctly understood. Ambition is a creature of self-interest and therefore altogether out of place in clinical investigation. The example set by the ambitious, young physician becomes an exemplar of what is prohibited in the professional ethics of clinical research, in sharp contrast to the entrepreneurial paradigm that endorses the competition that leads to impermissible experimentation on and sporting with the sick poor in the Royal Infirmary of Edinburgh.

Gregory's revolutionary professional ethics of clinical research is thus very much part of, and not autonomous from, his professional ethics in medicine. He should not be read as writing research ethics but the professional ethics of research. In a professional ethics of research patients become subjects, because there come under the power and "government" of professional Infirmary physicians. Professional physicians practice and therefore conduct research according to the three commitments that define the ethical concept of medicine as a profession. By making these commitments the professional physician-investigator takes on the ethical obligation to protect those subject to his power and government by providing only clinical investigation supported by experience-based hypotheses about previously incurable diseases, with the meaning Gregory sets out in the text just above, and supported by sympathy-based tenderness and steadiness in response to the felt experience of being a clinical research subject.

Gregory would reject the discourse of 'participant' now common in research ethics because it masks vulnerability to the investigator's organizational power over patients who are potential research subjects and who become research subjects. As Franz Ingelfinger (1980) showed, research subjects experience the subjugation to the power of the clinical investigator. Participants do not. Moreover, every patient is under the protection of the professional physician, as a function of the three commitments of the ethical concept of medicine as a profession. The patient who is also a research subject is under the same protection. This protection disappears in the discourse of 'participant' because this is not the discourse of Gregory's ethics in medicine but of respect for autonomy. From the perspective of Gregory's professional ethics of clinical research, the autonomy-based discourse of 'participant' is misleading and should be abandoned.

1.8 Conclusion: Gregory's Moral Revolution Against Entrepreneurial Medicine

Gregory's professional ethics in medicine should be interpreted as a moral revolution against the entrepreneurial paradigm of "interested" clinical practice that preceded *Lectures* for more than two millennia. His professional ethics of clinical research should be interpreted as a moral revolution against the "interested," ambitious, and predatory young clinical investigator. Gregory's closing words in *Lectures* powerfully summarize their legacy:

> I hope I have advanced no opinions in these Lectures that tend to lessen the dignity of a profession which has always been considered as most honourable and important. But, I apprehend, this dignity is not to be supported by a narrow, selfish, corporation-spirit; by self-importance; by a formality in dress and manners, or by an affectation of mystery. The true dignity of physic is to be maintained by the superior learning and abilities of those who profess it, by the liberal manners of gentlemen; and by that openness and candour, which disdain all artifice, which invite to a free enquiry, and thus boldly bid defiance to all that illiberal ridicule and abuse, to which medicine has been so much and so long exposed (Gregory 1772, [1772] 1998, 237–238).

The use of 'liberal manners of a gentleman' signals a change in the meaning of 'gentleman'. This word had designated a class-based station of economic, social, and political power and privilege. Gregory revolutionized the discourse of 'gentleman' to designate a social role in which an individual with power over others should think of and treat them as individuals for whom one has the welcome, sympathy-based responsibility to protect them. A man becomes a gentleman by making the three commitments that define the ethical concept of medicine as a profession.

1.8 Conclusion: Gregory's Moral Revolution Against Entrepreneurial Medicine

Power over others is thus guided and regulated by Baconian-science-based intellectual authority and sympathy-based moral authority. Individual-interest and guild-interest are no longer included in the concept of being a gentleman, or the concept of being a physician. A gentleman thus understood and therefore a physician as a professional is worthy of the intellectual and moral trust of patients who are no longer "the sick."

In Baker's terms, Gregory can also be read as a conservative revolutionary. He can be read as reaching back into Scottish Highland history and the ethical concept of the clan chief as obligated to protect all of the members of the clan that he leads. This was called 'paternalism' in the sense that the clan chief was the father of the clan who earned the trust of its members by sacrificing for them, in peace and in war (McCullough 1998). In this respect, Gregory' moral revolution against the long tradition of entrepreneurialism in the history of Western medicine can also be read as a counter-revolution.

As we will see in Chap. 3, Percival adds key components to the moral revolution in the history of medical ethics that Gregory started and Percival thereby completed. To set the stage for that account, in the next chapter I provide an intellectual biography of Percival apart from which his *Medical Jurisprudence* and *Medical Ethics* cannot be understood without succumbing to the twin perils of essentialism and presentism.

Chapter 2
An Intellectual Biography of Thomas Percival

2.1 A Methodological Note

Percival's writings were published in four volumes in 1807, edited by his son Edward Percival (Percival 1807). These volumes were reprinted in 1870 (Percival [1807] 1870). At least two facsimile editions are available in contemporary editions (Percival [1807] 2010; [1807] 2014). I have used the 2020 facsimile edition (Percival [1807] 2010). Call-outs to texts in the four volumes cite the original edition (Percival 1807).

The most comprehensive source for the life and times of Thomas Percival is *Memoirs of the Life and Writings Thomas Percival, M.D. to which is Added a Selection from his Literary Correspondence* (Percival, Edward 1807; Percival 1807, Vol. I, i–cclxii). His son Edward Percival (1783–1819), a physician who practiced in Dublin and Bath, wrote *Memoirs* as the introduction to *The Works, Literary, Moral, and Medical of Thomas Percival* in four volumes (Percival, Edward 1807). (For ease of reference, *Memoirs* will be cited as Percival, 1807, followed by lower-case Roman numerals, as in the original.)

Edward characterizes his *Memoirs* as an "account of Dr. Percival's literary life" (Percival 1807, Vol. I ccxxi). The *Memoirs* therefore go into considerable detail about Percival's writings, requiring the reader to search elsewhere for additional details about key events in Percival's life. I have therefore turned to other sources, including the entry, "Percival, Thomas," in *Dictionary of National Biography* (Lee 1895, Vol. XLIV), John Pickstone's scholarly work (Pickstone 1993), Espinasse's (1877) brief biography, and a master's thesis by Royden Hope (1947) for the University of Manchester. I will call on many of these sources for the account of Percival association with Manchester Infirmary that opens Chap. 3.

This book makes the case for Gregory and Percival as the co-inventors of professional ethics in medicine, an accomplishment upon which the global history of medical ethics pivots. I have therefore tried to inoculate my scholarly account from the effects of hagiography that, the reader will discover, appear in the *Memoirs*. The reader, I have every confidence, will judge whether I have succeeded.

2.2 Thomas Percival of Warrington and Manchester

2.2.1 The Percival Family in Warrington

Thomas Percival, M.D. (1740–1804), was born September 29, 1740, "N.S.," or the New Style calendar adopted by Parliament in 1752 or about two centuries after its commission by Pope Gregory XIII (1502–1585; papacy 1572–1585) of the Roman Catholic Church. This was the Gregorian calendar, adopted twelve years after Percival's birth. This momentous change in how the English recorded the passage of time presaged the momentous change that Dr. Percival (hereafter "Percival") made in the global history of medical ethics. In his *Memoirs of the Life and Writings of Thomas Percival, M.D.*, Edward Percival, Percival's son, places his father's birth in the family history from the time his grandfather, Peter Percival (d. 1701), settled in Warrington, a Lancashire suburb of Manchester in northwest England that is about twenty miles west of Manchester and the same distance east of Liverpool. The novels of Jane Austen (1775–1815) reveal the importance of "fortune" or inherited wealth, often in the form of landed estates, that came down to according to English inheritance law that favored first sons. Fortune figures in Edward's description of Percival's forebears in Thewall, Chester county.

> His remote ancestors were occupied in the cultivation of the patrimonial estate; a farm of moderate extent, which had been lineally transmitted to the present generation. The slender fortunes of his line were compensated by intellectual endowments, and hereditary worth (Percival 1807, Vol. I, i).

Readers of Austen's novels will know how to translate "slender fortunes:" the economic prospects of the Percival clan were, shall we say, modest, even straitened.

Not in line for the largess of inheritance that would come to his older brother, Percival's grandfather relocated, more by necessity than choice.

> His grandfather, Peter Percival, was the first who quitted the patrimonial habitation. Destined by birth to the scanty inheritance of a younger son, he was induced to seek a more ample fortune by embracing the profession of physic; and accordingly devoted himself to the usual methods of preparatory study. With the view to a more extended sphere of practice than his native village afforded, he fixed his residence at Warrington, in Lancashire; where he lived with decent hospitality and creditable fame (Percival 1807, Vol. I, ii).

Edward's polite language can be translated to mean that Peter Percival had to be prudent about where he set up a private medical practice. Doing so was an economically perilous undertaking at a time when physicians, unlike their successors now in high-income countries, could not be confident of economic security that ordinary working men and women struggled even harder to attain. However, the town of Warrington was growing and near a growing provincial city, Manchester, and thus economically promising. Peter married "Martha Wortley, the daughter of Mr. Wortley, of Sutton, in the same county … remarkable for the attainments of her understanding, and the exemplary virtue of her life" (Percival 1807, Vol. I, ii). As a feminine moral scientist and philosopher, Gregory could have written "the exemplary virtue of her life," with approval. Peter died in 1701.

Peter Percival's eldest son, Thomas (1691–1750), who became Percival's uncle, followed Grandfather Percival into medicine. Uncle Thomas learned to become a Baconian physician from Boerhaave himself at Leyden, to which Peter "removed himself" after study at the "free grammar school of Warrington; an institution well endowed, formerly much reported and held in great estimation" (Percival 1807, Vol. I, iii).

2.2.2 Percival's First Seventeen Years

Percival's father, Joseph, married Margaret Orred, "a lady of reputable family in Cheshire" (Percival 1807, Vol. III, iv). They had seven children, three of whom died young. Percival also had a powerful role model of Gregory's feminine virtues, his oldest sister, Elizabeth. Both of their parents died when Percival, their youngest and by then only other surviving child (Lee 1895, Vol. XLIV, 393), was only three years of age. Elizabeth undertook his rearing, becoming the "real mother of his understanding and manners" (Percival 1807, Vol. I, v). His "bachelor" Uncle Thomas helped to raise him (Hope 1947). In Uncle Thomas, Percival had as a surrogate father a living exemplar of the Baconian physician. Percival would later add Gregory as a literary exemplar.

> The excellent qualities of this lady [Elizabeth], a rare benevolence of temper, and undissembled probity of mind, were in no common degree congenial to the character which he was destined to unfold; whilst the image of her virtues seemed to be reflected in the youthful dispositions of her charge. The purity of her moral precepts, no less than the warmth of her affection, inspired his mind with indelible sentiment of filial regard; and to the latest hour of his life few reflections afforded him more grateful pleasure, than those associated with her kindness (Percival 1807, Vol. I, v).

At age ten, Percival inherited from his Uncle Thomas a "valuable library and moderate competency" (Nicholson 1885). Edward Percival puts it this way: Percival came into his "patrimonial fortune, which afforded him ample means for a liberal education" (Percival 1807, Vol. I, xi). After "the usual forms of elementary instruction, at a respectable seminary in the neighbourhood of Warrington" (Percival 1807, Vol. I, vi), Percival at the age of ten became a student in the free grammar school in

Warrington. There he was taught by the Oxford-educated Master of the school, Thomas Hayward (d. 1757). Percival studied Latin and Greek, the then-unquestioned foundations of a proper English education. Espinasse (1877) suggest that, impressed with his uncle, young Percival decided to follow him into medicine. He then spent twelve months at Manchester Grammar School (Hope 1947, 8).

2.2.3 Percival: The First Student at Warrington Academy

A committee was created to plan the Warrington Academy as early at 1754, when the committee published a letter with its plans for the Academy:

> Design for an academy: Proposal for Carrying into Execution A Plan for the Liberal Education of Youth, by Instructing them in the most important Branches of LITERATURE, as well as the Principles of Religion and Liberty (Tate Library Warrington Academy Papers 1754).

The committee solicited subscriptions (annual donations to create the Academy's funding) and a general meeting of the subscribers, to be known as a Society. Those who contributed two guineas became trustees, which appears to the have been the standard amount required to hold this oversight position. Twelve trustees were to be elected. "A proper number of Persons, of known Ability, [are to] be chosen by the Society, as soon as the State of the Fund will admit it, to be *Tutors* and *Teachers* ..." (Tate Library Warrington Academy Papers 1754). The Academy will be "open to all persons" (Tate Library Warrington Academy Papers 1754).

The Academy was planned to be self-governing under its own rules:

> That the *Committee*, assisted by the *Tutors*, shall form a proper System of Rules and orders for Government and Discipline of the Students, the Security of their Morals, and their better obtaining the Advantages, and answering the Ends of a Liberal Education (Tate Library Warrington Academy Papers 1754).

In 1757 the Warrington Academy opened and Percival became its first student. His study of Latin and Greek continued, to which were added Mathematics, *Belles Lettres*, and other subjects.

> The study of Ethics, however, which formed an important branch of academical discipline, attracted his early curiosity. Guided by an able master, he explored the various and fascinating regions of moral science; and imbibed a partiality for these pursuits, which, while it prompted his immediate industry, furnished the source of the most grateful occupations in his riper leisure (Percival 1807, Vol. I, viii).

The "master" was John Taylor (1694–1761), who, as we will see in greater detail below, was deeply influenced by Baconian moral science. Percival also studied with "a private instructor" (Percival 1807, Vol. I, viii), John Seddon (1725–1770). Seddon's influence on Percival's family was profound: "... soon after the period of Mr. Seddon's establishment at Warrington, the family of Mr. Percival was induced to quit communion with the church of England, and to espouse the tenets of Protestant dissent" (Percival 1807, Vol. I, ix).

The effect of this conversion to the ranks of dissent was to have an important bearing on the future career of Thomas Percival. From this time forward it greatly influenced his early education and his future outlook on life, and to the time of his death he strictly adhered to the Unitarian faith (Hope 1947, 12).

The trustees reported that by July, 1760, forty-four students were enrolled, with thirty-one attending at the opening of the Academy and ten of these students "preparing for the pulpit" (Tate Library Report 1760, 1). Rules approved included required attendance in class and at prayers, and a prohibition against going to "Taverns, or public Houses, or any Place of Public Diversion" (Tate Library Report 1760, 2). Distinct courses of study were approved for students intending to enter "the learned Professions" and those planning for "a life of Business and Commerce" (Tate Library Report 1760, 2). For 1761 the trustees reported that John Aikin (1713–1780), already a faculty member, would become the Divinity tutor and that Joseph Priestley (1733–1804), would succeed Aikin as tutor of languages and Belles Lettres (Tate Library Report 1761, 2). Percival had left for Edinburgh by that time.

The tutors were "Dissenters" and the Warrington Academy became a prominent Dissenters' school. Percival's intellectual formation in moral science fostered what Edward calls his "love of *moral* science" (Percival 1807, Vol. I, ccxxv). Percival's subsequent work in moral science and moral philosophy and his religious formation cannot be understood apart from Dissent in eighteenth-century England, especially the key figures of Taylor and Seddon, and the Warrington Academy, about which, more below.

2.2.4 Edinburgh, London, Leyden, and a Tour of the Netherlands and France

Percival put his Warrington-Academy studies to work in a critical reading of the Articles of the Church, assent to which the Oxford and Cambridge colleges required. This critical examination "served rather to confirm than remove his scruples (Percival E 1807, x)" and he gave up plans to attend Oxford, in a "deliberately arrived at" decision (Espinasse 1877, 178). He reached the same judgment about Cambridge. He turned his sights and plans north, to Scotland and the University of Edinburgh, for which he departed June 30, 1761 (Hope 1947, 18).

The University of Edinburgh distinguished itself in many ways. It was committed to *Lehrnfreiheit* or the freedom of its professors to teach what they saw fit, the origins of what is known today in universities in many countries as academic freedom. This commitment sustained a highly creative intellectual and academic environment. Edinburgh did not require allegiance to any prescribed beliefs. As a consequence, many students of great ability, such as Percival and Gregory before him, came to study medicine. Young men from the North American British colonies also came to study medicine, including young men who cultivated sentiments of independence from royal tyranny and its ever-ready minions of evil in Parliament in

London. Warrington Academy prepared him well for the academic, religious, and cultural pluralism that Percival met with in Edinburgh.

Warrington Academy also prepared him for the Baconian scientists and physicians on the medical faculty. Many had studied with Boerhaave and his colleagues in Leyden and were known as "Boerhaave's Men" (McCullough 1998). These included Robert Whytt (1714–1766), Professor of Theory of Medicine, who championed the study and treatment of "nervous ailments," making him a forerunner of psychiatrists and neurologists. John Rutherford (1695–1779), Professor of the Practice of Medicine, had brought students into the Royal Infirmary of Edinburgh, following Boerhaave's innovation, which Rutherford had experienced first-hand as a medical student in Leyden. William Cullen (1710–1790), Professor of Chemistry, taught clinical medicine and was revered by Edinburgh students as a great clinical teacher. Thomas Young (1726–1783) was Professor of Midwifery, an early academic "Man-Midwife" or obstetrician. He taught students about the use of the advanced technology of forceps to assist vaginal delivery. Man-midwives did not share this advanced technology with midwives, thus gaining market advantage with well-to-do pregnant women who preferred access to what is now known as operative vaginal delivery.

Whytt, Rutherford, and Cullen gave lectures preliminary to attendance by the students in the wards of the Royal Infirmary of Edinburgh. They adapted this practice from what they experienced in Leyden, where Boerhaave gave "prolegomena" to his lectures on the Institutes of Medicine that addressed topics in philosophy of medicine with emphasis on Baconian observational science. Rutherford uses 'patient' rather than 'the sick', or 'aegrotus', foreshowing Gregory's situating the concept of being a patient in his professional ethics in medicine. Whytt presented the concept of observed normal function: "In every disease, we are to suspect something wrong in the Machine & it shows always that there is a right performance of the function" (RCPSG 1/9/4. n.d., 2) Cullen's lectures were terse and included remarks on the temperament of the physician, which should for formed in response to "circumstances ... common to all men" (RCPSG 1/9/7 1768, 3). Young's lectures include admonitions such as "never propose Rude Questions to your patient" and "never be too officious and stay by the woman" (RCPSG 1/9/9 1768, 218–220). Young's approach invites the interpretation of it as a mixture of the discourses of *de cautelis* and *medicus politicus*. As they did for Gregory (McCullough 1998), these preliminary lectures further developed Percival's "study of Ethics" (Percival 1807, Vol. III, viii).

The intellectual life at Edinburgh extended beyond the extraordinary professors in the medical school and included David Hume (1711–1776). Percival had "the good fortune, in particular, to enjoy frequent and friendly intercourse with the rival candidates for historic fame, Mr. Hume and Dr. Robertson" (Percival 1807, Vol. III, xiii). "Dr. Robertson" was William Robertson (1721–1793), Principal (or president) of the University of Edinburgh and an accomplished historian, renowned for, among other works, *The History of Scotland during the Reigns of Queen Mary and King James VI* (Robertson 1759). "Mr. Hume" is, of course, David Hume but the Hume of *The History of England*, appearing in six volumes from 1754 to 1761 (Hume

2.2 Thomas Percival of Warrington and Manchester

[1778] 1983). The 'historic fame' referenced by Edward Percival should be read as fame in historiography of, respectively, Scotland and England.

Edward Percival was well aware of the controversy in response to Hume's irreligiosity:

> For the former of these [Hume] he [Percival] seems to have entertained a strong personal regard; nor did he afterwards suffer his veneration of the man and the philosopher to be diminished by his aversion from the polemic. "It was impossible to know Mr. Hume," (he declares in one of his moral dissertations) "without admiring his talents, and loving him for the suavity of his manners" (Percival 1807, Vol. I, xiii–xiv).

Their acquaintance was to be renewed when Percival visited Paris during Hume's time there as "secretary of the English embassy" (Percival 1807, Vol. I, xiv) and later chargé d'affaires from 1763 to 1766.

There was no established, much less required, medical curriculum at Edinburgh. Edward Percival reports that "[d]uring three *sessions*, Mr. Percival attended the lectures of the most distinguished professors of Edinburgh" (Percival 1807, Vol. III, xv). He then spent a year (1763–1764) in London, where he made many acquaintances. Percival returned to Edinburgh in the fall of 1764 (Hope 1947, 24).

> One friendship of particular intimacy may deserve notice, as it was cherished on each side by the reciprocation of an almost paternal and filial regard. The person to whom Mr. Percival was thus attached was the late Lord Willoughby de Parham, a nobleman of considerable learning and various accomplishments (Percival 1807, Vol. I, xv).

Lord Willoughby maintained a country home near Warrington, enabling both to continue their friendship when his lordship was not in London and engaged with his work in Parliament and the Royal Society and leadership of various charities.

Lord Willoughby died in 1765. Before his death Lord Willoughby had proposed Percival for membership in the Royal Society, of which his Lordship was then Vice-President. Percival was unanimously elected on March 7 of that year (Hope 1947, 24), "the youngest member (I am informed) ever introduced into that learned corporation" (Percival 1807, Vol. I, xvi). Percival had by then but one accomplishment in science or medicine, the essay *An Inquiry into the Resemblance between Chyle and Milk*, which Percival had presented to the Royal Medical Society of Edinburgh in 1763. Its first publication appears to have been in 1767, in Percival's first *Essays Medical and Experimental* (Percival [1767[1807]). There is no textual evidence that I could find to indicate that the electors of the Royal Society were aware of this work in 1765. John Pickstone (1944–2014) puts this honor in its historical context: "hardly the intellectual honor that such an election would become, but a mark of considerable intellectual and social respectability, especially in one so young" (Pickstone 1893, 164). *A Father's Instructions, Part the Second* is dedicated to the memory of Lord Willoughby (Percival 1807, Vol. I, 89).

In April of 1765 (Hope 1947), Percival "removed to the University of Leyden, with a view to complete his medical studies, and to be admitted to the degree of Doctor of Physic" (Percival 1807, Vol. I, xvi–xvii). He was awarded his M.D. after the public defense on July 6 of that year of "his inaugural dissertation *"De Frigore"*" (Percival 1807, Vol. III, xvii). He spent the balance of 1765 on a "tour through various parts of France and Holland," (Percival 1 807, xvii), an abbreviated Grand Tour. Percival returned to England and Warrington at the end of 1765.

Even though Boerhaave had died more than two decades before Percival studied at Edinburgh and Leyden, Boerhaave's influence was profound. At both universities, Percival would have studied Boerhaave's *Institutiones Medicae* (Institutes of Medicine) (Boerhaave 1747). The distinguished medical historian, Lester King (1908–2002), explains the genre of "Institutes" in the history of medical education:

> The word "Institutes" is not in any sense restricted to medicine. It would apply to almost any subject, for it indicates basic principles, a digest of fundamental information necessary to practice that subject. … In medicine, the Institutes were usually relatively brief, although there are exceptions to this, but they provided comprehensive coverage of the field. They furnished the entire background for medicine, what we today call a digest of the basic sciences, together with some principles of diagnosis and treatment. The Institutes traditionally comprised five divisions – physiology, pathology, semeiology (the study of signs), hygiene, and therapeutics – and whoever had a sound knowledge of these subjects could practice medicine with confidence. The information contained in the Institutes was usually presented in compact, dogmatic, and aphoristic form, without providing much in the way of detailed evidence or explanation (King 1970, 60).

Boerhaave's successors at Leyden lectured on the Institutes of Medicine, as did his professors at Edinburgh, including Cullen (1772).

Boerhaave opens *Institutiones* with an account of the "scope" (*scopus*) of the "Art" (*Ars*) of medicine, i.e., clinical application of the science (*scientia*) of medicine (Boerhaave 1747, 8). The scope or proper goals of the "Art" are "the avoidance of pain, disability, and death, as well as the conservation of present health and the restitution of its absence" (*omnum scopum Artis esse evitationem doloris, debilitaris, mortis; adeoque conservationem sanitates praesentis, absentis restitutionem*) (Boerhaave 1747, 8). The first part of the scope of medicine suggests that Boerhaave was an early advocate of what is now called preventive medicine. Note, too, that prevention and management of disability falls within the proper scope of medicine. There is also a section, the last, on "palliative care" (*curatio palliativa*)

Boerhaave sets out the content of *Institutiones* in succinct, numbered paragraphs in "aphoristic form," as King puts it. The 1,260 numbered aphorisms are designed to be memorized, allowing the physician to commit to memory the essential elements of medical science and practice, or at least be able to look up and rapidly absorb what he needed to take care of a sick individual. To facilitate this process, the index of thirty-five pages guides the "user from the back" to texts that are numbered in the order in which they appear, not the page number on which they appear. Cullen's (1772) *Institutions … for the use of STUDENTS* has 302 numbered paragraphs, but it is only Part 1 of a multipart course. Boerhaave's *Institutiones* and the texts entitled *Institutions* at Edinburgh would become the models for the Institutes format of *Medical Jurisprudence* and *Medical Ethics*, as we will see in Chap. 3.

2.2.5 Warrington and Marriage to Elizabeth Bassnett of London

Percival returned to Warrington in 1765. On March 24, 1766 (Hope 1947, 29), he married Elizabeth Bassnett (1747–1822), "the daughter and only surviving child of Nathanial Bassnett, esq; merchant, of London" (Percival 1807, Vol. III, xvii). She was also the "sole heiress" of her father's fortune (Thornber n.d.) They married in Liverpool at St. George's Church; she was 19; he was 26 (Howard 1997, Vol. 4, 64). This was a time of "studious leisure" (Percival 1807, Vol. III, xviii), the productivity of which was supported by his wife: "By this happy alliance, the most valuable exertions of Dr. Percival's life were called forth" (Percival 1807, Vol. I, xvii). Elizabeth Percival then disappears from the *Memoirs* and spent nearly four decades as his invisible helpmeet. When her husband died, she was 57. She died in Bath at the age of 75 (Howard 1997, Vol. 4, 64). Edward resided there until his death three years earlier, so she may have lived with him and his family or nearby. Unlike many other women of her time, Elizabeth Percival did not die in childbirth. Like many of other women of her time, at least four of her children died before she did, two of them very young, a loss with which she would live for the rest of her life.

I have been able to establish that they had at least seven children, four of whom predeceased both their parents and one of whom predeceased Elizabeth Percival: Thomas Bassnett Percival (1767–1798); Anne Percival (1768–1847); James Percival (1769–1793); Edward Cropper Percival (1783–1819), the author of *Memoirs*; Stanley Orred Percival (1789–1877); Maria Percival (1797?–1780); and Edward Bayley Percival (1798?–1780). In the "Preface" to the second part of *A Father's Instructions*, Percival lists five sets of initials (Percival 1807, Vol. I, 91). 'TBP' is Thomas Bassnett Percival, 'AP' is Anne Percival, and 'JP' is James Percival, who were alive at the time (1777). I have not been able to identify "FP" or "GBP".

Percival also wanted to start a clinical practice in a large city. He first considered London but decided upon nearby Manchester. "In the year 1767, he removed his family to that town, and commenced his professional career, with a degree of success, which, I believe, has seldom been paralleled" (Percival 1807, Vol. III, xviii).

This time in Percival's life was similar to the time in Gregory's life when he lived in Aberdeen. As Professor of Medicine at King's College, Gregory had no students. This was therefore a time of "studious leisure" that Gregory put to good use. For example, he helped to found the Aberdeen Philosophical Society with his cousin Thomas Reid, as described in Chap. 1. At the meetings of the Society Gregory presented papers that became his first book, *A Comparative View of the State and Faculties of Man with Those of the Animal World* (Gregory 1765).

Percival was similarly productive during his two years of "studious leisure" in Warrington, as he contemplated where he should move his new family and start to practice medicine.

> The leisure which Dr. Percival had hitherto enjoyed, had given him the opportunity of engaging in various philosophical and experimental enquiries, relating, for the most part, to the science of Physic. The "Essays" which he formed on the result of his investigations,

were sometimes presented to the Royal Society, and were afterwards inserted in the volumes of its Transactions; at other times, they were communicated to the public through the medium of the most current periodical journals. These miscellaneous pieces were, in the course of the present year [1767], collected and published in one volume, under the title of *Essays Medical and Experimental* (Percival 1807, Vol. III, xviii–xix).

2.2.6 Manchester: The English Enlightenment Commitment to Improvement Using Baconian Science

Percival considered settling in London but decided against this move (Espinasse 1877). It is possible, but not documented in my researches, that he did not welcome the challenges a Dissenter might encounter in London. Percival moved his family to Manchester in 1767 and resided there until his death in 1804.

> With such professional knowledge and skill, such culture and manners as his, Percival soon took the highest position among the physicians of Manchester, and abandoned his intention of settling in London (Espinasse 1977, 179).

Percival became an exemplar of the English enlightenment commitment to improvement, the relief of man's estate, with a focus on social institutions (Porter 1997, 2000). Edward explains:

> But amidst the active pursuits of his profession, of the retired occupations of his closet, Dr. Percival was not unmindful of the opportunities which came withing his reach, of engaging his services in schemes for the public benefit. From the period of his residence in Manchester, he had been a zealous supporter of the various institutions of benevolence which that wealthy and populous town comprehends (Percival 1807, Vol. I, xxxvii).

These institutions included, as one might imagine, Warrington Academy, "an institution which engaged in a peculiar manner the attention of the leading Dissenters in this kingdom" (Percival 1807, Vol. I, xxxviii). Percival served as a trustee for many years. Edward describes the faculty: "attracted by its singular fame, a band of literary characters assembled under its protection" (Percival 1807, Vol. I, xxxix), including especially Joseph Priestley. Percival was a strong supporter of Manchester Infirmary, becoming a subscriber in 1868 and continuing his support until his death (Hope 1947, 164). He also contributed his *Medical Jurisprudence* and then *Medical Ethics* to the improvement of this hospital for the working sick poor of the city, as we will see in Chap. 3.

In 1775, "Dr. Percival was induced, for the purposes of health, and for the pleasure of occasional retirement, to take a country residence in the neighbourhood of Manchester" (Percival 1807, Vol. I, xlii), Hart-Hill, in Salford, about three miles from Manchester. "His friends, both professional and mercantile, had similar retreats" (Pickstone 1993, 165). The Percival family home at Hart-Hill no longer stands. The rolling pastureland has been incorporated into Buile Park (Eccles Old Road n.d., a website that includes photographs of the rolling land around Hart Hill).

2.2 Thomas Percival of Warrington and Manchester

In 1775 the first of the three volumes of *A Father's Instructions* were completed that year. This and the many other works that followed are examined in the next section.

Honors came his way. In 1773 he was made an Honorary Fellow of the Medical Society of London (Hope 1947, 166). In 1777, "Dr. Percival was unanimously elected Fellow of the Royal Society at Paris; an honour which was conferred without solicitation, and accompanied by some flattering marks of distinction" (Percival 1807, Vol. I, lxii). Hope explains that the formal title was "Foreign Fellow" (Hope 1947, 167). In 1778 he was made a Fellow of the Royal Society of Edinburgh (Hope 1947, 166).

In May of 1780, Percival experienced a loss common to many parents of his time, the death of a child. His loss was more profound in that two of his six children, Maria age 3 and Edward Bayley not yet two years old, died (Percival 1807, Vol. I, ccxlviii–ccl) within two weeks of each other.

The next year, 1781, with others Percival founded the Literary and Philosophical Society of Manchester.

> This institution derived its origins from the stated weekly meetings for *conversation*, which Dr. Percival held at his own house; the resort of the literary characters, the principal inhabitants, and of occasional strangers. As these meetings became more numerous, it was in time found convenient to transfer them to a tavern, and to constitute a few rules for the better direction of their proceedings (Percival 1807, Vol. I, lxvii).

The English, Scottish, and Continental enlightenments flourished in coffee houses and taverns, essential social institutions. Intellectual societies often had rules, in part, to keep proceedings in line as spirit beverages fueled learned discourse. The rules of the Society may have been in Percival's thoughts, as he composed the enumerated *Medical Jurisprudence* and *Medical Ethics*.

The Society began, as many of its kind also did, to publish its proceeding, as "Memoirs" (Percival 1807, Vol. I, lxxi). Percival contributed a number of essays, which were gathered in his *Essays Medical, Philosophical, and Experimental* (Percival 1772a, 1776b, 1788–1789).

Starting in 1785, Percival joined with other Dissenters in Manchester to plan the creation of a "seminary for the education of Protestant Dissenting Ministers, similar to that which was on the eve of being dissolved in Warrington" (Percival 1807, Vol. I, lxxvi), i.e., the Warrington Academy. The Warrington Academy moved to Manchester in 1786 and became the Manchester Academy. In 1849 it became a member college of the University of London. In 1893 it relocated to Oxford, to become in 1996 a member college by royal charter of the University of Oxford, known as Harris Manchester College (Harris Manchester College, n.d.).

Another honor came to Percival June 2, 1786, through the good offices of his friend and correspondent, Benjamin Franklin (1706–1790). Percival was elected to membership in the American Philosophical Society of Philadelphia (Hope 1947, 203), founded in 1743 and still in existence (American Philosophical Society n.d.).

During the 1780s Percival rose to prominence in Manchester:

By the 1780s, Percival was the acknowledged leader of local culture, a figure of national significance, later a correspondent of such cosmopolitan figures as Benjamin Franklin. He was a founder of the Manchester Literary and Philosophical Society, a sponsor of Manchester New College (the successor of Warrington Academy), and a kind of super consultant to the Manchester Infirmary. He was a leading member of the Congregation of Cross Street Unitarian Chapel, which included much of Manchester's burgeoning mercantile wealth. He was in a position now to be a paternalist not just to his children (or via books) [*A Father's Instructions*, about which more, see below]; he was equipped and inclined to be a city father, a public paternalist, solving public problems rather larger than donkey-driving by the Bridgewater canal [referencing a story in *A Father's Instructions* about a cart-driver beating his donkey beside the canal] (Pickstone 1993, 166–167).

So did the Dissenters of Manchester: "… its dissenters may have been marginal to some aspects of English life, but they were powerful in Manchester, their chapel at least as rich as the local parish church" (Pickstone 1993, 172).

His son James, born in 1769, followed his father to the medical school of the University of Edinburgh. In 1793 he died there. His death had an impact on Percival's preparation of *Medical Jurisprudence*, as we will see in Chap. 3.

In 1796 Percival was instrumental, with others, in the creation of a Board of Health. One of its principal aims was improving the health of poor by directly causes of diseases in their "habitations," especially "infection" resulting from lack of "cleanliness and ventilation" (Percival 1807, Vol. I, cc). Gregory, as we saw in Chap. 1, was committed to improvement in health in its social dimensions by preventing famine. Percival continues in the English enlightenment commitment to improvement in health by preventing housing conditions that promote disease.

Percival identified three aims or "objects" of the Board, all directed to the health and well-being of the sick poor of Manchester:

The objects of the Board of Health are threefold:

I. To obviate the generation of diseases:
II. To prevent the spreading of them by contagion:
III. To shorten the duration of existing diseases, and to mitigate their evils, by affording the necessary aids and comforts to those who labour under them (Percival 1807, Vol. I, cclivii).

"On 25 Jan. 1796 he addressed the Manchester committee or board of health on certain evils which had been developed by the growth of the factory system, and recommended legislative interference with the conditions of factory labour" (Nicholson 1885). Espinasse suggests that "Percival may be regarded as one of the parents of factory legislation" (Espinasse 1877, 187) that limited working hours to twelve each day for children, for example.

In 1798 his eldest son, Thomas Basnett Percival, a clergyman, died at the age of thirty-two. His death deeply affected his father. As we will see in Chap. 3, his son's death played a role in the preparation of *Medical Ethics*.

On August 30, 1804, Percival died. He was aware that his life was ending and accepted it: "The spectacle of patient and submissive resignation which Dr. Percival exhibited during his last illness was truly impressive" ((Percival 1807, Vol. I, ccxviii). His remains, accompanied by his "three surviving sons, and his son-in-law," were interred "in the grave of his ancestors, in the burial-ground of the parochial church of Warrington" on September 3, 1804. The Literary and Philosophical Society of Manchester placed a tablet "over the chair of the President, in the hall where their meetings were held" (Percival 1807, Vol. I, ccxx). The tablet served as

> … a testimony of their grateful sense of his zeal, in promoting their various interests; of his frequent and valuable contributions to their Memoirs; of the Ability, Candour, and Urbanity with which he directed their discussions, and of the elegant Manners, virtuous Conduct, and dignified Piety, by which his Life was eminently distinguished (Percival 1807, Vol. I, ccxx).

2.3 Percival's Intellectual and Moral Formation

2.3.1 *The English National Enlightenment*

More than the calendar changed in England in the fourth decade of the eighteenth century, resulting in the above-noted "N.S." after Percival's birth date. The English enlightenment gathered momentum in ways that profoundly shaped the young Percival's intellectual development. Dissent became a key component of the English enlightenment, of which Percival self-consciously became a participant. In his scientific writings and in his professional ethics in medicine he became a leader of the English enlightenment.

It is commonplace in the anglophone philosophical literature to accept that there was a homogeneous cultural, intellectual, social, political, and economic movement in Western Europe during the "long eighteenth century" that came to be known as The Enlightenment. This movement was based on the appeal to Reason and the triumph of Reason over emotion, sentiment, and faith.

Immanuel Kant's (1724–1804) *What is the Enlightenment?* epitomizes the Reason-based understanding of The Enlightenment.

> This enlightenment requires nothing but *freedom* – and the most innocent of all that may be called "freedom": freedom to make public use of one's reason in all matters. Now I hear the cry from all sides: "Do not argue!" The officer says: "Do not argue drill!" The tax collector: "Do not argue pay!" The pastor: "Do not argue believe!" Only one ruler in the world says: "Argue as much as you please, but obey!" We find restrictions on freedom everywhere. But which restriction is harmful to enlightenment? Which restriction is innocent, and which advances enlightenment? I reply: the public use of one's reason must be free at all times, and this alone can bring enlightenment to mankind (Kant n.d.).

Reason alone has the capacity to release us from the irrational bonds of political and religious power. Only when liberated by Reason will we be free to pursue progress toward ever-greater freedom from the tyranny of all forms of unreason about the (alleged) human good. The roiling brew of emotions, or the passions, threatened to plunge us into irrationality. Reason, however, has the capacity to subdue the passions.

Isaiah Berlin (1909–1997) sounded a clarion-call with his warning that Kantian Reason paves the way toward tyranny, the antidote to which is a pluralism of views about the human good (Berlin 1958). Such a pluralism requires for its intellectual basis a pluralism about the capacities of reason, now, importantly, with a lower-case 'r'.

This pluralism can be found in eighteenth-century Western Europe, if we simply abandon the idea that there was a homogeneous phenomenon called The Enlightenment. Roy Porter and Mikláš Teich (2009) make the convincing case that there was no such intellectual, cultural, social, and political movement, Instead, there were multiple national enlightenments. Porter, separately, identified the "science of man" (Porter 1990, 12) as a central focus of some national enlightenments. As we saw in Chap. 1, the Scottish enlightenment was defined by the pursuit of Baconian moral science or the Baconian science of man. Hume's *Treatise of Human Nature* (published, as it happened, the year before and the year of Percival's birth) became the essential text of the Scottish enlightenment. The chief discovery reported in the *Treatise* was the principle of sympathy, a form of instinct or an automatic process of entering into the felt experience of others.

For Hume, reason did not have a capital 'R', because reason was, for the most part, a calculating machine by which humans match means to the end that sympathy "excites" us to pursue, the interests and well-being of others. One way reason matched the end of sympathy to its means, our "incitements," was to regulate sympathy so that its end stayed in view. The virtues play a major role in this regulatory function. Depending on context, reason invents these regulatory virtues, e.g., tenderness and steadiness to regulate the physician's sympathy in the clinical setting and in clinical research.

To subsume the *Treatise* and with it Gregory's *Lectures* under the Kantian elevation of reason to Reason in The Enlightenment distorts these seminal texts of the Scottish enlightenment beyond recognition. Kant's work needs to be retitled, much more modestly, as *What is the German Enlightenment?*

What Porter writes applies to the Scottish, and, as we shall see below, the English enlightenments:

> The new Enlightenment approaches to human nature ... dismissed the idea of innate 'sinfulness' as unscientific and without foundation [in Baconian experience, foundations in Reason having been rejected], arguing instead that passions such as love, desire, pride and ambition were not inevitably evil or destructive; properly channelled, they could serve as aids to human advancement (Porter 1990, 19).

The Scottish enlightenment was committed to the deployment of Baconian science and Baconian moral science to improve all aspects of society, by seeking relief of its adversities. The same would become true of the English enlightenment, as we shall see below. This drive for improvement was the eighteenth-century Scottish enlightenment's version of Bacon's "relief of man's estate."

> Francis Bacon in an earlier age had defined the aim of knowledge as the 'relief of man's estate', and this well defines the aims of the men of the Scottish Enlightenment, who in addition to (and often in conjunction with) their interest in what Hume called the 'science of man', were also interested in the improvement of agricultural techniques, improved civic planning and the creation of model villages, improvement of the design of prisons and hospitals, and improvement in taste and what they called 'refinement' (Daiches 1986, 5).

As we shall see below and in more detail in Chap. 3, Percival was deeply committed to the improvement of hospitals, a commitment at the heart of his professional ethics in medicine.

2.3.2 Warrington Academy

The first academy at Warrington was established in 1697 with Charles Owen, D.D., as tutor and ceased operations in 1746. The second academy, known down to our time as the Warrington Academy, opened in 1757 and continued in operation until 1783. Percival was the first student enrolled in the recrudesced Warrington Academy (Bright 1859; McLachlan 1931, 1943; Fulton 1933; Obrien 1989).

McLachlan characterizes The Warrington Academy as of the "more liberal" type. He explains the meaning of 'more liberal':

> ... the more liberal academies strove to maintain the principle of the open door, characteristic of the earlier academies, and admitted not only laymen as well as divinity students, but men of different religious opinions (not excluding Episcopalians) training for the ministry (McLachlan 1931, 4–5).

This commitment to religious pluralism defined 'liberal'. The commitment of Warrington Academy to a liberal education, even if strongly influenced by Dissent, was put into practice:

> Earlier, Warrington's reputation for scholarship combined with its undenominational outlook had found favour with many Anglicans: they were said to form at least a third of the students during the last period of the Academy (Wyckes 1986).

Lachlan reports that during its existence the Warrington Academy educated 21 men for medicine, 100 for commerce, and 55 for divinity. There was a three-year course "intended for a life of Business or Commerce" (McLachlan 1931, 209).

> Youths intended for business or the secular professions were not sent to the academics in order to escape contact with every form of religious teaching but to obtain this and much else without subscription to the Articles of the Anglican Church (McLachlan 1931, 25).

2.3.2.1 The Dissenting Academies and the Curriculum of the Warrington Academy

The Church of England has its origins in the defiance of the Roman Catholic Pope and his English Bishops by King Henry VIII (1491–1547; reign 1509–1547) and his making himself the head of this new church. This set loose decades of persecution, turmoil, violence, and warfare between Anglicans and Catholics that Queen Elizabeth I (1533–1603; reign 1558–1603) sought to end with the enactment by Parliament of the Act of Supremacy in 1558 and the Act of Uniformity in 1559. The Act of Supremacy was incorporated into the statutes of the universities of Oxford and Cambridge in 1659. This "effectively excluded Dissenters from Oxford and

Cambridge" (McLachlan 1931, 1). 'Dissenter' came to name faith communities that were "non-conformist" (McLachlan 1943; O'Brien 1989). "Those who broke away had two objectives, the reform of church government, and doctrinal reformation" (Obrien 1989, 2). They would not conform their consciences to the 39 articles of the Oath of Supremacy and therefore refused to subscribe to them. The Act of Toleration of 1689 allowed for freedom of worship of the non-conforming faith communities but did not change the exclusionary policies of the Oxbridge universities.

Official increased toleration of religious difference and the proliferation of Christian religious pluralism combined with the exclusionary Oxbridge policies made necessary the creation of academic institutions, known as "academies," for formal education after completion of grammar school (in Percival's case, at the age of seventeen). These academies were designed to prepare students for lives in commerce or to continue into the professions of law, medicine, and ministry at universities.

> Dissenters, being excluded from the universities by the demand for subscription to the Articles of the Church, were compelled to provide higher education for themselves, and, in particular, to maintain the supply of men for their ministry (McLachlan 1931, 17).

Academies were created on the basis of a foundation or endowment, by outside societies, or as freestanding academic institutions with their "own trustees and subscribers" (McLachlan 1931, 3–4). As noted above, 'subscribers' referred to those individuals with the wherewithal to provide annual donations that funded the academy's budget. This was a common source of revenue for charitable institutions at the time, notably the Infirmaries (McCullough 1998).

The curriculum for all included ancient languages, mathematics, logic, "natural history" and "natural philosophy" or Baconian science, moral philosophy, and "Belles Lettres" (McLachlan 1931, 210). The tutors with whom Percival studied were John Taylor and John Aikin in "Scripture Divinity" and classics, and John Holt for natural philosophy and mathematics (Tate Library Report 1758; Kendrick 1858; McLachlan 1931, 210) from 1757 to 1772. Holt also taught logic, metaphysics, and history. "Of his judgment Dr. Aikin entertained a very high opinion" (McLachlan 1943). Taylor and Aikin were considered "amongst the most eminent of the Dissenting Divines in England" (Bright 1859, 7).

'Scripture Divinity' took a Baconian approach to the sacred texts of Christianity; they were sources of evidence. Hence, the course included "lectures on the Evidences of Natural Religion" (McLachlan 1931, 25). The Unitarianism to which Percival subscribed at Warrington Academy was Baconian, accepting only evidence-based tenets, as we shall see below.

In an early experiment in what we now know in liberal arts colleges in the United States as the seminar style of teaching, Aiken schooled his students in critical appraisal of everything they were taught, including what he had taught them:

> To avoid even the appearance of dogmatism, it was his custom in every lecture to stop and say, "Gentlemen, have I explained the subject to your satisfaction?" He would then devote a little time to answering the questions and resolving the difficulties of his students (McLachlan 1931, 214).

2.3 Percival's Intellectual and Moral Formation 71

Thus did Aikin provide Percival with an exemplar of intellectual excellence, in the form of Gregory's intellectual virtue of candor.

Lord Willoughby of Parham (1713–1765), formally Hugh 15th Baron Willoughby of Parham, became the first president of Warrington Academy. He was English Presbyterian (Bright 1859, 3), further evidence of the Academy's commitment to religious pluralism. As we saw above, he also became an important and influential patron of Percival, such patronage being a necessity for advancement of those not born to noble blood.

The campus was romanticized by the very well-known poet, Anne Laetitia Barbauld (1743–1825), John Aikin's sister:

> Mark where its simple front yon mansion rears,
>   The nursery of men for future years (Bright 1859, 9).

The storied Mersey river (e.g., the "Mersey Beat" of a band of some accomplishment, two centuries later, from Liverpool where the Mersey empties into the Liverpool Bay on the Irish Sea), she adds in full romantic blush, "Reflects the ascending seats with conscious pride" (Bright 1859, 10). Bright takes the bloom off the flower when he reports the results of his visit to the campus comprising the "simple front" of the "ugly, mean old brick house" and a "narrow, dingy side" building (Bright 1859, 10). The Mersey may reflect the latter but Bright is skeptical (Bright 1859, 10). Perhaps the spare style of *Medical Jurisprudence* and *Medical Ethics* has its origins in these plain buildings.

2.3.2.2 Percival's Teachers at the Warrington Academy

John Aikin, John Taylor, and John Seddon had a profound influence on the intellectual formation of Percival during his years at Warrington Academy. The tutors of the Academy were published scholars, often on the press of William Eyres (1734–1809) of Warrington (Fulton 1933). Later, Percival published with Eyres, as did many other Dissenters.

John Aikin: Teacher of Jurisprudence. Aikin taught a third-year course on "Jurisprudence." The syllabus included Justinian's *Institutes* (in the original Latin) or the codification of law. Aiken's pedagogy was to study this legal text "so far as it is derived from the same sources with the doctrines of Natural Religion and Private Morality" (McLachlan 1931, 215). We will consider both in greater detail below. Aikin's teaching shaped Percival's understanding of his task in his 1794 *Medical Jurisprudence*, about which more in Chap. 3.

John Taylor: Teacher of Baconian Moral Science, Deism, and Dissent. John Taylor was born to a dissenting mother and his father was a merchant in Lancashire. He was an English Presbyterian who had studied divinity at the University of Glasgow, from which he held an honorary doctorate (Dissenting Academies Online-Taylor). Taylor came to Warrington Academy in 1857 from the Octagon Chapel, a dissenting congregation in Norwich. Taylor was one of the first tutors. His health was failing and he died four years later.

In his theological writings Taylor is committed to the concept of "natural religion" (Taylor 1762b, 12). By this he meant religious belief that could be established in the basis of evidence open to everyone. This is the discourse of Baconian religion. Baconian religion appeals to deism (the discoverable god of nature who is the author of creation and its evident order) supported by Baconian science, as we saw with Gregory in Chap. 2. Baconian Unitarian Dissent accepts the existence of Jesus Christ, based on the evidence of Scripture. Unitarian theism is distinctive because it excludes trinitarian theism (the God of revelation and incarnate in his son, Jesus Christ, blessed by the Holy Spirit). This is christianity with a deliberate lower-case 'c'. Thus, Taylor taught that we are "rational dependent beings and christians" (Taylor 1762b, 5). 'Rational' means an individual who conforms belief and judgment to evidence, including texts in Scripture that have the stature of evidence about god. 'Dependent' means that we are creatures of Nature's God, the god of deism. The use of lower-case 'c' in 'christian' is deliberate and signifies rejection of Christianity as promulgated by the Church of England and its theism. Here Taylor follows his teacher Thomas Dixon (1679/80–1729), an English non-conformist who opposed "all spiritual tyranny" (Dixon 1766, vii) and asserted against such tyranny that "[e]very man has a right to judge for himself, but not to prescribe for others" (Dixon 1766, iv).

'Rational' does *not* mean the deliverances of Reason as superior to Humean sympathy, a concept at work in Taylor's account of prayer. He recommends "*free* or *extempore* Prayer, in the just and rational sense of it" (Taylor 1762b, 16). "Rational prayer" should display "good order and connection" of "proper materials and language" (Taylor 1762b, 16). Rational prayer is an expression of what Dixon called "rational piety" (Dixon 1766, iii).

Spoken prayer is preferred because it promotes sympathy within the worshipping congregation:

> ... the Prayer which proceeds from the abundance of the heart and affections, is not only more lively in itself, but more affecting to others, who hear it, and most naturally suited to awaken their attention and penetrate and move their hearts (Taylor 1762b, 18–19).

The appeal to the concept of sympathy from the atheist, David Hume, would not have scandalized the Baconian Taylor, his students at Warrington, or readers of his book. Unitarian dissent, because it is Baconian dissent, is made of studier intellectual and spiritual stuff. Prayer should not exhibit the disorder of enthusiasts, theists whose beliefs lack an evidence base in nature and Scripture. Payer should conform to "natural plainness and simplicity" (Taylor 1762b, 52). The intellectual virtues of plainness and simplicity in prayer regulate sympathy and thereby prevent religious enthusiasm. For Taylor these and other virtues are inventions of reason and reason-based reflection on the products of sympathy. Instinct or sympathy unregulated is not a reliable source of knowledge of the virtues (Taylor 1762b). Taylor takes Francis Hutcheson (1694–1746) to task for not better appreciating this aspect of moral reasoning (Taylor 1759), which intellectual scolding would not apply to Hume and Gregory.

Religious belief, thus understood, should be put to work in life:

2.3 Percival's Intellectual and Moral Formation

These are the principles of religion, more just and important, which ought to be firmly established in the mind of every christian, to enable him to discharge the duties of his profession (Taylor 1762b, 22).

Baconian dissent is accountable to the discipline of evidence and well-regulated sympathy.

We should always interpret Scripture in a Sense consistent with the laws of natural Religion, or with the known Perfections of God, and the notions of Right and Wrong, Good and Evil, which are discernable in the Works of Creation and in the present Constitution of things (Taylor 1762a, 6).

An adherent to Baconian antipathy to bias of all forms, Taylor adds, as an antidote to "mean and selfish purposes" (Taylor 1762a, 11):

To the effectual Study of Scripture, it is necessary that our Minds and Hearts be unbyassed, unprejudiced, open to the Truth, and always quite free to discern and receive it (Taylor 1762a, 11).

Judgments about character and behavior based on results of Baconian moral science have intellectual and moral authority for everyone, including the individual about whom such judgments are made by others. That individual, as a matter of intellectual and moral integrity, should accept such judgments, which are, therefore, not paternalism, much less tyranny. This differs from judgments made without the results of Baconian moral science, such as those of Church of England, which were tyrannical.

Baconian dissent is not accountable to Christianity and therefore not accountable to ecclesiastical authority, especially that of the Church of England. Inasmuch as the monarch is the head of the Church of England and head of state, Baconian dissent is not accountable to the Church or state. Baconian dissent therefore entails religious liberty as a fundamental social and political value that promotes tolerant and peaceful pluralism.

And according to that rule [Baconian self-discipline] you sincerely endeavor to form your religious sentiments, leaving your fellow christians perfectly free to do the same, and living with them in peace, and in all offices of love and goodness, though they may happen in some things to differ from your judgment (Taylor 1762b, 78).

This is secular religion. No appeal is made to divine revelation, only to the evidence of nature and Scripture. Nor is there any intrinsic hostility toward any other faith community, including the state religion of England, with all of its power.

Taylor identifies the implications of Baconian dissent for other aspects of life:

It is not Speculation, but Practice and Experience, which renders a man skillful in business. So in religion, no Man can be truly wise and knowing but he who liveth wisely and virtuously (Taylor 1762a, 11).

In sharp contrast to the Oath of Supremacy, backed by theologically sanctioned state power, Taylor deploys the discourse of secular, evidence-based persuasion. Dissenters should live wisely and virtuously, as witnesses to natural religion and its truth. Such lives express the "principles of religion … as best adapted to our Circumstances or, all things considered, as the most likely to make Mankind wise and happy" (Taylor 1762a, 28–29). Part of the evidence base for persuasion is the exemplar of well-formed moral character.

Like other tutors at Warrington Academy, Taylor taught from the texts of others as well as from this own views. His principal text was *The Religion of Nature Delineated* by William Wollaston (1659–1724) (spelled "Woolaston" by Taylor). Edward Harwood (1729–1794), in his elegy for Taylor reports that Taylor's "last performance was a *Sketch of Moral Philosophy*, which he drew up for the use of his pupils, and as introductory to lectures on *Wollaston's Religion of Nature*" (Harwood 1716). Taylor *Sketch of Moral Philosophy* was published in 1760 (Taylor 1760).

Wollaston was a priest in the Church of England and a scholar of ancient Greek and Latin and classical history. *Religion of Nature* is full-throated in its Deism, which is announced in his title for the book. Truth, Wollaston holds, is accomplished when thought and speech conform to the full reality of things in the world, which are independent of us but not of God; he created them as the "author of nature" (Wollaston [1722] 1750, Sect 1, ¶ 22). We are capable of freedom of action, which is right when it conforms to the truth of things and wrong when it does not. The justification for this view of the normative is that God's creation reflects his providence, infusing his presence and goodness into nature and thereby vouchsafing the truth of things.

> X. *If there be moral good and evil, distinguished as before, there is religion; and such as may most properly be styled natural.* By *religion* I mean nothing else but an obligation to do (under which word I comprehend acts both of body and mind. I say, *to do*) what ought not to be omitted, and to *forbear* what ought not to be done. So that there must be religion, if there are things, of which some ought not to be done, some not to be omitted. But that there are such, appears from what has been said concerning moral good and evil: because that, which to omit would be evil, and which therefore being done would be good or well done, ought certainly by the terms *to be done*; and so that, which being done would be evil, and implies such absurdities and rebellion against the supreme being, as are mentioned under proposition the IVth. ought most undoubtedly *not to be done*. And then since there is *religion*, which follows from the distinction between moral good and evil; since this distinction is founded in the respect, which mens acts bear to truth; and since no proposition can be true, which expresses things otherwise than as they are in nature: since things are so, there must be religion, which is founded in nature, and may upon that account be most properly and truly called the *religion of nature* or *natural religion*; the great *law* of which religion, the law of nature, or rather (as we shall afterwards find reason to call it) of the Author of nature is (Wollaston [1722] 1750, Sect 1, ¶ 61).
>
> XI. *That every intelligent, active, and free being should behave himself, as by no act to contradict truth*; or, *that he should treat every thing as being what it is* (Wollaston [1722] 1750, Sect I, ¶ 62).

Wollaston provides a compelling summary, using a phrase that found its way into the Declaration of the Independence of the American States against the tyrant King George III:

> And so at last natural religion is grounded upon this strict and triple alliance or union of *truth, happiness* and *reason*; all in the same interest, and conspiring to the same methods, to advance and perfect human nature: and its truest definition is, *The pursuit of happiness by the practice of reason and truth* (Wollaston [1722] 1750, Sect III, ¶ XII.2).

Taylor prepared his account of moral reasoning in *A Sketch of Moral Philosophy* (Taylor 1760) for use with and by his students at Warrington Academy and "only as

2.3 Percival's Intellectual and Moral Formation

an introduction to the reading" (Taylor 1760, iv) of Wollaston's *Religion of Nature*. A philosophical "sketch" conveys the main points of a philosopher's view with limited argument. A sketch is not as spare as Ludwig Wittgenstein's (1889–1951) *Tractatus Logico-Philosophicus* (Wittgenstein 1922) and not as ample as Hume's *Treatise* (Hume [1739–1740] 2000).

Taylor seeks to elucidate "the Principles and Obligations of Virtue, or natural religion" (Taylor 1760, 5). He shares Wollaston's deism:

> For every Dispensation and Doctrine, which is of God, must necessarily be in Consistency with what He hath already discovered to us in the nature of Things, and certain Deductions of Reason from them (Taylor 1760, 6).

Reason grounded in and responsive only to the "nature of Things" aims to produce "Judgment … well settled in the true Principles of natural Reason" (Taylor 1760, 6). The "Principle" Taylor seeks must meet specified criteria: it should display "the … Force of Evidence" (Taylor 1760, 8), be "universal" (Taylor 1760, 9), and be "perfectly consistent with Liberty or Freedom of Choice" (Taylor 1760, 9). He then sets out a moral epistemology that requires reason and judgment to be disciplined to the truth in the nature of things and concludes:

> That right Action hath a real Foundation, not in the Prospect of Gain; nor in the Will, Power, Command, Law or Authority of any Being whatever; but in the different Nature of Things, as they are perceived by an intelligent Being. And that, the different Nature of Things being supposed, Obligation to right Action necessarily results; being taken away, there can be no reason or ground for it (Taylor 1760, 17).

This is Unitarianism as natural or Baconian religion, comprising Baconian deism, Dissent, and moral science. Right action is not a function of interest, either of an individual or a group. Right action is not a function of the views of others, including the preferences of others, state power, divine command of revealed traditions, statutory and common law, or the assertion of intellectual or moral authority by another person or by an institution such as the Church of England or by the monarch and others who exercise state power. Taylor used his *Sketches* and Wollaston's *Religion of Nature* to teach his students that, by being grounded in truth or the nature of things as created by God and not by them or any other human being, moral reasoning is autonomous. No one can force conformation of our moral reasoning to the nature of things; God's creation makes this available to everyone and gives the nature of things their moral worth, making conforming to the nature of things voluntary and rational (in the sense of following the logic of concepts).

Jerome Schneewind in his *The Invention of Autonomy* (Schneewind 1998) summarizes the philosophical and political accomplishment of thinkers such as Wollaston and Taylor. For "modern natural lawyers" simply substitute "Baconian Dissenters:"

> The modern natural lawyers held that by reasoning from observable facts we can find out how to cope with the moral and political problems that beset our lives. Experience gives us the evidence we need in order to infer that God exists and cares for us. Part of what we learn from it is that God has made the proper structure of our common life independent of any larger cosmic scheme. Even if there is some divine harmony in the universe, we cannot

appeal to it in determining how we ought to live. Once we understand that God governs us, [indirectly, by creating the "nature of things," the observable facts about ourselves in this world [the discoverable principles that constitute our nature] provide all the rational basis there can be for working out our proper direction. The empiricism of this approach seemed to the natural lawyers to take morality out of the disputed territory over which religious wars were fought and to link it instead to facts available to science (Schneewind 1998, 169).

Baconian Dissent commits to a discourse of peace, no small intellectual accomplishment and, given occasional physical attacks against Dissenters themselves and their meeting houses, also of considerable social and political significance. The Baconian moral scientific discourse of *Medical Jurisprudence* and *Medical Ethics* will become a discourse of peace, based on a professional ethics of cooperation, for the physicians, surgeons, apothecaries, managers, and trustees of Manchester Infirmary, as we will see in Chap. 3.

Wollaston and Taylor can be read as being self-consciously part of this broader eighteenth-century invention of autonomy on the basis of Baconian empirical method. 'Invention' is used in the sense described in Chap. 1 and succinctly stated by Schneewind, in his references Immanuel Kant's comments on the concept of a "slumbering monad" in the metaphysics of Gottfried Wilhelm Leibniz (1646–1716): "This monad he had not explained, but merely invented; for the concept of it was not given to him but was rather created by him" (Schneewind 1998, 3). This was perilous philosophical territory for Kant. It was welcome territory for a Baconian moral scientist.

Baconian Dissent and moral science were invented precisely to propel and secure the vast conceptual revolution that Schneewind describes:

During the seventeenth and eighteenth centuries established conceptions of morality as obedience came increasingly to be contested by emerging conceptions of morality as self-governance. On the older conception, morality is to be understood most deeply as one aspect of the obedience we owe to God. In addition, most of us are in a moral position in which we must obey other human beings. God's authority over all of us is made known to us by reason as well as by revelation and the clergy. But we are not all equally able to see for ourselves what morality requires. ... The new outlook that emerged at the end of the eighteenth century centered on the belief that all normal individuals are equally able to live together in a morality of self-governance. All of us, on this view, have an equal ability to see for ourselves what morality calls for and are in principle equally able to move ourselves to act accordingly, regardless of threats or rewards from others. ... The conception of morality as self-governance provides a conceptual framework for a social space in which we may each rightly claim to direct our own actions without interference from the state, the church, the neighbors, or those claiming to be better than we are. The older conception of morality as obedience did not have these implications (Schneewind 1998, 4).

Baconian Dissent and moral science established the autonomy of judgment and conscience required for self-government, in self-conscious defiance of the asserted authority of a state religion over morality, e.g., the Articles of the Church for attending the Oxbridge universities. As we will see in Chap. 3, Percival absorbed these lessons as Taylor engaged in the intellectual, moral, social, and political formation of his students as Baconian Dissenters. Warrington Academy understood itself to be engaged in such multidimensional formation. So did its descendants in the North

2.3 Percival's Intellectual and Moral Formation

American English colonies and, after them, in the United States, the liberal arts colleges. They were distinctive for the formation of citizens of the emerging and then new Republic, culminating in the President's course on ethics for senior students (McCullough 1999). This commitment has long since passed into history. Taylor deployed the invention of Baconian moral science to engage in the intellectual formation of students at Warrington Academy. Percival absorbed it and deployed it throughout the remainder of his life in his writings on morality.

John Seddon: Teacher of Rejection of Party-Interest as Incompatible with Baconian Moral Science. John Seddon (1725–1770) held ministry postings in Ormskirk and Hereford (Dissenting Academies Online-Seddon). He became rector of Warrington Academy in 1767. He had previously held the position of secretary (1757) while the Academy was being formed and also became its librarian when it opened in 1757. Like Taylor, Seddon was an English Presbyterian and was educated at the University of Glasgow, where he studied with Francis Hutcheson. Henry Arthur Bright in his *Historical Sketch* describes Seddon as a "practical and useful man, full of energy and intelligence" (Bright 1859, 9) and his epitaph characterized him as a man with "temperate zeal of civil and religious liberty" (Bright 1859, 9). This was Humean instinct well-tempered by intellectual and moral virtues of "cheerful piety, universal benevolence, [and] extensive knowledge" (Bright 1859, 9).

John Taylor devoted a book to disagreeing with Hutcheson (Taylor 1759) and there was friction between Taylor and Seddon as a result, and which may have begun as early as 1750, about the nature of prayer, which became public at a meeting of dissenting ministers in Warrington. At the Warrington Academy the dispute between the two deepened. For example, Taylor complained to the Trustees that "Mr. Seddon has invaded his province of moral philosophy by giving a course of lectures" (Bright 1859, 10). This was but one of a "series of misunderstandings between Dr. Taylor and the Trustees, which were only terminated the following year by Dr. Taylor's death" (Bright 1859, 10).

A major challenge for the Academy arose when moral and theological reasoning, shaped by unmanaged biases that originate in individual differences, was fracturing into different groups. Their differences were sometimes sharp, as in the case of the disagreement between Taylor and Seddon. The Trustees of the Academy had to deal with its aftermath.

> We need not enter further into this unhappy quarrel. Traces of its ill effects appear in many of Mr. Seddon's letters [to the Trustees], and it gave a blow to the Academy from which it never entirely recovered. The subscriptions from other places might be increased, but the Presbyterian body was no longer united. The friends of Dr. Taylor and many of his old congregation had lost confidence in the management of the Academy, and too often checked or thwarted the efforts of its supporters (Bright 1859, 11).

Bright documents this analysis further with a comment on this division by Joseph Priestley, who became a tutor at the Academy in 1761: "There had been an unhappy difference between Dr. Taylor and the Trustees, in consequence of which all of his friends, who were numerous, were our enemies" (Bright 1859, 10; citing *Dr. Priestley's Life*, p. 55; Rutt 1831, Vol. I, 61).

Seddon had earlier, in a 1755 letter to Lord Willoughby, expressed concern about fracturing of communities, using the phrase "little parties" to refer in a disparaging manner to factions that form within a larger community based on people sharing an interest, e.g., in the nature of public prayer as in the work of Taylor considered above.

> The tempers of Dissenters in London, and the disposition of their affairs, as your Lordship much better knows, is very peculiar, and renders it extremely difficult to address them in any publick affairs: their little parties, imagining separate interests, and prevailing jealousies on all sides, are not easily combined together; and measures that serve to gain any point of importance with one connexion, are the means of breaking with the other (Seddon letter of November 19, 1755 to Lord Willoughby).

Acting on shared "interest," i.e., shared self-interest, creates a group self-interest in the form of a "little party." "Party-interest" is formed when the interests of individuals happen to be shared, overlap, or are complementary. This interested division is antithetical to Baconian reasoning, as explained in Chap. 1. Such interested division is antithetical to Baconian Dissent. Priestley uses "the spirit of faction" to characterize different from discoverable "real interests" (Priestley 1765, 32). Seddon had first-hand experience with party-interest and, as a Baconian Dissenter, he rejected all forms of self-interest as injurious to organizations such as Warrington Academy. Percival was intellectually formed by this rejection of individual interest and party-interest, a position that he embraced for the rest of his life. As we shall see in Chap. 3, rejection of the pernicious effects on the well-being of patients at Manchester Infirmary of party-interest was a major motivation for Percival's writing of *Medical Jurisprudence* and *Medical Ethics*.

2.3.2.3 "Subjects Which Have a Connection ... Explained in a Regular System"

Joseph Priestley, later a renowned chemist and a founder of the form of Dissent known as Unitarianism in England, came to the Warrington Academy in 1761, where he served as tutor in Languages and *Belles Lett*ers for six years. He wrote a book on liberal education during this time (Priestley 1765). Having left already for his medical studies in Edinburgh, Percival was not one of Priestley's students. Percival became acquainted with Priestley when the former returned in 1765 to Warrington from Edinburgh and Leyden and started his medical practice. Percival would therefore have been well acquainted with Priestley's philosophy of education, which may have provided an antidote to the "parties" Taylor had created.

Priestley undertakes to describe a "proper course of studies for Gentlemen who are designed to fill the principal stations of active life, distinct from those which are adapted to the learned professions" (Priestley 1765, 1). Priestley is changing the meaning of 'gentleman' from its old meaning of a man with inherited wealth and social status he did nothing to earn to designate a man born well and raised properly to a man who is "designed" or formed intellectually and morally to take a "station" or position that is defined by responsibility for those subordinate the social and political power that define a social station or position. This process of intellectual

2.3 Percival's Intellectual and Moral Formation

and moral formation should be the same for all students and is "adapted" or specified in its content to whether a student intends to pursue commerce or one of the professions. The intellectually and morally well-formed man earns the social "station" or status of being a gentleman.

Priestley can be read as seeking, in the spirit of Enlightenment England, to improve the Academy curriculum described above around a general, integrated curriculum aiming to produce "MEN, PATRIOTS, CHIEFS, AND CITIZENS" (Priestley 1765, iii). Note the missing word, 'SUBJECT'. With these words Priestley trumpets the shift from a morality of obedience – to Crown and Church – to a morality of self-governance that Schneewind describes in the passage above.

Baconian reasoning prohibits a haphazard, unintentional, and therefore disorderly approach to science.

> In general the bulk of mankind are content with seeing how things are, without looking far into the causes or consequences of things. But a philosopher is not satisfied without endeavouring to see things, as much as possible, in all their connections and relations (Priestley 1765, 70).

The goal of teaching is improvement: "But it is the glory of human nature, that the operations of reason [*not* Reason], though variable, and by no means infallible, are capable of infinite improvement" (Priestley 1765, 150). Baconian pedagogy aiming at improvement should take a coherent, intended, and orderly approach to the curriculum:

> When subjects which have a connection are explained in a regular system, every article is placed where the most light is reflected upon it from the neighbouring subjects. The plainest things are discussed in the first place, and are made to serve as axioms, and as the foundation of those which are treated afterwards. Without this regular method of studying the elements of any science, it seems impossible ever to gain a clear and comprehensive view of it. But after a regular institution, any particular part of a plan of instruction may be enlarged at any time, with ease, and without confusion. With how much more ease and distinctness would a person be able to deliver himself upon any subject of policy or commerce, who had had the whole subject, and everything belonging to it explained to him in its proper connection, than another of the same abilities, who should only have dipped into the subject in a random manner, reading any treatise that might fall in his way, or adopting maxims from the company he might accidentally keep, and consequently, liable to be imposed upon the by the interested views with which men very often speak and write. For these are subjects, on which almost every writer or speaker is to be suspected, so much has his party and interest to do with everything relating to them (Priestley 1765, 16–17).

2.3.2.4 Condescension of Gentlemen of the Higher Social Classes to the Poor

Henry Grove (1684–1738) was a non-conforming minister in Taunton and then Somerset. He returned to Taunton Academy at the age of 23 to become tutor in ethics. Theologically, he was skeptical of the trinitarian concept of god. His collected sermons were published posthumously. A 1775 catalogue of the Warrington Academy lists Grove's twelve-volume sermons (n.a. 1775). Percival may have read the Grove text on condescension, in one of Grove's sermons with a commentary on Psalm VIII:

> [1] O LORD our Lord, how excellent is thy name in all the earth! who hast set thy glory above the heavens.
> [2] Out of the mouth of babes and sucklings hast thou ordained strength because of thine enemies, that thou mightest still the enemy and the avenger.
> [3] When I consider thy heavens, the work of thy fingers, the moon and the stars, which thou hast ordained;
> [4] What is man, that thou art mindful of him? and the son of man, that thou visitest him?
> [5] For thou hast made him a little lower than the angels, and hast crowned him with glory and honour.
> [6] Thou madest him to have dominion over the works of thy hands; thou hast put all things under his feet:
> [7] All sheep and oxen, yea, and the beasts of the field;
> [8] The fowl of the air, and the fish of the sea, and whatsoever passeth through the paths of the seas.
> [9] O LORD our Lord, how excellent is thy name in all the earth! (Bible, King James Version).

Grove invokes the deist argument from design for the existence of the creator god who intends good for his creation:

> It is implied in the words, that a serious reflection upon the incomparable greatness and majesty of God, as they are discovered by an attentive view of his works, will oblige us to admire and celebrate his condescending goodness in the peculiar care he takes in man. I have shown before that there is nothing unbecoming the perfections of God in his providential regard to this works, and particularly to man; but what is not unbecoming God, may be very great condescension in him; for condescension being always measured in the distance between the superior and inferior, whence this distance is infinite, the condescension must be infinite (Grove 1745, Vol. 4, 334–335).

In his essay, *On Truth*, Percival cites Grove's "moral philosophy" (Percival 1807, Vol. II, 20). Percival also cites Grove's "ethics" in Note VII of *Medical Ethics* (Percival 1803, 165). In his, Grove writes that benevolence includes condescension:

> A modest, yielding, obliging temper makes his conversation a pleasure, and benefit to his *equals*; and an affable, condescending, compassionate behaviour to *inferiors*, makes dependence and subjection easy, and his superior prudence, wealth, or power, their advantage. He readily informs the ignorant, incourages the well disposed, and kindly admonishes the thoughtless; instructs with patience, and reproves with gentleness (Grove 1749, 536).

Condescension guided by benevolence protects the "inferior" from the power of the "superior," just as God's benevolent condescension protects his creatures from his power, which includes the power of life and death. 'Condescension' and passages like this this may rankle the twenty-first century ear, in part because this word implies a claim of superiority over another void of the intellectual and moral authority to identify and act to protect the interests and welfare of another. This is precisely the opposite of Grove's usage, because the commitment of the creator god to man's good can be read out of creation itself, the nature of things. God's condescension is "as great as his majesty" (Grove 1745, Vol. 4, 345) and is therefore "deserving, in the highest degree, our admiration and praises" (Grove 1745, Vol. 4, 345). God's condescension has intellectual and moral authority for us and we have evidence for that in nature. God crosses an infinite gap, lowers himself infinitely, when he manifests himself in his creation, which is ordained by him to the good of humans.

Grove draws an important implication for the proper relationship between the rich and the poor: "It is reckoned a mark of great condescension for a very rich man to visit a poor man ..." (Grove 1745, Vol. 4, 335). The rich man committed to Baconian moral science has the intellectual and moral authority this commitment creates and the capacity to condescend to the poor, to close the vast social gulf between rich and poor at that time by caring for the poor. The moral exemplar for christians, of course, is Jesus in the text of the Gospels not the Jesus in the speculative metaphysics of the Trinity.

2.3.2.5 "You Do Constantly, Carefully, Impartially, and Conscientiously Attend to Evidence"

The English enlightenment shared with the Scottish enlightenment "the human impulse for improvement" (Porter 2000, 251). Porter's description of modernization in Scotland in the eighteenth century can be said of England as well: "Modernization did not only bring prosperity, it was a comprehensive force spreading civility to all departments of life" (Porter 2000, 255). Education was essential to this task and thus became essential to Dissenting communities, for whom civility was a public virtue that simultaneously protected them from the predatory power of the Church and state of England and fostered experienced-based cooperation that created the basis for the autonomy of Dissenters from church and state.

The Warrington Academy had an ethics curriculum, to which Percival was drawn, as noted earlier. In this school, ethics was more than a course of study. Porter summarizes a key feature of ethics in the Scottish enlightenment that shaped the task of intellectual and moral formation at the Academy:

> Early Enlightenment philosophers endowed ethics with a new, hopefully sounder basis in psychology. Morality had traditionally been cast as an objective system of divine laws or cosmic fitnesses: absolute right and wrong, duty and justice. Increasingly, virtue was refigured as a matter of heeding inner promptings – goodness lay not in obeying commandments but in harnessing motives (Porter 2000, 261).

"Harnessing motives" is achieved by properly regulating the "exciting" force of sympathy and thus becoming autonomous from "excitement" by others. This is the task of moral formation. The teachers at the Warrington Academy set themselves, quite self-consciously and without reservation, to the task of the moral formation of the Academy's students, Percival first among them to enroll, as Baconian Dissenters expected to become leaders in the improvement of the human condition using Baconian, evidence-based reasoning in all matters. John Taylor's "charge" to the Academy's students is Baconian through and through.

"The editor" of Taylor's *A Scheme of Scripture Divinity* prefaces the text of this "charge" with the following:

… much less did he think himself authorized, as a public Tutor, to impose his Sentiments on young Minds with an overbearing Hand. That he might do justice to his Pupils, and himself he always prefaced his Lectures with the following CHARGE, which does honor to the Author, and affords a noble Precedent to Seminaries of Learning (Taylor 1762, v–vi).

> I. I do solemnly charge you, in the name of the God of Truth, and of our Lord Jesus Christ, who is the Way, the Truth, and the Life, and before whose Judgment-Seat you must in no long time appear, that in all your Studies and Inquiries of a religious Nature, present or future, you do constantly, carefully, impartially and conscientiously attend to Evidence, as it lies in holy Scripture, or in the Nature of things, or the Dictates of Reason; cautiously guarding against the Sallies of Imagination, and the Fallacy of ill-grounded Conjecture.
> II. That you admit, embrace, or assent to the Principle, or Instinct, by me taught or advanced, but only so far as it shall appear to you to be supported and justified by proper Evidence from Revelation or the Reason of things.
> III. That, if at any time hereafter, any Principle or Sentiment, by me taught or advanced, or by you admitted and embraced, shall, upon impartial and faithful examination, appear to you to be dubious or false, you either suspect, or totally reject such Principle or Sentiment.
> IV. That you keep your mind always open to Evidence. – That you labour to banish from your Breast all Prejudice, Prepossession, and Party-Zeal. – That you study to live in Peace and Love with all your Fellow-Christians; and that you steddily assent for yourself, and freely allow to others, the unalienable right of Judgment and Conscience (Taylor 1762, vi–vii).

William Enfield (1741–1797), a Unitarian minister renowned for his elocution (Enfield 1792), preached a eulogy for John Aikin that exhibits the pedagogical spirit of Priestley and the other tutors at Warrington Academy. Aikin was opposed to "an unnatural conflict between Reason and Common Sense" (Enfield 1781, 8). Aikin "deliberated calmly, reasoned clearly, and formed a judgment for himself with caution and impartiality" (Enfield 1781, 5–6). Aikin was an "excellent man possessed of the most rational and steady PRINCIPLES of religion and virtue" (Enfield 1781, 6). For Percival, we might well imagine, Aikin was an exemplar of the Baconian Dissenter and moral scientist committed to a "most rational and steady" morality of self-governance in all matters.

2.4 Percival's Writings

Percival took full advantage of the learning and the leisure that his wealth afforded him to deploy Baconian method on an impressive range of subjects: natural science, clinical medicine, laboratory experimentation, clinical experimentation, climatology, environmental medicine epidemiology, public health, toxicology, philosophy of medicine, philosophy of science, philosophy of taste and art, philosophy of religion, the intellectual and moral formation of children, hospital management, and, last and far from least, professional ethics in medicine. In *The Works*, the presentation of his writings requires 1,898 pages. *Medical Jurisprudence* is not included.

The texts in these pages testify the Percival's commitment to mastering Baconian method "in all departments of life" (Porter 2000, 259). There is therefore some repetition in what follows, but the repetition has a scholarly point: the reader will experience Percival's intellectual progress in his dogged pursuit of this mastery, in which repetition of observation and experiment is essential. The process will readily be recognized, for it is followed today by scientists and physicians who seek to become independent investigators. Repetition achieves mastery, step by painstaking step, culminating, for Percival, in *Medical Jurisprudence* and *Medical Ethics*. The latter, as the reader will discover, repeats – and expands – the former.

Percival's writing vary in length. I have aimed to craft my interpretations in direct proportion to the length of the text being examined. I have also aimed to present the essentials of each text. The reader is thus prepared to read and interpret the texts in greater depth.

He wrote his first work in 1763, *An Inquiry into the Resemblance between Chyle and Milk*. He included this as Essay V in *Essays Medical and Experimental* (Percival [1767] 1807, Vol. III, 164–172), about which more see below.

He second work, *Dissertatio Medica Inauguralis De Frigore*, however, was the first published, when he was twenty-five and a medical student in Leyden. *Medical Ethics* appeared in 1803, a year before his death at age sixty-four.

2.4.1 Dissertatio Medica Inauguralis De Frigore *(1765)*

A '*dissertatio*' typically took the form of a disquisition in which an author undertakes the task of addressing a topic or question and then accomplishes this task, typically in two steps. The first is the "negative" argument in which positions that attempt, but fail, to address the topic or question – completely or only partially – are described in rejected (McCullough 1996). A *dissertation* differs from a *disputatio* in which an argument is made by examining positions *seriatim* and showing them to fail before turning to a defense of the author's position. Inasmuch as a dissertation was intended to convey mastery of its subject matter, its style is discursive and not aphoristic as in *Institutiones Medicae*.

'Frigore' is the ablative case of 'frigus, figoris' a neuter Latin noun, the general meaning of which is "cold, coldness, coolness" (Lewis and Short [1879] 1969, 782). It can also mean the chill of fever or the coldness of the dead body. Percival uses *de Frigore* to mean an exploration of the influences of external sources of cold on the functions of body e.g., how such sources of cold or chill in a person's physical environment can be productive of symptoms of diseases (Percival 1765).

'Chill', like 'fever', names a class of clinical conditions that were organized by signs and symptoms and not underlying pathology. 'Fever' was used in the history of Western medicine from the ancient world into the nineteenth century to name a general classification of diseases that has elevated body temperature, not a pathology, in common, for which treatment varied and therefore varied in its effectiveness (Bynum 1981). "During the early nineteenth century, British physicians also tended to believe that continued fever was a general disease that might assume various forms …" (Wilson 1993, 401).

From a Baconian perspective, the multiple uses of 'fever' reflected the lack of an experience-based, i.e., observationally based, clinical account of the causes of fever in its various forms. This meant that the only evidence base available supported classification of diseases generically. 'Fever' was apparently chosen because the heterogenous clinical entities thus generically grouped had elevated temperature as a sign or symptom. This experience-based classification was intended to guide clinicians to be more precise in their clinical observations, diagnoses, and treatment plans.

In the middle of the nineteenth century Carl Reinhold August Wunderlich (1815–1877) no longer uses 'fever' to name a class of diseases but to name a physiologic condition of the body, its temperature, that is a measurable indication of disease. "Early in his book, Wunderlich established two basic principles upon which the foundation of medical thermometry rests: first in healthy persons the temperature is constant (98.6—99.5 °F) and so an index of a sound condition; and second it undergoes variations in, and is thus an important index of, disease" (Reiser 1993, 834). Having a reliable measure and thus being able to identify a temperature associated with a sound condition permitted more clinically meaningful classifications of diseases by their various causes and organ systems affected, e.g., uterine cancer or tuberculosis.

'Frigus' is similar in Percival's use. 'Frigus' does not name a specific temperature range, as Wunderlich would late do for 'fever'. Percival opens with a consideration of five accounts of cold and, with dispatch, shows them to fail. This is the negative argument of his "*dissertatio*."

He then sets about the positive argument: investigating the principles of the "animal œcononomy" or physiology ("*Primum autem in principia œconomiae investiganda sunt*" (Percival 1807, Vil. II, 319)). As we saw in Chap. 1, this is the discourse of Baconian physiology that Gregory learned at Edinburgh and that was at a more developed level when Percival arrived two decades later. Principles (*principia*) are causal processes that are constituent process in things. The Baconians, Hume included, were realists about principles or causes. They also understood that direct observation of principles in the human body or in nature was rarely possible. Two important exceptions were direct observation by Hume of the mental physiology of impressions and ideas and of the moral physiology of sympathy as the double relation of impressions and ideas, as explained in Chap. 1. It was possible, following Baconian scientific method, to use careful, unbiased, precise observation to detect stable psychological patterns (Hume's regular and constant association of ideas), which observations counted, in degrees of reliability, as evidence for the existence and function of a principle. There were abundant Baconian scientific observations of the workings of physiologic sympathy, to which Percival meant his *De Frigore* to be an original and clinically significant contribution.

Percival invokes a Baconian appeal to experience or *experientia* (Percival 1807, Vol. II, 328), or "a trial, proof, experiment" (Lewis and Short [1859] 1969, 693). The multiple uses of '*frigore*' or 'cold' reflected the lack of an experience-based, i.e., observationally based, clinical account of the causes of lowered body temperature, or chill, in its various forms, which account becomes the evidence base for classification of diseases under the generic heading of chill. This experience-based classification should then be taken by clinicians to provide a reliable guide to more precise clinical observations, diagnoses, and treatment plans. Percival is not using '*de frigore*' to mean a body temperature lower than normal that can be a sign or symptom of pathology; that use comes later in the history of medicine, after Wunderlich changed the meaning of 'fever' from a general classification of diseases to body temperature higher than normal that can be sign or symptom of pathology.

Percival deploys Baconian observational method to create an observation-based classification of diagnoses associated with exposure to cold, based on observed causes as reported in the Baconian scientific literature. Baconian method is on full display and typified by a phrase that defines Baconian observational scientists: "as daily experience teaches us" ("*ut quotidiana nos docet experentia*") (Percival 1807, Vol. II, 328). 'Daily experience' means stable, repeated patterns revealed by careful, unbiased, precise observations. In further evidence of the impact of his teachers at Edinburgh, Percival advances an account based on the physiologic principle of sympathy. This principle explains how conditions external to the body can influence the function of organs and how affected organs can influence one another at a distance in the body. Sympathy, he holds, is communicated by vessels (*vasi*)) is the cause of "many great changes" ("*[m]ultae et magnae mutations*") (Percival 1807, Vol. II, 328). Again reflecting what he learned in Edinburgh, no doubt reinforced in Leyden, Percival claims that "this [s]ympathy is seen to be nothing other than greatly extended irritability" ("*Haec Sympathia nihil aliud esse videtur quam Irritabilitas magus extensa* ...) (Percival 1765, 328). Sympathy explains how other organs detect "irritability" or malfunction in an organ and become "irritated" or malfunction themselves. The sympathetic mechanism of chill is that external cold is communicated throughout the body by vessels. The balance of *De Frigore* is given over to a demonstration of how this is the case.

Throughout his disquisition Percival buttresses his clinical observational findings with references to pertinent, recent scientific sources. Then-familiar names of Baconian scientists appear, including Boerhaave, Hoffmann, and Whytt. Percival explores what we would now call environmental factors such as evaporation, humid air, and dry air. Percival then explores a number of clinical conditions, the role of chill-induced sympathetic responses in the origin of these conditions, and their clinical management, including intermittent fever, catarrh, diarrhea, rheumatism, and gangrene. This appears to be a defense of his claim about chill as a sympathetic process based on its clinical adequacy, the ability of chill as a sympathetic process to explain multiple conditions and clinical management of them. We would now say that one of Percival's main aims in *De Frigore* is to demonstrate the explanatory power of chill as a sympathetic process.

2.4.1.1 Percival's Adoption of the First Commitment of the Ethical Concept of Medicine as a Profession

The preparation and defense of *de Frigore* signals Percival's public debut as a Baconian physician, culminating the process of his intellectual formation that had begun at the Warrington Academy some years earlier. He publicly commits to becoming and remaining a scientifically and clinically competent physician, thus putting in place the first commitment of the ethical concept of medicine as a profession. In 1766, the next year, Gregory took up his position at the University of Edinburgh and initiated ethics lectures that culminated in *Lectures* in 1772, preceded by *Observations* in 1770. Percival's articulation of the first commitment of the ethical concept of medicine as a profession preceded Gregory's and is thus a conceptual invention that is independent of Gregory's.

2.4.2 Essays Medical, Philosophical, and Experimental

In the 1807 *Works* Percival's philosophical and scientific communications are gather into four parts with the title, *Essays Medical, Philosophical and Experimental*. Part I comprises his *Essays, Medical and Experimental (Percival 1772a)*. Part II comprises later essays that were included in the second edition of *Essays, Medical and Experimental (Percival 1773)*. Parts I and II comprise Volume III of *The Works (Percival 1807)*. Part III appeared as *Philosophical, Medical and Experimental Essays (Percival 1776b, 1788–1789)*, which title differs from that of the other three collections of essays. Part IV appeared as Volume II of *Essays Medical, Philosophical, and Experimental* (Percival 1788–1789). Parts III and IV comprise Volume IV of *The Works* (Percival 1807). The four parts into which the essays are organized in Volumes III and IV carry the introductory title, *Essays Medical, Philosophical, and Experimental*.

Baconian experimentation is undertaken to obtain observational evidence or evidence from designed experiments. Experiments are invented laboratory, clinical, or in-the-field processes, the outcomes of which cannot be reliably predicted. Hypotheses are formed to posit outcomes and are tested in the Baconian quest for reliability. The quest for certainty is utterly alien to Baconian science and also Baconian moral science and therefore appears nowhere in Percival's essays.

Observational studies can be conducted in the clinical setting, e.g., to describe the course of disease and influences on the course of disease such a chill or cold, e.g., Percival's observations on the effects of pump water or lead on individuals. Observational studies can be conducted in the community, as part of the science now known as public health. Percival reports on the health effects of those who work in and live near lead mines. He also makes a proposal for the preparation of bills of morality or the public health task of calculating mortality in a community and its causes. Outcomes are hypothesized and hypotheses are explored or tested.

2.4 Percival's Writings

Designed experiments can be conducted in the field, e.g., in Percival's exploration of the properties of pump water in Manchester and two towns. These include laboratory studies to ascertain the constituent properties of pump water, to gather evidence that allows reasoning to be guided by the truth of things, their nature. Percival's field research also includes auto-experimentation, to observe his own physiological responses to different quantities of Manchester pump water. Designed experiments can also be conducted in the clinical setting, e.g., administration of a remedy in a single case, e.g., Percival's case reports, or series of cases, Percival's clinical experiments on adults and children.

Percival calls these "trials," to mean that he tries a remedy in designed fashion, carefully observes results, analyzes or reasons about those results, and reports them precisely. Trials are designed experiments that can be repeated by others. He also makes reference to a clinical trial of a solution of wort that produces "mixed air" that has been prospectively approved by a group with what we would call prospective oversight and by the sponsor, thus anticipating prospective review and approval of human subjects research about which he goes into considerable detail in Medical Jurisprudence and Medical Ethics. This work anticipates many features of the current system of prospective review and approval of human subjects research by duly constituted entities such as Institutional Review Board and Research Ethics Committees, which system was created in the middle of the last century without awareness of Percival's remarkable precedent.

The words 'philosophical' and 'philosophy' referred to natural philosophy, which included observational and interventional experimental science, as just described, and philosophical reflections on Baconian method. 'Philosophy' did not refer to the autonomous discipline of academic philosophy that was created in the nineteenth century in a break of philosophical inquiry in metaphysics, epistemology, and ethics from the physical and biological sciences. We would classify reflections on Baconian method as philosophy of science, of which Percival's "Philosophical" essays are an example but a distinct example in that philosophy of medicine is tightly integrated with the biological (basic) and clinical sciences.

Percival states that he "communicated" this essay to the Royal Society, where they would have appeared in its Transactions and to other sources. In what follows, therefore, I have organized the essays into two groups, philosophical communications and scientific communications. The philosophical communications appear first, which is fitting inasmuch as they set the stage for his scientific communications by describing the commitment to Baconian scientific and medical reasoning that creates their intellectual authority.

2.4.2.1 Essays Medical, Philosophical, and Experimental: Part I

Philosophical Communications. One genre of Percival's intellectual work was essays on philosophy of science and medicine.

This collection of eight texts "attracted wide attention" (Lee 1895, 384). The first two essays, *"The Empiric"* and *"The Dogmatic,"* mount a defense of Baconian philosophy of medicine, described in Chap. 1. These two texts on Baconian philosophy of medicine are followed by scientific papers reporting on the results of laboratory and clinical experience.

Essay I. The Empiric or Man of Experience, being arguments against the use of theory and reasoning in physic, and Essay II. The Dogmatic or Rationalist; being arguments for the use of theory and reasoning in physic. The "Preface" is without a named author but ends with "Manchester, January 1, 1772" (Percival 1807, Vol. III, xix). This suggests that Percival is its author. He writes, of these first two, paired essays:

> The first and second Dissertations are the productions of his youth, and illustrate both the insufficiency of THEORY, and the danger of trusting EXPERIENCE alone in the practice of physic. The annals of medicine abound with instances of the fatal effects of empiricism, and hypothetical reasoning, founded on fictitious principles (Percival 1807, Vol. III, xiii).

The abstract theory of the dogmatic physician lacks evidence and is therefore speculation, a creature of imagination and productive of enthusiasm, strong beliefs originating independently of, and not correctable by, evidence. The hypotheses of the empiric may be generated by personal experience but are not tested by rigorous observation and experiment. Both divide physicians rather than "conciliate harmony" (Percival 1807, Vol. III, xiv) among physicians, the antidote to antiscientific competition for market share and reputation. Neither results in "improvement" (Percival 1807, Vol. III, xiv).

The Empiric appeared in an extract of *The Gentleman's Magazine and Historical Chronicle* in 1768 (Percival 1768a). The empiric embraces theories without an evidence base with their implications arrayed in elaborate systems. These provide no evidence-based explanations of disease and the effects of treatment. Worse, the empiric plays upon the "common propensities of mankind to search after hidden and undiscoverable causes, than to attend to the obvious phaenomena of nature" (Percival 1807, Vol. III, 3). "Creative imagination" (Percival 1807, Vol. III, 4) holds sway when it should have no such effect. He contrasts the theory of Georg Ernst Stahl (1659–1734), an advocate of vital force or vitalism. "Principles" of "corruption and decay" are posited to be in competition with principles of "life and health" (Percival 1807, Vol. III, Vol. 2, 6). Percival shows that this is contradictory thinking that "confutes itself" (Percival 1807, Vol. III, 7). He also shows that William Harvey's (1578–1657) "introduction of mechanics into medicine" (Percival 1807, Vol. III, 9) or the body as machine fails the test of adequacy, because there are many diseases that this theory cannot explain. Compared to Stahl's vitalism, the theory of body-as-machine has had "a more dangerous influence on the treatment of diseases" (Percival 1807, Vol. III, 22), e.g., smallpox. He concludes the first "dissertation" with a Baconian call to arms:

> But to watch with close attention the operations of nature, to treasure up a store of useful facts, to learn, by accurate observation, the diagnostics of diseases and by unbiassed experience, the true method of cure, requires unwearied labour, assiduity, and patience, at the same time that it admits of no pompous display of wit or knowledge (Percival 1807, Vol. III, 25).

2.4 Percival's Writings

In the experimental essays that follow the second "dissertation" Percival aims to demonstrate his mastery of these Baconian intellectual virtues. The repetition the reader will experience should remind the reader that successful character formation, mastery of virtues, requires life-long repetition or habit.

The reader is thus not surprised, when turning to the second dissertation, that Percival starts *The Dogmatic* with a quotation from Bacon: "Medicine not founded in philosophy is a weak thing" ("*Medicina, in philosophia non fundata, res infirma est*") (Percival 1807, Vol. III, 26). Percival invokes a key component of Baconian reasoning: disciplined reflection on experience aiming at the "concurring assistance of our judgment and understanding" (Percival 1807, Vol. III, 27) with the results of observation and experiment. This is the work of the "rationalist," who "has every advantage which the Empiric can boast, from reading, observation, and practice, accompanied with superior knowledge, understanding, and judgment" (Percival 1807, Vol. III, 35). This "superior knowledge, understanding, and judgment," no surprise, produce the experience-based theory of physiologic sympathy, explained in Chap. 1:

> By the laws of the animal œconomy, there subsists a certain sympathy between different parts of the body; by which the disordered state of one organ impairs the function of another (Percival 1807, Vol. III, 32).

The appeals to vital force and to the body-as-machine become unnecessary. The combination of experience and reflection, in a cycle of observation and experiment, define the "rationalist" physician. Percival does not use 'rationalist' as it is used to describe philosophers such as Descartes, who pursue the quest for certainty based on Reason alone. Percival uses 'rationalist' as a synonym for the Baconian physician.

A Father's Instructions. Part the Second. The texts included in *A Father's Instructions* are discussed at length below. The essay "Immortality" features a dialogue between Julius and Hiero. Julius wants a conclusive argument for immortality; Hiero, the Baconian, sticks with the evidence in nature, including human nature. Julius labels this "supposition:"

> I would banish all supposition, however probable, said Julius, and acknowledge the validity of no argument short of demonstration.
> Banish then your pretensions to philosophy, replied Hiero, and avow a general scepticism! For how few are the truths which admit of demonstration. Probability is almost the universal foundation of reasoning; and the wisest men are governed by it, both in their speculations, and in the most interesting transactions of life. The nature and force of evidence necessarily vary with its objects; and whatever be our inquiries or pursuits, we can expect only that kind and degree of it which they are capable of affording (Percival 1807, Vol. I, 181–182).

Hiero regrets the quest for certainty. Notice the calm and comfort that Hiero exhibits in the quest for reliability: making judgments, the reliability of which varies with the strength of the evidence. Notice, too, that Hiero's emphasis on the degree of strength is function of the subject matter. About some matters, the strength of evidence will be high but in others the strength of evidence will be lower. This anticipates by two centuries the development of formal tools of evidence-based reasoning. We will see in Chap. 3 how Percival in *Medical Jurisprudence* and *Medical*

Ethics will formalize the process for introducing evidence-based, probabilistic clinical judgment and practice based on it. Gregory proposed the same with his proposal to "lay medicine open" to sophisticated laypersons, as we saw in Chap. 1.

Here the difference between the English enlightenment and the enlightenments in Germany, France, and elsewhere on the Continent is on full display. There Reason, with a capital 'R', was thought to be able to deliver demonstrable truths, even if in the form of complex, abstract demonstrations, i.e., transcendental deductions in Kant's *Critique of Pure Reason* (Kant [1781] 1998). For the English, and the Scots — Hume principally among them — Kant is a speculative philosopher, a term used to dismiss all philosophical reasoning not based in evidence. In his injunction to the students at Warrington Academy always to be disciplined by evidence, included above, John Taylor did not need to add, so strong was his injunction, that his students should beware the siren call of Pure Reason.

Scientific Communications. For each of Percival's scientific communications I provide the date of its separate publication when I have been able to identify it.

Essay III. Experiments and Observations on Astringents and Bitters (1767). 'Astringent' may refer to a drug that shrinks or constricts bodily tissue, sometimes with an acerb, unpleasant taste or to both. Percival reports on forty-one laboratory experiments on astringents, starting with Peruvian bark (Percival 1767, 1807). This was cinchona, a plant indigenous to South America and used as a medicinal by people native to this region (Weatherall 1993). It was brought from Peru to Europe by Jesuit missionaries in the middle of the seventeenth century; hence the neologism, 'Jesuit's bark'. The cinchona plant's bark is a source of quinine. It was used to treat a form of intermittent fever or condition that is now called malaria (Weatherall 1993). Thomas Sydenham (1624–1689) used Jesuit's bark to treat "ague (or intermittent fever)" (Bynum 1993, 341) who thought that the drug "could stop the ague dead in its tracks" (Bynum 1993, 341). This observation played a major role in Sydenham's concept that drugs are "specific," a major contribution to nosology (Bynum 1993).

Percival deploys Sydenham's concept of drug specificity in his experiments on Peruvian bark.

> Physicians in general agree, that the PERUVIAN BARK is most powerful in its effects, when taken in substance. But as the stomach is frequently unable to bear it, and as many patients have almost invincible aversion to it in that form, it is of importance to determine, in what preparations the virtues of this valuable drug are least impaired, and whether it may not be administered under a form, that is elegant, palatable, and at the same time sufficiently efficacious (Percival 1807, Vol. III, 43–44).

The dose should have a concentration sufficient to produce its beneficial clinical effect of stopping intermittent fever but exhibit side effects that patients can tolerate as worth the trade-off for efficacious treatment. As a committed Baconian seeking to improve the care of patients with intermittent fever that was debilitating and could be fatal, Percival undertook what we would call laboratory experiments to determine the best part of the bark to use, in what concentration, and in what mixtures that might be palatable to patients, what he calls a "more agreeable and elegant preparation" (Percival 1807, Vol. III, 45). Reports of many experiments follow, including failed experiments or what we call experiments with negative results, prompting him to revise his approach and try again. The successful Baconian scientist must be undeterred by failure, no matter how discouraging, lest failure be taken personally and lead the investigator to abandon experimentation.

> I was neither mortified with my disappointment, at that time, nor am I now ashamed to acknowledge it. In a long course of experiments, which are undertaken with some particular view, and not made at random, instances of self-deception frequently and unavoidable occur; and in general they happily serve as a spur to industry (Percival 1807, Vol. III, 67).

He summarizes his results in seventeen concise findings that very nicely set the stage for other investigators to continue experimentation on a solid evidence base.

Essay IV. On the Uses and Operation of Blisters. This essay was probably published for the first time in this volume of essays. Blistering was used for, among other purposes, the treatment of pain.

> In many disorders, pain was believed to have no fixed abode: 'flying gout', for instance, would unpredictably migrate from limb to limb. Hence the prudent therapeutic indication was, by means of bloodletting and counter-irritants (blisters), to divert the pain-centre away from the trunk, and especially away from the vital organs, towards the extremities (Porter 1993, 1580).

Percival investigates the laboratory properties of blistering agents using cantharides (also known as Spanish fly), the secretions of blister beetles that are blistering agents. Percival wants to learn more about the "virtues and operations of blisters" (Percival 1807, Vol. III Vol. III, 119) and so he reports on clinical observations. Noting recent disputes among Italian physicians, Percival observes that there is no agreement on the "theory of action" of blistering (Percival 1807, Vol. III Vol. III, 120).

> Hence arises that diversity of opinion concerning the diseases in which they [blisters] are indicated, the time of their application, and the parts to which they ought to be applied. Nor can we ever hope for uniformity in this particular, amongst physicians, either with respect to their opinions or their practice, till a juster idea be formed of their mode of action, deduced from experience, and an attentive observation of their effects on the human body. When this is accomplished, a system of rules may be laid down for their right and advantageous application (Percival 1807, Vol. III Vol. III, 120).

This a clear, compact manifesto of Baconian clinical research. Percival then reports on a series of experiments. He uses the physiologic principle of sympathy to interpret his results, e.g., by suggesting that blistering of parts of the body "will seldom fail to afford relief, by lessening, or destroying the sense of that [original] irritation" (Percival 1807, Vol. III, 139). He follows Sydenham's clinically comprehensive observation of outcomes, to include both *juvantia* or clinically beneficial outcomes and *lædentia* or clinically harmful outcomes (Percival 1807, Vol. III Vol. III, 144).

Essay V. An Inquiry into the Resemblance between Chyle and Milk (1763). There is a note to indicate that Percival read this essay to the Royal Medical Society of Edinburgh in 1763. He was, as noted earlier, a medical student at the University of Edinburgh at the time.

Chyle is a substance obtained from "lacteal vessels" of the small intestine and therefore "must necessarily be composed of the food we eat" (Percival 1807 Vol. III, 165). Percival investigates chyle and milk in his next experimental essay. From the "great variety of authors" that Percival "consulted," he is able to identify but one experiment (Percival 1807, Vol. III, 164). He therefore relies on *a priori* reasoning and presents "four probable conclusions that may be deduced" (Percival 1807, Vol. III Vol. III, 165). In this youthful work, Percival's capacities as a Baconian scientist are not yet on display.

Essay VI. Experiments and Observations on Water; particularly on the hard pump water of Manchester (1769). Percival next reports on "chemical inquiry" of "pump water" in the City of Manchester (Percival 1769) (Percival 1807, Vol. III, 186). This report of laboratory experiments to ascertain the substances in the pump water and its resulting purity level appeared in 1771.

His concern is that "hard and impure water may be considered … as injurious to the human body" (Percival 1807, Vol. III Vol. III, 190). His concern is toxicological and clinical, but now directed toward a population of patients. Percival thus initiates his Baconian science of public health, to which, as we will see below, he made other contributions. His goal is to "discover some means of correcting its pernicious qualities" (Percival 1807, Vol. III Vol. III, 192). His investigations take him to pharmacy, the domain of apothecaries, a competitor group of practitioners. Baconian method is no respecter of guild boundaries, allowing Percival to assume that his findings, the findings of a physician who would *eo ipso* ordinarily be regarded as a competitor, should be taken with evidence-based authority by apothecaries. He will make the same assumption in *Medical Jurisprudence* and *Medical Ethics* about the reach of Baconian moral science and its capacity to generate an ethics of cooperation among physicians, surgeons, and apothecaries as an essential component of professional ethics in medicine. Following the approach of the other experimental essays, he concludes with a concise statement of his findings, twelve of them.

Essay VII. On the Disadvantages of Inoculating Children in Early Infancy (1768). Percival bases his experimental essay on "Inoculating children in early infancy" on clinical reports from other, reliable physicians (Percival 1768). He starts with an affirmation of the clinical benefits of inoculation against smallpox, because its "safety and utility" are well established and should serve to "remove every prejudice against it, whether political or religious" (Percival 1807, Vol. III Vol. III, 230). There is disagreement about childhood vaccination; whether infants should be inoculated "as soon as possible after birth," as proposed by "Dr. MATY, an ingenious physician in London" (Percival 1807, Vol. III Vol. III, 231). This is a reference to Matthieu Maty (1718–1776), a Dutch physician who settled in London in 1740 and became a member of the Royal Society. Among many other interests, he as an advocate for early childhood inoculation (Janssens 1981).

Percival conducts a review of the scientific literature on the subject, carefully assessing the evidence base for various claims. This allows Percival to take a dispassionate approach, guided only by evidence about the timing of infant inoculation based on its *juvantia* and *lædentia*. This approach has direct application to current controversies about childhood vaccination.

Percival concludes that infant inoculation is effective and safe when deferred to infants older than two or three months. However, he also concludes that delayed inoculation is clinically preferable: "But the fittest season for inoculation seems to be, between the age of two and four years, in healthy children, and three to six in those who are extremely tender and delicate" (Percival 1807, Vol. III, 246). The main reason is the "powers of nature are then sufficiently vigorous" (Percival 1807 Vol. III, 246).

Essay VIII. On the Efficacy of External Applications in the Angina Maligna, or Ulcerous Sore Throat (1770). There then follows a short essay on "ANGINA MALIGNA, or ulcerous sore throat" (Percival 1807 Vol. III, 248–253) written in 1770 (Percival 1771). Based on clinical observations of patients in his clinical practice, he proposes that this condition is a "distemper of the whole habit, and not almost entirely a local affection" that nonetheless appears to respond well to "… dulcified spirit of nitre to be given freely, in an infusion of rose leaves, mixed with port wine. It is cordial, antiseptic and gently diaphoretic, and thus answers several very important indications" (Percival 1807 Vol. III, 253).

Invocation of Historical Figures. In "The Empiric" Percival invokes Hippocrates in making his Baconian critique of "systems" or elaborate classifications of diseases with no evidence-based, much less according to their causes, such as physiologic sympathy among disordered organs. Percival writes: "The divine Hippocrates knew how to distinguish between theory and experience" (Percival 1807, Vol. III, 15. He repeats the use of 'divine Hippocrates' in his experimental essay on water (Percival 1807, Vol. III, 175). This is odd, inasmuch as the intellectual authority of Baconian scientific method and its results is self-generated and therefore not dependent on what authorities have said. Indeed, an historical figure becomes an authority for a Baconian if and only if that historical figure practiced Baconian method.

The theory of the four humors and their interaction to explain health and disease in Hippocratic medicine, as we saw in Chap. 1, was a fixed, unchanging account. Techné does not require an evidence base and is therefore immune to alteration by evidence. Indeed, the Hippocratic physician swears in the Oath to protect techné from change.

As we also saw in Chap. 1, Galvão-Sobrinho (1996) documents the practice of invoking the name of Hippocrates as a means to gain intellectual authority for one's view by association, without much regard for whether there is textual evidence in the Hippocratic corpus that the Hippocratic authors espoused the view in support of which they have been enlisted. Percival's goal, perhaps, is to bask in reflected glory. Percival was only 25 years of age when he wrote the twinned essays, "The Empiric" and "The Dogmatic." He had already been made a member of the Royal Society before having defended *de Frigore* in Leyden. It would not be surprising that he might discern the advantage of reflected glory to be gained by enlisting Hippocrates to his cause. Already Professor of Medicine at Edinburgh and 48 years of age Gregory in his Lectures also invokes the name of Hippocrates and for a reason similar to Percival's: "Hippocrates will always be held in the highest esteem, for his accurate and faithful description of diseases, for his candour, his good sense, and the simple elegance of his style" (Gregory 1772, [1772] 1998, 183). Gregory, however, perhaps with the confidence of an already accomplished physician, teacher, and writer, eschews honorific, even florid, adjectives such as "divine" that Percival deploys. Then too, a young, freshly minted member of the Royal Society may have had to contend, in a politic way (in Hoffmann's meaning, as explained in Chap. 1) with more senior, powerful Society members more resistant to Baconian science and medicine.

Percival's use of 'divine' to modify 'Hippocrates' contrasts with his use of 'ingenious' to modify 'Franklin' in "The Dogmatic" (Percival 1807, Vol. III, 31). This is a reference to the colonial American from the Province (soon to be Commonwealth) of Pennsylvania, Benjamin Franklin (1706–1790). In English, and Scottish, enlightenment discourse 'ingenious' names the disposition toward genius. 'Genius' names the role of disciplined imagination in scientific investigation. 'Imagination' names the capacity to join the concept of a property of one entity to the concept of another entity, e.g., joining the concept of having a single horn to the concept of horse to produce the concept of unicorn, as explained in Chap. 1. Undisciplined imagination is the bane of Baconian reasoning; disciplined imagination, by contrast, is essential to the deployment of Baconian reasoning in promising investigation. Disciplined imagination emanates from reason-based reflection on observed patterns in nature that are regular enough to be considered the result of a causal process. 'Genius' names the capacity to posit for the first time, in a scientifically plausible way, a connection of that observed pattern to a "principle" or causal process. This becomes a hypothesis to be tested. This is just what Franklin did when he hypothesized that lightning is a form of electricity, and tested his hypothesis against the observed pattern of the effects of lightning.

Percival makes reference to famous Baconian scientists. Boerhaave is invoked without honorifics. He needed none. So too for Hoffmann, Sydenham, and Whytt. In doing so, Percival appears to place himself in their company, or at least aspires to do so. In the experimental essays that follow "The Empiric" and "The Dogmatic" Percival can therefore be read as demonstrating the high level of genius and Baconian investigative method that warrants association with the likes of Boerhaave. Consider the first of these essays, "Experiments and Observations on Astringents and Bitters," considered above. First, Percival forms his hypothesis that Peruvian Bark has increased efficacy when boiled, reduced to a powder, and then diluted to prevent its nauseating side-effects. He then describes in detail no fewer than forty-four experiments that support seventeen "principal facts" or scientific findings. Genius-based hypothesis formation generates excitement that "naturally led" (Percival 1807, Vol. III, 107) him from experiments on Peruvian bark to experiments on tea and ink as astringents. When a hypothesis is rejected by the results of an experiment, Percival does not take this personally, as a Dogmatist or Empiric both would. The evidence-based rejection of a hypothesis has clinical significance because it becomes an antidote to enthusiasm and its product, what Gregory later described disparagingly as the "obstinate adherence" (Gregory 1772, [1772] 1998, 28) to a clinical practice that has been discredited by "experience" in the form of controlled laboratory experiments and limited clinical investigation.

> An obstinate adherence to an unsuccessful method of treating a disease, must be owing to a high degree of self-conceit, and a belief of the infallibility of a system. This error is the more difficult to cure, as it generally proceeds from ignorance. True knowledge and clear discernment may lead one into the extreme of diffidence and humility; but are inconsistent with self-conceit. It sometimes happens too, that this obstinacy proceeds from a defect in the heart. Such physicians see that they are wrong; but are too proud to acknowledge their error, especially if it be pointed out to them by one of the profession. To this species of pride, a pride incompatible with true dignity and elevation of mind, have the lives of thousands been sacrificed (Gregory 1772, [1772] 1998, 28–29).

Percival's politic youthful reserve may have restrained him from being as "warm," as the Scots put it, as Gregory in this passage. But Percival, I suspect, would not object to Gregory's condemnation of the serious clinical harm that enthusiastic physicians have caused.

2.4.2.2 Essays Medical, Philosophical, and Experimental: Part II

The Preface. In the Preface to these essays, Percival refers to Bacon from the outset, to explain the scientific method deployed in the essays that follow. This same method shapes all of Percival's scientific communications.

> The great Lord Veralum [Bacon] recommends the collection and collation of facts, observations, and experiments, as the best method of promoting the improvement of physic; and experience hath fully evinced the utility of such a plan. In this way, I am ambitious of contributing my mite to the general stock of medical knowledge; and shall think myself happy, if I can thus render the pursuit of my own instruction and amusement, subservient to the interests of my profession, and to the general good of mankind (Percival 1807, Vol. III, 257).

Improvement looms large, not for the investigator's benefit, but to "improve physic," which defines the "interests of my profession." Percival is at pains to state that "the experiments contained in these sheets were made with great care, and related with the strictest fidelity" (Percival 1807, Vol. III, 260) to the nature of things, truth, that Baconian method is designed to produce. The Dissenter commitment to serve society, especially the poor, defines "the general good of mankind."

Scientific Communications

Essay I. Observations and Experiments on the Colombo Root. Colombo root is an herb from the town of the same name in what was then known as Ceylon (Percival 1807, Vol. III, 264), now known as Sri Lanka. It was used for a variety of conditions in both adults and children, but there is a problem: "The Colombo-root, though a medicine of considerable efficacy, is not yet generally known in practice" (Percival 1807, Vol. III, 263).

Percival reports results of clinical observations of the efficacy of Colombo root for a variety of conditions. Methodologically, he remarks that he will not present cases, because "to enter into so minute a detail would be equally unnecessary and uninteresting" (Percival 1807, Vol. III, 270). This lapse in Baconian discipline is uncharacteristic of his other scientific communications, e.g., the exhaustive list of experiments on Jesuit's bark. He proposes, instead, to present "a few case histories, which exemplify the peculiar, or, if the expression be allowable, specific qualities of the Colombo-root" (Percival 1807, Vol. III. 270). This is another uncharacteristic departure, because the case histories provide only limited evidence for the plausibility of a hypothesis about these "specific qualities." He then returns to Baconian discipline when he reports on a series of experiments aimed at identifying the herb's qualities.

In a "P.S." Percival notes that this herb bears a "high price" that could encourage "adulteration" or dilution of the herb, which could reduce its clinical efficacy. Percival thus anticipates by two centuries the clinical ethical challenge of patients splitting expensive medications into multiple doses, to save money. This often results in sub-therapeutic dosing that, in turn, can worsen the course of the patient's disease.

Essay II. On the Preparation, Culture, and Use of the Orchis Root (1804). Orchis root is derived from various species of lily, "enumerated by Botanical writers" (Percival 1807, Vol. III, 285) (Percival 1804). Botanicals formed a considerable portion of remedies and were taught as a separate topic in medical schools and in textbooks complete with illustrations designed to facilitate accurate identification. Errors in identification could have unwelcome clinical results, including fatal results. Percival in this essay reports on laboratory experiments. The evidence from this is not strong and, as a good Baconian should, he calibrates his findings to the degree of support from the evidence he has gathered:

> From these observations, short and imperfect as they are, I hope it will sufficiently appear that the culture of the Orchis root is an object of considerable importance to the public, and highly worthy of encouragement from all patrons of agriculture (Percival 1807, Vol. III, 293).

Notice what Percival does not say, which an enthusiastic physician (a physician with strong beliefs about efficacy and safety of a remedy when that remedy lacks an evidence base sufficient to warrant the beliefs) would say: physicians should use his herb in the care of patients. Instead, Percival encourages the improvement of the agronomy of the Orchis root by the "RATIONAL FARMER," i.e., the farmer who is willing to follow Baconian method to improve crop output (Percival 1807, Vol. III, 292). The scientific improvement of agriculture was a major goal of the enlightenments in England and Scotland. Gregory, for example, was a member during his years in Aberdeen of its Gordon Mills Society for agricultural improvement, no small matter in a nation that experienced periodic famine and had short growing seasons (and still does) (McCullough 1998, 85). Percival's use of 'rational farmer' anticipates the creation in the late eighteenth century of "agricultural and mechanical" colleges to educate scientific farmers and ranchers, such as Texas A&M University in College Station, Texas, where students can major in such subjects as range science, now updated to ecosystem science and management, an essential fund of knowledge in the cattle industry on Texas ranches. Percival would approve; Gregory, too.

Essay III. Experiments and Observations of the Waters of Buxton and Matlock in Derbyshire (Percival 1772b). Percival returns to the subject of water quality and safety in an essay that includes laboratory experiments, clinical observations, and clinical experiments (Percival 1772b). For the first time, his experiments include auto-experimentation, which has a checkered history. While in Buxton, he auto-experiments with water from the St. Ann's well and then with water from Matlock, measuring his pulse as he consumes differing quantities at different times of the day. As it does now, measuring the patient's pulse was an essential component of physical examination. Changes in pulse played a major role in diagnosis at that time (Nicholson 1993). Percival reports his judgments on a scale of probability, given the limitations of auto-experimentation (Baker 2009).

Essay IV. Observations on the Medicinal Uses of Fixed Air (1772). To the best of my knowledge, this essay first appeared in *Essays, Medical and Experimental (Percival 1772a)*. The phrase 'fixed air' named preparations of air, gases including air more precisely, that occur naturally, such as the waters at Bath that "copiously exhale a mineral spirit" (Percival 1807, Vol. III, 307), or are prepared. In his essay, *Medicinal Uses of Fixed Air*, Percival reports on the use of fixed air – "streams of an effervescing mixture of chalk and vinegar; or, which I have lately preferred, of vinegar and pot-ash" and other concoctions – to treat various maladies. In the course of this essay, Percival refers to "trials" of fixed air. Percival refers to a trial by "Dr. Priestley." 'Trial' names a clinical experiment on patients, the meaning with which, we saw in Chap. 1, Gregory uses the word when he takes up the ethics of human subjects research.

Scurvy, which is now known to be caused by vitamin C deficiency secondary to malnourishment, was the scourge of Royal Navy crews on extended sea voyages. Seamen and officers alike were disabled by this condition, reducing both the seaworthiness and fighting effectiveness of warships at sea. In Percival's days its symptoms were well known but not its cause, although the limited diet available on long sea cruises was suspected to be the culprit. James Lind (1716–1794) is credited with performing a controlled clinical trial at sea in 1747 in sailors with the same diet of different remedies, including oranges, on a study population carefully selected to minimize clinical differences among the subjects (Lind 1772; Dunn 1997).

Malt wort infused with fixed air had reduced the incidence of scurvy on a long sea voyage led by Captain James Cook (1728–1779). Joseph Priestley's innovation was the inexpensive method of adding fixed air to drinking water. Percival describes Priestley's controlled clinical trial of fixed air based on wort.

> DR. PRIESTLEY, who suggested both the idea and the means of executing it, has, under the sanction of the College of Physicians, proposed the scheme to the Lords of the Admiralty, who have ordered trial to be made of it, on board some of his Majesty's ships of war (Percival 1807, Vol. III, 316).

The Admiralty had requested that Priestley submit his plans for producing the altered water, which was known as "Pyrmont water" (McBride 1991), to the Royal

College of Physicians. The College, in turn, recommended the use of Pyrmont water to the Admiralty. Priestley sent his papers to the Admiralty with a request that his new water be used on the forthcoming voyages of *HMS Resolution* and *HMS Adventure* (McBride 1991), which were to participate in Captain Cook's second voyage to the South Pacific. Percival's may be the first description of what has become known as prospectively reviewed and approved clinical research with human subjects. This passage sets the stage for Percival's proposal for prospective review and approval of such research in Manchester Infirmary in *Medical Jurisprudence* and *Medical Ethics*.

Essay V. On the Antiseptic and Sweetening Powers, and on the Varieties of Factitious Air (1772). To the best of my knowledge, this essay first appeared in *Essays, Medical and Experimental (Percival 1772a)*. Factitious air is manufactured air or fixed air. Percival explores the "property both of retarding and of correcting putrefaction" (Percival 1807, Vol. III, 321). Percival reports on a series of laboratory experiments to "explain the sweetening powers of fixed airs" (Percival 1807, Vol. III, 322), using air forced from animal lungs, it appears, mixed into "water and iron filings" (Percival 1807, Vol. III, 324).

Essay VI(a). On the Noxious Vapors of Charcoal (1772). To the best of my knowledge, this essay first appeared in *Essays, Medical and Experimental (Percival 1772a)*. When factitious or fixed air "produces any noxious effects," it is known as "MEPHITIC AIR" (Percival 1807, Vol. III, 330). Percival reports on cases in which individuals have breathed in the mephitic air of burning charcoal, which was used for indoor heating but without adequate exhaustion of the fumes. Percival prescribes a plan to respond to such exposure, beginning with the patient being "carried into the open air" (Percival 1807, Vol. III, 341). Subsequent clinical care should aim at relief of symptoms of the resulting "fever" (Percival 1807, Vol. III, 341). He also proposes prevention of disease and death from burning charcoal in a "confined" space: "a free draught of air by a chimney or some other way" (Percival 1807, Vol. III, 340).

Essay VII. On the Atrabilis (1772). To the best of my knowledge, this one-paragraph essay first appeared in *Essays, Medical and Experimental (Percival 1772a)*. Atrabilis is black bile, known to the ancients, as reported by Galen (b. 129 CE). Percival explores whether black bile is the outcome of diseases or their cause (Percival 1807, Vol. III, 342–343).

Essay VIII. On the Septic Quality of Sea Salt (1772). To the best of my knowledge, this essay first appeared in *Essays, Medical and Experimental (Percival 1772a)*. Percival reports on the investigation of preservation of meat from spoiling by Sir John Pringle (1701–1782), a renowned scientist, especially on putrefactive aspects of disease, which earned him the sobriquet, "father of military medicine." Percival proposes to explore why varying amounts of salt have different outcomes in preventing "the corruption of the flesh" (Percival 1807, Vol. III, 344).

Essay IX. On Coffee (1772). To the best of my knowledge, this essay first appeared in *Essays, Medical and Experimental* (Percival 1772a). There is appended in The Works a 1776 case report of a "physician" (referenced as Percival himself) (Percival 1807, Vol. III, 355–358), which must have been added later. Coffee had

2.4 Percival's Writings

been consumed in England for more than a century when Percival wrote his essay, seeking truth in the nature of coffee:

> Though coffee has been in general use for more than a century past, has been analyzed by fire, and variously investigated by writers of learning and reputation; yet neither chemistry nor experience have hitherto ascertained its true nature, or medicinal properties (Percival 1807, Vol. III, 351).

From his laboratory experiments and clinical reports, Percival classifies coffee as "slightly astringent and antiseptic," with "sedative powers" (Percival 1807, Vol. III, 354). The "MEDICINAL QUALITIES" of coffee appear to originate in a "grateful sensation" in the stomach (Percival 1807, Vol. III, 356).

Percival lists the twenty-seven "most important conclusions" or scientific findings of the preceding scientific communications after this essay. He starts with Colombo root and concludes with coffee.

Select Histories of Diseases with Remarks (1772). Percival appends to his Essays a series of case histories of patients he has attended, their diagnoses, and the clinical management of their diagnoses. These all conform to the Baconian standards of comprehensiveness and precision. The case histories describe deglutition (difficulty swallowing) ("read before the College of Physicians, August 9, 1769, and is published in the Medical Transactions, vol. II.") (Percival 1807, Vol. III, 365), dropsies, palsy, "obstinate" colics, successful treatment with warm baths, and miscellaneous cases. In the course of these communications, Percival draws some clinical conclusions about "the efforts which nature exerts to relieve herself" (Percival 1807, Vol. III, 376), limitations on inductive method to produce exceptionless "general laws of reasoning" (Percival 1807, Vol. III, 379), the use of medicine to "imitate by art the operations of nature" (Percival 1807, Vol. III, 379), and the search for diagnostic criteria,

Proposal for Establishing More Accurate, and Comprehensive Bills of Mortality, in Manchester. In his Preface to Part II Percival acknowledges his intellectual debt to the work of Richard Price (1723–1791) on calculating life expectancy in preparing this communication in the area of public health. Price's goal in *Observations on Reversionary Payments* is to establish a plan that creates "equitable assurances on lives" (Price 1773), in the form of annuities and pensions sustainable for the long run. His motivation, as reported in the Preface to the first edition and included in the third edition, is to prevent the financial "distress" that poorly structured "societies for the benefit of widows" are at risk for creating in the future (Price 1773, x). He has undertaken this book, which took more effort that he had anticipated, to provide these societies with reliable mathematical tools and information so that they can "reform themselves" and not become a burden on the crown's treasury should they fail (Price 1773, x). He is concerned that "bubbles" will be created that will be to the advantage of the "first annuitants" but not to those who follow them (Price 1773, x–xi). The former will be able to "plunder" funds (Price 1773, xi). His reader would have immediately recognized this as the discourse of men of "interest" and "party-interest." The self-interest of individuals (men of interest) or of a group allied around a shared interest (party-interest) should not be the animating principle of organization of these societies. There is, in my reading of *Observations*, the germ of the concept of the profession of medicine as a public trust that Percival advances in *Medical Jurisprudence* and *Medical Ethics*. (See Chap. 3.)

In the mathematical calculations required to create a financially sound annuity, Price warns against the "danger of happening to trust unskilful, or careless calculators" (Price 1773, 131). Funds should be held "in trust" (Price 1773, 414) for beneficiaries and for the "public benefit" of reducing the cost of assurances by the state (Price 1773, 126).

Percival states his goal in building on Price's work:

> The establishment of a judicious and accurate register of the births and burials, in every town and parish, would be attended with the most important advantages, medical, political, and moral (Percival 1807, Vol. III, 428).

The medical advantages would be evidence-based knowledge about such matters as the incidence of disease, the health of a community, and environmental impacts on a community's health status, such as the influence of "trade and manufactures on longevity" (Percival 1807, Vol. III, 428) The political advantages include a more accurate estimate of the population size and therefore "all calculations concerning the values of assurances on lives, reversionary payments, and every scheme for providing annuities for widows, and persons in old age" (Percival 1807, Vol. III), precisely the focus of Price's work.

The moral advantages reflect the intellectual capacity of Baconian moral science to make reliable moral judgments about how people choose to live and the impact of their choices on their health. Percival is therefore concerned about the "increase of vice or virtue" (Percival 1807, Vol. III, 429). Putting on his public health hat, Percival wants to have evidence about the "unfavourable influence of large towns on the duration of life" (Percival 1807, 430). He proposes a "a more exact and comprehensive register, than has hitherto been kept" (Percival 1807, Vol. III, 431), to improve current methods in Manchester. His registers are more comprehensive than Price's.

It is important to note that in his chapter on life expectancy, Price tales a dim view of hospitals: "… with respect to Hospitals in general, *as now constructed and regulated*, I cannot help fearing that they cause more distempers than they cure, and destroy more lives than they save" (Price 1773, 220). He cites in support John Aikin's (1747–1822), the son of Percival's tutor at Warrington Academy, *Thoughts on Hospitals* (Aikin 1771) and Percival's letter to Aikin on the same, about which more below. Suffice it to say that Price, reflecting the driving force of the English enlightenment, is calling for the improvement of hospitals and citing Aikin and Percival as leaders in this cause. In *Medical Jurisprudence* and *Medical Ethics* Percival will aim to improve the outcomes of patient care in Manchester Infirmary – and Infirmaries throughout Britain – by creating hospital registers and by writing regulations for self-governance of hospitals based on moral science. Hence, the use of 'Institutes' and 'Code', about which more in Chap. 3.

Observations and Experiments on the Poison of Lead (Percival 1774b). Percival, relying on other observers, describes the deleterious impact of the mining of lead and its use in manufacturing (Percival 1774b). His skills as a Baconian public health scientist are on display and extend to experiments to identify whether lead is contained in some of the glazed earthenware then in common use and in the mortars and pestles of apothecaries. He attaches an appendix with "melancholy examples" of lead poisoning (Percival 1807, Vol. III, 478). He includes case histories reported to him by letter from other physicians of the use of "Saturnine preparations" or treatments using lead. Having reviewed their mixed, sometimes deleterious outcomes, Percival exemplifies the evidence-based, measured tone of the Baconian clinical investigator:

> The facts which I have now adduced [in the reports of clinical colleagues], in conjunction with those contained in my Treatise on the Poison of Lead, afford a strong presumption, that Saturnine preparations, externally applied, are not as perfectly innocent as they are too generally asserted and believed to be. One positive proof, well authenticated [as in the letters he received], out-weighs a thousand negative ones; especially when such positive evidence is acknowledged but rarely to occur [and therefore is easy to miss] (Percival 1807, Vol. III, 481).

Percival's combination of his own experimental work with the meticulous, reliable clinical accounts of other physician-observers puts on full display the results of cooperation that only Baconian reasoning can create and sustain. This sets the stage for the ethics of cooperation that he will present as an essential component of professional ethics in medicine in *Medical Jurisprudence* and *Medical Ethics*.

2.4.2.3 Essays Medical, Philosophical, and Experimental: Part III

Scientific Communications

Essay I. Observations on the State of Population in Manchester and other Adjacent Places (1773). Percival seeks an accurate determination of the population of Manchester (Percival 1774b). He shares with Price a concern about "the declining state of population in this kingdom" (Percival 1807, Vol IV, 61). This is an urgent public health problem for any state or polity. Large cities are part of the problem: "[b]ut it must be acknowledged that large towns are injurious to the population" (Percival 1807, Vol. IV, 7). For example, Percival estimates childhood mortality by age five to be fifty percent (Percival 1807, Vol. IV, 7). He cites Franklin on probable causes. Because seamen have long exposure to "moisture" or high humidity, for which England is famous (or notorious), the high humidity in England cannot be the cause of poor health. Instead, Franklin hypothesizes that "putrid air" is the culprit (Percival 1807, Vol. IV, 27). Percival points to the Quaker community, Dissenters like Unitarians, to identify what we now call social determinants of health and diseases, including low poverty resulting from "more equal distribution of property" as well as the cultivation of the virtues of "diligence, cleanliness, temperance, and composure of mind" (Percival 1807, Vol. IV, 30). A Baconian scientist and moral scientist has the methodological authority to make the latter sort of observation based on the truth of things, in which case, the shared way of life of Quakers. This observation carries implicit approval rooted in Percival's public health concern to identify the causes of and thus seek to prevent the high rates of disease and death in urban settings. To view what Percival writes as paternalistic or arrogation of a supposed, but false, social and moral superiority would be a form of presentism.

Percival, like Gregory (McCullough 1998), is concerned about the excessive "confinement" of children. Gregory's target was the practice of keeping children indoors during cold weather. Percival targets schools and especially manufacturing with its "sedentary employment" of children that causes early mortality and ailments that "render their constitutions feeble and sickly" (Percival 1807, Vol. IV, 42). The root cause of these unacceptable outcomes is avarice, a vice in Baconian moral science: "But the love of money stifles the feelings of humanity" (Percival 1807, Vol. IV, 42). Avarice also contradicts the self-interests of manufacturers in a healthy workforce. The love of money also "makes men blind to see the very interest they so anxiously pursue" (Percival 1807, Vol. IV, 42). In *Medical Jurisprudence* and *Medical Ethics* Percival will appeal to both self-interest and humanity in what is probably the first account of the professionally responsible management of organizational resources in the history of medical ethics, as we will see in Chap. 3.

Essay II. On the Small-Pox and Measles (1775). Percival treats both smallpox and measles as contagious diseases that should be reported in bills or mortality so that a community can better understand the prevalence of these diseases and the ages at which they cause death. Childhood Inoculation should be used, in different age ranges depending on the child's "constitution" (Percival 1807, Vol. IV, 78), as he argued in his 1768 essay, *On the Disadvantages of Inoculating Children in Early Infancy*. (See above.) Percival undertakes what is recognizably a risk/benefit calculation to justify early childhood inoculation:

> The risque of receiving the natural small-pox by infection appears to be very great during the second year of life; and the fatality of this disease at this period is highly alarming. To avert such impending danger, the inoculation of health and vigorous children [who have low risk from the inoculation], at the *age of two of three months*, seems to be adviseable, especially in large towns (Percival 1807, Vol. IV, 76).

Note the use of 'seems to be adviseable' to reflect that the judgment is one of probability, not certainty, as required by Baconian scientific reasoning, here applied to public health practice.

Essay III. An Attempt to Account for the Different Quantities of Rain, which Fall at Different Heights over the Same Spot of Ground (1771). I read this essay as a window into Percival's intellectual development as he closed out his third decade. In the essay Percival displays a universal curiosity and disciplined adherence to Baconian observational method and reasoning to form hypotheses, as well as a touch of admirable whimsy in the topic. Consider how he opens the essay:

> It is a reflection which may mortify pride and humble arrogance, but which ought certainly to animate the spirit of patient attention, and console us under the disappointment of philosophical pursuits, that many of the most interesting laws of nature have remained undiscovered, till some happy coincidence of circumstances hath pointed them out to inquiry or observation (Percival 1807, Vol. IV, 85).

2.4 Percival's Writings

Percival's observations of the size of rain drops reaching the ground at different elevations indicate that rain drops increase in size as they descend from clouds. His inquiries, in which he cites Benjamin Franklin's inquiries into electricity, led him to this hypothesis:

> From what has been advanced, it appears probable to me, that the gradual discharge of the electrical fire [lightning originating in clouds] is the principal cause of the phenomenon I have attempted to explain (Percival 1807, Vol. IV, 93).

Already a correspondent of Franklin's, it comes as no surprise – and, one suspects, came as a delight to Percival – that Franklin wrote Percival from London, where he was at the time and where he received "your favour," Percival's essay sent by post (Percival 1807, Vol. IV, 98). Franklin gently agrees with Percival's hypothesis that the volume of water in rain drops increases as they fall, thus explaining different amounts of rain on surfaces of the earth that differ in elevation. However, Franklin disagrees with Percival's reasoning about the cause of this phenomenon, inasmuch as the increased volume can occur "several ways" (Percival 1807, Vol. IV, 100). This is a splendid example of the cooperative inquiry that Baconian methods require and thereby enable. At the age of thirty Percival has put in place the scientific basis for the ethics of cooperation that he will make a centerpiece of *Medical Jurisprudence* and *Medical Ethics*.

Essay IV. On the Solution of Human Calculi by Fixed Air (1776). Human calculi, known informally as stones, can be very painful and also cause tissue damage in the kidney and bladder. Given the avoidable risks of surgical management, Percival investigates a medical approach, using "fixed air," the properties of which he explored in *Essay II* of Part II, above.

Percival begins by noting that fixed air has been used to treat other diseases, with some measure of clinical success. He goes on the state that he has "a farther, and very interesting discovery to communicate, concerning the medicinal properties of this species of factitious air" on "human *calculus*" (Percival 1807, Vol. IV, 103). He explains how he arrived at his hypothesis that fixed air would be beneficial in partial dissolving of calculi: "Analogy seemed favourable to the hypothesis, and experiment has confirmed it" (Percival 1807, Vol. IV, 103). His report on the "discovery of a new lithontriptic medicine" (Percival 1807, Vol. IV, 110) is based on a series of laboratory experiments in which exposure to mephitic air reduced the size of calculi. The next step is clinical investigation: "Perhaps it may be questioned, whether fixed air can be conveyed, to the kidneys and bladder" (Percival 1807, Vol. IV, 111). He reports on the results of a "young gentleman," one of his patients who ingested "mephitic water" and excreted dissolved calculi in his urine (Percival 1807, Vol. IV, 119–120). He had characterized the experiments performed thus far that it is "highly probable" that fixed air can be circulated to the kidneys and bladder. The clinical experiment allows him "now to speak *decisively* to this point" (Percival 1807, Vol. IV, 119). Percival cites corroborating reports from Priestley and Pringle. His observations, combined with theirs, permit him to declare "the medicinal and lithontriptic qualities of fixed air, may now be regarded as practical truths, which have been established by experience" of the highest level, "incontrovertible evidence" (Percival

1807, Vol. IV, 122), reflecting the Baconian degrees of probability through which he progressed in his laboratory and then clinical "inquiries" or investigations.

Essay V. Experiments and Observations on the Nature and Composition of Urinary Calculi (1775). This short essay reports on Percival's laboratory investigation of the composition of a urinary calculus that he obtained from another physician, a bladder stone "of considerable size" that had "formed in less than twelve months" (Percival 1807, Vol. IV, 127). It is exemplary of the intellectual virtue of candor, as described by Gregory: the commitment to being open to new evidence and, when required by the evidence, to change one's thinking. Percival does not use 'candor', but he is committed to disciplining thought and speech to the nature of things or the truth, as he was taught to do at Warrington Academy. Percival, he tells his reader, had thought that the formation of a calculus "depends either upon some accidental *nucleus,* or upon a peculiar and often hereditary disposition to concrete in the animal fluids" (Percival 1807, Vol. IV, 129). His new experiments led to this conclusion: "I am now convinced, that hard waters actually contribute to the formation of it" from one of these two initial sources (Percival 1807, Vol. IV, 130). As we shall see in Chap. 3, Percival will count on candor, the discipline of conforming thought and speech to Baconian moral science, to support his argument professional ethics in medicine in *Medical Jurisprudence* and *Medical Ethics.*

Essay VI. Experiments and Observations on the Effects of Fixed Air on the Colours and Vegetation of Plants (1775). This essay, like the essay on rain, puts Percival's roving curiosity on full display, more precisely, his roving Baconian curiosity: "The influence of fixed air on vegetation is a new, curious, and very interesting object of inquiry" (Percival 1807, Vol. IV, 133). His interest in the effects on fixed air on flowers and other vegetation was sparked, Percival reports, by his reading of a scientific communication on the topic by Priestley. His description of Baconian curiosity is revealing:

> The preservation of flowers by mephitic air was an event which I little expected, at the commencement of these trials: And, as an active mind is seldom satisfied with the bare observance of effects, without inquiring into the causes which produce them, I was naturally led into a train of reasoning on this curious subject (Percival 1807, Vol. IV, 135).

The Baconian spirit of scientific reasoning is on further display when Percival offers "speculations," i.e., hypotheses suggested by his curiosity-driven exploratory investigation. Findings are to come after more investigation.

Essay VII. Miscellaneous Observations Concerning the Action of Different Manures (1770). As noted earlier, the English enlightenment was self-consciously committed to the improvement of all aspects of human life. This five-paragraph essays focuses on various substances that might "meliorate the soil" (Percival 1807, Vol. IV, 158) and thus improve crop yield. For someone like Percival, whose public health essays put on record his commitment to improving the health of urban population, increased crop yields were not an idle curiosity. The health of the community, especially of the poor, depended on improved agricultural output.

Essay VIII. Remarks on Different Absorbents (1776)

2.4 Percival's Writings

Percival revisits experiments from two years earlier on various absorbents, such as alum. Aware of the variation in purity in the samples he had tested, Percival admits that these experiments were "vague and indeterminate," the results of which fall short of "mathematical certainty" (Percival 1807, Vo. III, 162). He quickly adds that this standard is not required. Instead, advances in understanding absorbents or other *materia medica* require him to "found both our reasoning and practice on *data*, which approach nearly to truth" (Percival 1807, Vo. III, 162). He then proceeds in what has become a very familiar way by describing a series of experiments and their results.

Miscellaneous Observations, Cases, and Inquiries

The final scientific communication of Part III comprises a set of case reports, selected, it appears, for their clinical significance, for clinical interest in rare, unusual clinical events, or to generate hypotheses about the causes of various conditions. The first case reports on a matter of considerable clinical, and public health, significance, the accidental poisoning and subsequent deaths of three children who were given fresh yew-tree leaves for the treatment of worms. Dried leaves had first been administered by their mother. She then used fresh leaves, having relied on "the trifling and inefficacious means of relief, suggested to them [the parents] by their neighbours" (Percival 1807, Vol. IV, 181).

There follows the description of the case, beginning in 1751, of a twenty-four-year-old woman in her sixth month of pregnancy, who experienced some complications of pregnancy, including a "much distended" abdomen (Percival 1807, Vol. IV, 183). During the next twelve years she had chronic problems with "putrid" uterine discharges (Percival 1807, Vol. IV, 183), for which she received a variety of treatments. Percival reports on a three-week period in 1773 during which the fetal parts appeared in her stool. One possible explanation, which he does not consider, is that there had been an earlier attempt at induced abortion that perforated both the uterus and intestine, with the fetal parts being passed through the intestine. My colleague and academic partner in professional ethics in obstetrics and gynecology suggested (Frank A. Chervenak, M.D., personal communication August 2020) that his would be unrelated to the previous pregnancy. Treatment abated her pain but at home "she suddenly relapsed, and died in a few days" (Percival 1807, Vol. IV, 184).

The next cases are presented for the purpose of generating hypotheses about hitherto not-explained conditions, including "The Rarity of Air a Cause of Haemorrhages" (Percival 1807, Vol. IV, 185–186), electroshock for gout, poisonous mushrooms, pulmonary worms, military fever (tuberculosis), angina pectoris, typhus, apoplexy, and eye disease. There is also a description of the environmental effects of rapid drops in outdoor temperature. In the report on typhus Percival raises clinical concern about physicking with opium, which was possible because regulation of controlled substances was far in the future.

> The affection of the head [by typhus] is often relieved by opiates, but in some instances, is much aggravated by them; and I fear very serious mischief will arise from the incautious and indiscriminate use now made of them, by theorists of a certain sect (Percival 1807, Vol. IV, 195).

Baconian clinical judgment is at work in the use of 'incautious' and 'indiscriminate'. Both indicate failure to adhere to the discipline of evidence-based reasoning. 'Incautious' signals enthusiasm, the belief in clinical benefit without observation-based evidence. 'Indiscriminate' signals failure to undertake observations that would permit creation of evidence-based specific indications.

Hospital Improvement

Essay IX. On the Internal Regulation of Hospitals, Addressed to Mr. Aikin (1771). This essay precedes the just-described *Miscellaneous Observations, Cases, and Inquiries*. Percival's essay on hospitals' internal regulation, he informs his readers in a footnote, was included at the end of John Aikin's *Thoughts on Hospitals* (Aikin 1771). Aikin was the son of one of Percival's tutors at the Warrington Academy, also named John Aikin. Aikin *secundus* was a physician who, after attending Warrington Academy, took his M.D. at Leyden, just as Percival had.

Aikin's opening appeals to a "benevolent" principle. This is the moral physiological principle of sympathy, which was examined in depth in Chap. 1. As Hume explained in his report of this scientific discovery of the constitutive causal process of our moral physiology, the double relation of impressions in response to the plight of others is automatic and moves us into action to relieve the plight of others and, more generally, relieve "man's estate." Gregory could have written these words:

> To counterbalance the various evils and miseries of life, Providence has planted in our natures a benevolent principle, which, without waiting for duty to incite, or reason to approve, inclines us by an involuntary emotion to relieve the distresses of our fellow-creatures, and gives us the purest and most sensible pleasure for our reward.
>
> Never have the rights of humanity better understood, nor the feelings of compassion more indulged than in our age and country. Of this we have a pleasing proof in the rapid success attending every charitable institution. We have seen, within less than half a century, numerous edifices arise throughout the kingdom, dedicated to the support of the poor under the severe afflictions of disease and want – we have seen these amply maintained, carefully inspected, and diligently attended; and all this without any interference of the civil authorities, merely by the generous and disinterested zeal of individuals. In the Metropolis many new designs have been set on foot for the relief of particular diseases and calamities; in the country general Infirmaries have been established at almost every considerable town, upon the most liberal and extensive principles (Aikin 1771, 5–6).

Infirmaries put sympathy into action for the medical and surgical care of the sick poor. The "liberal and extensive principles" should guide the work of healthcare institutions. Putting these principles into practice does not occur by accident, a reality of which Aikin, as a physician, with high probability, was well aware. Aikin continues:

2.4 Percival's Writings

> Amidst the universal diffusion of this amiable spirit, one thing alone appears wanting to compleat the wishes of humanity; and this is, that a proper direction of the means, should accompany the well-meant intentions of doing good. Without due regard to this object the most benevolent designs may be frustrated, and instead of a blessing, prove an additional misfortune to the afflicted (Aikin 1771, 6–7).

Improvement of social institutions like the Infirmaries and practices like agriculture is not simply a matter of identifying the moral principle of sympathy and the invention of virtues to regulate sympathy – as in Gregory's professional ethics in medicine. Improvement requires the creation of practical measures, such as appropriate structures and proper directions. This practical concern about structures, we saw above, motivated Price's work on "financially distressed" reversionary societies. This practical concern also motivated Price's concern that hospitals, "*as now constructed and regulated*," constitute an obstacle to improvement. Aikin points to serious problems that need to be addressed, e.g., in the crowded wards "the peculiarly noisome effluvia so unfriendly to every vigorous principle of life" (Aikin 1771, 9). As we will see in Chap. 3, Percival's practical concern to improve Manchester Infirmary as it was regulated in the early 1790s took the form of the "Precepts" in *Medical Jurisprudence* and *Medical Ethics*.

Aikin then becomes the sympathy-driven voice of observation and experience put in service of the health and life of Infirmary patients. Aikin trains his sights on "the grand necessity of life, air, [which] is never to be had in a salutary degree of purity, frequently is vitiated so as to become a poison" (Aikin 1771, 9). He goes on to consider: "neatness" (Aikin 1771, 10); architectural design and the quality of construction; proper diet; cleaning and change of "bed-cloths" (Aikin 1771, 16); the different types of disease, e.g., sorted on the basis of treatability of fractures, and those who should attend them (anticipating specialization); and, at some length, diagnoses that justify denial of admission, e.g., "scrophula," which is a form of tuberculosis and that Aikin describes as a highly infectious "virus" that puts every patient in the Infirmary at risk. He considers many other diagnoses, analyzed for their risks for other patients and treatability (Aikin 1771, 33), on the assumption that the usefulness of an Infirmary is reduced if it does not prevent preventable mortality and misuses resources instead on incurable conditions. Aikin does not want an Infirmary misused with respect to the poor: "It is not poverty, but sickness, that demands the assistance of a hospital, and when diet and lodging are joined to medical relief, it is only that the end of curing a disease may be better accomplished" (Aikin 1771, 53). There are other charitable organizations to assist the poor who are not sick to the degree that Infirmary admission contributes to "the end of curing disease." He attacks as a form of "penurious œconomy" (Aikin 1771, 55) the practice of some Infirmaries that require a deposit for admission, as beyond the means of most patients.

Aikin emphasizes appropriate care of female and pregnant patients. Humanity mandates "relief of the distresses to which the weaker and softer sex are peculiarly [i.e., uniquely] liable" (Aikin 1771, 57). To meet this special need, it is necessary, he argues, to create lying-in hospitals for pregnant patients. His Baconian account of pregnancy merits attention:

> The chief source of error in the treatment of puerperal women has been considering the state of parturition too much a disease, rather than a regular operation of nature (Aikin 1771, 58).

The rules for the case of pregnant women should not be arbitrary but evidence based. He endorses home birth for indigent patients and lauds an experiment with this birth setting, attended by a "skilful practitioner" (Aikin 1771, 65), a trained midwife or perhaps a man-midwife.

Aikin goes on to address other topics, notably the need to train surgeons in Infirmaries and praises the medical school in Edinburgh for its leadership. Gregory, as we saw in Chap. 1, considered the sharp division of medicine and surgery to be incompatible with professional responsibility to protect the health and life of each patient. Aikin clearly shares this view, at which he arrived independently, inasmuch as *Lectures* was not yet published. Aiken may have had access to Gregory's *Observations*, privately published in 1770 (Gregory [1770] 1998).

Aikin emphasizes the importance of hospitals for "experimental practice" and defends experiments in medicine because they are its "original foundation" (Aikin 1771, 76). The conduct of a series of clinical experiments makes possible the accumulation of evidence to guide the creation of a "settled mode of practice" in a hospital but also by physicians elsewhere, who should accept the "authority" of properly conducted experiments, i.e., those that adhere to Baconian method (Aikin 1771, 77). Patients have benefitted from the "spirit of rational experiment" conducted in hospitals (Aikin 1771, 81). As we will see in Chap. 3, Percival will set out "institutes" or rules for making the "spirit of rational experiment" an essential component of the organizational culture of a hospital.

In this letter to Aikin, Percival proposes some "hints on the subject" of improving hospital care (Percival 1807, Vol. IV, 172). He focuses on "AIR, DIET and MEDICINE" (Percival 1807, Vol, IV, 172). He concludes:

> I have thus, my dear friend, very imperfectly drawn the outlines of a plan for rendering hospitals, upon their present establishment, more salutary to the sick and consequently more useful to the public, and I flatter myself that you will improve and finish it (Percival 1807, Vol. IV, 178).

I read his last clause to indicate that Percival sent his letter to Aikin before Aikin published *Thoughts*. As we will see in Chap. 3, Aikin's *Thoughts* has a strong, acknowledged, influence on *Medical Ethics*. In particular, the phrase "more useful to the public" does more than reflect Percival's commitment to public health. This phrase appears to be a source for Percival's concept in *Medical Ethics* that hospital polity should be directed to the common weal. Edward Percival in his *Memorial* states that Percival expanded this letter "to a more comprehensive form, in a memorial, addressed to the trustees of the Manchester Infirmary" (Percival 1807, Vol. I, xxvii). 'Memorial' appears to reference *Medical Jurisprudence*.

After the case reports, described above, Percival includes two "advertisements" from 1774 for a Lock Hospital recently created in Manchester. This was a specialized facility for the care of "female patients labouring under the venereal disease

2.4 Percival's Writings

(Percival 1807, Vol. IV, 203). The "advertisement" was a solicitation for charitable support of the new hospital.

The language used in the first advertisement uses the discourse of Baconian moral science:

> But humanity, whilst she mourns over the vices of mankind, incites us to alleviate the miseries which flow from them. The private hand of charity is never shut, when sickness, complicated with poverty, presents itself; and hospitals are established, in every part of the kingdom, for the reception of the wretched, whether innocent or guilty. A new institution, founded on these benevolent principles, and favourable to the interests of virtue, now claims the attention, and encouragement of the public … (Percival 1807, Vol. IV, 204).

John Aikin could have written these words; so, too, could Gregory have. Inasmuch as Percival included these advertisements in this collection of his essays, it is reasonable to infer that he wrote them. They bear the strong imprint of his intellectual commitments as a Baconian moral scientist. He also refers to these advertisements in *Medical Ethics*, as we will see in Chap. 3. As we saw earlier, the intellectual and moral authority of the Baconian moral scientist extends to making evidence-based moral judgments about others and their moral improvement. As evidence-based, the closing section of this advertisement is presented, and intended, to be non-judgmental.

> To the penitent sufferers it will afford a pleasing refuge, and give opportunity to confirm their wavering resolutions, and will restore them to health, to peace, and to usefulness. Happy will the governors be in dismissing such with this benevolent injunction: GO, AND SIN NO MORE (Percival 1807, Vol. IV, 204).

The point is biopsychosocial: the sin of licentiousness puts a woman's health and life at risk. The presentist will read this text and its injunction as judgmental, negative in tone. This would be a mistake; this text exemplifies the commitment to improvement, to the relief of man's estate, in all of its dimensions, from increased production in agriculture to reduction of venereal disease and, we would now say, its biopsychosocial consequences for patients.

The second advertisement continues in the same vein. Its core appeal succinctly presents the moral reasoning that Baconian moral science invented:

> The public has been already informed of the nature and design of this excellent INSTITUTION; which is founded on the wisest *policy*, approved by *reason*, and recommended by *humanity* (Percival 1807, Vol. IV, 205).

This summarizes, as well, the case for Manchester Infirmary and the case, as we shall see in Chap. 3, for *Medical Ethics*.

Percival also addresses hospitals in the final text in Part IV of *Essays Medical, Philosophical, and Experimental*: "Remarks Relative to the Improvement of the Manchester Infirmary" (1789). His topics include ventilation, cleanliness, "the condition of the beds and furniture" (Percival 1807, Vol. IV, 436), and heating. These improvements have a single purpose: the improved care of patients, including the prevention of contagion.

2.4.2.4 Essays Medical, Philosophical, and Experimental: Part IV

Scientific Communications

Essay I: On a New and Cheap Method of Preparing Pot-Ash, with Remarks (1780). This short essay was communicated to the Agricultural Society of Manchester. The topic is plant ashes soaked in water, a concentrated form of potassium used a fertilizer, a "rich manure" (Percival 1807, Vol. IV, 212). He offers some "general observations" (Percival 1807, Vol. IV, 216), inasmuch as he has not had the time to perform experiments. His goal is that of the Society, "to increase the productiveness of agriculture" (Percival 1807, Vol. IV, 220).

Essay II. On the Fatal Effects of Pickles Inpregnated with Copper (1785a). This essay reflects Percival's ongoing commitment to public health and the role of preventive medicine in promoting it in this essay on copper poisoning from "pickled samphire" (Percival 1807, Vol. IV, 223). Samphires are edible succulents that can be – and still are – pickled and therefore storable for future consumption. Percival describes a clinical case of a seventeen-year-old "young lady" (Percival 1807, Vol. IV, 222) who ingested vinegar from a preparation of pickled samphire that resulted in her death despite Percival's ministrations to her.

Essay III. Speculations on the Perceptive Power of Vegetables (1785b). This essay is the first of several presented to the Manchester Literary and Philosophical Society. It opens with a description of Baconian scientific method. The investigator should consider carefully the "kind of evidence which the subject admits of; and the degree of it" (Percival 1807, Vol. IV, 231). This scale runs from "but probable evidence" up to "the highest moral certainty" (Percival 1807, Vol. IV, 232). There is an intellectual risk: "For, as uncertainty is always painful to the understanding, very slight evidence, if the subject be capable of no other, sometimes amounts to credibility" (Percival 1807, Vol. IV, 232). Such is the case with the "powers, both of perception and enjoyment" of plants, which are like those of animals (Percival 1807, Vol. IV, 232). Hence the essay is entitled "Speculations." This title is warranted because he relies only on analogical reasoning about the structure and "instinctive œconomy of vegetables" (Percival 1807, Vol. IV, 236), as well as spontaneity and motion, but not experience. He concludes:

> Let us rather, with humble reverence, suppose, that vegetables participate, in some low degree, of the common elements of vitality: And that our great Creator hath apportioned good, to all living things "in number, weight, and measure" (Percival 1807, Vol. IV, 245).

In his *A Father's Instructions* he will make a similar case for ants, whose capacity for perception and enjoyment, analogical reasoning suggests, should be greater than that of plants.

Essay IV. Facts and Queries Related to Attraction and Repulsion (1789). This essay is a follow-up to an earlier presentation to the Manchester Literary and Philosophical Society about the "phænomena which take place between oil and water" (Percival 1807, Vol. IV, 249). Here he adds a "few miscellaneous facts" (Percival 1807, Vol. IV, 249). His method appeals to "analogy and observation"

(Percival 1807, Vol. IV, 253). As he cautions in the previous essay, the degree of resulting evidence is not the highest; nor is it the lowest, because analogy is complemented by observation.

Essay V. A Narrative of the Sufferings of a Collier, Who was confined more than seven Days without SUSTENANCE, and exposed to the CHOKE-DAMP, in a COAL PIT, not far from Manchester, with Observations on the Effects of Famine; on the MEANS of ALLEVIATING them; and on the ACTION of FOUL AIR on the HUMAN BODY (1784). Percival relates the narrative on the basis of a report from a reliable source about the miner's experience before rescue and his subsequent clinical course. Percival thus takes advantage of a natural experiment to describe one-person famine or prolonged deprivation of food. Percival also explores air in the mine. He calls the attention of the Society members to "the ease with which he [the collier] breathed, for a considerable space of time, air too impure for candles to burn in, and which the men, who went in search of him, durst not venture to inspire" (Percival 1807, Vol. IV, 285). Percival suggests the hypothesis that the mephitic air in the mine does not adversely affect the lungs so much as it does the nervous system.

Essay VI. A Physical Inquiry into the Powers and Operation of Medicines (Percival 1790b). Percival starts this essay with the following observation:

> Medicines are the instruments employed for the preservation of health and the cure of diseases: It must therefore, be an object of interesting speculation to the philosopher, and of practical importance to the physician, to investigate the *rationale* of their action on the human body (Percival 1807, Vol. IV, 301).

Edward Percival in his *Memoirs* emphasizes the "practical design" or intent of Percival in is scientific and clinical writing (Percival 1807, Vol, I, xxii), a design on display in this essay. The reader will recall from Chap. 1 that "the preservation of health and the cure of diseases" as the capacities of medicine come from Bacon and also Gregory, at the very beginning of *Lectures*. As we will see in the next chapter, there is a deliberate practical design – Institutes followed by precepts – to *Medical Jurisprudence* and *Medical Ethics*.

Percival aims to move beyond speculation to explore the hypothesis that medicines are "*the cause of a cause*" (Percival 1807, Vol. IV, 303). To establish the plausibility of this hypothesis, he appeals, no surprise, to the principle of physiologic sympathy. The organs of the body are "delicately adjusted to each other" by nerves (Percival 1807, Vol. IV, 302). Medicines taken by mouth affect the stomach, which in turn affects other organs either directly or by substances absorbed into the circulation: "The sympathy of the stomach to the whole animated system is so obvious to our daily experience, that it cannot require much illustration" (Percival 1807, Vol. IV, 304). The paradigm of physiologic sympathy firmly in place, he goes on to explore how medicines affect organs. In doing so, he displays what we would call the explanatory power of the paradigm of physiologic sympathy.

Essay VII. Experiments with the Solvent Powers of Camphor, and other Miscellaneous Communications (1787). Percival precedes his reports of experiments about the "SOLVENT POWER OF CAMPHOR," a neglected topic, with an account of nature that he takes from Bacon:

> No object or event stands single or detached in the great frame of nature. Each has its relations and dependencies, similitudes, contrarieties, and uses, which a well-informed mind can at once recognize, arrange and pursue; and which increasing knowledge may multiply to an extent beyond our present powers of comprehension (Percival 1807, Vol. IV, 322).

As he does in all of his experimental and medical essays, Percival undertakes, describes, and reports the results of experiments precisely to increase knowledge. He will do the same in *Medical Jurisprudence* and *Medical Ethics*, where, as we shall see in Chap. 3, he deploys Baconian moral science. The product is the conceptual framework of these two works.

Essay VIII. Medical Cautions and Remarks; Particularly Relative to Pulmonary Disorders (1789). Physicians are not infallible, Percival begins this essay ((Percival 1807, Vol. IV, 329). Admitting to errors should be routine but doing so is not. Errors are also taken personally, compounding the challenge of acknowledging and correcting them. In this context Percival proposes to "lay before the Medical Society a few cautions and remarks; assured of indulgence in that freedom, which is warranted by good attention, and the love of truth" (Percival 1807, Vol. IV, 332). To use his own language, sensible of the reactions he might provoke, he asks his colleagues to indulge him, to overlook their own reactions and focus on what he has to say. This is an implicit appeal to the professional intellectual virtue of candor.

Percival does not use 'caution' as it is used in the *de Cautelis* literature that we considered in Chap. 1. In the *de Cautelis* literature, cautions are motivated by the need to protect the physician who is subordinate to the power of the sick and others who pay the physician. By 'caution' he means to ask his colleagues to pause and consider the "painful disappointment" (Percival 1807, Vol. IV, 336) of failed treatments that leave the patient unimproved or worse off. Sympathy creates the response of a "painful" disappointment or distress that originates in observing the effects on the patient's health or even life of a failed course of treatment.

Essay IX. Observations on the Medicinal Uses of the OLEUM JECORIS ASELLI or Cod Liver Oil in the Chronic Rheumatism, and other Painful Disorders (1782). Percival opens with an acknowledgement of the "multiplicity of articles, which constitute the *Materia Medica*," which "has been a subject of complaint with some physicians (Percival 1807, Vol. IV, 354). He offers his observations on cod liver oil because, he notes, it is not much in use other than at Manchester Infirmary. There its use has had analgesic effects. Its taste is "nauseous, and leaves upon the palate a flavour, like that of tainted fish" (Percival 1807, Vol. IV, 357). When mixed with pleasant flavors, such as lemon juice, it is better tolerated. Indeed:

> But the hospital patients make no complaint of it; and such is their confidence in its efficacy, that they often solicit, as I before observed, to take it; and generally persevere, with steadiness, in the use of it (Percival 1807, Vol. IV, 357).

'Steadiness' is here used with Gregory's meaning of physically disciplining sympathy, to tame one's strong, physical, gut response to endure an unpleasant experience that is good for one's health. The same steadiness is needed when a physician experiences an instinctual, strong revulsion to the sight and smell of a suppurating wound that must be closely inspected, cleaned, inspected again, and then dressed.

2.4 Percival's Writings

Essay X. Hints toward the investigation of the Nature, Cause, and Cure of the Rabies Canina (Percival 1789a). From his letter to Aikin about the improvement of hospitals, considered above, we know that Percival uses 'hint' when he offers recommendations that lack a strong evidence base but appear to be promising if implemented. He is responding to a letter about a case. In language that Gregory would endorse, Percival invokes the intellectual virtue of candor:

> To your candour I can lay myself open without reserve; and from your judgment I shall be equally happy to receive either correction or confirmation of the following suggestions, relative, I. TO THE NATURE AND CAUSE; II. TO THE PREVENTION; III. TO THE CURE OF HYDROPHOBIA (Percival 1807, Vol. IV, 366).

He then proceeds through these three, the essential domains for improving physicians' understanding and management of a serious medical condition in the era before rabies vaccination and treatment and an era in which feral dogs were not uncommon.

Essay XI. Miscellaneous Facts and Observations Addressed to Doctor Simmons (1783–1789). 'Doctor Simmons' refers to Dr. Samuel Foart Simmons (1750–1813), a British physician who studied at Leyden and then returned to London to practice. Here Percival presents some cases, as he had under the same or similar headings in other parts of his four-part *Essays*. He opens by citing Bacon's approval of the use of "certain brief notes set down rather significantly than curiously" (Percival 1807, Vol. IV, 385). In this spirit he comments on the lymphatics, "reciprocal sympathy between the stomach and the lungs" (Percival 1807, Vol. IV, 393), and "arthritic vertigo" (Percival 1807, Vol. IV, 395).

Essay XII. Miscellaneous Practical Observations Communicated to Doctor Duncan (1789). 'Doctor Duncan' refers to Dr. Andrew Duncan (1744–1828), physician and professor at the University of Edinburgh. He also co-founded the Royal Society of Scotland. Percival describes clinical cases of administration of various remedies. As we have seen throughout this review of his *Essays*, well prepared and reported case reports provided an important source of observational evidence before the era of structured clinical trials. The case reports in this Essay could be classified as efficacy trials, attentive to complications. The first case reports concern "flowers of zinc" (Percival 1807, Vol. IV, 400) or zinc oxide, which Percival used for respiratory disorders, including hoarseness and asthma. He goes on to report on the use of "poppy heads" (Percival 1807, Vol. IV, 450), perhaps as a source of opium, for colic and treatment with mercury or blisters of *hydrocephalus internus*, which, justifiably, he calls an "alarming malady" (Percival 1807, Vol. IV, 414).

Essay XIII. An Account of an Earthquake in September 1777. Percival reports some observations of an earthquake and its aftermath in Manchester. He speculates on "electric fluid" as a cause (Percival 1807, Vol. IV, 419). He then adds this comment:

> But in whatever manner such awful and tremendous events may be accounted for, the pious philosopher, when he contemplates them, extends his view beyond all secondary causes; and directing them to the great Author of the universe, regards the laws of nature only as the exertion of his divine energy (Percival 1807, Vol. IV, 419).

Note the absence of a theistic response, such as an appeal to God's mercy. Here we see how closely allied Percival's Unitarianism is to Baconian deism. Percival's Unitarianism is itself therefore Baconian.

There then follows texts not separately numbered as essays. "Observations on the Silk Cotton of Sumatra" contains Percival's speculations on the use in the "manufactures of Manchester" of a form of silk sent to him by the Archbishop of York (Percival 1807, Vol. IV, 420). "On the Acid Tar" (1783) (Percival 1807, Vol. IV, 423) explores the properties of coal tar as revealed in experiments on it, noting its corrosive powers but speculating that it might replace vinegar. Reflecting the low level of evidence, Percival forms a hypothesis: "I am persuaded that it might be employed to advantage, both in pharmacy and the arts, as a cheap and active menstruum" (Percival 1807, Vol. IV, 424) or solvent.

"Observations on the Structure and Polity of Prisons" (1787) (Percival 1807, Vol. IV, 427) addresses the origin in architecture, ventilation, crowding in prisons and how resulting contagion might be prevented. Percival uses 'polity' the refer to the governance of an institution organized to fulfill an important social function, including organizational structure and the power relationships it creates and sustains. He will apply this concept to hospitals and make ethics an essential component of their polity, as we will see in Chap. 3.

2.4.3 Writings on Political Philosophy: Baconian Polity

An Inquiry into the Principles and Limits of Taxation, as a Branch of Moral and Political Philosophy (Percival 1790a). In this essay on a central topic in public policy, taxation, Percival sets out an account of a legitimate polity. The Dissenters' concern with governance of the church, which Percival became aware of while a student at Warrington Academy, becomes in his maturity concern with the governance of the state. His account of legitimate governance creates the philosophical framework for his investigation into ethically justified tax policy, tax collection, and expenditures from the public treasury created by tax revenues. Tax policy, tax collection, and public expenditures are ethical justified when they occur in a legitimate polity, because it is only in a legitimate policy that there is "establishment of just authority" (Percival 1807, Vol. II, 249).

By 'polity' Percival means a society that organizes itself under just government. The reason is practical: no individual has the capacity to protect himself from monetary, political, and social predators, e.g., those who would take his property without his consent but may have far superior power and violent means to do so. He has in mind the English sovereign and tyrants in other countries, present and past. In a legitimate policy, government exists to enable, sustain, and protect the "public good" ((Percival 1807, Vol. II, 256). A polity that exists to serve the interests of the monarch or tyrant or of "factions" (Percival 1807, Vol. II, 245) at the expense of others is not legitimate. The "public good" entails that no one should exploited (experience the burdens of public policy without experiencing the opportunity for

2.4 Percival's Writings

offsetting benefit). This is precisely the position that a sympathy-based Baconian moral scientist would take and we know from all that we have learned about Percival's intellectual formation through his first five decades of life that Percival is indeed a sympathy-based Baconian moral scientist. This commitment is on display when Percival invokes the "moral feelings of the mind" (Percival 1807, Vol. II, 247).

The public good is not to be established on the "unstable foundation of arbitrary will" (Percival 1807, Vol. II, 234), i.e., separated from the sympathy-based moral reasons that justify a polity and therefore subject to enthusiasm of Parliament and the monarchy. In the discourse of Baconian science, we saw above, enthusiasm in science and medicine takes the form of beliefs that lack a basis in evidence, i.e., the nature of things or truth. In the discourse of Baconian moral science, enthusiasm in morality takes the form of beliefs that lack a basis in evidence about human nature. The intellect and judgment of the Baconian scientist and moral scientist is under "rational control" (Percival 1807, Vol. II, 242), i.e., the discipline of evidence regulated by Gregory's intellectual virtue of candor.

As a Baconian Dissenter and deist, we also saw above, Percival is committed to the metaphysics of deism: there is a Creator god, who is not the God of any religion. The Creator has both intellect and will, which latter the Creator exercises rationally, i.e., under the constraint of his intellect. Percival's deism rejects voluntarism, the view that God's will is unconstrained by his intellect.

> For the Deity himself is bounded, in the exercise of power, not only by physical impossibilities, but by the rectitude of his divine nature (Percival 1807, Vol. II, 242).

The Creator's intellect is thus the source of "natural law" that by the power of the Creator's will structures all of creation. Natural law can therefore be discovered in the nature of humans, other living things, and inanimate objects.

Three natural rights, Percival claims at the outset, define human nature: to "life, liberty, and property" (Percival 1807, Vol. II, 231).

> Life is the gift of GOD, and held under his disposal and authority; Liberty is essential to the perfection of a rational, a moral, and accountable agent; and Property results from the exercise of those powers and faculties, which the Deity has bestowed, which duty calls forth into action, and which are necessary to well-being, and even to self-preservation (Percival 1807, Vol. II, 231).

He then links these natural rights to the concept of the public good of a polity, by identifying the implications of natural law:

> Yet, though government, in this sense [the "social state" that originates in the law of nature], is of divine authority, it is so constituted by its adaptation to the interests and felicity of its subjects. The rights of the people, therefore, are not only antecedent to, but included in, those of the magistrate; and consequently there can never subsist a legitimate competition between them (Percival 1807, Vol. II, 233).

His readers would instantly draw the conclusion, which Percival, I suspect, with confidence in his reader's intellects, that Percival here rejects the divine right of kings. These natural rights also become the basis for this rejection of the enslavement of persons. By analogy to the Deity being "bounded," the magistrate or instruments of government power are bounded by the public good. Any exercise of government power inconsistent with individuals' "interests and felicities," the latter deriving from the exercise of their natural rights, is illegitimate.

Percival brings this ethical framework to bear on taxation, which, to be a legitimate exercise of government power, must meet the standard of "equity," which derives from "principles of reason, justice, and patriotism" (Percival 1807, Vol. II, 234). Equity requires that the burdens of taxation be bearable, where 'bearable' means taking into account the economic resources of individuals who are to be taxed, to prevent exploitation. Citing the "feudal" system, a paradigm of exploitation, Percival rejects a tax scheme in which the "excise falls chiefly on the lower tenantry and labouring poor" (Percival 1807, Vol. II, 240) and that allows the wealthy to escape their tax obligations for reasons of self-interest and not the public good. Taxes must be equitably assessed, collected, and spent. Invoking patriotism to defend inequitable taxation will fail; patriotism is tied to the public good, not the interests of the wealthy. His argument appeals to the task of reason to match ends, the common weal, with means, taxation and public expenditure.

> A just government is obliged to the most scrupulous attention to the original ends of its institution. Nor can even wise and legitimate *ends* be pursued by *means* inconsistent with equity, because no policy can ever supersede the laws of morality: and this rather dignifies, than derogates from, sovereign dominion (Percival 1807, Vol. II, 242).

Percival summarizes his conclusion much as he summarizes finding in his scientific communications, but with more emphasis:

> And, from what has been advanced, I presume, it may be inferred, that a *tax* can be of no *moral obligation*, when the claim to allegiance is absolutely forfeited [by interest-based claims]; that it is of *imperfect obligation* from mere general allegiance [consent of the governed independently of the public good]; and that to give it *full* and *complete* validity, should be a LEVY MADE ON THE COMMUNITY BY LAWFUL AUTHORITY; ACCORDING TO PRESCRIBED FORMS; IN AN EQUITABLE MODE AND PROPORTION; AND FOR THE PUBLIC WEAL (Percival 1807, Vol. II, 249).

As we shall see in Chap. 3, the political philosophy for a morally legitimate polity that Percival in this essay brings to bear on tax policy will also be brought to bear on the morally legitimate polity of a hospital that originates in professional ethics in medicine and on morally legitimate criminal law that intersects with professional ethics in medicine, topics that Percival takes up in Chapter I and Chapter IV of *Medical Ethics*, respectively. He calls this "political ethics" (Percival 1803, 108).

2.4.4 Biographical Memoirs

Percival's wrote two "Biographical Memoirs." These are obituaries that provide personal and intellectual portraits of two men who were important in his life.

A Tribute to the Memory of Charles de Polier, Esq.; Addressed to the Literary and Philosophical Society of Manchester (1782). Percival here offers a memoir of this friend and fellow member of the Literary and Philosophical Society of

2.4 Percival's Writings

Manchester. Charles de Polier (1753–1782) died young. Born in France, he came to Manchester in 1779 and was one of the founders of the Society. Of their first meeting, Percival writes:

> By the laws of hospitality he was entitled to our attention as a stranger. But his personal accomplishments, and the charms of his conversation, soon superseded the ordinary claims of custom, and converted formal civility into esteem and friendship (Percival 1807, Vol. II, 198).

As I read this memorial, Percival offers de Polier to his children and readers as a moral exemplar of properly formed character of intellectual and moral excellence in a life lived for the public good. Virtue-based moral philosophy requires exemplars, in which spirit Percival starts:

> The contemplation of moral and intellectual excellence affords the most pleasing and instructive exercise to a well-constituted mind. By exalting our ideas of human character, it expands and heightens the principle of benevolence; and at the same time is favourable to piety, by raising our views to the Supreme Author of all that is fair and good in man (Percival 1807, Vol. II, 191).

Percival continues to present this exemplar of having a "sense of rectitude, … inviolable integrity, and sacred regard to the truth" (Percival 1807, Vol. II, 195). De Polier exhibited honor emanating from "the constitution of his mind" (Percival 1807, Vol. II, 195). De Polier's intellectual and moral virtues "were strengthened by habit, regulated by reason, and sanctioned by religion" (Percival 1807, Vol. II, 195). This can be read as a succinct statement of proper intellectual and moral formation that originates in sympathy disciplined by habit and regulated by the inventions of reason, i.e., by the virtues of tenderness and steadiness. Religion "sanctions" or approves of this intellectual and moral formation but does not originate it. This is just the order that a Baconian Dissenter who is also a moral scientist would express. This order of ethical appeals also appears in the "Discourse" by his son, Thomas Bassnett, that Percival appends to both *Medical Jurisprudence* and *Medical Ethics*.

Biographical Memoirs of Thomas Butterworth Bayley, Esq. (1802). Thomas Butterworth Bayley (1744–1802), as Percival describes him in this memorial, was an improver exemplary of the English enlightenment to improvement (Percival 1802). Percival, again as a virtue-based moral philosopher should, offers Bayley as a moral exemplar to this children and readers. Percival describes his as a "gentleman." In using 'gentleman' Percival does not mean a man with wealth with a home in London for the season and an estate in the country. Instead, 'gentleman' means an earned moral and social status. An individual earns the title, 'gentleman' by taking seriously the "rank and duties of a gentleman" because sympathy requires that individual to do so for the sake of the common weal (Percival 1807, Vol. II, 290). Bayley did so by becoming a Magistrate, in which capacity he presided over the county Court of Assize and oversaw the construction of a "GOAL and PENITENIARY HOUSE" in Manchester (Percival 1807, Vol. II, 291). This building was "commodious" with single rooms and "well-ventilated" to prevent contagion (Percival 1807, Vol. II, 291–292). Bayley established a "BOARD OF HEALTH" to address the "state of the great body of the poor" with a laudatory mission:

> To ameliorate the condition of the indigent; to prevent the generation of diseases; to obviate the propagation of them by contagion; and to mitigate those which exist, by providing comforts and accommodations for the sick ... (Percival 1807, Vol. II, 292).

Bayley extended the scope of his commitment to the poor "by promoting the moral and religious instruction of the rising generation amongst the poor" (Percival 1807, Vol. II, 293). Recall that Baconian moral science creates the basis for reliable claims about moral formation in the virtues of sympathy, to which formation "moral and religious instruction" contributes.

Bayley opposed enslavement of persons and took the lead in the House of Commons in 1788 when he was the first to sign a petition to the House to abolish enslavement of persons. Percival provides a Humean description of this event:

> On taking the pen, he lifted up his hands to Heaven, and with an elevated voice exclaimed, "May God grant his blessing on this virtuous effort in favour of oppressed humanity!" A profound silence ensued; one sympathetic emotion seemed to pervade the whole assembly; and every heart was in union with the devout aspiration (Percival 1807, Vol. II, 297).

As we shall see in Chap. 3, the opening paragraph of *Medical Jurisprudence* and *Medical Ethics* invokes sympathy and its virtues of tenderness, steadiness, condescension, and authority to create the "union" of the physicians and surgeons in the ethics of cooperation of a profession of medicine

Percival's philosophy of religion is on display. He had learned at Warrington Academy that religious life should be based on conviction, i.e., being convinced of truth using Baconian method. For Baconian scientists and moral scientists like Percival truth was found in the nature of things where the deists' Creator had put it. Dissenters were also respecters of well-formed conscience, including conscience formed by other religions, even the Church of England with which Bayley was in "communion" (Percival 1807, Vol. II, 301).

The Dissenter John Seddon (1719–1769) of Manchester (not to be confused with John Seddon of Warrington Academy, his second cousin) puts forward a test of religiously formed conscience:

> Truth is unchangeable, the condition of divine favour a fixed unalterable thing. Persons may as well attempt to extinguish the sun with a sponge, or pluck the stars from the firmament, as think of recommending themselves to a righteous GOD, by any thing but real virtue of heart and life. Every species of religion which does not lay the main stress upon moral excellence, or goodness of heart and life, is false religion; and that which excludes and contemns virtue is worse than atheism (Seddon 1766, vi).

Respect for all individuals of well-formed conscience is principled pluralism.

> His devotion was sincere and fervent, but devoid either of enthusiasm or superstition. To the communion of the Church of England he was cordially attached, not from the prejudice of *early education*, but from mature reflection and deliberate judgment (Percival 1807, Vol. II, 301).

Religiosity that meets the Baconian criteria of "mature reflection and deliberate judgment" commands respect because mature reflection and deliberate judgment are essential for forming and sustaining a virtuous character. Note a key point in Percival's philosophy of religion: religion commands respect when it satisfies criteria that originate independently of it, such as promoting moral excellence. Religion and Baconian science are reconciled by requiring the former to become accountable to the latter, thus becoming Baconian religions, as exemplified in the works of John Taylor that were analyzed earlier in this chapter. This is how Percival understood what it meant to be a Dissenting Unitarian.

In *Medical Ethics* Percival will make an analogous point about when state power that affects health and life commands respect by physicians and surgeons: when that power conforms to professional ethics in medicine, as we shall see in Chap. 3.

The criteria for assessing any religion arise, not from faith or faith traditions, but from the truth of things. This is because all "mature reflection and deliberate judgment" is grounded in the truth of things. And, the truth of things is observed by using the tools of Baconian science, including moral science. Religion that commands respect requires a deism that passes muster in Baconian science. The result is to eliminate the potential for conflict between deist religion and science, in a fell swoop. This allows him to say, in a February 10, 1785, letter to his son Thomas Basnett Percival, then a student at Cambridge: "Religion and Ethics, considered in intellectual view, hold the first rank in dignity among the sciences" (Percival 1807, Vol. I, xcviii).

Pickstone (1993) reads Percival to be following Bishop Joseph Butler (1692–1752):

> He stood for the defence of Christian religion against skepticism and secular rationalism, not by setting religious ethics *against* secular ethics (as would later become popular), but by accepting the possibility of secular ethics to which religious belief was superadded. Butler's secular ethics – the supposed subject of man's intrinsic moral sense – was largely classical in its derivation, largely *stoical* (Pickstone 1993, 166).

There is an element of stoicism in Percival's moral writing, as explained later. Here I want to differ from Pickstone: Percival's ethics is secular because it is the product of secular Baconian science applied the secular truth of things. To repeat, religious belief that commands respect must be compatible with Baconian science, an idea that was *not* classical in origin. Butler also emphasized the limits on "knowledge of divine design, limits that had to be continuously in mind when making moral arguments" (Garrett 2018). Butler would, I think, have been skeptical of the robust confidence of Baconian deists to read out the truth of things.

2.5 The Moral Formation and Development of Children

2.5.1 A Father's Instructions

In 1775 Percival published the first of three parts of a work directed to the moral formation and development of children with a lengthy but highly informative title, *A Father's Instructions Adapted to the Different Periods of Life, from Youth to Maturity, and Designed to Promote the Love of Virtue; a Taste for Knowledge, and*

Attentive Observations of the Works of Nature. A Father's Instructions was remarkably successful in that it appeared in many subsequent editions in Britain well into the nineteenth century. On this side of the Atlantic Ocean it appeared seven decades later with the title, *Parental Instructions, or, Guide to Wisdom and Virtue Designed for Young Persons of Either Sex, Selected Mainly from the Writings of an Eminent Physician* (Percival 1846). This is sustained, positive reception of one's literary contributions that most authors can only wish were their own.

Percival explains that he has gathered these "Lessons of Wisdom and Virtue" (Percival 1807, Vol. I, 6) as an *aide-memoire* for his four children to recall in the future, after he has died, the stories as he related them at their home near Manchester, Hart-Hill.

> Adieu! My dear children. May you be wise, virtuous, and happy! And thereafter may we meet, to part no more, in those regions of the blessed, where our knowledge and felicity will be for ever increasing; and where we shall enjoy together the glorious presence of our common Father, the Parent of the Universe! (Percival 1807, Vol. I, 6).

Note the order: happiness will be a function of wisdom and virtue. Wisdom will be the product of Baconian science and virtue the product of Baconian moral science, the virtues that regulate sympathy and thus are worth cultivating. Note, too, that intellectual improvement that the "felicity" that accompanies it, will continue in the afterlife.

2.5.1.1 The Genre of Paternal Advice

The genre of paternal advice to children was well established. Thomas Scott (1705–1775), known for this hymn writing. for example, wrote such a book all in verse (Scott 1748). Gregory had written a similar text, *A Father's Legacy to his Daughters* (1774), published posthumously. This work also had a very successful publishing history (McCullough 1998). In his lectures on medical practice to Edinburgh medical students on the clinical diagnosis and management of gout, he notes that are two kinds: acute and hereditary. He tells his students, with remarkable frankness, that he has hereditary gout and expects to die from it. Gregory therefore brought to his parenting of his surviving daughters a keen awareness of his impending mortality. He was also widowed. He wrote *A Father's Legacy* as a set of instructions for life that would guide his daughters after he died (McCullough 1998).

Gregory bases his advice to his daughters on sympathy and its virtues. Men, he explains, because they work in the world of commerce or a world in which "interest" is primary, are at risk of becoming hard-hearted. Women, by contrast, are at risk of dissipation or undisciplined feelings. He encourages his daughters to continue in the Church of England, in which he, a deist, had raised them, because religion has the capacity of "checking dissipation, and rage for pleasure" (Gregory 1774, 9). Religion steadies moral development. Religion encourages proper moral formation and religious tolerance. Religion also fortifies women again the "man of false manners," a man of interest who feigns the virtues in order to take advantage of women.

2.5 The Moral Formation and Development of Children

Similarly, Percival cautions against "affectation in all of its odious forms" and "false airs" (Percival 1807, Vol. I, 30). Gregory recommends the cultivation of the regulatory virtues of sympathy that sustain its proper function of direct engagement with the plight or others, the virtues of tenderness and steadiness (McCullough 1998).

In the preface of "Part the Second" (Percival 1807, Vol. I, 87), Percival raises the prospect of his own death:

> Soon, however, the connection in which we now rejoice will be dissolved. The frequent interruptions of my health, and the natural delicacy of my condition, warn me of the precarious tenure on which I hold the dearest blessings of life; and heighten my connection to you, and to my friends, whilst they render me indifferent to almost every other enjoyment (Percival 1807, Vol. I, 91–92).

He wants to "improve the fleeting period of our union; to cherish the generous sympathies which the filial and paternal relations inspire; and to discharge our reciprocal duties with assiduity, delight, and perseverance" (Percival 1807, Vol. I, 92). This is a wonderful expression of the eighteenth-century Enlightenment commitment to improvement accomplished by cultivating sympathy and its virtues.

In his preface to "Part the Third," entitled "To the Author's Sons and Daughters," death has become a real presence in their lives:

> Since I last addressed you, my dear children, our family circle has been contracted by the death of your two excellent brothers. In deploring their loss, we become more sensible of the warmth and of the value of our attachment to each other, whilst mutual sympathy in sorrow draws closer the bands of mutual amity and love. Dear to us all, inexpressibly dear, is their memory: and this tender recollection is an incense which may ascent to heaven (Percival 1807, Vol. I, 253).

James Percival had died in 1793, while he as a medical student at the University of Edinburgh (Percival 1807, Vol. I, clxxx). Thomas Bassnett Percival had died in 1798 at thirty-one years of age. Percival does not mention Maria and Edward Bayley Percival, who had died earlier, in 1780. Humean sympathy and its virtues bound his family together and animate almost every page of *Instructions*.

2.5.1.2 Percival's Three Goals

Gregory's *Legacy* might have been available to Percival when he wrote what would become the first of three parts of *Instructions*. There certainly echoes of Gregory in "The Preface" in which Percival explains his goals. Percival is mindful that, with the publication of this book, his "Tales and Reflections will fall into other hands, besides those of the author's children, for whose use they were intended" (Percival 1807, Vol. I, 7). *Instructions* has three aims:

> The first and leading one is to refine the feelings of the heart, and to inspire the mind with the love of moral excellence (Percival 1807, Vol. I, 7).
>
> The second design of this little work is to awaken curiosity, to excite the spirit of inquiry, and to convey, in a lively and entertaining manner, a knowledge of the works of God (Percival 1807, Vol. I, 7).

The third end proposed is to promote a more early acquaintance with the use of words and idioms (Percival 1807, Vol. I, 8).

Our moral lives are a function of the "feelings of the heart," or sympathy, as his readers would readily recognize and that Gregory emphasizes. These feelings should be regulated by the virtues of tenderness and steadiness, the feminine virtues to which Percival will make repeated reference in the texts that follow. Virtue displays "beauty" in contrast to the "deformity of vice" (Percival 1807, Vol. I, 7). Here Percival may be echoing the ancient wisdom that beauty is the fundamental metaphysical category, as for example, in the beauty of the sun that draws people out of Plato's cave (Plato 2000). The second end requires "strict attention ... to truth and nature" of what Taylor taught Percival at Warrington Academy: truth is in the nature of things, put there by the Creator god. Knowledge of the works of God echoes Gregory's view that religion is essential for the moral formation of women. The third end reflects the view that there is a truth of things about taste. We now take for granted that *de gustibus non disputandum est* (in matters of taste there should be no disputes). From Gregory and Percival's perspective, this is a mistake. Gregory took the view that taste is disciplined by nature in some cases, e.g., the physician avoiding styles of dress that terrify children (McCullough 1998). Percival's goal in encouraging the development of a "most proper and expressive" vocabulary was to prevent the use of "vulgar and familiar forms of speech" (Percival 1807, Vol. I, 8) that gratuitously hurt others, in violation of the requirements of sympathy.

2.5.1.3 Genres Included

The texts of *Instructions* display a remarkable range of genres. Percival includes all or parts of poems, historical and biblical narratives, fables, and fictional narratives. The texts in the first part are usually short, easily committable to memory. The fables feature delightfully named characters, such as Mendaculus:

> Mendaculus was a youth of good parts, and of amiable dispositions; but by keeping bad company he had contracted, in an extreme degree, the odious practice of lying. His word was scarcely ever believed by his friends; and he was often suspected of faults, because he denied the commission of them; and punished for his offences, of which he was convicted only by his assertions of innocence (Percival 1807, Vol. I, 69–70).

Mendaculus' vice of mendacity almost came to a very bad end, when, one day he was riding with his father when his father's horse threw him and Mendaculus "had not the strength to afford the necessary help" (Percival 1807, Vol. I, 70). He went into the nearby town for help but no one believed him. He returned to the accident site but his father was not there, having been rescued by a passing coach and taken home to recover, but only as Mendaculus later learned. Mendaculus reformed himself and "he soon found, by sweet experience, that truth is more easy and natural than falsehood" (Percival 1807, Vol. I, 71). Percival thus is an optimist about the potential for moral self-reform. A short text, "The Honour and Advantage of a

Constant Adherence to Truth" (Percival 1807, Vol. I, 27–28) reinforces the lessons of Mendaculus.

The texts in the second and third part tend to be longer, including some quite lengthy disquisitions. In some of these longer texts the narrator is one "Euphronius," Percival himself, thinly disguised. Percival repeats a number of themes, as an effective pedagogue should, inasmuch as repetition encourages memory and mastery.

2.5.1.4 Sympathy for Animals and the Ethics of Animal Experimentation

Sympathy extends beyond humans to include horses, conveyed in a riveting account of a man beating his horse. This story explained how vices not only harm others but also the vicious person, by causing "degradation" of character (Percival 1807, Vol. I, 70). Our sympathy extends even to ants: "For the sensations of many insects are at least as exquisite as those of animals of more enlarged dimensions" ((Percival 1807, Vol. I, 12). Birds have "the same natural right to liberty" as humans (Percival 1807, Vol. I, 13).

Percival provides an account of the ethics of animal experimentation based on humanity and its virtue of tenderness, as the antidote to the inherent risk of cruelty in animal experimentation:

> Beware, my son, said Euphronius, of observing spectacle of pain and misery with delight. Cruelty, by insensible degrees, will steal into your heart; and every generous principle of your nature will then be subverted. The philosopher, who has in contemplation the establishment of some important truth, or the discovery of what will tend to the advancement of *science*, and to the good and happiness of mankind, may perhaps be justified, if he sacrifice to his pursuits the life or enjoyment of an inferior animal. But the emotions of humanity should never be stifled in his breast; his trials should be made with tenderness, repeated with reluctance, and carried no farther than the object in view unavoidably requires. Wanton experiment on living creatures, even those, which are merely subservient to the gratification of curiosity, merit the severest censure. They degrade the man of letters into a brute; and are fit amusements only for the cannibals of New Zealand (Percival 1807, Vol. I, 51).

This is a robust ethics of animal experimentation. It also informs Percival's professional ethics of clinical research with human subjects, as we will see in Chap. 3. Sympathy for animals requires that investigation using them advance science, contribute to the good of human beings, show tender regard by preventing and minimizing pain, undertaking repetition for the purpose of replication with the minimum number of animals required to establish findings reliably, and using only the number of animals required to test a hypothesis. "Wanton experiments" use animals for "the gratification of curiosity:" there are no offsetting benefits making such use prohibited by sympathy and its virtue of tenderness. Only the unjustified misery and death of animals and moral deformity of the experimenter follows from failure to adhere to the sympathy-based moral requirements of the ethics of research with animal subjects. The context for his remarks about the "cannibals of New Zealand" is his views on different races, about which more below when he takes up enslavement of persons. This is a compelling example of how a comprehensive ethics of research with animal subjects can be elucidated without reference to the contentious concept of animal rights.

2.5.1.5 The Regulatory Virtues of Tenderness and Steadiness

Sympathy or humanity – Percival uses the terms interchangeably – should be cultivated by conforming to its regulatory virtues. These are invented by reason, to implement its role of moderating the passions (Percival 1807, Vol. I, 3), as he puts it in the title of a one-paragraph text: "It is the Office of Reason and Philosophy to Moderate, not to Suppress, the Passions" (Percival 1807, Vol. I, 36). Chief among the virtues are tenderness and steadiness, which Percival has taken from Gregory's professional ethics in medicine. For example, he writes of the "permanent tenderness" of parents (Percival 1807, Vol. I, 20). He summarizes the role of virtues in moral formation:

> An assemblage of virtues constituted his [Philander, a friend of Euphronius] moral character. His heart was tenderness and humanity itself; his friendship warm, steady, and disinterested [i.e., not based on self-interest]; his benevolence universal; and his integrity, inviolate (Percival 1807, Vol. I, 33).

2.5.1.6 Percival's Adoption of the Second Commitment of the Ethical Concept of Medicine as a Profession

Sympathy regulated by the virtues of tenderness and steadiness turns our attention and concern to others and blunts self-interest. The result is the ethical obligation to make the protection and promotion of others one's primary concern and motivation (the result of the "excitement" caused by properly regulated sympathy), keeping self-interest systematically secondary. Percival thus adopts the second commitment of the ethical concept of medicine as a profession invented by Gregory and described in Chap. 1.

2.5.1.7 Condescension and Authority

Percival includes William Enfield's poem, "Compassion for the Poor" (Percival 1807, Vol. I, 17–18) that explains how compassion incites us to respond to the indigent: "Hard is the fate of the infirm and poor." Sympathy moves us to alleviate that plight. Our sympathetic response brings us down from our higher socioeconomic status. This is condescension. In Johnson's *A Dictionary of the English Language* (Johnson 1755), 'condescension' is defined as "voluntary humiliation; decent from superiority; voluntary submission to equality with inferiours" (Johnson 1755). The reader should beware the presentist inclination dismiss condescension as an illicit sense of superiority over and disdain for those "beneath" us, upon whom we look down our distinguished noses.

2.5 The Moral Formation and Development of Children

Percival also uses the story, "True Elevation of the Mind Displayed in Condescension and Humanity" (Percival 1807, Vol. I, 216–217), to explain condescension. This story is about the life and death of Sir Philip Sidney (1554–1586), "one of the brightest ornaments of Queen Elizabeth's court," who displayed "the most undaunted and enterprising courage" in a battle near Zutphen in The Netherlands in 1586, in which Netherlandish forces aided by the English were defeated by Spanish forces. Sidney was severely wounded in the leg by musket-fire. He was removed to the rear and became dehydrated from blood loss. He was about to consume drink that had been brought to him, "but as he was putting the vessel to his mouth, a poor wounded soldier, who happened to be carried by him at that instant, looked up to it with wishful eyes" (Percival 1807, Vol. I, 217). Sir Sidney refused the drink and gave it to the soldier saying, "*Thy necessity is yet greater than mine*" (Percival 1807, Vol. I, 217). He died several weeks later from his wound.

The person who condescends has real authority and power over the one to whom the person condescends. Sir Sidney did not cease to be a member of the English aristocracy and thus in a position of social superiority, as well as military superiority, over the wounded soldier. But he put these lofty stations aside to do what sympathy and its virtue of tenderness required of him, the story is meant to convey to Percival's reader. Real authority and power are not expressed in "stern reproof" and are never "harsh" (Percival 1807, Vol. I, 91) but, like Sir Sidney's, display tender regard for those under one's authority. Condescension, as a virtue of sympathy, protects those under one's authority from abuse of one's power over them. This becomes a solution to the anomaly of unaccountable power for the entrepreneurial paradigm that was identified in Chap. 1.

Percival's account of the concept of power bears directly on the concept of ethically justified authority. Power is the ability to forms one's will into a decision and then execute that decision, oneself or through others:

> *Power*, abstractly considered, is of little estimation; and may either dignify or degrade the possessor. If you wish to derive honour from it, be careful to render it subservient to the happiness of all around you; and enjoy with gratitude, not with affected superiority, the exalted privilege of doing good (Percival 1807, Vol. I, 170).

Percival rejects "self-love" and the "*levelling principle*" that self-love generates (Percival 1807, Vol. I, 52):

> Numbers of mankind are influenced by a *levelling principle*, which cannot brook superior excellence; and they wage secret war with whatever rises above their own mediocrity as a kind of moral or intellectual usurpation (Percival 1807, Vol. I, 52).

The Levellers were a faction emerged from the first the English Civil War (1642–1651) that supported popular sovereignty. Percival is committed to self-governance on the basis of our natural rights, as we saw above. At the same time, Percival is committed to the superiority of intellectual authority of Baconian reasoning over speculative reasoning. This superiority should never become self-serving, although it comes at a price: "It is evident, therefore, that, in the present condition of things, envy and detraction are the price which must be paid for pre-eminence in virtue" (Percival 1807, Vol. I, 54)

2.5.1.8 Opposition to Enslavement of Persons

Percival wrote on the abomination of the enslavement of persons thirty years before Parliament, in 1807, enacted the Abolition of the Slave Trade Act. Every individual possesses the capacity for "pre-eminence in virtue." This is no accidental, hereditary virtue, unlike hereditary titles and lands. The truth of things is that virtue is acquired, by hard, sustained work. Claims to pre-eminence in intellectual and moral virtue by virtue of the circumstances of one's birth are without foundation in human nature. From the perspective of the nobility, this is heretical thinking but not on the surface of the words. Percival was a sophisticated revolutionary.

> May not thousands of suffering Negroes, in our West-Indian colonies, possess the seeds of similar virtue, choked only in their growth of depressing servitude? What a compound aggregate of evil, beyond all estimate, does the practice of slavery present to our view, when we contemplate the moral and intellectual excellence which it has probably prevented: and the depravity, ignorance, and misery it has actually produced (Percival 1807, Vol. I, 77).

He continues:

> Life and liberty, with the powers and enjoyments dependent on them, are the common and unalienable gifts of bounteous heaven. To seize them by force, is rapine; to exchange for them the wares of Manchester or Birmingham, is improbity; for it is to barter without reciprocal gain (Percival 1807, Vol. I, 78).

Enslavement of persons not only violates the enslaved person's unalienable rights, a phrase that appears in the American Declaration of Independence, enslavement of persons violates the morality of exchanges in a just marketplace. For Percival, economics is not neutral but subject to justice. In the ethics of economics markets exist for the public weal. All living things, human beings most of all, are "in that state of freedom for which nature formed" them (Percival 1807, Vol. I, 143). Every failure to respect and support that freedom is an injustice, an "improbity."

The perpetrators of enslavement of persons, not those persons themselves, produce its abhorrent outcomes for enslaved persons. In another text Percival reviews the "striking variety of the human species" (Percival 1807, Vol. I, 101), more or less by the continent on which they were thought to be commonly found. He describes the "Negroes of Africa" (Percival 1807, Vol. I, 101) by what we would regard as racialist – or racist – stereotypes of visual appearance. The text, however, reads like a Baconian scientific report of facial appearance, in parallel to the "countenances" of the other varieties of human beings that Percival also describes in the same way (Percival 1807, Vol. I, 100). Appearance, however, is not the nature of a human being; his or her "intellectual and moral powers" (Percival 1807, Vol. I, 101), reason and sympathy, are. Race or appearance does not diminish these powers. Oppressors, however, can damage the development of these powers. The intellectual and moral powers of "these wretched people are uncultivated; and they are subject to the most barbarous despotism" (Percival 1807, Vol. I, 101). The text that follows makes clear that Negroes are not wretched by nature; their wretched condition has been imposed on them by "savage tyrants" of the slave trade.

Percival thus undermines the central tenant of racism, that one's own race is inherently superior and the others inherently inferior. This is a demonstrably false belief. He condemns the racists slavers, the purported owners, sellers, and the depraved abuses of persons that are intrinsic to enslavement: "this infernal commerce is carried on by the humane, the polished, the Christian inhabitants of Europe" (Percival 1807, Vol. I, 102). His third purpose in writing *Instructions* was to support "a more early acquaintance with the use of words and idioms" (Percival 1807, Vol. I, 8). Here Percival instructs his young reader in the deployment of elegant sarcasm, deployed in an full-bore attack on the vaunted but false superiority of the slavers over enslaved persons, signaled by the use of 'infernal' and then turning 'humane', 'polished', and 'Christian' into barbed condemnation. This is high verbal art of righteous anger.

He describes the "striking proof of the ideas of horror, which the captive negroes entertain of the state and servitude they are to undergo," a report of one Dr. Goldsmith. This is Oliver Goldsmith (1728–1774), an Irish polymath: acclaimed novelist, playwright, and poet, as well as naturalist and prolific writer in other genres. Percival refers to him as "Dr.," because Goldsmith studied medicine at Edinburgh and practiced for a time. The story from which Percival quotes is reported in Goldsmith's account of sharks (Goldsmith 1806). Goldsmith relates the report of a slaver ship captain about the Middle Passage. Enslaved Africans jumped overboard when, temporarily freed of their shackles belowdecks and taken above to the main deck, they had the chance to do so (Percival 1807, Vol. I, 102).

The scientific, observational tone with which Percival describes what he understood the mortality rate of enslaved persons during the Middle Passage to be turns chilling: "Fourteen hundred thousand unhappy beings, who are now in the European colonies, in the New World, are the unfortunate remains of nine millions of slaves, who have been conveyed thither" (Percival 1807, Vol. I, 102). In the context of the polite, restrained style of his writings, 'unhappy' and 'unfortunate' are barely masked fighting words or what Gregory in a similar understatement called "warm" words (McCullough 1998).

What Percival writes about the vice of sensuality applies all the more to moral consequences of the vicious institution of enslavement of persons for its practitioners: "a vice which contaminates the body, depresses the understanding, deadens the moral feelings of the heart, and degrades the human species from the exalted rank which they hold in the creation" (Percival 1807, Vol. I, 134). *Instructions* puts on display the exemplary use of "words and idioms" to express moral outrage without ever having to raise one's voice. Percival was confident that he did not need to express his moral outrage explicitly. He counts on the sympathetic response of his children and readers to put himself or herself in Percival's place as he or she reads Dr. Goldsmith's account and experiences, by the workings of sympathy, Percival moral outrage for themselves and for their moral instruction.

In summary, Percival makes an argument against enslavement of persons to which there is no available philosophical response and does so with measured forcefulness that, on my reading of the texts, underscores the moral outrage that sympathy causes him to experience from just thinking about the subject and that he wants his reader to experience without being prompted. This is just how our moral physiology works.

Sympathy also puts us in the place of the enslaved person. Enslavement causes "misery," a state of physical, intellectual, and moral deprivation that can drive humans to so despair of their future that taking their own lives becomes a morally acceptable option. Enslavement is false to the nature of things in philosophically grotesque ways. Enslavement of persons denies that the possession of the capacity for "moral and intellectual excellence" is the same in all of us, which denial can only be believed if one embraces the philosophically grotesque belief that one race of human beings is inferior in these and all other respects. Enslavement egregiously violates the "unalienable" rights that we all possess.

Enslavement is also false to the truth of market exchanges in which individuals sell their property for money or barter. Offering stolen goods as one's legitimate property violates the requirements of just markets. Offering for sale what can have no price – what is, in the precise meaning of 'priceless', priceless – is fraud. Finally, slavers are also depraved, the lowest form of life in the discourse of a virtue-based moralist, which point Percival makes with unrivaled and therefore enviable disgust. To repeat: "this infernal commerce is carried on by the humane, the polished, the Christian inhabitants of Europe" (Percival 1807, Vol. I, 102). Percival can be read as participating in the moral revolution against the enslavement of persons under the sanction of English law.

2.5.1.9 Baconian Philosophy of Religion

Percival instructs his reader to eschew "speculative doctrines of religion" (Percival 1807, Vol. I, 46), i.e., those that lack an evidence base in nature or scripture. The reason: "as they have no influence on the moral conduct of mankind, [they] are comparatively of little importance" (Percival 1807, Vol. I, 46). They are also a source of endless differences. He does not say, and probably does not need to say, that these differences have become violent.

> An intemperate zeal, therefore, for such points of faith betrays a weak understanding, and contracted heart: and that zeal may justly be deemed intemperate, which exceeds the value of its object, and which abates our benevolence toward those who do not adopt the same opinions with ourselves (Percival 1807, Vol. I, 46).

To limit benevolence to those who agree with us, i.e., who share a self-interest, is to foster party-interest, which is incompatible with sympathy, the well-spring of benevolence. Anyone who is "intemperate" has lost control of sympathy and become self-indulgent, a vice. The use of "weak understanding" and "contracted heart" echo the language that Gregory uses to describe someone who does not submit to the intellectual virtue of candor. When that someone is a physician, clinical calamity ensues:

> It sometimes happens too, that this obstinacy proceeds from a defect in the heart. Such physicians see that they are wrong; but are too proud to acknowledge their error, especially

if it be pointed out to them by one of the profession. To this species of pride, a pride incompatible with true dignity and elevation of mind, have the lives of thousands been sacrificed (Gregory 1772, [1772] 1998, 28–29).

2.5.1.10 Percival's Adoption of the Third Commitment of the Ethical Concept of Medicine as a Profession

We saw above an important implication of sympathy regulated by its virtues of tenderness and steadiness: Percival's adoption of the second commitment of the ethical concept of medicine as a profession. With his express and powerful opposition to "party-interest" or shared, overlapping, or complementary self-interest of a group Percival adopts the third commitment of the ethical concept of medicine as a profession: the commitment to the primacy of the ethical obligation to protect and promote the interests of other, keeping group self-interest systematically secondary.

Percival also adds to the conceptual scope of the third commitment. As we saw in Chap. 1, Gregory railed against the "corporation spirit" or the guild interests of the members of the Royal Colleges, especially those in London. The concept of a "party-interest" includes the shared interests of guild members. But it also includes the interests of an individual that happen to be shared, overlap, or complement the interests of others. Family members can have kin-based, shared interests, as did, for example, the Coan School physicians in ancient Greece before it took on recruits from outside the family. When these physicians recruited young men outside the family, as we saw in Chap. 1, they used the *Oath* to invent loyalty to the masters. In response to the uncertain and fragile nature of this undertaking, they solemnized the party-interests in a "written covenant." Individuals with a shared interest in retaining their power in an organization can also have party-interests. Percival responds to instances of both family-interest party-interest at Manchester Infirmary in *Medical Jurisprudence* and *Medical Ethics*, as we will see in the next chapter.

2.5.1.11 Theodicy

A major topic in philosophy of religion is theodicy or the problem of evil: How is evil in God's creation compatible with his omniscience, omnipotence, and benevolence? The German philosopher Gottfried von Leibniz's (1646–1716) only published book was on this topic (Leibniz 1985). Percival takes up this topic in "On the Divine Permission of Evil, Natural and Moral" (Percival 1807, Vol. I, 260–299).

Percival distinguishes among three types of evil:

Evil may be considered under the three following views:

 I. As purely physical, or appertaining solely to the material system of nature.
 II. As physical, but influencing or dependent on human agency.
 III. As moral in its origin, nature, and effects (Percival 1807, Vol. I, 262).

Purely physical evil "counteracts the design of the Creator, by disturbing the order or subverting the œconomy of nature" (Percival 1807, Vol. I, 262). He dismisses this concept as inconsistent with "the supreme wisdom and uncontrolable power of the Sovereign of the universe" (Percival 1807, Vol. I, 262) and therefore a "gross absurdity" (Percival 1807, Vol. I, 262). He goes on to argue that the problem of purely physical evil reflects the myopic perspective of human beings of the adverse impacts on them alone of events like earthquakes and volcanic eruptions: "Shall the pride of man arrogate to himself every blessing of heaven?" (Percival 1807, Vol. I, 265). No, Percival answers, because many other life-forms are affected and not always or all for the worse. All things considered, in the literal meaning of this too-casually used phrase, purely physical evil does not occur. From the perspective of the "system of nature … absolute evil has no existence in the works of God" (Percival 1807, Vol. I, 266).

Percival takes a similarly comprehensive approach to the problem of evil in the second of the three meanings of evil he educes. Human life in all of its stages, including life after death, must be considered. The "happiness of man" (Percival 1807, Vol. I, 268) is a continuous process, not a single state. Happiness therefore should not be equated with a single, or even multiple, instances of evil of the second kind. Conceptualizing happiness as a state is conceptual error that prevents us from understanding God's benevolence expressed in a "progressive plan" for the "structure of the human frame" (Percival 1807, Vol. I, 269). The "pain, the labour, and the danger, which he [man] has to encounter, are not to be denominated evils; since he is gifted with the power of rendering them subservient to his highest interest and everlasting good" (Percival 1807, Vol. I, 273).

Percival elaborates on the third type of evil: "Moral evil consists in a corruption of the appetites, passions, and affections, and in a consequent perversion of the will" (Percival 1807, Vol. I, 287). Put another way, moral evil is a function of the failure to cultivate the virtues that regulate sympathy toward the good of others, the moral good, and cultivate, instead, gratification of self-interest, moral evil. Human beings are also free to pursue "moral excellence" and therefore may pursue "moral turpitude" (Percival 1807, Vol. I, 295). Moral turpitude generates confusion of judgment, in which material things, "comfortable subsistence, plenty, future provision for offspring" and the like (Percival 1807, Vol. I, 295) are, erroneously, taken to have "intrinsic value" that warrants "unremitting arduous pursuit" (Percival 1807, Vol. I, 295). All of these matters fall under the scope and exercise of our freedom. Percival thus asks, and leaves for this reader to answer: "But shall the man, who has wilfully brought upon himself intellectual darkness, impute to God, the depravity to which it gives occasion?" (Percival 1807, Vol. I, 291).

2.5.1.12 A Persistent Theme: Stoicism

Percival makes frequent reference to Cicero (106-43 BCE), one of the leading Stoics, a school of thought that flourished during the four centuries before the Common Era. Stoicism was more than a school of thought, as Dick Baltzly explains:

When considering the doctrines of the Stoics, it is important to remember that they think of philosophy not as an interesting pastime or even a particular body of knowledge, but as a way of life. They define philosophy as a kind of practice or exercise (*askêsis*) in the expertise concerning what is beneficial (Aetius, 26A). Once we come to know what we and the world around us are really like, and especially the nature of value, we will be utterly transformed (Baltzly 2019).

The concept of a Baconian scientist of nature and of man is also more than a concept. It is a way of life in which an individual becomes transformed from a young person into an adult who should be taken seriously by committing to the discipline of conforming to the truth of things, the product of the Creator god. This is as it should be in a book of *Instructions* or intellectual and moral formation.

The Baconian scientist's way of life is on display in the virtues of intellectual and moral self-discipline that should be cultivated and the vices to be avoided. These virtues are on full, repeated, and progressive display in the "experimental" essays examined earlier in this chapter. Percival's discussion of enslavement of persons, for example, portrays this evil practice as without ethical justification of any kind. But he goes on to make clear that slavers are depraved, human beings profoundly bent by the vices that must be in place for an individual to contemplate becoming a slaver, much less actually being one. Rejection of willful moral self-degradation is one of the hallmarks of the stoic way of life. More to the point, rejection of willful moral degradation is one of the hallmarks of the Baconian moral scientist's way of life.

2.5.1.13 Appetites

The slaver has an appetite for tyranny over others. Percival addresses the appetites in a "Sketch of a Discourse on the Use and Abuse of the Appetites" (Percival 1807, Vol. I, 322–327). Below the title, Percival cites 1 Corinthians 31: "Whether therefore ye eat, or drink, or whatsoever ye do, do all to the glory of God." The Baconian Dissenter and deist can embrace this instruction: "The innocent state of the appetites implies the indulgence of them according to the simplicity and original intention of nature" (Percival 1807, Vol. I, 323). The appetites, it can be said, should be regulated by steadiness, to prevent overindulgence, at the one extreme, and abject self-denial resulting in malnutrition, at the other extreme. Percival illustrates this point with reference to temperance, an especially important virtue when physicians might be offered a "cordial" during home visit, and then on the next home visit, and the next.

> For the boundary of temperance being once passed, the rational is degraded into the brutal nature; and appetite and may become the habitual pander of folly and vice (Percival 1807, Vol. I, 323).

Percival returns to the topic of temperance in *Medical Jurisprudence* and *Medical Ethics*.

The virtues with which Percival opens *Medical Jurisprudence* and *Medical Ethics* – tenderness, steadiness, condescension, and authority – and upon which the

"Institutes" that follow build can be read as the virtues of medical self-restraint, another hallmark of stoicism that transforms the entrepreneurial physician into the professional physician. Piety, conforming oneself to the will of the Creator god as expressed in the truth of things about human nature, should be considered the "consummation" of morality generally (Percival 1807, Vol. I, 369). By analogy, these four virtues should be considered the "consummation" of medical morality.

2.5.1.14 Whimsy

Percival's *Instructions* encompass almost 400 pages of *The Works*. While in the first part the entries are short, they become longer in parts "the second" and "the third." Some go on for many pages and tax even the adult reader. Younger readers would therefore be forgiven for wondering why they have to work through so many pages as *Instructions* progresses.

There is textual evidence that Percival was a master teacher in that he includes "maxims." In the first part this section is entitled, "Maxims" (Percival 1807, Vol. I, 74–75). In "part the third" Percival betrays a surprising and welcome whimsy with this title: "Maxims, Ironical and Ludicrous" (Percival 1807, Vol. I, 363–368). There is a dose of drollery now and then, too.

Some samples from the first set of maxims:

> Swearing is a proof of courage; because it shews that we neither *fear* the disapprobation of wise men, nor the displeasure of God (Percival 1807, Vol. I, 74).
>
> To unite inconsistencies displays a great genius. Be therefore a rake in appearance, though a wise man in reality (Percival 1807, Vol. I, 74).
>
> Liberty and health are but fictitious blessings; for they are unfelt while possessed, and prized only when lost (Percival 1807, Vol. I, 75).

Some examples from the second set of maxims:

> Overlook your own failings; be rigid towards the failings of others; for it is wiser to give indulgence to one fool than to many (Percival 1807, Vol. I, 363).
>
> Acquire the character of a wit, and you may be at liberty to play the fool (Percival 1807, Vol. I, 364).
>
> To do one thing, and think of another; or to do two things at once; may be regarded as marks of a superior compass of mind (Percival 1807, Vol. I, 364).
>
> *Homo sum, humani nihil á me alienum puto*. This maxim furnishes an everlasting apology for meddling in other men's affairs (Percival 1807, Vol. I, 365).
>
> Ask for everything, and you may get something (Percival 1807, Vol. I, 365).
>
> If all be well that ends well, the event consecrates the means (Percival 1807, Vol. I, 367).

2.5.2 *Moral and Literary Dissertations; Chiefly Intended as a Sequel to A Father's Instructions (1788)*

In "The Preface" Percival explains that his purpose in the essays gathered in this collection is "teaching his elder children the most important branches of ethics, viz., VERACITY, FAITHFULNESS, JUSTICE, and BENEVOLENCE, in a *systematic* and *experimental* manner, by EXAMPLES" (Percival 1807, Vol. II, v). The use of 'experimental' signals that these are works in moral science, explicated in the context of historical and fictitious examples of exemplars: "The mode of exemplification pursued in the present work has necessarily occasioned some deviation from each of these great originals … (Percival 1807, Vol. II, vii). As a moral scientist, Percival will therefore be concerned with both conceptual clarity and an account of how we are motivated to act rightly: "To promote the love of truth, and to excite aversion of duplicity and falsehood, are objects which merit the most serious attention in the business of education" (Percival 1807, Vol. II, vi).

A Socratic Discourse on Truth. This essay is dedicated to "T.B.P," his son Thomas Bassnett Percival (*A Socratic Discourse on Truth and Faithfulness*. Percival 1781). In it Percival proposes to "take a particular view of TRUTH, and of her inseparable companion FAITHFULNESS" (Percival 1807, Vol. II, 4) and. He then clarifies the key concepts:

> I presume you will concur with me in opinion, that MORAL TRUTH is the *conformity of our expressions to our thoughts*; and FAITHFULNESS, *that of our actions to our expressions*: And that LYING or FALSEHOOD *is generally a mean, selfish, or malevolent, and unjustifiable, endeavor to deceive another, by signifying or asserting that to be truth or fact, which is known or believed to be otherwise; and by making promises, without any intention to perform them* (Percival 1807, Vol. II, 4).

This is a more ample account of lying than the spare account: representing as true what one knows to be false. To this Percival adds that the motivation to lie arises, not in the interests of the liar's interlocutor, but in the self-interest of the liar in deliberately harming the interests of the liar's interlocutor. The essay becomes a dialogue among Philocles (the name of a 5th century BCE Athenian tragic poet), Sophron (the name of a 5th century BCE writer of prose dialogues said to be favored by Plato), and Euphronius (Euphronius or Euphronio, a late six and early fifth century BCE Athenian red-figure vase painter and Percival's avatar). They explore many variations of false statements of the historical and fictitious figures and analyze them against the criteria set out in the concept of lying above.

Vows, Faithfulness, and Honor. Vows can be a form of lying:

> Nor can even vows, however solemn, be binding, when the object of them is the commission of a crime: for though appeals to the Deity are sacred pledges of our sincerity, they make no change in the nature of legality of our actions (Percival 1807, Vol. II, 9).

Truth is in the nature of things. In the case of human actions, truth is the discoverable component of actions. The vow of loyalty to commit a crime includes in its nature committing a crime, which includes in its nature the intention to harm the interests of the one against whom the crime is committed as well as the interests of the polity, the common good. In such cases, despite its external appearances, such a vow is lying. Its appearances are deceptive.

In the "Appendix" to this essay, Percival elaborates on the concepts of honor and faithfulness in a section entitled, "True and False Honour." Faithfulness, Sophron says, is "founded on certain ideas of HONOUR, which originally spring from the best natural principles" (Percival 1807. Vol. I, 8). In the "Appendix" he elaborates:

> The genuine principle of honour, in its full extent, may be defined, a quick perception and strong feeling of moral obligation, particularly with respect to probity and truth, in conjunction with an acute sensibility to shame, reproach, and infamy (Percival 1807, Vol. II, 203).

Percival is changing the meaning of 'honor', as Gregory did before him. In the introduction to the French translation of *Lectures* (Gregory 1787), Verlac points out that the basis of medical ethics is not *amour propre*. The latter is self-directed, a kind of self-love or vanity that requires satisfaction when it is offended. *Amour propre* does not originate in the "best natural principles" but in base self-interest. *Amour propre* was the basis for dueling at that time. Verlac states that the basis of medical ethics, for Gregory, is "pleasure of the practice of duty" (Gregory 1787, xxiv). *Amour propre* is fragile, all too readily injured, causing distress in response to personal psychosocial injury. At the beginning of *Lectures* Gregory rejects without qualification the man of "interest," thus rejecting all forms of mere self-interest, including vanity. For Percival, honor is not directed to oneself but to others, as sympathy requires. Honor is thus a "strong feeling of moral obligation." Failure to fulfill one's obligations, "especially of probity and truth," in a properly formed moral character, naturally provokes "an acute sensibility to shame, reproach, or infamy." These serve as preventive of such failure in the future. Self-regard, by contrast, generates "… *spurious honour*, which, by a perversion of the laws of association, *puts evil for good, and good for evil*; and, under the sanction of a name, perpetrates crimes without remorse, and even without ignominy" (Percival 1807, Vol. II, 204). Percival uses what is, for him, strong language, when he goes on to reject dueling, which had been outlawed in the previous century but persisted:

> To this empirical morality *duelling* owes its rise, which, with fatal confidence, pretends to cure the indecorums of social intercourse, whilst it destroys the lives of individuals, subverts the peace of families, and violates the most sacred laws of the community. It is astonishing that this practice, which originated in the dark ages of ignorance, superstition, and disorder, should be continued in his enlightened period, though condemned by the polity of every state [as incompatible with the common weal], and utterly repugnant to the spirit and precepts of Christianity (Percival 1807, Vol. II, 204).

The "indecorums of social intercourse" are indeed harms but they are momentous harms only from the perspective of a man whose character has become bent by the degrading gravitational force of *amour propre*. A "cure" is needed, the spur of "an acute sensibility to shame, reproach, or infamy," which risks none of the calamitous outcomes of dueling. Percival returns to the morality of dueling, at some considerable, in *Medical Jurisprudence*, and especially in *Medical Ethics*, as we will see in Chap. 3.

2.5 The Moral Formation and Development of Children

Percival, like Gregory before him, therefore, has changed the meaning of 'gentleman'. This is not a social station of wealth, privilege, and power. Nor is it, as Thomas Gisborne (1758–1846), one of Percival's correspondents about *Medical Jurisprudence* (see Chap. 3), would have it, an "office" defined by its duties (Gisborne 1794). The social role makes the gentleman duty-bound, as one would expect a moral realist like Gisborne, to say. That is, a self-interested individual is not required to change by taking on the social station of gentleman, which he has come to by inheritance and not by anything in his character that he has properly formed. He can fulfill the duties of his social station or office by rote and not from virtue.

Percival would point out that Gisborne has it exactly backward: a properly formed moral character, in which honor originates in sympathy-based ethical obligations, is the necessary and sufficient condition for becoming a gentleman. Hereditary privilege has nothing to do with becoming a gentleman. Nor does rote fulfillment of duties. Becoming a gentleman by virtue of birth to and then the death of someone else (usually but not always one's father, or perhaps older brother) is neither a necessary nor a sufficient condition for becoming a gentleman. A man earns the moral status of being a gentleman by succeeding in proper intellectual and moral formation. Becoming a gentleman is open to all men willing to conform their character to the truth of things. The meaning of 'gentleman' is autonomous from how English society happened to have organized itself in the middle of the eighteenth century. Gisborne accepts the hierarchy of monarch, peerage, and commoners (with its multiple levels of businessmen, lawyers, physicians, clergy, and laborers). Percival's concept of being a gentlemen levels this sociopolitical hierarchy in a fell swoop. Percival's disagreement with Gisborne runs very deep. Gisborne's interest in practical ethics, in being useful, may have influenced Percival, but that is all.

Baker points out that moral revolutionaries introduce new discourses, as Gregory and Percival do when they replace 'the sick' with 'patient'. Moral revolutionaries also change the meaning of existing discourse, such as 'honor' and 'gentleman'. The essentialist thinks that such changes of discourse do not occur, because the concepts referred to by 'honor' and 'gentleman' are timeless. Thus does the essentialist set up himself or herself and his or her readers and students for egregious misinterpretation of historical texts, about which more in Chap. 4.

In the "Appendix" Percival elaborates on his treatment of insincere vows. Percival has pointed out that vows "make not change in the nature or legality of actions" (Percival 1807, Vol. I, 9). He continues: "… and it would be the grossest superstition to suppose, that the violation of GOD's ordinances can be either honourable of acceptable to him" (Percival 1807, Vol. I, 9). In "Fealty to Magistrates" in the Appendix, Percival comments on the related topic of the obligations in their exercise of their power by magistrates over those subordinate to their power, an analogous relationship the faithful have to God's ordinances. "The commands of the MAGISTRATES, and of the LEGISLATURE, are not binding, when they oppose the known and acknowledged obligations of morality …" (Percival 1807, Vol. I, 207). This follows directly from his Baconian moral science: morality is based in the truth of things, the principle of sympathy and the regulatory functions of reason as the constituent components of human nature. Morality thus is autonomous from state power. It follows that state power is accountable to the findings of Baconian moral science about our civic lives. This is the basis for autonomous assessment of law against the standards of Baconian, sympathy-based morality. Percival invokes this ethical framework, which he presents after descriptions of "obedience to imperial mandates, founded on cruelty and injustice" (Percival 1807, Vol. I, 208):

> Instances like these afford the most irrefragable evidence, that fealty to magistrates must always be regarded as conditional obligation; and that implicit obedience to their commands may involve us in high degrees of guilt and infamy (Percival 1807, Vol. I, 209).

Earned guilt and infamy, just as in the earned "shame, reproach, and infamy" of dishonor and unfaithfulness should be avoided as morally abhorrent. His children certainly knew, and many of this readers would have known, that Percival himself was a moral exemplar of the autonomy of morality from the state when he refused to assent to the Articles of the Church, which assent was required to attend the Oxbridge universities.

The autonomy of morality from the state has important implications for what Percival will have to say about the immorality and illegality of abortion in *Medical Ethics*, as we will see in Chap. 3. In contemporary medical ethics and health policy, a physician's dissent from fulfilling professional responsibility to a patient, e.g., prescribing contraception or offering termination of pregnancy after diagnosis of a fetal anomaly, is classified as a claim of conscience. These claims, like all claims to the exercise of power, are subject to the justified limits of "the known and acknowledged obligations of morality." Claims of conscience *simpliciter* made to exercise the power to limit the scope of ethically justified and legally sanctioned clinical practice do not command moral respect. Only claims of conscience based in the obligations of morality and that "known and acknowledged" in Baconian moral science have moral authority for others, including patients, professional colleague, and the state. Ethically justifiable freedom of conscience must be an expression of properly formed intellectual and moral character expressed as conscience, based on truth of things put in them by Creator.

Is There an Obligation to Express all of our Thoughts? Philocles asks: "If truth … be an agreement between our words and our thoughts, are you under an obligation to express all your thoughts?" (Percival 1807, Vol. II, 21). Sophron answers in the negative, citing the virtue of prudence, which "often forbids it; and it is no violation of truth to conceal those thoughts, or that knowledge, with which another has no right to be acquainted" (Percival 1807, Vol. II, 21). This is especially the case when "improper or treacherous questions are asked" (Percival 1807, Vol. II, 22). Percival thus offers an alternative to Kant's account of an individual bent on murder who asks the whereabouts of his intended victim (Kant & Wood 1996). The interrogated individual should remain silent. Percival might add that an abstract concept of lying, prescinding from predictable consequences, is "speculative" and therefore not to be taken seriously.

Later in the essay, quoting from Hawkesworth, Percival provides a practical account of prudence, i.e., the virtue of identifying and then acting to protect one's

2.5 The Moral Formation and Development of Children

legitimate self-interests, but understood now as self-interests the pursuit of which benefits others and not just oneself. There is an echo here of Hoffmann on enlightened self-interest. (See Chap. 1.)

> But to use the words of an excellent moralist, "as every action may produce effects, which human sagacity cannot foresee; we should not lightly venture to the verge of evil, not strike at others, though with a reed, lest, like the rod of Moses, it become a serpent in our hands (Percival 1807, Vol. II, 27).

The "excellent moralist" was John Hawkesworth (1715–1773), a London-born writer and editor. He published an account of James Cook's Pacific voyages (Abbott 1970). He also wrote fiction with moral take-home lessons like those in *A Father's Instructions*. He was described as a "zealous promoter of the interests or religion and morality" (Allibone 1891, 811) Hawkesworth's take-home lesson is that prudence creates the ethical obligation to remain well on the safe side of risking harm to others by lying.

Equivocation. Philocles raises the issue of equivocation.

> Philocles now pursued the subject, by inquiring into the nature of EQUIVOCATION; which Sophron defined to be a mean expedient to avoid declaration, without verbally telling a lie. An equivocation, said he, consists of such expressions as admit of more than one meaning. The speaker uses them in one sense, and designs that the hearer should understand them in another (Percival 1807, Vol. II, 27).

Euphronius, Percival's voice, asks a question about clinical practice.

> Can you acquit me, Philocles, said I, of the criminality of equivocation, when in the exercise of my professional duties, I study, by cheerful looks and ambiguous words to remove from my patients the horror of despair, to mitigate the apprehensions of danger, and to deceive them into hope; that by administering a cordial to a drooping spirit, I may smooth the bed of death, or revive even expiring life? For there are maladies which rob the philosopher of fortitude, and the Christian of consolation (Percival 1807, Vol. II, 28–29).

Percival here appears to accept Gregory's admonition not to abandon the dying, as had been the norm and practice since the Hippocratic text instructed the physician to leave off the treatment of the sick when disease or injury has "overmastered" them.

> Let me here exhort you against the custom of some physicians, who leave their patients when their life is despaired of, and when it is no longer decent to put them to farther expence. It is as much the business of a physician to alleviate pain, and to smooth the avenues of death, when unavoidable, as to cure diseases. Even in cases where his skill as a physician can be of no further avail, his presence and assistance as a friend may be agreeable and useful, both to the patient and to his nearest relations (Gregory 1772, [1772] 1998, 35–36).

Gregory includes smoothing the avenues of death in his definition of medicine: "Medicine, or the art of preserving health, of prolonging life, of curing diseases, and of making death easy" (Gregory 1772, [1772] 1998, 109).

Philocles responds:

> From my heart I acquit you, answered Philocles, with his wonted humanity. You do a kindness, not a wrong, to the person whom you thus deceive; and may reasonably presuppose

his future approbation of that conduct, which meets the present acquiescence of all his friends (Percival 1807, Vol. II, 29).

The criteria for lying, set out in its definition above, are not met by equivocation directed to what, following Engel (1977), we would call the biopsychosocial benefit of the patient.

Philocles' response opens with an invocation of the basis of his response: the requirements of sympathy and its virtues, especially tenderness. The problem with this response is that Philocles overlooks the challenge to physicians of telling patients that they are gravely ill. Gregory surfaces the powerful forces of self-protection that arise, describes the duty that must nonetheless be fulfilled, and prescribes how it should be fulfilled:

> To a man of a compassionate and feeling heart, this is one of the most disagreeable duties in the profession: but it is indispensible. The manner of doing it, requires equal prudence and humanity. What should reconcile him the more easily to this painful office, is the reflection that, if the patient should recover, it will prove a joyful disappointment to his friends; and, if he die, it makes the shock more gentle (1772, Gregory [1772] 1998, 35).

The recognition of the duty becomes the means to prevent understandable self-interest from becoming the basis for equivocation, which would, by Percival's account, be an unacceptable basis for the separation of thought from expression. It is worth noting that David Oken (1961), in one of the articles cited frequently in the literature on medical paternalism in what now can be called the "classical period" of bioethics (1960s-1970s), noted in the qualitative portion of his study that the most common reason physicians gave for not telling patients about a cancer diagnosis was the impact on themselves of having to do so. It is not enough to appeal, as Philocles does, to humanity. One must also, as Gregory does, appeal to duty as the discipliner of self-interest. Percival returns to communicating bad news in *Medical Ethics*, as we will see in Chap. 3.

Secrecy. The topic of secrecy is addressed and bears on the professional obligation of confidentiality, which he also addresses in *Medical Jurisprudence* and *Medical Ethics*. (See Chap. 3.) The question put to Sophron is this: "whether SECRECY, in certain cases, be not a breach of faithfulness or veracity?" (Percival 1807, Vol. II, 29). Sophron responds:

> To betray the confidence that is reposed in us, whether we have tacitly or by a promise bound ourselves to fidelity, evinces a weak understanding and a bad heart. Levity, an eagerness to communicate, or the desire of seeming to be important, are the most frequent causes of the breach of secrecy; but it is to be feared, that it sometimes originates from baseness or malevolence (Percival 1807, Vol. II, 46).

The vocabulary in the first sentence echoes Gregory's account of the reasons some physicians might have had for resisting his moral science of sympathy and its plainly feminine virtue of tenderness: "The insinuation that a compassionate and feeling heart is commonly accompanied with a weak understanding and a feeble mind, is malignant and false" (Gregory 1772, [1772] 1998, 21). The challenges of maintaining secrecy in the open wards of Manchester Infirmary occupies Percival's attention in *Medical Jurisprudence* and *Medical Ethics*, as we will see in Chap. 3.

2.5.2.1 On the Influence of Habit and Association

Percival, we know from ample textual evidence, was a student of Hume's works. In his first *Treatise* Hume provides a Baconian, observational account of the association of ideas, the process by which human beings build up reliable beliefs. Hume reports his findings, which include the "constant conjunction:" between "our correspondent impressions and ideas" (Hume [1739–1740] 2000, 9). There is also a "uniting principle" or uniting cause of the "bond of union" among our ideas (Hume [1739–1740] 2000, 12). These associations are of three types: "RESEBLANCE, CONTIGUITY in time or place, and CAUSE AND EFFECT" (Hume [1739–1740] 2000, 13).

In *Miscellaneous Observations on the Influence of Habit and Association* Percival's approach to the topic of habit and association is that of the physician-philosopher or Baconian scientist:

> The laws of HABIT and ASSOCIATION form a most important branch of both physiology and ethics. And as *the proper study of mankind is man*, every fact must be deemed interesting, which tends to elucidate either the animal, intellectual, or moral œconony of his nature (Percival 1807, Vol. II, 71).

He tells his reader that, concerning his observations, "no particular regard has been paid to system in the arrangement of them: and I have attempted only, as LORD VERALUM [Bacon] expresses it, "to write certain brief notes, set down rather significantly than curiously"." (Percival 1807, Vol. II, 71). Reflecting the lower degree of reliability of such observations, he uses the locution, "I am persuaded" (Percival 1807, Vol. II, 75), about his findings or comments on the findings of others.

His catalogue of physiological habits and associations includes "MUSCULAR ACTIONS" (Percival 1807, Vol. II, 71–73) and "PARALYTIC AFFECTIONS of the organs of speech" (Percival 1807, Vol. II, 73). Some of these associations have adverse impact on mental physiology.

> In the foregoing examples, the force of habit and association is clearly manifest: and man, whilst under the influence of their authority, however despotic or perverted [as in mental disorders], still retains a capacity for action and enjoyment, though he ceases to be a rational or moral agent. But the supposition of their operation stops at once all the movements of the mind, and seems to annihilate every energy of the understanding, the affections, and the will (Percival 1807, Vol. II, 82–83).

He further explores the "progressive influence of particular associations on the judgment as they gradually acquire the force of habit, by time, and vividness, by frequent renewal" (Percival 1807, Vol. II, 85). These associations can sometimes form without meeting the conditions for reliable associations among ideas that Hume describes. For example, when the association among our ideas has "no natural or proper connection," we become at risk for "credulousness," which "lays the mind open to impressions of error, as well as of truth" (Percival 1807, Vol. II, 89). A physician who abandons Baconian method for the products of imagination (associating ideas without an evidence base) becomes "speculative" and a predator on the health and lives of patients.

Some imagined associations threaten our moral and religious integrity, He explains: "LUDICROUS ASSOCIATIONS, not founded on truth or nature, are peculiarly unfavourable to the principles and practice of virtue and religion" (Percival 1807, Vol. II, 92).

> When the mind has been habituated to the assemblage of ludicrous ideas, they recur on very improper occasions, not only spontaneously, but even in spite of every effort of the judgment and will. In this state, elevation of thought and dignity of character are unattainable; and seriousness, when assumed, is always marked with some glaring and risible inconsistency (Percival 1807, Vol. II, 94).

False associations of ideas produced by an imagination undisciplined by the truth of things may be considered ludicrous associations when their possessor takes no responsibility for the well-being of others. When the possessor of false associations does have such responsibility, false associations are not benign, given the "force of evil habits and the pernicious influence of false associations" (Percival 1807, Vol. II, 111).

These are non-trivial matters in our intellectual and moral lives generally. False associations can result in what Gregory called dissipation, which distorts and damages the operations of sympathy.

> … the power of habit, and the propensity to combine ideas together, are essential to the just constitution of the mind; and that without their well-regulated aid, knowledge would be unattainable, virtue a transient emotion or desultory act, and life itself a scene of indifference and insipidity (Percival 1807, Vol. II, 111).

Reliable, evidence-based associations are required by a "just mind," the grounding of thought in the truth of things that is then equipped to guide judgment and behavior for the public good. This will become important when Percival addresses the topic of when a physician or surgeon should retire in *Medical Jurisprudence* and *Medical Ethics*. (See Chap. 3.) The association of ideas also plays a major role in his account of lunacy and insanity in *Medical Ethics*.

2.5.2.2 On Inconsistency of Expectations in Literary Pursuits

This essay aims to persuade its reader that, for sustained proper intellectual and moral formation over the course of a lifetime, the *vita contemplativa* (the contemplative life) and the *vita activa* (the active life) should not be understood to be mutually exclusive. He starts with examples "of men occupied chiefly, if not solely, in the walks of literature" and then makes the case that "the taste for knowledge may be cultivated successfully in the busy scenes of active life" (Percival 1807, Vol. II, 117).

> Man is evidently constituted for two great ends; the attainment of virtue, and of knowledge. All his mental endowments have reference to one or other of these final causes: on them, therefore, must depend the *perfection* and *felicity* of his nature (Percival 1807, Vol. II, 119).

Citing Seneca, Percival puts forth the view that attaining these ends requires both the *vita contemplativa* and the *vita active*:

Just and weighty, therefore, is the maxim of another ancient moralist, with which I shall conclude these reflections, that *we should not rest satisfied with the WORDS of wisdom, without the WORKS; nor turn philosophy into an idle pleasure, which was given us for a salutary remedy* (Percival 1807, Vol. II, 123).

2.5.2.3 On the Beauties of Nature and on a General Taste for the Fine Arts

These two essays are about taste:

> The sensibility to beauty, which, when cultivated and improved, we term Taste, is universally diffused through the human species: and it is most uniform with respect to those objects, which, being out of power, are liable to variation, from accident, caprice, or fashion (Percival 1807, Vol. II, 127).

Percival, like Gregory, did not subscribe to the view *de gustibus non disputandum est*, i.e., matters of taste should not be disputed. Both subscribed to the evidence-based view that because there is are non-idiosyncratic, transcultural standards for making aesthetic judgments. Percival takes the view that there are non-variant responses of the experience of beauty to events in nature, such as "the verdant lawn, the variegated landscape, the boundless ocean, the starry firmament" (Percival 1807, Vol. II, 127). The mechanism, he says, is a "secret sympathy" (Percival 1807, Vol. II, 129).

This view of the experience of beauty as grounded in nature, the truth of things, has, Percival adds, implications beyond aesthetics:

> Scepticism and irreligion are hardly compatible with the sensibility of the heart, which arises from a just and lively wisdom, harmony, and order, subsisting in the world around us: and emotions of piety must spring up spontaneously in the bosom that is in unison with animated nature (Percival 1807, Vol. II, 132).

In support of the claim that "scepticism and irreligion are hardly compatible with the sensibility of the heart," Percival cites Gregory's *Comparative View of the State and Faculties of Man with Those of the Animal World* (Gregory 1765). *Comparative View* was a success: "London read the book, Aberdeen read the book, and so did Edinburgh …" (Stewart 1901, 112). Percival had read the book, too. This is further textual evidence that Percival read Gregory's works.

Gregory's commitment to the Baconian moral science of sympathy is on full display in *Comparative View*. Hume had emphasized sympathy as a "social principle" and Gregory agrees:

> The next distinguishing principle of mankind, which was mentioned, is that which unites them into societies, and attaches them to one another by sympathy and affection. This principle is the source of the most heart-felt pleasure which we can ever taste (Gregory 1765, 59).

Gregory develops a comprehensive philosophy of religion in *Comparative View*. Gregory took the view that religion formed an individual in the virtues such as tenderness by disciplining what he called "good dispositions" by giving them "steadiness" (Gregory 1772, [1772] 1998, 233). He then takes up infidelity, building on this account of dispositions and the virtues:

> Absolute infidelity, or settled Scepticism in Religion is not proof of a bad Understanding or a vicious disposition, but is certainly a very strong presumption of the want of Imagination and sensibility of Heart. Many philosophers have been infidels, few Men of taste and sentiment (Gregory 1765, 165–166).

Percival may well have had this passage in mind.

In the second, short essay, Percival elaborates on the moral significance of taste:

> The analogy of physical to moral beauty, and the connection subsisting between a good heart and a just relish for the general works of nature, have, I trust, been fully established (Percival 1807, Vol. II, 133).

When this connection is broken, "reason itself is liable to abuse; and philosophy and religion have been rendered subservient to scepticism and superstition" (Percival 1807, Vol. II, 138).

Miscellaneous Observations on the Alliance of Natural History, and Philosophy, with Poetry

This essay presents a philosophy of art grounded in the view that truth is in the nature of things and thus, more generally, in nature. Poetry therefore should be judged according to its deployment of the "alliance of natural history, and philosophy [in the sense of what we call the natural sciences] with poetry."

> The maxim of Lord Veralum [Bacon], that "knowledge is power," is no less applicable to poetry than philosophy. For whenever we engage in this delightful pursuit as an art, or as a science, it is evident that the ability to convey and the capacity to relish its peculiar pleasures, must be exactly proportioned to our acquaintance with the means either of communicating or enjoying them. The works of creation are the great storehouse where these means are to be sought; and an inquisitive attention to every surrounding object is essential to the poet, and highly useful to the lover of poetry (Percival 1807, Vol. II, 141).

To this end, Percival comments on the "HARMONY of the SPHERES" (Percival 1807, Vol. II, 148), trees, mountains, snow, and mists. There is also a delightful account of the "polity of Rooks" in which Percival observes sympathy among birds when one of the flock is injured, falls in a river, and drowns "amidst the moans of his whole fraternity" (Percival 1807, Vol. II, 162).

2.5.2.4 Of the Intellectual and Moral Conduct of Experimental Pursuits

Percival provides a Baconian philosophy of observational and experimental science and the interpretation of their findings.

> We should recollect, that though the operations of nature are simple, uniform, and regular, they are only discoverable to be such, when fully unfolded to our understandings: and that, when we endeavor to trace her laws by artificial arrangements, combinations, or

decompositions, which is all that *experiment* can accomplish, success may be sometimes frustrated by circumstances so minute, as to elude the most sagacious observation (Percival 1807, Vol. II, 180).

To guard against hubris in science, Percival emphasizes the importance of "judicious and comprehensive analogies" (Percival 1807, Vol. II, 186), because incomplete descriptions of findings may mask dissimilarities that would invalidate the analogy. He also emphasizes caution in deploying the "inductive method of reasoning" (Percival 1807, Vol. II, 187).

2.6 Conclusion: Percival: Life-Long Committed Baconian Scientist

Percival was a life-long Baconian scientist. The writings that we have examined in this chapter provide consistent, strong textual evidence in support of this claim. He was therefore also a Baconian Dissenter and Deist.

2.6.1 Dissenter and Deist

The Baconian Dissenter claims autonomy of properly formed conscience from illegitimate authority, i.e., authority not directed to the common good. Dissenters of the Percivalian type were pluralists about what should count as a well-formed conscience. They were in strong agreement that the well-formed conscience is autonomous from state authority and therefore power, including the ecclesiastical authority and power of the Church of England.

Properly formed conscience is properly formed character; conscience is not idiosyncratic or self-interested but directed to the good of others. Judgments about the good of others are grounded in the nature of things. Deism is the view that there is evidence in the nature of things, especially the evident order of nature, for the existence of a Creator god who is benevolent.

The nature of things, the truth of things, is discoverable using the methods of Baconian science and moral science. Applied to human nature these sciences discover that our nature comprises two capacities, instinct and reason. Instinct takes the form of sympathy, a causal principle of our moral physiology that incites us to care about and for others as our primary concern and motivation. There is no Reason with a capital 'R'. Reason with the lower-case 'r' is inert; it cannot incite us to action for the benefit of others. Having an idea of what one should do lacks motive force; the plight of another mirrored in us by properly function sympathy has the motive force that the moral life required. The moral life requires both good reasons or justification and motivation to action. Sympathy properly regulated by virtues supplies both.

Reason with a lower-case 'r' matches means to ends, based on reflection about experience, i.e., evidence. For reason to do its work in a sustained fashion we need the intellectual virtue of candor: being open to change in our evidence-based ideas required by new evidence. For sympathy to direct us in a sustained way to care for others requires that sympathy be regulated, so that we do not over-respond (enthusiasm) or under-respond (dissipation, hard-heartedness). Gregory shows that the regulators of the principle of sympathy are the professional virtues of tenderness and steadiness, which are feminine virtues.

Percival adds two new regulatory professional virtues when organizational hierarchy gives one power (the ability to form and then to effect one's will, directly or through others) over another: condescension and authority. Power is justified when it is exercised to care for others and thus promotes the common good or common weal. Power always creates risk of distorting effects of power on those over whom power is held and exercised. Power that creates these distorting effects is tyrannical power. In the Infirmary, physicians and surgeons had power over patients, though not absolute power. This was called "government." To prevent tyrannical power, the government of the patient must be regulated by the virtues of condescension and authority. Physicians and surgeons should close their social gulf with their Infirmary patients and know what they are doing when they engage the patient's clinical condition. When in the hospital physicians, surgeons, apothecaries, managers, and trustees submit to the discipline of properly regulated sympathy, the resulting hospital polity will be just because all exercises of power will be cooperative toward the common weal of a hospital, the health and lives of its patients.

Baconian sciences also establish that our nature is structured by unalienable (they cannot be separated from us, made other than our nature, the meaning of 'unalienable') rights to life, liberty, and property. When we exercise these rights, directed by sympathy properly regulated by tenderness and steadiness, we become justifiably autonomous from state authority and power.

2.6.2 *Baconian Philosophy of Religion and Its Implications for Baconian Philosophy of Medicine*

Percival is committed to the view that religion is accountable to the truth of things as explained by Baconian observational and experimental science. Religion is also accountable to the truth of scripture. The concept of the Trinity, for example, is not a truth of scripture. In other words, religion is accountable to deistic Baconian science. The Dissenter John Seddon of Manchester (not to be confused with John Seddon of Warrington Academy) expresses concern for what happens in the absence of such accountability:

> It has been a very common thing, in the Christian world, to censure and condemn persons not *believing enough*; but little or no notice has been taken of the other extreme, *believing too much*. There has been a violent cry against *heresy*; but men have been seldom warned

against *Credulity, implicit Faith, and admitting principles without reason or evidence.* The latter, however, has been greatly prejudicial to true religion (Seddon 1766, iii).

Percival's Unitarianism is spare, even austere in its theism that is constrained by the truth in things in nature and Scripture.

Percival's Baconian philosophy of religion provides deist Dissent autonomy from the state and the state church. The directly parallel Baconian philosophy of science provides deist Baconian science or nature, man, and morals autonomy from the state. In the next chapter we will see how in Percival's philosophy of medicine Baconian professional ethics in medicine provides autonomy of professional ethics in medicine from the state. This is not a social contract in which society grants the profession of medicine autonomy in exchange for the commitment to use special knowledge and skills for patients and the self-regulation to sustain that commitment. In social contract theory the profession of medicine has no intrinsic autonomy from the state but only negotiated autonomy.

2.6.3 *Improvement of Medicine and Healthcare Institutions*

The English enlightenment was committed to improvement in all aspects of human life, to relieve man's estate. Price instructed his contemporaries that improvement requires attention to the structure and direction of organizations, whether reversionary funds, hospitals, or schools. With his colleague, John Aikin, Percival was committed to the improvement of hospitals in their structure, including the physical structure of their architecture, and their direction by managers and trustees. The texts of Percival that we have considered in this chapter provide ample evidence of Percival's commitment to improvement of hospitals and, especially, the lot of the working sick poor who receive medical and surgical care in Manchester Infirmary, a general hospital, as well as specialty hospitals for the mentally ill and for prostitutes.

As we will see in the next chapter, the hospital polity that developed at Manchester Infirmary during its first four decades was what Percival would, and did, judge to be an unjust polity, because it was based on party-interest. The resulting unacceptable clinical care of patients was an anomaly that a party-interest-based hospital polity was not able to change. *Medical Jurisprudence* and *Medical Ethics* can be read as Percival's revolutionary response to this anomaly with the new paradigm of professional ethics in medicine.

2.6.4 Discourse of Peace

Dissenters had many decades of experience with discourses of antipathy, exclusion, and oppression. They also had experience with the violence of mob rule addressed to their houses of worship and persons. They had very good reason to embrace a discourse of peace. Baconian moral science created a discourse of peace based on the commitment to a pluralism of well-formed conscience and the genuine respect for difference that this commitment fostered.

By the 1790s the Manchester Infirmary was in turmoil that spilled into the public arena, as we will see at the beginning of the next chapter. The physicians, surgeons, and apothecaries who worked at or wanted to work at the Infirmary needed a discourse of peace. So did the managers and trustees who were responsible for the finically responsible administration of the Infirmary. We will see that *Medical Jurisprudence* and *Medical Ethics* promoted an ethics of cooperation in patient care and clinical research, a discourse of peace for a professional hospital polity. Persons with well-formed conscience respect differences with others who are also scientifically and morally serious and are thus well disposed to cooperation. In *Medical Jurisprudence* and *Medical Ethics* physicians, surgeons, and apothecaries morally formed by making the three commitments of the ethical concept of medicine as a profession are thereby disposed to cooperation.

2.6.5 Inventing New Words and Changing the Meaning of Existing Words

Baker explains that one of the defining features of moral revolutions is how their proponents invent new words and also change the meaning of existing words. In the course of their co-invention of professional ethics in medicine, Gregory and Percival invent the concept of being a patient: a human being who is presented to a clinician who has made the three commitments of the ethical concept of medicine and is therefore a professional, trustworthy clinician who has available forms of clinical management that are reliably predicted to benefit the patient clinically. Like Gregory's and Percival's ethics of animal experimentation, no appeal to rights is made in their invention of the ethical concept of being a patient. A defining feature of their moral revolution against the long tradition of entrepreneurial medicine is the replacement of 'the sick' ('*aegrotus*') by 'patient'.

Both also change the meaning of 'gentleman'. This word in their hands means a social role that one has earned in virtue of one's proper intellectual and moral formation, like de Polier and Bayley. The opportunity to become a gentleman is thus open to all men willing to do the life-long work of proper intellectual and moral formation. No one is born to the social status of being a gentleman. As we will see in the next chapter, Gisborne thought the opposite. One of the interesting aspects of changing the meaning of an existing word so radically is that a long-familiar word becomes socially revolutionary. Given what Percival has to say about inalienable rights and his condemnation of enslavement of persons, it is fair to say that he was a leveler of British social hierarchy and therefore a republican. Gisborne's conservative acceptance of the hierarchy of English society marks a sharp contrast. Recall from Chap. 2 that Warrington Academy prepared its students to be citizens, not subjects. Gisborne's conservative social and political philosophy could not be at a farther remove from Percival's.

Percival joins Gregory in changing the meaning of 'honour'. Instead of a form of *amour propre* or fragile, easy-to-take-offense self-regard, honor is directed to the protection of others, as sympathy requires. Honor is thus a "strong feeling of moral obligation," not self-interest. Failure to fulfill one's obligations, "especially of probity and truth," in a properly formed moral character, naturally provokes "an acute sensibility to shame, reproach, or infamy" (Percival 1807, Vol. II, 204) not offense based on preening self-regard. Percival is self-consciously changing the meaning of 'honour': Self-regard generates "… *spurious honour*, which, by a perversion of the laws of association, *puts evil for good, and good for evil*; and, under the sanction of a name, perpetrates crimes without remorse, and even without ignominy" (Percival 1807, Vol. II, 204). He also calls out "illusions of false honour" (Percival 1807, Vol. II, 204). Percival uses what is, for him, strong language, when he goes on to reject dueling, which, despite having been outlawed, continued on the basis of lethal honor. He returns to the subject of dueling, at some length, in *Medical Jurisprudence* and *Medical Ethics*.

2.6.6 Hospital Polity

For Taylor Warrington Academy was a just academic polity because it followed the rules, which he set out, for proper intellectual and moral formation. The medical polity of a hospital should be just, i.e., directed to the common good or common weal. The common weal comprises the health and lives of patients and members of the community and not the individual self-interest or party-interest of physicians, surgeons, apothecaries, managers, or trustees. To secure the autonomy of the hospital, it should self-governing under agree-upon rules of conduct. As we saw in the case of the rules for the Warrington Academy, the rules should be directed to the "end" of institution, in the case of a hospital, the scientifically and clinically competent care of patients by professional clinicians. Such care has as its priority the protection and promotion of the health and life of each patient, the outcome that defines the common weal of a hospital. The rules of the Academy were also created to provide for the "Security of their [students'] Morals" (Warrington Academy Papers, Vol. I 1754). As we will see in Chap. 3, *Medical Jurisprudence* and *Medical Ethics* are directed to the "moral security" of a hospital's patients.

2.6.7 A Way of Life

Percival began his intellectual development at the Warrington Academy and brought it to a high degree of development in his writings. In Baconian discourse, the textual evidence presented in this Chapter for this claim supports this interpretation of his intellectual biography as having a very high probability of being reliable. 'Reliable' means that this interpretation can be built on with a high degree of confidence, setting the stage for the interpretation of *Medical Jurisprudence* and *Medical Ethics* in the next chapter.

For Percival, becoming a Baconian moral scientist combined intellectual commitment and accomplishment. Taking his cue from stoicism as a way of life, becoming a Baconian moral scientist was therefore a way of life for him. I take this to be the point of presenting Euphronius as a moral exemplar in *A Father's Instructions*. Euphronius epitomizes the life structured by the intellectual and ethical obligations of the Baconian scientist of nature, man, and morals.

Chapter 3
Thomas Percival Joins Gregory's Moral Revolution Against the Long Tradition of Entrepreneurial Medicine in the History of Western Medicine

3.1 How Events at Manchester Infirmary Resulted in Percival Writing *Medical Jurisprudence* and Then *Medical Ethics*

Eighteenth-century Manchester and environs emerged as a rapidly growing center of the textile industry. By 1717, Manchester was estimated to have a population in excess of 12,000, which had increased to more than 17,000 by 1758, and to more than 70,000 in 1801 (Chaloner 1959). Chaloner attributes this growth to "immigration," "a natural increase" resulting from the number of births exceeding the number of deaths, and "increasing supplies of food" (Chaloner 1959, 42–43). Periodic food shortages occurred, sometimes accompanied by social unrest, including violent unrest (Chaloner 1959, 43–45). Despite increasing employment in cotton factories ('manufactures'), including the employment of children, many lived in poverty. Poor housing conditions contributed to persistent, preventable morbidity and mortality.

Charities were created to respond to the needs of the poor. These included healthcare organizations. In his monumental study, *Medicine and Industrial Society*, John Pickstone (1944–2014) (1985) provides a detailed account of the creation and history of the various types of healthcare organizations – a general hospital, Manchester Infirmary; various specialized hospitals for care of patients with fever (then equated to typhus) (Fever Hospital), sexually transmitted infections (Lock Hospital), and mental illness (Lunatic Hospital); and dispensaries that provided out-patient care, especially care for the sick poor in their homes – that came into existence in Manchester and the surrounding area during the eighteenth century.

© The Author(s), under exclusive license to Springer Nature Switzerland AG 2022
L. B. McCullough, *Thomas Percival's Medical Ethics and the Invention of Medical Professionalism*, Philosophy and Medicine 142, https://doi.org/10.1007/978-3-030-86036-3_3

Manchester Infirmary was founded in 1752 by the surgeon Charles White (1728–1813) and Joseph Bancroft, a Manchester mercantilist. The first building (1753) had a capacity of twelve patients. Expansion in 1755–1756 added more than one hundred beds. In 1790 White helped to found St. Mary's Hospital in Manchester, leaving the Infirmary to do so, after a dispute, described in greater detail below.

As was then common, the Infirmary's budget came from subscriptions, with subscribers who each year gave two guineas (a gold coin with a fixed value of a bit more than one pound sterling) having a vote in the governance of the hospital. Trustees, who contributed a larger amount and served on the governing Board, recommended individuals for admission to this hospital principally for the working sick poor (Pickstone 1985). The original staff was three physicians and three surgeons.

> The new Infirmary was built on land known as Daub-holes, which today is known as Piccadilly, and included a pond. In 1779, in an attempt to increase subscriptions, the Infirmary built a set of baths, with special rates for trustees. These baths proved extremely popular with trustees and other members of the public who paid a fee. In the early days the Infirmary also engaged in a small-pox inoculation programme. The Infirmary did not admit pregnant women, children, lunatics or sufferers from infectious diseases. These exclusions led to the development of specialised voluntary hospitals, many closely associated with MRI [Manchester Royal Infirmary]. The Manchester Lunatic Hospital, which later became Cheadle Royal Hospital opened next to the Infirmary in 1766, and was managed by the Infirmary Board. More controversial was the founding in 1790 of the Lying-in Hospital, now known as St Mary's (The Manchester Royal Infirmary n.d.).

Appointments by the trustees to the medical staff were uncompensated but nonetheless highly valued because the imprimatur of the trustees added to one's reputation and helped therefore to build and sustain a successful clinical practice (Rise 1986; McCullough 1998). During the latter third of the eighteenth century two families of surgeons, the Halls and the Whites, who constituted the clinical staff or "honorary" appointments to the Infirmary, gained increasing power. "By 1780, the day-to-day control of the Infirmary lay increasingly with its surgeons" (Pickstone and Butler 1984, 228). By 1787, these two families, the Whites and Halls, controlled four of the six honorary positions. Newly arrived physicians, including surgeons and man-mid-wives, to Manchester were blocked by the White and Hall surgeons from appointments. These physicians, including John Ferriar (1761–1815) who became a friend of Percival's, in late 1788 called for "Rule 13, which limited the size of the honorary staff" to be rescinded (Pickstone and Butler 1985, 235).

A group of trustees supported this change at a December, 1788, meeting of the Board but the Whites and the honorary staff physicians objected at a public meeting of the Infirmary Board (Pickstone and Butler 1985, 235) and in the press:

> Our conduct having hitherto met with the approbation of the Trustees, it is to be hoped that they will not permit a rule to be broken which has sufficed ever since the institution of the Charity. As we do not apprehend that the alteration will produce any real advantage to the Infirmary, we are determined to resist it (Renaud 1898, 30).

This letter was signed by the six individuals with honorary appointments, in a united front: the physicians, John Cowling (d. 1804?) and Alexander Eason (1735–1796), and surgeons Thomas White and Charles White (1728–1813) and Edward Hall (1731–1791) and Richard Hall (1752–1801). Renaud describes the letter, quite reasonably, as an "ultimatum" that signaled "war" between these honorary physicians and surgeons and the trustees "involving a vital question touching the present administration and future government of the Infirmary" (Renaud 1898, 30).

Accounts of these events continued to be published in the *Manchester Mercury*. All those who subscribed to support the Infirmary were eligible to vote on matters of governance. The Halls and Whites "mustered enough support to reverse the December decision by a vote of 114 to 62" (Pickstone and Butler 1985, 236). It was proposed and approved by the Board that Ferriar and another physician be appointed to the home service in 1789. A typhus epidemic interrupted these events, although it was not severe in Manchester. In 1790 William Simmons (1762–1830), a surgeon and man-midwife, asked to be appointed to the Infirmary home service. "Extending the home-patient service in this way was a direct threat to the Halls and Whites, who had dominated midwifery in Manchester" (Pickstone and Butler 1985, 237). They left Manchester Infirmary and launched a new lying-in charity, St. Mary's, later that year.

The Board published Simmons' request and White's reply, spilling the dispute into the public arena, including letters in the *Mercury* pro and con (Pickstone and Butler 1985, 238). The Board appointed a committee to undertake a comprehensive review of the matter. Members included Simmons and others who "had direct personal interest in expansion" (Pickstone and Butler 1985, 240). The committee recommended expansion and at a September 23, 1790, meeting of subscribers 271 voted for expansion while 142 were opposed (Pickstone and Butler 1985, 241). Four new honorary faculty were appointed, including Ferriar. The new lying-in hospital started by the Whites and Halls "soon established a dominant role in the care of the pregnant poor" (Pickstone and Butler 1985, 242).

In effect, with the departure of the Whites and Halls, the Infirmary was creating a new medical staff. Governance by these two families, allied with the two physicians in their interest to control the Infirmary, ended. One unintended consequence of the work of Ferriar and his colleagues to "open up" the Infirmary (Pickstone and Butler 1985, 235) was a shift in governing power from the honorary faculty to the trustees. Granshaw explains the result: "Donors, as hospital governors, had far greater power over affairs in the hospital than the doctors whom they appointed" (Granshaw 1993, 1186). This was all the more the case for the trustees, those who gave the higher amount required to achieve this status.

The trustees turned to Percival for guidance (Pickstone and Butler 1985; Pickstone 1993). He had been elected as an honorary physician in 1779 but had resigned in October 1780. In a letter to the trustees and published in the *Mercury* Percival explained that he possessed "neither the strength of constitution nor the leisure from the necessary duties of life to fulfil with fidelity the trust reposed in him" (Pickstone and Butler 1985, 230). He may have been referring to failing eyesight but also "violent headaches" (Brockbank, 86). Pickstone writes:

The Infirmary Trustees were keen to supervise the physicians and surgeons and insisted that their attendance be recorded. In 1792, they asked Thomas Percival for detailed guidance on acceptable professional behaviour to ensure that the embarrassing arguments of 1790 did not happen again. Percival's advice was duly incorporated in the Infirmary rules, and he published a version privately in 1794. In 1802, a second edition became generally available as *Medical Ethics*, a work of great influence in Britain and especially in the United States (Pickstone and Butler 1985, 242).

Medical Ethics carries a publication date of 1803. However, textual evidence from its "Notes and Illustrations" suggest that the text was near complete in June of 1802. The first "Note" describes the Manchester Infirmary and includes admissions and outcomes data for a decade ending "the 24th of June 1802" (Percival 1803, 135). Percival was an experienced data scientist, as we saw in Chap. 2 in his essays on mortality tables and in his major role in public health in Manchester. It is therefore plausible to assume that he would want to report the most current data in *Medical Ethics* and would therefore have included the admissions and outcomes data just before he sent his manuscript to the press. The hypothesis that Percival had completed *Medical Ethics* by late June of 1802, however, is not compatible with two citations in "Note XVI" to the *Courier* on March 9, 1803 (Percival 1803, 225) and April 23, 1803 (Percival 1803, 224). This was probably *The Courier and Evening Gazette*, then published in London. *Medical Ethics* was published in that same year.

Pickstone proposes that the trustees had confidence in Percival for a good reason: "we remind ourselves that Percival was a widely-read *moralist*, and that his moralizing for children was clearly linked to his moralizing for doctors" (Pickstone 1993, 169). *A Father's Instructions*, as we saw in Chap. 2, was indeed widely read. As we will see in the next section, Percival draws on two of the genres of texts in *A Father's Instructions* to write *Medical Jurisprudence* and *Medical Ethics*.

In their memorial notice after Percival's death, the Board indicates the high and sustained regard that they had for Percival. Renaud writes:

> At their quarterly meeting the Board of Trustees recorded … their wish to testify their great respect for the talents and virtues of the late Dr. Percival, Physician Extraordinary to these Charities; that they feel a cordial sympathy with his family, his friends, and the public at large, in the removal of so venerable a character; that they, in a particular manner, lament the great loss which this institution has suffered by that afflicting event, and that they desire with heartfelt gratitude to record his name amongst the distinguished and zealous patrons and friends of these important Charities (Renaud 1898, 74).

Percival, I believe, would have welcomed the influence of his work, and of Baconian moral science, in the use by the Board of 'cordial sympathy' and 'so venerable a character'.

Percival might have interpreted what Pickstone, above, characterizes as the "embarrassment" (Pickstone and Butler) of the trustees to be an outcome of the failure of family-interest and party-interest as the basis for the governance of the Infirmary. The antidote was to be professional ethics in medicine and its ethics of cooperation.

Pickstone (1985) focuses on the role of J.L. Philips (1761–1814), Treasurer of the Infirmary starting in 1793 and textile manufacturer with his brother. "He was one of Manchester's largest manufacturers, a cultivated man who in his youth had been friendly with the local radicals in the Literary and Philosophical Society" (Pickstone 1985, 30). He had opposed the expansion. Pickstone examined pamphlets from the expansion dispute annotated by Philips.

> Because some of the pamphlets survive with annotations by Philips we can be sure that he was not impressed by claims of medical altruism. He regarded the Infirmary surgeons and physicians as self-interested. Philips was convinced that the best interests of the hospital were represented by its lay trustees (Pickstone 1985, 30).

For Philips, the power of governance of and responsibility for Manchester Infirmary should shift to the trustees. This can be seen as the birth of the modern hospital in which considerable power is vested in the governing board and the managers they appoint. Pickstone points out that in 1801 there was a dispute: "… yet another dispute: at the Infirmary, in 1801, the medical committee was up in arms about the powers of the lay governors" (Pickstone 1993, 174). Such disputes "became very common in the new century" (Pickstone 1993, 174). As we shall see later in this chapter, preventing such disputes – and contention generally – became a major concern for Percival.

In *Medical Jurisprudence* and *Medical Ethics* Percival calls for the creation of a hospital polity based on professional ethics in medicine. Only such a polity is directed to the common good or common weal of a hospital: the protection and promotion of the health-related interests of its patients. As we will see in this chapter, Percival holds the physicians, surgeons, and apothecaries of a hospital accountable for sustaining this ethically justified hospital polity. As we will also see, Percival also holds the trustees accountable for sustaining this ethically justified hospital polity. In effect, Percival responds with professional ethics in medicine to the power struggle that broke out at Manchester Infirmary in the wake of the proposal to expand the honorary medical staff between physicians and surgeons, on the one hand, and the trustees and managers, on the other.

3.2 Medical Jurisprudence

Based on what is known about the events that led to the Infirmary trustees for guidance, we can say with confidence that Percival was asked to provide ethically justified, practical guidance for managing and preventing disputes that had arisen from clashing interests, especially party-interest – the shared interest of the six honorary medical staff in retaining their control over the Infirmary by excluding newcomers – in conflict with the individual self-interest of Ferrriar and the others in gaining appointments that would help them build their practices. At least one trustee, Philips, was concerned that the dispute was driven by these forms of self-interest rather than the best interests of the Infirmary, i.e., fulfilling its role as a Charity devoted to the healthcare of the sick poor. Percival's commitment to Baconian moral science made him a foe of self-interest in all of its forms, individual-self-interest and party-interest alike, in favor of a primary commitment to the care of patients. His commitment to practical advice in *A Father's Instructions* and its sequel, *Literary and Moral Dissertations*, made him a foe of speculative, theoretical moral philosophy, in favor of making a difference in the moral formation and moral lives of his readers, of all ages.

3.2.1 A "Code"

Medical Jurisprudence is subtitled *A Code of Ethics and Institutes*. Johnson's *Dictionary* helps us to understand how Percival might be using 'code'. The *Dictionary* defines a code as "A book. A book of the civil law" (Johnson 1755, 401). A book of the civil law contains enumerated statutes, clearly and concisely stated. The many writings examined in Chap. 2 suggest that Percival understood 'code' to mean a set of ethically justified rules, clearly and concisely stated so that they serve as a practical, i.e., applicable, basis for moral judgment and behavior based on it. The ethical justification, it should now be abundantly clear, will appeal to Baconian moral science: the principle of sympathy and its regulatory virtues, which are adapted to the clinical care of patients. The practical rules identify the implications of Baconian moral science for each successive topic. The topics addressed in *Medical Jurisprudence* can be read, in my view, as what Percival judged to be ethical problem list at the Infirmary for its physicians, surgeons, apothecaries, managers, and trustees. This mirrors Gregory in *Lectures*, in which he addressed what he took to be the problem list in clinical practice and research (McCullough 1998).

3.2.1.1 Three Models

Percival had ready to hand three models, from which he drew guidance: Justinian's *Institutes of Justinian* (Justinian 2002); William Cullen's *Institutions of Medicine* (Cullen 1772), which he had studied at Edinburgh in Cullen's lectures; and Samuel Farr's *Elements of Medical Jurisprudence* (Farr [1788] 1814).

Institutes of Justinian. Recall from Chap. 2 that at Warrington Academy Percival had taken Aikin's course on jurisprudence, which included what Percival now calls "ethics" or moral science and its implications or "institutes." Aikin and his students read Justinian's (d. 565 CE) *Institutes* (Justinian 2002). Percival surely knew the opening of Justinian's *Institutes* with its compact conceptual framework:

> Justice is the set and constant purpose which gives to every man his due. Jurisprudence in the knowledge of things divine and human, the science of the just and the unjust. Having laid down these general definitions, and our object being the exposition of the law of the Roman people, we think that the most advantageous plan will be to commence with an easy and simple path, and then proceed to details with a most careful and scrupulous exactness of interpretation (Justinian 2002, 3).

3.2 Medical Jurisprudence 155

I read Percival in the first three sections of *Medical Jurisprudence* to be taking his readers –physicians, surgeons, apothecaries, managers, and trustees – to be in need of "an easy and simple path" so that they can focus on what needs to be done for the patients of the Infirmary and to keep individual self-interest and party-interest systematically secondary. The first three sections of *Medical Jurisprudence* concern "jurisprudence" in one of the meanings that Percival would have learned from Aikin: moral science and its practical implications, in this case, for clinical practice.

Cullen's Institutions of Medicine. Recall also from Chap. 2 that Percival had attended William Cullen's lectures on the "Institutions of Medicine" at the University of Edinburgh. We noted then that the style of these lectures, and his text (Cullen 1772), is typical for texts in the *Institutiones Medicae* literature. Cullen opens with a brief account of the science of physiology and then presents compact disquisitions, with topics reduced to their essentials, with not a word wasted. These identify the implications of physiology for clinical practice. The first three sections of *Medical Jurisprudence* open with a compact account of an ethical framework. There then follow concise, practical guidances that identify the clinical implications of the ethical framework.

Here I present the opening paragraph of each section and then a summary of the topics covered. *Medical Ethics* addresses these same topics, as well some additional topics, so detailed exposition of the topics will be postponed to the next section, which provides a detailed historically based, philosophical analysis of Percival's professional ethics in medicine.

The first item of Section I sets out the ethical framework for this section.

SECTION I. OF PROFESSIONAL CONDUCT, RELATIVE TO HOSPITALS
OR OTHER MEDICAL CHARITIES
HOSPITAL PHYSICIANS and SURGEONS should minister to the sick, with due impressions of the importance of their office; reflecting that the ease, the health, and the lives of those committed to their charge depend on their skill, attention, and fidelity. They should study, also, in their deportment, so as to unite *tenderness* with *steadiness*, *condescension* with *authority*, as to inspire the minds of the patients with gratitude, respect, and confidence (Percival 1794, 3).

There then follow numbered items that address Percival's problem list for hospital practice: limiting patients' choices of clinician; the affective dimension of patient care; clinical conversations with a patient in the presence of other patients; maintaining confidentiality in an open ward; the role of clergy; advising patients about the need for a last will and testament (also taken up in Section IV); resource management; injury to reputation; professional charges; the boundary between medicine and surgery; clinical investigation; recording data about cases and their periodic review; hospital architecture; consultations; advance notice for some operations; dispensaries; and specialty hospitals.

Section II is based on section I, as the first sentence makes clear.

SECT. II
OF PROFESSIONAL CONDUCT IN PRIVATE, OR GENERAL PRACTICE

> I. THE *moral rules of conduct*, prescribed towards hospital patients, should be fully adopted in private or general practice. Every case, committed to the charge of a physician or surgeon, should be treated with attention, steadiness, and humanity: Reasonable indulgence should be granted to the mental imbecility and caprices of the sick: Secrecy, and delicacy when required by peculiar circumstances, should be strictly observed. And the familiar and confidential intercourse, to which the faculty are admitted in their professional visits, should be used with discretion, and with the most scrupulous regard to fidelity and honour (Percival 1794, 23).

There then follow numbered items that address Percival's problem list for private practice: temperance, an important topic in that physicians making home visits to the well-to-do would be offered a "cordial;" "gloomy prognostications" or "crepe hanging" (McCullough et al. 1998); interference with other physicians, an intrinsic hazard created by the practice of patients summoning more than one physician; the boundary between physic and surgery; consultations; academic qualifications; punctuality; scheduling visits; covering another physician or surgeon who is away; compensation, a vexing problem when the well-to-do did not pay and physicians had little recourse; gratuitous treatment of clinicians and their families and clergy; quack medicines; secret nostrums; and conflicts among clinicians.

Section III addresses the professional relationship of physicians and surgeons with apothecaries.

> SECT. III.
> OF THE CONDUCT OF PHYSICIANS TOWARDS APOTHECARIES
> I. IN the present state of physic, in this country, where their profession is properly divided into three distinct branches, a connection peculiarly intimate subsists between the physician and the apothecary, and various obligations necessarily result from it. On the knowledge, skill, and fidelity of the apothecary, depend, in a very considerable degree, the reputation, the success, and the usefulness of the physician. As these qualities, therefore, justly claim his attention and encouragement, the possessor of them merits his respect and patronage (Percival 1794, 36).

There then follow numbered items that address Percival's problem list: the responsible management of this relationship; conferring with apothecaries; cooperation between physician or surgeon and the apothecary; effective communication to the apothecary; and compensation of apothecaries.

The fourth section concerns the role of the physician or surgeon in the intersection of law and medicine:

> SECT. IV.
> OF THE KNOWLEDGE IF LAW REQUISITE FOR PHYSICIANS AND SURGEONS
> GENTLEMEN of the faculty of physic, by the authority of different parliamentary statutes, enjoy an exemption from serving on inquests or juries; from bearing armour; from being constables or church-wardens; and from all burdensome offices, whether leet or parochial. These privileges are founded on reasons highly honourable to medical men; and should operate as incentives to that diligent and assiduous discharge of professional duty, which the legislature has generously presumed to occupy the time and to employ the talents of physi[61]cians and surgeons, in some of the most important interests of their fellow citizens. It is perhaps on account of their being thus excused from many civil functions, that Sir William Blackstone, in his learned Commentaries, judges the study of the law to be less essential to them, than to any other class of men. He observes that "there is no special

3.2 Medical Jurisprudence

> reason why gentlemen of the faculty of physic should apply themselves to the study of the law, unless in common with other gentlemen, and to complete the character of general and extensive knowledge, which this profession, beyond others, has remarkably deserved." But I apprehend it will be found that physicians and surgeons are often called upon to exercise appropriate duties, which require not only a knowledge of the principles of jurisprudence, but of the forms of regulations adopted in our courts and judicature. The truth of this observation will sufficiently appear from the following brief detail of some of the principal cases, in which the science of law is of importance to medical practitioners (Percival 1794, 43–44).

This is the longest of the four section, encompassing fifty-four pages. Percival addresses; advising patients who are seriously ill about the importance of a last will and testament; lunatics, or those who are legally *non compos mentis*; homicide in its various legal forms; abortion; infanticide, especially in the context of bastardy or being born out of wedlock, an event with very serious social and legal consequences for mother and child; dueling, including the attendance by a physician or surgeon at a duel; homicide by poisoning; rape; nuisances, including what we would now call environmental harms and crimes; and judicial testimony.

For each topic Percival provides a primer on the law. In *Medical Ethics* at one point he characterizes this as "political ethics" (Percival 1803, 108). He makes relevant distinctions in the manner of Justinian, who, for example, starts with a distinction between public and private law and then distinguishes three categories of private law:

> Of private law then we may say that it is of threefold origin, being collected from the precepts of nature, from those of the law of nations, of from those of the civil law of Rome (Justinian 2002, 3).

Similarly, Percival draws on English law to distinguish among the classifications of homicide and natural law for his treatment of the law on abortion.

Farr's Elements of Medical Jurisprudence. Percival cites Dr. Samuel Farr's *Elements of Medical Jurisprudence* (Farr [1788] 1814) in *Medical Jurisprudence*. Farr tells his reader that he has taken, and to some extent, adapted, his text from Faselius' *Elementa Medicinæ Forensis* (Faselius 1767). Faselius describes the purpose of his book:

> There is a kind of medical knowledge, which is not so much concerned in the cure of diseases, as in the detection of error, and the conviction of guilt. A physician, a surgeon or a coroner, is often called upon to make a deposition of what he knows concerning some particular transactions in a court of judicature. Such persons then should be well acquainted with the animal œconomy; and with those views of the science, which, in foreign countries, have been dignified with a peculiar name, as the medicine of the courts, legal medicine, or medical jurisprudence (Farr [1768] 1814, 1).

Each section provides a conceptual framework for its topic, such as rape, infanticide, and homicide, with relevant legal distinctions and then provides a primer on clinical findings pertinent to the topic, to which the physician or surgeon could testify with authority. As we will see when we take up Chapter IV of *Medical Ethics*, Percival does not follow this approach.

'Medical jurisprudence', as Percival learned the phrase at Warrington Academy and used it as the title of *Medical Jurisprudence*, did not have the narrow meaning that Farr gave to it and that continued to be its meaning in the work of Theodoric Beck (1823) and the literature that continues to this day. For Percival the scope of 'medical jurisprudence' included Farr's approach but also, as Aikin had taught Percival, moral science and its implications for judgment and behavior. For this component of medical jurisprudence Percival adopted the "Institutes of Medicine" style in which, in the manner of Justinian, Boerhaave, and Cullen, in which the essentials are presented first followed by their implications in the form of compact guidance or "precepts." Johnson's *Dictionary* has a definition for precept: "A rule authoritatively given; a mandate; a commandment; a direction" (Johnson 1755, 1550). When a rule or direction is justified by an ethical framework, it is "authoritatively given" and therefore becomes a precept of professional ethics in medicine. The definition of the verb, 'institute', in Johnson's *Dictionary* as a verb is "to fix; to appoint; to enact; to settle; to prescribe" and as a noun: "established law; settled order; precept; maxim; principle" (Johnson 1755, 1105). "Institutes" prescribe the behavior of physicians and surgeons by "precepts" organized by appropriate headings into a "code."

The use of 'code', therefore, does *not* mean that moral science – or moral philosophy based on moral science – is codified; these are presumed as the "Institutes" of the "Precepts" that follow in each of the four chapters. This means that the reader is presumed to be familiar with moral science and therefore needs only a concise summary of the aspects of moral science relevant to medical practice. Judgment and behavior, by contrast, *are* codified. This codification takes the form of an ethically justified, concise set of guidances, so that physicians will have a reliable approach to the problems addressed in each numbered paragraph or paragraphs in the first three sections. *Medical Jurisprudence* and, after it, *Medical Ethics* engage in the quest for reliability, not the quest for certainty. In the final section, criminal law is reduced to its essentials, much in the manner of the opening of *Justinian's Institutes* (Justinian 2002) followed by concise guidance for providing medical or surgical evaluation of alleged criminal behavior about the medical or surgical dimensions of which a court of law or coroner's enquiry requires expert evaluation by a physician. That physician is presumed to be knowledgeable both about the distinction between naturally caused or human caused events such as the death of an infant immediately after birth and how applicable criminal law applies to medical or surgical findings. It is therefore a mistake to read *Medical Jurisprudence* as reducing moral science and moral philosophy based on it to a (mere) code. In the phrase in its title, 'code of ethics and institutes', 'code of ethics' is the subjective genitive (ethics is the origin of a code of judgment and behavior deriving from ethics) and 'code of institutes' is the objective genitive (institutes and precepts constitute the code, the codified judgment (institutes) and behavior (precepts)).

The title page of *Medical Jurisprudence* lists no author. However, the unsigned "advertisement" at the end of the text explains the inclusion of Thomas Bassnett Percival's "Discourse" on "Hospital Duties" (separately paginated) in which he refers to Thomas Bassnett as his son. The advertisement is dated "MANCHESTER Feb 24, 1794" (Percival 1794, not paginated: 21). Assigning authorship to Percival presents no challenge to readers, then and now.

3.2 Medical Jurisprudence

Percival circulated the privately published, "anonymous" text of *Medical Jurisprudence* to a select group of friends, acquaintances, and other moralists. It was common practice at the time to privately publish a text and seek responses to it. It was also common to publish, or permit to be published, an anonymous text, to test public reaction. Gregory had followed the latter practice by permitting the publication of his ethics lectures, probably edited by his son, James Gregory (1753–1821) (McCullough 1998), as *Observations on the Duties and Offices of a Physician, and on the Method of Prosecuting Enquiries in Philosophy* (Gregory 1770, [1770] 1998). He followed two years later with a revised version, published under his own name, *Lectures on the Duties and Qualifications of a Physician* (Gregory 1772, [1772] 1998).

Percival also reports that he circulated "to many other respectable friends … copies of the Medical Ethics … subsequently to the first circulation of the scheme" before its publication (Percival 1803, 140). The use of 'first circulation' refers to *Medical Jurisprudence*. The use of 'the Medical Ethics' could also refer to *Medical Jurisprudence*.

Brockbank reports that the Infirmary copy of *Medical Jurisprudence* has notes in Percival's hand:

> In the Infirmary copy is the following note in Percival's handwriting at the beginning of the book: "The completion of 'Medical Jurisprudence' [as Percival proposed to call the work until his friends persuaded him that 'Medical Ethics' was more suitable] has been long suspended, and it is uncertain when the undertaking will be resumed. A title page, an introduction, a fifth and sixth section, and an appendix, containing notes and illustrations, are wanting to finish this little work. Manchester, March 17th, 1794." At the end of the book is another note: "Two sections wanting. Section V. on the powers, privileges, honours, and emoluments of the faculty. Section VI. on the moral, religious, and political character of physicians" (Brockbank 1904, 91).

Percival did not complete the planned fifth and sixth sections, although he mentions "the powers, privileges, honours, and emoluments of the faculty" in *Medical Jurisprudence*, Section IV, number XVI, adding that the laws relating to these "can require no pleas to recommend them to attention" (Percival 1794, 89). For *Medical Ethics* he did prepare a title page and a dedication. There follow four "Chapters" and the planned appendix with "notes and illustrations."

Percival was surely well aware that his project had been solicited by the Infirmary trustees after a very public controversy that resulted in a wholesale reconstitution of the medical staff of the Infirmary after the Whites and Halls split off to start their lying-in hospital. Pickstone's account of the Infirmary Treasurer Philips, related above, indicates that the trustees took a keen interest in *Medical Jurisprudence* and incorporated it into the rules of the Infirmary. Percival's personal notes, quoted above, indicate that he intended to continue the project and publish it. Given what we learned about Percival in Chap. 2, it is reasonable to say that Percival was aware that readers of such a text would be acquainted with the controversy that engendered it. A prudent, indeed politic, author might seek critical input of others, with the aim of improving the text and also gaining stamps of approval that could be acknowledged in the new book. Put another way, Percival may have been creating the opportunity to gain for his potentially controversial text the approval of authorities many of whose names, or even all of them, readers would recognize. (Readers acquainted with prefaces of books published by academic philosophers in the United States can see this practice continued to this day, especially in the acknowledgement of comments on earlier drafts by very well-known academic philosophers.) Some of the responses he received will be examined in the next section.

3.3 Delay in Completing *Medical Ethics*

Medical Ethics appeared nine years after *Medical Jurisprudence*. Percival' personal notation, cited by Brockbank above, indicates that there had been delay, in Percival's estimation, of the preparation of *Medical Jurisprudence* in the form in which it was privately published. This occurred four years after the controversy about expanding the honorary staff of the Infirmary had been settled by a vote of the subscribers.

Percival had retired from the Infirmary in 1780 because of poor eyesight, which became so poor that he needed to hire secretaries to help him with his writing, by reading texts to him, taking dictation, and then reading it back to him for corrections. We know from Chap. 2 that Percival was a prolific writer. Functional blindness surely slowed his productivity. We also saw in Chap. 2 that Edward Percival, in his *Memorial*, reports that his father experienced chronic headaches, which sometimes became severe and debilitating.

As we saw in Chap. 2, in the Preface to the second part of *A Father's Instructions* in 1777 had already signaled to his children concern about his health, which he described: "… frequent interruptions of my health, and the natural delicacy of my condition, warn me of the precarious tenure on which I hold the dearest blessings of life …" (Percival 1807, Vol. I, 91).

The death of children from disease and of wives from complications of pregnancy and childbirth was common in the eighteenth century. Percival's wife survived him but at least four of his children predeceased him. Baconian moral science was not an abstraction for Percival. He made it an essential component of the intellectual and moral formation of his children. A reader of the poetry, tales, fables, and precepts that he taught them, as well as the essays, readily detects great warmth (a very positive word in eighteenth-century British moral science) for his children. It is easy to imagine therefore what were probably personally and intellectually very happy times for him as he sat with his children at Hart-Hill and showed them ants and birds and taught them sympathetic regard for all life forms. In the discourse of moral science, Percival had life-long tender regard for his children. There is therefore every reason to believe that he felt their deaths keenly, as profound losses.

In 1780, less than a year since his appointment to the Infirmary's medical faculty, as we saw in Chap. 2, his three-year-old daughter, Maria, and his infant son, Edward Bayley died within two weeks of each other in May of that year. Both were taken by what we now call "Whooping Cough." Only once in more than forty years as a philosopher-medical-educator in the clinical setting have I heard the sound of severe

3.3 Delay in Completing *Medical Ethics*

whooping cough in a child, who survived that admission. I was terrified by that sound and haunted by it still; I do not know how parents cope with the loss of a child compounded by the memory of the sound of failing, terminal struggle to breathe in one child and then another without the ability to stop any of it, in the space of but three harrowing weeks.

Maria died first, from "the Hooping Cough, complicated with Hectic Fever and Pulmonary Consumption" (Percival 1807, Vol. I, ccxlix). His inscription to Maria's memory includes:

> Afflictive long will be thy loss;
>   yet, sweet the Memory of thy dawning virtues (Percival 1807, Vol. I, ccxlix)

His infant son, Edward Bayley was taken next. He died of "Hooping Cough, and Acute Asthma." Percival's inscription, the product of self-discipline that leaves me in awe, includes:

> A Mother's solace, and a Father's Hope!
>   Pity the parting pang
>   so soon renewed!
>   Forgive the Sigh
>   that faintly utters
>   "LET THY WILL BE DONE!"

Perhaps Percival had acquired a second reason to continue his retirement at Hart-Hill: to begin his remaining life's work of living with the "afflictive" loss of these little children.

Four years after publication of *Medical Jurisprudence*, Thomas Basnett Percival died in 1798, as the reader will recall learning from Chap. 2. He was Percival's first-born child. Pickstone writes that by the end of the 1790s "Percival's world was now darkening" (Pickstone 1993, 170). This statement provides an accurate clinical characterization: Percival was blind. This statement, sad to say, suggests the burden of the iron grip of the deaths of three of his children. His closeness to and intellectual regard for Thomas Bassnett is evident in his inclusion as an "appendix" to *Medical Jurisprudence* a 1791 *Discourse* on the hospital duties of physicians, which he also appends, *in memoriam*, to *Medical Ethics*. Finally, in the dedication of *Medical Jurisprudence* to his son Edward, Percival writes, "Sensible that I begin to experience that pressure of advancing years, I regard the present publication as the conclusion, in this way, of my professional labours" (Percival 1803, ix–x).

3.4 Medical Ethics, or a Code of Institutes and Precepts, Adapted to the Professional Conduct of Physicians and Surgeons

3.4.1 Title Change

The title of *Medical Ethics* makes four changes in the title of *Medical Jurisprudence or a Code of Ethics and Institutes, Adapted to the Professions of Physic and Surgery*. 'Medical jurisprudence' becomes 'medical ethics'. After 'code', 'of ethics' is deleted and, after 'institutes', 'and precepts' is added. 'The professions of' is replaced by 'professional conduct' after 'adapted to'.

Percival explains the first change in the "Preface:" "This work was originally entitled, "MEDICAL JURISPRUDENCE;" but some friends objected to the term JURISPRUDENCE, it has been changed to ETHICS" (Percival 1803, 7). 'Ethics', of course, already appeared in the subtitle of *Medical Jurisprudence*. Percival has moved it to the main title. This change made the 1803 book the first to be entitled 'Medical Ethics' in the global history of medical ethics.

The institutes and precepts are adapted from what exists already, Baconian moral science as already modified by John Gregory for medicine and surgery: the principle of sympathy and its regulatory professional virtues for clinical practice and research, tenderness and steadiness. Percival makes a further adaptation: two new regulatory professional virtues required to manage power differentials and class differences between physicians and surgeons and their patient: authority and condescension. This adaptation continues in the precepts for three clinical settings: hospital practice, private practice, and relationships with apothecaries. The use of 'adapted' signals that Percival is not codifying medical ethics, i.e., reducing medical ethics to a set to rules, the justification for which is not provided, thus stripping medical ethics of its ethics. Percival is committed to the ethics of medical ethics, which he has taken from Gregory and then expanded with two new professional virtues. No reduction to a form of non-ethics occurs. Instead, he is codifying judgment and behavior, or as he puts it in his title, "conduct." As we shall see in Chap. 4, in doing so, he adds significantly to the scope and content of professional ethics medicine invented by Gregory three decades earlier.

The use of the plural in 'professions of medicine and surgery' in the title of *Medical Jurisprudence* reflects the division between medicine and surgery that still existed in the early 1790s. Each had its separate college in London and Edinburgh. In Glasgow they formed one Royal College, suggesting the plausibility of a single profession.

Gregory laments this division. He opens his consideration of this topic with a reflection on the situation in France:

> There have arisen at different periods, and particularly in France, about twenty years ago, great disputes about the boundary of physic and surgery, and the proper subordination of surgery to medicine. A dispute hurtful to mankind, and which has been often conducted in

a manner unworthy of scholars and gentlemen. I shall embrace this opportunity of giving my sentiments concerning it (Gregory 1772, [1772] 1998, 43).

He then turns to Great Britain:

> The separation of physic from surgery in modern times, has been productive of the worst consequences. The physicians and surgeons, formed into separate societies, had separate interests to support, which, in many cases, clashed with each other (Gregory 1772, [1772] 1998, 43–44).

The Royal College were guilds, based on party-interest sanctioned by the crown. They were not professions, as Gregory and Percival used this word.

Gregory's moral revolution in inventing professional ethics in medicine was to reform physic into the profession of medicine. Gregory meant for his reformation to include surgery, because there is but one science of medicine:

> But it must be apparent to every sensible and ingenuous observer, that the diseases of the human body are so intimately connected, that it is impossible to understand some of them perfectly, and be entirely ignorant of all the rest; and hardly possible to understand any of them, without some knowledge of Anatomy, and of the Animal œconomy, both in its sound and morbid state (Gregory 1772, [1772] 1998, 45).

Gregory then identifies the implication that there is but one, Baconian, science of medicine, i.e., for both physic and surgery.

> Every distemper, external as well as internal, falls under the cognizance of the physician, and it is a reflection on him to be ignorant of any of them; neither is it possible to fix any such precise boundaries between external and internal diseases, as to render the distinction in any degree useful, or applicable in practice. Suppose a person to break his leg, and a fever and gangrene to ensue; the question occurs, whether the limb should be immediately amputated, or to ['whether we should' substituted for 'to' in errata] wait for some time till the effects of certain medicines, given with a view to stop the progress of the mortification, are known. It is evidently the business of a physician, in this case, to judge from the symptoms, from the habit of body, and from other circumstances, whether the delay is prudent or not. As to the performance of the operation itself, that is a different question. The genius and education requisite to make a good physician, are not necessary to make a good operator. What is peculiarly necessary to make a good operator, is a resolute, collected mind, a good eye, and a steady hand. These talents may be united with those of an able physician; but they may also be separated from them (Gregory 1772, [1772] 1998, 46–47).

Gregory goes on to refer to each "branch" of "the profession" (Gregory 1772, [1772] 1998, 49). Percival will use 'branch' as well. Gregory then and adds: "Every department of it is respectable, when exercised with capacity and integrity" (Gregory 1772, [1772] 1998, 49). Gregory was not making a descriptive but normative claim, given the deep divisions that still existed when he published *Lectures*.

In the title to *Medical Jurisprudence* Percival uses "the Professions of Physic and Surgery" (Percival 1794, 1 [not numbered]). This does not go as far as Gregory but shares with him being a normative claim. This is textual evidence that Gregory and Percival were fomenting a moral revolution from "interested" entrepreneurial guilds, the Royal Colleges, into a profession based on the ethical concept of medicine as a profession.

Change was afoot in surgery itself. The Scottish surgeon, John Hunter (1728–1793), who trained in hospital-based apprenticeships, in his London practice in the last third of the eighteenth century undertook to improve surgery by research, which he published (Lawrence 1993, 974).

> He amassed a huge collection of anatomical, pathological, and embryological specimens which was subsequently given to the newly established Royal College of Surgeons. He was made a member of the Royal Society in 1767 [two years after Percival], and remained eminent among London surgeons, with an appointment at St. George's Hospital and a considerable private practice, until his death (Lawrence 1993, 974–975).

Hunter propelled forward the scientific development of surgery, a first step toward its becoming a profession by making possible the first commitment of the ethical concept of medicine as a profession: becoming scientifically and clinically competent. Hunter's work had important consequences:

> At the turn of the nineteenth century, London surgeons strove for equal status with physicians. Like that of the Paris surgeons before them, their strategy lay in emphasizing that surgery was no longer an empirical craft, but a science resting on a secure body of theoretical knowledge. John Hunter's work, with its stress on studying the normal as well as the pathological, and the relationship of structure to function as an essential prelude to surgery, served its purpose well (Lawrence 1993, 975).

It seems reasonable to assume that Percival was aware of Hunter and his work and its implications for surgery as a profession. In any case, Percival was leading change, not following others, when in the title of *Medical Ethics* he uses "the Professional Conduct of Physicians and Surgeons" (Percival 1803, i [not paginated]). This, too, is a normative claim. I read Percival as "adapting" Gregory's reformation of medicine into a profession to how physicians and surgeons comport themselves. In Chapter I Percival will go into considerable detail about the "institutes and precepts" that put this adaptation into effect, by creating sustained accountability of physicians and surgeons to each other, a revolutionary idea for its day.

The title of *Medical Ethics* in an understated way – and therefore easy to miss – signals Percival's manifold moral revolution. There is a new category of behavior, professional conduct, based on Gregory's Baconian moral science of medicine, that itself is expanded or "adapted" to professional conduct of physicians *and* surgeons. Surgeons are explicitly included; Percival is leading the transition of medicine and surgery away from being guilds with their guild-interests. This is a revolution against individual entrepreneurial self-interest and guild-interest. As we will see in Chapter I, Percival's also mounts a revolution against what had been an organizational culture of party-interest that had prevailed for decades in the Manchester Infirmary. He proposes, for the first time, a replacement: an ethically justified hospital polity, what is now called an organizational culture of professionalism (McCullough et al. 2020).

3.4.2 Format: Four Chapters, "On Hospital Duties," and Notes and Illustrations

The format of *Medical Ethics* follows that of *Medical Jurisprudence*. The "sections" of the latter have become "chapters." The first three address professional ethics in hospital practice, private practice, and in relationships with apothecaries. The fourth addresses medical jurisprudence in the specific sense of knowledge of law that physicians need to have when using medical knowledge in legal processes. Unlike *Medical Jurisprudence*, *Medical Ethics* includes a "Contents" section, of six detailed pages, that guides the reader to the numbered sections of each chapter and thereby introduces the reader to the scope of the book. Percival adds "Notes and Illustrations," to supplement the "aphoristic form of this code of Medical Ethics" (Percival 1803, 4). Between the text of *Medical Ethics* and the "Notes and Illustrations" Percival includes "On Hospital Duties" (this time consecutively paginated) by his son Thomas Bassnett, as Percival had in *Medical Jurisprudence* but now also as a memorial to Thomas Bassnett.

3.4.3 Dedications to Sir George Baker and to Edward Cropper Percival

Following the title page, Percival dedicates *Medical Ethics* to Sir George Baker (1722–1809). Baker was physician to King George III (1738–1820; reign 1760–1820), including during his period of mental illness that may have been caused by porphyria. Baker started his medical studies in Leyden in 1745 but returned to complete his medical studies at Cambridge in 1756 (Waldron 1973). "In his day Baker was renowned both as a physician and scholar" (Waldron 1973, 178). He was twice elected President of the Royal College of Physicians (Waldron 1973). Baker discovered that lead in cider and other sources was the cause of Devonshire colic, the course of which involved severe abdominal pain often followed by death (n.a., 1968; Waldron 1973). Recall from Chap. 2 that Percival had also taken an active interest in cases of lead poisoning caused by contamination of water supplies by effluvia from mills. In his dedication Percival states that Baker has "honoured with this sanction and improved by his communications" the text of *Medical Ethics* (Percival 1803, no pagination v).

In a May 9, 1794, letter Dr. Baker sent his comments on *Medical Jurisprudence*, part of which letter Edward Percival includes in *Works* (Percival 1807, Vol. I, clxxxvi–clxxxvii). Baker stars with an encomium. Using 'practitioners' Dr. Baker then identifies lack of cooperation among physicians, and, it appears from the use of 'practitioners', between physicians and surgeons, and sees Percival's text on this subject as a powerful antidote:

> WHAT I have seen of Medical Jurisprudence meets with my entire approbation; and I hope that you will soon have time to complete the whole work. The dignity of Physic cannot any

where be well supported without harmony and due subordination among those practitioners whom neighbourhood has connected; nor can the evils which are apt to arise in their common intercourse be more probably everted than by the voluntary subscription of the Faculty to such laws as you have proposed (Percival 1807, Vol. I, clxxxvi–clxxxvii).

As we will see below in the analysis of the text of *Medical Ethics* a professional ethics of cooperation – more than Baker's "harmony" and without his "subordination" – is one of the book's central themes, as it was in *Medical Jurisprudence*.

Percival also dedicates the book, which he describes as "this little Manual of MEDICAL ETHICS" (Percival 1803, vii), to his son, Edward Percival, who will, four years later, publish his edition of his father's *Works*, analyzed in Chap. 2. Percival signals the loss of his second son, James, a medical student who had died ten years previously.

Percival returns to this loss in the "Preface," where he describes James as "an ornament to the healing art" (Percival 1803, 2). Percival then acknowledges "a second family loss, equally afflictive" (Percival 1803, 2), the death his eldest son, Thomas Bassnett Percival, a clergyman who had died five years previously. Percival had used "afflictive long" to describe the death of his daughter, Maria, at three years of age (Percival 1807, Vol. I, ccxlix). 'Afflictive' is a word that is clinical in its origin, 'affliction'. In his *Dictionary* Johnson defines 'afflictive': "That which causes affliction; painful; tormenting" (Johnson 1755, 94) and 'affliction': "The cause of pain or sorrow; calamity" and "The state of sorrowfulness; misery: opposed to prosperity" (Johnson 1755, 94). 'Afflictive' names a chronic psychological condition, in this context, the permanent loss of a loved one that torments one for life. After these two passages about the deaths of James and Thomas Basnett, Percival never returns to the theme of personal loss. Percival had appended Thomas Bassnett's "On Hospital Duties" to *Medical Jurisprudence*, which text is analyzed later in this chapter. He appends it also to *Medical Ethics* but now as a memorial.

Gregory uses 'afflictive' once in *Lectures*. The context in which he does so is instructive.

> There are, besides, some peculiar circumstances in the profession of a physician, which should naturally dispose him to look beyond the present scene of things, and engage his heart on the side of religion. He has many opportunities of seeing people, once the gay and the happy, sunk in deep distress; sometimes devoted to a painful and lingering death; and sometimes struggling with the tortures of a distracted mind. Such afflictive scenes, one should imagine, might soften any heart not dead to every feeling of humanity, and make it reverence that religion which alone can support the soul in the most complicated distresses; that religion, which teaches to enjoy life with chearfulness, and to resign it with dignity (Gregory 1772, 68–69).

Perhaps Percival's subsequent silence about his repeated personal losses is explained by how his Dissenting Unitarianism taught him to live with permanent loss of his children, four of them, with "cheerfulness" and "dignity." This is Dissenting stoicism of a piece with the spare theism of his Unitarianism.

James at first followed his older brother into the ministry but then undertook medical studies in Edinburgh. Percival says that his "solicitudes are naturally transferred" (Percival 1803, viii).

Percival then sets out a concise account of what he calls "professional ethics:"

> It is the characteristic of a wise man to act on determinate principles; and of a good man to be assured that they are conformable to rectitude and virtue. The relations in which a physician stands to his patients, to his brethren, and to the public, are complicated, and multifarious; involving much knowledge of human nature, and extensive moral duties. The study of professional Ethics, therefore, cannot fail to invigorate and enlarge the understanding; whilst the observance of the duties which they enjoin, will soften your manners, expand your affections, and form you to their propriety and dignity of conduct, which are essential to the character of a GENTLEMAN (Percival 1803, viii–ix).

First, a man must form his character properly, "on determinate principles." In Baconian moral science these are the principles, in lexical order, of sympathy and reason. To become "conformable to rectitude and virtue" a man forms his character further by adopting the habits prescribed by the regulatory virtues of tenderness and steadiness. Physicians have ethical obligations, again in lexical order, "to his patients, to his brethren, and to the public." Routinely fulfilling these ethical obligations strengthens, secures, proper moral formation, the moral formation of a gentleman. That is, the moral status of "gentleman" is the function of a man's commitment to the principles and virtues of Baconian moral science. One is not born to this moral status; one earns it. As we saw in Chap. 2, it follows that any man can earn this moral status if he is willing to do the initial and then life-long moral work required.

The dedication closes with his frank acknowledgement of his own infirmities and, obliquely, his death. This will be his final publication: "Sensible that I begin to experience that pressure of advancing years, I regard the present publication as the conclusion, in this way, of my professional labours" (Percival 1803, ix–x).

3.4.4 Preface

In the "Preface" that introduced *Medical Ethics* Percival informs his reader about the intellectual and personal journey he had taken from *Medical Jurisprudence* to *Medical Ethics*. He notes that *Medical Jurisprudence* was "composed in the spring of 1792" and that "the substance of it constitutes the code of laws, by which the practice of that comprehensive institution in now governed" (Percival 1803, not paginated 1). *Medical Jurisprudence* has become the "Institutes and Precepts" of professional ethics in medicine for the Manchester Infirmary. The first of the "Notes and Illustrations" is referenced here and describes the components and mission of the Manchester Infirmary (Percival 1803, 135–139).

Percival means for *Medical Ethics* to have broader reach.

> The author was afterwards induced, by an earnest desire to promote the honour and advancement of his profession, to enlarge the plan of his undertaking, and to frame a general system of MEDICAL ETHICS; that the official conduct and mutual intercourse of the faculty might be regulated by precise and acknowledged principles of urbanity and rectitude (Percival 1803, not paginated 1).

Percival explains that he sent the privately published *Medical Jurisprudence* to "his numerous correspondents; by most of whom it was warmly encouraged; and by many of them was honoured with valuable suggestions for its improvement" (Percival 1803, not paginated 1–2). Note II in "Notes and Illustrations" lists the names of twenty-five men to whom Percival sent the text. There were also "many other respectable friends" to whom the text was sent (Percival 1803, 140). With his thanks to those who responded, he indicates that circulating *Medical Jurisprudence* privately served to gain acceptance for it, as explained above.

> And I record not only with *gratitude*, but as the necessary *sanction* of my work, the names of those who have honoured it with their approbation or assistance (Percival 1803, 139).

In Volume I of *Works* Edward Percival includes some of this correspondence. They amply document the "approbation" and "sanction" that Percival reports.

Percival cites works by Thomas Gisborne (1758–1846) and John Gregory, as well as the *Statuta Moralia* of the Royal College of Physicians. Percival describes Gisborne's *Enquiry into the Duties of Men* as "a work that reflects the highest honour on the abilities and philanthropy of the author; and which may be justly regarded as the most complete system extant of PRACTICAL ETHICS" (Percival 1803, 5) and notes that Gisborne's "chapter concerning physicians contains a reference to these institutes" (Percival 1803, 5), i.e., *Medical Jurisprudence*. He then adds, crucially:

> And it treats so largely of the duties of the faculty, as to seem, at first view, to supersede the use of the present manual. But the two publications differ not only in their plan, but in many of their leading objects; and it may be hoped they will rather illustrate than interfere with each other (Percival 1803, 6).

Gisborne was a clergyman and abolitionist. His *The Principles of Moral Philosophy Investigated* (Gisborne 1795) was a response to William Paley's (1743–1805) approach in *Principles of Moral and Political Philosophy* (Paley [1785] 2013). Gisborne's use of the same title signals his intent to replace Paley's account with the correct account. Gisborne took himself to have shown that Paley's work is but a catalogue of errors.

> The principle of morals assumed by Mr. Paley, whether that principle be general or particular expediency, is totally devoid of proof. The conduct of the Almighty affords no ground for inferring that he wills us to regulate our actions by the one or the other. Reason rejects the former as totally inapplicable by man; and each of them as leading to consequences subversive to itself. And revelation forbids us to listen to doctrines, either of which arms every man with unlimited authority to violate at his discretion her most sacred laws (Gisborne 1795, 61).

The proper philosophical method is to "in the first place, investigate, by reference to natural reason alone, the primitive rights and obligations of mankind" and show that the results "fully accord with the general tenor of Revelation" (Gisborne 1795, 68). From the perspective of Baconian moral science this is investing far too much confidence in the poor powers of reason. Moreover, the products of reason are made accountable to revelation, the reverse of Percival's Dissenting deism, as described in

Chap. 2. Gisborne's "plan" differs sharply from Percival's Baconian method of moral science, as noted previously in this Chapter and Chap. 2.

In his *An Enquiry into the Duties of Men* Gisborne (1794) proposes to apply this approach to moral reasoning in the following manner:

> To apply moral truths to practical purposes; to point out their bearings on modern opinions and modern manners; and to deduce from them rules of conduct by which the inhabitants of this country in particular, each in his own respective station, may be aided in acquiring the knowledge and encouraged in the performance of their several duties, are objects of unequivocal utility. They are the objects which it is my wish to attain, as far as I am able, in the present work (Gisborne 1794, Vol. I, 1).

Gisborne takes for granted and therefore as his starting point the then-current class structure with the sovereign at its head and his or her subjects beneath them, divided into the peerage and the commoners and their various, given "stations." In the manner of a moral realist, Gisborne uses natural reason to read out the duties that constitute basic social roles into one of which one individual is born, the sovereign, and into the second of which everyone else is born as peer or commoner.

Gisborne describes "the general duties of Englishmen as subjects and fellow-citizens:" The first duty of a subject as such is to fulfil the engagements into which he has entered with his country" (Gisborne 1794, Vol. I, 75). Gisborne starts with the duty of a physician to be properly trained, in order to become competent. When he turns to duties in clinical practice, Gisborne, without acknowledgement (which may not have violated scholarly standards at the time) calls for physicians to comport themselves just as Gregory had already argued more than two decades earlier: cultivate "punctuality; display" the "utmost delicacy" with female patients; maintain secrets; and exercise "prudent control" over the sick (Gisborne 1794, Vol. II, 132–134). The physician should cultivate "steadiness which is necessary to secure a compliance with his instructions" (Gisborne 1794, Vol. II, 13), betraying a fundamental misunderstanding of the professional virtue of steadiness and conflating it with the professional virtue of authority. The goal is to "bespeak his sympathy with the suffer," which so dilutes the principle of sympathy as to trivialize it. This approach, Gisborne claims, will render the "general behavior" of the physician "most beneficial, as well as most amiable" (Gisborne 1794, Vol. II, 133). Gregory and Percival would reject this: sympathy and its professional virtues create ethical obligations not something "amiable," because sometimes, as in the case of giving patients bad news, obligations are unpleasant. Worse, having explicitly rejected Paley's "particular" expediency, Gisborne seems to invoke it.

The difference between Gisborne's moral-realist role-related practical medical ethics and Percival's Baconian moral scientific professional ethics in medicine runs deep. For Gisborne, the obligations or duties to of physicians to their patients originate in our various, pre-ordained, fixed social roles. For Percival, the obligations or duties of physicians to their patients originate in the principle of sympathy and its professional regulatory virtues of tenderness, steadiness, condescension and authority. Committing to these duties or obligations, in turn, creates the social role of the physician; that role is not a given, as Gisborne assumes. Gisborne uses the discourse of sympathy and its virtues. However, he does not do so as a Baconian moral scientist, but as a social contract theorist, in which the social contract is based on our natural rights discoverable by Reason. Percival needn't have worried that Gisborne's medical ethics might "interfere" with *Medical Ethics*. Methodologically and in its content Gisborne's moral philosophy had little or no influence on Percival's *Medical Ethics*. Put another way, Percival can be read to compliment Gisborne on the remarkable scope of his practical ethics, which encompasses several volumes. But Percival does not compliment what Gisborne actually has to say, for good reason.

Gisborne, as Percival notes, makes reference to *Medical Jurisprudence* on the topic of communicating with a surgery patient during the procedure and about truthful communication more generally. I defer consideration of Gisborne's comments to the later section of this chapter below on this topic.

As we will see when we turn to the text of Chapter I, Section I, Percival's debt to Gregory is evident. Percival builds on Gregory's Baconian-moral-science account of the principle of sympathy and its regulatory professional virtues of tenderness and steadiness (properly understood, see Chap. 1). Percival then adds to Gregory's invention of professional medical ethics. *Medical Ethics* does more than "illustrate" *Lectures* but complements it.

Percival may have mentioned the *Statuta Moralia* of the Royal College of Physicians because Dr. Baker, the dedicatee of *Medical Ethics*, had referenced it in the letter discussed above (Percival 1807, Vol. I, clxxxvi–clxxxvii). Baker describes the relationship between the two texts:

> In our statute book at the College of Physicians, we have a chapter 'De Conversatione Morali,' some parts of which are similar to your Medical Jurisprudence; but your laws are fuller and more comprehensive. With respect to them, I can truly say, that I find much to admire, and nothing to criticize (Percival 1807, Vol. I, clxxxvii).

Statuta Moralia, however, is a guild document, based on guild-interest. Percival would *not* share this view. He was breaking, sharply, from rules or institutes based on party-interest, whether the guild-interest of the royally chartered guilds or the party-interest of the Whites, the Halls, and their two physician comrades trying to protect their power and privilege in Manchester Infirmary. Percival's experience as a Baconian Dissenter might have cautioned him to mute the reading of *Medical Ethics* as rejecting the medical counterpart to the Anglican articles of faith. After all, Percival would have been reasonable to assume that Dr. Baker – and the membership of the Royal College of Physicians – might take an interest in the successor to *Medical Jurisprudence*.

In the "Preface" to *Medical Ethics* Percival explains what he understands 'jurisprudence' in Justinian's sense: "According to the definition of Justinian, however, Jurisprudence may be understood to include moral injunctions as well as positive ordinances. *Juris præcepta sunt hæc honeste vivere; alterum non lædere; suum cuique tribuere*.-INST. JUSTIN. Lib. i. p. 3" (Percival 1803, 7). ("The precepts of justice are to live honestly, not to injure another, and to grant to each what is due.") In this meaning of 'medical jurisprudence' *Medical Ethics* remains a work of medical jurisprudence.

Finally, Percival reports that a project intended to be included in *Medical Ethics* will not be completed:

> It was the author's original intention to have treated of the POWERS, PRIVILEGES, HONOURS, and EMOLUMENTS of the FACULTY. But he now conceives, that this would lead him into a field of investigation too wide and digressive; and therefore chooses to confine himself to what more strictly belongs to Medical Ethics (Percival 1803, 4).

3.4.5 The Text of Medical Ethics: Chapter I: Of Professional Conduct, Relative to Hospitals, or Other Medical Charities

II. Ethical Framework for Institutes and Precepts: Baconian Moral Scientific Professional Ethics in Hospital Practice

> I. HOSPITAL PHYSICIANS and SURGEONS should minister to the sick, with due impressions of the importance of their office; reflecting that the ease, the health, and the lives of those committed to their charge depend on their skill, attention, and fidelity. They should study, also, in their deportment, so to unite *tenderness* with *steadiness*, and *condescension* with *authority*, as to inspire the minds of their patients with gratitude, respect, and confidence (Percival 1803, 9).

This opening text is verbatim the same as in *Medical Jurisprudence*. 'Office' is from the Latin *officium*: a service, including an obligatory service (Lewis and Short [1879] 1969, 1260), in this case to patients in the Manchester Infirmary. The life and health of the patient are "committed" to the "charge" of the physician, to protect and promote. This obligatory service is to be discharged with "skill" or the first commitment of the ethical concept of medicine as a profession, to become and remain scientifically and clinically competent. This obligatory service is to be discharged with "fidelity," the second and third commitments of the ethical concept of medicine as a profession, to the protection of the ease, life, and health of the patient as the physician's or surgeon's primary concern and motivation, keeping individual self-interest and party-interest systematically secondary. "Attention" is the disciplined focus on the patient's clinical needs, as Gregory describes it:

> Sympathy produces an anxious attention to a thousand little circumstances that may tend to relieve the patient; an attention which money can never purchase: hence the inexpressible comfort of having a friend for a physician (Gregory 1772 [1172] 1998, 19).

Four professional virtues regulate sympathy and therefore direct the physician's skill, attention, and fidelity to the patient. The first two are from Gregory: the professional virtues of tenderness and steadiness. Tenderness generates the physician's sympathy-based experience of the patient's experience, directly entering into the affective life of the patient. This experience is steadied, prevented from going to the extremes, either of loss of control or hard-heartedness, as we saw in Chap. 2. Johnson's *Dictionary* reflects these meanings from Gregory's Baconian moral science of medicine. Tenderness is "susceptibility of the softer passions; kind attention; anxiety for the good of another; soft pathos of expression" (Johnson 1755, 2034). 'Soft' would have been readily understood to be a feminine trait. Gregory genders tenderness feminine, in Rosemary Tong's meaning (Tong 1993; McCullough 1998). Steadiness is "state of being not tottering or not easily shaken; firmness; constancy; consistent unvaried conduct" (Johnson 1755, 1934). Steadiness characterizes women of learning and virtue, as we saw in Chap. 1. Tenderness and steadiness in synergy result in kind attention and anxiety for the good of another, or attention, as consistent, unvaried, and effective conduct.

Percival adds two professional virtues that are designed to responsibly manage the power and class differences that exist between physicians and surgeons, from the comfortable middle class, and patients in the Infirmary, the working sick poor in the regimented, hierarchical environment of the hospital or the sick poor in their homes for treatment of infection of physician-assisted home birth, often mired in poverty. Like Gregory, Percival was very concerned that these class differences not become an obstacle to professional patient care, should the physician or surgeon react in a class-conscious way and treat the patient as a social inferior to be lorded over.

Engelhardt (1996) distinguished two meanings of 'authority' of physicians. The first, "an authority," means that the physician or surgeon possesses a fund of knowledge that is superior to those of Infirmary and at-home patients, because of the difference in education of physicians and of apprenticeship in a hospital or surgery lectures in a medical school that included them in its curriculum. It is crucial always to keep in mind that authority in Baconian science of medicine comes in degrees, as a function of the probability that a physician's or surgeon's fund of knowledge is based on the results of Baconian experience, which come in degrees of probability as we saw in Chap. 2. Gregory was aware of this limitation when he made the case that laying medicine open, making physicians accountable to scientifically sophisticated laypersons, will support the claim to authority: "The objection to laying medicine open to the world, like other sciences, from its tendency to multiply quacks, and to lessen the authority of the physician, is not well founded" (Gregory 1772, [1772] 1998, 230); just the opposite.

The second, "in authority" means that the physician or surgeon exerts influence or, perhaps, control over the patient. In the home environment, control is an impossible goal. In the regimented environment of the Infirmary, physicians and surgeons did indeed gain power – what was then called 'government' – over patients. Gregory addressed the professional ethics of government of patients:

> The government of a physician over his patient should undoubtedly be great. But an absolute government very few patients will submit to. A prudent physician should, therefore, prescribe such laws, as, though not the best, are yet the best that will be observed; of different evils he should chuse the least, and, at no rate, lose the confidence of his patient, so as to be deceived by him as to his true situation. This indulgence, however, which I am pleading for, must be managed with judgment and discretion; as it is very necessary that a physician should support a proper dignity and authority with his patients, for their sakes as well as his own (Gregory 1772, [1772] 1998, 22–23).

Johnson's *Dictionary* defines authority variously: "legal power; influence; credit; power; rule; support; justification; countenance; testimony; weight of testimony; credibility" (Johnson 1755, 186). Percival appears to draw on some of these definitions to understand being *an* authority to mean justified credibility. Percival appears to draw on some of these definitions to understand being *in* authority as justified exercise of power to influence patients.

A presentist reading of Percival's use of 'condescension' will egregiously misread the text. In contemporary discourse to condescend to someone is not acceptable because a false sense of superiority leads to the treatment of another as intrinsically inferior, which is taken to be disrespectful. A sense of superiority is claimed on the basis of education, nationality, sex, gender, religion, socioeconomic status or any other difference falsely believed to make one superior to the "other." Percival uses 'condescension' as an antidote to a false sense of superiority, based mainly on class differences, that is bound to bias clinical judgment and decision making by causing the physician or surgeon to focus only on himself rather than the patient.

Johnson's *Dictionary* captures Percival's use: "voluntary humiliation; decent from superiority; voluntary submission to equality with inferiours" (Johnson 1755, 440). The professional virtue of condescension requires descent from socioeconomic superiority in a voluntary submission to equality as a human being with the patient. Recall from Chap. 2 that Percival's scathing critique of slavers' denial of the intrinsic equality of all human beings. The focus become and remains the ease, health, and life of the patient. Being in authority derives its intellectual justification when the physician or surgeon justifiably acts as *an* authority. Condescension, as a professional virtue regulating sympathy, provides moral authority for the power of being *in* authority over patients. Recall also from Chap. 2 Henry Grove on condescension to the poor as a virtue to be cultivated: "It is reckoned a mark of great condescension for a very rich man to visit a poor man …" (Grove 1745, Vol. 4, 335).

In doing so, condescension severs the connection between being *in* authority and social class. England was then a very class-conscious society, as evidenced in the table of contents of Gisborne's *Enquiry into the Duties of Men* (Gisborne 1796). Gisborne took this social hierarchy for granted, because people were born into it. Percival, the Baconian moral scientist and moral revolutionary held that an individual has to earn authority as a physician over others by becoming a Baconian physician or surgeon (thus making the first commitment of the ethical concept of medicine as a profession) and exercising that authority over others, not for self-interest or party-interest, but for the well-being of the patent, as required by tenderness, steadiness, and condescension functioning in synergy (thus making the second and third commitments of the ethical concept of medicine as a profession). When this occurs, the power of the physician over the patient is directed to the protection, not the abuse, of the patient.

The result is a conceptual basis for the "Institutes and Precepts" that follow in *Medical Ethics* that: draws its intellectual and moral authority from Baconian moral science; is, as Percival learned from Aikin, Taylor, and Seddon at Warrington Academy, open to anyone who forms his character according to the principle sympathy and its four professional virtues that adapt Baconian moral science to medicine and surgery; is, like Baconian Dissent, independent of religious beliefs and therefore requires no assent to external moral authority such as the Church of England or the state; is, like Baconian Dissent, autonomous from theological and state power; is therefore secular in that, as deist, it neither requires nor is intrinsically hostile to the theologies of faith communities and traditions; and is not a function of being born into a social class with its defining duties.

This is Baconian moral scientific professional ethics in medicine, shaped by Baconian Dissent and deism. The professional virtue of authority as *an* authority implements the first commitment of the ethical concept of medicine as a profession: to become and remain scientifically and clinically competent. The professional virtues of tenderness, steadiness, and condescension keep the physician's focus on the patient's well-being and thereby implement the second and third commitments: to the protection and promotion of the patient's health-related interests as the physician's primary concern and motivation, keeping individual self-interest and party-interest systematically secondary. These four professional virtues regulate the "incitement" by sympathy of the physician and surgeon to care for the patient, guided by commitments that make the physician and surgeon intellectually and morally trustworthy.

Percival completes the moral revolution against the entrepreneurial paradigm that Gregory began. Percival does so by adding to Gregory's account two new professional virtues that "adapt" sympathy to the care of the sick poor in the Infirmary and in the Infirmary's home services.

I.II. Government of Infirmary Patients in their Choice of Physician or Surgeon

As explained in Chap. 2, patients were admitted to the Infirmary on the recommendation of a subscriber or trustee, as was common for infirmaries in Britain at the time (Risse 1986). Physicians and surgeons on the "faculty" were not compensated and rotated clinical responsibility on a schedule, so that they could maintain their private practices. For the smooth running of the Infirmary and therefore for the clinical benefit of its patients, maintaining the schedule of rotations was essential. It still is. Recall from Chap. 2 Price's emphasis on the regulation of hospitals as essential to their being safe and effective (Price 1773, 220).

The timing of admission was a function of the patient's condition and approval of a subscriber or trustee. An individual might find himself or herself a patient when the patient's preferred physician or surgeon was not on rotation. To gain access to their favored clinician, patients might declare themselves well enough to leave, with the goal of returning when their favored clinician would be back in the rotation (Risse 1986; McCullough 1998).

Percival starts by noting that the "choice of a *physician*, or *surgeon*, cannot be allowed to hospital patients, consistently with the regular and established succession of medical attendance" (Percival 1803, 10). The polity of the hospital, committed to the well-being of its patients as its common weal or common good, does not admit unjustified interruption of its regulated environment. Here Percival follows Gregory: "The government of a physician over his patient should undoubtedly be great. But an absolute government very few patients will submit to" (Gregory 1772, [1772] 1998, 22). Occasional consultation by the patient's "favourite practitioner" should be allowed as "just and humane" (Percival 1803, 10). This sympathy-based practice will help to put a patient's mind at ease, setting an ethically justified limit on being *in* authority over patients. In addition, this practice will prevent a "deceitful plea" to be discharged (Percival 1803, 10). Percival emphasizes in his the moral writings analyzed in Chap. 2 that lying warps moral character. Finally, self-discharge "may be the occasion of irreparable loss of time in the treatment of diseases" (Percival 1803, 7), which can result in preventable, unnecessary clinical harm to the patient who seeks to self-discharge. Competent clinical care rules this out as ethically unacceptable.

Note Percival's argument that lying damages moral formation. Baconian moral judgments about character and behavior have intellectual and moral authority for any individual about whom such judgments are made. Baconian moral judgments by a physician about a patient therefore have intellectual moral authority for the patient. As a consequence, the patient as a matter of intellectual and moral integrity, should accept physician-imposed constraints on his or her autonomy. This is all the more the case for the exercise of positive, autonomy-based rights that are intrinsically limited.

From the perspective of Percival's professional ethics in medicine in this section, we can critically appraise the anti-paternalism of bioethics. Anti-paternalism makes two related assumptions. (1) The moral judgments of physicians about patients have no intellectual or moral authority for the patient, indeed for anyone, including the physician. This view was part and parcel of the general rejection of authority in the United States in 1960s, because all claims to authority were suspect. Physicians were considered moral predators because their claim to be *an* authority was rejected. (2) Interference with autonomy is ethically impermissible because all external constraints infringe on Millian liberty and only external restraints based on the harm principle are ethically permissible. The first assumption rejects the first commitment of the ethical concept of medicine as a profession, because it is impossible to become trustworthy on the basis of scientific and clinical competence. Percival would have us, correctly, reject the first assumption. This means that anti-paternalism comes down to the second assumption (McCullough 2011). Thus does respect for patient autonomy, in a fell swoop, become the lexically ordered first principle of medical ethics.

I.III. "Attention to the Feelings and Emotions of the Patients"

Percival urges the view that attention to the "symptoms of their diseases" is but one component of the care of patients. Sympathy and its professional regulatory virtue of tenderness require attention to the feelings of patients. For example, some patients may exhibit "extreme timidity with respect to venæsection" and this "contraindicates" its use in some cases (Percival 1803, 11). Physicians and surgeons should become aware of the "prejudices of the sick" but not condemn them, to prevent the patient from simply falling silent about them, which will not prevent them preying upon the patient psychologically: "they will operate secretly and forcibly on the mind, creating fear, anxiety, and watchfulness" (Percival 1803, 11). For 'watchfulness' read 'distrust'. Such psychological turmoil increases the risk of a poor outcome, which the first commitment of the ethical concept of medicine as a profession rules out as unacceptable.

Gregory emphasizes taking seriously patients with "nervous ailments" (Gregory 1772, [1772] 1998, 23). Their psychological disturbances are real and need to be addressed. Percival's concern is more clinically comprehensive: the psychological dimensions of illness generally and the need to identify and address them clinically. Percival thus anticipated George Engel's biopsychosocial concept of health and disease, discussed in Chap. 2. From Engel's (1977) perspective, Percival should be read as warning against the clinical perils of biomedical reductionism: it increases the risk of poor outcomes.

I.IV. Discussions about Patients

Then, as now, discussion about the patient's clinical condition, its diagnosis, and its clinical management, occurred. Disagreements would not have been uncommon, perhaps more so then than now, given competing theories of disease and the consequent lack of a stable clinical nomenclature. Medical students were also often present, because Manchester Infirmary was also a teaching hospital. Students need to be taught, including correction of their errors of clinical reasoning and judgment. Percival's point is that "misapprehension" is sure to result. He makes the psychologically reliable clinical observation that "misapprehension may magnify real evils, or create imagery ones" (Percival 1803, 11). It follows from I.III. that the physician has a sympathy-based ethical obligation to prevent this psychological morbidity, both in itself and as a potential confounder of clinical management. Percival states what follows from this ethical analysis: no such discussions are to occur with anyone, "either with the house surgeon, the pupils of the hospitals, or any medical visitor" (Percival 1803, 11). Such discussions must occur where the unacceptable psychological risk to the patient is prevented. Today, this takes the form of discussing cases unreservedly in conference rooms or outside the patient's room with the door shut and voices lowered. Percival would approve.

I.V. Confidentiality

The architecture of infirmaries was open, with large wards. This allowed for ventilation and also efficient use of limited personnel to observe many patients at once. Open architectural spaces also make maintenance of confidentiality – access to information about patients by persons without authorized access – a considerable challenge, perhaps at times an impossibility. Percival calls for an strong ethical obligation: "*Secrecy*, also, when required by peculiar circumstances, should be strictly observed" (Percival 1803, 11). 'Peculiar circumstances' refers to clinical conditions, the careless revelation to others of which is reliably predicted to be harmful to the patient.

Secrecy regarding female patients is even more important. Gregory underscores to the risks of violating confidentiality with respect for female patients:

> Secrecy is particularly requisite where women are concerned. Independent of the peculiar tenderness with which a woman's character should be treated, there are certain circumstances of health, which, though in no respect connected with her reputation, every woman, from the natural delicacy of her sex, is anxious to conceal; and, in some cases, the concealment of these circumstances may be of consequence to her health, her interest, and to her happiness (Gregory 1772, [1772] 1998, 26–27).

For 'peculiar' read 'special' or 'distinctive'. Percival follows Gregory on this topic. He also adds that to "neglect or sport" with the "feelings" of female patients is "cruelty" (Percival 1803, 11). Gregory also condemns sporting with patients. To sport with another human being, or animal (as in fox hunting), is to cause physical and/or psychological harm with no offsetting clinical benefit to that individual and therefore only from self-interest. Doing so is antithetical to sympathy and its professional regulatory virtue of tenderness. Acting with cruelty is a vice that damages moral formation, Percival adds. Physicians and surgeons should form the moral character of students as a bulwark against such cruelty: "Let these considerations be forcibly and repeatedly urged on the hospital pupils" (Percival 1803, 11).

I.VI. "Moral and Religious Influence of Sickness"

Percival continues his emphasis on the psychosocial aspects of illness by emphasizing that these dimensions of illness are "so favourable to the best interests of men and of society, that is justly regarded as an important object in the establishment of every hospital" (Percival 1803, 11–12). Clergy should therefore become involved in patient care, but with a constraint: "the sacred offices will be performed with propriety, discrimination, and greater certainty of success" (Percival 1803, 12). Recall from Chap. 2 that Baconian Dissenters were deists and that they held religious beliefs to standards of evidence in nature and scripture. Percival is bringing this view on the proper relationship between religion and science to characterize professional ethics of spiritual care in the clinical setting.

Gregory had taken the view that clergy whose views and practices were not consistent with Baconian moral science should not be permitted to participate in patient care:

> Neither is it proper that he [the physician] should withdraw when a clergyman is called to assist the patient in his spiritual concerns. On the contrary, it is decent and fit that they should mutually understand one another and act together. The conversation of a clergyman, of cheerful piety and good sense, in whom a sick man confides, may sometimes be of much more consequence in composing the anguish of his mind, and the agitation of his spirits, than any medicine; but a gloomy and indiscreet enthusiast may do great hurt; may terrify the patient, and contribute to shorten a life that might otherwise be saved (Gregory 1772, [1772] 1998, 36).

Percival takes a similar view in the limits he calls for physicians and surgeons to set on the clinical role of clergy:

> The character of a physician is usually remote either from superstition or enthusiasm: And the aid which he is now exhorted to give, will tend to their exclusion from the sick wards of the hospital, where their effects have often been known to be not only baneful, but even fatal (Percival 1803, 12).

We saw in I.II. that Baconian moral science makes the physician *an* authority about the moral formation of patients and puts them *in* limited authority over patients. We saw in I.V. that Baconian moral science makes medical educators *an* authority about the moral formation of "pupils" and puts medical educators *in* authority over learners. Here Percival continues with the standard claim of Baconian moral science to make its practitioners *an* authority about the moral formation of others: clergy purveying "superstition" (beliefs incompatible with evidence) and "enthusiasm" (beliefs that lack evidence) lack intellectual and moral authority with respect to the well-being of patients. To fulfill the sympathy-based ethical obligation to protect patients from the clinically harmful outcomes of superstition and enthusiasm, Baconian physicians and surgeons have the ethical obligation to exercise power as *in* authority, by excluding anti-religious – now authoritatively understood in Baconian terms Percival learned at Warrington Academy – clergy from the Infirmary wards. Percival's Justinian "easy and simple path" turns out to be deceptively simple in this and in many other sections of *Medical Ethics*.

I.VII. Advising a Patient who is Seriously Ill to Complete a Last Will and Testament

For those who died *in testate*, or without a will, the complexities of English inheritance law could leave a man's wife and children destitute. Sympathy and its professional regulatory virtue of tenderness create an ethical obligation to prevent such harmful consequences. These are not only financial but clinical in that destitution can result in malnutrition and disease or even starvation and death. For patients who are seriously ill, "on the bed of sickness and death" (Percival 1803, 12), someone should alert them to the need to execute a last will and testament, especially if the patient will leave an estate, however modest.

Gregory was clear that the physician has an ethical obligation to inform gravely ill patients about their condition: "To a man of a compassionate and feeling heart, this is one of the most disagreeable duties in the profession: but it is indispensible. The manner of doing it, requires equal prudence and humanity" (Gregory 1772, [1772] 1998, 35). Fulfilling this ethical obligation remains challenging to this day. Out of self-protection, a physician might prefer someone else to be the bearer of bad news. This may explain Percival's proposal for who should be this messenger:

> This kind office will be best performed by the house surgeon, whose frequent attendance on the sick diminishes their reserve, and entitles him to their familiar confidence. And he will doubtless regard the performance of it as a duty. For whatever is right to be done, and cannot by another be so well done, has the full source of moral and personal obligation (Percival 1803, 12–13).

Another who cannot give bad news as well is, of course, the physician. But the physician could learn to fulfill this ethical obligation "well" and come to see doing so as a "duty." It is therefore fair to criticize Percival for letting his brethren – and himself – off the hook without sufficient justification.

I.VIII. Professionally Responsible Hospital-Resource Management

3.4 Medical Ethics, or a Code of Institutes and Precepts, Adapted to the Professional... 179

The formulary, which included medications and spirit beverages, was a major cost center in infirmaries (Risse 1986; McCullough 1998). The Manchester Infirmary would not have been an exception, making cost control important for the hospital managers and for the trustees. Percival makes a case for the use of expensive wines and drugs, limited to "diseases of extraordinary malignity and danger" (Percival 1803, 13). Percival advances two lines of argument, both of which are designed, as I read them, to be used verbatim by physicians and surgeons dealing with managers understandably pre-occupied by cost.

Percival first makes a cost-savings argument: in evidence-based clinical judgment, a single dose of an expensive drug may be more effective than multiple doses of a less expensive version that is not clinically as potent and the multiple doses of the cheaper drug will have a higher cumulative cost, even though their unit-cost of lower than that of the single-dose drug. This is a cost-savings argument and appeals only to economic rationality. This is a line of reasoning that every manager and trustee would understand and therefore have to accept. Percival here takes his cue from Hoffmann's politic physician: the cost-savings argument very effectively aligns the physician's or surgeon's ethical obligation with the legitimate organizational interest in responsible cost control. In such circumstance, there is no intrinsic conflict between ethical obligations to patients and the legitimate economic interests of the hospital. Put more generally, Percival here rejects the view that economic considerations and professional ethics in medicine are necessarily at odds with each other.

Percival's second line of argument applies when there is no cost-saving to be achieved but there is some probability to prevent the patient's death. Cost-saving in this limited clinical circumstance is ethically obligatory for the hospital to assume as a charity directed to the well-being of its patients.

> If the case, however, were far from otherwise, no œconomy, of a fatal tendency, ought to be admitted into institutions, founded on principles of the purest beneficence, and which, in this age and country, when well conducted, can never want contributions adequate to their liberal support (Percival 1803, 13–14).

Here Percival uses 'beneficence' as an ethical principle that creates the *prima facie* ethical obligation of the physician or surgeon to provide clinical management that in deliberative clinical judgment is predicted to result in net clinical benefit (McCullough, Coverdale, and Chervenak 2020). 'Purest beneficence' means that there should be no admixture of economics and professional ethics in medicine when a patient's death can be prevented.

Risse (1986) points out that patients with a high risk of mortality were not admitted into infirmaries, to keep their mortality rates low so that the infirmary and its subscribers and trustees would gain a social reputation for successful medical care. This is an echo of the appeal to reputation in the Hippocratic *Oath*, as explained in Chap. 1. Manchester Infirmary did not admit patients who were gravely ill or who had infections that could increase the mortality risk for other inpatient. At Manchester Infirmary Percival reports that for the decade ending in June 1802, the morality rate was about 5% (Percival 1803, 135), consistent with that Risse reports (Risse 1986).

The Dispensary home service provided care for this high-risk population at home, as part of its charitable mission to care for the sick poor. Percival reports the ten-year mortality for the same period for this service as 8%. These outcomes data are important because the economic impact of Percival's appeal to "purest beneficence" for Infirmary in-patients who became gravely ill was probably small enough to be manageable economically by the hospital's managers. The limitation of this, the first text on professionally responsible hospital-resource management, to "disease of extraordinary malignity and danger" (Percival 1803, 13) has major implications that only become clear in this context.

This section speaks directly to the trustees and managers. As noted above, power had shifted to them after the dispute between the Whites, the Halls, and their physician allies, on the one hand, and the newcomers such as Ferriar, on the other. In this Section Percival implicitly accepts that power but puts ethically justified limits on it, so that the power of the trustees and managers is guided by "purest beneficence," which sympathy requires in clinical cases in which the risk of death is high and preventable but at a high cost to the formulary. Percival wants to prevent an intrinsic risk of managerial power and the power of the purse: the managers and trustees generating new individual self-interest or new party-interest in the Infirmary, a development that would be antithetical to its mission to serve the common weal. Percival, as a good Baconian moral scientist, assumes that he has the intellectual tools to undertake the moral instruction of the managers and trustees in leadership ethics, just as the undertakes the moral instruction of physicians, surgeons, and apothecaries and, as we have seen just above and will see later when he considers lock hospitals for prostitutes, the moral instruction of patients. The comprehensive scope of Baconian moral science in medicine is on full display in *Medical Ethics*.

By undertaking the moral instruction of the managers and trustees, Percival establishes the autonomy of physicians and surgeons from managerial control in cases in which it is necessary to prevent an "œconomy, of a fatal tendency" (Percival 1803, 13). In less serious cases, by implication, physicians and surgeons should be willing to accept managerial control. Percival's claim of ethically justified autonomy, limited to clinically serious, high-risk-of-mortality, cases, is therefore a claim of limited professional autonomy. This has important implications for Chapter IV of *Medical Ethics*, especially Percival's account of the medical jurisprudence of abortion. This also stands in contrast with the approach proposed by James Gregory (1753–1821), John Gregory's son. He proposed in 1800 that hospital managers should see to it that the resources required by physicians to fulfill their ethical obligations to their patients be made routinely available, a more sweeping claim of autonomy from organizational leaders and managers than that proposed by Percival. There is no textual evidence that Percival was aware of James Gregory's book (Gregory 1800; McCullough 2009, 412).

I.IX–X. Public Charges by a Physician or Surgeon against another Physician or Surgeon

As we saw above in the account of how Percival came to write *Medical Jurisprudence*, disputes among physicians could and did spill into the public arena.

One such public arena was called "flyting," the printing and distribution of broadside and pamphlets, sometimes authored anonymously, used to attack the reputation of another physician or surgeon (Baker 1993a, b; Pickstone 1993; Baker and McCullough 2009a). This practice constituted a straightforward violation of the Hippocratic *Oath*. This practice also violated the guild rules of the Royal College of Physicians of London, its *Statuta Moralia*:

> No colleague will accuse by name another either of ignorance, malpractice, wickedness, or an ignominious crime; nor heap public abuse … (Clark 1964, Vol. I, 414).

Percival in Section IX has a similar provision but with an important addition: "except under the restriction contained in the succeeding article" (Percival 1803, 14). Here is the restriction:

> No *professional charge* should be made by a physician or surgeon, either publicly or privately, against any associate, without previously laying the complaint before the gentlemen of the faculty belonging to the institution, that they may judge concerning the reasonableness of its grounds, and the measures to be adopted (Percival 1803, 14).

Charges against another physician or surgeon should be considered "*professional*," i.e., a matter to be governed by professional ethics in medicine. The first commitment of the ethical concept of medicine as a profession comes to bear: charges should be evidence-based and then subject to peer-review for their evidence base. If there is an evidence base, sanctions should be considered by the medical faculty. This is professional self-regulation for the benefit of patients, not self-interested self-regulation. Charges lacking an evidence base harm not only the physician or surgeon against whom they are also lodged but patients, by promoting the same "misapprehension" that discussion of cases within earshot or sight of patients promotes. (See I.IV., above.) Sympathy and its professional regulatory virtue of tenderness prohibit creating this risk for patients. Charges with an evidence base should lead to improvement, a topic to which Percival turns in I.XIII. (See below). It turns out that Dr. Baker understated the difference between the guild rules in *Statuta Moralia* and the ethically justified "institutes" or rules in *Medical Jurisprudence* in his letter to Percival about the comparison of the latter to the former (Percival 1807, Vol. I, clxxxvi–clxxxvii). So does Percival in his Preface to *Medical Ethics*. Perhaps Percival's choice to dedicate his new text to Dr. Baker was politic.

I.XI. The Boundary Between Medicine and Surgery.

This is among the shortest sections in Chapter I:

> A proper *discrimination* being established in all hospitals between the *medical* and *chirurgical* cases, it should be faithfully adhered to by the physicians and surgeons, on the admission of patients (Percival 1803, 14).

Percival may be taking Gregory's account of the boundary between physic and surgery, examined above, as the basis for the requisite "*discrimination*." The boundary is defined by the fund of knowledge and, especially, the manual skill set of the "operator" that differs from that of the physician. Percival will return to the relationship between medicine and surgery in the next section, in Section XXIII, and also at the end of Chapter II where he addresses the professional responsibility to retire from practice.

I.XII. "Trials" in the Hospital to Improve Medical and Surgical Clinical Management

The commitment to improvement, as we saw in Chap. 1, helped to define the English enlightenment. Percival takes the view that creating "new *remedies* and *new methods of chirurgical treatment*" (Percival 1803, 15) should be undertaken in the hospital. Doing so will advance the "public good," a defining component of "hospital polity." Doing so will also advance the clinical care of the sick poor, "who, being the most numerous class of society, are the greatest beneficiaries up the healing art" (Percival 1803, 15). This is perhaps the earliest expression of the ethical justification of clinical research on medically indigent subjects in public hospitals. Manchester Infirmary was already a teaching hospital for medical "pupils." Percival now proposes that it become a research hospital, not for the benefit of the well-to-do but for the benefit of its target population, thus contributing to the "public good."

Percival rejects an undisciplined approach to clinical research:

> But in the accomplishment of this salutary purpose, the gentlemen of the faculty should be scrupulously and conscientiously governed by sound reason, just analogy, or well-authenticated facts. And no such trials should be instituted, without a previous consultation of the physicians or surgeons, according to the nature of the case (Percival 1803, 15).

The appeal to "reason, just analogy, or well-authenticated facts" is transparently Baconian, as we should by now expect of Percival. This appeal permeates his "experimental" and "medical" essays, as we saw in Chap. 2. This appeal also draws on Aikin's account of "experimentation" (Aikin 1771, 76–79). 'Just analogy' means the disciplined exercise of genius, as this capacity is explained in Chap. 1. There should also be what we now call prospective review and that Percival calls "previous consultation." As we saw in Chap. 1, Gregory had proposed a professional ethics of clinical research based on the prohibition against "sporting" with the sick poor and a Humean version of the Golden Rule (RCSE C36 1771, 9). Percival is no mere revolutionary. He expands the boundaries of his revolution in both clinical and research ethics when he turns to creating what can be called his professional ethics of cooperation and accountability in an organizational culture of professionalism in the Manchester Infirmary – and every other hospital.

I.XIII–XVIII. Percival's Professional Ethics of Cooperation and Accountability in an Organizational Culture of Professionalism

The concept of organizational culture is a cluster concept, a concept with multiple, related components. Some may apply in some circumstances; some in others. These components include the express mission and values of the organization, its actual values as expressed in budgets and strategic decisions, what leadership encourages and rewards, what leadership discourages and punishes, what leadership tolerates, and what leadership tolerates that should not be tolerated (McCullough et al. 2020). Percival in these six sections can be read as expressing the value of professional cooperation as key to an organizational culture of professionalism.

In Section XIII Percival calls for "unreserved intercourse" to "advance professional improvement" (Percival 1803, 15). He wants there to be "free communication," i.e., free of individual self-interest and party-interest and the biases they generate. This is a revolutionary proposal, aimed at reforming the "interested" organizational culture that the Whites, Halls, and their physician allies had created into a disinterested, professional organizational culture. He starts with what is bound to catch the attention and then the commitment of the physician and surgeons to his reform: "whatever is extraordinary or interesting in the course of their hospital practice" (Percival 1803, 15). These cases are to be written up and deposited in a "register," which we now know as a registry or database. In effect, the register creates an evidence base that will become indispensable for the "unreserved intercourse" among the faculty and bring intellectual discipline and therefore intellectual authority to the sustained conversation that he envisions. This conversation will become essential for cultivating the intellectual virtue of authority.

In Section XIV he describes what information should be included in the register and how it should be organized so that it makes scientific and clinical sense and thus "advance[s] professional improvement." This section is a direct descendent of the work that Percival did on improving hospital bills of mortality and the gathering of public health data that were explored in Chap. 2. These scientific publications were well known and it is therefore reasonable to assume that his physician and surgeon readers, as well as the hospital managers and trustees, would make the connection. Percival was asking his colleagues to do something with which they would already have become familiar and adapt to a setting they knew well, the wards of the Infirmary. The scope of information to be included is very comprehensive and includes what we would call environment determinants of disease as well as social determinants such as "the influence of particular trade and manufacturers on health and life" (Percival 1803, 16).

Section XV takes up the task of analyzing hospital data and then using the results to establish evidence-based clinical policies. The first step is for each physician and surgeon to scrutinize the "comparative success" (Percival 1803, 16), or outcomes, of patients with similar conditions in their hospital-based and private practices. They should then undertake a "diligent investigation" (Percival 1803, 16). He directs his colleagues to a central task that will use this information: identifying who should be admitted to the hospital, which will be patients reliably predicted to have improved outcomes or "success" from admission. Percival cites his friend and reader of *Medical Jurisprudence*, John Aikin and his *Thoughts on Hospitals*, which Percival knew well and had commented on, as we saw in Chap. 2. Hospital admission should be used to help patients to obtain "speedy relief" and thereby fulfill "the intention of the charity to relieve as great a number as possible" (Percival 1803, 17).

This signals a potential change in emphasis from the standard practice of infirmaries to exclude from admission those with a high mortality risk, to promote the reputation of the hospital as worthy of its charitable support from those with the financial wherewithal to subscribe and the more considerable wherewithal to contribute the higher amount that qualified the donor to become a trustee. The goal has become the common weal or common good of the hospital, to use its limited resources to obtain good outcomes for the largest number of patients. Good reputation becomes the product of effective use of philanthropic resources not a goal unto itself. The reader should keep in mind that neither Aikin nor Percival is proposing to abandon the most seriously ill to their own devices. The Manchester Infirmary was a complex charity, with a program of home care for these patients. Admitting contagious patients, Aikin and Percival are presuming, would not reduce their risk of mortality and only increase the risk of mortality for less seriously ill patients. For "institutions, founded on our principles of the purest beneficence" (Percival 1803, 13), this policy was ethically permissible.

"Principles of purest beneficence" define the concept of "whole medical polity of the hospital" (Percival 1803, 18), which Percival introduces in Section XVI. Indiscriminate admission would undermine this ethical justified polity, because it would be based on sympathy for an individual patient rather than sympathy for all of the patients in the hospital.

Section XVI makes reference to Notes and Illustrations III, which Percival addresses the "SITUATION, CONSTRUCTION, AND GOVERNMENT OF HOSPITALS" (Percival 1803, 140–147). Percival complements these sections on the role of physicians and surgeons in the government of a hospital by taking seriously Price's admonition: "… with respect to Hospitals in general, *as now constructed and regulated*, I cannot help fearing that they cause more distempers than they cure, and destroy more lives than they save" (Price 1773, 220). Percival's approach throughout Note III emphasizes the mission of a hospital, to provide safe and effective clinical care of his patients. To this end, a hospital should be sited in a place that minimizes health risks to patients, unlike the Manchester Infirmary:

> The hospital at Manchester is three-fourths of the year involved in smoke, by being erected on the eastern side of the town; an evil which might easily have been avoided, by the choice of an opposite site (Percival 1803, 142).

The "structure and accommodation" (Percival 1803, 142) should promote ventilation, to ensure "adequate supplies of fresh air" (Percival 1803, 142) that has enough flow to prevent infection but not so much that it activates "prejudices against a flow of cool air" (Percival 1803, 144) on the part of patients. He invokes the professional virtues of tenderness and authority to justify this matter of "structure and accommodation:"

> These prejudices, if they are to be deemed such, claim not only tenderness, but indulgence. For, though silenced by authority, as I have before observed [Section III], they will operate secretly and forcibly on the mind, creating fear, anxiety, and watchfulness (Percival 1803, 144).

Sympathy and its professional regulatory virtue of tenderness make these outcomes ethically impermissible. Increasing the risk of their occurrence is the exercise of authority untempered by tenderness, which is not permissible. Note the use of 'watchfulness', to indicate suspicion and consequent distrust.

3.4 Medical Ethics, or a Code of Institutes and Precepts, Adapted to the Professional...

The section on government of the hospital comes next and is addressed to the managers and trustees, just as Section VIII was. Percival had served on committees at the Manchester Infirmary and in the town and therefore had first-hand experience of their role in creating and sustaining cooperation (Baker and McCullough 2009a). The ethics of cooperation should be understood as Percival's antidote to individual self-interest and party-interest, which, had they been left unchallenged at Manchester Infirmary in the late 1780s and early 1790s, might have destroyed the Infirmary as a charity directed to the common weal. The trustees should elect "nine gentlemen of talents, respectability, and independence, to give dignity and authority to their proceedings," (Percival 1803, 144), with 'gentlemen' understood as explained earlier. This group should be known as the "COUNCIL of the Infirmary" (Percival 1803, 144). Terms should be limited to three years. Physicians and surgeons should not be eligible to serve in this capacity. Here Percival implicitly acknowledges the power structure (Granshaw 1993) that had emerged at Manchester Infirmary after the dispute described above. Percival's proposed council would have the power to prevent the private differences among clinicians that became embarrassing public differences. "The Council should be a board of arbitration, for adjusting whatever differences or disputes may arise between the several members of the Infirmary" (Percival 1803, 145). This should be read as complementary to the ethics of cooperation that Percival has set out in these sections, one goal of which is to prevent and thereby minimize such "differences and disputes." The council becomes the backstop, to prevent differences and disputes from becoming disabling as they had at Manchester Infirmary under the Whites, the Halls, and their physician allies. The physicians and surgeons should have a formal advisory role:

> The physicians and surgeons of the Infirmary should be requested to form themselves into a committee, to aid the council with their experience, knowledge, and advice; and to take into consideration whatever laws or regulations may be proposed, relative to their peculiar departments, before they be referred to the decision of the general body of the trustees (Percival 1803, 146).

Here Percival appears to invoke the limited professional autonomy implicit in Section VIII. This clinical committee should "take into consideration" whether new "laws and regulations" (Percival 1803, 146) proposed by the managers and trustees would result in an "œconomy of fatal tendency" (Percival 1803, 13) or what he would call a "false œconomy." In effect, Percival provides for the organizational culture of professionalism that he has proposed the physicians and surgeons to create now to become the responsibility of the trustees. This is shared professional responsibility by the clinicians and the organizational leaders for the intellectual and moral integrity of an infirmary's organizational culture of professionalism. Percival's proposals for the administrative structure and function of a hospital go far beyond Aikin's *Thoughts on Hospitals* (Aikin 1771). Percival thus proposes what has become a familiar structure in American hospitals, a Board of Trustees as the governing body, advised by and consulting with the Medical Executive Committee and in which refusal to adopt policies proposed by the latter puts a steep burden of proof on the former. This is a little known and underappreciated legacy of *Medical Ethics*.

In Section XVII Percival next adds accountability to his account of an organizational culture of professionalism. A committee of clinicians should be established to promote the data collection and analysis for which has just called. Over time, this committee will be able to bring consistent scientific and clinical discipline with proposed improvements "reduced to a definite and consistent form" (Percival 1803, 19). I read this to be anticipating continuous quality enhancement by almost two centuries. Percival is a student of human nature. Over time, the committee will identify the clinically superior physicians and surgeons by appealing, not to reputation or self-regard or self-promotion, but evidence. Those who are less capable will be exposed and this risks the excitement of "jealousy" (Percival 1803, 19). Percival points out that, as a result of the rigorous process that he proposes and its gradual and then sustained effect on organizational culture, those inclined to jealousy will find themselves alone.

Percival in Section XVIII returns to the "professional conduct of physicians and surgeons," by pointing out that the sustained "intercourse," data collection and analysis, and accountability that should define a professional hospital polity will promote consultations of physicians with surgeons.

> The harmonious intercourse which has been recommended to the gentlemen of the faculty, will naturally produce *frequent consultations*, viz. of the physicians on medical cases, of the surgeons on chirurgical cases, and of both united in cases of a compound nature, which, falling under the department of each, may admit all elucidation by the reciprocal aid of the two professions (Percival 1803, 19).

Gregory, we saw earlier, had lamented the fraught boundary between physic and surgery. In Section XI Percival had called for a "proper *discrimination* being established in all hospitals between the *medical* and *chirurgical* cases" (Percival 1803, 14). In Section XVIII Percival this "proper discrimination" does *not* mean that the way for the two disciplines to maintain the boundary between them is to retreat each into its separate camp and hermetically seal itself off from the other. Percival would regard that siloed approach as anathema. Instead, via "frequent consultations" they should cooperate to improve the care of patients with medical problems, with surgical problems, and with problems of a "compound nature."

I.XIX–XXII and Section XXIV. A Guidebook to Clinical Consultations

Having encouraged consultations and accountability, Percival turns to the practical task of prescribing a process for consultations. In the context of the previous six section and Note III, Percival's goal is to prevent disputes, because these impede patient care. In Dr. Baker's letter to Percival about *Medical Jurisprudence*, considered above, Baker references *De Conversatione Morali, Statutis Pænalibus*, a chapter in *Statuta Moralia Collegii Regalis Medicorum Londinensium* (Royal College of Physicians of London 1771). This text also describes a process for consultations but preserves the hierarchy of senior physician over junior. The latter may speak first but this order can be abandoned at the discretion of the senior physician. Percival calls for discussion in ascending order of priority, the goal of which is to oblige the senior physician or surgeon to listen to others participating in the consultation, as a means to professional improvement and thereby improving patient care. The senior physician retains the discretion to alter the treatment plan "as future contingences may require, or a further insight into the nature of the disorder may shew to be expedient" (Percival 1803, 20). Participants should be concise, an important clinical skill. Participation should be limited to those directly involved or others but only with "the unanimous consent of the gentlemen present" (Percival 1803, 21). No consultation should occur without "due notice" (Percival 1803, 20).

Section XXII closes with a proviso about the need for examination of the patient before the consultation convenes:

> If an examination of the patient be previously necessary, the particular circumstances of danger or difficulty should be carefully concealed from him, and every just precaution used to guard him from anxiety or alarm (Percival 1803, 21).

This proviso relates to the proviso in Section IV about not having discussion of cases with awareness of the patient. Sympathy and tenderness create the ethical obligation not to risk psychological harm from an examination, the results of which may or may not alter treatment planning.

Section XXIV addresses the intersection of consultations and the obligation of religious worship of clinicians. Consultations should not be held on Sundays, "except in cases of urgent necessity" (Percival 1803, 22). Here Percival proposes to manage what is known as a conflict of commitment: an incompatibility between professional ethical obligations in patient care and personal ethical obligations of the physician or surgeon to others than patients. This differs from conflict of interest: an incompatibility of professional ethical obligations in patient care and the self-interests of the physician or surgeon. Ethical obligations constrain judgment and behavior for the benefit of others; self-interests do not. Conflicts of commitment are therefore more ethically demanding than conflicts of interest. The bar for making personal obligations secondary to professional obligations therefore should be set high. Percival does so: in a medical or surgical emergency, by definition, treatment cannot safely be delayed. All three commitments of the ethical concept of medicine as a profession require timely and effective responses to medical and surgical emergencies, without exception. Percival does not explain his proposed policy. Its origin is in his view that religion is accountable to the truth of things. Baconian medicine is about the truth of things in the clinical and research settings, This has the clear implication that the life of the patient takes priority. Note that Percival took the same position in Section VIII regarding expensive medical treatment necessary to prevent imminent death.

I.XXIII and XXV. Surgical Operations

In Section XXIII requires that "[n]o important operation" occur without consultation among the physicians and surgeons and "the acquiescence of a majority of them" (Percival 1803, 21). This becomes another aspect of his proposed organizational culture of accountability of physicians to surgeons and of surgeons to physicians, in the limited case of an "important" operation. The use of 'important' suggests high-risk surgery that may also have educational value. The latter is supported by inviting "two surgeons of the town" to attend "[a]s a hospital is the best school of practical surgery" (Percival 1803, 22). Section XXV calls for scheduling operations in advance, so that those who will observe can plan to do so.

At the turn of the nineteenth century general anesthesia was in the future of surgery. Patients therefore were conscious although analgesia was used, which may have altered cognitive function. Surgeons were prized for their speed, so any disruption, including from the patient, increased the risk of poor outcomes. Recall also from Chap. 1 Hume's description of the sounds and smells (from cautery, for example) of surgery and how they can incite terror in a patient. Percival knew his Hume and this is perhaps the source Percival's concern about the clinically adverse effects of noise: "A decorous silence ought to be observed" (Percival 1803, 21).

Sympathy and its virtue of tenderness require that the patient's experience of surgery be addressed and Percival does so. A physician or surgeon should communicate truthfully with the patient when the procedure is going well:

> It may be humane and salutary, however, for one of the attending physicians or surgeons to speak occasionally to the patient; to comfort him under his sufferings; and to give him assurance, if consistent with truth, that the operation goes on well, and promises a speedy and successful termination (Percival 1803, 21–22).

The physician or surgeon's steadiness will further re-assure the patient. If such assurance cannot be truthfully given, "decorous silence," perhaps, becomes steady silence in support of the patient. This sheds light on an implicit assumption that may be present in Section IV about discussions in front of patients and the misapprehension they may promote. Silence, Percival appears to hold, does not create this risk.

Percival's sympathy-based concern about the sounds and sights of surgery applies to patients waiting for their procedures and to how surgeons should be attired as they move from one surgery to the next:

> When several operations are to take place in succession, one patient should not have his mind agitated by the knowledge of the sufferings of another. The surgeon should change his apron, when besmeared; and the table or instruments should be freed from all marks of blood, and every thing that may excite terror (Percival 1803, 22–23).

Recall that, like Gregory, Percival addresses what he takes to be the ethical problem list in hospital practice. He includes auditory and visual sources of "terror" for this reason, reminding his reader of the broad scope of sympathy-based ethical obligations in the care of Infirmary patients.

I.XXVI–XXXI. Clinical Practice in other Organizational Settings

The final six sections of Chapter I provide guidance to the behavior of physicians and surgeons in the other clinical programs of the complex charity conducted by the subscribers and trustees of Manchester Infirmary: dispensaries or home healthcare, "an ASYLUM for FEMALE PATIENTS labouring under SYPHILIS" (Percival 1803, 24) or lock hospitals, and "ASYLUMS for INSANITY" (Percival 1803, 26) or lunatic hospitals (Granshaw 1993) – 'lunatic' in its ancient meaning of being too much under the influence of the moon and thus mentally disturbed to some or even a great degree.

In Section XXVI Percival follows the implications of the sections that have come before: The ethical obligations of "gentlemen of the faculty" in dispensaries are essentially the same as those they have in hospital care. However, physicians will be seeing some patients in their homes, which are the homes of the poor. In terms of architecture, ventilation, food, and many other respects the social distance from the Infirmary to these homes is considerable. The psychosocial challenges will also be more acute.

> But greater *authority* and greater *condescension* will be sound requisite in domestic attendance on the poor. And human nature must be intimately studied, to acquire that full ascendancy over the prejudices, the caprices, and the passions of the sick, and of their relatives, which is essential to medical success (Percival 1803, 24).

Percival reflects the broad scope of clinical management, to include challenging unfounded health beliefs, as described by Andrew Wear:

> In the eighteenth century, there was added to simple charity, a sense that the poor needed to be educated, to be enlightened out of their 'ignorance' and 'superstitions' in matters of health (Wear 1993, 1296).

Addressing the "medical ignorance" (Wear 1993, 1296) of the sick poor required condescension, to bridge the socioeconomic gap between practitioner and patient. Here we detect again the influence of Grove that direct engagement with the sick poor where they live will require more condescension, closer to that of the divine than to the human. As the social gap between physician and patient narrows by the self-conscious condescension of the physician, the risk of abuse of the physician's power diminishes. Condescension creates a restraint on the physician's power over patients in the Infirmary and in their homes as part of the home-care program of the Dispensary. The professional regulatory virtue of condescension becomes an antidote to initial social distance, and with it, the power differential between physician and patient. The potential to abuse that social power is thereby responsibly managed.

The homes of the sick poor will have none of the structural and administrative advantages for the exercise of authority that exist in the regimented environment of the hospital. Physicians will therefore have to be even more attentive to the psychosocial dimensions of health and disease, including the beliefs of patients that lack an evidence base, the precise meaning of 'prejudice' in the discourse of Baconian medicine and moral science. Failure to recognize and address such beliefs and behavior based on them will doom plans of care to failure. Grove provides the needed guidance. The condescending physician "… instructs with patience, and reproves with gentleness" (Grove 1749, 536).

In Note IV, cited in Section XVI, Percival addresses patients "ill of contagious fevers" (Percival 1803, 147). He proposes seven "REGULATIONS FOR THE ADMISSION OF PATIENTS INTO THE HOUSE OF RECOVERY" and fifteen "INTERNAL REGULATIONS FOR THE HOUSE OF RECOVERY" (Percival 1803, 147–152). Most concern the structure and government of the house of recovery. One regulation in the first set of regulations continues the theme of "government" of patients.

> III. The physicians shall be requested to form the necessary regulations, for the domestic government of families of home patients, afflicted with fever (Percival 1803, 148).

This government is directed to the recovery of the patient, a process under the direction of the physician but the control of the patient and his or her family. This remains true for out-patient clinical management.

The moral instruction of patients is part of home care aiming at "medical success" (Percival 1803, 23). This is all the more the case for lock hospitals. Percival understands prostitution of women as, in part, a function of moral failings, but never a loss of intrinsic worth. This moral reality should, however, not lead to blame and dismissal. Here the reader should recall the same point made by Percival about the catastrophic moral error of slavery of denying equal, intrinsic moral worth, that we examined in Chap. 2.

> Yet whoever reflects on the variety of diseases to which the human body is incident, will find, that a considerable part of them are derived from immoderate passions, and vicious indulgences. Sloth, intemperance, and irregular desires, are the great sources of those evils, which contract the duration, and imbitter the enjoyment, of life. But humanity, whilst the bewails the vices of mankind, incites us to alleviate the miseries which flow from them. And it may be proved that a LOCK HOSPITAL is an institution founded on the most benevolent principles, consonant to sound policy, and favourable to reformation and to virtue (Percival 1803, 24).

The regimented environment of a hospital supports the ethical obligation to care for these women that sympathy in natural response to their plight generates.

Presentist inclinations must be avoided in response to what might seem condescending (in the twenty-first-century meaning). As a Baconian moral scientist, Percival is justified in making intellectually and morally authoritative claims about the formation, and deformation, of moral character. He also views deformed character as a contagion. Percival refers to the female patients of a lock hospital in a way that might trouble the twenty-first-century reader: "Over such objects pity sheds the generous tear; austerity softens into forgiveness; and benevolence expands at the united pleas of frailty, penitence, and wretchedness" (Percival 1803, 25). The "generous tear," "forgiveness," and expanded "benevolence" are the products of correctly functioning sympathy for these patients and strongly motivate the physician to help them.

Here Percival cites "two Reports, intended to promote the establishment of a Lock Hospital in Manchester, I 1774" (Percival 1803, 25). He included these in his *Essays Medical, Philosophical, and Experimental*, which are described in Chap. 2. The first of these, we saw in Chap. 2, makes a direct appeal to sympathy and I repeat it here:

> But humanity, whilst she mourns over the vices of mankind, incites us to alleviate the miseries which flow from them. The private hand of charity is never shut, when sickness, complicated with poverty, presents itself; and hospitals are established, in every part of the kingdom, for the reception of the wretched, whether innocent or guilty. A new institution,

founded on these benevolent principles, and favourable to the interests of virtue, now claims the attention, and encouragement of the public ... (Percival 1807, Vol. IV, 204).

Percival goes on in Section XVII to instruct his readers – all of whom would have been men – that "extraordinary" self-discipline will be required. Students should not be expected to be capable of such self-discipline and should therefore not be allowed into a lock hospital: "The strictest decorum should be observed in the conduct towards the female patients; no young pupils should be admitted into the house ..." (Percival 1803, 26). Strict decorum is required to maintain a professional relationship with the female patient that is asexual. Students do not have the requisite experience and self-control to accomplish this task.

In Sections XXVIII and XXIX Percival points out an epidemiological fact about mental illness: wealth does not confer immunity from mental illness and its biopsychosocial demands on families. He then points out clinical realities: the needs of patients with mental illness can outstrip the ability of families to meet those needs and mental illness has a systemic effect on "rational and moral character" (Percival 1803, 26). Mental illness also presents myriad scientific and clinical challenges to physicians.

Hospitals play a major role in addressing these challenges, because they permit close and longitudinal study of patients and how they respond to treatment. To support the improvement of mental health care, Percival, no surprise, calls for the creation and study of "registers" adapted to the distinctive clinical circumstances of lunacy. Such data may have helped "on a late melancholy occasion ... felt by the whole kingdom" (Percival 1803, 28), the mental illness of King George III (1765–1810) (Peters 2011), in the management of which Dr. Baker participated. Percival identifies the professional regulatory virtues of sympathy that should guide the physician investigating mental illness:

> Certain cases of *mania* seem to require a *boldness of practice*, which a young physician of sensibility may feel a reluctance to adopt. On such occasions he must not yield to timidity, but fortify his mind by the councils of his more experienced brethren of the faculty. Yet, with this aid, it is more consonant to probity to err on the side of caution than of temerity (Percival 1803, 29).

In Section XXI Percival cites Note V, "CAUTION AND TEMERITY IN PRACTICE" (Percival 1803, 152–154). Temerity is a professional virtue related to steadiness: providing clinical care to the mentally ill, about whose condition, Percival notes, so little is known, will require going beyond the bounds of current experience, but carefully. Aikin adds another dimension, the risk to one's reputation of failed experiments (Aikin 1771, 81).

As we saw in Chap. 1, Gregory cautioned against desperate measures in such clinical circumstances:

> Desperate remedies should be used in some cases, where every other method has been provided ineffectual. In such circumstances we should have recourse to medicines which under more favourable circumstances might be thought dangerous (RCPE, Gregory J, 1766, 13).

The use of potentially dangerous remedies should be measured, attentive always to the lack of efficacy and manifestation of serious risk. The physician should have good reason for a clinical experiment, guided by the ethical constraints Percival sets out in Section XII, where he presents his professional ethics of clinical research. At the same time, the physician should have the fortitude to venture beyond Baconian experience, but always disciplined by careful observation and unbiased analysis of outcomes. This disciplined willingness to venture into the clinically unknown Percival calls boldness. Undisciplined venturing into the clinically unknown Percival would have classified as the vice of recklessness. He quotes Bacon that "boldness should never be blind" (Percival 1803, 153) but guided by past experience, recorded in the hospital registers, as the basis for "just analogy" or hypothesis formation. Basing new remedies on "theoretical dogmas, or on pride which disclaims authority" (Percival 1803, 153) is impermissible boldness, or recklessness. Temerity can become an unwillingness to be bold, an outcome of "once burned, twice shy." Boldness disciplined by steadiness, especially in response to initial or even repeated failure, is the "caution" that Percival recommends.

Percival closes Chapter I with a brief consideration of other kinds of healthcare organizations:

> Hospitals for the small-pox, for inoculation, for cancers, &c. &c. are established in different places; but require no professional duties, which are not included under, or deducible from, the precepts already delivered (Percival 1803, 29).

3.4.6 The Text of Medical Ethics: Chapter II: Of Professional Conduct in Private, or General Practice

II.I. Ethical Framework for Institutes and Precepts: Baconian Moral Scientific Professional Ethics in Private Practice, Adopted from Hospital Practice

> I. THE *moral rules of conduct*, prescribed towards hospital patients, should be fully adopted in private or general practice. Every case, committed to the charge of a physician or surgeon, should be treated with attention, steadiness, and humanity: Reasonable indulgence should be granted to the mental imbecility and caprices of the sick: Secrecy, and delicacy when required by peculiar circumstances, should be strictly observed. And the familiar and confidential intercourse, to which the faculty are admitted in their professional visits, should be used with discretion, and with the most scrupulous regard to fidelity and honour (Percival 1803, 30).

Percival continues in the style of "Institutes" by referring back to Chapter I, Section I, in which he sets out his Baconian moral scientific professional ethics in hospital practice. This, we saw above, is based on the principle of sympathy from Hume, two professional regulatory virtues that Gregory invents, tenderness and steadiness, and two new professional regulatory virtues for hospital practice that Percival invents, condescension and authority. Condescension creates the ethical obligation to put bridge the socioeconomic and cultural gap between a physician or surgeon, from the (sometimes comfortable) middle class, and the patient, a member of the social class of deserving sick poor. The "deserving" sick poor were willing to work, even if for poverty wages. In the Manchester Infirmary physicians and surgeons had power, granted to them by the trustees and managers, over the sick, a power that was expressed in and reinforced by the hierarchical structure of the hospital. Authority creates the ethical obligation of physicians to use this power competently, on the basis of Baconian science. Combined with tenderness and steadiness, authority creates the ethical obligation to use this power for the clinical benefit of each patient and thereby the common weal of the hospital. Power should never be used for individual self-interest or party-interest.

The professional regulatory virtue of authority secures the first commitment of the ethical concept of medicine as a profession, to become and remain scientifically and clinically competent. The professional regulatory virtue of condescension focuses the physician on the clinical needs of the patient, blunting self-interest. Tenderness and steadiness make meeting these needs the physician's or surgeon's priority. Condescension, tenderness, and steadiness secure the second and third commitments of the ethical concept of medicine as a profession, to make the protection and promotion of the patient's health-related interests the primary concern and motivation (incitement in Baconian moral scientific discourse), keeping individual self-interest (the second commitment) and party-interest (the third commitment) systematically secondary.

The private practice of medicine occurred in the homes of those who could afford to pay the physician's or surgeon's fees. The well-to-do also came from a higher socioeconomic class than physicians or surgeons, except those, like Percival, with inherited wealth and those who were very successful economically, like the surgeon families of the Whites. The well-to-do often would consider purchasing the services of several practitioners, in their presence, thus incentivizing competition for market share and thus "exciting" self-interest of individual practitioners and party-interests of physicians against surgeons and vice versa. The well-to-do also paid the piper and therefore called the tune. And they sometimes did not pay the piper, about which practitioners could do little, given the power imbalance. Gregory had complained about this; Percival does too, in his own way.

This setting of unequal power and incentives to become subservient was ripe for the deployment the cautions of the *de Cautelis* literature and of the enlightened self-interest of the politic physician. Percival, we shall see, eschews the discourses of *de Cautelis* and *medicus politicus* in favor of the discourse of the professional ethics in medicine that he sets out in Chapter I. Does he do so completely?, is a question that will be taken up below, in analysis of pertinent sections of Chapter II.

If a physician were dismissed from service to a household, the immediate financial consequences might not be trivial. If word got around, reputation might be injured, followed by dismissal from other households. There was none of the economic security that has existed in the United States and other high-income countries since the end of World War II. Loss of market share could be economically calamitous. Obstetricians used forceps to assist delivery, a technology that can become death-dealing for the fetus in the birth canal. Some obstetrician induced "still-birth," having first dismissed household staff and other attendants from the pregnant woman's bedchamber, to prevent the dire reputational and socioeconomic consequences of a bastard child. Some man-midwives, as obstetricians were then known, would respond with threats of blackmail should their services no longer be required (McCullough 1998).

In the setting of a physician or surgeon providing services to someone who was wealthier, condescension is not applicable. It thus does not appear in the list of virtues that Percival sets out: "attention, steadiness, and humanity" (Percival 1803, 30). Gregory, recall, had held that the "government" of the patient by the physician should be "great," but, as a student of human nature, Gregory knew that government of the patient could not be "absolute" (Gregory 1772 [1772] 1998, 22–23).

> A prudent physician should, therefore, prescribe such laws, as, though not the best, are yet the best that will be observed; of different evils he should chuse the least, and, at no rate, lose the confidence of his patient, so as to be deceived by him as to his true situation. This indulgence, however, which I am pleading for, must be managed with judgment and discretion; as it is very necessary that a physician should support a proper dignity and authority with his patients, for their sakes as well as his own (Gregory 1772, [1772] 1998, 23).

Percival follows suit, calling for "indulgence" in response to patients' characteristics that might impede the exercise of authority in the form of recommendations or suggestions to patients. The "peculiar" circumstances in which "secrecy, and delicacy" (Percival 1803, 30) are obligatory may refer to the blackmail of female patients. Percival's readers may have recognized that Percival's language mirrors Gregory's:

> Secrecy is particularly requisite where women are concerned. Independent of the peculiar tenderness with which a woman's character should be treated, there are certain circumstances of health, which, though in no respect connected with her reputation, every woman, from the natural delicacy of her sex, is anxious to conceal; and, in some cases, the concealment of these circumstances may be of consequence to her health, her interest, and to her happiness (Gregory 1772, [1772] 1998, 26–27).

Gregory in this passage refers, albeit obliquely, to the practice of blackmail described just above (McCullough 1998), suggesting that Percival does, as well. The professional ethics of medicine that Percival described in Chapter I, as he makes abundantly clear, depends on "familiar and confidential discourse" as an necessary condition and a jointly sufficient condition (with others such as the use of registers and the faculty committee to review important cases).

Percival in Chapter I had invented an organizational culture of professionalism for Manchester Infirmary – and any other hospital that wanted to adopt it – complete with its structural components. These would not be available in the setting of private practice. Notwithstanding, by proposing to "adopt" the "moral rules of conduct" (Percival 1803, 30) from Chapter I, Percival aims to invent an organizational culture of professionalism for private medical and surgical practice, in revolution against the self-interested organizational culture of entrepreneurial medicine. We turn now to his account of how he carried out this "adoption."

II.II. Temperance

It was common for physicians to be offered a "cordial" or spirit beverage in the homes of patients. Repeated acceptance during the course of home visits would result in inebriation. The resulting altered mental status would be completely incompatible with the first commitment of the ethical concept of medicine as a profession. Both cognitive skills of diagnosis and treatment planning and the manual skills of surgery would become impaired. The resulting risks to the "well being, and even to the life, of a fellow-creature" (Percival 1803, 31) is not acceptable. Percival refers to Note VI, in which he quotes from Gregory, Tacitus, and Gisborne in support (Percival 1803, 154–156). It is striking that temperance is the first item of the problem list in the ethics of private practice that Gregory addresses. Temperance is essential for sustaining the first commitment of the ethical concept of medicine as a profession.

II.III. Gloomy Prognostications

In contemporary medical and surgical discourse, especially the latter, "gloomy prognostications" (Percival 1803, 31) are known as "crepe hanging." This is the misleading practice of exaggerating the challenges of a procedure that a surgeon has performed many times and safely, as a hedge against a poor outcome ("recall that I informed you about the risk") and to encourage gratitude for a procedure the challenges of which were well in hand form beginning to end. The patient is misled, not to protect the patient from bad news, but in the self-interest of the surgeon in reducing professional liability, on the one hand, and increasing the ranks of grateful patients who will sing the surgeon's praises and thus, perhaps, result in additional referrals (McCullough et al. 1998).

Percival is well aware of the distinction between self-serving "gloomy prognostications" and being honest with patients about their condition and its clinical management. The latter disclosure is ethically obligatory to ensure "timely notice of danger" (Percival 1803, 31), always to "the friends of the patient …, and even to the patient himself, if absolutely necessary" (Percival 1803, 31). His approach is very close to Gregory's:

> In this and other similar cases, it may be proper for a physician, in the most prudent and gentle manner, to give a hint to the patient of his real danger, and even solicit him to set about his necessary duty. But, in every case, it behooves a physician never to conceal the real situation of the patient from the relations. Indeed justice demands this; as it gives them an opportunity of calling for further assistance, if they should think it necessary (Gregory 1772, [1772] 1998, 34–35).

Percival describes the fulfillment of the ethical obligation to provide bad news to the patient's friends and, especially, to the patient as "peculiarly alarming" and therefore "assigned to any other person of sufficient judgment and delicacy" (Percival 1803, 31). Gregory describes this obligation:

> To a man of a compassionate and feeling heart, this is one of the most disagreeable duties in the profession: but it is indispensible. The manner of doing it, requires equal prudence and humanity (Gregory 1772, [1772] 1998, 35).

This is not medical paternalism, which is the interference with the patient's autonomy based on the clinical judgment that disclosure of information, especially bad news, risks harm to the patient (Beauchamp and Childress 2019, 230–231). Like Gregory, Percival is concerned with the affective effects on the physician.

Percival identifies a further ethical obligation of the physician to patients in the end-stage of a life-taking disease or injury:

> For the physician should be the minister of hope and comfort to the sick; that by such cordials to the drooping spirit, he may smooth the bed of death; revive expiring life; and counteract the depressing influence of those maladies, which rob the philosopher of fortitude, and the Christian of consolation (Percival 1803, 31–32).

Gregory also uses "smooth:" "It is as much the business of a physician to alleviate pain, and to smooth the avenues of death, when unavoidable, as to cure diseases" (Gregory 1772, [1772] 1998, 35). The "avenues of death" were smoothed with the liberal use of laudanum, a liquid form of opium that numbs pain and can make a patient indifferent to pain and, in large doses, suppresses respiratory drive sufficient to cause death.

Percival refers the reader to a "long note" (Percival 1803, 167), Note VII: "A PHYSICIAN SHOULD BE THE MINISTER OF HOPE AND COMFORT TO THE SICK" (Percival 1803, 156). He starts with a long passage from Gisborne's *Enquiry into the Duties of Men* (Gisborne 1794), the key claim of which is this: "But truth and conscience forbid the physician to cheer him by giving promises, or raising expectations, which are known, or intended to be, delusive" (Percival 1803, 158). This includes being honest about uncertainties. To convey a "positive falsehood" when "misled by mistaken tenderness" (Percival 1803, 158) is impermissible. Percival then takes the reader through a concise history on the topic from the ancient world to Francis Hutcheson (1694–1746).

Percival responds, especially to Gisborne, with an argument that applies "in cases of real emergency" (Percival 1803, 166). By this he means cases, which "seldom occur" (Percival 1803, 166), such as: "… the father of a numerous family, or one whose life is of the highest importance to the community, who makes enquiries which, if faithfully answered, might prove fatal to him" (Percival 1803, 166). The patient in such rare cases "has the strongest claim, from the trust reposed in his physician, as well as from common principles of humanity, to be guarded against whatever would be detrimental to him" (Percival 1803, 166). Sympathy and its professional regulatory virtue of tenderness create the ethical obligation to respect this claim.

Recall, from the text of II.III that Percival describes being honest with gravely ill patients as "alarming." In arguing for respect for the claim of patients in the rare circumstances he describes, Percival is emphatic about the affective effects of respecting this claim: the physician or surgeon "will therefore generously relinquish every consideration, referable only to himself" (Percival 1803, 166).

Percival's view came to be known as the "therapeutic privilege" (Beauchamp and Childress 2019, 126–127). Beauchamp and Childress concisely state the main line of reasoning that Percival advances: "Attempts to justify the therapeutic privilege are beneficence- and nonmaleficence-based because non-disclosure is aimed at the patient's good and at preventing harm from occurring" (Beauchamp and Childress 2019, 126). Percival adds a crucial necessary condition: non-disclosure can never be used as a matter of self-protection for the physician or surgeon. In his now-classic study of communicating bad news to patients, David Oken (1961) found in his qualitative study that the most common reason for not telling patients a cancer diagnosis (at a time when mortality rates were very high, given the very limited effectiveness of treatment) was precisely self-protection. In this context, Percival's justification for rare invocation of therapeutic privilege was prescient.

In his *Discourse on Truth and Faithfulness*, examined in Chap. 2, Percival departs from the definition of lying as knowingly representing as true that which is false:

> I presume you will concur with me in opinion, that MORAL TRUTH is the *conformity of our expressions to our thoughts*; and FAITHFULNESS, *that of our actions to our expressions*: And that LYING or FALSEHOOD *is generally a mean, selfish, or malevolent, and unjustifiable, endeavor to deceive another, by signifying or asserting that to be truth or fact, which is known or believed to be otherwise; and by making promises, without any intention to perform them* (Percival 1807, Vol. II, 4).

In the rare cases in which Percival exempts the physician from the "alarming" duty to be honest, the physician does not engage in behavior that is "mean, selfish, or malevolent." Percival explicitly excludes justification based on self-interest. This behavior is meant to "smooth the bed of death" (Percival 1803, 32) psychologically and not solely by means of analgesia, sedation, and death. Thus does the physician show tender regard for the well-being of the patient, at the farthest remove from malevolence.

Over the past two decades or so a strong consensus has emerged that the risk to harm to patients from conveying bad news that concerned Percival is more a function of how patients are informed rather than whether they are informed. There are now step-wise process for conveying bad news (Baile et al. 2000). These are being used in medical education (Lenzi et al. 2005).

II.IV–XIV. Inventing Rules for Cooperation for "the Good of the Patient" (Percival 1803, 37)

The changing of the guard, with the support of the trustees of Manchester Infirmary and their full confidence in Percival, created an unprecedented opportunity for him to complement Gregory's professional ethics in medicine with new concepts, to invent a professional ethics of hospital practice. The ethics of cooperation became an essential component of this new organizational culture of professionalism. Percival could invent new rules with a level of confidence that the trustees would implement them and oblige the physicians and surgeons of the Infirmary to cooperate.

Percival gives no indication in any of his writings that he was a naïf. He must have been fully aware of the formidable challenge of inventing rules for cooperation in the private-practice setting. He was taking on a paradigm of entrepreneurialism, described in Chap. 1, in which physicians, surgeons, and apothecaries regarded each other as competitors in an unforgiving, small market in which practitioners had only the power of persuasion and, if they were willing to use it, blackmail. Failure had calamitous reputational, personal, and economic consequences.

Notwithstanding, Percival set to work and invented rules in these sections for cooperation in private practice. This cooperation was not based on party-interest, e.g., cooperating in setting fees with the hope that a competitor would not undercut one. Instead, Percival deploys his Baconian moral scientific professional ethics in medicine: "as the good of the patient is the sole object in view" (Percival 1803, 37).

II. IV. "Officious Interference"

'Officious' in "officious interference" for Percival means a self-interested assertion of authority and power over another practitioner. Such a practitioner is a "professional busy-body" (Percival 1803, 32), a very strong phrase for the usually circumspect Percival. It is not quite as strong as the language that we saw him, in Chap. 2, use to condemn the practice of enslaving persons. To use the discourse of his Table of Contents, "Proper conduct respecting interference in cases under the charge of another" (Percival 1803, xii) should replace officious interference. Proper conduct aims to respect and preserve "the trust reposed in the physician or surgeon employed" (Percival 1803, 32) by the patient. Self-interested interference, especially when motivated by self-aggrandizement, is antithetical to the obligations of sympathy and the commitment to experience-based patient care. To preserve this trust, differences between physicians should be based on "experience and practical knowledge, not on speculative or theoretical differences of opinion" (Percival 1803, 33). Here Percival expresses the discipline and consequent reliability of what is now known as evidence-based reasoning as the basis for an ethics of cooperation. Sometimes a physician is incompetent, i.e., "When artful ignorance grossly imposes on credulity; when neglect puts to hazard an important life; or rashness threatens it with still more imminent danger" (Percival 1803, 33). In such cases interference becomes an ethical obligation and therefore far from the nosiness of the busy-body.

II.V. Succeeding a Physician or Surgeon in Attending a Patient

Section V addresses the situation in which a patient calls for a physician after having already been attended by another practitioner. Here Percival appeals to what Gregory called the intellectual virtue of candor: to be open to new evidence from whatever source it comes, especially from a competitor (Gregory 1772, [1772] 1998, 28–29). If a Baconian critical appraisal supports the previous plan of care, it should be endorsed by the new physician. If such a plan of care has not met with success, this outcome should become the point of departure for new treatment planning. In Note VIII, Percival notes that (Michel de) Montaigne (1553–1592) "treats, with great humor, of physic and physicians; and makes it a charge against them, that they perpetually direct variations in each others prescriptions" (Percival 1803, 168). Experience-based reasoning about the clinical judgment and practice of the preceding attending physician and in one's own clinical judgment becomes the antidote to this ridicule.

II.VI. The Boundary between Medicine and Surgery

Section VI calls for the boundary between medicine and surgery to be "steadily maintained" (Percival 1803, 34), reinforcing the same point in Chap. 1, Section XI. Here he refers to the "two professions" (Percival 1803, 34), perhaps referring to the actual state of affairs that he aims to reform, for the benefit of patients:

> Experience has fully evinced the benefits of the discrimination recommended, which is established in every well regulated hospital, and is thus expressly authorized by the faculty themselves, and by those who have the best opportunities of judging of the proper application of the healing heart. No physician or surgeon, therefore, should adopt more than one denomination, or assume any rank or privilege is different from those of his order (Percival 1803, 34).

Section VII calls for consultations to be "promoted, in difficult or protracted cases, as they give rise to confidence, energy, and more enlarged views in practice" (Percival 1803, 34–35). The intellectual virtue of candor should guide such consultations. This can result in diagnoses or treatment plans that had not yet been identified but are supported in experience-based clinical judgment, or "more enlarged views in practice" (Percival 1803, 34–35). Questioning the patient should be initiated by the senior physician, with younger physicians following.

II.VIII. "Special Consultations"

Section VIII concerns the need for "special consultations" (Percival 1803, 35), i.e., when the patient has objected to continued attendance by a physician. His successor "should pay only two or three visits; and sedulously guard against all future unsolicited interference" (Percival 1803, 35). This can be a delicate clinical situation, to be managed by meeting the patient's needs, on what may be longer visits than normal. The goal appears to be to avoid "officious interference" with the previous physician from that physician's perspective. Compensation should be adequate: "For this consultation a double gratuity may reasonably be expected from the patient, as it will be found to require an extraordinary portion both of time and attention" (Percival 1803, 35). This was long before the era of "usual and customary fees" and also in an era in which physicians and surgeons were not always successful in collecting their fees. Percival makes the case for the legitimate self-interest of the physician: the extra time such visits will require, to get up to speed and identify, recommend, and initiate a treatment plan.

Section VIII also addresses the still-common situation in which a physician is summoned "through the anxiety of the family, or solicitation of friends to visit a patient, who is under the regular direction of another physician, to whom notice of this call has not been given" (Percival 1803, 36). The physician should see the patient and identify a treatment plan but then should make no changes without consultation with the patient's regular physician, unless it is too late in the day to do so, in a so clinically urgent case that delay in initiating the treatment plan would be clinically dangerous.

II.IX. Theoretical Discussions

"Theoretical discussions" (Percival 1803, 36) concern discussions of hypotheses that might explain the patient's condition or discussions of treatments for novel conditions based on analogy to known conditions and their clinical management. Recall that in Chapter I, Section IV Percival admonishes his reader not to have any discussions within earshot or eyesight of hospital patients, lest unnecessary "apprehension" (Percival 1803, 11) be provoked. In Section IX Percival wants to prevent causing "perplexity" among consultants and consumption of time with no consequent clinical benefit for patients. In Note IX Percival extends this prohibition to "any reasonings on the nature of the case, and of the remedies prescribed, either with the patient or his friends" (Percival 1803, 169). He then tells a moral tale, perhaps to leaven – but also reinforce – his admonition:

> It is said by my lamented friend Mr. Seward, in his entertaining anecdotes, that the late Lord Mansfield [jurist 1705–1793] gave this advice to a military gentleman, who was appointed governor of one of our islands in the West-Indies, and now expressed his apprehensions of not being able to discharge his duties as chancellor of his province. "When you decide, never give reasons for your decision. You will in general decide well; yet may give very bad reasons for your judgment" (Percival 1803, 169).

Percival here refers to William Seward's book of anecdotes (Seward 1798).

II.X. Rules for Hospital Consultations Apply

In Section X Percival aims to "remove all grounds of dispute amongst medical gentlemen" (Percival 36). A gentleman, we now know, is a man who has formed his moral character on the basis of the virtues of sympathy. It is incompatible for such an individual to act primarily from individual self-interest or party-interest. The rules for hospital consultation that Percival sets out in Chapter I are designed to remove individual self-interest and party-interest to a systematically secondary status, as required by the second and third commitments of the ethical concept of medicine as a profession. The rules of hospital consultation therefore apply in private practice and he refers his reader to Sections XIX, XX, and XXI in Chapter I. He makes one adaptation, the definition of seniority, for the order in which practitioners should speak in consultations:

> And the *seniority* of a physician may be determined by the period of his public and acknowledged practice as a physician, and that of a surgeon by the period of his practice as a surgeon, in the place where each resides. This arrangement, being clear and obvious, is adapted to remove all grounds of dispute amongst medical gentlemen: And it secures the regular continuance of the order of precedency, established in every town, which might otherwise be liable to troublesome interruptions by new settlers, perhaps not long stationary (Percival 1803, 36–37).

II.XI Regular Academical Education

Section XI addresses consultations with practitioners without a "regular academic education" (Percival 1803, 370. Gregory had taken up this topic and writes:

> As a doctor's degree can never confer sense, the title alone can never command regard; neither should the want of it deprive any man of the esteem and deference due to real merit. If a surgeon or apothecary has had the education, and acquired the knowledge of a physician, he is a physician to all intents and purposes, whether he has a degree or not, and ought to be respected and treated accordingly (Gregory 1772, [1772] 1998, 49–50).

Percival shares Gregory's warranted skepticism about degrees, at a time when one could purchase a medical degree and when medical students were not able or willing to pay the hefty additional fees some universities charged for the degree itself (McCullough 1998). Like all aspects of patient care, consultation should be guided by a single ethical imperative, whether the practitioner meets the standards of Baconian, experience-based medicine, i.e., has made the first commitment of the ethical concept of medicine as a profession:

> … as the good of the patient is the sole object in view, and is often dependent on the personal confidence, the aid of an intelligent practitioner ought to be received with candour and politeness, and his advice adopted, if agreeable to sound judgment and truth (Percival 1803, 37–38).

In Note X Percival relates Samuel Johnson's account of the life of Thomas Sydenham (1624–1689), author of a famous textbook on medicine that earned him the sobriquet, the English Hippocrates. Percival quotes Johnson "that Sydenham was made a physician by accident and necessity" (Percival 1803, 170). Sydenham had attended Oxford but did not obtain a degree. Percival's point is that a physician would be very unwise indeed to rule out consulting with the likes of Sydenham because that individual did not have what would then have been called an "ornament" of medical education, a degree.

II.XII. Punctuality

In Section XII Percival urges physicians and surgeons to be punctual when "the faculty … are to hold consultation together" (Percival 1803, 38). A respectful five-minute waiting period should be observed before proceeding. There then follow what are now familiar rules:

> No visits should be made but in concert, or by mutual agreement: No statements or discussion of the case should take place before the patient or his friends, except in the presence of each of the attending gentlemen of the faculty, and by common consent: And no *prognostications* should be delivered, which are not the result of previous deliberation and concurrence (Percival 1803, 38).

II.XIII Number of Visits to the Sick and Attendance on Gravely Ill Patients

Section XIII calls for physicians and surgeons to limit the number of visits to patients.

> *Visits* to the sick should not be *unseasonably repeated*; because, when too frequent, they tend to diminish the authority of the physician, to produce instability in his practice, and to give rise to such occasional indulgences, as are subversive of all medical regimen (Percival 1803, 38).

Percival also takes exception to the view of Sir William Temple that a physician may leave off the continued care of desperately ill patients "without any hope of deserving" the fees he might still collect (Percival 1803, 39). Following Gregory, Percival provides an argument for what physicians and surgeons should not abandon gravely ill patients:

> For the offices of a physician may continue to be highly useful to the patient, and comforting to the relatives around him, even in the last period of a fatal malady; by obviating despair, by alleviating pain, and by soothing mental anguish. To decline attendance, under such circumstances, would be sacrificing, to fanciful delicacy and mistaken liberality, that moral duty which is independent of, and far superior to, all pecuniary appreciation (Percival 1803, 39).

Recall that laudanum was used to alleviate pain and sooth mental anguish and was clinically effective with respect to these outcomes, even if it could shorten life by causing death. There is an implicit endorsement of physician-assisted suicide in the meaning of active euthanasia, introducing into the patient's body a life-taking pathology that was not previously present and then not disrupting the course of that pathology as it progresses to death.

II.XIV. Officiating for Another Physician or Surgeon

Section XIV takes up what a physician or surgeon should charge when he "officiates for another" (Percival 1803, 39), i.e., takes over the patients care "during any considerable length of time" (Percival 1803, 39). This "additional practice" (Percival 1803, 39) should be compensated in the usual amount. However, when covering for another physician or surgeon for a "short duration" (Percival 1803, 39), no fee should be charged. Percival here and above when he addresses fees in the context of a consultation is aiming to promote cooperation by proposing simple rules aimed at eliminating the potential for controversy and contention, which always risk unnecessary and therefore impermissible harm to the patient.

II.XV–XX., XXV. Fees and their Waiver
II.XV. An Agreed-Upon Fee Schedule

Section XV calls for physicians and surgeons to agree on a fee schedule for the very same reason. This fee schedule should take into account the "pecuniary acknowledgement of their patients" (Percival 1803, 40), i.e., their ability to pay based on their financial resources. Here Percival is responding to the unmanaged variation in fees and the collection of them, including "mean" fees paid by the "affluent" that are "both unjust and degrading" (Percival 1803, 40). It is crucial that physicians and surgeons keep their incomes in perspective. Remuneration should never be allowed to become a physician's or surgeon's primary concern and motivation, in violation of the second commitment of the ethical concept of medicine as a profession. It is especially important that young physicians, who are entering practice and need an income, to keep their moral priorities straight:

> To a young physician, it is of great importance to have clear and definite ideas of the ends of his profession; of the means for their attainment; and of the comparative value and dignity of each. Wealth, rank, and independence, with all the benefits resulting from them, are the ends which he holds in view; and they are intersecting, wise, and laudable. But knowledge, benevolence, and active virtue, the means to be adopted in their acquisition, are of still higher estimation. And he has the privilege and felicity of practicing an art, even more intrinsically excellent in its mediate than in its ultimate objects. The former, therefore, have a claim to uniform pre-eminence (Percival 1803, 40–41).

In Note XI Percival provides an historical perspective on fees, in the context of which he addresses what a physician or surgeon should do to collect fees from patients who do not pay but can afford to do so. When repeated, this problem can result in "accumulated claims from long-protracted and often expensive attendance" (Percival 1803, 179). Refusal to pay has no moral authority for the physician or surgeon when this failure results from "from prejudice, from captiousness, from parsimony, or from dishonesty" (Percival 1803, 179). In only such circumstances is it ethically justified to pursue recourse in court:

> Under such circumstances considerations of benevolence, humanity, and gratitude, are wholly set aside: For when disputes arise, they must be suspended or extinguished; and the question at issue, can alone be decided on the principles of *commutative justice* (Percival 1803, 179).

For a Baconian moral scientist of professional ethics medicine, the first of these two sentences is extraordinary. It is not hard to imagine the moral pain Percival might have experienced as he wrote it. The burden of proof to set aside the ethical obligations of sympathy is very, very steep indeed. The non-payment of fees must be chronic to the point of considerable adverse impact on the legitimate self-interest in being adequately compensated for one's services. The motives of the patient who does not pay must be inconsistent with moral formation and behavior based on sympathy and its regulatory virtues. In contemporary practice in the United States these strict burdens of proof have been eliminated by the levelling effect of contract law. Patients or third-party payers who do not pay per agreement to do so are in breach of contract *simpliciter*.

II.XVI. Gratuitous Care of Members of the Profession and their Families

Percival is concerned that when a physician or surgeon cares for a family member, his "solicitude" as a spouse or parent "obscures the judgement, and is accompanied with timidity and irresolution, [of] medical men, under the pressure of sickness, either as affecting themselves or their families" (Percival 1803, 41). This creates what we would now call a conflict of commitment, between the ethical obligations to a patient and the ethical obligations to a family member when a family member becomes a patient. Physicians and surgeons therefore are "peculiarly dependent upon each other" (Percival 1803, 41) to care for each other's family members. Visits should occur in response to an invitation. Physicians or surgeons who live at a distance should have their travel costs met by the physician or surgeon who requests them to attend to a family member.

II.XVII. Attention to the Physician or Surgeon who Invites Attendance on Family Members

The physician or surgeon who invites attendance on a family member has "dear and important interests … at stake," such that "the mind of a husband, a father, or a friend, may receive a deep and lasting wound, if the disease terminate fatally, from the adoption of means he could not approve, or the rejection of those he wished to be tried" (Percival 1803, 42). Sympathy will incite a powerful, tender response to a fellow practitioner.

Tenderness to a fellow practitioner and candor create the ethical obligation to listen to his suggestions, because, as a physician, he "will not lightly sacrifice his judgment; but will urge, with proper confidence, the measures he deems to be expedient" (Percival 1803, 42). While Percival does not use 'steadiness', he invokes the concept when he recommends that the requesting physician "leaves the final decision concerning them to his more responsible coadjutor" (Percival 1803, 42). This will require stoical self-discipline.

II.XVIII. Gratuitous Care of Clergy

Clergy's stipends, from the aristocrats who employed them or from the church, were modest. Housing was modest, as well. The reader will recall from Chap. 2, O'Brien's comment on the narrow building at Warrington Academy. Narrow buildings signaled modest socioeconomic status, perhaps even economically straitened circumstances. Clergy lived in narrow, often mean homes, which Percival refers to as *res angusta domi* or the "straitened condition of home." Making gratuitous care a general rule will have the result that "the feeling of individual obligation may be rendered less oppressive" (Percival 1803, 42). General rules about fees, also addressed in the previous section, become powerful tools to tamp down individual self-interest that could adversely affect patient care. This general rule has broader application: "Military or naval subaltern officers, in narrow circumstances, are also proper objects of professional liberality" (Percival 1803, 43). There is a justified exception, those clergy who can afford a physician's or surgeon's fee: "But such of the clergy as are qualified, either from there stipends or fortunes, to make a reasonable remuneration for medical attendance, are not more privileged than any other order of patients" (Percival 1803, 42–43).

II.XIX. Fees for Consultation by Letter

It was common for individuals to write to physicians, especially well-known physicians, to ask for medical advice (McCullough 1998). This practice anticipated practice-at-a-distance – telemedicine, computer-linked conferencing – by two centuries. Percival uses 'patient' in this context, because the patient has been presented to a physician or surgeon, but at a distance. These consultations take "more trouble and attention than a personal visit" (Percival 1803, 43). Percival states that it is reasonable to expect double one's usual fee for the practical reason that "this has long been the established practice of many respectable physicians" (Percival 1803, 43). Follow-up correspondence "may justly be regarded in the light of ordinary attendance, and may be compensated, as such, according to the circumstances of the case, or of the patient" (Percival 1803, 43).

II.XX. "Acts Due to the Public"

Physicians and surgeons can be asked to certify absence due to illness of patients that excuses "the absence of persons who hold situations of honour and trust in the army, the navy, or the civil departments of government" (Percival 1803, 43). This also applies to jury duty, constables, church-wardens and others. These certifications "should be considered as acts due to the public, and therefore not compensated by any gratuity" (Percival 1803, 43), because the physician has the ethical obligation to use his knowledge and skill for "the good of the community" (Percival 1803, 44). These certifications should without exception be based on the truth about the patient's condition. Becoming an "accessary, by untruths or prevarication, to the evasion of this duty, is at once a high misdemeanour against social order, and a breach of moral and professional honour" (Percival 1803, 44).

II.XXV. Gratuitous Care by Wealthy Physicians

A wealthy physician (note that Percival does not make reference to wealthy surgeons), i.e., a man with a "fortune" earned or inherited (as in Percival's own case), may elect not to charge other individuals with fortunes for his services. A central theme of the sections in Chapter II on fees is to establish practices that will discourage the pursuit of individual self-interest by undercutting competitors' fees. In addition, Percival appeals to the English idea of property: one should be paid what one has earned through one's labor. In Section XXV he takes a dim view of social solidarity among the wealthy, a class of which he himself had been a member for the previous fifty years:

> A wealthy physician should not give advice *gratis* to the affluent; because it is an injury to his professional brethren. The office of physician can never be supported but as a lucrative one; and it is defrauding, in some degree, the common funds for its support, when fees are dispensed with, which might justly be claimed (Percival 1803, 47).

II.XXI–XXII. Quack Medicines and Nostrums

Medicines and "nostrums" were prepared in the absence of any regulatory authority of government to certify their components, effectiveness, safety, and labeling, as does the U.S. Food and Drug Administration. Much of medical practice was empiric, in the sense that practitioners used medicines, botanicals, and elixirs to "cure" the sick where 'cure' meant any symptomatic relief but could not explain how or why the cure occurred. In the absence of effective licensing laws anyone could offer healing services.

Quacks were practitioners with no formal education. Johnson's *Dictionary* defines a quack as "a boastful pretender to arts which he does not understand" sometimes making public claims in support of his or her practices. More pejoratively, the *Dictionary* adds: "An artful tricking practitioner in physick" (Johnson 1755, 1614). Nostrums were medicines and other remedies prepared without any quality controls and in ignorance of the properties of their components, accompanied by claims to effectiveness without an "experience" or evidence base. A practitioner could prepare a nostrum, put his name on it, and perhaps make money from doing so, no small matter of self-interest given the modest incomes of most physicians and surgeons. Quack remedies and nostrums could be clinically dangerous, even fatal.

Gregory addresses the appeal of secret remedies:

> Experience shews, that men are naturally attached to whatever has an air of mystery and concealment. A vender of a quack medicine does not tell more lies about its extraordinary virtues, than many people do who have no interest in the matter; even men of sense and probity. A passion for what is new and marvellous, operates more or less on the imagination; and, in proportion as that is heated, the understanding is perplexed. When a nostrum is once divulged, its wonderful qualities immediately vanish, and in a few months it is generally forgotten. If it be really valuable, the faculty perhaps adopt it: but it never recovers its former reputation (Gregory 1772, [1772] 1998, 59–60).

Percival, as a Baconian physician committed to the well being of patients takes a stance against quack medicines in Section XXI: "The use of *quack medicines* should be discouraged by the faculty, as disgraceful to the profession, injurious to health, and often destructive even of life" (Percival 1803, 44). He explains the psychology of why patients may want to used such remedies in their self-physicking, for which there were self-care manuals, such as the very popular *Domestic Medicine* (Buchan 1769). Physicians should not express "displeasure" toward or abandon patients who uses quack medicines, especially when dealing with a patient with "a credulity that is insurmountable" (Percival 1803, 45). Medications whose contents are known should not be offered as quack medicine, because this would be deceptive.

In Section XXII Percival takes a stronger view on nostrums:

> No physician or surgeon should dispense a secret *nostrum*, whether it be his invention, or exclusive property. For if it be of real efficacy, the concealment of it is inconsistent with beneficence and professional liberality. And if mystery alone give it value and importance, such craft implies either disgraceful ignorance, or fraudulent avarice (Percival 1803, 45).

This is some of the strongest language that Percival uses in *Medical Ethics*. He plainly and forcefully rejects the entrepreneurial paradigm, in which dispensing nostrums would be supported. Note that he picks up Gregory's point about human psychology that the sick can be persuaded by an "air of mystery" about the "new and marvelous" (Gregory 1772, [1772] 1998, 59–60). Percival could have added that duping patients for one's own economic gain and perhaps in the process perhaps putting the patient's health or life at risk would be sporting with patients, which is impermissible in Baconian moral science. He may have been confident that his reader could draw this inference for himself.

II.XXIII. *Esprit du Corps*

In Section XXIII Percival takes up the topic of *Esprit du Corps*, the strong sense of fellow feeling that binds soldiers together in a common cause. They become brothers in arms, a fraternity. Fellow feeling among physicians is a component of being a profession but only when embracing fellow feeling serves to "to promote the honour and interest of the association, so far as they are consistent with morality, and the general good of mankind" (Percival 1803, 46). Percival rejects an understanding of the concept of '*esprit du corps*' as self-serving, a kind of party-interest. Only then will medicine be a profession with earned "respectability" that physicians and surgeons should protect from injury (Percival 1803, 46). He closes the section with details about this obligation. The physician or surgeon "should avoid all contumelious representations of the faculty at large; all general charges against their selfishness or improbity; and the indulgence of an affected or jocular scepticism, concerning he efficacy and utility of the healing art" (Percival 1803, 46). Read out of context this passage could be interpreted as an expression of party-interest of the sort that animates the *Statuta Moralia* of the Royal College of Physicians. Percival would respond that such a reading is ruled out by an *esprit du corps* that is "consistent with morality, and the general good of mankind" (Percival 1803, 46).

The concept of *esprit du corps* does not mean fellow feeling based on party-interest as in the guild entrepreneurial paradigm. An ethically justified *esprit du corps* means a sense of loyalty and cohesiveness around the common purpose of serving the "good of the patient" (Percival 1803, 37). *Esprit du corps*, properly understood, should be understood as shared sympathy-based fellow feeling for patients. Like the Scots whose fellow feeling created and sustained a nation independent of the state of the United Kingdom, the *esprit de corps* of physicians creates a profession, an analog of a nation, that is independent from the state. Percival is putting in place the concept that a profession of medicine, properly understood to be based on Baconian moral science, enjoys a degree of autonomy from the state. This becomes a central theme of Chapter IV, as we will see later.

II.XXIV. Managing Disputes

As we saw in the analysis of Percival's professional ethics in hospital practice, an ethics of cooperation is essential to professional ethics in medicine. The commitment to scientific and clinical competence requires cooperation to improve hospital practice. Percival takes advantage of the hospital structure to propose the creation and maintenance of a data base, the hospital register, and using the results of analyzing this data base, the outcomes of the deliberations of proposed committee of the gentlemen of the faculty. He then proposes that the trustees serve as adjutors of disputes that cannot be managed by this process of peer review and that should become progressively rarer. Prevention of "controversy, and even contention" (Percival 1803, 46) becomes an essential component of the ethics of cooperation.

Percival carries his revolution to a distinctive level when he proposes a parallel structure for private practice in Section XXIV: "arbitration of a sufficient number of physicians or of surgeons, according to the nature of the dispute; or to the two orders collectively, if belonging both to medicine and surgery" (Percival 1803, 46). Gregory had proposed accountability in the form of laying medicine open to review and improvement by scientifically sophisticated laypersons (McCullough 1998). Percival calls for self-regulation, a more realistic, practical proposal. To encourage this arbitration process, its proceedings and results should be kept private, as publicizing it "may be personally injurious to the individuals concerned, and can hardly fail to hurt the general credit of the faculty" (Percival 1803, 46). 'Credit' here means the reservoir of earned trust the self-regulation based on Baconian clinical science should create over time. The contemporary safety culture in medicine in many countries adopts a confidential approach for an additional reason: to encourage speaking up without fear of retaliation so that all of the pertinent clinical information is identified and taken into account in the sustained effort to reduce errors (doing the wrong thing clinically or doing the clinically right thing the wrong way).

II.XXVI–XXVII. Unavoidable, Unsolicited Involvement in a Case under the Supervision of Another Physician

Section XXVI proposes to manage the challenge of unsolicited involvement in a case under the supervision of another practitioner when such involvement cannot be avoided because advice is solicited by a patient or the patient's friends. The physician should fulfill his professional responsibility to provide competent advice but also the ethical obligation not to jeopardize the patient's well being by disrupting the plan of care by the patient's physician, which plan of care has not been critically assessed. Percival's proposal to set sail safely past the Scylla and Charybdis this situation creates is the following:

> Under such circumstances, his observations should be delivered with the most delicate propriety and reserve. He should not interfere in the curative plans pursued; and should even recommend a steady adherence to them, if they appear to merit approbation (Percival 1803, 47).

In section XXVII Percival takes up the related problem of a physician who is attending to a patient who resides in the country and who "may be desired to see a neighbouring patient, who is under the regular direction of another physician, in consequence of some sudden change or aggravation of symptoms" (Percival 1803, 47). The delay that will result in the physician of record being summoned could result in loss of health or life. Again, the good of the patient is the primary concern. Cooperation should be maintained with this commitment foremost in mind:

> The conduct to be pursued, on such an occasion, is to give advice adapted to present circumstances; to interfere no farther than is absolutely necessary with the general plan of treatment; to assume no future direction, unless it be expressly desired; and, in this case, to request an immediate consultation with the practitioner antecedently employed (Percival 1803, 47–48).

II.XXVII. Critical Self-Appraisal to Improve Patient Care

In the private practice setting no structured review of cases of the kind Percival elaborates in Chapter I is possible. Percival proposes a revolutionary idea: the physician should re-create the process of peer-review of "every interesting and important case, especially when it hath terminated fatally" (Percival 1803, 48). The physician should serve as his own peer-reviewer of each component of the process of care and the outcome in the same "calm reflection" (Percival 1803, 48) used by the hospital committee. This will require considerable intellectual discipline. I read Percival to have reached back to his Warrington Academy days and taken a page from the ancient Greek philosophers, especially Plato, about the perils of self-deception: "Let no self-deception be permitted in the retrospect; and if errors, either of omission or commission, are discovered, it behoves that they should be brought fairly and fully to the mental view" (Percival 1803, 48). The results should guide future practice. Percival here implicitly invokes the concept of a virtue: a habit that shapes character so that the ethically obligatory becomes routine and not a constant struggle with the distraction of individual self-interest. The intellectual virtue of authority, in the sense of being *an* authority, requires the habit of critical self-appraisal for the claim to be an authority to be justified and therefore trusted by patients. This habit becomes constitutive of the commitment to become and remain scientifically and clinically competent.

II.XXIX. Supporting Moral Formation of Patients

Percival in Chapter I had addressed "vicious conduct," i.e., habits based on vices, which should be understood as either the unconstrained indulgence of self-interest or, as in the practice of enslaving persons (see Chap. 2) or prostitution, deformations of character that have been imposed on one by the irresistible power of others. A Baconian moral scientist knows that sympathy remains intact, although badly damaged. Moral reformation is therefore a realistic goal.

When moral reformation will promote the patient's well-being, physicians and surgeons should undertake it. Doing so will also serve as an antidote to the self-interested negative reaction a physician may have to a patient, a not-unheard-of phenomenon in contemporary medicine with respect to patients who abuse alcohol and drugs or engage in other self-destructive behavior that has left their health badly damaged and driven off their social supports. Percival proposes a remedy: "And his councils, or even remonstrances, will give satisfaction, not disgust, if they be conducted with politeness; and evince a genuine love a virtue, accompanied by a sincere interest in the welfare of the person to whom they are addressed" (Percival 1803, 49).

II.XXX. Conflict of Commitment with Religion of the Physician

A conflict of commitment exists for a physician when fulfilling ethical obligations to a patient is not compatible with fulfilling ethical obligations to others than the patient. This includes religious obligations to God, including ritual observance of "the sabbath" (Percival 1803, 49). Note the lower-case 's' in 'sabbath', recognizing, perhaps, a pluralism of sabbaths. Percival had addressed this topic in Chapter I, where he took the view that this conflict of commitment should be managed in favor of religious obligations, with the exception of clinical emergencies that immediately threaten a patient's health or life. Here he expresses the constraint in similar terms: "The observance of the sabbath is a duty to which medical men are bound, so far as is compatible with the urgency of the cases under their charge" (Percival 1803, 49). Otherwise, visits can be scheduled so as not to interfere with religious worship. Inasmuch as this is an ethically justified plan for responsible management of the conflict of commitment, other physicians and surgeons should respect it. Practitioners "should not be induced to forgo this important privilege, by the expectation of a call from their physician or surgeon" (Percival 1803, 49–50).

In Note XII, "PUBLIC WORSHIP, SKEPTICISM, AND INFIDELITY" (Percival 1803, 179–199), Percival goes to considerable length to make the case for the compatibility of religious belief and being a Baconian physician. He points out that one peril of being a medical student is that the "taste for recreation" (Percival 1803, 180) may weaken one's resolve to attend church services. The habit of regular religious worship is the antidote. He points to the moral exemplars of Sir Thomas Browne (1605–1682) and John Locke (1632–1704), both physicians, as "examples of wise and conscientious Christians" (Percival 1803, 184). The "imputation of scepticism and infidelity" (Percival 1803, 185) against physicians is based on the assumption that the commitment of Baconian science requires the scientist and therefore the scientific physician to become an atheist. He cites Thomas Gisborne and, especially, Gregory on this topic.

In *Lectures* Gregory devotes more words to this topic than the many others he addressed. Percival, it turns out, does the same. Both therefore regard the imputation of atheism to be a serious topic for professional ethics in medicine. The imputation was often expressed as "*Ubi tres medici, duo athei*," or "Wherever there are three physicians there are two atheists." (Kocher 1947). The intellectual biography in Chap. 2 strongly supports the view that Percival would reject this imputation. He recruits Gregory's arguments to that effect.

Percival writes: "Though his [Gregory's] excellent lectures are, doubtless, in the hands of most physicians, yet I am tempted to make a transcript of them …" (Percival 1803, 189), which he proceeds to do. Gregory's argument is that Baconian deism, the view that there is a creator god, is not only compatible with Baconian science but required by it. Religion, Percival continues, promotes true associations, a concept he explained in his essay *Miscellaneous Observations on the Influence of Habit and Association* (Percival 1807, 71–111), examined in Chap. 2. These associations include "[t]enderness, humanity, sympathy, friendship, and domestic love" (Percival 1803, 196). Percival concisely summarizes the findings of this detailed analysis of the proper relationship between Baconian medicine and religion, expressed in the discourse of Dissent that he learned from Taylor and Seddon at Warrington Academy: "Rational theism leads the mind, by fair and necessary induction [from experience, as in his scientific essays examined in Chap. 2], to extend its views to revelation" (Percival 1803, 196). Rational theism for Percival becomes an evidence-based, spare deistic theism, the variant of Unitarianism to which he was committed.

II.XXXI–XXXII. "A Physician who is Advancing in Years" (Percival 1803, 50) and the Profession of Medicine as a Public Trust

Percival closes Chapter II with a topic with which he had direct experience, "[a] physician who is advancing in years" (Percival 1803, 50). His reader would have been well aware that he had resigned from the faculty of Manchester Infirmary, publicly, more than two decades earlier and had withdrawn from medical practice. Percival had also, recall, become blind. His son, Edward reports that his father had been experiencing debilitating headaches as he was completing work on *Medical Ethics* (Percival 1803, ccxvii). But there is nary a whisper from Percival about his personal condition. This is exemplary uncomplaining self-discipline that the stoic emperor and philosopher, Marcus Aurelius (121–180 CE), would have recognized and admired. It is reasonable to assume, in my judgment, that Percival took solace from the ancient intellectual and moral company in which he therefore found himself in his final years.

Section XXXI takes up the challenge for the physician, who, "yet unconscious of any decay in his faculties, may occasionally experience some change in the wonted confidence of his friends" (Percival 1803, 50). Patients may give a hint of their concern and "may now request that he will join in consultation, perhaps with a younger coadjutor" (Percival 1803, 50). Because the good of the patient comes first, the older physician should "admit this change without dissatisfaction or fastidiousness, regarding it as no mark of disrespect; but as the exercise of a just and reasonable privilege in those by whom he is employed" (Percival 1803, 50). There are considerable advantages to accepting the involvement of a younger colleague, especially in that it "may promote the successful management of a difficult and protracted case" (Percival 1803, 50). Both physicians should be guided by "candour" and for the older physician "impartiality" (Percival 1803, 50), i.e., not take the change and need for assistance personally, a requirement that will take considerable self-discipline. Percival then makes explicit the professional ethics of cooperation that will unite to the older and younger physician in their care of the former's patients: "co-operating, by [50] mutual concessions, in the benevolent discharge of professional duty" (Percival 1803, 50–51).

In Note XIII Percival cites Bacon's *Essay of Youth and Age* (Bacon 2010) to make the case that a team of older and younger businessmen draws on the traits of each to get a better result. The younger businessman will bring an inclination toward innovation and a general willingness to try new things. Tempered by experience, including the experience of failure, the older physician will bring caution that risks "mediocrity of success" (Percival 1803, 201). Bacon concludes:

> Certainly it is good to compound employments of both; for that will be good for the present, because the virtues of either age may correct the defects of both; and good for succession, that young men are learners, while men in age are actors (Percival 1803, 201).

Section XXXII takes up a challenge that every older physician or surgeon must confront unless death obviates the need:

> The commencement of that period senescence, when it becomes incumbent on a physician to decline the offices of his profession, it is not easy to ascertain; And the decision on so nice a point must be left to the moral direction of the individual. For, one grown old in the useful and honourable exercise of the healing art, may continue to enjoy, and justly to enjoy, the unabated confidence of the public. And whilst exempt, in a considerable degree, from the privations and infirmities of age, he is under indispensable obligations to apply his knowledge and experience, in the most efficient way, to the benefit of mankind (Percival 1803, 51).

The decision to retire is not a personal but professional decision, guided by the commitment "to the benefit of mankind" as the antidote to individual self-interest.

Percival calls for the physician to become self-aware and self-assess, following the model set out in Section XXVIII for critical self-appraisal of one's clinical practice, especially cases with bad outcomes:

> As age advances, therefore, a physician should, from time to time, scrutinize impartially the state of his faculties; that he may determine, *bona fide*, the precise degree in which he is qualified to execute the active and multifarious offices of his profession (Percival 1803, 50–51).

Ever practical, Percival identifies checklists for both physicians and surgeons. First the physician's:

> And whenever he becomes conscious that his memory presents to him, with faintness, those analogies, on which medical reasoning and the treatment of diseases are founded; that diffidence of the measures to be pursued perplexes his judgment; that, from a deficiency and the acuteness of his senses, he finds himself less able to distinguish signs, or to prognosticate events; he should at once resolve, though others perceive not the changes which have taken place, to sacrifice every consideration of fame or fortune, and to retire from the engagements of business (Percival 1803, 52).

Here Percival invokes the professional virtue of self-sacrifice: when individual self-interest becomes incompatible with the three commitments of the ethical concept of medicine as a profession, especially the commitment to scientific and clinical competence, then individual self-interest must be sacrificed. The good of the patient should always be the primary concern and motivation. The physician "should at once resolve" (Percival 1803, 51) – without hesitation – to retire.

Second is the surgeon's checklist:

> To the surgeon under similar circumstances, this rule of conduct is still more necessary. For the energy of the understanding often subsists much longer than the quickness of eye-sight, delicacy of touch, and steadiness of hand, which are essential to the skilful performance of operations (Percival 1803, 52).

Neither checklist has gone out of date.

Section XXXII ends with a crucial, revolutionary conceptual claim: the profession of medicine is a public trust:

> Let both the physician and surgeon never forget, that their professions are public trusts, properly rendered lucrative whilst they fulfil them; but which they are bound, by honour and probity, to relinquish, as soon as they find themselves unequal to their adequate and faithful execution (Percival 1803, 52).

Percival here forcefully rejected the entrepreneurial paradigms based on individual self-interest, party-interest, or guild-interest. The profession of medicine is a public trust: the fund of knowledge and skills of physicians and surgeons are to be maintained and improved for each the patient's good and thereby for the common weal now and for the indefinite future. As a public trust, the profession of medicine is not the private property of a physician or surgeon to use for his own benefit. In this context, 'honour' should be read as earlier explained, with Percival's reformed meaning of it: the sense of self-worth that derives from the life of service to patients and not from prickly, self-interested *amour propre*.

Note XIV reinforces this conceptual point, which is at the very heart of Percival's professional ethics in medicine. Percival includes a letter sent to Dr. William Heberden (1710–1801) from Percival about *Medical Jurisprudence*, dated August 28, 1794. Heberden reports that he is now in his 85th year and remarks that he retired some years earlier. His reasoning reflects that of *Medical Jurisprudence*, in which "trust" is invoked repeatedly and anticipates Section XXXII of *Medical Ethics*: "because I was willing to give over, before my presence of thought, judgment, and recollection were so impaired, that I could not do justice to my patients"

(Percival 1803, 203). Percival endorses this judgment: "It is an observation of Bacon, that letters written by wise men, are the best of human works" (Percival 1803, 205).

3.4.7 The Text of Medical Ethics: Chapter III: Of the Conduct of Physicians Towards Apothecaries

The task of apothecaries was "to prepare and furnish drugs to physicians' prescriptions" (Gelfand 1993, 1126). They were thus subordinate, at least in physicians' thinking and practice, to physicians. Edward Shorter (1993) uses 'the traditional period' to describe the period in the history of Western medicine before the nineteenth century "or that which existed before the infusion of science into medical practice" (Shorter 1883, 783).

> The 'traditional' physicians may in most countries be divided into two groups: the elite consultant physicians in the cities, and the great mass of starveling practitioners elsewhere. This distinction cleaved traditional physicians into those of high or low social standing the bearers of the 'gold-headed canes' and the country apothecaries. In England, the fellows of the Royal College of Physicians stood out clearly against the surgeon-apothecaries who were the forebears of the nineteenth-century 'general practitioner' (Shorter 1993, 783–784).

The hierarchical structure had the consultant physicians at its apex, with physicians who struggled for market share and some measure of economic security next, then the surgeons, and finally the apothecaries.

Gelfand points out that "the traditional professional hierarchy in which learned physicians, in principle, presided over artisanal subordinates, the barber-surgeon and the apothecary" began to break down already in the eighteenth century in England (Galfand 1993, 1126). Their supposed subordinates began to challenge the prerogatives and privileges of physicians with respect to who was competent to do what.

> These 'new men' (the professional [i.e., guild] medical groups were exclusively male) had ambitious designs on the practice of medicine; apothecaries, in particular, not content merely to prepare and furnish drugs to physicians' prescriptions, provided increasing competition in diagnosing and treating disease during the course of the seventeenth century. In 1704, their existing status as medical practitioners received legal confirmation when the House of Lords found in favor of William Rose, an apothecary, against the College of Physicians. The Rose case virtually ended the physicians' efforts to regulate other healers (Gelfand 1993, 1126).

The result, no surprise, was increased competition, consistent with the entrepreneurial paradigm.

We saw in the analysis of the first two chapters of *Medical Ethics* that Percival rejected the entrepreneurial paradigm of individual self-interest of physicians and surgeons and their party-interest – writ large in the Royal College or small writ in the claim to power and control of the Manchester Infirmary by the Whites and the Halls with, it is worth noting, their physician allies who were subordinate to these surgeons' power. The basis of his "Institutes," as he makes clear in Section I of *Medical Jurisprudence* and Chapter I of *Medical Ethics* is professional ethics in medicine. In the hospital setting, professional ethics requires the ethics of cooperation for the good of the patient. Percival's moral revolution thus ejects the entrepreneurial model from the hospital setting. Inasmuch as private practice is to be conducted on the paradigm of hospital practice, private practice requires the ethics of cooperation. Thus, in Chapter II Percival is at pains to provide detailed guidance that aims to prevent "contention" and "controversy" that only undermine cooperation. The basis for the "Precepts" in Chapter III of Percival's "Institutes" will also be professional ethics in medicine and its ethics of cooperation. As in Chapters I and II Percival aims to provide a clinically comprehensive account of the physician-apothecary relationship.

Chapter III opens with a reference to the "three distinct branches" of the "profession" of "physick," the prevention, diagnosis, and treatment of diseases and injuries (Percival 1803, 53). The collapse of the hierarchy of physicians, surgeons, and apothecaries had fostered the competition that defines the entrepreneurial paradigm. In Chapter III Percival opens a third front in his moral revolution, to bring the physician-apothecary relationship into an intra-professional relationship that banishes both competition and hierarchy.

III.I. Respect for and Patronage of Apothecaries

> I. IN the present state of physic, in this country, where their profession is properly divided into three distinct branches, a connection peculiarly intimate subsists between the physician and the apothecary; and various obligations necessary result from it. On the knowledge, skill, and fidelity of the apothecary, depend, and a very considerable degree, the reputation, the success, and the usefulness of the physician. As these qualities, therefore, justly claim his attention and encouragement, the possessor of them merits his respect and patronage (Percival 1803, 53).

The use of 'branches' is instructive, for its suggests that physicians, surgeons, and apothecaries are branches of a single tree. They are not to understand themselves in a hierarchy with physicians in charge. Nor are they competitors, lest they pull the tree apart. As branches of a single tree, they flourish or die together.

Physicians and apothecaries have a "connection peculiarly intimate" (Percival 1803, 53) or an especially intimate relationship. The "skill, and fidelity of the apothecary" (Percival 1803, 43) are necessary conditions for the "reputation, success, and usefulness of the physician" (Percival 1803, 53). Respect for the apothecary and patronage, in the sense of professional developmental support, as Percival will explain, aim to build a cooperative relationship.

III.II. Apothecary as Precursor

Apothecaries usually had lower fees than physicians. They also settled in small towns, where they could eke out a living but physicians could not. It was therefore likely that a patient would summon an apothecary, after having tried self-physicking and not being satisfied with the result. The apothecary therefore had more and more direct clinical experience with the patient, thus becoming source of "very important information," including "the rise and progress of the disease, with the hereditary constitution, habits, and disposition of the patient" (Percival 1803, 53). It is "expedient" for the physician to "confer" with the apothecary, to save time in gathering clinically pertinent information. Inasmuch as this prevents delay in attending to the patient, "expediency become a moral duty" (Percival 1803, 53). Here Percival weds the clinically practical to professional responsibility, a hallmark of his thinking throughout *Medical Ethics*. The apothecary, between the physician's visits, becomes key to putting the treatment plan into effect, usually a form of self-care under the physician's directions and using the apothecary's preparations. Another hallmark of Percival's thinking is the importance of professional moral formation to good patient care. To this end, Percival makes the case that, to fulfill this crucial role it is important that the apothecary is a "man of honour, judgment, and propriety" (Percival 1803, 54). Well-timed joint visits should be made, to sustain the "opportunity of executing his peculiar [special] trust" (Percival 1803, 54).

III.III. Cooperation, Decorum, and Etiquette

We saw in Chapters I and II that sustained conversation about science and cases is essential for the cooperation that fuels professional development and assumption of responsibility. This becomes the model that Percival wants physicians and apothecaries to adopt. In the social setting decorum and etiquette are expected forms of verbal regard and deferential behavior that make social interchange pleasant, especially as a refuge from the interested world of commerce. At the same time, no one was fooled. There were men of "false manners," who used decorum and etiquette to gain advantage, sometimes predatory financial and sexual advantage (McCullough 1998). Decorum and etiquette therefore did not invite unreserved trust.

Percival calls for professional "decorum" and "etiquette" (Percival 1803, 55). These are patterns of comportment designed to cement a cooperative relationship into place and then sustain "a deeper interest in the success of the curative plans proposed" (Percival 1803, 55). But the commitment goes beyond interest, to honor, as properly understood, and earned reputation: "his honour and reputation will be directly involved in the purity and excellence of the medicines dispensed, and in the skill and care with which they are compounded" (Percival 1803, 55). This is all directed to the good of the patient: "The patient will find himself the object of watchful and unremitting care, and will experience that he is connected with his physician, not only personally, but by a sedulous representative and coadjutor" (Percival 1803, 55).

III.IV. Inspection of Drugs

Percival recognizes that he is now in new territory for professional ethics in medicine. As a result, he appears less than fully confident that apothecaries will commit themselves to Baconian medicine and its professional ethics. He signals this by the use of 'interest' in the previous section. In Section IV, he anticipates President Ronald Reagan's (1911–2004; presidency 1981–1989) famous statement to Mikhail Gorbachev, the last leader of the Union of Soviet Socialist Republics, when they were negotiating a nuclear arms treaty: "trust but verify." Percival's version goes as follows: "The duty and responsibility of the physician, however, are so intimately connected with these points, that no dependence on the probity of the apothecary should prevent the occasional inspection of the drugs, which he prescribes" (Percival 1803, 55).

Percival cites a London law that requires "a stated examination of the simple and compound medicines kept in the shops" (Percival 1803, 56). Percival makes a case for this to become policy in "every provincial town, throughout the kingdom" (Percival 1803, 56). He offers a justification that appeals to reputation, properly understood as reputation for acting for the good of the patient, from which compensation should follow, keeping compensation a systematically secondary consideration, as required by the second commitment of the ethical concept of medicine as a profession:

> Nor will any respectable apothecary object to this necessary office, when performed with delicacy, and at seasonable times; since his reputation and emolument will be increased by it, probably in the exact *ratio*, thus ascertained, of professional merit and integrity (Percival 1803, 56).

III.V. Visiting a Patient in the Country

In Chapter II Percival addresses visits to patient who live in the country. He continues to explore this topic, now in the physician-apothecary relationship. Percival acknowledges the role of apothecaries as "the guardians of health through large districts" (Percival 1803, 56). Percival fills in the details of the "patronage" that he called for physicians to deploy for the benefit of apothecaries: "… no opportunities should be neglected of promoting their improvement, or contributing to their stock of knowledge, either by the loan of books, the direction of their studies, or by unreserved information on medical subjects" (Percival 1803, 56057). Apothecaries will then be able to improve their practices, which will benefit the towns they serve:

> For practical improvements usually originate in towns, and often remain unknown or disregarded and situations, where gentlemen of the faculty have little intercourse, and where sufficient authority is wanting to sanction innovation (Percival 1803, 57).

Thus does Percival expand the scope of the English enlightenment commitment to improvement.

III.VI. The Apothecary's Profit

Profit is the excess of price over cost. Apothecaries often charged more for the drugs and elixirs they prepared than the cost of their ingredients. The net difference might, at first glance, appear to be profit. Percival takes up this matter by including text from Adam Smith's (1723–1790) *Wealth of Nations* (Smith [1776] 2000). Percival uses this text to rebut the claim that the profit of apothecaries is "something uncommonly extravagant" (Percival 1803, 57). Smith makes the case that much of the difference between cost of ingredients and the price of apothecaries is a function of the cost of their labor, for which they are justified in seeking reasonable compensation.

Physicians should embrace this line of reasoning, as Percival explains, referring to apothecaries as "this profession:"

> And a physician, who knows the education, skill, and persevering attention, as well as the sacrifice of ease, health, and sometimes even of life, which this profession requires, should regard it as a duty not to withdraw, from those who exercise it, any sources of reasonable profit, or the honourable means of advancement in fortune (Percival 1803, 58).

Percival then decries two "practices injurious to the interests of this branch of the faculty" (Percival 1803, 58) that should cease because, presumably, they create competition that undermines the financial viability of an apothecary's practice and thus the good of patients:

> Two practices prevail in some places injurious to the interest of this branch of the faculty, and which ought to be discouraged. One consists in suffering prescriptions to be sent to the druggist, for the sake of a small saving an expence: The other in receiving an annual stipend, usually degrading in its amount, and in the services it imposes, for being consulted on the slighter indispositions to which all families are incident, and which properly fall within the province of the apothecary (Percival 1803, 58–59).

III.VII. Requests to Treat Patients of an Apothecary when he is Absent

Percival addresses this topic in the relationship of physicians and surgeons in private practice in Chapter II, Section XIV. Percival's concern is for the patient, that he or she would experience unnecessary disruption to the course of treatment initiated by the apothecary. In addition, out of self-interest accepting such invitations could be "liable to abuse," i.e., stealing the patient from the apothecary out of economic self-interest. Percival has already made abundantly clear that it is never ethically permissible to make self-interest the primary concern and motivation of the physician, in violation of the second commitment of the ethical concept of medicine as a profession. Percival's judgment is firm:

> Indeed this practice is so liable to abuse, and requires, in its exercise, so much caution and delicacy, that it would be for the interest and honour of the faculty to have it all together interdicted. Physicians are the only proper substitutes for physicians; surgeons for surgeons; and apothecaries for apothecaries (Percival 1803, 59).

III.VIII. The Apothecary's Recommendation of a Physician

Sometimes an apothecary will be asked by a patient or patient's family member to recommend a physician. The patient or family may have a preference. The good of the patient should guide the apothecary's response, the ethical obligation to protect which is fulfilled by doing one's best to ensure that the physician is competent. The first commitment of the ethical concept of medicine as a profession should guide the apothecary:

> It will then behove him to learn fully whether the patient or his friends have any preference or partiality; and this he ought to consult, if it lead not to an improper choice. For the maxim of Celsus is strictly applicable on such an occasion: *ubi par scientia, melior est amicus medicus quam extraneus* (Percival 1803, 59).

The passage from Celsus may be translated as: "Where the two are equal in knowledge and skill, the physician who is a friend is better than a physician who is a stranger."

When the patient or family has no preference, the commitment to competence should continue to guide the apothecary:

> But if the parties concerned be entirely indifferent, the apothecary is bound to decide according to his best judgment, with a conscientious and exclusive regard to the good of the person for whom he is commissioned to act. It is not even sufficient that he selects the person on whom, in sickness, he reposes his own trust; for in this case friendship justly gives preponderancy; because it may be supposed to excite a degree of zeal and attention which might overbalance superior science or abilities. Without favour or regard to any personal, family, or professional connections, he should recommend the physician whom he conscientiously believes, all circumstances considered, to be best qualified to accomplish the recovery of the patient (Percival 1803, 59–60).

This passage is worth quoting in full because it displays key elements of Percival's professional ethics in medicine. Ensuring that the physician displays Baconian scientific and clinical competence is essential, as Percival emphasized from *de Frigore* when he was twenty-five years old and in *The Empiric* and *The Dogmatic*, which were analyzed in Chap. 2. The apothecary should put aside his personal experience as the patient of his preferred physician, to prevent biased judgment. The goal is to recommend the "best qualified" physician, where 'best qualified' means a physician who has mastered Baconian scientific and clinical competence.

III.IX. Supporting Apothecaries' Widows and Children and Impoverished Apothecaries who have Retired

We saw in Chap. 2 the considerable interest that Percival took in reversionary funds, to which individuals contributed, to create a common fund for the benefit of widows and children and retired folks. Percival identified a role for the expertise of the physician: calculating mortality as accurately as possible, so that these funds would have the most reliable scientific data to guide them in setting the fees that needed to be paid in and annuities to be disbursed. Percival had also learned a key concept of insurance: the cost of insurance is lower when risk is borne by a large rather than small population of beneficiaries. A larger fund is also likely to better managed.

> One comprehensive establishment seems to be more eligible than many on a smaller scale. For it would be conducted with superior dignity, regularity, and efficiency; with fewer obstacles from interest, prejudice, or rivalship; with considerable saving in the aggregate a time, trouble, and expence; with more accuracy in the calculations relative to its funds, and consequently with the utmost practicable extension of its dividends (Percival 1803, 60–61).

Percival starts *Medical Ethics*, we saw above, with professional ethics in hospital practice because he grasps, implicitly, that sustaining the commitment of physicians, surgeons, and apothecaries to professional ethics in clinical practice and research requires a supportive organizational culture. A major goal of an organizational culture of professionalism is to keep self-interest systematically secondary. Creating economically sound and well-managed "relief" and "retirement" funds is directly analogous: An apothecary can have confidence that, should he die young, his widow and children will enjoy some level of economic security and, should he live long enough to retire, his retirement will also enjoy some level of economic security. Being concerned about the economic welfare of one's family and of oneself and one's family in one's retirement is a legitimate form of individual self-interest. Providing for the economic welfare of one's widow and children, Percival would add, is an ethical obligation generated by sympathy for them. Providing for one's retirement is a matter of prudence, a virtue that is essential to proper moral formation. Providing for one's retirement is thus not an ethically trifling matter. Creating relief and retirement funds supports the apothecary, during his years of active practice, in fulfilling his ethical obligations to his family – mitigating conflicts of commitment that could create incentives to put income first and thus unjustifiably increase prices – and in acting prudently. Finally, the goals of these funds are achievable only through voluntary, sustained cooperation. These funds thus become exemplars of the professional ethics of cooperation that Percival makes central to *Medical Ethics*. These funds become a key component in what might be called an implicit organizational culture of cooperation in private practice, not only of apothecaries, but also physicians and surgeons.

3.4.8 The Text of Medical Ethics: Chapter IV: Of Professional Duties, in Certain Cases Which Require a Knowledge of Law

Catherine Crawford provides a concise account of the relations between law and medicine in eighteenth-century England. The regulation of medicine was attempted via licensure by the Royal Colleges in London, under their royal charters. Their authority, however, encompassed only the London area. Another aspect of the relationship between law and medicine was the provision of expert testimony: "It was not uncommon for midwives, surgeons, and physicians to provide expert testimony in early modern English courts …" (Crawford 1993, 1626). In criminal proceedings, English juries, composed of laypersons, were finders of fact "under a comparatively free system of proof" (Crawford 1993, 1627). Crawford provides a capsule summary of expert medical testimony that serves to put the content of Chapter III in context:

> Medical investigation was nowhere obligatory, though it could be arranged by the coroner (the local official responsible for investigating sudden or suspicious deaths), by the parties, or by the magistrate conducting proceedings (if any of these chose). But neither medical experts nor their findings had official status in English common law. Medical practitioners contributed to inquests and trials in the role of witness and testified on much the same footing as other witnesses, frequently without payment and under *sub pœna* [under penalty]. Their evidence was given orally and, like other testimony, it had only as much authority as the jury of lay people was willing to give it in each instance. Although questions of law were governed by precedent and resolved by judges, questions of fact – which included most

medico-legal questions – were not. Any judgment that contained a determination of fact had to be given to a jury, which deliberated in private and did not ordinarily give reasons for its verdict. As the rules of evidence gradually developed, judges could control what jurors heard, but not the way jurors *weighed* what they heard (Crawford 1993, 1627–1628).

In Chapter IV Percival takes up the professional responsibilities of physicians serving as expert witnesses to the fact finders. This is the longest chapter in *Medical Ethics*, at fifty-three pages. The reader will recall from Chap. 2 and earlier in this chapter that John Aikin taught a course on jurisprudence at Warrington Academy, which was as much as course on ethics as on law. Percival also had the more immediate model of Farr's *Elements of Medical Jurisprudence* (Farr [1788] 1814), which we examined earlier in this chapter in connection with *Medical Jurisprudence*.

Farr entitles his "Introduction" as "Institutes &c" or the intellectual basis for the chapters that follow, which address a wide range of clinical conditions that might come before a coroner or criminal court. Farr is concise, as an Institutes should be, as illustrated in this passage, cited at the beginning of this chapter:

> There is a kind of medical knowledge, which is not so much concerned with the cure of diseases, as in the detection of error, and the conviction of guilt. A physician, a surgeon, or a coroner, is often called upon to make a deposition of what he knows concerning some particular transactions in a court of judicature. Such persons then should be well acquainted with the animal œconomy; and with those views of the science, which, in foreign countries, have been dignified with a peculiar name, as the medicine of the courts, legal medicine, or medical jurisprudence (Farr [1788] 1814, 1).

In each subsequent chapter Farr provides a detailed account of clinical examinations and findings pertinent to the topic of each chapter.

Percival aims to acquaint his reader with the essential legal concepts used in medical jurisprudence of which an expert witness needs to be aware, e.g., the distinction among manslaughter and murder, and the physician's role as an expert witness in cases in which these terms apply legally. This task takes up about half of Chapter IV, in which he defines such key terms as: personal and real property (Percival 1803, 64); sudden death (Percival 1803, 71); capital crimes (Percival 1803, 72); justifiable homicide and excusable homicide (by "misadventure" or by self-defense) (Percival 1803, 73); manslaughter (Percival 1803, 73, 77); malpractice that is criminal (Percival 1803, 74); physical assault (Percival 1803, 75); murder or felonious homicide, "which in atrocity exceeds every other" (Percival 1803, 75–76); abortion (Percival 1803, 78–79); infanticide, especially of bastard children (Percival 1803, 79–84); stillbirth vs. infanticide (Percival 1803, 85–86); duelling, including attendance at a duel by a surgeon (Percival 1803, 87–95); homicide by poison (Percival 1803, 95–99); rape, including statutory rape (Percival 1803, 99–103); nuisances or what we would call environmental harms and crimes, e.g., contamination of water supply by a lead smelter, which was examined in Chap. 2 (Percival 1803, 103–105); and fires (Percival 1803, 106).

The "Notes and Illustrations" in Chapter IV provide additional detail, mainly historical and philosophical, on the topic to which the note makes reference. Two of Percival's intellectual commitments at work. He maintains the style of "Institutes" that aims to provide the essentials of professional ethics in medicine. He also situates the topic referenced in its historical and philosophical context in the Notes. There his considerable erudition is on display.

Note XVI on "duelling" (Percival uses two ls) (Chapter IV, Section XII) provides this dual context (Percival 1803, 214–228). He begins by tracing the history of resolving disputes in Ancient Rome and among the Germans: "Velleius Paterculus informs us, that questions, decided amongst the Romans by legal trial, were terminated amongst the Germans by arms or judicial combat" (Percival 1803, 214). He then describes the rules of "honour" understood in its morally decrepit sense of fragile self-regard. The history is then complemented by the use of extended quotation from philosophers, including (no surprise) Lord Verallum or Bacon, Lord Shaftsbury (Anthony Ashley Cooper, Third Earl of Shaftsbury, 1671–1713), William Paley, and Benjamin Franklin.

He also takes up other such matters as advising patients in "imminent danger" about the need for a last will and testament, to protect their "fortune" (Percival 1803, 63), which he also addresses in Chapter II, Section II. He addresses the concept and clinical assessment of the capacity to make decisions or *compos mentis* (Percival 1803, 64–68). Capacity can wax and wane and is also specific to the task at hand. He makes clear to readers what is at stake, legally, for a patient whose capacity has become a matter of judgment by a court:

> And before he becomes accessary to his deprivation, as it were, of all legal existence, he will weigh attentively the whole circumstances of the disorder, the original cause of it; the degree in which it subsists; its duration, and probable continuance. For if the malady be not fixed, great, and permanent, this solemn act of law must be deemed inexpedient, because it cannot be reversed without difficulty: and when insanity has been once formally declared, there may be grounds of apprehension, that the party will be consigned to neglect and oblivion (Percival 1803, 67–68).

He calls for physicians to participate in inspection of "[h]ouses for the reception of lunatics," as provided by law (Percival 1803, 69–70).

Percival uses the balance of Chapter IV to do more: He situates his primer on medical jurisprudence in the context of what he calls "political ethics" to explain the relationship between physicians and surgeons, on the one hand, and coroner's courts and criminal courts, on the other. He then describes the scientific responsibilities of the Baconian expert witness. Throughout, he invokes professional ethics in medicine to criticize the law, in a striking display of the autonomy of professional medical ethics from state power and of the accountability of law to professional medical ethics. Rather than work through the details of the primer, section by section, as in the examination of Chapters I–III, I will examine three overarching themes that shape Chapter IV of *Medical Ethics*: his political ethics, Baconian expert witnessing, and the autonomy of professional ethics in medicine from state power as expressed in law.

3.4.8.1 Political Ethics

Political ethics functions as the basis for the many critical remarks that Percival makes about English criminal law and its penalties. In the manner of a text on "Institutes," and as he did in the previous three chapters, he sets out the conceptual framework for Chapter IV in its first section. Later in Chapter IV he uses the phrase 'political ethics' to explicate this conceptual framework further. A search of all four volumes of *Works* reveals that the only text in which Percival uses 'political ethics' is Chapter IV, Section XIX (Percival 1803, 108) of *Medical Ethics*. Without using the phrase, Percival articulates a political ethics in some of his other writings, which were examined in Chap. 2.

Two components of Percival's political ethics shape Chapter IV. The first is that our moral lives are defined by our duties to each other, a view required by Baconian moral science in which human beings are bound together by the "fellow feeling" that expresses sympathy and "incites" us to care for each other. This explains the inclusion of the Latin quote from Cicero on page 2 of *Medical Ethics*, the verso page of the title page. Cicero explains that our moral lives are shaped by *officia* (plural of *officium*) or duties.

> For no phase of life, whether public or private, whether in business or in the home, whether one is working on what concerns oneself alone or dealing with another, can be without its moral duty; on the discharge of such duties depends all that is morally right, and in their neglect all that is morally wrong in life (Cicero 1913, 7; Percival 1803, not paginated ii).

Cicero bases these duties on self-preservation as the paramount value. Sympathy-based moral science will agree that our moral lives are shaped by *officia* but not follow Cicero on his primary principle of self-preservation. As we saw in Chap. 2, moreover, Percival deploys Baconian moral science and its detection of the "truth of things" as the basis for what is morally right and morally wrong. Section I of Chapter IV can therefore be read as invoking Baconian moral science to identify reciprocity as basis for the physician's ethical obligation to serve as an expert witness: the truth of things is that physicians and surgeons have been granted exemptions from important civic responsibilities and therefore have reciprocal ethical obligations:

> I. Gentlemen of the faculty of physic, by the authority of different parliamentary statutes, enjoy an exemption from serving on inquests or juries; from bearing armour; from being constables or church-wardens; and from all burdensome offices, weather leet or parochial. These privileges are founded on reasons highly honourable to medical men; and should operate as incentives to that diligent and assiduous discharge of professional duty, which the legislature has generously presumed to occupy the time, and to employ the talents, of physi[61]cians and surgeons, in some of the most important interests of their fellow-citizens. It is perhaps on account of their being thus excused from many civil functions, that Sir William Blackstone, in his Learned commentaries, judges the study of the law to be less essential to them, than to any other class of men. He observes that "there is no special reason why gentlemen of the faculty of physic should apply themselves to the study of the law, unless in common with other gentleman, and to complete the character of general and extensive knowledge, which this profession, beyond others, has remarkably deserved." But I apprehend it will be found that physicians and surgeons are often called upon to exercise

appropriate duties, which require not only a knowledge of the principles of jurisprudence, but of the forms of regulations adopted in our courts of judicature (Percival 1803, 61–62).

In *A Father's Instructions* Percival explains how reciprocity emerges from working the earth, from the state of nature in which human beings existed before the formation of governments and states. In the state of nature, the earth does not "produce spontaneously the sustenance and comforts of life."

> In the culture of the ground, not only industry, but observation, invention, knowledge, and social assistance are required. Arts thus originate; civil polities are formed; an interchange of commodities is established; commerce is extended; and by the reciprocity of wants and supplies, the productions of nature are multiplied and universally diffused (Percival 1807, Vol. I, 274).

Sympathy, properly regulated by such virtues as tenderness and condescension, creates the ethical obligation to meet the "wants" of others, what they need but do not have, and the "supplies" that one has produced. So powerful and effective is the resulting fellow feeling that "the productions of nature are multiplied and universally diffused" (Percival 1807, Vol. I, 274).

Baconian moral science provides the basis for the second component of Percival's political ethics: a "just sense of moral or political duty" (Percival 1807, Vol. II, 237). He explains the meaning of these words in his essay, *An Inquiry into the Principles and Limits of Taxation, as a Branch of Moral and Political Philosophy* from 1790, which was examined in Chap. 2. A just sense of moral or political duty will exist in a legitimate polity, a government directed consistently to the public good. The public good is founded in the truth of things and not in the "unstable foundation of arbitrary will" (Percival 1807, Vol. II, 234). I read this as a gesture in the direction of Plato's character in *Republic*, Thrasymachus, who posits that justice is the will of the stronger (Plato 2000). Plato has Socrates show the hapless Thrasymachus that this comes to the exercise of "arbitrary will" and is therefore no foundation for justice at all. Percival, obliquely, also references the arbitrariness of monarchical power, which England had experienced in an extreme form during the mental illness of King George III earlier in the eighteenth century and to which Percival makes reference.

Baconian investigation into the truth of things reveals the natural rights that have been given to us by the creator god of deism, "life, liberty, and property" (Percival 1807, Vol. II, 231). Inasmuch as these rights originate in the creator god, they are directed to the good of god's subjects. The concept of human good and the rights that protect it originate independently of state power:

> Yet, though government, in this sense [the "social state" that originates in the law of nature], is of divine authority, it is so constituted by its adaptation to the interests and felicity of its subjects. The rights of the people, therefore, are not only antecedent to, but included in, those of the magistrate; and consequently there can never subsist a legitimate competition between them (Percival 1807, Vol. II, 233).

Percival then argues, on the basis of these natural rights, that a legitimate government and therefore legitimate laws must satisfy a standard of "equity" that derives from "principles of reason, justice, and patriotism" (Percival 1807, Vol. II, 234). By 'reason' he means the deployment of Baconian method to identify the truth of things (not Reason). 'Justice' is met when sympathy-based ethical obligations are routinely fulfilled. 'Patriotism' Percival takes from Priestley's injunction that was examined in Chap. 2: fidelity to a state that protects natural rights and promotes fellow feeling.

These philosophical reflections position Percival to persuade his reader to adopt his political ethics or an account of a "just government:"

> A just government is obliged to the most scrupulous attention to the original ends of its institution. Nor can even wise and legitimate *ends* be pursued by *means* inconsistent with equity, because no policy can ever supersede the laws of morality: and this rather dignifies, than derogates from, sovereign dominion (Percival 1807, Vol. II, 242).

The laws of a just government, in this case taxation, must satisfy four criteria: laws must be made "by lawful authority; according to prescribed forms; in an equitable mode and proportion; and for the public weal" (Percival 1807, Vol. II, 249, capitalization removed).

Political ethics concerns the duties that we owe to each other in a polity that meets these four criteria for a just government. This is the meaning with which Percival deploys "political ethics" in Chapter IV:

> But in criminal prosecutions, which affect the life of the person accused, scruples will be apt to arise in one who, by the advantages of a liberal education, has been accustomed to serious reflection, yet has paid no particular attention to the principles of political ethics. It is incumbent, therefore, on gentlemen of the faculty, to settle their opinions concerning the right of the civil magistrate to inflict capital punishment; the moral and social ends of such punishment; the limits prescribed to the exercise of the right; and the duty of a citizen to give full efficiency to the laws (Percival 1803, 108–109).

Put another way, political ethics, as properly understood in Baconian moral science, is based on the truth of things. Percival takes the view that the "moral and social" end, or purpose, of "penal law" is, not vengeance, but the prevention of crime (Percival 1803, 84). The critical appraisal of the text of criminal law and criminal punishment in cases at the intersection of law and medicine should be undertaken on this basis.

Percival deploys such critical appraisals in Chapter IV, especially pertaining to abortion (which at that time was outlawed after quickening or the pregnant woman's detection of the movement of the fetus in utero) and infanticide of bastard children. Percival considers both to be crimes. His critical appraisal is therefore directed to whether then-current criminal law fulfills the end of preventing these crimes. For physicians and surgeons a key issue will be whether punishment of women found guilty of these crimes is consistent with Baconian clinical judgment, or Baconian science, and therefore clinical ethical judgment, or Baconian moral science. When punishment does not meet this test, it becomes cruel. We know from the texts examined in Chap. 2 that Percival judges cruelty wrong not only because of the harm done to the animal or human who is harmed but also because of the harm done to the moral character of the perpetrator.

With respect to abortion, Percival's concern is that the law does not recognize that the pregnant woman may have a "moral or salutary end" and therefore does not act with "malice against mankind" (Percival 1803, 78).

> On the like grounds we may reason concerning the cases of death, occasioned by drugs designed to produce abortion. This purpose is not always unlawful: For the configuration of the *pelvis* in some females is such as to render the birth of a full-grown child impossible, or inevitably fatal. But even in such instances the guilt of manslaughter may be incurred by ignorance of the drastic quality of the medicine prescribed, or want of due caution in the dose administered (Percival 1803, 78).

As we saw in Chap. 2, in considering Percival's concept of lying, intent is crucial. The woman's intent is therefore crucial and the law must take this into account. When her intent is to protect her own health from serious harm or even her life or is to use a medicine for her own health, but, from ignorance of lethal dosage for her fetus, she commits no crime. The reason is that the law should not be preventing women from acting to prevent their own serious loss of health or death or maintaining their health. However, "when no moral or salutary end as in view, the simple act itself, if fatal in the issue, falls under the denomination of murder: (Percival 1803, 78).

With respect to infanticide, Percival criticizes both the text of the law and the punishment it prescribes.

> The statute, indeed, which makes the concealment of the birth of a bastard child full proof of murder, confounds all distinctions of innocence and guilt, as such concealment, whenever practicable, would be the wish and act of all mothers, amiable or vicious, under the same unhappy predicament. Law, however, which is the guardian and bulwark of the public weal, must maintain a steady, and even rigid watch, over the general tendencies of human actions: And when these are not only clearly understood, but interpreted according to the rules of wisdom and rectitude, that may justly be constituted a civil crime, which, if permitted, might give occasion to atrocious guilt, though in its own nature innocent (Percival 1803, 84–85).

If the woman's intent in "concealment" is to prevent others from learning about a natural stillbirth, then her act is "amiable." If her intent is to conceal death that she caused, then her act is "vicious." The failure to make this intention-based distinction is not conceptually adequate and is therefore not acceptable; the law should be changed, making the former a civil, and not criminal, wrong.

Having earlier reviewed the plight of women who give birth to a bastard child, he comments on the punishment prescribed in applicable law.

> The measure of punishment, however, should be proportionate, as nearly as possible, to the temptations to offend, and to the kind and degree of evil produced by the offense. If inadequate to the former, it will be nugatory; and if too severe for the latter, it will defeat itself, by furnishing a just plea for superseding its execution (Percival 1803, 85).

His conclusion is acerbic: "A revision of our sanguinary statutes is much wanted" (Percival 1803, 85).

Recall Percival's criteria for a just polity. The laws of a just government must be made "by lawful authority; according to prescribed forms; in an equitable mode and proportion; and for the public weal" (Percival 1807, Vol. II, 249, capitalization removed). It follows from Percival's critical appraisal of English criminal law on abortion and infanticide that these laws are not "in an equitable mode and proportion" with respect for preventing abortion and infanticide and therefore do not promote the "public weal." By punishing women whose intent is to protect their own health or lives, the criminal law of abortion harms the "public weal." In its "sanguinary" aspect, the criminal law of infanticide harms the "public weal" by too often carrying out capital punishment.

Throughout Chapter IV Percival understands the medical, political, and moral aspects of human life to be interconnected. A medical critique of criminal law has political or policy implications based on the moral aspects of the criminal law. He had already made this connection in his argument for improved bills of mortality in Manchester, from *Proposals for Establishing More Accurate and Comprehensive Bills of Mortality, in Manchester*, which was examined in Chap. 2:

> The establishment of a judicious and acute register of the births and burials, in every town and parish, would be attended with the most important advantages, medical, political, and moral (Percival 1807, Vol. III, 428).
>
> In a political view, exact registers of human mortality are of still greater consequence, as the number of people and progress of population in the kingdom, may, in the most easy and unexceptionable manner, be deduced from them (Percival 1807, Vol, III, 429).

The progress of the kingdom itself is enabled by critical appraisal of criminal law, when it intersects with medicine, on the basis of political ethics.

3.4.8.2 Baconian Testimony

Percival reminds his reader of the oath he will take in court:

> It is the injunction of the law, sanctioned by the solemnity of an oath, that in judicial testimony, *the truth, the whole truth, and nothing but the truth* shall be delivered. A witness, therefore, is under a sacred obligation to use his best endeavours that his mind be clear and collected, unawed by fear, and uninfluenced by favour or enmity (Percival 1803, 108).

The pathway to the truth, the truth of things, is Baconian scientific method. From his first scientific endeavor, *de Frigore*, when he was twenty-five years old through his many "medical" and "scientific" essays, Percival's commitment to using Baconian, "experienced"-based, scientific method and thereby to the first commitment of the ethical concept of medicine as a profession was unwavering. It comes as no surprise, therefore, that he insists that physicians and surgeons who provide expert testimony at inquests and trials meet standards of Baconian scientific investigation and reporting its results in terms that a lay jury can be expected to understand.

> When a physician or surgeon is called to give evidence, he should avoid, as much as possible, all obscure and technical terms, and the unnecessary display of medical erudition. He should deliver, also, what he advances, in the purest and most delicate language, consistent with the nature of the subject in question (Percival 1803, 106).

Percival reminds his reader of the paramount importance of this commitment in clinical practice.

3.4 Medical Ethics, or a Code of Institutes and Precepts, Adapted to the Professional... 227

> But whatever be the indulgence of the law towards medical practitioners, they are bound by a higher authority than that of the most solemn statute, not to exercise the healing art without due knowledge, tenderness, and discretion: And every rash experiment, every mistake originating from gross inattention, or from that ignorance which necessarily results from defective education, is, in the eye of conscience, a crime both against God and man (Percival 1803, 75).

Just as "due knowledge," produced by Baconian scientific discipline, should guide clinical practice, so too should it guide expert witnessing. Consider the approach he recommends in cases of alleged criminal homicide by poisoning:

> When the particular drug, or other mean employed, can be accurately ascertained, its deleterious qualities should be fully investigated; and these should be cautiously compared with the effects ascribed to it, in the case under consideration. It may often be expedient, also, to examine the body of the sufferer by dissection; and this should be accomplished as expeditiously as possible; that the changes imputed to death may not be confounded with those which are imputed to poison. But on such points reference can alone be made to the knowledge and experience of the practitioner ... (Percival 1803, 97–98).

The professional ethics of cooperation that shapes Chapters I–III applies when "two or more gentlemen of the faculty are to offer their opinions or testimony" (Percival 1803, 107). Percival's professional ethics of cooperation has as its goal the good of the patient, to which end contention and controversy should be prevented. In court testimony the goal becomes preventing "contrariety" (Percival 1803, 107) that will only confuse the jury and undermine the oath to be truthful. The professional ethics of cooperation in professional ethics in medicine sets the standard for expert witnessing. Percival provides a compelling example of failure to meet this professional ethical standard.

> Several years ago, a trial of considerable consequence occurred, relative to a large copper work; and two physicians of eminence were summoned to the assizes, to bear testimony concerning the salubrity or insalubrity of the smoke issuing from the furnaces. The evidence they offered was entirely contradictory. One grounded his testimony on the general presumption that the ores of copper contain arsenic; and consequently that the effluvia, proceeding from the roasting of them, must be poisonous because arsenical. The other had made actual experiments on the ore employed in the works under prosecution, and on the vapours which it yielded: He was thus furnished with full proof that no arsenic was discoverable in either. But the affirmative prevailed over the negative testimony, from the authority of the physician who delivered it; an authority which he probably would not have misapplied, if he had been antecedently acquainted with the decisive trials made by his opponent (Percival 1803, 107–108).

It is not, I believe, too great a stretch to say that in proposing to make the professional ethics of cooperation a legal standard, Percival anticipates by two centuries the proposal for science courts to replace the adversarial system in American common law and to replace interests-based testimony with obligations-based testimony (Chervenak et al. 2010).

As we saw in Chap. 2, Baconian investigations yield results that range along a continuum of probability, as Percival explains in *Medical Cautions and Remarks Particularly Relative to Pulmonary Disorders*, examined in Chap. 2.

> Many of the principles of physic may be deemed demonstrative; but the application of them rests on no other evidence than probability. In different cases this evidence varies in degree; and we are justified in acting according to that degree, which every individual case affords. The same observation may be extended to politics and morality; sciences which are often clearly understood in theory, but egregiously misused in the conduct of life ((Percival 1807, Vol. IV, 330).

Percival applies this framework to expert testimony, The physician or surgeon must guard against a strong sympathetic response to the horror of a crime and concomitant revulsion for the individual accused of it.

> When professional testimony is required, in cases of such peculiar malignity as to excite general horror and indignation, a virtuous mind, even though scrupulous and timid, is liable to be influenced by too violent impressions; and to transfer to the accused that dread and aversion, which, before conviction, should be confined to the crime, and as much as possible withheld from the supposed offender (Percival 1803, 112).

Percival then implicitly invokes the professional virtue of steadiness that regulates the correlative of sympathy, revulsion, that is achieved by submitting to the discipline of Baconian science:

> If the charge, for instance, be that of a parricide, accomplished by poison, and accompanied with deliberate malice, ingratitude, and cruelty; the investigation should be made with calm and unbiased precision, and the testimony delivered with no colouring of passion, nor with any deviation from the *simplicity of truth*. When *circumstantial proofs* are adduced, they should be arranged in the most lucid order, that they may be contrasted and compared, in all their various relations, with facility and accuracy; and that their weight may be separately and collectively determined in the balance of justice. For, in such evidence, there subsists a regular graduation from the slightest presumption to complete moral certainty. And if the witness possesses sufficient information in this branch of philosophical and juridical science, he will always be competent to secure himself, and on many occasions the court also, from fallacy and error (Percival 1803, 112–113).

3.4.8.3 The Autonomy of Professional Ethics in Medicine from State Power

In both his political ethics, the critical appraisal of criminal law that this political ethics supports, and in his insistence that expert testimony strictly adhere to Baconian scientific method, Percival claims the autonomy of professional ethics in medicine and therefore the profession of medicine from state power. It follows that criminal law, when it intersects with medicine and surgery, is accountable for its legitimacy to professional ethics in medicine. This brings to prominence the role of Baconian Dissent in Percival's Baconian moral scientific professional ethics in medicine.

We saw in Chap. 2 that Percival understood that the commitment to Baconian investigation of the truth of things in natural, medical, and moral science produced revolutionary findings. For example, the authority of state power does not derive from the divine right of kings but from the common weal and the consistency of deployment of state power to this, its proper end. State power is therefore accountable to the truth of things as identified in Baconian science and moral science. This is precisely the reasoning of Dissent that Percival learned at Warrington Academy and that he applied when he dissented from the Articles of Faith at the Oxbridge universities and went north, to Scotland, to start his medical education. Political ethics and Baconian moral science working in the intersection of law and medicine can be read as forms of Baconian Dissent from illegitimate authority when it claimed by the state – or anyone else for that matter.

The autonomy of the profession of medicine has important implications for how Percival understood the place of the medical profession in the idea of a "social union" devoted to "public justice" and "social order" (Percival 1803, 110). These derive from the sympathy-based commitment to meet the needs of others with one's supplies as a matter of reciprocity and the commitment to respect and implement the natural rights to life, liberty, and property. Percival does not use 'social contract' to signal that the social union is not built solely on natural rights and the need to protect them with the power of the state. The social union becomes the basis of the polity expressed in state power. In the social union thus understood, justified state power is directed to the common weal, which derives from sympathy-based reciprocity, and not simply to protection of natural rights. In this social union, the profession of medicine – properly understood, we now know, as clinical practice and research based on professional ethics in medicine – is autonomous from state power and enters into the polity of the social union on this basis. Others should respect this autonomy because, quite simply, is it based on the truth of things and the principle of sympathy and its professional regulatory virtues. Gisborne takes the view that the physician has "virtually promised" to fulfill his duties and that it is therefore "universally expected" that he do so (Gisborne 1795, Vol. II, 132). In other words, an implicit contract exists between the physician and the patient. For Percival explicitly making the commitments that define the ethical concept of medicine as a profession creates the physician-patient relationship, independent of any social contract – implicit or explicit. These commitments generate the autonomy of the profession of medicine from the state, with which autonomy medicine enters the social union or, in another discourse, the social contract. This marks another difference between Percival and Gisborne on social and political philosophy.

3.5 A Discourse, Addressed to the Gentlemen of the Faculty, the Officers, the Clergy, and the Trustees of the Infirmary at Liverpool, on Their Respective Hospital Duties. By The Rev. Thomas Bassnett Percival, Ll. B.

Percival appends this "Discourse" by his son to both *Medical Jurisprudence* and *Medical Ethics*. The discourse was an "Anniversary Sermon Preached in May 1791; for the Benefit of the Infirmary at Liverpool." In the "Advertisement" to *Medical*

Jurisprudence, dated February 24, 1794, Percival informs his reader: "The foregoing SERMON is inserted, by permission, as an APPENDIX to a work, which has long remained unfinished in the press" (Percival 1794, not paginated: 120). In Note XX in *Medical Ethics* Percival further explains two reasons for including this text.

His son was qualified to prepare and present it:

> THIS Anniversary Discourse was addressed to the gentlemen of the faculty; the officers; the clergy; and the trustees of the Infirmary, at Liverpool, for the benefit of the charity; And I believe was highly approved by the judicious audience, before whom it was delivered. As the preacher assumed topics of exhortation, not before adopted by divines on such occasions, it may be proper to state, that he was peculiarly qualified, from his knowledge of the polity of hospitals, to execute with ability so delicate and so arduous a task. After passing several years at St. John's College, in Cambridge, in the pursuits of general science, he removed to Edinburgh to engage in the study of physic. But notwithstanding his acquisitions in the HEALING ART, to which he applied himself with great assiduity, he uniformly discovered a predilection for THEOLOGY. It became expedient, therefore, not to oppose the strong direction of his mind. He returned to Cambridge; and when he had taken the degree of LL. B. was admitted into holy orders. (Percival 1803, 238–239).

Including this discourse also became a memorial to its author:

> Being appointed to the chaplaincy of the British company of merchants at St. Petersburgh, he removed thither; and executed the duties of that honourable and important station with exemplary fidelity, and with the general approbation of the factory. In this office he died, after a lingering and painful illness, on the 27th of May, 1798, in the thirty-second year of his age (Percival 1803, 239).

In the Preface to *Medical Ethics* Percival informs his reader that he began work on *Medical Jurisprudence* in "the spring of 1792" (Percival 1803, not paginated: 1). Thomas Bassnett's discourse is dated as having been delivered in May, 1791. It thus predates *Medical Jurisprudence* and therefore, of course, *Medical Ethics*.

The reader will recall from Chap. 2 that Percival read his *A Father's Instructions* to his children before he published them. Thomas Bassnett was therefore well acquainted with his father's Baconian moral science. Its influence appears in the frequent appeals in the "Discourse" to sympathy of the "feeling mind" (Percival 1803, 119) and its regulatory virtue of tenderness. Thomas Bassnett nicely combines sympathy and the fellow feeling that it produces, so that no one is a stranger, in the phrase 'social sympathy' (Percival 1803, 120). 'Condescension' becomes 'Christian condescension' (Percival 1803, 125).

Using words that Gregory and his father could have written, Thomas Bassnett addresses the "ill-founded opinion, that compassion is not the true virtue of a surgeon. This branch of the profession has been charged with harness of heart … (Percival 1803, 125). He responds with an account of "true compassion:"

> And a distinction should ever be made between true compassion, and that unmanly pity which enfeebles the mind; which shrinks from the sight of woe; which inspires timidity; and deprives him, who was under its influence, of all capacity to give relief. Genuine compassion rouses the attention of the soul; gives energy to all its powers; suggests expedients in danger; incites to vigorous action and difficulty; and strengthens the hand to execute, with promptitude, the purposes of the head. The pity which you should repress, is a turbulent emotion. The commiseration which you should cultivate, is a calm principle. It is

benevolence itself directed forcibly to a specific object. And the frequency of such objects diminishes not, but augments its energy: For it produces a tone or constitution of mind, constantly in unison with suffering; and prepared, on every call, to afford the full measure of relief (Percival 1803, 125–126).

It is instructive that Thomas Bassnett became an Anglican priest and that, out of his love for his son, complemented by Baconian deist convictions, Percival accepted this choice, on which, as explained above, Thomas Bassnett's mind was firmly set. Throughout the "Discourse" Thomas Bassnett's method is to appeal, first, to Baconian moral science in a manner instantly recognizable from his father's writings, complemented with Christian scripture, going beyond his father's spare Unitarian christianity.

> Appear, therefore, to your patients to be actuated by that fellow-feeling, which nature, education, and Christianity require. Make your cases, in a reasonable degree, your own; *and whatsoever ye would that men should do unto you, do ye even so unto them* (Percival 1803, 126).

Notice the order of the appeals. The first three are secular: fellow feeling from Baconian moral science; nature from Baconian science; and education in the sense of moral formation. Christianity comes fourth. Throughout the "Discourse" Thomas Bassnett cites Christian scripture only after arguments based on moral science. The scriptural passages reinforce the moral scientific claims. Appeals to scripture also complement the moral scientific claims: the former add to the latter and are not made independently of the latter. Thomas Bassnett's "Discourse" can, therefore, be read as deploying a double-pronged argument by persuasion, first the results of Baconian moral science that everyone must accept as a matter of intellectual and moral excellence, and, second, an appeal to persons of faith in the Christian state church. His father had complete confidence in the first prong and would accept the second, but only as a source of evidence from scripture, in the manner Percival learned at Warrington Academy. Here Thomas Bassnett's theism differs from his father's.

Thomas Bassnett's "Discourse" may have influenced *Medical Ethics*. Consider the former on clinical innovation and research in a hospital, which is addressed in Chapter I, Section XII:

> For every improvement in the healing art is a public good, beneficial to the poor as well as to the rich, and to the former in a proportionably greater degree, as they are more numerous, and consequently more frequently the objects of it. On this point, however, peculiar delicacy is required; and as the discretionary power, with which you are entrusted, is almost without controul, it should be exercised what the nicest honour and probity. When novelties in practice are introduced, be careful that they are conformable to reason and analogy; That no sacrifice be made to fanciful hypothesis, or experimental curiosity; that the infliction of pain or suffering be, as much as possible, avoided; and that the end in view fully warrant the means for its attainment (Percival 1803, 122–123).

The first sentence of this passage recalls Percival's ethics of experimentation with animals, which we examined in Chap. 2. In *Medical Ethics* Percival makes a similar case, as we saw above. Thomas Bassnett's claim that "the discretionary power, with which you are entrusted, is almost without control" would, I think, have caught

Percival's eye. Yes, that power should be regulated by "the nicest honour and probity" but that is a slender reed from which to hang the protection of the patients in the Infirmary from ambitious physicians of the sort that Gregory sought to rein in with his research ethics, described in Chap. 1. This may have prompted Percival to start *Medical Ethics* as he did, with an account of an organizational culture of professionalism that incorporates into its structure and governance "the nicest honour," where 'honour' is properly understood, as explained above, and "probity," or well-founded clinical judgment, hypothesis formation, and hypothesis testing (as Percival exhibits in his "experimental essays" examined in Chap. 2) required by accountability to the committee of gentlemen who will prospectively oversee clinical innovation and research.

The anonymous editor of the 1827 second edition of *Medical Ethics* characterizes the relationship between it and Thomas Bassnett's discourse in an interesting way: "Every important rule regarding the guardianship of hospitals, advanced in Mr. Percival's Sermon, is a recapitulation of the Ethics" (Percival 1807, xx).

3.6 Conclusion

Thomas Percival wrote the first book in the global history of medical ethics entitled, *Medical Ethics*. This chapter has provided an historically based philosophical interpretation of this text and its predecessor, *Medical Jurisprudence*. The intellectual biography of Percival in Chap. 2 revealed him to have been a Baconian scientist in his scientific or "experimental" and clinical or "medical" essays, starting with his 1763 *On the Resemblance between Chyle and Milk* and 1765 inaugural dissertation, *De Frigore*. He presented many of these works to scientific groups and published them in the scientific journals of this day. This intellectual biography also revealed Percival to have been a Baconian moral scientist in his "moral writings," i.e., writings on moral science. He wrote *Medical Ethics* and *Medical Jurisprudence* before it as a Baconian scientist and moral scientist, committed also to Baconian Dissent and deism.

3.6.1 *Professional Ethics in Medicine: Three Commitments*

As a Baconian moral scientist, Percival adopted Gregory's account of the secular ethical concept of medicine as a profession. Medical science is founded in the truth of things. It therefore makes no appeal to divinity, revelation, or the theology of any faith community. Medical science is also deist: no intrinsic hostility exists between medicine and religion. It is false that *ubi tres medici, duo athei* (wherever there are three doctors, there are three atheists).

Three commitments of the physician define the secular ethical concept of medicine as a profession: to becoming and remaining scientifically and clinically competent; to making the protection and promotion of the patient's health and life the physician's primary concern and motivation, requiring individual self-interest to be systematically relegated to secondary status; and to making the protection and promotion of the patient's health and life the physician's primary concern and motivation, requiring group self-interest or party-interest to be systematically relegated to secondary status. Fulfilling these commitments makes medicine a public trust, for the improvement of which physicians are responsible, so that they pass better medicine on to their successors and their successors' patients. There is no religious test for making or sustaining these three commitments. Professional ethics in medicine is therefore transreligious.

When physicians and surgeons form their professional character to the intellectual virtue of candor they become and remain scientifically and clinically competent. This is the source of physicians and surgeons having intellectual authority, being *an* authority about health and its preservation and restoration (Engelhardt 1996). Physicians and surgeons form their professional character to the virtues of tenderness, steadiness, condescension, and authority by committing to the patient's health and life and the primary concern and motivation and keeping all forms of -interest secondary. This is the source of physicians and surgeons having moral authority, being *an* authority about what patients should do about their health and its preservation and restoration (Engelhardt 1996). When physicians and surgeons gain candor-based authority and use it with tenderness, steadiness, authority, and condescension they become intellectually trustworthy, and not tyrannical, wielders of power over patients. Trustworthy clinicians are justifiably *in* authority, though with limits on their government of their patients. The long tradition of entrepreneurial medicine had no response to the anomaly it generated: rampant intellectual distrust. Professional ethics in medicine as a set of commitments that define a way of life provides the antidote to intellectual distrust.

Percival starts *Medical Ethics* uniquely, with professional ethics in hospital practice. I read Percival to have understood that undertaking and sustaining the way of life defined by professional ethics in medicine will have little chance of succeeding should physicians, surgeons, and apothecaries have to labor alone. A supportive organizational culture increases the chances of sustained success in the intellectual and moral formation for which Percival calls in *Medical Ethics*. I think that he got this exactly right.

3.6.2 Baconian Moral Scientific Professional Ethics in Medicine

The opening paragraph of both *Medical Jurisprudence* and *Medical Ethics* – they are identical in their wording – announces that Percival makes Baconian moral science the basis for everything that follows. In an undeniable reference to Gregory, he invokes his two inventions: two professional regulatory virtues of sympathy, tenderness and steadiness. Percival then adds two inventions of his own: professional regulatory virtues of sympathy, condescension and authority. Percival's professional medical ethics is Baconian moral scientific professional ethics in medicine. The result is Baconian moral scientific professional ethics in medicine. That it is Baconian means that it is transnational and transcultural. The long tradition of entrepreneurial medicine had no response to the anomaly it generated: rampant moral distrust. Professional ethics in medicine as a set of commitments that define a way of life provides the antidote to moral distrust.

3.6.3 "Institutes" and "Precepts" of Professional Ethics in Medicine

Percival learned from his study at Edinburgh of the Theory of Medicine and of the *Institutions of Medicine*, as taught by Cullen, and from his study of Boerhaave's *Institutiones Medicae* in Leyden that medicine has both theoretical and practical components. By mastering both, the medical student enters the way of life of the Baconian physician. From Gregory and from his own "experimental and medical" writings Percival learned mastery of the theory of medicine, the "truth of things" of medical morality. From his "literary" and "moral" writings, he learned mastery of the practical aspects of morality: following the many rules he sets out in those writings, guided by moral exemplars of doing so. He brought to *Medical Jurisprudence* and *Medical Ethics* the intellectual tools and way of life of a Baconian moral scientist, shaped by Baconian Dissent and deism. These tools prepared him to join and uniquely expand Gregory's moral revolution against the long tradition of entrepreneurialism in Western medicine.

Medical Ethics describes itself as a "Code" of Institutes and Precepts" (Percival 1803, [1803] 2022, i). A Code is a set of justified rules. Its first component is justification. The three commitments that Gregory invented as the content of the ethical concept of medicine as a profession provides the conceptual framework for professional ethics in medicine. Failure to make and sustain these commitments will result in "an acute sensibility to shame, reproach, or infamy" (Percival 1807, Vol. II, 204), which serves as a powerful correction to losing one's moral way.

The ethical concept of medicine as a profession becomes the "Institutes" section of Percival's "Code." In the opening paragraph of *Medical Ethics* Percival made Gregory's professional ethics in medicine his "Institutes." Percival makes a key addition, the professional virtues of condescension and authority. The theory of professional ethics in medicine thus reliably in place, he devotes himself to the "Precepts" of professional ethics in medicine: the ethically justified rules for the reliable, practical application of the theory in the organizational culture of a hospital, in private practice, in cooperation with apothecaries, and in political ethics, the proper relation of physicians and surgeons to state power. The precepts of the "Code" translate the institutes into clinical practice, research, and the professional organizational culture of a hospital. *Medical Ethics* thus becomes what Percival calls "Practical Ethics" (Percival 1803, [1803] 2022, 5). The result is that "everything belonging to it [professional ethics in medicine] [is] explained to him [the reader] in its proper connection" (Priestley 1765, 17). The "Code" with its constituent "Institutes" and "Precepts" create the practical ethics to carry into effect Percival's moral revolution against the long tradition of entrepreneurialism in the history of Western medicine.

3.6.4 Deism and Dissent in Percival's Professional Ethics in Medicine

3.6.4.1 Deism: Medicine and Religion

In Chap. 2 we saw that Percival concisely summarizes the proper relationship between Baconian medicine and religion – the latter is accountable to the former as the only reliable account of the truth of things – in the discourse of deistic Dissent that he learned from Taylor and Seddon at Warrington Academy: "Rational theism [the theism of Dissenting Unitarians of the Percivalean persuasion] leads the mind, by fair and necessary induction [from experience, as in his scientific essays examined in Chap. 2], to extend its views to revelation" (Percival 1803, 196).

Percival uses 'rational theism' to underscore that religions and their theologies are accountable to the truth of things, the identification of which is the task of Baconian science and moral science. 'Rational theism' becomes Percival's Dissenting, Unitarian variant of deism. Theologies are held to account to rational theism; only those parts of theology compatible with rational theism command intellectual and moral respect that are the basis for toleration and pluralism, as we saw in Chap. 2. Because religion is accountable to Baconian science and moral science and because professional ethics in medicine is based on Baconian science and moral science, deist professional ethics in medicine is transreligious.

3.6.4.2 Dissent: Medicine and Society

Dissenter deists who adopted Baconian science and moral science, as Percival surely did, use Baconian science and moral science to hold to account all forms of power – organizational, social, ecclesiastical, and political – to account for the intellectual and moral authority of that power. Hospitals must have a just polity, which they do when their trustees, managers, and professional medical staff commit to protect and promote the good of the patient. Only a gentleman who earns this social status has intellectual and moral authority, because earning the title of "gentleman" requires him to be committed to the common weal and not to self-interest or party-interest. The Articles of Faith of the Church of England do not pass this test of accountability and so have no intellectual or moral authority, a radical implication of Baconian deism that Percival expressed only by subscribing to the rational theism of Unitarianism, an alternative religion, and by refusing to assent to the Articles of Faith. Political power has intellectual and moral authority for those subjected to it when it conforms to the criteria for a just polity set out in political ethics. Holding all forms of power to account to Baconian Dissent means that it is autonomous from forms of power that do not meet the meet the intellectual and moral truth of things.

The resulting relationship of medicine and society is that the profession of medicine, properly understood, is autonomous from society. This is not the negotiated autonomy of social contract theory, as we saw in Chap. 2 and in earlier discussion in this chapter of the differences between Percival and Gisborne. It is not the case that social contract theory grants this status in response to the unique fund of knowledge and skills that society needs. The autonomy of the profession of medicine precedes social contract theory. Social contract theory therefore cannot serve as the basis for professional ethics in medicine.

There is a parallel autonomy in the polity of the hospital. Chapter I, Section VIII on the responsible use of formulary resources is addressed to the hospital managers and trustees. Percival's argument calls them to account for potentially preventable death from an "œconomy, of fatal tendency" (Percival 1803, 13). This means that the trustees and managers should respect the experienced-based clinical judgment of physicians and surgeons, which clinical judgment is autonomous from the power of the trustees and managers.

Pickstone and Butler describe the Infirmary as a "relatively democratic organization" (Pickstone and Butler 1985, 248). Percival sought to make it more democratic, perhaps sensing the shift in power to the trustees and managers, discussed earlier. Percival would have it that the polity of a hospital should be self-governance based on an ethics of cooperation required by professional ethics in medicine in an organization setting. The first commitment of the ethical concept of medicine as a profession creates the common clinical component: Baconian clinical science. The second and third commitments create the common focus on each patient's health and life: Baconian moral science. Baconian clinical and moral science creates the autonomy of physicians, surgeons, and apothecaries from the trustees and managers that an ethics of cooperation requires. His proposals in Notes III for various hospital committees aim to secure this autonomy, as a practical matter in the administrative structure of a hospital.

3.7 A Professional Colleague's Instructions

Before *Medical Ethics* Percival was an accomplished moralist, especially in his capacity an instructor of children, starting with his own at Hart-Hill, on their moral formation. As we saw, *A Father's Instructions* enjoyed considerable success, which helped to make Percival a public figure to whom the Trustees of Manchester Infirmary could turn with confidence to help them manage the clashing interests that emerged during the eventually successful effort to expand the number of honorary physicians at the Infirmary. Pickstone, in a passage included in Chap. 2, succinctly states how *A Father's Instructions* prepared him for undertaking *Medical Ethics*: "He was in a position now to be a paternalist not just to his children (or via books); he was equipped and inclined to be a city father, a public paternalist, solving public problems …" (Pickstone 1993, 167).

In inventing a professional ethics in medicine that has an ethics of cooperation at its core, Percival did more, much more, than become a "public paternalist." Joining Gregory, Percival revolted against the entrepreneurial paradigm, in which physicians, surgeons, and apothecaries engaged in fierce, economically high-stakes competition that unnecessarily put at risk the health and lives of sick people. Physicians, surgeons, and apothecaries practiced an environment of "interest, prejudice, or rivalship" (Percival 1803, 60–61). Contention and disagreement were their stock and trade, expressed in flytes or in letters to the Manchester *Mercury* during the 1789–1790 dispute described at the beginning of this chapter. The "good of the patient" was not "the sole object in view" (Percival 1803, 37); it was not in view at all. Endemic intellectual and moral distrust defined the entrepreneurial paradigm. Intellectual and oral distrust could not be remedied with more individual self-interest, guild-interest, or party-interest; they only fed fuel to the fire. The paradigm of professional ethics in medicine and its ethics of cooperation banished the discourse of rivalship that defines the entrepreneurial paradigm and replaced it with the discourse of cooperation, which is a discourse of peace designed to prevent rivalship from evolving into the controversy and contention that disrupted the charitable mission of Manchester Infirmary for almost two years.

Percival uses 'colleagues' twice in *Medical Ethics*. The first usage occurs in Chapter I, Section IX:

> No physician or surgeon, therefore, should *reveal* occurrences in the hospital, which may injure the reputation of any one of his colleagues; except under the restriction contained in the succeeding article (Percival 1803, 14).

We saw above that he added "restriction," which does not appear in *Statuta Moralia*, to deploy the accountability ingredient in the ethics of cooperation that should define an organizational culture of professionalism in a hospital with a just polity. The second occurrence of 'colleague' is in a footnote to Chapter I, Section XXIII, in which Percival refers to "the time when I was desired, by them and my other colleagues, to frame a code of rules for the Manchester Infirmary" (Percival 1803, 23). In Chapter III he refers to the apothecary three times as the physician's 'coadjutor' (Percival 1803, 4250, 53). Percival's discourse of 'colleague' and 'coadjutor' signals the force of his moral revolution against the entrepreneurial paradigm by replacing its discourse of rivalship and subordination, respectively, with a single professional ethics of medicine and therefore a single profession of medicine.

Contra Pickstone *Medical Ethics* is not a paternalistic tract for physicians, surgeons, and apothecaries. *Medical Ethics* can be subtitled, *A Professional Colleague's Instructions to Physicians, Surgeons, and Apothecaries on the Professional Life of Caring for Patients*.

Chapter 4
The Place of Percival's *Medical Ethics* in the History of Medical Ethics

In this, the final, chapter I will attempt to place Thomas Percival *Medical Ethics* and the professional ethics in medicine that it expounds in the history of medical ethics. I will begin with what Percival achieved, the co-invention with John Gregory, of medical professionalism defined as professional ethics in medicine. I will then turn to how *Medical Jurisprudence* and then *Medical Ethics* were received in the nineteenth century and interpreted in the twentieth century. Percival's influence was strongest in the United States, where in mid-nineteenth-century the newly formed American Medical Association formulated the first national code of medical ethics in the history of the United States, acknowledging the influence of Gregory and Percival. I will close the chapter and therefore this book with a reflection on Gregory and Percival's legacy for contemporary professional ethics in medicine.

4.1 Achievement: *Medical Ethics* and the Invention of Medical Professionalism

> Dr. Percival's valuable and truly classic work was republished in 1803, and completed what Dr. Gregory had omitted (Ryan 1836, 46).

Michael Ryan (1800–1840) was an Irish physician who wrote a major treatise on medical jurisprudence (Ryan 1836). This includes a history of medical ethics, one of the first, in which he deploys extensive passages from both Gregory's *Lectures* and Percival's *Medical Ethics*. Howard Brody, Zahra Meghani, and Kimberly Greenwald have edited a contemporary edition and introduced it with a comprehensive scholarly account of Ryan's work (Brody et al. 2009). In the single sentence above, Ryan points to the central claim of this book: Gregory and Percival co-invented medical professionalism, based on the ethical concept of medicine as a profession. Gregory started a moral revolution against the entrepreneurial paradigm, based on Baconian science and Baconian moral science. Percival completed this moral revolution by writing Baconian moral scientific professional ethics in medicine that "completed what Gregory had omitted." The result is a comprehensive account of professional ethics in medicine in clinical practice, innovation and research, in the organizational culture of a hospital or what Percival calls the "polity" of a hospital, and in the relationship of the profession of medicine to state power. Percival complemented Gregory's professional ethics in medicine by adding to it the hospital duties of physicians and surgeons as the paradigm duties of physicians that should also govern in private practice. Percival also makes implicit elements of Gregory's professional ethics in medicine explicit, e.g., the professional regulatory virtues of condescension and authority.

Gregory and Percival shared a revolutionary starting point: Both were Baconian scientists and physicians as well as Baconian moral scientists. Gregory and Percival learned Baconian medical science at the University of Edinburgh, which had eclipsed Leyden, after the death of Boerhaave, as the premier center for Baconian medical science, a status it would enjoy well into the nineteenth century. Clinical judgment and practice were to be based solely on the results of experience, either in the form of the findings of either careful observation or controlled experiments. We saw in Chap. 2 that Percival had deployed Baconian scientific method on many topics in clinical practice. As a result, Percival demonstrated his commitment to become and remain a scientifically and clinical competent physician.

This commitment is on display from his second scientific work in *de Frigore* (Percival 1765) and his earliest works in philosophy of science and philosophy of medicine, the paired essays, "The Empiric" and "The Dogmatic." Gregory had invented this commitment as the first commitment of the ethical concept of medicine as a profession. Percival complements Gregory's contribution by exploring implications more comprehensively – not only in clinical practice but also in public health and in environmental medicine.

One of Gregory's first topics in *Lectures* is men of "interest," physicians committed to the pursuit of self-interest, which was the functioning norm of the entrepreneurial paradigm that had preceded his work for centuries. Gregory advances antidotes that shape his moral revolution against entrepreneurial medicine. Baconian medicine forswears all forms of bias, i.e., clinical judgment and practice not based on experience (with 'experience' used in its technical meaning in Baconian philosophy of science and medicine). This includes, especially, bias that originates in self-interest. Thus, Gregory condemns the use of nostrums and secret medicine. They lack an experience base and therefore illicitly take advantage of the air of mystery that promotes patients' compliance and therefore future sales. The intellectual virtue of candor requires physicians to be open to information, regardless of its source but also to subject new information to experience-based appraisal, now known as critical, evidence-based appraisal (Guyatt et al. 2000).

4.1 Achievement: *Medical Ethics* and the Invention of Medical Professionalism

Percival complements Gregory's approach to candor. In Chapter I of *Medical Ethics* Percival calls for the creation of an organizational culture of cooperation based on and promoting candor. The faculty of Manchester Infirmary – and of every other infirmary and healthcare organization – should commit to accountability for the scientific and clinical evidence-base of clinical practice and also of clinical innovation and research, In the process they will master Baconian self-discipline that will guide them in their private practices. There they will be accountable to themselves but with the rigor that the hospital committee would have required. In both settings, the physician or surgeon who achieves this self-discipline will not be a man of "interest." Instead, he will be committed to using his Baconian scientific and clinical competence for the "good of the patient" and to keeping individual self-interest systematically secondary. This commitment requires experience-based cooperation for the good of the patient. This is the second commitment of the ethical concept of medicine as a profession that Gregory had invented and that Percival complements with a professional culture of accountability and cooperation.

This second commitment is also required by the principle of sympathy and its professional regulatory virtues. Gregory identifies two such virtues: tenderness, or the direct engagement with the lived experience of the patient, especially the affective dimensions of that experience; and steadiness, preventing the double relation of impressions and ideas from becoming loss of control, on the one hand, or hardheartedness, on the other. Gregory also saw sympathy as a principle that, when thus regulated, would close the socioeconomic gap between physicians and their patients in the Royal Infirmary of Edinburgh, while still permitting effective "government" of patients to achieve for them the clinical benefits of treatment of their conditions. Gregory also called for physicians to seek government over patients, to the limited extent that the constraints of human nature and self-care of private patients in implementing regimen permitted.

Percival invents two professional regulatory virtues that explicitly capture the need to close socioeconomic gaps and to assert sufficient control to increase the probability of success of regimen: condescension and authority. Condescension, a virtue that Percival probably absorbed from Grove, as we saw in Chap. 2, obligates the physician to bridge socioeconomic and other clinically irrelevant differences and come "down" to the patient's level. Percival's readers would know that the paradigm of condescension occurred when God become man in the form of his beloved son, Jesus. If the God of Christianity could bridge an infinite divide, physicians could bridge a finite divide, however personally challenging that task might prove to be. Percival also makes explicit that the professional regulatory virtue of authority includes being both *an* authority – having superior knowledge about clinical medicine and its organization in Manchester Infirmary – and *in* authority – having superior knowledge of moral formation, the virtues that patients should cultivate and the vices they should avoid and putting that knowledge to work in plans of care and in hospital policy, e.g., the moral regimen for patients with mental illnesses and for prostitutes in the lock hospital.

Gregory had the outline of a professional ethics for clinical research, as we saw in Chap. 1, but he did not include it in *Lectures*. The conceptual basis is sympathy and its prohibition of sporting with the sick poor, a form of cruelty. Gregory also wanted accountability, by "laying medicine open" to critical appraisal by sophisticated laypersons, a radical proposal for its time. Percival sets the professional ethics of clinical innovation and research in the context of the hospital, where it can best be conducted and conducted for those who will gain the most from it, the sick poor, if only because, as Thomas Bassnett Percival points out in his "Discourse," there are many more poor folk than the well-to-do. Percival brings the professional ethics of accountability to bear by proposing prospective review and oversight of clinical innovation and research by members of the faculty of the hospital. This was a revolutionary proposal but made less radical and perhaps therefore more politic by putting physicians and surgeons in charge.

Gregory had lamented the gulf between physicians and surgeons, especially as it represented entrenched, divisive guild-interests. He proposed that physicians and surgeons should close this gulf by establishing priority for managing a clinical case based on the skill set that the patient's presenting condition, as required by Baconian, experienced-based clinical judgment. Gregory explains this cooperation in the example of a patient with gangrene. The work-up and diagnosis of the patient is a medical, not surgical, judgment. The clinical judgment that the patient's condition requires surgical management is also a medical judgment. The planning for and carrying-out of surgical management is a surgical judgment. Gregory counts on the professional intellectual virtue of candor to guide this revolutionary improvement in cooperation designed to close the gap between physicians and surgeons for the clinical benefit of patients.

Percival takes Gregory's anti-corporation-spirit revolution one step further: cooperation that the good of the patient requires should be formalized in the hospital setting as a matter of professional responsibility. The system of accountability for the Baconian scientific and moral quality of patient care that Percival describes in Chapter I requires formalized cooperation among physicians, among surgeons, between physicians and surgeons, and between physicians and apothecaries. Scientific and moral cooperation is a function of making the three commitments of the ethics concept of medicine as a profession. When professional accountability and cooperation exist, an ethically justified hospital polity exists, because professional accountability and cooperation are necessarily directed to the good of the patient. Both provide a powerful antidote to men of interest who can exist and succeed only by evading accountability and cooperation. Both provide a powerful antidote to self-governance based on party interest, a built-in risk of power in an organizational setting. Ethically justified self-governance by physicians and surgeons in a hospital is a direct function of a system of accountability and cooperation and justified by implementing it.

Percival expands the scope of conflicts of interest by expanding the scope of 'interest'. For Gregory, 'interest' included both individual self-interest and the interests of the merchant guilds known as the Royal Colleges. He used 'corporation spirit' to describe this guild-interest, referring to the creation by charter of royal corporations with legally sanctioned, though limited, powers. Percival expands the concept of group self-interest into the concept of party-interest: a form of group self-interest that comes into existence whenever individuals discover that they have interests in common that that they can prosecute more effectively if they band together. The members of the Royal College have a party-interest, but a party interest can exist in the absence of royal sanction. Percival had in mind the party-interest of the Halls, Whites, and their physician colleagues in medicine at Manchester Infirmary and how they misused this party-interest to block improvement of patient care. The resulting polity of the Manchester Infirmary, from its founding four decades earlier, had become a polity of party-interest and therefore an ethically impermissible polity. Every moral writing we examined in Chaps. 2 and 3 supports the view that this would have been Percival's moral judgment and a motivation for him to join in the effort to improve the polity of Infirmary into a professional polity. This helps to explain why he starts *Medical Ethics* with the hospital duties of physicians and surgeons.

Gregory's proposal for routine, candor-based cooperation takes an implicit step toward the view that physicians, surgeons, and apothecaries constitute a single profession. Percival makes this step explicit. He was not yet prepared to do so in 1792 when he began work on *Medical Jurisprudence*. Recall that its title references "The Professions of Physic and Surgery," perhaps because there were only the beginnings of uniting them into one profession at the time, perhaps influenced by the London surgeon, John Hunter, "considered by many in Britain" to be "the greatest living exponent of scientific surgery" (Lawrence 1993, 974). Actual integration of medicine and surgery, however, belongs to the nineteenth century. In this context, the change in title in *Medical Ethics* to include "The Professional Conduct of Physicians and Surgeons" goes well beyond Gregory and can be read as a revolutionary leading of change. In Chapter III, Percival uses 'three distinct branches' (Percival 1803, 53) to include physicians, surgeons, and apothecaries into one profession. At the same time, he also described medicine and surgery as "the two professions" (Percival 1803, 19). Nonetheless, the idea that medicine and surgery should be considered one profession is indisputably conveyed in the title of *Medical Ethics* in a clear departure from the title of *Medical Jurisprudence*. This locution also implies that the continued separation of medicine and surgery serves to encourage the formation of party-interests by physicians and surgeons still wed to the entrepreneurial paradigm, i.e., most physicians and surgeons at the time. The title of *Medical Ethics* can therefore be plausibly read as Percival signaling how thoroughgoing he intended his professional ethics in medicine to be. As we saw at the end of Chap. 3, Percival's use of 'colleague' to mean professional colleagues tracks revolutionary conceptual change. Gregory had used 'colleague' once in *Lectures*, but to refer to faculty members who supervised medical students' inaugural dissertations (Gregory 1772, [1772] 1998 213).

Percival's account of medicine as a profession includes something not found in Gregory's Lectures: the limited autonomy of medicine from managers and trustees of Manchester Infirmary and from the state, both its criminal laws and its official religion, the Church of England. The former appears in Chapter I, Section VIII, in which, as we saw in Chap. 3, Percival undertakes the moral instruction of the managers and trustees of Manchester Infirmary about the professionally responsible use of the hospital formulary, a major cost center at the time – and still to this day. He limits his case only to patients with the gravest conditions, which makes sense in terms of preventing imminent mortality when there is potentially effective treatment available in the formulary. It also makes sense in politic terms, as explained in Chap. 2 in the analysis of the *medicus politicus* literature: Percival understands that if he proposed to drain the resources of the formulary indiscriminately, he would meet justified resistance because the managers and trustees have the ethical obligation to steward the hospital's resources for the good of all of its patients. It is also politic to make one's first argument non-rejectable: the managers and trustees have an ethical obligation to the hospital to be economically rational about resource use and a cost-saving argument is the epitome of economic rationality (and still is in healthcare organizations). Any use of the formulary that will save money must be approved. Percival then appeals to "purest beneficence," a clinical judgment that is experienced-based and therefore the exclusive purview of physicians and surgeons who have made a clinical judgment in the process of accountability that Percival describes in Chapter I. Physicians and surgeons have autonomy over matters over which they, justifiably, have exclusive purview. Because they are the only ones who function as *an* authority, they are the only ones *in* authority.

In Chapter IV, in effect, physicians are the only ones who function as *an* authority about the clinical variations in capacity to make decisions about testamentary documents, whether an individual is *compos mentis*, and whether a lunatic retains sufficient decision-making capacity. Physicians are also the only ones who are *an* authority about the complex cognitive and affective aspects of a woman's decision to self-administer an abortifacient or not to report a stillbirth of a bastard child. Percival acknowledges that the instruments of juridical justice function as *in* authority about the administration of criminal law. However, when the criminal law intersects with medicine, the administration of criminal law is accountable to the experienced-based clinical judgment of physicians and surgeons. To this extent, the profession of medicine is *an* authority that is autonomous from the state.

At barely the age of twenty-one, Percival asserted his autonomy, as a Baconian Dissenter, from the state church, the Church of England. He did so on the basis of the Baconian identification of the truth of things and the spare deism that it requires, as he has been taught to do by his tutors at Warrington Academy. There is a powerful easy-to-miss expression of Percival the Dissenter in the text of *Medical Ethics*: 'christian' has the lower-case 'c', except in passages that he quotes faithfully from the original source. The general lesson from this experience is this: Baconian science and moral science possess intellectual and moral autonomy from state power – or any form of power exercised without the experience-based discipline of Baconian scientific and moral scientific reasoning – including especially Christian ecclesiastical power, now with an upper-case 'C'. Here the difference between his son's "Discourse" and the text of *Medical Ethics* becomes instructive for what the latter does not include: an appeal to Christian scripture or teaching in any form.

Medical Ethics is a secular text in two senses. It makes no appeal theological sources of morality. At the same time, as a text compatible with deism – because Baconian science and moral science are compatible with deism, as Gregory argued

4.1 Achievement: *Medical Ethics* and the Invention of Medical Professionalism

and as Percival himself did in texts analyzed in Chap. 3 – *Medical Ethics* is not intrinsically hostile to theology, Christian theology in particular and, for that matter, non-Christian theology. The result is the same as that sought by Gregory: there is no religious or theological test required to make the three commitments of the ethical concept of medicine as a profession. As a result, professional ethics in medicine is transreligious. This explains the absence from *Medical Ethics* of theological references found in his son's "Discourse;" the omission is required by Baconian science and moral science and is therefore deliberate. This omission also comes to define the variant of Unitarianism to which Percival subscribed. In a Baconian moral scientific professional ethics in medicine such appeals become unnecessary.

There is one further way in which Percival completes Gregory's co-invention by adding to it something altogether new. The three commitments required the ethical concept of medicine will be very difficult to make and sustain in a moral revolution against the paradigm of entrepreneurial medicine in the absence of a supportive organizational culture. The reader will recall from Chap. 3 that 'organizational culture' names a cluster concept that includes the express mission and values of the organization, its actual values as expressed in budgets and strategic decisions, what leadership encourages and rewards, what leadership discourages and punishes, what leadership tolerates, and what leadership tolerates that should not be tolerated. An organizational culture of professionalism will be structured and led with the goal of sustaining physicians in the three commitments of the ethical concept of medicine. I read Percival to have understood this point implicitly, as a result of witnessing the organizational culture of party-interest that the Halls, Whites, and their physician allies had created at the Manchester Infirmary. Trustee Philips, we saw in Chap. 3, came to the same observation and pushed for change.

Percival understood that revolutionary change was required to create, perhaps for the first time in its history, a hospital polity at Manchester Infirmary directed to the good of the patient. This explains why Chapter I of *Medical Ethics* addresses the hospital duties of physicians and surgeons. These must be designed to create an ethically justified hospital polity that, in turn, requires organizational structures of professional self-government. This polity must also be strong enough that its intellectual and moral discipline can be carried into private practice, in which hospital physicians and surgeons should become exemplars of professional ethics in medicine. Other physicians and surgeons engaged in only private practice can follow these exemplars to reform themselves from entrepreneurial practitioners into professional physicians. To paraphrase Price on hospitals, Percival set himself the task to scientifically and morally "construct and regulate" a profession of medicine worthy of the name. Percival's ambition thus expresses the English enlightenment commitment to improvement, in a far-reaching way.

Percival's achievements in *Medical Ethics* culminate in the transformative claim at the end of Chapter II that medicine is a public trust. Physicians, surgeons, and apothecaries should make the three commitments that define the ethical concept of medicine as a profession in order to earn the title of "professional." Making these commitments directs clinical judgment, clinical practice, clinical innovation and research, and therefore the polity of a hospital to the good of the patient. The scope of these commitments includes present patients, of course. But, in the English enlightenment drive to improve social institutions such as the medical profession, hospitals, and dispensaries, the scope of these commitments also includes future patients. To achieve this improvement, social institutions must be preserved and strengthened for the good of *future* patients. This is the meaning in which the medical profession is a public trust: it is preserved and strengthened to serve patients and thereby the general weal, today and for all tomorrows. Like the assets of a reversionary fund, the assets of scientifically and clinically competent practice, innovation, research, and an organizational culture of professionalism are to be held in trust for future patients. Thus does the profession of medicine, and its members, become intellectually and morally trustworthy. The concept of medicine as a public trust thus becomes the antidote to the long tradition of intellectual and moral distrust generated by the entrepreneurial paradigm in the forms described in Chap. 1. Percival, complementing Gregory's invention, created the conceptual vocabulary of "public trust" to put a full stop to that tradition and co-invents medical professionalism.

4.2 Reception

The reception of Percival's *Medical Ethics* concerns what those who came after him thought of the book and its proposals. The reception of *Medical Ethics* begins with that of his son, Edward and continues in England through the second edition (Percival 1827) and third edition (Percival 1849), as well as in Michael Ryan's history of medical ethics (Ryan 1836). I have been able to identify additional sources that document this reception until the end of the nineteenth century. The reception in the United States dates from the early nineteenth century and culminates in the *Code of Medical Ethics* of 1847 of the then-fledgling American Medical Association.

4.2.1 Reception in England

In his *Memoirs* Edward Percival remarks on the completion and publication of *Medical Ethics*. (As noted at the beginning of Chap. 2, Edward's biography of his father can become hagiographic.)

> In the spring of 1803, his work was completed and sent to the press; and nearly the whole of a large impression [Edward's footnote: "A thousand copies"] was sold and circulated in a few months. The voice of the public declared in its favour; and the testimonies of the best judges have stamped a value on the performance, which amply gratified the author's expectations. As the work last noticed [*A Father's Instructions*, third part 1803] seemed to complete Dr. Percival's scheme of *moral* enquiry; so this latest production of his pen may be regarded as the conclusion of that plan of *professional* research and disquisition which he had commenced in the outset of his career (Percival 1807, Vol. I, ccix).

4.2 Reception

The second edition of *Medical Ethics*, anonymously edited, contains the text with added commentary on sections that were of interest to the editor. He notes that the 1803 book "has long since been out of print" (Percival 1827, xviii–xix). Percival sought to characterize "what sort of character he *ought to be*" (Percival 1827, xxi, emphasis original), the editor quotes from Percival. The editor then states his goal: "painting what sort of character he *ought not to be*" (Percival 1827, xxi). This goal is motivated, the reader learns, by the editor's highly critical view of then-contemporary physicians and their colleges.

> In the observations, which we have made upon certain physicians and others it cannot be supposed, that we have meant to reflect upon men of Dr. Percival's character, but upon a race which has multiplied throughout the country, successful in the most inaccountable manner, beyond their merits, though exceedingly and altogether different in learning and conduct from the several great and eminent examples who, with the author of the Medical Ethics, adorned the profession at the beginning of this century (Percival 1827, xxv).

The editor's comments can become acerbic. For example, after Section VI of Chapter I, on the "*moral* and *religious* influence of sickness" (Percival 1827, 4), the commentary begins with "We are sorry to say, that the injunctions of Dr. Gregory and Dr. Percival require to be much strengthened" (Percival 1827, 5). He explains the need when he claims that physicians have "tolerated, if not encouraged, a vile system of intrusion on the religious principles of their patients" (Percival 1827, 6). The editor presents no evidence of this "intrusion." The sustained negative tenor of the editor's comments invites classification of them as a screed utterly incompatible with the intellectual standards that Percival set for himself in *Medical Ethics*. The reader would be justified to reach the judgment that Percival would not have welcomed this reception of his work.

The editor of the third edition of *Medical Ethics* explains the need for it.

> As the late Dr. Percival's Code of Medical Ethics is commonly quoted as a work of authority, not only in this country, but also in America [about which more below], and as the original edition has now become scarce, it was thought that it might be usefully republished (Percival 1849, 1).

The reader's curiosity concerning omission of mention of the second edition is immediately satisfied in the footnote:

> A new edition was published in 1827, but the Editor's notes are of such a nature as to render the book absolutely mischievous (Percival 1849, 1).

Here the editor does credit to Percival's restrained style, even on subjects that clearly aroused his moral anger such as enslavement of persons, as we saw in Chap. 2. The use of 'mischievous' would, I think, have pleased Percival with its elegant dismissal of the "Editor's notes" in a fell swoop.

The editor provides a capsule summary of Percival's literary and medical stature:

> Dr. Percival held a distinguished rank both as a literary character, and a physician. In the latter capacity he displayed quick penetration, discriminating judgment, patient attention, and above all, says Abp. Magee, a deep sense of responsibility. As an author he obtained considerable reputation in the philosophical and religious world, particularly by his "Essays, Medical and Experimental," and his last work entitled, "Medical Ethics," in which,

it is said, while delineating the requisites and qualifications of the medical practitioner, he unconsciously displayed the most exact portraiture of himself (Percival 1949, 14–15).

"Abp Magee" refers to The Rev. William Conner Magee (1821–1891), Archbishop of York. Edward Percival includes an excerpt from a "biographical tribute" in his *Memoir* (Percival 1807, Vol. I, ccxxii–ccxxv). The editor's second and final sentences are adapted from this text. Magee adds:

> Indeed, in that most valuable treatise [*Medical Ethics*], which he expressly dedicated as a 'paternal legacy' to a much-beloved son, and which may now be regarded as his bequest to his brethren of the faculty, and to the public, he has left behind him a monument to professional integrity and honour, which will exhibit him to those of after-times, that his life and conduct have done to his cotemporaries, one of the worthiest objects of their admiration and esteem (Percival 1807, Vol. I, ccxxv).

Michael Ryan includes an extensive passage from Gregory's *Lectures* and then remarks:

> Such are the chief of the duties of medical men, according the amiable and revered Dr. Gregory, the observance of which cannot fail to promote the honor and dignity of the profession (Ryan 1836, 62–63).

This section opened with Ryan's characterization of *Medical Ethics* as a "valuable and truly classic work" (Ryan 1836, 46).

In his *Profiles of Warrington Worthies* the physician James Kendrick (1809–1882) provides single-paragraph portraits of his chosen subjects. Kendrick describes Percival: "An eminent physician, moral essayist, and philosopher. Author of 'A Father's Instructions to his Children'; 'Medical Ethics' &c" (Kendrick 1858, 9), indicating the positive reception of the latter. Pickstone pairs the two titles as well, remarking: "… we remind ourselves that Percival was already [at the time he wrote *Medical Ethics*] a widely-read *moralist*, and that his moralizing for children was clearly linked to his moralizing for doctors" (Pickstone 1993, 169).

Robert Angus Smith (1817–1884) was a Scottish chemist who made his scientific career in Manchester. In his history of science in Manchester he characterizes Percival and his *Medical Ethics* as follows:

> There is no attempt in Dr. Percival's book to prove himself the wisest man under the sun and possessed of every virtue, but he shows himself a wise and practical man, as his position in Manchester might be expected to prove him; and he gives rules for the behavior of medical men towards their patients and each other which are dictated by the highest feelings and the most refined perception and taste. So far as these are concerned, it seems scarcely possible to go beyond Dr. Percival and we could imagine this treatise to be a code of morals and manners to all succeeding generations (Smith 1883, 37).

Charles West (1816–1898) was a fellow of the Royal College of Physicians. He played an instrumental role in the establishment of the Hospital for Sick Children in London in 1851 (now the Great Ormond Street Hospital for pediatrics). He tells his reader that the title of his book, *The Profession of Medicine*, is taken from a lecture that he gave in 1850 at St. Bartholomew's Hospital in London (West 1898). He states that his thoughts, almost a half-century later remain essentially unchanged (West 1898, vii).

> An old man's opinions on these subjects will, I am sure, meet with indulgence, and all the more, since in the main they correspond with those of Dr. Gregory, as expressed in his lectures *On the Duties and Qualifications of a Physician*, published in 1772; and with those of Dr. Percival in *Medical Ethics*, which appeared in 1803 (West 1896, vii–viii).

West adds:

> For myself, I can only hope that if Gregory and Percival were my critics, they would approve of what I have tried to do, and that my book may, in some measure, answer the end ["of lessening human suffering"] now, which theirs accomplished a century ago (West 1898, x).

New standards for professional behavior were articulated first by John Gregory and then by Thomas Percival. Their works provided many American and Canadian doctors who studied in Edinburgh and London with the intellectual foundation from which to formulate formal codes of ethics when the American and Canadian medical associations were created in 1847 and 1867, respectively (MacDougal and Langley n.d.)

4.2.2 Reception in the United States

In the United States positive reception came quickly, with the way paved by two leaders of nineteenth-century American medical ethics, as Robert Baker explains:

> *Medical Ethics* was immediately treated as authoritative, especially by the Americans. Two of Gregory's students, Samuel Bard (1742–1821), a founder of New York's Columbia Presbyterian Hospital, and Benjamin Rush (1724–1813), cofounder of a number of Philadelphia medical institutions, had heralded the importance of medical ethics for the American medical profession (Baker 1993b, 865).

Medical Ethics was a source also for the codes of conduct prepared by state medical societies, sometimes known as "Medical Police." The first of these, the *Boston Medical Police* "borrowed extensively from Percival's *Medical Ethics*" (Baker 1993b, 865). By mid-century, others followed in other states (Baker 2013; Burns 1974, 1977).

When the editor of the third edition of *Medical Ethics* remarked on the reception of it in the United States, he referenced and quotes from the "Note to 1847 Convention" by Drs. John Bell, Isaac Hays, and the other committee members who had prepared the American Medical Association's new 1847 *Code of Ethics*. This "Note" underscores the fact the *Medical Ethics* was well known in the United States by the mid-1840s. Percival's book and its ideas were well received in the United States because of the moral authority and intellectual respect they had attained by the middle of the nineteenth century, as Baker points out (Baker 1993a, 2019). The "Note" reads

> Doctor Hays, on presenting this report, stated that justice required some explanatory remarks should accompany it. The members of the Convention, he observed, would not fail to recognize in parts of it, expressions with which they were familiar. On examining a great

number of codes of ethics adopted by different societies in the United States, it was found that they were all based on that of Dr. Percival, and that the phrases of this writer were preserved, to a considerable extent, in all of them. Believing that language which had been so often examined and adopted, must possess the greatest merits for such a document as the present, clearness and precision, and having no ambition for the honours of authorship, the Committee which prepared this code have followed a similar course, and have carefully preserved the words of Percival wherever they convey the precepts it is wished to elucidate (American Medical Association [1847] 1999, 315; Percival 1849, 1).

Robert Baker, in his masterful *Before Bioethics*, sets out the history of this reception of *Medical Ethics* in the United States in the first half of the nineteenth century. The medical societies in the several states played a major role in the successful reception of *Medical Ethics* (Baker 2013). Baker explains that these medical societies frequently included 'medical police' in their names. Baker explains the meaning of this phrase: "… the expression "medical police"" simply described regulations for self-government of "medical practitioners" (Baker 2013, 102). Percival would agree, especially with reference to creating an ethically justified hospital polity, as explained earlier in this Chapter. Such was the positive reception of *Medical Ethics* that it became the "primary source, or ur-text, for the *Boston Medical Police*" (Baker 2013, 102). The Connecticut Medical Society produced a shortened version of this text that was then adopted by medical societies in other states and cities. The result was that "… the Connecticut version of the *Boston Medical Police* became a template for instruments of medical society self-governance in early nineteenth-century America" (Baker 2013, 104).

The positive reception of *Medical Ethics* in the United States was propelled forward by the wonderfully named "The Secret Kappa Lambda Society of Hippocrates" (Ambrose 2005; Baker 2013, 136–140). Kentucky was the second state, after the original thirteen colonies, admitted to the union in 1802. Lexington was the home of Transylvania University, founded in 1780 as Transylvania Seminary (a common origin for many early American liberal arts colleges founded in the eighteenth century and earlier) and which still exists. Transylvania had a medical school from 1799, when it became a university, to 1859, the first medical school in what was then known as the West in the United States, the land west of the Appalachian Mountains. The meaning persists in the use of 'Midwest' to describe the prairie states west of the Appalachians. This mountain range contained a vast forest (and still does); hence the name Transylvania, from the Latin for "across the forest."

Dr. Samuel Brown (1769–1857) served as "he first Professor of the Theory and Practice of Medicine" in Transylvania's Medical Department (Ambrose 2005, 48). In 1820 he founded a fraternity, the form of secret society then increasingly common at American colleges. These societies typically used Greek letters in their titles. Dr. Brown meant for Kappa Lambda to be "a traditional medical society in a fraternity format" (Baker 2013, 137). Dr. Samuel Jackson (1787–1872), a professor at the Philadelphia College of Pharmacy, started a chapter in that city, as a medical society using the Greek letters of a fraternity (Baker 2013, 137). The constitution of the Philadelphia society called for its members "to engraft medical ethics on moral precept" (Baker 2013, 137).

4.2 Reception

In pursuit of this last goal, "engrafting medical ethics on moral precept," in 1821, the parent Kappa Lambda Society in Lexington published a fifteen-page pamphlet, *Extracts from the Medical Ethics ... by Thomas Percival, MD*, distributing packets of twenty copies to the Philadelphia society and to the Kappa Lambda branches that had sprouted in Baltimore, the District of Columbia, and New York City (Baker 2013, 137–138).

The Society produced a revision of *Extracts* in 1823, which was then incorporated into the "Ethical Code" of the Philadelphia Society (Kappa Lambda Society 1823; Percival 1823). Drs. John Bell and Isaac Hays, who served on the committee that drafted the 1847 Code and prepared the "Note to the 1847 Convention" quoted above, played a central role in this process.

Ambrose explains that the positive reception of *Medical Ethics* explains why the authors of *Extracts* turned to Percival:

> In the English-speaking medical world, Percival's small book, titled *Medical Ethics, or, A Code of Institutes and Precepts*, became the manual for future medical ethicists. He had compiled it in an effort to prevent the perennial disagreements among the medical staff at the Manchester Infirmary (Ambrose 2005, 50).

As we saw in Chap. 3, there was one major dispute and then others subsequently, but they were between the medical staff and the trustees.

In the United States in the twentieth century some receptions of *Medical Ethics* were based on failure to meet the scholarly standard of getting the text right. One such reception of *Medical Ethics* treats it as an text in etiquette, not professional ethics. Chauncey Leake (1896–1978) was a pharmacologist who was a leader in American medical education, who played a key role in the development of programs in bioethics and also medical humanities at both the University of California at San Francisco and the University of Texas Medical Branch in Galveston, on our coast (Brody 2014). He edited an edition of *Medical Ethics* for the American audience (Leake 1927) and also, it appears, to inspire the study of medical ethics. He has some kind words for Percival's work:

> A study of Percival's "Code" (1803) is fundamental for an appreciation of modern "medical ethics." ... He sincerely did his best to promote the idealism and dignity of the ancient profession of medicine. Let us do no less (Leake 1827, 57).

For the most part, however, Leake treats *Medical Ethics* as a catalogue of errors, especially the failure to distinguish medical ethics from medical etiquette:

> The term "medical ethics," introduced by Percival, is really a misnomer. Based on Greek traditions of good taste, and on Percival's "Code," it refers chiefly to the rules of etiquette developed in the profession to regulate the professional contacts of its members *with each other*. Toward this, society often evinces a respect not warranted by considerations of its own welfare. Unfortunately Percival was persuaded that "medical ethics" was the proper title for his system of professional regulations. All similar and subsequent systems of general professional advice, whether official or not, have received the same title. As a result, confusion has developed in the minds of many physicians between what may be really a matter of ethics and what may be concerned with etiquette (Leake 1827, 1 2).

He then calls for medical ethics to be focused on "the philosophical analysis of the principles of ethical theory made by recognized ethical scholars" (Leake 1827, 3).

The "chief positions" that one will discover upon such analysis are "idealism" and "hedonism" (Leake 1827, 3). Robert Baker (1993) points out that Leake's interpretation was the received view for quite some time after the appearance of his edition of *Medical Ethics*. He then shows, in a close reading of the text of *Medical Ethics* that there is no textual evidence for Leake's reading and textual evidence that requires a fair-minded reader to reject Leake's interpretation.

Leake's interpretive errors are egregious. He makes no effort to place *Medical Ethics* in its historical context: Baconian moral science. He also fails to understand that Percival's many rules were precepts for the behavior of physicians and surgeons that instantiate his professional ethics of accountability and cooperation and that these rules therefore structure an organizational culture of professionalism. Percival wrote professional etiquette, a set of precepts, for professional cooperation for the good of the patient, not etiquette *simpliciter*. Finally, Leake misses altogether what is plain from the title of *Medical Ethics*: Percival seeks to unite physicians, surgeons, and apothecaries into a single profession based on cooperation aimed at the good of patient by preventing conflict with which patients can impermissibly pay with their health and lives.

A second reception of *Medical Ethics* misreads it as a text in service of monopoly control of the medical marketplace. Baker (1993) goes on the consider the subsequent influence of Leake's reception of *Medical Ethics* as a set of rules for etiquette, or the intra-professional behavior of physicians and surgeons, that is not really ethics: "What passes for professional ethics, is really intra-professional etiquette" (Baker 1993a, 182). Two sociologists built on Leake's reading to offer a different reception of *Medical Ethics*, Jeffrey Berlant (1975) and Ivan Waddington (1984). They claimed that *Medical Ethics* was the handmaiden of the drive in the nineteenth century by physicians and surgeons, and their instruments, the Royal Colleges, for monopoly control of the medical and surgical marketplace. Both therefore treat Percival as conservative, aiming to maintain the power of physicians and surgeons over clinical practice. As Berlant puts it, medical ethics was deployed by Percival as "… a means of legitimatizing the monopolistic privileges of the profession to the powers that be and to the public" (Berlant 1975, 59).

Baker identifies many of the presentist errors of this reception of Percival as a conservative defender of the medical profession's powers and privileges in service to the interests of the Royal Colleges. I want to add that this reception of Percival has no basis in his texts. As we saw in Chap. 3, Percival rejects the party-interest of the Royal Colleges. It is true to the text to read Percival as also maintaining that medicine and surgery have justified, limited ethically justified autonomy from the state. Limited autonomy is ethically justified when it conforms to the ethical concept of medicine as a profession, i.e., when powers and privileges, especially of self-regulation, are exercised for the good of the patient. The exercise of power to pursue party-interest in the form of monopoly control is ethically illegitimate.

Baker summarizes the critique of the reception of *Medical Ethics* by Leake, Berlant, and Waddington and what Baker calls the "revisionist reading" of *Medical Ethics* as having four components, the first three of which apply here:

4.2 Reception

...(1) that the subject of *Medical Ethics* ... is primarily the regulation of intra-professional relationships, not the practitioner-patient relationship; (2) that these regulations are properly considered etiquette, not an ethic; and (3) that their interest is essentially conservative, i.e., to preserve the monopolistic powers of the profession (Baker 1993a, 184).

All three readings fail. These received views of *Medical Ethics* should be rejected, because they have been discredited by textual and philosophical scholarship.

Edmund Pellegrino prepared an edition of *Medical Ethics* for *Classics of Medicine Library* in 1985. This edition includes a facsimile of the text as originally published in 1803: *Medical Ethics*, Thomas Bassnett Percival's "Discourse," and the "Notes and Illustrations" to both. Pellegrino also prepared an introduction, "Thomas Percival's Ethics: The Ethics Beneath the Etiquette" (Pellegrino 1985). Pellegrino points out that Percival is a student of "Baconian experimentalism" (Pellegrino 1985, 16). However, he confines the influence of Baconian science and philosophy of science to this genre of Percival *oeuvre*. Instead, Pellegrino identifies Cicero and Gisborne as major influences on Percival's moral writings. We also saw in Chap. 3 that Gisborne's philosophical method differs from Percival, substantively.

Medical Ethics begins with a quote from Cicero, about the ubiquitous nature of our moral obligations to each other: they structure every private and public aspect of our moral lives. Cicero's first principle of self-preservation, however, cannot be found in *Medical Ethics*, as we saw in Chap. 3. To be sure, Percival agrees without reservation with what Cicero says:

For no phase of life, whether public or private, whether in business or in the home, whether one is working on what concerns oneself alone or dealing with another, can be without its moral duty; on the discharge of such duties depends all that is morally right, and in their neglect all that is morally wrong in life (Cicero 1913, 7).

By including it at the beginning of *Medical Ethics*, Percival clearly endorses Cicero's claim that the moral life is primarily one of obligation to others. The moral life in medicine is primarily one of obligation to patients, colleagues, the community, and the law, as we saw in Chap. 3. Percival disagrees with Cicero on the origins of the ethical obligations of physicians. Their ethical obligations originate in the principle of sympathy and its professional regulatory virtues of tenderness, steadiness, condescension, and authority. Percival has an intellectual debt to Cicero for the idea that our moral lives are through and through lives of obligation to others but no intellectual debt to Cicero for the origin of our moral lives.

Pellegrino claims that one of the hallmarks of Percival's work in moral philosophy is "the close integration of faith and reason" (Pellegrino 1985, 19). Pellegrino does not explain other than to say that "[p]hilosophy and theology were, for him, complementary and not antagonistic as they were to many Enlightenment thinkers" (Pellegrino 1985, 19). We saw in Chaps. 2 and 3 that Percival was a Baconian Dissenter, which meant that religion should be based on the truth of things, the result of which is to make religion Baconian. Percival calls this "rational theism" (Percival 1803, 198) in *Medical Ethics*, as we saw in Chap. 3.

Pellegrino summarizes the main features of *Medical Ethics*:

> Percival's *Ethics* is not, strictly speaking, a formal treatise on ethics. It does not systematically examine the rectitude of medical actions on the basis of a moral theory, nor does it derive its principles of expose the presuppositions upon which they are based. It is a work, rather, of medical morals – as series of maxims or moral aphorisms devised to guide the conduct of the "good" physician. It presupposes an ethics – one which is rooted in the principle of beneficence, and in the duties of a virtuous man, and a Christian, should impose upon himself in recognition of this principle when he is a physician (Pellegrino 1985, 26–27).

Pellegrino missed the message in the title of *Medical Ethics*: it is code, a set of rules, of Institutes – capsule summaries of its conceptual framework – and precepts – Pellegrino's "moral aphorisms" that find their ethical justification in the ethical framework. As we in Chap. 3, Chapter I, Section I is an Institute that encapsulates Gregory's Baconian moral scientific professional ethics and adds to it two new professional regulatory virtues of sympathy. *Medical Ethics* does indeed "presuppose an ethics" but it is Baconian moral science and Gregory's professional ethics in medicine. For Percival, as for Gregory, there is no "moral theory" autonomous from Baconian science. Pellegrino's misreading of the text of *Medical Ethics* and the works on moral philosophy in which he situates *Medical Ethics* result in a missed opportunity to identify Percival's commitment to and self-identity as a moral scientist.

Lisbeth Haakonssen (1997) takes seriously Percival's commitment to the improvement of medicine by deploying Baconian method in observational and experimental investigations. This commitment defined the "new scientific and reforming physicians who believed the 'dignity' of their profession, in fact its only *raison d'être*, depended on the progressive development of a public body of scientific knowledge" (Haakonssen 1997). She is correct that Percival counted himself as committed to this endeavor. As we saw in Chap. 2 Percival aimed to contribute to scientific knowledge and to put it to work, e.g., in addressing pollution of the water supply and consequent poisoning of people from the effluents of lead smelters and in addressing the health of the sick poor of Manchester by advocating for a Board of Health to address their needs using scientifically based public health measures such as improved housing and limiting child labor.

Haakonssen identifies the significance of this goal for the "implied contract with society:"

> The reformist physicians insisted on the acquisition of scientific knowledge as an essential part of the particular duties of a physician and of his implied contract with society. Ultimately it was scientific knowledge that bound the profession together, equipped it as a profession, and served as its brightest ornament (Haakonssen 1997, 123).

From this emerged in Percival's work, according to Haakonssen, a concept of medicine as a profession: "A profession was thus primarily a voluntary association characterized by a set of duties and rights" (Haakonssen 1997, 123). This, she adds, is the context in which Percival's invocation of the *esprit de corps* of physicians, in Chapter II, Section XXIII.

Haakonssen turns to the work of the jurist, William Blackstone (1723–1780), whom Percival had read and cites, as we saw in Chap. 3. Blackstone invokes the concept of an implicit contract to explain that everyone who takes up an "office" enters a social role constructed of duties, the chief of which is the competent and diligent discharge of those duties (Haakonssen 1997, 124). Haaksonssen elaborates:

> The legal notion of implied contract was no more than a formalization of a much more general understanding of the ethics of social relations (Haakonssen 1997, 124).
> … entering the fraternity of physicians is a tacit agreement. Implied contract, on the other hand, is not an event but a moral relation between two or more parties (Haakonssen 1997, 125).

The "particular role of office" in which an individual "at the time" may find himself in generates the duties or obligations of that individual (Haakonssen 1997, 125).

As we have seen in Chap. 3, Chapter I, Section I of *Medical Ethics* expresses in a concise rendition the "Institute" of the book, the Baconian moral science of the principle of sympathy and its four professional regulatory virtues of tenderness, condescension, and authority. These generate the ethical obligations that Percival sets out the numbered precepts that follow. Together the precepts in the four chapters of *Medical Ethics* define the duties or obligations of physicians and surgeons in hospital practice, private practice, and in their contributions to the administration of justice and of physicians and apothecaries. In other words, *Medical Ethics* defines the social role of the physician, surgeon, and apothecary in the single profession of medicine. The concept of an "unformulated and implied contract inherent in any office" (Haakonssen 1997, 126) or social role *presupposes* that the ethical obligations of physicians, surgeons, and apothecaries that originate in the three commitment that define the ethical concept of medicine as a profession. Baconian moral scientific professional ethics in medicine defines the social role of the professional physician, surgeon, or apothecary. The concept of an implied contract became a mechanism that the law can use to enforce the duties of obligations originating in professional ethics in medicine, which Percival acknowledges (Percival 1803, 177). Haakonssen is committed to the view, like Gisborne's as we saw in Chap. 3, that there is a broader tacit compact, the social contract that generates social roles that, in turn, originate duties or obligations. This way of thinking is alien to *Medical Ethics* in which sympathy and its professional regulatory virtues originate duties that, in turn, generate social roles in which those duties are discharged.

More generally, Baconian Dissent does not need to invoke social contract theory. Baconian dissent has intellectual, moral, and therefore social and political authority independent of all authorities in eighteenth-century England, especially Church of England and the constitutional monarchy. Far from entering into a social contract, Baconian Dissent dissents – from the divine right of kings, from ecclesiastical authority, from unjust laws of taxation, and from the practice of enslaving persons.

Worse, social contract theory is like all contracts: wary agreement between self-interested parties with no professional responsibility to protect the other party's interests. Social contract theory for medicine as a profession re-instates the entrepreneurial, pre-Gregory and pre-Percival paradigm. Gregory and Percival would have, correctly, rejected social contract theory as not compatible with the revolutionary new paradigm of medicine as a profession. Based on the review in Chap. 1 of Baker's historical account of moral revolutions, an appeal to social contract theory, as the basis for professional ethics in medicine, should be interpreted to be a counter-revolution, albeit an unwitting one and one that Percival would reject.

4.3 Influence

The preceding account of the reception of *Medical Ethics* in the United States is also a story of the influence of Percival's book on the creation of the 1847 *Code of Ethics* of the American Medical Association. That influence starts with city and state medical societies known as "Medical Police" adopting or adapting *Medical Ethics*, continues with the creation of *Extracts* by physicians who would play a leadership role in the formation of the new American Medical Association, and culminates in the 1847 *Code of Ethics*. Readers will find Baker's detailed account of this history enormously informative (Baker 2013).

In *Before Bioethics* (2013) Baker makes many invaluable scholarly contributions to the history of medical ethics that preceded the invention of the field of bioethics in the late 1960s and early 1970s. Chief among these for present purposes is Baker's close comparative reading of the text of the *Code of Ethics* and *Medical Ethics*. Here is the, by now very familiar, Section I of Chapter I of *Medical Ethics*

> I. HOSPITAL PHYSICIANS and SURGEONS should minister to the sick, with due impressions of the importance of their office; reflecting that the ease, the health, and the lives of those committed to their charge depend on their skill, attention, and fidelity. They should study, also, in their deportment, so to unite *tenderness* with *steadiness*, and *condescension* with *authority*, as to inspire the minds of their patients with gratitude, respect, and confidence (Percival 1803, 9 not paginated).

Baker replicates this opening paragraph of *Medical Ethics* and, with strikethroughs to indicate deletions and italicized text to indicate additions, shows his reader that substantial changes have been made.

> A ~~hospital p~~[P]hysicians ~~and surgeons~~ should *not only be ever ready to obey the calls of the sick, but his mind ought also to be imbued with the greatness of his mission, and of the responsibility he habitually incurs in its discharge. These obligations are the more deep and enduring, because there is no tribunal other than his own conscience, to adjudge penalties for carelessness and neglect.* Physicians should, *therefore*, minister to the sick, with due impressions of the importance of their office; reflecting that the ease, the health, and the lives of those committed to their charge depend on their skill, attention, and fidelity. They should study, also, in their deportment, so to unite *tenderness* with *steadiness*, and *condescension* with *authority*, as to inspire the minds of their patients with gratitude, respect, and confidence (Baker 2013, 145; American Medical Association [1847] 1999, 324).

This is the first paragraph of the *Code of Ethics*' "Chapter I: Of the Duties of Physicians to their Patients and of the Obligations of Patients to their Physicians." Percival's key move, to start with hospital duties in the context of an organizational culture of accountability and cooperation, i.e., an organizational culture of professionalism, has disappeared. Along with it disappears the basis of duties in private practice on conscience professionally formed and made exemplary in the hospital's organizational culture. Recall that in *Medical Ethics* Section I of each Chapter functions as the introductory material in an "Institutes" that encapsulate the conceptual framework for the proposed codification of behavior that follows. By not starting with hospital duties, the *Code of Ethics* offers a tenuous conceptual framework as a replacement.

The disappearance of the conceptual basis for Percival's Institutes appears to have first occurred in *Extracts from the Medical Ethics of Dr. Percival*:

I. PHYSICIANS and SURGEONS should minister to the sick, with due impressions of the importance of their office; reflecting that the ease, the health, and the lives of those committed to their charge depend on their skill, attention, and fidelity. They should study, also, in their deportment, so to unite *tenderness* with *steadiness*, and *condescension* with *authority*, as to inspire the minds of their patients with gratitude, respect, and confidence (Percival 1823, 9 not paginated).

This drops the first word, 'HOSPITAL', of the first sentence of Chapter I, Section I, in *Medical Ethics*. The conceptual framework of *Medical Ethics* is further removed in *Extracts*, because all of the remaining Sections, II–XXI of Chapter I are excised. Section II of *Extracts* is *Medical Ethics* Chapter II, Section I, less its first sentence: "THE *moral rules of conduct*, prescribed towards hospital patients, should be fully adopted in private or general practice" (Percival 1803, 30). The same is true of the second section of the first chapter of the *Code of Ethics*.

There is no textual evidence to explain the thinking of Dr. Brown and possible co-authors in Lexington in the writing of the first version of *Extracts* or of Drs. Bell and Hays in their preparation of the revision of 1823. But it is clear that the methodological break is decisive in *Extracts* and that the *Code of Ethics* inherits that break. The first hospital in Lexington, Kentucky, St. Joseph's, was not established until 1877. It would therefore have made little sense for Dr. Brown and the other members of the original branch of Kappa Lambda to adopt Percival's conceptual model. Samuel Jackson in Philadelphia was not based at the medical school of the University of Pennsylvania until 1825 and started teaching at the Philadelphia Hospital under 1842 (Penn People n.d.). Perhaps it made no more sense to him to adopt hospital duties as the paradigm of physicians' professional responsibility. Against this reading is the fact that the Philadelphia Kappa Lambda Society included in its membership many prominent physicians of Philadelphia, including members of the medical faculty at the University of Pennsylvania.

There is another source of potential difference between *Medical Ethics* and *Extracts*. In late eighteenth-century England – and certainly Scotland – the discourse of Baconian moral science would have been instantly recognizable to Percival's readers, especially physicians readers such as Ferriar who had attended the University of Edinburgh, the center of Baconian science and moral science in Britain – and the world, for that matter. Two decades later in the United States this assumption could not so reliably be made. The discourse of Baconian moral science remained attractive but was becoming disconnected from Baconian moral science itself, especially as increasing numbers of physicians trained in the new American medical schools and not in Edinburgh. We therefore cannot confidently assume that the authors and readers of the *Extracts* or, two decades later, the *Code of Ethics* would understand the discourse of Baconian moral science of the final sentence of the first section of each document and Percival and his contemporary readers understood it. In less than a half-century, we are now at some remove from Percival *Code of Institutes and Precepts*.

There is textual evidence for this change in the phrase, 'greatness of his mission'. Percival would have made clear that this means attending to the good of the patient. And 'greatness of his mission' can be read to refer to fulfilling the ethical obligations created by the virtues of tenderness, steadiness, condescension, and authority. 'Greatness of mission', however, can also appeal to self-regard and false honor. Percival would warn against it use for this reason only. In his characteristic understated way, in which he expresses his confidence that his reader does not need such appeals, Percival, in my reading of this work, would not use this phrase. *Extracts* starts to increase the distance from Percival's Baconian moral scientific professional ethics in medicine. The *Code of Ethics* increases the distance.

In Chapter II Percival makes an appeal to the "tribunal" of "conscience" understood in the context of Chapter I, as we saw in Chap. 3. Percival appeals to conscience formed by submitting to the discipline of experience-based Baconian scientific medicine. The *Code of Ethics* cannot make this appeal, because, following the *Extracts*, its authors have stripped away Percival's account of properly formed conscience in the private practice setting. The *Code of Ethics* leaves its reader unable to understand how the "tribunal" of conscience should be a tribunal of *professional* conscience of the kind that Percival describes in Chapter II, Section XXVIII.

Recall that *Medical Ethics* includes in its title "Or a Code of Institutes and Precepts" (Percival 1803, I no pagination). The "Institutes" comprise the conceptual framework, concisely stated, which is the first Section of Chapters I–IV, with the first Section of Chapter I expressing in concise form the Baconian moral scientific basis for this content. The format of an "Institutes" is to follow the concisely stated conceptual framework with numbered sections that provided compact, practical guidance to clinical judgment and practice. The latter comprise the "Precepts." The *Extracts* are aptly named: the first Section of Chapter I and all of the Sections of Chapter II have been removed from *Medical Ethics* and edited into a single document of thirty-two sections. The title has been omitted, thus erasing the format of an "Institutes." When the American Medical Association committee worked up its ethics statement, the *Extracts* provided an attenuated conceptual framework and thirty-one precepts. Calling it a 'Code' marked a significant departure from *Medical Ethics*, because the result is a set of Precepts without the Institutes that explain and justify them.

There is another respect in which *Code of Ethics* marks a departure from *Medical Ethics*, the addition of "the Obligations of Patients to their Physicians" (American Medical Association [1847] 1999, 324). In the "Introduction to the 1847 Code of Ethics," John Bell makes an argument that echoes, distantly, Percival's appeal to reciprocity in his political ethics, described in Chap. 3.

> Every duty or obligation implies, both in equity and for its successful discharge, a corresponding right. As it is the duty of the physician to advise, so he has a right to be attentively and respectfully listened to. Being required to expose his health and life for the benefit of

the community, he has a just claim, in return, on all its members, collectively and individually, for aid to carry out his measures, and for all possible tenderness and regard to prevent needlessly harassing calls on his services and the unnecessary exhaustion of his benevolent sympathies (American Medical Association [1847] 1999, 317–318).

Physicians freely commit to provide clinical care of their patients. Recall that in the outpatient setting, the success of a plan of care is a function of the patient's disciplined implementation of it. The duty to care for patients effectively is therefore a function of the patient's implementation of the plan of care, of their self-physicking under the physician's direction. This fits Percival's appeal to reciprocity in his political ethics. The addition of the appeal to "equity" or fairness toward the physician is less clearly connected to Percival's professional ethics in medicine. 'Equity' in the *Code of Ethics* means that the physician's duty creates a correlative right of the physician against the patient to do his or her part.

The same line of reasoning applies in public health, including the physician's response to contagion. The *Code of Ethics* makes it clear in its Chapter III that physicians have the duty to stay and care for patients: "… and when pestilence prevails, it is their duty to face the danger, and to continue their labors for the alleviation of suffering, even at the jeopardy of their own lives" (American Medical Association [1847] 1999, 333). Note that the *Code of Ethics* does *not* claim an independent right that obligates patients but a right that is derived from the freely assumed duty. This is the ethically justified moral instruction of patients that Percival makes repeatedly. The final claim to be free of "needlessly harassing calls" to prevent "unnecessary exhaustion of his benevolent sympathies" would, I think, give Percival pause, because it expresses self-interest, even the peevish self-interest of *amour propre*.

The professional regulatory virtues of tenderness and steadiness, especially the latter, which the *Code of Ethics* itself invokes, as we saw above, should prevent the exhaustion of sympathy and the study of human nature should prepare physicians to respond in a professional manner by taking "harassing calls" to be behavioral signs of distress that tenderness incites the physician to relieve. Like the appeal to the "greatness" of the physician's work on behalf of patients, this text is at risk of being read as an appeal to over-weaning self-regard and thus antithetical to properly understood honor. The influence of Percival's professional ethics in medicine on the *Code of Ethics* may be in the adoption of its discourse but cut off from its conceptual basis. To use Alasdair MacIntyre's (1981) discourse, perhaps *Extracts* broke *Medical Ethics* into shards that then are shattered still further in the *Code of Ethics*.

4.4 Gregory's and Percival's Legacy for Contemporary Professional Ethics in Medicine

Percival wrote Baconian moral scientific professional ethics of medicine, shaped by Baconian deism and Dissent. In doing so, Percival "completed" Gregory's invention of Baconian moral scientific professional ethics in medicine and therefore medical professionalism. In the history of medical ethics their co-invention of professional ethics in medicine is their legacy to us.

They gave us professional ethics in medicine that is transreligious, transcultural, and transnational, an accomplishment that we should never take for granted. Baconian deism and Dissent secure the transreligious aspect: there are no tests of faith for becoming a professional physician. The practitioners of Baconian moral science in Edinburgh came from a particular nation, Scotland, but the method they refined and applied did not originate in Scotland but England. Already, in the hands of a Hume or Gregory, Baconian moral science became transnational. Gregory's students were multinational and his work took root in the American Colonies and then the United States, as well as in France, Germany, and Spain. Percival's work came to the United States. By the end of the nineteenth century Gregory and Percival's co-invention of medical professionalism had become transnational. Their moral revolution was becoming successful in meeting many of the criteria for success that Baker identifies (Baker 2019). Finally, Gregory's invention occurred at the University of Edinburgh that, with its absence of tests of theological orthodoxy and according its faculty and students alike to pursue *lehrnfreiheit*, became a distinctively multi-cultural university. As a Dissenter, Percival was an unequivocal foe of cultural hegemony, as we would put it. The international dissemination of their books provides further evidence for the transcultural nature of their co-invention.

This means that the ethical concept of becoming a patent is transnational, transreligious, and transcultural. The concept of being a patient in professional ethics in medicine does not originate in the patient but in the professional relationship created by making the three commitments of the ethical concept of medicine as a profession. As a result, to be a patient does not require that one is a person (Ruddick and Wilcox 1982), a rational, self-conscious entity that is capable of giving itself value and thus possessing autonomy (Engelhardt 1996). To say the least, the concept of being a person invokes complex metaphysics, which is not always acknowledged in the literature of medical ethics and bioethics that invokes the concept of being a person as the basis for the ethical principle of respect for autonomy. The ethical concept of being a patient in professional ethics in medicine is *not* a metaphysical concept nor is it required to be. Professional ethics in medicine, and therefore professional ethics in obstetrics and gynecology, is thus completely free of the metaphysical challenges that plague medical ethics and bioethics and are frequently ignored.

The most common way to express the ethical concept of being a patient in the literature of medical ethics and bioethics is to invoke the concept of a right, the claim of an individual against others to be treated in a specified way. The discourse of rights comes with another metaphysical problem: what kind of entity has rights that originate in it? There is no agreement on the authoritative method for addressing question. There is therefore no convincing answer to the question. This is not a problem for professional ethics in medicine, and therefore for professional ethics in medicine's specialties, because the ethical concept of being a patient is beneficence-based. Beneficence-based reasoning does not require invocation of the concept of a right. Indeed, doing so conflates the ethical principles of beneficence and respect for autonomy, a major methodological error in ethical reasoning from which professional ethics in medicine is immune.

Gregory and Percival appealed to Hume's scientific discovery of sympathy: a constitutive, causal process in individuals that incentivizes them naturally to enter into the lives of others and respond to their vulnerability to disease, injury, and death. Hume's "experimental method of reasoning into moral subjects" (Hume [1739–1740) 2000, 1) has a robust metaphysics. Principles are real, constitutive, causal processes in human beings. Baconian moral physiology took for granted that every human being possessed the principle of sympathy. Differences in its expression were a function of the degree to which one had cultivated, or failed to cultivate, the virtues that regulate sympathy. The concept of fixed, unchanging human and animal traits dated back to Ancient Greece.

Two centuries later the metaphysics of Baconian moral science have become deeply problematic. Hume, Gregory, and Percival did their work before Charles Darwin (1809–1882) did his work on evolution. A core concept of evolutionary biology is the variation of traits. Not all members of a species exhibit all of the traits thought to be typical of that species. Evolutionary biology transforms the essentialist concept of species in Aristotle into a cluster concept.

This conceptual transformation means that some human beings lack sympathy and are therefore heartless. In the professional discourse of psychiatry such individuals are classified as sociopathic, a personality disorder for which there is no effective treatment.

As the heirs to the scientific revolution that Darwin and others launched, we cannot appeal to cognitive or affective capacities that are constitutive of the nature of all human beings and therefore the same in all of us. Instead, we have to appeal to what the experience of clinical practice would be like for physicians and their patients and what the experience of clinical innovation and research would be like for clinical investigators and their research subjects if so many physicians failed to commit to the ethical concept of medicine as a profession that the profession of medicine ceased to exist.

The history of medicine tells us what these experiences would be like, because the best guide to the future is the past. As explained in Chap. 1, before Gregory and Percival co-invented the ethical concept of medicine as profession: the long tradition of entrepreneurial medicine had produced epidemic intellectual and moral distrust of the sick toward medical practitioners of all kinds, and especially toward physicians and surgeons (Porter and Porter 1989). The sick stayed away from medical practitioners because the sick did not trust physicians or surgeons to know what they were doing and did not trust that physicians and surgeons were doing what they did primarily for the benefit the sick individual. This intellectual and moral distrust was corrosive for the sick and also, crucially, for physicians who found themselves the object of distrust.

The practice of medicine, as every physician and trainee knows, is very cognitively and affectively demanding, especially when risk of morbidity and disability increase, when a patient suffers functional decline, and when a patient dies. The demands of clinical innovation and research are equally high, especially when unexpected adverse events occur or when clinical investigation does not yield the definitive results hoped for from it. These demands would become impossible to manage in an atmosphere of epidemic distrust. Epidemic distrust would doom advocacy and health policy to failure.

Making and sustaining the commitment to the ethical concept of medicine, to medical professionalism, becomes an essential and powerful antidote to intellectual and moral distrust and therefore becomes the only reliable source for the successful management of the demands of clinical practice and research, which, in turn, is essential for patient safety and quality. This is crucial in clinical practice and research with patients with experience-based distrust of physicians, especially female patients, patients of color, and patients who have been abused by physicians or other healthcare professionals. Put simply, the sustained commitment to the ethical concept of medicine as a profession creates the intellectual and moral excellence of medicine. The experience of this intellectual and moral excellence makes being a physician a way of life with value for physicians, their patients, their families, and society.

Clinical practice now must conform to and support the requirements of an organizational culture of patient safety and quality. Team care should not become a mere slogan, because team care is the indispensable means by which an organizational culture of safety and quality is created and sustained. Team care requires an ethics of cooperation based on the shared commitment to the ethical concept of medicine as a profession. The ethics of cooperation as a component of professional ethics in medicine is part of Percival's legacy to us.

Percival was explicit about creating an ethics of cooperation among physicians, surgeons, and apothecaries in the Royal Infirmary of Manchester. In the first Chapter of *Medical Ethics* Percival goes into considerable detail about the creation of registers (registries and databases about the processes and outcomes of clinical care and research), the creation of regular clinical conferences to review challenging cases (thus anticipating tumor boards and morbidity and mortality conferences by a century), and a committee to oversee clinical research (thus anticipating Institutional Review Boards and Research Ethics Committees by a century-and-a-half). These forms of cooperation are required, Percival maintained, by the commitment to the ethical concept of medicine as a profession.

Gregory and Percival wrote professional ethics in medicine to unify medicine and surgery, the boundaries of which were then hotly contested, for which patient's paid dearly (McCullough 1998). The desired unification of medicine and surgery required an ethics of cooperation, which commitment to the ethical concept of medicine as a profession creates. Gregory paints a compelling portrait of the clinical consequences of physicians spurning cooperation and accountability:

> An obstinate adherence to an unsuccessful method of treating a disease, must be owing to a high degree of self-conceit, and a belief of the infallibility of a system. This error is the more difficult to cure, as it generally proceeds from ignorance. True knowledge and clear discernment may lead one into the extreme of diffidence and humility; but are inconsistent with self-conceit. It sometimes happens too, that this obstinacy proceeds from a defect in the heart. Such physicians see that they are wrong; but are too proud to acknowledge their

error, especially if it be pointed out to them by one of the profession. To this species of pride, a pride incompatible with true dignity and elevation of mind, have the lives of thousands been sacrificed (Gregory 1772, 28–29).

Finally, the transnational, transcultural, and transreligious nature of the ethical concept of medicine as a profession makes possible the creation of international societies of physicians in the various specialties, such as the International Federation of Gynecology and Obstetrics (FIGO) (International Federation of Gynecology and Obstetrics n.d.), World Association of Perinatal Medicine (World Association of Perinatal Medicine n.d.), the International Academy of Perinatal Medicine (International Academy of Perinatal Medicine n.d.), as well as transnational non-governmental organizations such as the World Medical Association (World Medical Association n.d.) and the World Health Organization (World Health Association n.d.). These international and transnational organizations issue statements on a wide range of ethical challenges in clinical practice, clinical innovation and research, and health policy and advocacy. The global intellectual and moral authority of such statements for physicians in all nations and cultures, religious and non-religious alike, originates in the ethical concept of medicine as a profession. FIGO, for example, has made its commitment to the ethical concept of medicine as a profession explicit (FIGO Committee for the Ethical Aspects of Human Reproduction and Women's Health. Professionalism in Obstetric and Gynecologic Practice 2017).

These justifications for committing to the ethical concept of medicine as a profession do not comprise what in ethical reasoning is known as a "principled argument" or an appeal to concepts that originate in the "moral point of view" that is taken to apply in all circumstances because it invokes timeless philosophical concepts such as the common morality. A principled argument is in the tradition of the quest for certainty and requires physicians to consider the ethical concept of medicine as a profession to be timeless and adherence to it required by unassailable argument.

Principled ethical reasoning differs from the ethical reasoning of Gregory and Percival, because these two physician-ethicists made their cases for professional ethics in medicine in the tradition of the quest for reliability, in two ways. The first is the style of persuasion of Gregory and Percival. In an argument of persuasion, one offers, as I have here, a set of considerations, none of which is "principled" and therefore decisive. Instead, their ethical reasoning aims to persuade because the destructive consequences of longstanding corrosive intellectual and moral distrust for physicians, their patients, and clinical innovators and investigators and their subjects, organizational culture, and health policy and advocacy of not having a profession of medicine should be judged unacceptable. The discourse of persuasion characterizes the quest for reliability. Gregory and Percival learned the quest for reliability from Bacon in science and from Hume in Baconian moral science. They continued this quest in their professional ethics in medicine.

The second is the pragmatic nature of professional medical ethics. The American physician-philosopher, William James (1842–1910), invented a form of pragmatism that is distinctive for its emphasis on truth as something that is made, especially the truth of social practices and institutions such as the profession of medicine (James [1896] 1907). When physicians make and sustain the three commitments that define the ethical concept of medicine as a profession, they make it true that there is a profession of medicine. When physicians do so they transform the concept of medicine as a public trust into a social and political reality. The profession of medicine that physicians thereby will into existence and sustain turns Gregory and Percival's conceptual full stop to the long tradition of entrepreneurialism into an actual full stop. Put another way, the profession of medicine is not some timeless idea that, because it is timeless, sustains itself and is thus immune from intellectual and moral damage that results when enough physicians abandon the ethical concept of medicine as a profession. Philosophers engaged in the quest for certainty must be committed to timeless ideas but the history of ideas and concepts, including the histories of medical ethics and of professional ethics in medicine, makes such a commitment implausible. Medical professionalism is the invention of two remarkable British physician-ethicists of the eighteenth century, John Gregory and Thomas Percival. Their invention will not sustain itself but it is very much worth sustaining when we consider medical practice and research that is not professional or, worse, unprofessional. The long tradition of the entrepreneurial paradigm in the history of Western medicine shows us what that looked like and what it would look like again. The argument from persuasion concludes: Physicians and their patients – all of us – should not want to give up physicians and their patients only to return to the sick, ever-distrustful – "watchfulness" is Percival's word (Percival 1803, 11) – of entrepreneurial Hippocratic, guild, cautious, or politic practitioners and their customers, growing ever more hard-hearted and distrustful, respectively.

4.5 Painters Before and After Cimabue

Let me conclude with a personal reflection. The Italian film director, Franco Zeffirelli (1923–2019), made a documentary about the 1966 flooding of Florence, *Florence: Days of Destruction*. Its black-and-white graininess finishes the removal of color from Florence that the flood had initiated. The film is narrated by the Welsh actor Richard Burton (1925–1984) (Zeffirelli 1966; Burton et al. 1966). Zeffirelli, a Florentine, included a sequence that showed the water damage from the River Arno in the church of Santa Croce to *Crucifix* (c. 1268–1271), which has been traditionally attributed to Cimabue (c.1240–1302). He was a Florentine painter and mosaicist and "who may have been Giotto's [d. 1337] teacher" (Janson 1965, 267).

I had finished my Art History 101–102 sequence of courses at Williams College with soon-to-be legendary faculty Whitney Stoddard (1913–2003) and William Pierson, Jr. (1911–2008). French art, twentieth-century American art, and before-the-members-saw-them retrospectives of Franz Kline (1910–1962) at the Museum of Modern Art and of Paul Klee (1879–1940) at the Solomon R. Guggenheim Museum with S. Lane Faison (1907–2006) were to come. These were pedagogically ancient times at small liberal arts colleges that were tucked away in New England villages, far from the fleshpots of towns and cities. All introductory courses came in two required semesters. So ancient were those times that it was necessary to plead with the grazing dinosaurs to move to the side so that one could enter Lawrence Hall, the home of the Department of Art History, for amazing lectures of side-by-side slides of the "monuments" of art history in a the packed darkened lecture hall (even at 8 am on Saturdays) and small-group sessions led by faculty (not teaching assistants!). I was thus embarked on becoming an Art History major and a little-known (unknown, to be precise) member of the Williams Art History Mafia (Kinzer 2004).

With my head full of images from their lectures and the Janson *History of Art* (Janson 1965) the visual impact of the damage shocked (and still does on reviewing), as I watched the documentary broadcast by my local public broadcasting television station in Boston. Mud inches deep on the floor of the church and paintings and sculptures soaked with water and mired in still-wet mud required no words to convey the extent and severity of the damage. In one sequence, the camera pans to the Cimabue (as one is taught to say in Art History courses), taken down from the wall of the church and resting on a cleared space of floor. More than three-quarters of the paint was dissolved off the wood base. There was enough of Christ's remaining, partial face still to see his eyes just closing followed by his head arcing toward the earth at the moment of his death.

With the rarest of magnificent theatrical voices – think of James Earl Jones with the ancient accent of Wales – Burton delivers these lines of the script, written from the perspective of a Florentine:

> This is the greatest single loss caused by the flood in Florence. It is the famous Crucifixion painted by Cimabue at the end of the thirteenth century. This is not only a rare and marvelous piece, but it is considered a turning point in the history of art. In school the first thing one is taught about art is that painters are divided into those who came before Cimabue and those who painted afterwards (author's transcription).

In the global history of medical ethics there were writers on medical ethics who came before Gregory and Percival and their moral revolution against the long tradition of entrepreneurialism in the history of Western medicine, culminating in their co-invention of professional ethics in medicine and thereby of medical professionalism, and writers on medical ethics who came after their singular accomplishment. The history of global medical ethics pivots on Gregory and Percival.

Bibliography

Bibliographical Note

The bibliography that follows this brief introduction comprises four additional sections. Section II comprises Percival's privately and publicly published works. The former is *Medical Jurisprudence*. Section III includes manuscript resources, including information about the libraries in which they are deposited. Section IV lists online sources. Section V lists primary and secondary sources that I consulted and which played an invaluable role in developing my historically based, philosophical interpretation of *Medical Jurisprudence* and *Medical Ethics* as the products of a Baconian scientist of nature and of man or of morals, committed to Baconian deism and Dissent.

Privately and Publicly Published Works of Thomas Percival

Two printers played an important role in publishing Percival's writings. William Eyres (1734–1809) was a Warrington publisher, noted especially for the quality of his typography. He also published John Aikin (1713–1780), a noted Dissenter and one of Percival's teachers at Warrington Academy (Kendrick 1858). Joseph Johnson (1738–1809) was Dissenter and quite successful London publisher of books by such Dissenters such as Joseph Priestley (1733–1804), in addition to Percival (Tyson 1975). These and other publishers played an essential role in the development of the philosophical, political, religious, and scientific literature of Dissent in eighteenth-century England.

Kappa Lambda Society. 1823. *Extracts from the Medical Ethics of Dr. Percival*. Philadelphia: Published privately for the Kappa Lambda Secret Society of Hippocrates by Clark & Fraser, Printers, 33 Carter's Alley.

Leake, Chauncey, ed. 1927. *Percival's Medical Ethics*. Baltimore: Williams and Wilkins.

Percival, Edward. 1807. *Memoirs of the Life and Writings of Thomas Percival, M.D*. In *The Works, Literary, Moral, and Medical of Thomas Percival, Volumes I–IV*, ed. Edward Percival, Vol. I, i–cclxii. Printed by Richard Cruttwell, St. James-Street, Bath; for J. Johnson, St. Paul's Church-Yard, London.

Percival, Thomas. 1763. *An Inquiry into the Resemblance Between Chyle and Milk*. First published in *Essays Medical, Philosophical, and Experimental, Part I*. Thomas Percival. (Percival 1807, Vol. III, 164–172)

Percival, Thomas. 1765. *Dissertatio Medica Inauguralis De Frigore*. Submitto Thomas Percival. Lugduni Batavorum, Apud Theodorum Haak.

Percival, Thomas. [1767] 1807. *Essays Medical and Experimental: On the Following Subjects, viz. I. The Empiric. II. The Dogmatic. Or, Arguments for and against the Use of Theory and Reasoning in Physick. III. Experiments and Observations on Astringents and Bitters IV. On the Uses and Operation of Blisters. V. On the Resemblance between Chyle and Milk*. London: Printed for J. Johnson and B. Davenport, in Pater Noster Row. In Percival, Thomas T*he Works, Literary, Moral, and Medical of Thomas Percival* as *Essays Medical, Philosophical, and Experimental Part I,* ed. Edward Percival, Vol. III, 1–23 with a Preface xii–xix). London: J. Johnson, St. Paul's Church-Yard.

Percival, Thomas. 1767. Experiments on the Peruvian bark by Thomas Percival M.D. F.R.S. Received February 5, 1767. *Philosophical Transactions (1683–1775)*. 57: 221–233.

Percival, Thomas. 1768a. Extract from the essays medical and experimental. *The Gentleman's Magazine and Historical Chronicle*. Volume XXXVIII, 369–371. London: Printed at St. John's Gate for D. Henry; and sold by F. Newbery, The Corner of St. Paul's Churchyard, Ludgate Street. https://books.google.com/books?id=0Bs9AAAAYAAJ&pg=PA370&lpg=PA370&dq=%22the+empiric+or+man+of+experience%22&source=bl&ots=7GUFe9TiwP&sig=ACfU3U3me4EpfJmlkjik9bUsckruCAfOmA&hl=en&sa=X&ved=2ahUKEwjfibfh6fzpAhV1tDEKHaIrATwQ6AEwAHoECAcQAQ#v=onepage&q=%22the%20empiric%20or%20man%20of%20experience%22&f=false. Accessed 4 Sept 2020.

Percival, Thomas. 1768b. *On the Disadvantages which Attend the Inoculation of Children in Early Infancy*. London: J. Johnson in Pater-noster-Row and T. Cadell, (Successor to Mr. Millar) in the Strand.

Percival, Thomas. 1769. *Experiments and Observations on Water; Particularly on the Hard Pump Water of Manchester*. London: Printed for J. Johnson in Pater-Noster-Row.

Percival, Thomas. 1771, October 12. Copy of a Letter from Thomas Percival, of Manchester, M.D., F.R.S. On the Efficacy of External Applications in the Angina Maligna. *The Gentleman's Magazine for January* 1771: 764–765.

Percival, Thomas. 1772a. *Essays Medical and Experimental. The Second Edition, Revised and Considerably Enlarged, to Which is Added an Appendix.* London: Printed for J. Johnson, 72 St. Paul's Churchyard.

Percival, Thomas. 1772b. Experiments and Observations of the Waters of Buxton and Matlock in Derbyshire, by Thomas Percival, M.D. and F.R.S. Read June 25, 1772. *Philosophical Transactions, Giving Some Accounts of the Present Undertakings, Studies, and Labors of the Ingenious, in Many Considerable Parts of the World.* Volume LXII, 455–464. London: Printed for Lockyer Davis, in Holbourn. Printer for the Royal Society.

Percival, Thomas. 1772c. The History and Cure of a Difficulty in Deglutition, of Long Continuance, Arising from a Spasmotic Affection of the Œsophagus. *Medical Transactions, Published by the College of Physicians in London. Volume the Second.* 90–104. London: Printed for S. Baker and J. Dodsley.

Percival, Thomas. 1774a. *Further Observations on the State of Population in Manchester and other Adjacent Places.* Manchester: Printed for the author.

Percival, Thomas. 1774b. *Observations and Experiments on the Poison of Lead.* London: Printed for J. Johnson.

Percival, Thomas. 1776a. Published anonymously. *A Father's Instructions: to his Children: Consisting of Tales, Fables, and Reflections; Designed to Promote the Love of Virtue, a Taste for Knowledge, and an Early Acquaintance with the Works of Nature.* London: Printed for J. Johnson, St Paul's Church-Yard.

Percival, Thomas. 1776b. *Philosophical, Medical, and Experimental Essays.* London: Printed for J. Johnson, 72 St. Paul's Churchyard.

Percival, Thomas. 1777. *A Father's Instructions to his Children, Consisting of Tales, Fables and Reflections, etc.* London: J. Johnson.

Percival, Thomas. 1781. *A Socratic discourse on Truth and Faithfulness; in Which the Nature, Extent, and Obligation, ... of These Moral Duties are Explained ...: Being the Sequel to "A Father's Instructions."* Warrington: Printed by W. Ashton.

Percival, Thomas. 1782. *A Tribute to the Memory of C. de Polier, addressed to the Literary and Philosophical Society of Manchester.* Manchester. Read November 13, 1782 Memoirs of the Manchester Literary and Philosophical Society, 1785. 287–296 Warrington: Printed by W. Eyres for T. Cadel in the Strand, London.

Percival, Thomas. 1785a. A History of the Fatal Effects of Pickles Impregnated with Copper, Together with Observations on that Mineral Poison. *Medical Transactions, Published by the College of Physicians in London. Volume the Third.* 80–98, London: Printed for J. Dodsley, P. Elmsley, and Leigh and Sotheby.

Percival, Thomas. 1785b. *Speculations on the Perceptive Power of Vegetables: Addressed to the Literary and Philosophical Society of Manchester.* Warrington: W. Eyres.

Percival, Thomas. 1788–1789. *Essays Medical, Philosophical, and Experimental. Fourth Edition.* Warrington: Printed by W. Eyres, for J. Johnson, No. 72 St. Paul's Churchyard, London. Volume I 1788, Volume II 1789.

Percival, Thomas. 1789a. *Hints Towards the Investigation of the Nature, Cause and Cure of the Rabies Canina; Addressed to Dr. Haygarth* [by T. Percival]. (Copy of

Dr. Haygarth's Proposal for Obviating the Effects of the Bite of a Mad Dog.). Manchester. No publisher identified.

Percival, Thomas. 1789b. *Moral and Literary Dissertations (Chiefly Intended as the Sequel to "A Father's Instructions") ... To Which are Added a Tribute to the Memory of C. de Polier, and an Appendix, etc.* Warrington. No publisher identified.

Percival, Thomas. 1790a. *An Inquiry into the Principles and Limits of Taxation as a Branch of Moral and Political Philosophy.* [Extracted from vol. 3 of the Memoirs of the Literary and Philosophical Society of Manchester.] Warrington. No publisher identified.

Percival, Thomas. 1790b. *A Physical Inquiry into the Powers and Operation of Medicines.* No city identified: No publisher identified.

Percival, Thomas. 1790c. *A Short View of the Grounds and Limits of the Obligation to Pay Taxes. Addressed to the Manchester Literary and Philosophical Society.* Printed by W. Eyres, Warrington.

Percival, Thomas. 1794. *Medical Jurisprudence or A Code of Ethics and Institutes, Adapted to the Professions of Physic And Surgery.* Manchester: published privately, no information about printer.

Percival, Thomas. [1794] 2022. *Medical Jurisprudence or A Code of Ethics and Institutes, Adapted to the Professions of Physic and Surgery.* Manchester: published privately, no information about printer. In McCullough, Laurence B. 2022. Thomas Percival's *Medical Ethics* and the Invention of Medical Professionalism: With Three Key Percival Texts, Two Concordances, and a Chronology, 291–336. New York: Springer.

Percival, Thomas. 1802. *Biographical Memoirs of Thomas Butterworth Bayley, Esq., F.R.S., &c &c of Hope Hall Near Manchester.* Manchester: Printed for W. Shelmerdine.

Percival, Thomas. 1803. *Medical Ethics or, a Code of Institutes and Precepts, Adapted to the Professional Conduct of Physicians and Surgeons: I: In Hospital Practice. II: In Private or General Practice. III: In relation to Apothecaries. IV: In Cases which may require a Knowledge of Law. To which is added, An Appendix; Conataining a discourse on Hospital Duties; Also, Notes and Illustrations. By Thomas Percival, M.D. F.R.S.AND A.S. LOND, F.R.S AND B.M.S. EDINB &c. &e.* Manchester: Printed by S. Russell, for J. Johnson, St, Paul's Church Yard, and R. Bickerstaff, Strand, London.

Percival, Thomas. [1803] 1807. *Medical Ethics or, A Code of Institutes and Precepts, Adapted to the Professional Conduct of Physicians and Surgeons: I: In Hospital Practice. II: In Private or General Practice. III: In Relation to Apothecaries. IV: In Cases Which may Require a Knowledge of Law. To Which is Added, An Appendix; Conataining A Discourse on Hospital Duties; Also, Notes and Illustrations. By Thomas Percival, M.D. F.R.S.AND A.S. LOND, F.R.S AND B.M.S. EDINE &c. &e.* Manchester: Printed by S. Russell, for J. Johnson, St, Paul's Church Yard, and R. Bickerstaff, Strand, London. In *The Works, Literary, Moral, and Medical of Thomas Percival, Volumes 1–IV*, ed. Edward Percival, Vol.

II, 355–572. Printed by Richard Cruttwell, St. James-Street, Bath; for J. Johnson, St. Paul's Church-Yard, London.

Percival, Thomas. [1803] 1985. *Medical Ethics or, a Code of Institutes and Precepts, Adapted to The Professional Conduct of Physicians And Surgeons by Thomas Percival, M.D.*, Introduction by Edmund Pellegrino, M.D. Birmingham: The Classics of Medicine Library.

Percival, Thomas. [1803] 2022. *Medical Ethics or, A Code of Institutes and Precepts, Adapted to the Professional Conduct of Physicians and Surgeons: I: In Hospital Practice. II: In Private or General Practice. III: In relation to Apothecaries. IV: In Cases which may require a Knowledge of Law. To Which is Added, An Appendix; Conataining a Discourse on Hospital Duties; Also, Notes and Illustrations. By Thomas Percival, M.D. F.R.S.AND A.S. LOND, F.R.S AND B.M.S. EDINB &c. &e.* Manchester: Printed by S. Russell, for J. Johnson, St, Paul's Church Yard, and R. Bickerstaff, Strand, London. In McCullough, Laurence B. 2022. Thomas Percival's *Medical Ethics* and the Invention of Medical Professionalism: With Three Key Percival Texts, Two Concordances, and a Chronology, 336–434. New York: Springer.

Percival, Thomas. 1804. On the Preparation, Culture, and Use of the Orchis Root by J. Percival, M.D. *The Philosophical Magazine: Comprehending the Various Branches Science, the Liberal and Fine Arts, Agriculture, Manufactures, and Commerce.* Vol. XVIII, 158–163. London: Printed for Alexander Tilloch.

Percival, Thomas. 1806. *A Father's Instructions Tenth Edition, with the Addition of the Third Part.* London: J. Johnson.

Percival, Thomas. 1807. *The Works, Literary, Moral, and Medical of Thomas Percival, Volumes 1–IV*, ed. Edward Percival. Printed by Richard Cruttwell, St. James-Street, Bath; for J. Johnson, St. Paul's Church-Yard, London.

Percival, Thomas. 1823. *Extracts from the Medical Ethics of Dr. Percival.* Philadelphia [Clark & Raser, printers]. Note: This is the U.S. National Library of Medicine citation. https://collections.nlm.nih.gov/ext/mhl/27710910R/PDF/27710910R.pdf. Accessed 4 Sept 2020.

Percival, Thomas. [1823] 2022. *Extracts from the Medical Ethics of Dr. Percival.* Philadelphia [Clark & Raser, printers]. In McCullough, Laurence B. 2022. Thomas Percival's *Medical Ethics* and the Invention of Medical Professionalism: With Three Key Percival Texts, Two Concordances, and a Chronology, 435–443. New York: Springer.

Percival, Thomas. 1827. *Medical Ethics Or, A Code of Institutes and Precepts, Adapted To The Professional Conduct Of Physicians And Surgeons by the Late Thomas Percival, M.D. F.R.S. and A.S. Lond, F.R.S. And B.M.S. EdinB &c. &e. With Additions, Illustrative of the Past and Present State of the Profession and its Collegiate Institutions, in Great Britain. Published by W. Jackson.* Editor not identified. Manchester: W. Jackson.

Percival, Thomas. 1849. *Medical Ethics Or, A Code of Institutes and Precepts, Adapted To The Professional Conduct Of Physicians And Surgeons by the Late Thomas Percival, M.D., F.R.S.* Third Edition. Editor not identified. Oxford: John Henry Parker. London: John Churchill, Princes Street, Soho.

Percival, Thomas. [1807] 1870. *The Works, Literary, Moral, and Medical of Thomas Percival, Volumes I–IV*, ed. Edward Percival. Printed by Richard Cruttwell, St. James-Street, Bath; for J. Johnson, St. Paul's Church-Yard, London. London: J. Johnson. Reprint.

Percival, Thomas. [1807] 2010. *The Works, Literary, Moral, and Medical of Thomas Percival, Volumes I–IV*, ed. Edward Percival. Printed by Richard Cruttwell, St. James-Street, Bath; for J. Johnson, St. Paul's Church-Yard, London. Whitefish, Montana, USA: Facsimile edition by Kessinger Publishing's Rare Reprints

Percival, Thomas. [1807] 2014. *The Works, Literary, Moral, and Medical of Thomas Percival, Volumes I–IV*, ed. Edward Percival. Printed by Richard Cruttwell, St. James-Street, Bath; for J. Johnson, St. Paul's Church-Yard, London. Cambridge: Facsimile edition by Cambridge University Press.

Percival, Thomas. 1846. *Parental Instructions, or, Guide to Wisdom and Virtue Designed for Young Persons of Either Sex, Selected Mainly from the Writings of an Eminent Physician*. New York: Harper & Bros.

Manuscript and Unpublished Sources

Aberdeen University Library

AUL 2206/45: 1743. "Medical Notes," including "A proposal for a medicall society," by John Gregory.

Edinburgh University Library

EUL E.B. 6104 ED 11744. 1744. "Practical remarks on the sympathy of the parts of the body by the late Dr. James Crawford Professor of Medicine in the University of Edinburgh," article in *Medical Essays and Observations, Revised and Published by a Society in Edinburgh*, Vol. V, Part II.

Tate Library, Harris Manchester College of the University of Oxford

Warrington Academy Papers. 1754. Published letter of July 11, 1754.

Report of the Progress that has been made in the Establishment of the Academy at Warrington with an Abstract of the LAWS for the Governance of the STUDENTS. 1758. Report of first meeting of trustees of Warrington Academy 30 June 1757.

A Report of the State of the Academy at Warrington Drawn up by the Trustees at their Annual Meeting July 10 MDCCLX. 1760.

A Report of the State of the Academy at Warrington Drawn up by the Trustees at their Annual Meeting. 1761.

Royal College of Physicians of Edinburgh

RCPE, Gregory J, 1766. 1766. "Lectures on Medicine," by John Gregory. This librarian's note reads: "This may be the copy used by Gregory to lecture, 1766–73. The additions and interpolations strongly suggest original work."

Royal College of Physicians and Surgeons of Glasgow

RCPSG 1/9/4. n.d. "Clinical lectures by Dr. Whytt," reporter unknown.
RCPSG 1/9/9. 1768. "Lectures by Dr. Young Professor of Midwifery in the College of Edinburgh. Nov. 22 1768," Two Vols., by J.M. Foster.

Royal College of Surgeons of Edinburgh

RCSE C36 1771. 1771. "Clinical lectures by Dr. Gregory 1771 & Dr. Cullen 1772."

Online Sources

Bible, King James Version. n.d. https://quod.lib.umich.edu/cgi/k/kjv/kjv-idx?type=DIV2&byte=2198535. Accessed 4 Sept 2020. 1 Corinthians 31. https://quod.lib.umich.edu/cgi/k/kjv/kjv-idx?type=DIV2&byte=5099399. Accessed 11 July 2020.

American Medical Association. n.d. Code of medical ethics. Why does the medical profession need a code of ethics? https://www.ama-assn.org/delivering-care/ethics/why-does-medical-profession-need-code-ethics. Accessed 4 Sept 2020.

American Philosophical Society. n.d. https://www.amphilsoc.org/grants/lewis-and-clark-fund-exploration-and-field-research. Accessed 4 Sept 2020.

Eccles Old Road. Uncovering Salford's Lost Heritage. Hart Hill. https://ecclesoldroad.uk/place/hart-hill/. Accessed 4 Sept 2020.

Harris Manchester College, n.d. http://www.hmc.ox.ac.uk/discover/our-history/. Accessed 4 Sept 2020.

The Manchester Royal Infirmary. n.d. Archive Unit. https://archiveshub.jisc.ac.uk/search/archives/b489e047-e6b1-3992-aaa3-5e40e2147729?component=7d7aa227-54f0-3f6f-baef-6433404be16c. Accessed 4 Sept 2020.

Royal College of Physicians of Edinburgh. n.d. https://www.rcpe.ac.uk/. Accessed 4 Sept 2020.

Royal College of Surgeons of Edinburgh. n.d. https://www.rcsed.ac.uk/. Accessed 4 Sept 2020.
Royal College of Physicians and Surgeons of Glasgow. n.d. https://rcpsg.ac.uk/. Accessed 4 Sept 2020.
Royal College of Physicians of London. n.d. https://www.rcplondon.ac.uk/. Accessed 4 Sept 2020.
Royal College of Surgeons of England. n.d. https://www.rcseng.ac.uk/. Accessed 4 Sept 2020.

Other Published Primary and Secondary Sources

No author identified. 1775. *A Select Catalogue of Books in the Library Belonging to Warrington Academy*. Warrington: Printed by William Eyres.
No author identified. 1968. Sir George Baker (1722–1809) Discoverer of the Pathogenesis of Devonshire colic. *Journal of the American Medical Association* 204(6): 541.
Abbott, John L. 1970. John Hawkesworth: Friend of Samuel Johnson and editor of Captain Cook's Voyages and of the Gentleman's Magazine. *Eighteenth Century Studies* 3(3): 339–350.
Aikin, John. 1771. *Thoughts on Hospitals, with a Letter to the Author by Thomas Percival*. London: Printed for Joseph Johnson, 72 St. Paul's Churchyard.
Allibone, Samuel Austin. 1891. *A Critical Dictionary of English Literature and British and American Authors Living and Deceased from the Earliest Accounts to the Latter Half of the Nineteenth Century*. Vol. I. Philadelphia: J.B. Lippincott Company.
Ambrose, Charles T. 2005. The Secret Kappa Lambda Society of Hippocrates (and the Origin of the American Medical Association's Principles of Medical Ethics). *Yale Journal of Biology and Medicine* 78(1): 45–56.
American Medical Association. Code of Ethics. [1847] 1999. In *The American Medical Ethics Revolution: How the AMA's Code of Ethics Has Transformed Physicians' Relationships to Patients, Professionals, and Society*, eds. R.B. Baker, A.L. Caplan, L.L. Emanuel, and S.H. Latham, 324–334. Baltimore: Johns Hopkins University Press.
Audi, Robert. 2015. Intuition and its Place in Ethics. *Journal of the American Philosophical Association* 1(1): 57–77.
Bacon, Francis. 2010a. *Essay on Youth and Age*. Whitefish: Facsimile edition by Kessinger Publishing's Rare Reprints, extracted by Bacon's *Essays or Counsels, Civil or Moral*.
Bacon, Francis. 1875b. *The New Organon*. In *The Works of Francis Bacon, Vol. IV*, ed. J. Spedding, R.L. Ellis, and D.D. Heath, 265–270. London: Longman, Cumpers, and Co.

Bacon, Francis. 1875c. *Of the Dignity and Advancement of Learning*. In *The Works of Francis Bacon, Vol. IV*, ed. J. Spedding, R.L. Ellis, and D.D. Heath, 273–498. London: Longman, Cumpers, and Co.

Bacon, Francis. 1875d. Preface, The Great Instauration. In *The Works of Francis Bacon, Vol. IV*, ed. J. Spedding, R.L. Ellis, and D.D. Heath, 13–21. London: Longman, Cumpers, and Co.

Bacon, Francis. 1875e. Preparative Toward a Natural and Experimental History. In *The Works of Francis Bacon, Vol. IV*, ed. J. Spedding, R.L. Ellis, and D.D. Heath, 249–263. London: Longman, Cumpers, and Co.

Baile, W.F., R. Buckman, R. Lenzi, G. Glober, E.A. Beale, and A.P. Kudelka. 2000. SPIKES-A Six-Step Protocol for Delivering Bad News: Application to the Patient with Cancer. *Oncologist* 5(4): 302–311.

Baker, Robert. 1993a. Deciphering Percival's Code. In *The Codification of Medical Morality: Historical and Philosophical Studies of the Formalization of Western Medical Morality in the Eighteenth and Nineteenth Centuries: Volume One: Medical Ethics and Etiquette in the Eighteenth Century*. Eds. Robert Baker, Dorothy Porter, Roy Porter, 179–211. Dordrecht: Kluwer Academic Publishers (now Springer).

Baker, Robert B. 1993b. The History of Medical Ethics. In *Companion Encyclopedia of the History of Medicine*, eds. W.F. Bynum and R. Porter, 852–887. London/New York: Routledge.

Baker, Robert B. 2009. The Discourses of Practitioners in Nineteenth- and Twentieth-Century Britain and the United States. In *The Cambridge World History of Medical Ethics*, eds. R.B. Baker and L.B. McCullough, 446–464. New York: Cambridge University Press.

Baker, Robert B. 2013. *Before Bioethics: A History of American Medical Ethics from the Colonial Period to the Bioethics Revolution*. New York: Oxford University Press.

Baker, Robert B. 2019. *The Structure of Moral Revolutions: Studies of Changes in the Morality of Abortion, Death, and the Bioethics Revolution*. Cambridge, MA: MIT Press.

Baker, Robert B, and Laurence B. McCullough. 2009a. The Discourses of Philosophical Medical Ethics. In *The Cambridge World History of Medical Ethics*, eds. R.B. Baker and L.B. McCullough, 281–309. New York: Cambridge University Press.

Baker, Robert B, and Laurence B. McCullough. 2009b. What is the History of Medical Ethics? In *The Cambridge World History of Medical Ethics*, eds. R.B. Baker and L.B. McCullough, 3–16. New York: Cambridge University Press.

Baltzly, Dirk. 2019. Stoicism. *The Stanford Encyclopedia of Philosophy* (Spring 2019 Edition), ed. Edward N. Zalta. https://plato.stanford.edu/archives/spr2019/entries/stoicism/. Accessed 4 Sept 2020.

Beaton, James. 2000. The Royal College of Physicians and Surgeons of Glasgow: A short history. *Proceedings of the Royal College of Physicians and Surgeons of Glasgow* 30: 63–68.

Beauchamp, Tom L, and James F. Childress. 2019. *Principles of Biomedical Ethics*, 8th ed. New York: Oxford University Press.

Beck, Theodoric Romeyn. 1823. *Elements of Medical Jurisprudence*. Albany: Webster and Skinner.

Berlant, Jeffrey. 1975. *Profession and Monopoly: A Study of Medicine in the United States and Great Britain*. Berkeley: The University of California Press.

Berlin, Isaiah. 1958. *Two Concepts of Liberty*. Oxford: The Clarendon Press.

Boerhaave, Hermann. 1747. *Institutiones Medicae*. Parisiis apud Guillelum Cavalier, Patrem, via Jacobeâ, sub Signo Lilii Aurei.

Bright, Henry Arthur. 1859. *A Historical Sketch of Warrington Academy*. Liverpool: T. Brakell, Printer, Cook Street. Facsimile Reproduction by Book Renaissance. www.ren-books.com.

Brockbank, Edward Mansfield. 1904. *Sketches of the Lives and Work of the Honorary Medical Staff of Manchester Infirmary from its Foundation in 1752 until 1830 When it Became the Royal Infirmary*. Manchester: Manchester University Press.

Brody H. 2014. Chauncey Leake and the Development of Bioethics in America. *Kennedy Institute of Ethics Journal* 24(1): 73–95.

Brody, H., Z. Meghani, and K. Greenwald. eds. 2009. *Michael Ryan's Writings on Medical Ethics*. Dordrecht: Springer.

Buchan, William. 1769. *Domestic Medicine*. Edinburgh: Balfour, Auld, and Smellie.

Burns, Chester R. 1974. Reciprocity in the development of Anglo-American medical ethics, 1765–1865. In *Proceedings of the XXIII International Congress of the History of Medicine*, Vol. 1, 813–819 London: Wellcome Institute for the History of Medicine.

Burns, Chester R. 1977. Historical Introduction to 1975 reprint Thomas Percival: Medical Ethics or Medical Jurisprudence? In *Legacies in Ethics and Medicine*, ed. Chester R. Burns, 284–299. New York: Science History Publications.

Burton, Richard, Furio Colombo, and Franco Zeffirelli, Roman Vlad, Radio audizioni Italia, and Committee to Rescue Italian Art. 1966. *Florence: Days of Destruction*. Committee to Restore Italian Art. https://umaryland.on.worldcat.org/oclc/959295493. Accessed 4 Sept 2020.

Bynum, William. 1981. Cullen and the Study of Fevers in Britain 1760–1820. *Medical History* (Supplement No. 1): 135–147.

Bynum, William. 1993. Nosology. In *Companion Encyclopedia of the History of Medicine*, eds. W.F. Bynum and R. Porter, 335–356. London/New York: Routledge.

Carter, J.J., and J.H. Pittock. 1987. *Aberdeen and the Enlightenment: Proceedings of a Conference Held at the University of Aberdeen*. Aberdeen: Aberdeen University Press.

Castro, Rodrigo. 1662. *Medicus-politicus sive de officiis medicus-politicus tractatus quattuor distinctis libris ....* Ex Bibliopolio Zachariae Hertelli, Hambrugi (Germany).

Chaloner, W.H. 1959. Manchester in the Latter Half of the Eighteenth Century. *Bulletin of the John Rylands Library* 42 (1): 40–60.

Chervenak, J.L., F.A. Chervenak, and L.B. McCullough. 2010. A New Approach to Professional Liability Reform: Placing Obligations of Stakeholders Ahead of Their Interests. *American Journal of Obstetrics and Gynecology* 203: 203. e1–203.e2037.

Chervenak, Frank A., McCullough, Laurence B., and Thomas E. Baril. 2006. Ethics, a Neglected Dimension of Power Relationships of Physician Leaders. *American Journal of Obstetrics and Gynecology* 195(3): 651–656.

Cicero. 1913. *De Officiis, with an English Translation by Walter Miller*. New York: The Macmillan Company.

Clark, Sir G. 1964. *A Short History of the Royal College of Physicians of London*. Oxford: The Clarendon Press.

Cohen, Roger. 2014, April 7. From Death into Life. *The New York Times*. https://www.nytimes.com/2014/04/08/opinion/cohen-from-death-into-life.html. Accessed 4 Sept 2020.

Craig, W.S. 1976. *History of the Royal College of Physicians of Edinburgh*. Oxford: Blackwell Scientific Publications.

Crawford, Catherine. 1993. Medicine and the Law. In *Companion Encyclopedia of the History of Medicine*, eds. W.F. Bynum and R. Porter, 1619–1640. London/New York: Routledge.

Cullen, William. 1772. *Institutions of Medicine: Part 1: Physiology. For the use of Students in the University of Edinburgh*. Edinburgh: Printed for Charles Elliott, Edinburgh, and T. Cadell, *Strand*, London.

Cullen, William. 1816. *First Lines on the Practice of Physic*, 2 Vols. Edinburgh: Printed for Bell and Bradfute, and Adam Black. First published by Cullen in 1777

Daiches, D. 1986. *The Scottish Enlightenment: An Introduction*. Edinburgh: The Saltire Society.

Descartes, René. [1641] 2017. *Meditations on First Philosophy, with Selections from the Objections and Replies*, ed. John Cottingham. Cambridge Texts in the History of Philosophy. Cambridge: Cambridge University Press.

Digby, K. 1669. *Of the Sympathetick Powder: A Discourse in a Solemn Assembly in Montpelier*. London: John Williams.

Dissenting Academies Online. Seddon, John. https://dissacad.english.qmul.ac.uk/sample1.php?parameter=personretrieve&alpha=639. Accessed 4 Sept 2020.

Dissenting Academies Online. Taylor, John. https://dissacad.english.qmul.ac.uk/sample1.php?parameter=personretrieve&alpha=1458. Accessed 4 Sept 2020.

Dixon, Thomas. 1766. *The Sovereignty of Divine Administration, Vindicated; or a Rational Account of Our Blessed Saviour's Remarkable Temptation in the Wilderness; the Possessed at Carparnaum; the Daemonies at Gadara, and the Destruction of the Swine: with Free Remarks upon several other Important Passages in the New Testament. With a Preface by the Reverend John Seddon of Manchester*. London: Printed for Becket and De Hondt in the Strand; J. Gore in Liverpool' and Messieurs Clarke and Haslingden in Manchester.

Dunn, P.M. 1997. James Lind (1716–94) of Edinburgh and the Treatment of Scurvy. *Archives of Disease in Childhood: Fetal Neonatal Edition* 76(1): F64–F65.

Emanuel, Ezekiel J., and Linda L. Emanuel. Four Models of the Physician-Patient Relationship. *Journal of the American Medical Association* 267(16): 2221–2226.

Enfield, William. 1781. *A Funeral Sermon Occasioned by the Death of the Late Rev. John Aikin, DD, Professor of Divinity in Warrington*. London: Printed by W. Eyres for J. Johnson, No. 72 St. Paul's Churchyard.

Enfield, William. 1792. *The Speaker: Or, Miscellaneous Pieces, Selected from the Best English Writers, and Disposed under Proper Heads, with a View to Facilitate the Improvement of Youth in Reading and Speaking*. London: J. Johnson, St. Paul's Churchyard.

Engel, George L. 1977. The Need for a New Medical Model: A Challenge for Biomedicine. *Science* 196: 129–136.

Engelhardt, Jr., H.T. 1985. The Foundations of Bioethics. New York: Oxford University Press.

Engelhardt, Jr., and H. Tristram. 1996. *The Foundations of Bioethics*, 2nd ed. New York: Oxford University Press.

Espinasse, Francis. 1877. *Lancashire Worthies*. London: Simkin, Marshall, & Co.

Farr, Samuel. [1788] 1814. *Elements of Medical Jurisprudence or A Succinct and Compendious Description of such Tokens in the Human Body as are Requisite to Determine the Judgment of a Coroner, and Courts of Law, in cases of Divorce, Murder, Rape, &c. to which are added Directions for Preserving the Public Health*, 2nd ed. London: Printed for J. Callow, Medical Bookseller, 10, Crown-Court, Princes-Street, Soho.

Faselius, Johann Friedrich. 1767. *Elementa Medicinae Forensis*. Ienae: Impens. 10. Wilh. Hartung.

Feinberg, Joel. 1984. *Harm to Others: The Moral Limits of the Criminal Law*. New York: Oxford University Press.

FIGO Committee for the Ethical Aspects of Human Reproduction and Women's Health. Professionalism in Obstetric and Gynecologic Practice. 2017. *International Journal of Gynaecology and Obstetrics* 36: 249–251.

Foot, Philippa. 1978. The Problem of Abortion and the Doctrine of Double Effect. In *Virtues and Vices and Other Essays*, Philippa Foot, 19–32. Oxford: Oxford University Press.

Fulton, John F. 1933. Warrington Academy (1757–1786) and its Influence Upon Medicine and Science. *Bulletin of the Institute of the History of Medicine* 1(2): 50–80.

Galvão-Sobrinho, Carlos R. 1996. Hippocratic Ideals, Medical Ethics and the Practice of Medicine in the Early Middle Ages: The Legacy of the Hippocratic Oath. *Journal of the History of Medicine and Allied Sciences* 51(4): 438–455.

Garrett, Aaron. 2018. Joseph Butler's Moral Philosophy. In *The Stanford Encyclopedia of Philosophy* (Spring 2018 Edition). Ed. Edward N. Zalta. https://plato.stanford.edu/archives/spr2018/entries/butler-moral/. Accessed 4 Sept 2020.

Gelfand, Toby. 1993. The History of the Medical Profession. In *Companion Encyclopedia of the History of Medicine*, eds. W.F. Bynum and R. Porter, 1119–1150. London/New York: Routledge.

Gevitz, Norman. 1993. Unorthodox Medical Theories. In *Companion Encyclopedia of the History of Medicine*, eds. W.F. Bynum and R. Porter, 826–851. London/New York: Routledge.

Gisborne, Thomas. 1785. *The Principles of Moral and Political Philosophy Investigated, together with Remarks on the Principle Assumed by Mr. Paley as the Basis for all Moral Conclusions, and on other Positions by the Same Author*, 2nd ed. London: Printed by T. Bensley for D. White and Son, Horace's head, Fleet-Street.

Gisborne, Thomas. 1794. *An Enquiry into the Duties of Men in the Higher and Middle Classes of Society in Great Britain Resulting from their Respective Station, Professions and Employment*. London: B&J White.

Goldsmith, Oliver. 1806. A History of the Fishes. In *The Works of Oliver Goldsmith: with an Account of his Life and Writings, A New Edition*. Volume the Ninth: 1–254. London: J. Johnson.

Gracia, Diego. 2009. The Discourses of Practitioners in Nineteenth- and Twentieth-Century Spain. In *The Cambridge World History of Medical Ethics*, eds. Baker, Robert B., and Laurence B. McCullough, 427–431. New York: Cambridge University Press.

Gracia, Diego. 2010. Philosophy: Ancient and Contemporary Approaches. In *Methods in Medical Ethics*, 2nd ed., ed. J. Sugarman and DP Sulmasy, 55–72. Washington, DC: Georgetown University Press.

Granshaw, Lindsay. 1993. The Hospital. In *Companion Encyclopedia of the History of Medicine*, eds. W.F. Bynum and R. Porter, 1180–1203. London/New York: Routledge.

Gregory, James. 1800. *Memorial to the Managers of the Royal Infirmary*. Edinburgh: Murray and Cochrane.

Gregory, John. 1765. *A Comparative View of the State and Faculties of Man with Those of the Animal World*. London: J. Dodsley.

Gregory, John. 1770. *Observations on the Duties and Offices of a Physician, and on the Method of Prosecuting Enquiries in Philosophy*. London: W. Strahan and T. Cadell.

Gregory, John. [1770] 1998. *Observations on the Duties and Offices of a Physician, and on the Method of Prosecuting Enquiries in Philosophy*. London: W. Strahan and T. Cadell. In *John Gregory's Writings on Medical Ethics and Philosophy of Medicine*, ed. Laurence B. McCullough, 93–159. Dordrecht: Kluwer Academic Publishers (now Springer).

Gregory, John. 1772. *Lectures on the Duties and Qualifications of a Physician*. London: W. Strahan and T. Cadell.

Gregory, John. [1772] 1998. *Lectures on the Duties and Qualifications of a Physician*. London: W. Strahan and T. Cadell. In *John Gregory's Writings on Medical Ethics and Philosophy of Medicine*, ed. Laurence B. McCullough, 161–245. Dordrecht: Kluwer Academic Publishers (now Springer).

Gregory, John. 1774. *A Father's Legacy to his Daughters*. London: W. Strahan and T. Cadell. Edinburgh: J. Balfour.

Gregory, John. 1778. *Vorlesungen über die Pflichten und Eigenschaften eines Artzes. Aus dem Englischen nach der neuen und verbesserten Ausgabe.* Anonymous translation. Leipzig, Germany: Caspar Fritsch.

Gregory, John. 1788. *The Works of the Late Dr. John Gregory, M.D.* London: A. Strahan and T. Cadell; Edinburgh: W. Creech.

Gregory, John. 1789. *Lexioni Sopra I Doveri e la Qualita di un medico.* Padovano FF, trans. Florence: Gaetano Cambiagi., 1789.

Gregory, John. 1797. *Discours sur les dévoirs, les qualités et les connaissances du médicin, avec un cour d'études,* trans. Verlac B. Paris: Crapart & Briands.

Gregory, John. 1803. *Discurso sobre los deberes, qualidades y conocimientos del medico, con el método des sus estudios.* Madrid: Imprenta Real.

Gregory, John. 1805. *Lectures on the Duties and Qualifications of a Physician, Revised and Corrected by James Gregory, M.D.* Ed. James Gregory. Edinburgh: W. Creech; London: T. Cadell and W. Davies.

Gregory, John. 1817. *Lectures on the Duties and Qualifications of a Physician.* Philadelphia: M. Carey and Son, 1817.

Gregory, John. 1820. *On the Duties and Qualifications of a Physician, New Edition.* London: J. Anderson.

Grove, Henry. 1745. *Sermons and Tracts: Being the Posthumous Works of the late reverend Mr Henry Grove of Taunton in four volumes.* London: James Waugh.

Grove, Henry. 1749. *A System of Moral Philosophy.* London: Printed and sold by J. Waugh, at the Turk's Head in Lombard-Street.

Guyatt GH, Haynes RB, Jaeschke RZ, et al. 2000. Users' Guides to the Medical Literature: XXV. Evidence-Based Medicine: Principles for Applying the Users' Guides to Patient Care. Evidence-Based Medicine Working Group. *Journal of the American Medical Association.* 284(10): 1290–1296.

Haakonssen, L. 1997. *Medicine and Morals in the Enlightenment: John Gregory, Thomas Percival, and Benjamin Rush.* Amsterdam: Editions Rodopi.

Harwood, Edward. 1761. *A Sermon Occasioned by the Death of the Rev. John Taylor, D.D., Late of Norwich, Professor of Divinity and Morality in the Academy in Warrington, Lancashire; with some account of his Character and Writings.* London: Printed for J. Waugh at the Turk's-Head in Lombard Street; and W. Fenner, at the Angel & Bible in Pater-Noster-Row.

Hippocrates. 1923. *Decorum.* In *Hippocrates,* with an English translation by W.H.S. Jones, 267–301. The Loeb Classical Library. Cambridge, MA: Harvard University Press.

Hoffmann, Friedrich. 1749. *Medicus Politicus, sive Regulae Prudentiae secundun quas Medicus Juvenis Studia sua et Vitae Rationem Digere Debet.* In F. Hoffmann *Operum Omnium Physico-Medicorum Supplementum in Duas Partes Distributum,* apud Fratres de Tournes, Genevae.

Hope, Royden Birtley. 1947. *Dr. Thomas Percival, A Medical Pioneer and Social Reformer.* Manchester University Library: Thesis submitted for the Degree of Master of Arts of the University of Manchester.

Howard, Joseph Jackson. 1997. *Visitation at England and Wales, Notes, Volume 4 1902.* Bowie: A Facsimile Reprint by Heritage Press.

Hume, David. [1778] 1983. *The History of England.* In *Six Volumes.* Indianapolis: Liberty Fund. Liberty Fund Classics.

Hume, David. 1987. Of National Characters. In *David Hume: Essays Moral, Political, and Literary*, ed. E.F. Miller, 197–215. Indianapolis: Liberty Classics.

Hume, David. [1739–1740] 2000. *A Treatise of Human Nature*, ed. David Fate Norton and Mary J. Norton. Oxford: Oxford University Press.

Ingelfinger, Franz J. Arrogance. 1980. *New England Journal of Medicine* 303(26): 1507–1511.

International Academy of Perinatal Medicine. n.d. https://iaperinatalmedicine.org/#. Accessed 4 Sept 2020.

International Federation of Gynecology and Obstetrics. n.d. https://www.figo.org/. Accessed 4 Sept 2020.

James, William. [1896] 1907. The Will to Believe and Other Essays in Popular Philosophy. New York: Longmans Green and Co. Originally published 1896.

Janson, H.W., with Dora Jane Janson. 1965. *History of Art: A Survey of the Major Visual Arts from the Dawn of History to the Present Day.* Englewood Cliffs: Prentice-Hall, Inc. and New York: Harry N. Abrams, Inc.

Janssens, U. 1981. Matthieu Maty and the adoption of inoculation for smallpox in Holland. *Bulletin of the History of Medicine* 55(2): 246–256.

Johnson, Samuel. 1755. *A Dictionary of the English Language.* London: J&P Knapton. A Digital Edition of the 1755 Classic: https://johnsonsdictionaryonline.com/. Accessed 4 Sept 2020.

Definition of 'affliction': https://johnsonsdictionaryonline.com/affliction/. Accessed 4 Sept 2020.

Definition of 'afflictive': https://johnsonsdictionaryonline.com/afflictive/. Accessed 4 Sept 2020.

Definition of 'authority': https://johnsonsdictionaryonline.com/page-view/?i=186. Accessed 4 Sept 2020.

Definition of 'code': https://johnsonsdictionaryonline.com/page-view/?i=401, accessed 4 Sept 2020.

Definition of 'condescension': https://johnsonsdictionaryonline.com/page-view/?i=440. Accessed 11 4 Sept 2020.

Definition of 'institute': https://johnsonsdictionaryonline.com/page-view/?i=1105. Accessed 4 Sept 2020.

Definition of 'precept': https://johnsonsdictionaryonline.com/page-view/?i=1550. Accessed 4 Sept 2020.

Definition of 'quack': https://johnsonsdictionaryonline.com/quack-noun/. Accessed 4 Sept 2020.

Definition of 'steadiness': https://johnsonsdictionaryonline.com/page-view/?i=1934. Accessed 4 Sept 2020.

Definition of 'tenderness': https://johnsonsdictionaryonline.com/page-view/?i=2034. Accessed 4 Sept 2020.

Johnson, Samuel. *Sydenham.* 1812. In *The Works of Samuel Johnson, L.L.D. A New Edition*, ed. Arthur Murray, Vol. XII, 152–160. New York: Published by William Turrell.

Jollimore, Troy. 2020. Impartiality. *The Stanford Encyclopedia of Philosophy* (Summer 2020 Edition). Ed. Edward N. Zalta. https://plato.stanford.edu/archives/sum2020/entries/impartiality/. Accessed 4 Sept 2020.

Jonas, Hans. 1966. *The Phenomenon of Life: Towards a Philosophical Biology.* Evanston: Northwestern University Press.

Jonsen, Albert R. 2000. *A Short History of Medical Ethics.* New York: Oxford University Press.

Jouanna, Jacques. 2001. *Hippocrates*, trans DeBevoise MB. Baltimore: Johns Hopkins University Press.

Justinian. 2002. *The Institutes of Justinian Translated into English with an Index by J.B. Moyle, D.C.L.* Union: The Lawbook Exchange, Ltd.

Kant, Immanuel. [1781] 1998. *Critique of Pure Reason.* Trans. Paul Geyer and Allen Wood. Cambridge Edition of the Works of Immanuel Kant. Cambridge: Cambridge University Press.

Kant, Immanuel. n.d. *What is Enlightenment?* Trans. Mary C. Smith. http://www.columbia.edu/acis/ets/CCREAD/etscc/kant.html/. Accessed 4 Sept 2020.

Kant, I., and A. Wood. 1996. On the Supposed Right to Lie from Philanthropy. In *Practical Philosophy*, ed. M. Gregor, 605–616. The Cambridge Edition Works of Kant. Cambridge: Cambridge University Press.

Kappa Lambda Society. 1823. *Extracts from the Medical Ethics of Dr. Percival.* Philadelphia: Published privately for the Kappa Lambda Secret Society of Hippocrates.

Kass, Leon. 1997. The Wisdom of Repugnance. *The New Republic* 216 (22): 17–26.

Kendrick, James. 1858. *Profiles of Warrington Worthies, Collected and Arranged by James Kendrick, M.D.* Warrington: Printed by John Haddock and Son, at the "Old Warrington Press."

King, Lester S. 1970. Precursors of Boerhaave's Institutiones Medicae. In *Boerhaave and his Time*, ed. G.A. Lindeboom, 60–68. Leiden: E.J. Brill.

Kinzer, Stephen. 2004, March 31. Legacy; One College's Long Shadow: Looking Back at the Williams Mafia. *The New York Times.* https://www.nytimes.com/2004/03/31/arts/legacy-one-college-s-long-shadow-looking-back-at-the-williams-mafia.html. Accessed 4 Sept 2020.

Kocher, Paul. 1947. The Physician as Atheist in Elizabethan England. *Huntington Library Quarterly* 10(3): 229–249.

Kuhn, Thomas. 1962. *The Structure of Scientific Revolutions.* Chicago: University of Chicago Press.

Kuhn, Thomas. 2012. *The Structure of Scientific Revolutions*, 50th Anniversary ed. Chicago: University of Chicago Press.

Lawrence, Ghislaine. 1993. Surgery (traditional). In *Companion Encyclopedia of the History of Medicine*, eds. W.F. Bynum and R. Porter, 961–983. London/New York: Routledge.

Leake, Chauncey, ed. 1927. *Percival's Medical Ethics.* Baltimore: Williams and Wilkins.

Lee, S, ed. 1895. Dictionary of National Biography. 15 Waterloo Place, London: Smith, Elder & CO.

Leibniz, G.W. 1985. *Theodicy: Essays on the Goodness of God, the Freedom of Man, and the Origin of Evil*. Chicago: Open Court Publishing.

Lenzi R, W.F. Baile, J. Berek, et al. 2005. Design, Conduct and Evaluation of a Communication Course for Oncology Fellows. *Journal of Cancer Education* 20(3): 143–149.

Lewis, Charlton T., and Charles Short. [1879] 1969. *A Latin Dictionary Founded on Andrews' Edition of Freund's Latin Dictionary Revised, Enlarged, and in Great Part Rewritten*. Oxford: At the Clarendon Press.

Lind, James. 1772. A Treatise on the Scurvy. *In Three Parts. Containing an Enquiry into the Nature, Causes, and Cure of that Disease. Together with a Critical and Chronological View of What has been Published on the Subject*, 3rd ed. London: Printer for S. Crowder, G. Wilson, and D. Nichols, T. Cadell, T. Becket and Co. G. Pearch and W. Woodfall.

MacDougal, Heather, and G. Ross Langley. n.d. Medical Ethics: Past, Present and Future. For Royal College of Physicians and Surgeons of Canada. http://www.royalcollege.ca/rcsite/bioethics/primers/medical-ethics-past-present-future-e,. Accessed 4 Sept 2020.

MacIntyre, Alasdair. 1981. *After Virtue*. South Bend: University of Notre Dame Press.

Maty, M. 1752. Extract of a letter to Dr. Maty FRS from Geneva Concerning the Introduction and the Success of Inoculation in the City, read June 18 1752. *Philosophical Transactions of the Royal Society* 47: 503.

McBride, William M. 1991. "Normal" Medical Science and British Treatment of the Sea Scurvy, 1753–75. *Journal of the History of Medicine and Allied Sciences* 46(2): 158–177.

McCullough, Laurence B., and Frank A. Chervenak. 1994. *Ethics in Obstetrics and Gynecology*. New York: Oxford University Press.

McCullough, Laurence B. 1996. *Leibniz on Individuals and Individuation: The Persistence of Premodern Ideas in Modern Philosophy*. Dordrecht: Kluwer Academic Publishers (now Springer).

McCullough, Laurence B. 1998. *John Gregory and the Invention of Professional Medical Ethics and the Profession of Medicine*. Dordrecht: Kluwer Academic Publishers (now Springer).

McCullough, Laurence B. 1999. The Liberal Arts Model of Medical Education: Its Importance and Limitations. In *Building Bioethics*, ed. Loretta Kopelman, 95–108. Dordrecht: Kluwer Academic Publishers.

McCullough, Laurence B. 2006. The Ethical Concept of Medicine as a Profession: Its Origins in Modern Medical Ethics and Implications for Physicians. In *Lost Virtue: Professional Character Development in Medical Education*, eds. N. Kenny N and W. Shelton, 17–27. New York: Elsevier.

McCullough, Laurence B. 2009. The Discourses of Practitioners in Eighteenth-Century Britain. In *The Cambridge World History of Medical Ethics*, eds. R.B. Baker and L.B. McCullough, 403–413. New York: Cambridge University Press.

McCullough, Laurence B. 2011. Was Bioethics Founded on Historical and Conceptual Mistakes About Medical Paternalism? *Bioethics* 25(2): 66–74.

McCullough LB, Jones JW, Brody BA. 1998. Informed Consent: Autonomous Decision Making of the Surgical patient. In *Surgical Ethics*, eds. Laurence B. McCullough, James W. Jones, and Baruch A. Brody, 15–37. New York: Oxford University Press.

McCullough, Laurence B., Coverdale, John H., and Frank A, Chervenak. 2020. *Professional Ethics in Obstetrics and Gynecology*. Cambridge/New York: Cambridge University Press.

McLachlan, H. 1931. *English Education Under the Test Acts: Being a History of Non-Conformist Academies 1662–1820*. Manchester: Manchester University Press.

McLachlan, H. 1943. *Warrington Academy: Its History and Influence*. Manchester: Printed for the Chetham Society.

Meyers, Sylvia Harcstark. 1990. *The Bluestocking Circle: Women, Friendship, and the Life of the Mind in Eighteenth-Century England*. Oxford: The Clarendon Press.

Nicholson, Albert. 1885. Percival, Thomas. *Dictionary of National Biography, 1885–1900*. Volume 44. https://en.wikisource.org/wiki/Percival,_Thomas_(1740-1804)_(DNB00). Accessed 4 Sept 2020.

Nutton, Vivian. 2009 The Discourses of European Practitioners in the Tradition of the Hippocratic Texts. In *The Cambridge World History of Medical Ethics*, eds. R.B. Baker and L.B. McCullough, 359–362. New York: Cambridge University Press.

Obrien, P. 1989. *Warrington Academy 1757–1786: Its Predecessors and Successors*. Wigan: Owl Books.

Oken, David. 1961, April 1. What to Tell Cancer Patients. A Study of Medical Attitudes. *Journal of the American Medical Association* 175: 1120–1128.

Paley, William. [1785] 2013. *The Principles of Moral and Political Philosophy*. Cambridge Library Collection. Cambridge: Cambridge University Press.

Pellegrino, Edmund D. 1985. Thomas Percival's Ethics: The Ethics Beneath the Etiquette. In *Medical Ethics or, a Code of Institutes and Precepts, Adapted to The Professional Conduct of Physicians And Surgeons by Thomas Percival, M.D.*, Introduction by Edmund Pellegrino, M.D., 1–52. Birmingham: The Classics of Medicine Library.

Pellegrino, Edmund D. 2006. Toward a Reconstruction of Medical Morality. *American Journal of Bioethics* 6(2): 65–71.

Penn People. n.d. Samuel Jackson. https://archives.upenn.edu/exhibits/penn-people/biography/samuel-jackson. Accessed 4 Sept 2020.

Pernick, Martin. 2009. Bioethics and History. In *The Cambridge World History of Medical Ethics*, eds. R.B. Baker and L.B. McCullough, 16–20. New York: Cambridge University Press.

Peters, Timothy. 2011. King George III, Bipolar Disorders, Porphyria and Lessons for Historians. *Clinical Medicine (London)* 11(3): 261–264.

Pickstone, John V. 1985. *Medicine and Industrial Society: A History of Hospital Development in Manchester and its Region, 1752–1946*. Manchester: Manchester University Press.

Pickstone, John V. 1993. Thomas Percival and the Production of Medical Ethics. In *The Codification of Medical Morality: Historical and Philosophical Studies of the Formalization of Western Medical Morality in the Eighteenth and Nineteenth Centuries: Volume One: Medical Ethics and Etiquette in the Eighteenth Century*. Eds. Robert Baker, Dorothy Porter, Roy Porter, 161–178. Dordrecht: Kluwer Academic Publishers (now Springer).

Pickstone, J.V., and Butler, S.V.F. 1984. The Politics of Medicine in Manchester, 1788–1792: Hospital Reform and Public Health Services in the Early Industrial City. *Medical History* 28(3): 227–249.

Plato. 1924. *Plato's Euthyphro, Apology, Crito*. Ed. with notes by John Burnet. Oxford: Clarendon Press.

Plato. 2000. *The Republic*. Ed. G.R.F. Ferrari, trans. Tom Griffith. Cambridge Texts in the History of Political Thought. Cambridge: Cambridge University Press.

Plato. 2010. *Plato – Meno and Phaedo*. Eds. David Sedley and Alex Long. Cambridge: Cambridge University Press.

Porter, Roy. 1990. *The Enlightenment*. London: Macmillan Press LTD.

Porter, Roy. 1993. Pain and Suffering. In *Companion Encyclopedia of the History of Medicine*, eds. W.F. Bynum and R. Porter, 1574–1591. London/New York: Routledge.

Porter, Roy. 1997. *The Greatest Benefit to Mankind: A Medical History of Mankind*. New York/London: W.W. Norton & Company.

Porter, Roy. 2000. *The Creation of the Modern World: The Untold Story of the British Enlightenment*. New York: W.W. Norton.

Porter, Dorothy, and Roy Porter. 1989. *Patient's Progress: Doctors and Doctoring in Eighteenth-Century England*. Stanford: Stanford University Press.

Porter, Roy, and Mikuláš Teich. 1981. *The Enlightenment in National Context*. Cambridge: Cambridge University Press.

Price, Richard. 1773. *Observations on Reversionary Payments; On Schemes for Providing Annuities for Widows, and Persons in Old Age; On the Methods of Calculating Assurances on Lives; And on the National Debt*. 3rd ed. Printed for T. Cadell, The Strand, London.

Priestley, Joseph. 1765. *An Essay on the Course of Liberal Education for Civil and Active Life. With plans of lectures on I. The Study of History and General Policy. II. The History of England. III. The Constitution and Laws of England. To which are added, remarks on a code of education, proposed by Dr. Brown, in a late treatise, intitled, Thoughts on civil liberty, &c. By Joseph Priestley, LL.D. Tutor in the Languages and Belles Lettres in the Academy at Warrington*. London: Printed for C. Henderson under the Royal Exchange; T. Becket and De Hondt in the Strand; and by J. Johnson and Davenport, in Pater-Noster-Row.

Rachels, James. 1975. Active and Passive Euthanasia. *New England Journal of Medicine* 292(2): 78–80.

Rather, L.J. 1965. *Mind and Body in Eighteenth-Century Medicine: A Study Based on Jerome Gaub's De Regimine Mentis*. Berkeley: University of California Press.

Rawls, John. 1971. *A Theory of Justice: Original Edition*. Cambridge, MA: The Belknap Press of Harvard University Press.

Reid, Thomas. 1990. *Practical Ethics: Being Lectures and Papers on Natural Religion, Self-Government, Natural Jurisprudence, and the Law of Nations*, ed. K. Haakonssen. Princeton: Princeton University Press.

Reiser, S.J. 1993. The Science of Diagnosis: Diagnostic Technology. In *Companion Encyclopedia of the History of Medicine*, eds. W.F. Bynum and R. Porter, 826–851. London and New York: Routledge.

Renaud, F. 1898. *A Short History of the Rise and Progress of the Manchester Royal Infirmary. Chronologically Arranged*. Manchester: J.E. Cornish, 16, St. Ann's Square.

Rhodes, Rosamond. 2019. A Defence of Medical Ethics as Uncommon Morality. *Journal of Medical Ethics* 45(12): 792–793.

Risse, G.B. 1986. *Hospital Life in Enlightenment Scotland: Care and Teaching at the Royal Infirmary of Edinburgh*. Cambridge: Cambridge University Press.

Robertson, William. 1759. *The History of Scotland during the Reigns of Queen Mary and King James VI*. In Two Volumes. London: Printed for A, Millar, in the Strand.

Royal College of Physicians. n.d. History of the Royal College of Physicians. https://www.rcplondon.ac.uk/about-us/who-we-are/history-royal-college-physicians. Accessed 4 Sept 2020.

Royal College of Physicians of London. 1771. *Statuta Moralia Collegii Regalis Medicorum Londinensium. De Conversatione Morali, Statitis Pœnalibus. Statutes of Morality, Belonging to the College of Physicians in London. Being translated from the Latin. Concerning Moral Conversation and Penal Statutes*. https://www.google.com/books/edition/The_ancient_physician_s_legacy_to_his_co/bF9ZAAAAcAAJ?hl=en&gbpv=1&bsq=moralia. Accessed 4 Sept 2020.

Royal College of Physicians of Edinburgh. n.d. History of the College. https://www.rcpe.ac.uk/heritage/history-college. Accessed 4 Sept 2020.

The Royal College of Surgeons of Edinburgh. n.d. History and Vision. https://www.rcsed.ac.uk/the-college/about-us/history-and-vision. Accessed 4 Sept 2020.

Ruddick, W., and W. Wilcox. 1982 Operating on the Fetus. *Hastings Center Report* 12(5): 10–14.

Rush, Benjamin. [1789] 1805. *Observations on the Duties of a Physician, and the Methods of Improving Medicine. Accommodated to the Present State of Society and Manners in the United States*. In *Medical Inquiries and Observations*, 2nd ed., Benjamin Rush, Vol. I, 345–408. Philadelphia: J. Conrad & Co.

Rutt, J.T. 1831. *Life and Correspondence of Joseph Priestley*, 2 vols. London: R. Hunter, 72 St. Paul's Churchyard.

Ryan, Michael. 1836. *A Manual of Medical Jurisprudence and State Medicine, Compiled from the Latest Legal and Medical Works of Beck, Paris, Christison, Fodere, Orfila, etc*. 2nd ed. London: Sherwood, Gilbert, and Piper, Paternoster Row.

Schneewind, Jerome B. 1998. *The Invention of Autonomy: A History of Modern Moral Philosophy.* Cambridge: Cambridge University Press.

Science Museum Group Collection. n.d. Royal College of Surgeons of England 1745. Available via https://collection.sciencemuseumgroup.org.uk/people/cp20377/royal-college-of-surgeons-of-england. Accessed 4 Sept 2020.

Scott, Thomas. 1748. *A Father's Instructions to his Son.* London: printed for R. Dodsley at Tully's Head in Pall-Mall, and sold by M. Cooper in Pater-Noster-Row.

Seddon, John. 1766, January 2. Preface. In *The Sovereignty of the Divine Administration; or a Rational Account of our Blessed Saviour's remarkable Temptation in the Wilderness, the Possessed at Carparnaum, the Demoniacs at Gadora, and the Destruction of the Swine: With Free Remarks upon several other Important Passages in the New Testament. With a Preface by the Reverend MR JOHN SEDDON OF MANCHESTER*, Thomas Dixon, iii–vii. London: Becket and de Hondt.

Seward, William. 1798. *Anecdotes of Distinguished Persons, Chiefly of the Present and Two Preceding Centuries.* London: Printed for T. Cadell Jun. and W. Davies in the Strand.

Shorter, Edward. 1993. The Doctor-Patient Relationship. In *Companion Encyclopedia of the History of Medicine*, eds. W.F. Bynum and R. Porter, 783–800. London/New York: Routledge.

Smith, Adam. [1776] 2000. *The Wealth of Nations*, edited with Notes, Marginal Summary, and Enlarged Index, by Edwin Cannan. Introduction by Robert Reich. New York: The Modern Library.

Smith, R. Angus. 1883. *A Centenary of Science in Manchester.* London: Taylor and Francis.

Stewart. 1901. *The Academic Gregories.* Edinburgh: Oliphant, Anderson & Ferrer.

Strawson, P.F. 1959. *Individuals: An Essay in Descriptive Metaphysics.* London: Methuen.

Taylor, John. 1759. *An Examination of the Scheme of Morality Advanced by Dr Hutcheson.* London: J. Waugh and W. Fenner.

Taylor, John. 1760. *A Sketch of Moral Philosophy; Or, An Essay to Demonstrate the Principles of Virtue and Religion upon a New, Natural, and Easy Plan.* London: Printed for J. Waugh, at the Turk's-head in Lombard street; and W. Fenner, at the Angel and Bible in Pater-Noster-Row.

Taylor, John. 1762a. *A Scheme of Scripture Divinity, Formed on the Plan of the Divine Dispensations. With a Vindication of the Sacred Writings.* London: Printed for J. Waugh, at the Turks' Head in Lombard-Street; and W. Fenner, at the Angel and Bible in Pater-Noster-Row.

Taylor, John. 1762b. *The Scriptural Account of Prayer in an Address to Dissenters of Lancashire Occasioned by a new Liturgy some Ministers of that County are composing for the Use of a Congregation in Liverpool*, 2nd ed. London: Printed for J. Waugh, at the Turks' Head in Lombard-Street; and W. Fenner, at the Angel and Bible in Pater-Noster-Row.

Thornber, Craig. n.d. Thomas Percival 1740–1804. *Cheshire Antiquities*. https://www.thornber.net/cheshire/ideasmen/percival.html. Accessed 4 Sept 2020.

Tong, Rosemary. 1993. *Feminine and Feminist Ethics*. Belmont, California: Wadsworth Publishing Company.

Tyson, Gerald P. 1975. Joseph Johnson, an Eighteenth-Century Book Seller. *Studies in Bibliography* 28: 1–16.

Vérsenyi, Laszlo. 1963. *Socratic Humanism*. London: Yale University Press.

Von Staden, Heinrch. 1996. "In a Pure and Holy Way:" Personal and Professional Conduct in the Hippocratic Oath. *Journal of the History of Medicine and Allied Sciences* 51(4):406–408.

Waddington, Ian. 1984. *The Medical Profession in the Industrial Revolution*. Dublin: Gill & Macmilan.

Waldron, H.A. 1973. Sir George Baker. *Journal of the Royal College of Physicians of London* 7 (2): 177–184.

Wear, Andrew. 1993. The History of Personal Hygiene. In *Companion Encyclopedia of the History of Medicine*, eds. W.F. Bynum and R. Porter, 1283–1308. London/New York: Routledge.

Weatherall. M. 1993. Drug Therapies. In *Companion Encyclopedia of the History of Medicine*, eds. W.F. Bynum and R. Porter, 915–938. London/New York: Routledge.

West, Charles. 1896. *The Profession of Medicine: Its Study, and Practice; Its Duties and Rewards*. London: Kegan, Paul, Trench, Trübner, & Co, Ltd.

Whitehead, Alfred North. [1929] 1978. *Process and Reality: An Essay in Cosmology. Gifford Lectures Delivered in the University of Edinburgh During the Session 1927–1928*. Corrected edition edited by David Ray Griffin and Donald W. Sherburne. New York: The Free Press.

Wilson, L.G. 1993. Fevers. In *Companion Encyclopedia of the History of Medicine*, eds. W.F. Bynum and R. Porter, 382–411. London/New York: Routledge.

Wittgenstein, L. 1922. *Tractatus Logico Philosophicus*. With an Introduction by Bertrand Russell. New York: Harcourt, Brace, & Company, Inc., London: Kegan, Paul, Trench, Turner & Co. Ltd.

Wollaston, W. 1750. *The Religion of Nature Delineated*. London: J and P Knapton, London, prepared by John Clarke. Online text based on facsimile edition by Kessinger Publishing. Originally published in 1722. Available via http://fair-use.org/william-wollaston/the-religion-of-nature-delineated/. Accessed 4 Sept 2020.

World Association of Perinatal Medicine. n.d. http://www.wapm.info/. Accessed 4 Sept 2020.

World Health Organization. n.d. https://www.who.int/. Accessed 4 Sept 2020.

World Medical Association. n.d. https://www.wma.net/. Accessed 4 Sept 2020.

Wyckes, David L. 1986. Sons and Subscribers: Lay Support and the College. In *Truth, Liberty, Religion: Essays Celebrating Two Hundred Years of Manchester College*, ed. Barbara Smith, 31–77. Oxford: Manchester College.

Zeffirelli, Franco. 1966. *Florence: Days of Destruction*. Produced by RAI (*Radiotelevisione italiana*, owned by the Italian government). Directed by Franco Zeffirelli. Narrated by Richard Burton. 50 minutes.

**Part II
Three Key Texts – *Medical Ethics*, *Medical Jurisprudence*, and *Extracts* – Two Concordances, and a Chronology**

Chapter 5
Three Key Texts – *Medical Ethics, Medical Jurisprudence*, and *Extracts*

1794

Medical Jurisprudence or A Code of Ethics and Institutes, Adapted to the Professions of Physic and Surgery

Citation to Original Publication:

Percival, Thomas. 1794. *Medical Jurisprudence or A Code of Ethics And Institutes, Adapted To The Professions Of Physic And Surgery*. Manchester: published privately, no information about printer.

Citation to Publication in this Volume:

Percival, Thomas. [1794] 2022. *Medical Jurisprudence or A Code of Ethics And Institutes, Adapted To The Professions Of Physic And Surgery*. Manchester: published privately, no information about printer. In Laurence McCullough, Thomas Percival's *Medical Ethics* and the Invention of Medical Professionalism: With Three Key Percival Texts, Two Concordances, and a Chronology: 291–336. New York: Springer.

MEDICAL JURISPRUDENCE

OR

A CODE OF

ETHICS AND INSTITUTES,

ADAPTED TO THE PROFESSIONS OF

PHYSIC AND SURGERY

[1794]

[title page; not paginated: 1]

------ *QUICQUID DIGNUM SAPIENTE*

BONO-QUE EST

Hor. Lib I. Ep IV.

Nulla enim vitae pars, neque publicis, neque privatis, neque forensibus, neque domesticis in rebus, neque si tecum agas quid, neque si cum altero contrabas, vacare officio potest: In toque colendo sita vitae est bonestas omnis, et in negligendo turpitudo.

Cic. De Off. Lib I, Cap ii.

["For no phase of life, whether public or private, whether in business or in the home, whether one is working on what concerns oneself alone or not dealing with another, can be without its moral duty; on the discharge of such duties depends all that is morally right, and in their neglect all that is morally wrong in life" (Cicero 1913, 7).]

[not paginated: 2]

MEDICAL JURISPRUDENCE

OR

A CODE OF ETHICS AND INSTITUTES,

ADAPTED TO THE PROFESSIONS OF

PHYSIC AND SURGERY

SECTION I.
OF PROFESSIONAL CONDUCT, RELATIVE TO HOSPITALS OR OTHER MEDICAL CHARITIES

I. HOSPITAL PHYSICIANS and SURGEONS should minister to the sick, with due impressions of the importance of their office; reflecting that the ease, the health, and the lives of those committed to their charge depend on their skill, attention, and fidelity. They should study, also, in their deportment, so as to unite *tenderness* with *steadiness*, and *condescension* with *authority*, as to inspire the minds of the patients with gratitude, respect, and confidence.

[not paginated: 3]

II. The *choice* of a *physician* or *surgeon* cannot be allowed to hospital patients, consistently with the regular and established succession of medical attendance. Yet personal confidence is not less important to the comfort and relief and the sick-poor, than of the rich, under similar circumstances: And it would be equally just and humane, to inquire into and to indulge their partialities, by occasionally calling into consultation the favourite practitioner. The rectitude and wisdom of this conduct will be still more apparent, when it is recollected that patients in hospitals not unfrequently request their discharge, on a deceitful plea of having received relief; and afterwards procure another recommendation, that they may be admitted under the physician or surgeon of their choice. Such practices involve them in a degree of falshood; produce unnecessary trouble; and may be the occasion of irreparable loss of time in the treatment of diseases.

III. The *feelings* and *emotions* of the patients, under critical circumstances, require to be known and to be attended to, no less than the symptoms of their diseases. Thus, extreme *timidity*, with respect to venæsection, contraindicates its use, in certain cases and constitutions. Even the *prejudices* of the sick are not to be contemned, or [4] opposed with harshness. For though silenced by authority, they will operate secretly and forcibly on the mind, creating fear, anxiety, and watchfulness.

IV. As misapprehension may magnify real evils, or create imaginary ones, no *discussion* concerning the nature of the case should be entered into before the patients, either with the house surgeon, the pupils of the hospital, or any medical visitor.

V. In the large wards of an Infirmary the patients should be interrogated concerning their complaints, in a *tone* of *voice* which cannot be *overheard*. Secrecy, also, when required by peculiar circumstances, should be strictly observed. And females should always be treated with the most scrupulous *delicacy*. To neglect or to sport with their feelings is cruelty; and every wound thus inflicted tends to produce a callousness of mind, a contempt of decorum, and an insensibility to modesty and virtue. Let these considerations be forcibly and repeatedly urged on hospital pupils.

VI. The moral and religious influence of sickness is so favourable to the best interests of men and of society, that it is justly regarded as an [5] important object in the establishment of every hospital. The institutions for promoting it should, therefore, be encouraged by physicians and surgeons, whenever seasonable opportunities occur. And by pointing out these to the officiating clergyman, the sacred offices will be performed with propriety, discrimination, and greater certainty of success. The character of a physician is usually remote from either superstition or enthusiasm: And the aid, which he is now exhorted to give, will tend to their exclusion from sick wards of the hospital, where their effects have often been known to be not only baneful, but even fatal.

VII. It is one of the privileges which softens the lot the poor, that they are exempt from the solicitudes attendant on the disposal of property. Yet there are exceptions to this observation: And it may be necessary that a hospital patient, on the bed of sickness and death, should be reminded, by some friendly monitor, of the importance of a *last will* and *testament* to his wife, children, or relatives, who otherwise, perhaps, might be deprived of his effects, of his expected prize money, or of some future residuary legacy. This kind office will be best performed by the house-surgeon, whose frequent attendance on the sick diminishes their reserve, and entitles him to [6] their familiar confidence. And he will doubtless regard the performance of it as a duty. For whatever is right to be done, and cannot by another be so well done, has the full force of moral and personal obligation.

VIII. The physicians and surgeons should not suffer themselves to be restrained, by parsimonious considerations, from prescribing *wine*, and *drugs* even of *high price*, when required in diseases of extraordinary malignity and danger. The efficacy of every medicine is proportionate to its purity and goodness; and on the degree of these properties, *cæteris paribus*, both the cure of the sick, and the speediness of its accomplishment must depend. But when drugs of an inferior quality are employed, it is requisite to administer them in larger doses, and to continue the use of them a longer period of time; circumstances which more than counterbalance any savings in their price. If the case, however, were far otherwise, no œconomy, of a fatal tendency, ought to be admitted into institutions, founded on the purest beneficence, and which, in this age and country, when well conducted, can never want contributions adequate to their liberal support [7].

IX. The medical gentlemen, of every charitable institution, are in some degree responsible for, and the guardians of, the honour of each other. No physician or surgeon, therefore, should reveal occurrences in the hospital, which may injure the reputation of his colleagues; except under the restriction contained in the succeeding article.

X. No professional charge should be made by a physician or surgeon, either publicly or privately, out of the hospital, against any associate, without previously laying the complaint before the gentlemen of the faculty belonging to the institution, that they may judge concerning the reasonableness of its grounds; and the proper measures to be adopted.

XI. A proper *discrimination* being established in all hospitals between the *medical* and *chirurgical cases*, it should be faithfully adhered to, by the physicians and surgeons, on the admission of patients.

XII. Whenever cases occur, attended with circumstances not heretofore observed, or in which the ordinary modes of practice have been attempted without success, it is for the public good, an in an especial degree advantageous to [8] the poor, who, being the most numerous class of society, are the greatest beneficiaries of the healing art, that *new remedies* and *new methods* of *chirurgical treatment* should be devised. But in the accomplishment of this salutary purpose, the gentlemen of the faculty should be scrupulously and conscientiously governed by sound reason, just analogy, or well authenticated facts. And no such trials should be instituted, without a previous consultation of physicians or surgeons, according to the nature of the case.

XIII. To further professional improvement, a friendly and unreserved intercourse should subsist between the gentlemen of the faculty, with a free communication of whatever is extraordinary or interesting in the course of their hospital practice. And an account of every case or operation, which is rare, curious, or instructive, should be drawn up by the physician or surgeon, to whose charge it devolves, and entered in a register, kept for the purpose, but open only to the physicians and surgeons of the charity.

XIV. Hospital registers usually contain only a simple report of the number of patients admitted and discharged. By adopting a more comprehensive plan, they might be rendered subservient to medical science, and beneficial to [9] mankind. The following sketch is offered, with deference, to the gentlemen of the faculty. Let the register consist of three tables; the first specifying the number of patients admitted, cured, relieved, discharged, or dead; the second the several diseases of the patients, with their events; the third the sexes and ages of the patients. The ages should be reduced into classes; and the tables adapted to the four divisions of the year. By such an institution, the increase or decrease in sickness; the attack, progress, and cessation of epidemics; the comparative healthiness of different situations, climates, and seasons; the influence of particular trades and manufactures on health and life; with many other curious circumstances, not more interesting to physicians than to the community, would be ascertained with sufficient precision.

XV. By the adoption of the *register*, recommended in the foregoing article, physicians and surgeons would obtain a clear insight into the comparative success of their hospital and private practice; and would be incited to a diligent investigation of the causes of such difference. In particular diseases it will be found to subsist in a very remarkable degree: And the discretionary power of the physician or surgeon, in the admission of patients, could not be exerted with [10] more justice or humanity, than in refusing to consign to lingering suffering, and almost certain death, a numerous class of patients, inadvertently recommended as objects of these charitable institutions. "In judging of diseases with regard to the propriety of their reception into hospitals," says an excellent writer," the following general circumstances are to be considered.

"Whether they be capable of speedy relief, because, as it is the intention of the charity to relieve as great a number as possible, a quick change of objects is to be wished; and also because the inbred disease of hospitals will almost inevitably creep, in some degree, upon one who continues a long time in them, but rarely attack one, whose stay is short."

"Whether they require in a particular manner the superintendance of skilful persons, either on account of their acute and dangerous nature, or any singularity or intricacy attending them, or erroneous opinions prevailing among the common people concerning their treatment."

"Whether they be contagious, or subject in a particular degree to taint the air, and generate pestilential diseases." [11]

"Whether a fresh and pure air be peculiarly requisite for their cure, and they be remarkably injured by any violation of it."*

[Bottom of page 12]: *See Dr. Aikin's Thoughts on Hospitals, p. 21.

XVI. But no precautions relative to the reception of patients, who labour under maladies incapable of relief, contagious in their nature, or liable to be aggravated by confinement in an impure atmosphere, can obviate the evils arising from *close wards*, and the false œconomy of crowding a number of persons into the least possible space. There are inbred diseases which it is the duty of the physician and surgeon to prevent, as far as lies in their power, by a strict and persevering attention to the whole medical polity of the hospital. This comprehends the discrimination of cases admissible, air, diet, cleanliness, and drugs; each of which articles should be subjected to rigid scrutiny, at stated periods of time.

XVII. The establishment of a *committee* of the *gentlemen* of the *faculty*, to be held monthly, would tend to facilitate this interesting investigation, and to accomplish the most important objects of it. By the free communication of remarks, various improvements would be sug-[12]gested; by the regular discussion of them, they would be reduced to a definite and consistent form; and by the authority of united suffrages, they would have full influence over the governors of the charity. The exertions of individuals, however benevolent or judicious, often give rise to jealousy; are opposed by those who have not been consulted; and prove inefficient, by wanting the collective energy of numbers.

XVIII. The harmonious intercourse, which has been recommended to the gentlemen of the faculty, will naturally produce *frequent consultations*, viz. of the physicians on medical cases, of the surgeons on chirurgical cases, and of both united in cases of compound nature, which falling under the department of each, may admit of elucidation by the reciprocal aid of the two professions.

XIX. In consultations on medical cases, the junior physician present should *deliver* his *opini*on first, and the others in succession, according to seniority: The same should be observed in chirurgical cases; and a majority should be decisive in both: But if numbers be equal, the decision should rest with the physician or surgeon, under whose care the patient is placed. No decision, however, should restrain the acting [13] practitioner from making such variations in the mode of treatment, as future contingencies may require, or a further insight into the nature of the disorder may shew to be expedient.

XX. In consultations on mixed cases, the junior surgeon should deliver his opinion first, and his brethren afterwards in succession, according to seniority. The junior physician present should deliver his opinion after the senior surgeon; and the other physicians in the order above prescribed.

XXI. In every consultation, the case to be considered should be *concisely stated* by the physician or surgeon, who requests the aid of his brethren. The opinions relative to it should be delivered with brevity, according to the preceding arrangement, and the decisions collected in the same order. – The order of seniority, among the physicians and surgeons, may be regulated by the dates of their respective appointments in the hospital.

XXII. Due *notice* should be given of a consultation, and no person admitted to it, except the physicians and surgeons of the hospital, and the house surgeon, without the unanimous consent of [14] the gentlemen present. If an examination of the patient be previously necessary, the particular circumstances of danger or difficulty should be carefully concealed from him, and every precaution used to guard him from anxiety or alarm.

XXIII. No important operation should be determined upon, without a consultation of the physicians and surgeons, and the acquiescence of a majority of them. Twenty-four hours notice should be given of the proposed operation, except in dangerous accidents, or when peculiar circumstances occur, which may render delay hazardous. The presence of a *spectator* should not be allowed during an operation, without the express permission of the operator. All extra-official interference in the management of it should be forbidden. A decorous *silence* ought to be observed. It may be humane and salutary, however, for one of the attending physicians or surgeons to speak occasionally to the patient; to comfort him under his sufferings; and to give him assurance, if consistent with truth, that the operation goes well, and promises as speedy and successful termination.* [15]

[Bottom page 15, continued to bottom page 16] * The substance of the five preceding articles (XIX. XX. XXI. XXII. XXIII.) was suggested by Dr. Ferriar and Mr. [15] [continued at bottom of page 16] Simmons, at the time when I was desired to frame a code of rules for the Manchester Infirmary. The alterations, now made, are intended to adapt them to general use.

As a hospital is the best school for practical surgery, it would be liberal and beneficial to invite, in rotation, two surgeons from the town, who do not belong to the institution, to be present at each operation.

XXIV. It is an established usage, in some hospitals, to have a *stated day* in the week for the performance of operations. But this may occasion improper delay, or equally unjustifiable anticipation. When several operations are to take place in succession, one patient should not have his mind agitated by the knowledge of the sufferings of another. The surgeon should put on a fresh apron, whenever it is besmeared; and the table and instruments should be freed from all marks of blood, and everything that might excite terror.

XXV. Dispensaries afford the widest sphere for the treatment of diseases, comprehending, not only such as ordinarily occur, but those which are so infectious, malignant, and fatal, as to be excluded from admission into infirmaries. Happily, also, they neither tend to [16] counteract that spirit of independence, which should be sedulously fostered in the poor, nor to preclude the practical exercise of those relative duties, the "charities of father, son, and brother," which constitute the strongest moral bonds of society. Being institutions less splendid and expensive than hospitals, they are well adapted to towns of moderate size; and might even be established, without difficulty, in populous country districts. Physicians and surgeons, in such situations, have generally great influence: And it would be truly honourable to exert it in a cause subservient to the interests of medical science, of commerce, and of philanthropy.

The duties which devolve on gentlemen of the faculty, engaged in the conduct of Dispensaries, are so nearly similar to those of hospital physicians and surgeons, as to be comprehended under the same professional and moral rules. But greater *authority* and greater *condescension* will be found requisite in domestic attendance on the poor. And human nature must be intimately studied, to acquire that full ascendancy over the prejudices, the caprices, and the passions of the sick, and of their relatives, which is essential to medical success [17].

XXVI. Hospitals, appropriated to particular maladies, are established in different places, and claim both the patronage and the aid of the gentlemen of the faculty. To an ASYLUM for FEMALE PATIENTS, labouring under SYPHILIS, it is to be lamented that discouragements have been too often and successfully opposed. Yet whoever reflects on the variety of diseases to which the human body is incident, will find that a considerable part of them are derived from immoderate passions, and vicious indulgences. Sloth, intemperance, and irregular desires are the great sources of evil, which contract the duration, and imbitter the enjoyment of life. But humanity, whist she bewails the vices of mankind, incites us to alleviate the miseries which flow from them. And it may be proved that a LOCK HOSPITAL is an institution founded on the most benevolent principles, consonant to sound policy, and favourable to reformation and to virtue. It provides relief for a painful and loathsome distemper, which contaminates, and its progress, the innocent as well as the guilty, and extends is baneful influence to future generations. It restores to virtue and to religion those votaries whom pleasure has seduced, or villainy betrayed; and who now feel, by sad experience, that ruin, misery, and disgrace *are the wages of sin*. Over such objects pity sheds the generous tear; au-[18]sterity softens into forgiveness; and benevolence at the united pleas of frailty, penitence, and wretchedness.*

*[Bottom page 19] * See two Reports, intended to promote the establishment of a Lock Hospital in Manchester, in the year 1774, and inserted in the author's Essays, Medical, Philosophical, and Experimental.

No *peculiar rules* of conduct are required are requisite in the medical attendance on LOCK HOSPITALS. But as these institutions must, from the nature of their object, be in a great measure shut from the inspection of the public, it will behove the faculty to consider themselves as responsible, in a particular degree, for their right government; that the moral, no less than the medical purposes of such establishments, may be fully answered. The strictest decorum should be observed in the conduct towards the female patients; no young pupils should be admitted into the house; every ministering office should be performed by nurses properly instructed; and books adapted to the patients should be put into their hands, and given them on their discharge. To provide against the danger of urgent want, a small sum of money, and decent clothes should at this time be dispensed to them; and, when practicable, some mode should be pointed out to obtaining a reputable livelihood [19].

XXVII. ASYLUMS for INSANITY possess accommodations and advantages, of which the poor must, in all circumstances, be destitute; and which no private family, however opulent, can provide. Of these schemes of benevolence all classes of men may have equal occasion to participate the benefits; for human nature itself becomes the mournful object of such institutions. Other diseases leave man a rational and moral agent, and sometimes improve both the faculties of the head, and the affections of the heart. But lunacy subverts the whole rational and moral character; extinguishes every tender charity; and excludes the degraded sufferer from the enjoyments and advantages of social intercourse. Painful is the office of a physician, when he is called upon the minister to such humiliating objects of distress: Yet great must be his felicity, when he can render himself instrumental, under Providence, in the restoration of reason, and in the renewal of the lost image of God. Let no one, however, promise himself this divine privilege, if he be not deeply skilled in the philosophy of human nature. For though casual success may sometimes be the result of empirical practice, the *medicina mentis* can only be administered with steady efficiency by him, who, to a knowledge of the animal œconomy, and of the physical causes which regulate or disturb its movements, [20] unites an intimate acquaintance with the laws of association; the controul of fancy over judgment; the force of habit; the direction and comparative strength of opposite passions; and the reciprocal dependences and relations of the moral and intellectual powers of man.

XXVIII. Even thus qualified with the pre-requisite attainments, the physician will find that he has a new region of medical science to explore. For it is a circumstance to be regretted, both by the faculty and the public, that the various diseases which are classed under the title of insanity, remain less understood than any others with which mankind are visited. Hospital institutions furnish the best means of acquiring more accurate knowledge of their causes, nature, and cure. But this information cannot be attained, to any satisfactory extent, by the ordinary attention to single and unconnected cases. The synthetic plan should be adopted; and a regular *journal* should be kept of every species of the malady which occurs, arranged under proper heads, with a full detail of its rise, progress, and termination; of the remedies administered, and of their effects in its several stages. The age, sex, occupation, mode of life, and if possible hereditary constitution of each patient should be noted: And when the event proves fatal, the brain, and other organs [21] affected, should be carefully examined, and the appearances on dissection minutely inserted in the journal. A register like this, in the course of a few years, would afford the most interesting and authentic documents; the want of which, on a late melancholy occasion, was felt and regretted by the whole kingdom.

XXIX. Lunatics are, in great measure, secluded from the observation of those who are interested in their good treatment; and their complaints of ill-usage are so often false or fanciful, as to obtain little credit or attention, even when well founded. The physician, therefore, must feel himself under the strictest obligation of honour, as well as of humanity, to secure to these unhappy sufferers all the *tenderness* and *indulgence*, compatible with steady and effectual government.

XXX. Certain cases of *mania* seem to require a *boldness of practice*, which a young physician of sensibility may feel a reluctance to adopt. On such occasions he must not yield to timidity, but fortify his mind by the counsels of his more experienced brethren of the faculty. Yet, with this aid, it is more consonant to probity to err on the side of caution than of temerity [22].

Hospitals for the small-pox, for inoculation, for cancers, &c. &c. are established in different places; but require no professional duties, which are not included under, or deducible from, the precepts already delivered.

SECT. II
OF PROFESSIONAL CONDUCT IN PRIVATE, OR GENERAL PRACTICE

I. THE moral *rules* of conduct, prescribed towards hospital patients, should be fully adopted in private or general practice. Every case, committed to the charge of a physician or surgeon, should be treated with attention, steadiness, and humanity: Reasonable indulgence should be granted to the mental imbecility and caprices of the sick: Secrecy and delicacy when required by peculiar circumstances, should be strictly observed. And the familiar and confidential intercourse, to which the faculty are admitted in their professional visits, should be used with discretion, and with the most scrupulous regard to fidelity and honour [23].

II. The strictest *temperance* should be deemed incumbent on the faculty; as the practice both of physic and surgery at all times requires the exercise of a clear and vigorous understanding: And on emergencies, for which no professional man should be unprepared, a steady hand, an acute eye, and an unclouded head, may be essential to the well being, and even to the life, of a fellow-creature. Phillip of Macedon reposed with entire security on the vigilance and attention of his general Parmenio. In his hours of mirth and conviviality he was wont to say, "Let us drink, my friends; we may do it with safety, for Parmenio never drinks!" The moral of this story is sufficiently obvious when applied to the faculty; but it should certainly be construed with great limitation by their patients.

III. A physician should not be forward to make gloomy prognostications; because they savour of empiricism, by magnifying the importance of his services in the treatment or cure of the disease. But he should not fail, on proper occasions, to give to the friends of the patient timely notice of danger, when it really occurs, and even to the patient himself, if absolutely necessary. This office, however, is so peculiarly alarming, when executed by him, that it ought to be declined, whenever it can be assigned to any other person of [24] sufficient judgment and delicacy. For the physician should be the minister of hope and comfort to the sick; that by such cordials to the drooping spirit, he may smooth the bed of death, revive expiring life, and counteract the depressing influence of those maladies, which rob the philosopher of fortitude, and the christian of consolation.

IV. *Officious interference*, in a case under the charge of another, should be carefully avoided. No meddling inquiries should be made concerning the patient; no unnecessary hints given, relative to the nature or treatment of his disorder; nor any selfish conduct pursued, that may directly or indirectly tend to diminish the trust reposed in the physician or surgeon employed. Yet though the character of the professional busy-body, whether from thoughtlessness or craft, is highly reprehensible, there are occasions which not only justify, but require a spirited interposition. When artful ignorance grossly imposes on credulity; when neglect puts to hazard an important life; or rashness threatens it with still more imminent danger; a medical neighbour, friend, or relative, apprized of such facts, will justly regard his interference as a duty. But he must be careful that the information, on which he acts, is well founded; that his motives are pure and honourable; and that his judgment of the mea-[25]sures pursued is built on experience and practical knowledge, not on speculative or theoretical differences of opinion. The particular circumstances of the case will suggest the most proper mode of conduct. In general, however, a personal and confidential application to the gentlemen of the faculty concerned should be the first step taken; and afterwards, if necessary, the transaction may be communicated to the patient or to his family.

V. When a physician or surgeon is called to a patient, who has been before under the care of another gentleman of the faculty, a consultation with him should be requested, if he live in the same town: His practice, also, should be treated with candour, and even justified, so far as probity and truth will permit. For the want of success in the primary treatment of a case is no impeachment of professional skill or knowledge; and it often serves to throw light on the nature of a disease, and to suggest to the subsequent practitioner more appropriate means of relief.

VI. In large and opulent towns, the *distinction* between the *provinces* of *physic* and *surgery* should be steadily maintained. This distinction is sanctioned both by reason and experience. It is founded on the nature and objects of the two [26] professions; on the education and acquirements requisite for their most beneficial and honourable exercise; and tends to promote the complete cultivation and advancement of each. For the division of skill and labour is no less advantageous in the liberal than in the mechanic arts: And both physic and surgery are so comprehensive, and yet so far from perfection, as separately to give full scope to the industry and genius of their respective professors. Experience has fully evinced the benefits of the discrimination recommended, which is established in every well regulated hospital, and is thus expressly authorized by the faculty themselves, and by those who have the best opportunities of judging of the proper application of the healing art. No physician or surgeon, therefore, should adopt more than one denomination, nor assume any rank or privilege different from those of his order.

VII. *Consultations* should be *promoted*, in difficult or protracted cases, as they give rise to confidence, energy, and more enlarged views in practice. On such occasions no rivalship or jealousy should be indulged: Candour, probity, and all due respect should be exercised towards the physician or surgeon first engaged: And as he may be presumed to be best acquainted with the patient and with his family, he should deliver all [27] the medical directions agreed upon, though he may not have precedency in seniority or rank. It should be the province, however, of the senior physician, first to propose the necessary questions to the sick, but without excluding his associate from the privilege of making farther inquiries, to satisfy himself, or to elucidate the case.

VIII. As circumstances sometimes occur to render a *special consultation* desirable, when the continued attendance of another physician or surgeon might be objectionable to the patient, the gentleman of the faculty, whose assistance is required, in such cases, should pay only two or three visits; and sedulously guard against all future unsolicited interference. For this consultation a double gratuity may reasonably be expected from the patient, as it will be found to require an extraordinary portion both of time and attention.

IX. *Theoretical discussions* should be avoided in consultations, as occasioning perplexity and loss of time. For there may be much diversity of opinion, concerning speculative points, with perfect agreement in those modes of practice, which are founded not on hypothesis, but on experience and observation [28].

X. The rules, prescribed for hospital consultations may be adopted in private or general practice:*

[Bottom page 29] * See articles XIX, XX, and XXI. section I

And the *seniority* of a physician may be determined by the period of his public and acknowledged practice as a physician, and that of a surgeon by the period of his practice as a surgeon, in the place where each resides. This arrangement, being clear and obvious, is adapted to remove all grounds of dispute amongst medical gentlemen: And it secures the regular continuance of the order of precedency, established in every town, which might otherwise be liable to troublesome interruptions by new settlers, perhaps not long stationary.

XI. A regular *academical education* furnishes the only presumptive evidence of professional ability, and is so honourable and beneficial, that it gives a just claim to pre-eminence among physicians, in proportion to the degree in which it has been enjoyed and improved: Yet as it is not indispensably necessary to the attainment of knowledge, skill, and experience, they who have really acquired, in a competent measure, such qualifications, without its advantages, should not be fastidiously excluded from the privileges of fel-[29]lowship. In consultations, especially, as the good of the patient is the sole object in view, and is often dependent on the personal confidence, the aid of an intelligent practitioner ought to be received with candour and politeness, and his advice adopted, if agreeable to sound judgment and truth.

XII. *Punctuality* should be observed in the visits of the faculty, when they are to hold consultation together. But as this may not always be practicable, the physician or surgeon, who first arrives at the house of appointment, should wait five minutes for his associate, before his introduction to the patient, that the unnecessary repetition of questions may be avoided: No visits should be made but in concert, or by mutual agreement: No statement or discussion of the case should take place before the patient or his friends, except in the presence of each of the attending gentlemen of the faculty, and by common consent: And no *prognostications* should be delivered, which are not the result of previous deliberation and concurrence.

XIII. *Visits* to the sick should not be *unseasonably repeated*; because, when too frequent, they tend to diminish the authority of the physician, to produce instability in his practice, and to give [30] rise to such occasional indulgences, as are subversive of all medical regimen.

Sir William Temple has asserted, that "an honest physician is excused for leaving his patient, when he finds the disease growing desperate, and can, by his attendance, expect only to receive his fees, without any hopes or appearance of deserving them." But this allegation is not well founded: For the offices of a physician may continue to be highly useful to the patient, and comforting to the relatives around him, even in the last period of a fatal malady; by obviating despair, by alleviating pain, and by soothing mental anguish. To decline attendance, under such circumstances, would be sacrificing, to fanciful delicacy, and mistaken liberality, that moral duty which is independent of, and far superior to, all pecuniary appreciation.

XIV. Whenever a physician or surgeon *officiates* for another, who is sick or absent, during any considerable length of time, he should receive the fees accruing from such additional practice: But if this fraternal act be of short duration, it should be gratuitiously performed; with an observance always of the utmost delicacy towards the interest of any other member of profession, who may be previously connected with the family, on which attendance is given [31].

XV. Some general rules should be adopted by the faculty, in every town, relative to the *pecuniary acknowledgments* of their patients; and it should be deemed a point of honour to adhere to this rule, with as much steadiness, as varying circumstances will admit. For it is obvious that a medium fee, as suited to the general rank of patients, must be an inadequate gratuity from the rich, who often require attendance not absolutely necessary; and yet too large to be expected from that class of citizens, who would feel a reluctance in calling for assistance, without making some decent and satisfactory retribution.

But in the consideration of fees, let it ever be remembered, that though mean ones from the affluent are both unjust and degrading, yet the characteristical beneficence of the profession is inconsistent with sordid views, and avaricious rapacity. To a young physician it is of great importance to have clear and definite ideas of the ends of his profession; of the means for their attainment; and of the comparative value and dignity of each. Wealth, rank, and independence, with all the benefits resulting from them, are the primary ends which he holds in view; and they are interesting, wise, and laudable. But knowledge, benevolence, and active virtue, [32] the means to be adopted in their acquisition are of still higher estimation. And he has the privilege and felicity of practising an art, even more intrinsically excellent in its mediate than in its ultimate objects. The former, therefore, have a claim to uniform pre-eminence.

XVI. All members of the profession, including apothecaries, as well as physicians and surgeons, together with their wives and children, should be attended *gratuitously* by any one or more of the faculty whose assistance may be required. For as solicitude obscures the judgment, and is accompanied with timidity and irresolution, medical men, under pressure of sickness, either as affecting themselves or their families, are peculiarly dependent upon each other. But visits should not be obtruded officiously; as such unasked civility may give rise to embarrassment, or interfere with that choice, on which confidence depends. Distant members of the faculty, when they request attendance, should be expected to defray the charges of traveling. And if their circumstances be affluent, a pecuniary acknowledgement should not be declined: For no obligation ought to be imposed, which the party would rather compensate than contract. This rule may be applied, *mutatis mutandis*, to medical attendance on the clergy [33].

XVII. As the first *consultation* by *letter* imposes much more trouble and attention than a personal visit, it is reasonable, on such an occasion, to expect a gratuity of double the usual amount. And this has been long the established practice of many respectable physicians. But a subsequent epistolary correspondence, on the further treatment of the same disorder, may justly be regarded in the light of ordinary attendance, and may be compensated, as such, according to the circumstances of the case, or of the patient.

XVIII. The use of *quack medicines* should be discouraged by the faculty, as disgraceful to the profession, injurious to health, and often destructive even of life. Patients, however, under lingering disorders, are sometimes obstinately bent on having recourse to such as they see advertised, or hear recommended, with a boldness and confidence, which no intelligent physician dares to adopt, with respect to the means that he prescribes. In these cases, some indulgence seems to be required to a credulity that is insurmountable: And the patient should neither incur the displeasure of the physician, nor be entirely deserted by him. He may be apprized of the fallacy of his expectations, whilst assured, at the same time, that diligent attention shall be paid to the process of the experiment he is so unadvi-[34]sedly making on himself, and the consequent mischiefs, which may arise, obviated as timely as possible. Certain active preparations, the nature, composition, and effects of which are well known, ought not to be prescribed as quack medicines.

XIX. No physician or surgeon should dispense a secret *nostrum*, whether it be his invention, or exclusive property. For if it be of real efficacy, the concealment of it is inconsistent with beneficence and professional liberality. And if mystery alone give it value and importance, such craft implies either disgraceful ignorance, or fraudulent avarice.

XX. As diversity of opinion and opposition of interest, may in the medical, as in other professions, sometimes occasion *controversy*, and even *contention*; whenever such cases unfortunately occur, and cannot be immediately terminated, they should be referred to the arbitration of a sufficient number of physicians or of surgeons, according to the nature of the dispute; or to the two orders collectively, if belonging both to medicine and surgery. But neither the subject matter of such references, nor the adjudication, should be communicated to the public; as they may be personally injurious to the individuals concerned, and can hardly fail to hurt the general credit of the faculty [35].

SECT. III.
OF THE CONDUCT OF PHYSICIANS TOWARDS APOTHECARIES

I. IN the present state of physic, in this country, where the profession is properly divided into three distinct branches, a connection peculiarly intimate subsists between the physician and the apothecary; and various obligations necessarily result from it. On the knowledge, skill, and fidelity of the apothecary, depend, in a very considerable degree, the reputation, the success, and the usefulness of the physician. As these qualities, therefore, justly claim his attention and encouragement, the possessor of them merits his respect and patronage.

II. The apothecary is, and almost every instance, the præcursor of the physician; and being acquainted with the rise and progress of the disease, with the hereditary constitution, habits, and disposition of the patient, he may furnish very important information. It is in general, there-[36]fore, expedient, and where health or life are at stake expediency becomes a moral duty, to confer with the apothecary, before any decisive plan of treatment is adopted, to hear his account of the malady, of the remedies which have been administered, of the effects produced by them, and of his whole experience considering the *juvantia* and *lædentia* in the case. Nor should the future attendance of the apothecary be superseded by the physician: For if he be a man of honour, judgment, and propriety of behaviour, he will be a most valuable coadjutor through the whole course of the disorder, by his attention to varying symptoms; by the enforcement of medical directions; by obviating misapprehensions in the patient, or his family; by strengthening the authority of the physician; and by being at all times an easy and friendly medium of communication. To subserve these important purposes, the physician should occasionally make his visits in conjunction with the apothecary, regulating by circumstances the frequency of such interviews. If often repeated little substantial aid can be expected from the apothecary, because he will have no intelligence to offer which does not fall under the observation of the physician himself: Nor any opportunity of executing his peculiar trust, without becoming burdensome to [37] the patient by multiplied calls, and unseasonable assiduity.

III. This amicable *intercourse* an *co-operation* of the physician and apothecary, if conducted with the *decorum* an attention to *etiquette*, which should always be steadily observed by professional men, will add to the authority of the one, to the respectability of the other, and to the usefulness of both. The patient will find himself the object of watchful and unremitting care, and will experience that he is connected with his physician, not only personally, but by a sedulous representative and coadjutor. The apothecary will regard the free communication of the physician as a privilege and mean of improvement; he will have a deeper interest in the success of the curative plans pursued; and his honour and reputation will be directly involved in the purity and excellence of the medicines dispensed, and in the skill and care with which they are compounded.

The duty and responsibility of the physician, however, are so intimately connected with these points, that no dependence on the probity of the apothecary should prevent the occasional inspection of the drugs, which he prescribes. In London, the law not only authorizes, but enjoins [38] a stated examination of the simple and compound medicines kept in the shops. And the policy that is just an reasonable in the metropolis, must be proportionally so in every provincial town, throughout the kingdom. Nor will any respectable apothecary object to this necessary office, when performed with delicacy and at seasonable times; since his reputation and emolument will be increased by it, probably in the exact *ratio* of professional merit and integrity, hereby discovered.

IV. When a physician is called to visit a patient and the country, he should not only be *minute* in his *directions*, but should *communicate* to the apothecary the *particular view*, which he takes of the *case*; that the indications of cure maybe afterwards pursued with precision and steadiness; and that the apothecary may use the discretionary power committed to him, with as little deviation as possible from the general plan prescribed. To so valuable a class of men as the country apothecaries, great attention and respect is due. And as they are the guardians of health through large districts, no opportunities should be neglected of promoting their improvement, or contributing to their stock of knowledge, either by the loan of books, the direction of their studies, or by unreserved information on medical [39] subjects. When such occasions present themselves, the maxim of our judicious poet is strictly true,

······The worst avarice is that of sense.POPE

For practical improvements usually originate in towns, and often remain unknown or disregarded in situations, where gentlemen of the faculty have little intercourse, and where sufficient authority is wanting to sanction innovation.

V. It has been observed, by a political and moral writer of great authority that "apothecaries' profit is become a bye-word, denoting something uncommonly extravagant. This great apparent profit, however, is frequently no more than the reasonable wages of labour. The skill of an apothecary is a much nicer and more delicate matter then that of any artificer whatever; and the trust which is reposed in him is of much greater importance. He is the physician of the poor in all cases, and of the rich when the distress or danger is not very great. His reward, therefore, ought to be suitable to his skill and his trust, and it arises generally from the price at which he sells his drugs. But the whole drugs which the best employed apothecary in a large market town, [40] will sell in a year, may not perhaps cost him above thirty or forty pounds. Though he should sell them, therefore, for three or four hundred, or a thousand per cent. profit, this may frequently be no more than a reasonable wages of his labour charged, and the only way in which he can charge them, upon the price of his drugs."*

[Bottom page 41] *See Smith's Wealth of Nations, book I. chap. x.

The statement here given exceeds the emoluments of the generality of apothecaries, in country districts. And a physician, who knows the education, skill, and persevering attention, as well as the sacrifice of ease, health, and sometimes even of life, which this profession requires, should regard it as a duty not to withdraw, from those who exercise it, any sources of reasonable profit, or the honourable means of advancement in fortune. Two practices prevail in some places injurious to the interest of this branch of the faculty, and which ought to be discouraged. One consists in suffering prescriptions to be sent to the druggist, for the sake of a small saving in expence. The other in receiving an annual stipend, usually degrading in its amount and in the services it imposes, for being consulted on the slighter indispositions to which all families are incident, and which properly fall within the province of the apothecary [41].

In the County of Norfolk, and in the city of London, benevolence institutions have been lately formed, for providing funds to relieve the widows and children of gentlemen of the faculty, and occasionally also members of the profession who become indigent. Such schemes merit the sanction and encouragement of every liberal physician and surgeon. And were they so extended, their usefulness would be greatly increased, and their permanency almost with certainty secured. Subscribers from every part of Great Britain, should be admitted, if they offer satisfactory testimonials of their qualifications. One comprehensive establishment seems to be more eligible than many on a smaller scale. For it would be conducted with superior dignity, regularity, and efficiency; with fewer obstacles from interest, prejudice, or rivalship; with considerable saving in the aggregate a time, trouble, and expence; with more accuracy in the calculations relative to its funds, and consequently with the utmost practicable extension of its dividends [42].

SECT. IV.
OF THE KNOWLEDGE OF LAW REQUISITE FOR PHYSICIANS AND SURGEONS

I. GENTLEMEN of the faculty of physic, by the authority of different parliamentary statutes, enjoy an exemption from serving on inquests or juries; from bearing armour; from being constables or church-wardens; and from all burdensome offices, whether leet or parochial. These privileges are founded on reasons highly honourable to medical men; and should operate as incentives to that diligent and assiduous discharge of professional duty, which the legislature has generously presumed to occupy the time and to employ the talents of physicians and surgeons, in some of the most important interests of their fellow-citizens. It is perhaps on account of their being thus excused from many civil functions, that Sir William Blackstone, in his learned Commentaries, judges the study of the law to be less essential to them, than to any other class of men. He observes that "there is no special [43] reason why gentlemen of the faculty of physic should apply themselves to the study of the law, unless in common with other gentleman, and to complete the character of general and extensive knowledge, which this profession, beyond others, has remarkably deserved."*

[Bottom page 44] * Vol. I, sect. I. introduction

But I apprehend it will be found that physicians and surgeons are often called upon to exercise appropriate duties, which require not only a knowledge of the principles of jurisprudence, but of the forms of regulations adopted in our courts and judicature. The truth of this observation will appear from the following brief detail of some of the principal cases, in which the science of law is of peculiar importance to medical practitioners.

II. When a physician attends upon a patient, under circumstances of imminent danger, his counsel may be required about the expediency of a *last will* and *testament*. It behoves him, therefore, to know whether, in cases of intestacy, the daughters, or younger children, of the sick person would be legally entitled to no share of his fortune: Whether the fortune would be equally divided, when such equality would be improper or unjust: whether diversity of claims and ex-[44]pensive litigations would ensue, without a will, from the nature of the property in question: And whether the creditors of the defunct would, by his neglect, be defrauded of their equitable claims. For it is a culpable deficiency in our laws that real estates are not subject to the payment of debts by simple contract, unless expressly charged with them by the last will and testament of the proprietor; although credit is often founded, as Dr. Paley well observes, on the possession of such estates. This excellent moralist adds, "He, therefore, who neglects to make the necessary appointments for the payment of his debts, as far as his effects extend, sins in his grave; and if he omits this on purpose to defeat the demands of his creditors, he dies with a deliberate fraud in his heart."*

[Bottom page 45] * See Paley's Principles of Moral and Political Philosophy, book III. part I. chap. xxiii.

Property is divided by the law into two species, *personal* and *real*; each requiring appropriate modes of transfer or alienation, with which a physician should be well acquainted. It may also be required of him to deliver an opinion, and even a solemn judicial evidence, concerning the *capacity* of his patient to make a *will*, a point sometimes of difficult and nice decision [45]. For various disorders obscure, without perverting, the intellectual faculties. And even in delirium itself there are lucid intervals, when the memory and judgment become sufficiently clear, accurate, and vigorous, for the valid execution of a testament. In such cases the will should commence with the signature of the testator, concluding with it also, if his hand be not, after continued mental exertions too tremulous for subscription; and it should be made with all possible conciseness, and expedition."*

[Bottom page 46] * "In the construction of the statute, 29, Car. II. c.3. it has been adjudged that the testator's name, written with his own hand, at the beginning of the will, as I John Mills, do make this my last will and testament; is a sufficient signing, without any name at the bottom; though the other is the safer way." See Blackstone's Comment. book II. chap. xxiii.

If the patient be surprised by sudden and violent sickness, the law authorizes a *nuncupative will* in the disposal of personalty. But to guard against fraud, the testamentary words must be delivered with an explicit intention to bequeath; the will must be made at home, or among the testator's family and friends, unless by unavoidable accident; and also in his last sickness: for [46] if he recover, it is evident that time is given for a written will.*

[Bottom page 47] *Id. Book II. c. 32.

The law excludes from the privilege of making a will *madmen, idiots*, persons in their *dotage*, or those who have stupified their understandings by drunkenness. But there is a high degree of hypochondriacism, which not unfrequently falls under the cognizance of a physician, and on which he may be required to decide, whether it amounts to mental incapacity for the execution of a last will and testament. To define the precise boundaries of rationality is perhaps impossible; if it be true, according to Shakespear, that "the lunatic, the lover, and the poet are of imagination all compact." But a partially distempered fancy is known to subsist with general intelligence: And a man, like Mr. Simon Browne, believing the extinction of his rational soul by the judgment of God, may uniformly evince, in every other instance, very distinguished intellectual powers; and be capable of directing his concerns, and disposing of his property, with sufficient discretion. To preclude one, so affected, from being a testator, seems inconsistent either with wisdom or justice; especially if the will, which has been made, discover, in its essential parts, no traces of a disturbed [47] imagination or unsound judgment. But whenever false ideas, of a *practical kind*, are so firmly united as to be constantly and invariably mistaken for truth, we properly denominate this unnatural alliance INSANITY. And if it give rise to a train of subordinate wrong associations, producing incongruity of behaviour, incapacity for the common duties of life, or unconscious deviations from morality and religion, MADNESS has then its commencement.*

[Bottom page 48] * See Author's Moral and Literary Dissertations, p. 127, second edit.

III. A lunatic, or *non compos mentis*, in the eye of the law, is one who has had understanding, but has lost it by disease, grief, or other accident. The king is the trustee for such unfortunate persons, appointed to protect their property, and to account to them, if they recover, for their revenues, or, after their decease to their representatives. The Lord Chancellor, therefore, grants a commission to inquire into the state of mind of the insane person; and if he be found *non compos*, he usually commits the care of his person, with a suitable allowance for his maintenance, to some friend, who was then called his committee." †

[Bottom page 48] †See Blackstone's Comment. Book I, chap. viii.

The physician, who has been [48] consulted about the case, will doubtless be called upon to deliver an opinion concerning his patient. And before he becomes accessory to his deprivation, as it were, of all legal existence, he will weigh attentively the whole circumstances of the disorder; the original cause of it; the degree in which it subsists; its duration; and probable continuance. For if the malady be not fixed, great, and permanent, this solemn act of law must be deemed inexpedient, because it cannot be reversed without difficulty. And when insanity has been once formally declared, there may be grounds of apprehension that the party will be consigned to neglect and oblivion. With regard to the waste or alienation of property by the person thus afflicted, little risque is incurred, if he be put under the ordinary restraint of a proper curator. For whilst his mind remains in the state of alienation, he is incapable of executing any act with validity; and the next heir, or other person interested, may set it aside, on the plea of his incapacity. But the use of guardians or committees of a lunatic is chiefly to renew, in his right, under the direction of the court of chancery, any lease for lives or years, and to apply the profits for the benefit of the insane person, of his heirs, or executors [49].

IV. In the case of *sudden death*, the law has made provision for examining into the cause of it, by the *coroner*, an officer appointed for the purpose, who is empowered to summon such evidence as is necessary, for the discharge of his inquisitorial and judicial functions. On these occasions, the attendance of a physician or surgeon may often be required, who should be qualified to give testimony consonant to legal, as well as to medical knowledge. To this end, he must not only be acquainted with the signs of natural death, but also of those which occur, when it is produced by accident or violence. And he should not be a stranger to the several distinctions of homicide, established in our courts of judicature. For the division of this act into *justifiable*, *excusable*, and *felonious*, will aid his investigation, and give precision to the opinion which he delivers.

V. When a crime, which the law has adjudged to be capital, is attempted to be committed by force, the resistance of such force, even so as to occasion the death of the offender, is deemed *justifiable homicide*. Mr. Locke, in his Essay on Government, carries this doctrine to a much greater extent; asserting, that "all manner of force, without a right upon a man's person, puts him in a state of war with the aggressor, [50] and of consequences, being in such a state of war, he may lawfully kill him that puts him under this unnatural restraint." *

[Bottom page 51] * Essay on Government, part II. ch. iii.

But Judge Blackstone considers this conclusion as applicable only to a state of uncivilized nature; and observes, that the law of England is too tender of the public peace, too careful of the life of the subjects, to adopt so contentious a system; nor will suffer with impunity any crime to be *prevented* by death, unless the same, if committed, would also be punished by death. †

[Bottom page 51] † Blackstone's Comment. book IV. ch. xiv

VI. With cases of justifiable homicide, however, gentlemen of the faculty are seldom likely to be professionally concerned. But *excusable homicide* may frequently fall under their cognizance, and require their deliberate attention, and accurate investigation. It is of two sorts; either *per infortunium*, by misadventure; or *se defendendo*, upon a principle of self-preservation. Death may be the consequence of a lawful act, done without any intention of hurt. Thus if an officer, in the correction of a soldier by the sentence of a court martial, happens to occasion his death, it is only misadventure; the punishment being lawful [51]. But if the correction be unwarrantably severe, either in the manner, the instrument, or the quality of punishment, and death ensues, the offender is at least guilty of manslaughter, and in some circumstances, of murder. A surgeon, therefore, is usually present, when soldiers are chastised with the lash; and on his testimony must depend the justification of the mode and degree of punishment inflicted. When medicines administered to a sick patient, with an honest design, to produce the alleviation of his pain, or cure of his disease, occasion death, this is misadventure, in the view of the law; and the physician or surgeon, who directed them, is not liable to punishment criminally, though a civil action might formerly lie for neglect or ignorance. But it hath been holden that such immunity is confined to *regular* physicians and surgeons. Sir Matthew Hale, however, justly questions the legality of this determination; since physic and salves were in use; before licensed physicians and surgeons. "Wherefore he treats the doctrine as apocryphal, and fitted only to qualify and flatter licenciates and doctors in physic; though it may be of use to make people cautious how they meddle too much in so dangerous an employment." The college of physicians, however, within their jurisdiction, which extends seven [52] miles round London, are vested by charter with the power of fine and imprisonment *pro mala praxi*. Yet, doctor Groenevelt, who was cited, in the year 1693, before the Censors of the College, and committed to Newgate, by a warrant from the president, for prescribing *cantharides* in substance, was acquitted on the plea that bad practice must be accompanied with a bad intention, to render it criminal. This prosecution, whilst it ruined the doctor's reputation and injured his fortune, so that he is said to have died in want, excited general attention to the remedy, and afterwards established the use of it: though it must be acknowledged that his doses were two bold and hazardous. But whatever be the indulgence of the law towards medical practitioners, they are bound by a higher authority than that of the most solemn statute, not to exercise the healing art without due knowledge, tenderness, and discretion: And every rash experiment, every mistake, which originates either from gross inattention or defective education, is, in the eye of conscience, a crime both against God and man.

It must frequently devolve on the faculty to decide concerning the nature and effects of blows, strokes, or wounds inflicted, and how far the death of the sufferer is to be ascribed to them, or to some antecedent or subsequent disease. In [53] homicide, also, *se defendendo*, the manner and time of the defence are to be considered. For if the person assaulted fall upon the aggressor, when the fray is over and he is running away, this is revenge and not defence. And though no witness were present, the situation of the wound or of the blow would afford, if in the back of the assailant, presumptive evidence of *felonious homicide*.

VII. This crime, the most atrocious of all others, is considered by the law under the three heads of *suicide, manslaughter*, and *murder*; concerning each of which the faculty are occasionally obliged to give professional evidence. A *felo de se* is one who has deliberately put an end to his existence, or committed any unlawful malicious act, the immediate consequence of which proved death to himself. To constitute this act a crime, the party must have been of years of discretion, and in the possession of reason. A physician, therefore, may be called upon, by the coroner, to state his opinion of the mental capacity of defunct. And the law will not authorize the plea, that every melancholic or hypochrondriac fit deprives a man of the power of discerning right from wrong. Even if a lunatic kills himself in a lucid interval, Sir M. Hale affirms that he is a *felo de se*. And the physician, who has attended [54] him, is best qualified to judge of the degree, the duration, or periodical seasons of such returns of sanity. But there are cases of temporary distraction, when death maybe rushed upon apparently with design, but really from the influence of terror, or the want of that presence of mind, which is necessary to the exercise of judgment, and the discrimination of actual from imaginary evil. Of this kind the reader will find an affecting instance, related by Dr. Hunter, in the Medical Observations and Inquiries published by a Society of Physicians, In London." *

[Bottom page 55] * Vol. VI. p. 279.

VIII. *Manslaughter* is defined "the unlawful killing of another, without malice, express or implied, which may be either voluntarily, upon a sudden heat; or involuntarily, but in the commission of some unlawful act." Yet though this definition is delivered from Sir Matthew Hale, by the excellent commentator on the laws of England, so often quoted, it is not sufficiently precise and comprehensive. For when a person does an act lawful in itself, but which proves fatal to a fellow citizen, because done without due circumspection, it may, according to circumstances, be either misadventure, manslaughter, or murder. Thus when a workman [55] kills any one, by flinging down a stone or piece of timber into the street, if the accident be in a country village, where there are few passengers, and if he give warning by calling out to them, it is only misadventure: But if it be in London or any other populous town, where persons are continually passing, it is manslaughter, though warning be loudly given: And it is murder, if he know of their passing, and yet gives no warning at all; for this is malice against all mankind.*

[Bottom page 56] * Blackstone's Comment. book. IV. ch. xiv.

On the like grounds we may reason concerning the cases of death, occasioned by drugs designed to produce abortion. This purpose is not always unlawful: For the configuration of the *pelvis* in some females, is such as to render natural parturition impossible, or inevitably fatal. But even in such instances, the guilt of manslaughter may be incurred by ignorance of the drastic quality of the medicine prescribed, or want of due caution in the dose administered. And when no moral or salutary and is in view, the simple act itself, if fatal in the issue, falls under the denomination of murder. †

[Bottom page 56] † See Burn's Justice of Peace, vol. I. page 216.

"If a woman be quick with child, and, by a potion or otherwise, killeth it in her womb, this is a great misprision, yet no murder: [56] But if the child be born alive, and dieth of the potion or other cause, this is murder."*

[Bottom page 57] * Id. vol. II. p. 110.

The procuring of abortions was common amongst the Romans; and it is said, was liable to no penalty before the reigns of Severus and Antoninus. Even those princes made it criminal only in the case of a married woman, practicing it to defraud her husband of the comforts of children, from motives of resentment. For the *fœtus* being regarded as a portion of the womb of the mother, she was supposed to have an equal and full right over both. The false opinion may have its influence in modern, as well as in ancient times; and false it must be deemed, since no female can be privileged to ensure her own bowels, much less the *fœtus*, which is now well known to constitute no part of them. To extinguish the first spark of life is a crime of the same nature, both against our Maker and society, as to destroy an infant, a child, or a man; these regular and successive stages of existence being the ordinances of God, subject alone to his divine will, and appointed by sovereign wisdom and goodness as the exclusive means of preserving the race, and multiplying the enjoyments, of mankind. Hence the father of physic, in the oath enjoined on [57] his pupils, and which some universities now impose on medical graduates, obliged them solemnly to abjure the practice of administering the πεσσος φθοριος. But in weighing the charge against any person, of having procured an abortion, the methods employed should be attentively considered by the faculty; as this effect has often been ascribed to causes inadequate to its production. Even the pessary, so sanctimoniously forbidden by Hippocrates, has little of that activity and power, which superstition has assigned to it.

IX. The law of England guards, with assiduous care, the lives of infants, when endangered by motives which counteract, and too often overbalance, the strong operations of maternal love. In cases of *bastardy*, therefore, it is declared, by a statute passed in the reign of James the first, that "If any woman be delivered of any issue of her body, male or female, which being born alive, should by the laws of this realm be a bastard, and she endeavour privately, either by drowning, or secret burying thereof, or any other way, either by herself, or the procuring of others, so to conceal the death thereof, as that it may not come to light whether it was born alive or not, but be concealed, she shall suffer death, as in case of mur-[58]der; except she can prove, by one witness at least, that the child was born dead." *

[Bottom page 59] * Burn's Justice, vol. I. p. 216.

This law, though humane in its principle, is much too severe in its construction. To give certainty to punishment, by facilitating conviction, is doubtless an essential object of jurisprudence. And it has been well observed, that the statute, which made the possession of the implements of coining a capital offense, by constituting such possession complete evidence of guilt, has proved the most effectual mean of enforcing the denunciation of law against this dangerous and tempting crime.†

[Bottom page 59] † See Paley's Moral and Political Philosophy, 4to. p. 350
But the analogy, which the able moralist has drawn between this ordinance and that relating to bastardy, is not fully conclusive. For possession, in the former case, clearly implies a specific purpose, for which the legislature, with sufficient wisdom and justice, has provided a specific punishment. Whereas secrecy in the mother, concerning the death of her illegitimate offspring, hardly amounts to the lowest degree of presumptive evidence of felonious homicide. Gentlemen of the faculty have often melancholy experience, of the distraction [59] and misery, which females suffer under these unhappy circumstances. And when it becomes their painful office to deliver evidence on such occasions, justice and humanity require, that they should scrutinize the whole truth, and *nothing extenuate, nor set down aught in malice*. "What is commonly understood to be the murder of a bastard child by the mother," says Dr. Hunter, "if the real circumstances were fully known, would be allowed to be a very different crime in different circumstances. In some (it is hoped to be *rare*) instances, it is a crime of very deepest dye. … But, as well as I can judge, the greatest number of what are called murders of bastard children, are of a very different kind. The mother has an unconquerable sense of shame, and pants after the preservation of character: So far she is virtuous and amiable. She has not the resolution to meet and avow infamy. In proportion as she loses the hope either of having been mistaken with regard to pregnancy, or of being relieved from her terrors by a fortunate miscarriage, she every day sees her danger greater and nearer, and her mind overwhelmed with terror and despair. In this situation many of these women, who are afterwards accused of murder, would destroy themselves, if they did not know that such an action would [60] infallibly lead to an inquiry, which would proclaim what they are so anxious to conceal. In this perplexity, and meaning nothing less than the murder of the infant, they are meditating different schemes for concealing the death of the child; but are wavering between difficulties on all sides, putting the evil hour off, and trusting too much to chance and fortune. In that state often they are overtaken before they expected; their schemes are frustrated; their distress of body and mind deprives them of all judgment and rational conduct; they are delivered by themselves wherever they happen to retire in their fright or confusion; sometimes dying in the agonies of childbirth, and sometimes being quite exhausted they faint away, and become insensible of what is passing; and when they recover a little strength, find that the child, whether still-born or not, is completely lifeless. In such a case, is it to be expected, when it would answer no purpose, that a woman should divulge the secret? Will not the best dispositions of mind urge her to preserve her character? She will therefore hide every appearance of what has happened as well as she can, though if the discovery be made, that conduct will be set down as a proof of her guilt." … "Here let us suppose a case, which every body will allow to [61] be very possible: An unmarried woman, becoming pregnant, is striving to conceal her shame, and laying the best scheme that she can devise, for saving her own life and that of the child, and at the same time concealing the secret; but her plan is at once disconcerted by her being taken ill by herself, and delivered of a dead child.

If the law punishes such a woman with death for concealing her shame, does it not require more from human nature, than weak human nature can bear? In a case so circumstanced, surely the only crime is the having been pregnant, which the law does not mean to punish with death; and the attempt to conceal it by fair means should not be punishable with death, as that attempt seems to arise from a principle of virtuous shame." *

[Bottom page 61] * Med. Obs. and Inq. Vol. VI. p. 271. et seq.

The observations, here quoted, have a just claim to attention, from the extensive experience which the author possessed, and still more from his intimate knowledge of the female character. Yet to the moral and political philosopher, Dr. Hunter may appear to have exalted the sense of shame into the principle of virtue; and to have mistaken the great end of penal law, which is not vengeance, but the prevention of crimes. The [62] statute, indeed, which makes the concealment of the birth of a bastard child full proof of murder, confounds all distinctions of innocence and guilt, as such concealment, whenever practicable, would be the wish and act of all mothers, virtuous or vicious, under the same unhappy predicament. Law, however, which is the guardian and bulwark of the public weal, must maintain a steady, and even rigid watch, over the general tendencies of human actions: And when these are not only clearly understood, but interpreted according to the rules of wisdom and rectitude, that may justly be constituted a civil crime, which, if permitted, might give occasion to atrocious guilt, though in its own nature innocent. The measure of punishment, however, should be proportionate, as nearly as possible, to the temptations to offend, and to the kind and degree of evil produced by the offence. If inadequate to the former, it will be nugatory; and if too severe for the latter, It will defeat itself, by furnishing a just plea for superseding its execution.*

[Bottom page 63] * "L' atrocité des loix en empêche l'exécution. Lorsque la peine est sans mesure, on est souvent obligé de lui prefférer l'inpunité." – MONTESQUIEU.

A revision of our sanguinary statutes is much wanted; and it would be happy if means [63] could be devised of suppressing the punishment, by obviating the crime, when it is merely positive or municipal. This we have seen accomplished with respect to the coinage of money, by the simple introduction of a standard weight in the payment of gold. And a sagacious legislator might doubtless discover and adopt similar improvements, in other branches of penal jurisprudence.

Much observation is required to discriminate between a child still born, and one that has lived after birth only a short space of time. Various appearances, also, both internal and external, may be mistaken for marks of violent death. Even the swimming of the lungs in water, a test on which so much reliance is placed, will, on many occasions, be found fallacious. But these are points of professional science, which do not strictly fall under the subject of this section; and the reader is particularly referred to the paper already quoted, and also to the *Elementa Medicinæ Forensis Joh. Fred. Faselii*; or to a valuable epitome of the same work in English by Dr. Farr.* [64]

[Bottom page 64] *Elements of Medical Jurisprudence; or a succinct and compendious Description of such Tokens in the Human Body, as are requisite to determine the Judgment of a Coroner, and of Courts of Law, in Cases of Divorce, Rape, Murder, &c. London, Becket, 1788 [64].

X. *Duelling* is another species of felony, even though the consequences of it should not prove fatal: And gentlemen of the faculty are peculiarly interested in the knowledge of the laws relating to it; because they are not only liable to be summoned on the trial of the parties, if either or both of them be wounded, but are frequently professional attendants on them in the field of combat. It is astonishing that a practice, which originated in ages of Gothic ignorance, superstition, and barbarism should be continued in the present enlightened period, though condemned by the ordinances of every state, and repugnant to the spirit and percepts of christianity. In the usages of the ancient Germans, evident traces of it may be discovered. But it was employed by them either as an appeal to the justice, or to the prescience of the Gods. Velleius Paterculus informs us, that questions, decided amongst the Romans by legal trial, were terminated amongst the Germans by arms or judicial combat.*

[Bottom page 65] * Vellei Paterculi. lib. II. cap. cxviii.

Tacitus describes it as a species of divination, by which the future events of important wars were explored. A captive from the enemy was compelled to fight with a man selected from their own nation. Each was accoutred with his proper weapons; and the [65] presage of success was determined by the issue of the battle.*

[Bottom page 66] * Vide Tacit. de Situ, Morib. et Populis Germaniæ, sect. x.

A law is quoted by Stiernhöok, which shews, that judicial combat was, at first appropriated to points respecting personal character, and that it was only subsequently extended to criminal cases, and to questions relative to property. The terms of the law are, "If any man shall say to another these reproachful words, 'you are not a man equal to other men,' or, 'you have not the heart of a man,' and the other shall reply, 'I am a man as good as you.' let them meet on the highway. If he who first gave offence appear, and the person absent himself, let the latter be deemed worse than he was called; let him not be admitted to give evidence and judgment either for man or woman, and let him not have the privilege of making a testament. If the person offended appear, and he who gave the offence be absent, let him call upon the other thrice with a loud voice and make a mark upon the earth, and then let him who absented himself be deemed infamous, because he uttered words which he durst not support. If both shall appear properly armed, and the person offended shall fall in the combat, let a half compensation be paid for his death. But [66] if the person who gave the offense shall fall, let it be imputed to his own rashness. The petulance of his tongue hath been fatal to him. Let him lie in the field without any compensation being made for his death.*

[Bottom page 67] * Lex Uplandica apud Stiern. – Robertson's History of Charles V. vol. I. note 22.

Montesquieu, on the authority of Beaumanoir, whom he quotes with great respect, deduces the rise and formation of the articles, relative to the point of honour, from the following particular judicial usages. The accuser declared, in the presence of the judge, that such a person had committed such an action: The accused made answer that *he lied*, upon which the judge gave orders for the duel. Thus it became an established rule, that whenever the lie was given to a person, it was incumbent on him to fight. *Gentlemen* combated on horseback, completely armed. *Villeins* fought on foot, and with bastons. The baston, therefore, was regarded as an instrument of affront, because to strike a man with it was to treat him as a villein. For the like reason, a box on the ear or blow on the face were deemed contumelies, to be expiated with blood; since villeins alone were liable to receive such disgraceful blows, as it [67] was peculiar to them to fight with their heads uncovered.*

[Bottom page 68] * See Montesquieu, Liv, XXVIII. c. xx.

Practices like these were so congenial to the proud and martial spirit of the times, as well as to the superstition which prevailed, that they became universal throughout Europe. But it is evident that they could not fail to subvert the regular course of justice, diminish the authority of government, and violate the sacred ordinances of the church. For the clergy uniformly remonstrated against, and even anathematized them, as adverse to christianity; and the civil power frequently interposed, to set bounds to usage, which its authority was too feeble to suppress. Henry I. of England, in the twelfth century, prohibited trial by combat, in all questions concerning property of small value. Louis VII. of France issued an edict to the same effect. St. Louis, who was a distinguished legislator, considering the rude age in which he reigned, attempted a more perfect jurisprudence, by substituting trial by evidence, in place of that by combat. And afterwards it became the policy of every monarch, who possessed power or talents, to explode this relic of Gothic barbarism. By degrees the practice became less and less frequent; courts of judicature, acquired [68] an ascendancy; law was studied as a science, and administered with greater regularity; and the ferocious manners of the inhabitants of Europe yielded to the arts of peace, and to the benefits of social and civilized life. But an event occurred, in the year 1528, which both revived the practice of single combat, and gave a new form to it, more absurd and fatal. The political and personal enmity, which subsisted between the Emperor Charles V. and Francis I., led the former to commission the French herald, sent to him with a denunciation of war, to acquaint his sovereign, that he should from that time consider him not only as a base violator of public faith, but as a stranger to the honour and probity of a gentleman. Francis instantly sent back the herald, with a *cartel* of defiance, giving the emperor *the lie*, and challenging him to single combat. Charles accepted the challenge, but it being impracticable to settle the preliminaries, this romantic and ridiculous enterprize of course was never accomplished. The transaction, however, excited such universal attention, and reflected so much splendour and dignity on this novel mode of single combat, that every gentleman thought himself entitled, and even bound in honour to draw his sword, and to demand satisfaction of his adversary, for affronts trivial [69] and even imaginary.*

[Bottom page 70] * See Robertson's History of Charles V. book V.

The best blood in Christendom was shed; personages of the first distinction were devoted to death; the ease, the familiarity, and the confidence of private intercourse were interrupted; and war itself was hardly more destructive to life, and to its dearest enjoyments, then this fatal and seductive frenzy.†

[Bottom page 70 to bottom page 71] † The History of Lord Herbert of Cherbury, who lived in the reigns of Queen Elizabeth and James I., fully exemplifies the folly and danger of adopting false principles of honour. During the abode of this romantic nobleman at the Duke of Montmorencie's, about twenty-four miles from Paris, it happened, one evening, that a daughter of the Duchess de Ventadour, of about ten or eleven years of age, went to walk in the meadows, with his lordship, and several other gentlemen and ladies. The young lady wore a knot of ribband on her head, which a French chevalier snatched away, and fastened to his hatband. He was desired to return it, but refused. The lady then requested Lord [70] Herbert to recover it for her. A race ensued; and the chevalier, finding himself likely to be overtaken, made a sudden turn, and was about to deliver his prize to the young lady, when Lord Herbert seized his arm, and cried out, "I give it to you." `Pardon me,` said the lady, `it is he who gives it me.` "Madam," replied Lord Herbert, "I will not contradict you, but if the chevalier do not acknowledge that I constrain him to give the ribband, I will fight with him." And the next day he sent him a challenge, "being bound thereto," says he, "by the oath taken when I was made knight of the bath." See the Life of Lord Herbert of Cherbury; also Percival's Moral and Lit. Dissert. p. 299, second edit. [71]

Evils of such magnitude required adequate remedies; and all the terrors of law were every where exerted to repress them. Sir Francis Bacon, when attorney-general, in the reign of James I., delivered a charge, before the court of star chamber, touching duels, which gives a clear and animated view of the light in which they were then regarded. "The first motive," he says, [70] "is a false and erroneous imagination of honour and credit; and therefore the king, and his proclamation, doth mostly aptly call them *bewitching duels*. For if one judge of it truly, it is no better than a sorcery, that enchanteth the spirits of young men; and a kind of satanical illusion and apparition of honour against religion, against law, and against moral virtue. Hereunto maybe added, that men have almost lost the true notion and understanding of fortitude and valor. For fortitude distinguisheth of the grounds of quarrels whether they be just; and not only so, but whether they be worthy; and setteth a better price upon men's lives van to bestow them idly. Nay, it is weakness and disesteem of a man's self, to put a man's life upon such liedger performances: a man's life is [71] not to be trifled away; it is to be offered up and sacrificed to honourable services, public merits, good causes, and noble adventurers. It is in expence of blood, as it is in expence of money; it is no liberality to make a profusion of money upon every vain occasion; nor no more is it fortitude to make effusion of blood, except the cause be of worth." *

[Bottom page 72] Bacon's Works, 4to. Birch's edit. vol. II. p. 565.

The decree of the Star Chamber against Priest and Wright, the objects of Sir Francis Bacon's charge, was, that they should both be committed to prison; that the former should be fined £500. and the latter 500 marks, and that at the next assizes they should publicly acknowledge their high contempt of, and offence against God, the king's majesty, and his laws, shewing themselves penitent for the same. Though this judgment appears to have been founded in wisdom and equity, yet, happily for our country, the court, which passed the sentence, has been long suppressed; and we are now governed not by arbitrary will, but by known and fixed laws. Those which subsist against duelling I shall quote on the authorities of Foster, Blackstone, Hawkins, and Burn. "Deliberate duelling, if death ensueth, is in [72] the eye of the law murder; for duels are generally founded in deep revenge; and though a person should be drawn into a duel, not upon a motive so criminal, but merely upon the punctilio of what the swordsmen falsely call honour, that will not excuse; for he that deliberately seeketh the blood of another upon a private quarrel, acteth in defiance of all laws human and divine."*

[Bottom page 73] * Sir Michael Foster's Reports, 8vo p. 297.

"Express malice is when one, with a sedate deliberate mind formed design, doth kill another. This takes in the case of deliberate duelling, where both parties meet, avowedly, with an intent to murder; thinking it their duty as gentlemen, and claiming it as their right, to wanton with their own lives and those of their fellow-creatures, without any warrant or authority from any power either human or divine, but in direct contradiction to the laws both of God and man. And, therefore, the law has justly fixed the crime and punishment of murder on them, and on their seconds also." †

[Bottom page 73] † Blackstone's Comment. book IV, chap xiv.

"The law so abhors all duelling in cold blood, that not only the principal who actually kills the other, but also his seconds, are guilty of murder, whether they fought or not: and it [73] is holden that the seconds of the party slain are also guilty as accessaries."*

[Bottom page 74] * I Hawkins, 82; and Burn's Justice, vol. II. p. 509.

From variations in the moral and intellectual character of man, it is impossible to ascertain the precise period, when the passions maybe supposed to become cool, after having been violently agitated. Judgment, therefore, must be founded on the circumstances of deliberation, which are delivered in the course of evidence. In many cases, it has been determined that death, in consequence of an appointment and meeting, a few hours subsequent the provocation, is murder.†

[Bottom page 74] † See Legg's ca Kelyng, 27. Eden's Principles of Penal Law, p. 224.

XI. Before a surgeon engage professionally to *attend* a *duellist* to the *field* of *combat*, it behoves him to consider well, not only how far he is about to countenance a deliberate violation of the duties of morality and religion; but whether, in the construction of law, he may not be deemed an aider and abettor of a crime, which involves in it such turpitude, that death is alike denounce against the principal and the accessary. Does he not voluntarily put himself into a predicament familiar, and many essential points, to that of the *second*, who is expressly condemned [74] by the legislature of this country? Both are apprized of the purpose to commit an act of felony: Both take an interest in the circumstances attendant upon it: And both are present during the execution; the one to regulate its antecedents, the other to alleviate its consequences. But I suggest these considerations with much diffidence: And though I observe some passages, in Sir Michael Foster's Discourse concerning Accomplices, which seem to confirm them; yet candour obliges me to quote the following, apparently adverse, opinion of this excellent judge. "In order to render a person an accomplice and a principal in felony, he must be aiding and abetting at the fact, or ready to afford assistance, if necessary. And therefore, if A happeneth to be present at a murder, for instance, and taketh no part in it, nor endeavoureth to prevent it, nor apprehendeth the murderer, nor levieth hue and cry after him, this strange behaviour of his, though highly criminal, will not of itself render him either principal or accessary."*

[Bottom page 75] * Foster's Crown Law, 8vo. p. 350.

But whatever be the objections against the attendance of a surgeon in the field of combat, they cannot be construed to extend to the afford-[75]ing of all possible assistance, to any unfortunate sufferer, in an affair of honour; provided such assistance be not preconcerted, but required as in ordinary accidents or emergencies. For in the offices of the healing art, no discrimination can be made, either of occasions or of characters: And it must be acknowledged, that many of the victims of duelling have been men, from their talents and virtues, possessing the justest claim to assiduous and tender attention. That lives of such inestimable value to their friends, to their families, and to the public, should be at the mercy of any profligate rake, who wantonly gives affronts, or idly fancies he receives them, is a great aggravation of the folly, as well as of the guilt of duelling. This reflection seems to shew the propriety of a change in the penal code, respecting it; and that the punishment inflicted should be confined to the aggressor; strict inquisition into the circumstances of the case being previously made, by the coroner, or some magistrate authorized and bound to exercise this important trust. And he may, with reason, be regarded as the aggressor, who either violates the rules of decorum, by any unprovoked rudeness or insult; or who converts into an offence, what was intended only as convivial pleasantry [76].

XII. A physician has no special interest in an acquaintance with the statutes relative to duelling. But as he possesses the rank of a gentleman, both by his liberal education and profession, the *law of honour*, if that may be termed a law which is indefinite and arbitrary, has a claim to his serious study and attention. As a philosopher, also, it becomes him to trace its origin, and to investigate the principles on which it is founded: And as a moralist, duty calls upon him to counteract its baneful influence and ascendancy. For in principle, it is distinct from virtue; and as a practical rule, it extends only to certain formalities and decorums, of little importance in the transactions of life, and which are spontaneously observed by those, who are actuated with the true sense of propriety and rectitude. Genuine honour, in its full extent, may be defined a quick perception and strong feeling of moral obligation, in conjunction with an acute sensibility to shame, reproach, or infamy. In different characters, these constituent parts of the principle are found to exist in proportions so diversified, as sometimes to appear almost single and detached. The former always *aids and strengthens virtue*; the latter may occasionally *imitate her actions*,*

[Bottom page 77] * Addison's Cato

when fashion happily [77] countenances, or high example prompts to rectitude.

But being connected, for the most part, with a jealous pride and capricious irritability, it will be more shocked with the *imputation*, then with the *commission* of what is wrong. And thus it will constitute that spurious honour, which, by a perversion of the laws of association, *puts evil for good, and good for evil* ; and, under the sanction of a name, perpetrates crimes without remorse, and even without ignominy.*

[Bottom page 78] * See the Author's Mor. And Lit. Diss. p. 295.

XIII. *Homicide* by *poison* is another very important object of medical jurisprudence. When it is the effect of inadvertency, or the want of adequate caution, in the use of substances dangerous to health and life, the law regards it as a misdemeanor: When it is the consequences of rashness, of wanton experiment, or of motives unjust, though not malicious,†

[Bottom page 78] † "If an action unlawful itself be done deliberately, and *with intention of mischief*, or great bodily harm to particulars, or of mischief indiscriminately, fall it where it may, an death ensue against or beside the original and intention of the party, it will be murder. But of such *mischievous intention* doth not appear, which is matter of fact, and *to be collected from circumstances*, and the act was done heedlessly and incautiously, it will be manslaughter: not accidental death, because the act which ensued was unlawful." Foster, p. 261 [78].

it becomes [78] manslaughter: And when the express purpose is to kill, by means of some deleterious drug, it constitutes a most atrocious species of murder. In cases of this nature, the faculty are called upon to give evidence concerning the nature of the poison, the symptoms produced by it, and the actual fatality of its operation. I do not know whether the period of this fatal operation be extended, as in the infliction of blows and wounds, to a year and a day. But if it be, the most nice and accurate investigation of the progressive advances of disease and death will be incumbent on the physician or surgeon, who was consulted on the occasion. No subject has given rise to more misconception and superstition, than the action of poisons. Numberless substances had been classed as such, which, if not inert, or at least innoxious; and powers have been ascribed to others, far exceeding their real energy. Even Lord Verulam, the great luminary of science, in his charge against the Earl of Somerset, for the murder of Sir Thomas Overbury, in the tower of London, seems to give credit to the story of Livia, who was said to have poisoned the figs upon the tree, which her husband was wont to gather with his own hands. And he seriously states, that "Weston chased the poor prisoner with poison after poison; poisoning salts, poisoning meats, [79] poisoning sweet-meats, poisoning medicines and vomits, until at last his body was almost come, by the use of poisons, to the state that Mithridates's body was by the use of treacle and preservatives, that the force of the poisons was blunted upon him: Weston confessing, when he was tried for not dispatching him, that he had been given enough to poison twenty men." *

[Bottom page 80] * Bacon's Works, vol. II. p. 614.

In this criminal transaction the truth probably was, what has been judiciously suggested by Rapin, that the lieutenant of the tower, refusing to be concerned in the crime, yet not daring to discover it, from the fear of the Viscount Rochester's resentment, seized the victuals sent from time to time for the prisoner, and threw them into the house of office. Sir Thomas Overbury, however, fell a victim at last to an empoisoned glyster.

When the particular drug, or other mean employed, can be accurately ascertained, its deleterious qualities should be fully known; and these should be cautiously compared with the effects ascribed to it, in the case under consideration. It may often be expedient, also, to examine the body of the sufferer by dissection; and this should be accomplished as expeditiously as [80] possible; that the changes imputed to death may not be confounded with those which are imputed to poison. But on such points reference can alone be made to the knowledge and experience of the practitioner, and to the lights which he may acquire by consulting Faselius and other works of a similar nature. I shall, therefore, close this article with a few passages of the charge of Mr. Justice Buller to the grand jury, relative to the trial of Capt. Donellan, for the murder of Sir Theodosius Boughton, at the Warwick assizes, in March 1781. "In this case, gentlemen," he says, "you will have two objects to consider, first, whether the deceased did die of *poison*? secondly, whether the person suspected did assist in *administering* the poison? With respect to the first of these considerations, you will, no doubt, *hear the sentiments of those who are skilled in the nature and effects of poison*, which is of various sorts and most subtle in its operation. From the information of such persons you will be able to form an opinion of the effects which *different poisons* have on *different persons*; and also the effects the same *poisons* have on persons of *different habits and constitutions*. If you find he did get his death by poison, the next case is, to consider, who gave him that poison. Where poison is knowingly given, and death ensues [81], it is wilful murder; and if one is present, when poison is given by another, he is not an accessary, but a principal."*

[Bottom page 82] * Hist. Sketches of Civ. Lib., p. 209.

XIV. In all civilized countries, the honour and chastity of the female sex are guarded from violence, by the severest sanctions of law. And this protection is at once humane, just, and necessary to social morality. It is consonant to humanity that weakness should be secured against the attacks of brutal strength: It is just that the most sacred of all personal property should be preserved from invasion: And it is essential to morality that licentious passion should be restrained; that modesty should not be wounded; nor the mind contaminated, in some instances, before it is capable of forming adequate conceptions of right and wrong. The crime of *rape*, therefore, subjects the perpetrator to condign punishment by every code of jurisprudence, ancient or modern. Amongst the Jews death was inflicted, if the damsel was betrothed to another man: And if not betrothed, a fine, amounting to 50 shekels of silver, was to be paid to her father by him who had *laid hold of the virgin*, and she was to become his wife: And because *he had humbled her, he might not* [82] *put her away all his days*:*

[Bottom page 83] * Deuteronomy xxii. 28, 29.

For the privilege of divorce was authorized by the Jewish institutions. The Romans made this offence capital, superadding the confiscation of goods. Even the carrying off a woman from her parents or guardians, and cohabiting with her, whether accomplished by force, or with her full consent, were made equally penal with a rape, by an imperial edict. For the Roman law seems to have supposed, that women never deviate from virtue, without being seduced by the arts of the other sex. And, therefore, by imposing a powerful restraint on the solicitations of men, they aimed at a more effectual security of the chastity of women. *Nisi etenim eam solicitaverit, nisi odiosis, artibus circumvenerit, non faciet eam velle in tantum dedecus sese prodere.* But the English law, as Judge Blackstone has observed, does not entertain such sublime ideas of the honour of either sex, as to lay the blame of a mutual fault on one only of the transgressors. And it is, therefore, essential to the crime of rape, that the woman's will is violated by the execution. But, by a statute of Queen Elizabeth, if the crime be perpetrated on a female child under the age of *ten* years, the consent or non-consent is immaterial, as she is supposed to be of insufficient [83] judgment. Sir Matthew Hale is even of opinion, that such profligacy committed on an infant under *twelve* years, the age of female discretion by common law, either with or without consent, amounts to a rape and felony. But the decisions of the courts have, generally, been founded on the statute above-mentioned.

A male infant, under the age of fourteen years, is deemed, by law, incapable of committing, and therefore cannot be found guilty of a rape, from a presumed imbecility both of body and mind. This detestable crime, being executed in secrecy, and the knowledge of it being confined to the party injured, it is just that her single testimony should be adducible in proof of the fact. Yet the excellent observation of Sir Matthew Hale merits peculiar attention. "It is an accusation," he says, "easy to be made, and harder to be proved; but harder to be defended by the party accused, though innocent." He then relates two extraordinary cases of malicious prosecution for this crime, which had fallen under his own cognizance; and concludes, "I mention these instances, that we may be more cautious upon trials of offences of this nature, wherein the court and jury may, with so much ease, be imposed upon, without great care and vigilance; the heinous-[84]ness of the offense many times transporting the judge and jury with so much indignation, that they are overhastily carried to the conviction of the person accused thereof, by the confident testimony of sometimes false and malicious witnesses." Collateral and concurrent circumstances of time and place;*

[Bottom page 85] * These circumstances are particularly adverted to in the Mosaic Law. See Deut. xxii. 25, 26, 27.

appearances of violence on examination, &c. are, therefore, necessary to be added to the mere affirmative evidence of the prosecutor. And the inspection of a surgeon is often required, to ascertain the reality of the alleged violence. On such occasions, his testimony should be given with all possible delicacy, as well as with the utmost caution. Even external signs of injury may originate from disease, of which the following example has been communicated to me, by a very ingenious surgeon in Manchester.

A girl, about six years of age, was admitted into the Manchester Infirmary, on account of a mortification in the female organs, attended with great soreness and general depression of strength. She had been in a bed with a young man, and there was reason to suspect, that he had taken criminal liberties with her. The [85] mortification increased, and the child died. The young man, therefore, was apprehended, and tried at the Lancaster Assizes; but was acquitted on sufficient evidence, that many instances of a similar disease had appeared about the same period, in which there was no possibility of injury or guilt. In one case, Mr. Simmons, the gentleman to whom I am indebted for this information, opened the body after death. The disorder had been a *typhus*, accompanied with the mortification of the *pudenda*. There was no evident cause of this extraordinary symptom, discoverable on inspection. The lumbar glands were of a dark colour; but all the *viscera* were sound.

XV. Concerning *nuisances*, the investigation and testimony of the faculty may be required, whenever they are of a nature offensive by the vapours which they emit; or injurious to the health of individuals, or of the community. The law defines any thing that worketh hurt, inconvenience, or damage, to be a nuisance.*

[Bottom page 86] * See Blackstone's Comment. Book III. ch. xiii.; and Book IV. ch. xiii.

Thus if a person keeps hogs, or other noisome animals, so near the house of another, that the stench incommodes him, and renders the air unwholesome, this is a nuisance; because it deprives him [86] of the enjoyments and benefits of his habitation. A smelting house for lead, the smoke of which kills the grass and corn, and injures the cattle of a neighbouring proprietor of land, is deemed a nuisance. Dye-houses, tanning-yards, &c. are nuisances, if erected so near a water-course, as to corrupt the stream. But a chandler's factory, even when situated in a crowded town, is said to be privileged from action or indictment, because candles are regarded as a necessary of life. Hawkins, however, questions the authority of this opinion, since the making of candles may be carried on in the country without annoyance.*

[Bottom page 87] * I Hawk. 199. Burn's Justice, vol. III. p. 239.

But this is hardly possible in a populous neighbourhood: And as Lord Mansfield has adjudged, that, in such cases, what makes the enjoyment of being and property uncomfortable is, in the view of the law, a nuisance;†

[Bottom page 87] † Burron Mansfield, 333. Burn U. S.

various works and trades, essential to the happiness and interest of the community, may fall under this construction. But chemistry, mechanics, and other arts and sciences, furnish methods of diminishing, or obviating almost every species of noisome vapour. And there can be no doubt that vitriol works, aqua fortis works, marine acid bleaching works, the singeing of velvets, &c. may be carried on with very little inconvenience [87] to a neighbourhood, by means neither difficult nor expensive. The same observation may be applied to the business of the dyer, the fell-monger, the tanner, the butcher, and the chandler. And as these with many other disgustful trades are, in some degree, necessary in large towns, justice and policy require, that they should only be prosecuted as nuisances, when not conducted in the least offensive mode possible. To guard against arbitrary powers in municipal government, and to render the decision and investigation of such points perfectly consistent with the liberty of the subject, the reference should be made to a jury; or at least, any individual should be allowed an appeal to one, if he think himself aggrieved.

The frequency of fires, in large manufacturing towns, makes it expedient that magistrates, or commissioners, should be authorized to scrutinize rigidly into the causes of them, when they occur; to punish neglect or carelessness, as well as malicious intention; and to enforce suitable measures of prevention. The plans, proposed for this last very important purpose, by Mr. Hartley and Lord Stanhope, have been proved to be effectual, and are not expensive. The adoption of them, therefore, or of other means, which may hereafter be discovered, should be [88] required, under a heavy penalty, in cases deemed by insurers *doubly hazardous*.

XVI. The laws, which specially relate to the *powers, privileges, honours,* and *emoluments* of the *faculty*, can require no pleas to recommend them to attention. But as they will fall under the subject-matter of the following section, the present shall be closed with a few observations on *judicial testimony*, as it concerns physicians and surgeons.

It is a complaint made by coroners, magistrates, and judges, that medical gentlemen are often reluctant in the performance of the offices, required from them as citizens qualified, by professional knowledge, to aid the execution of public justice. These offices, it must be confessed, are generally painful, always inconvenient, and occasion an interruption to business, of a nature not to be easily appreciated or compensated. But as they admit of no substitution, they are to be regarded as appropriate debts to the community, which neither equity nor patriotism will allow to be cancelled.

When a physician or surgeon is called to give evidence, he should avoid, as much as possible, all obscure and technical terms, and the un-[89]necessary display of medical erudition. He should deliver, also, what he advances, in the purest and most delicate language, consistent with the nature of the subject in question. When two or more gentlemen of the faculty are to offer their opinions or testimony, it would sometimes tend to obviate contrariety, if they were to confer freely with each other, before their public examination. Intelligent and honest men, fully acquainted with their respective means of information, are much less likely to differ, than when no communication has previously taken place. Several years ago, a trial of considerable consequence occurred, relative to a large copper work; and two physicians of eminence were summoned to the assizes, to bear testimony concerning the salubrity or insalubrity of the smoke issuing from the furnaces. The evidence they offered was entirely contradictory. One grounded his testimony on the general presumption that the ores of copper contain arsenic; and consequently that the effluvia, proceeding from the roasting of them, must be poisonous because arsenical. The other had made actual experiments on the ore, employed in the works under prosecution, and on the vapours which it yielded: He was thus furnished with full proof that no arsenic was discoverable in either. But the affirmative prevailed over the negative testimony, from the authority of the physician who delivered it; an [90] authority which he probably would not have misapplied, if he had been antecedently acquainted with the decisive trials made by his opponent.

XVII. It is the injunction of the law, sanctioned by the solemnity of an oath, that in judicial testimony, *the truth, the whole truth,* and *nothing but the truth* shall be delivered. A witness, therefore, is under a sacred obligation to use his best endeavours that his mind be clear and collected, unawed by fear, and uninfluenced by favour or enmity. But in criminal prosecutions, which affect the life of the person accused, scruples will be apt to arise in one who, by the advantages of a liberal education, has been accustomed to serious reflection, yet has paid no particular attention to the principles of political ethics. It is incumbent, therefore, on gentlemen of the faculty, to settle their opinions concerning the right of the civil magistrate to inflict capital punishment; the moral and social ends of such punishment; the limits prescribed to the exercise of the right; and the duty of a citizen to give full efficiency to the laws.

The magistrate's *right* to inflict punishment, and the ends of such punishment, though intimately connected, are in their nature distinct. The right is clearly substitution or [91] transfer of that which belongs to every individual, by the law of nature, viz. instant self-defence, and security from future violence or wrong. The ends are more comprehensive, extending not only to complete security against offence, but to the correction and improvement of the offender himself, and to counteract the disposition of others to offend. Penal laws are to be regulated by this standard; and the lenity or severity, with which they are executed, should, if possible, be exactly proportionate to it. In different circumstances, either personal or public considerations may preponderate: And in cases of great moral atrocity, or when the common weal is essentially injured, all regard to the reformation of a criminal is superseded; and his life is justly forfeited to the good of society. In the participation of the benefits of the social union, he has virtually acceded to its conditions; and the violation of its fundamental articles renders him a rebel and an enemy, to be expelled or destroyed, both for the sake of security, and as an awful warning to others. When capital punishments are viewed in this light, the most humane and scrupulous witness may consider himself as sacrificing private emotions to public justice and social order; and that he is performing an act at once beneficial to his country and to mankind. For political and [92] moral œconomy can subsist in no community, without the steady execution of wise and salutary laws: And every atrocious act, perpetrated with impunity, operates as a terror to the innocent, a snare to the unwary, and an incentive to the flagitious. The criminal, also, who evades the sentence of justice, like one infected with the pestilence, contaminates all whom he approaches. He, therefore, who, from false tenderness, or misguided conscience, has prevented conviction, by withholding the necessary proofs,*

[Bottom page 93] * "The oath administered to the witness, is not only that what he deposes shall be true, but that he shall also depose the whole truth: *So that he is not to conceal any part of what he knows, weather interrogated particularly to that point or not.*" Blackstone, B. III. ch. xxiii.

is on accessary to all the evils which ensue. The maxim, that *it is better ten villains should be discharged than a single person suffer by a wrong adjudication*, is one of those partial truths which are generally misapplied, because not accurately understood. It is certainly eligible that the rules and the forms of law should be so precise and immutable, as not to involve the innocent in any decision obtained by corruption, or dictated by passion and prejudice; though this should sometimes furnish an outlet for the escape of actual offenders. The plea, also, may have some validity, in crimes of a nature chiefly political, (with which, however, the faculty can [93] professionally have no concern,) such as coining and forgery, or in cases wherein the punishment much exceeds the evil or turpitude of the offence. For Lord Bacon has well observed, that "over great penalties, besides their acerbity, deaden the execution of the law."*

[Bottom page 94] * See proposal for amending the Laws of England. Bacon's Works, 4to. vol. ii. p. 542.

And when they are discovered to be unjustly inflicted, its authority is impaired; its sanctity dishonored; and veneration gives place to disgust and abhorrence.

But the dread of *innocent blood being brought upon us*, by explicit and honest testimony, is one of those superstitions which the nurse has taught, in which a liberal education ought to purge from the mind. And if, in the performance of our duty, innocence should unfortunately be involved in the punishment of guilt, we shall assuredly stand acquitted before God and our own consciousness. The convict himself, lamentable as his fate must be regarded, may console himself with the reflection, that, though his sentence be unjust, "he falls for his country, whilst he suffers under the operation of those rules, by the general effect and tendency of which the welfare of the community is maintained and upheld."† [94]

[bottom page 94] † Paley's Mor. and Polit. Phil. B. VI. ch. ix. p. 553. 4to.

XVIII. When professional testimony is required, in cases of such peculiar malignity as to excite general horror and indignation, a virtuous mind, even though scrupulous and timid, is liable to be influenced by too violent impressions; and to transfer to the accused that dread and aversion, which, before conviction, should be confined to the crime, and as much as possible withheld from the supposed offender. If the charge, for instance, be that of a parricide, accomplished by poison, and accompanied with deliberate malice, ingratitude, and cruelty; the investigation should be made with calm and unbiased precision, and the testimony delivered with no colouring of passion, nor with any deviation from *the simplicity of truth*. When *circumstantial proofs* are adduced, they should be arranged in the most lucid order, that they may be contrasted and compared, in all their various relations, with facility and accuracy; and that their weight may be separately and collectively determined in the balance of justice. For, in such evidence, there subsists a regular graduation from the slightest presumption to complete moral certainty. And if the witness possesses sufficient information in this branch of philosophical and juridical science, he will always be competent to secure himself, and, on many occasions, the court also, from fallacy and error. The Mar-[95]quis de Beccaria has laid down the following excellence theorems, concerning judicial evidence: "When the proofs of a crime are dependant on each other, that is, when the evidence of each witness, taken separately, proves nothing; or when all the proofs are dependant upon one, the number of proofs neither increases nor diminishes the probability of the fact; for the force of the whole is no greater than the force of those on which they depend; and if this fails, they all fall to the ground. When the proofs are independant of each other, the probability of the fact increases in proportion to the number of proofs; for the falsehood of one does not diminish the veracity of another.....The proofs of a crime may be divided into two classes, perfect and imperfect. I call those perfect, which exclude the possibility of innocence; imperfect, those which do not exclude this possibility. Of the first, one only is sufficient for condemnation; of the second, as many are required as form a perfect proof; that is to say, each of these, separately taken, does not exclude the possibility of innocence; it is nevertheless excluded by their union.*

[Bottom page 96] * Beccaria's Essay on Crimes and Punishment, chap. xiv.

AN

APPENDIX

A DISCOURSE,

ADDRESSED TO THE

GENTLEMEN OF THE FACULTY;

THE OFFICERS;

THE CLERGY; AND THE TRUSTEES OF THE INFIRMARY

AT LIVERPOOL,

ON THEIR RESPECTIVE HOSPITAL DUTIES,

BEING AN

ANNIVERSARY SERMON

Preached in May 1791, before the GOVERNORS of the INSTITUION.

For the Benefit of the Charity

BY THE

Rev. THOMAS BASSNETT PERCIVAL, LL. B.

Of Saint John's College, Cambridge; Chaplain to the Marquis of Waterford; to the Company of British Merchants, and to the Embassy, at Saint Petersburg. [not paginated: 1]

...."LO! A GOODLY HOSPITAL ASCENDS,

IN WHICH THEY BADE EACH LENIENT AID BE NIGH,

THAT COULD THE SICK-BED SMOOTH OF THAT SAD COMPANY.

IT WAS A WORTHY EDIFYING SIGHT,

AND GIVES TO HUMAN KIND PECULIAR GRACE,

TO SEE KIND HANDS ATTENDING DAY AND NIGHT,

WITH TENDER MINISTRY, FROM PLACE TO PLACE:

SOME PROP THE HEAD; SOME, FROM THE PALLID FACE,

WIPE OFF THE FAINT COLD DEWS WEAK NATURE SHEDS;

SOME REACH THE HEALING DRAUGHT; THE WHILST TO

    CHACE

THE FEAR SUPREME, AROUND THEIR SOFTENED BEDS,

SOME HOLY MAN BY PRAYER ALL OPENING HEAVEN DISPREDS."

Thomson's Castle of Indolence; Canto II. [not paginated: 2]

A

DISCOURSE

ADDRESSED TO THE

GENTLEMEN OF THE FACULTY;

THE OFFICERS;

THE CLERGY; AND THE TRUSTEES OF THE INFIRMARY,

AT LIVERPOOL

ON THEIR RESPECTIVE HOSPITAL DUTIES;

By the Rev. THOMAS B. PERCIVAL, LL.B. &c.

Let us not be weary in well doing, for in due season we shall reap if we faint not. – Galations vi.

9.

IF we consider the circumstances of man, as placed in this great theatre of action; as connected with his fellow-creatures by various ties and relations; and with God himself, his creator and judge: If we consider the powers and faculties with which he is endowed, and that these are talents committed to his trust, capable of indefinite degrees of improvement, and which the Lord, at his coming, will demand with usury; we shall see the fullest reason for the apostolical injunction, *be not weary in well doing*; and rejoice in the assurance, that *in due season we shall reap, if we faint not*. The sphere of human duty has no limits to its extent. Every advance [not paginated: 3] in knowledge widens its boundaries; every increase of power and wealth multiplies and diversifies the objects of it; and length of years evinces their unceasing succession. Therefore, W*hatsoever thy hand findeth to do, do it with all thy might*. Vigour and perseverance are essential to every noble pursuit; and no virtuous effort is in vain. To be discouraged by opposition; to be alarmed by danger; or overcome by difficulty, is a state of mind unfitted for the christian warfare.

But the present interesting occasion calls for a specific application of the precept, contained in our text. What is just and true, concerning the whole duty of man, must be equally just and true of every individual branch of moral and religious obligation. And it can require no deep research, no abstruse investigation, to work conviction on our minds, that the higher is the object we have in view, the more active and incessant should be our exertions in the attainment of it. The institution, which now claims your most serious attention, is founded on the *wisest policy*; adapted to the noblest purposes of *humanity*; and capable of being rendered subservient to the *everlasting welfare* of mankind.

The *wisdom* of such charitable foundations can admit of no dispute. On the lower classes of our [4] fellow-citizens alone, we depend for food, for raiment, for the habitations in which we dwell, and for all the conveniences and comforts of life. But health is essential to their capacity for labour; and in this labour, I fear, it is too often sacrificed. An additional obligation, therefore, to afford relief, springs from so affecting a consideration. He, who at once toils and suffers for our benefit, has a multiplied claim to our support; and to withhold it would be equally chargeable with folly, ingratitude, and injustice.

But *humanity* prompts, when the still voice of wisdom is not heard. Sickness, complicated with poverty, has pleas, that, to a feeling mind are irresistible. *To weep with those that weep* was the character of our divine master; and, to the honour of our nature, we are capable of the same generous sympathy. Vain and idle, however, are the softest emotions of the mind, when they lead not to correspondent actions. And he who views the naked, without clothing them, and those who are sick, without ministering unto them, incurs the dreadful denunciation, *Depart from me, ye cursed, into everlasting fire, prepared for the devil and his angels. For in as much as ye did it not to one of the least of these my brethren, ye did it not unto me* [5].

It were an easy and pleasing task to enlarge on these general topics. But they come not sufficiently "home to men's business and bosoms." And honoured as I am, by being thus called to the privilege of addressing you, I feel it incumbent on me to be more appropriate, by suggesting to your candid attention, the distinct and relative duties attached to the several orders, which compose this most excellent community. Permit me, therefore, to claim your indulgence, whilst I offer, with all deference and respect, but with the plainness and freedom of gospel sincerity, a few words of exhortation,

I. TO THE FACULTY;
II. TO THE OFFICERS AND SUPERINTENDANTS;
III. TO THE CLERGY;
   And lastly, TO THE GENERAL BODY OF TRUSTEES AND CONTRIBUTORS.

I. TO THE FACULTY. As man is placed by Divine Providence in a situation which involves a variety of interests and duties, often complicated in mixed together, the motives which influence human actions must necessarily be mixed and complicated. And wisdom and virtue consist in the selection of those which are fit and good, and in the arrangement of all, by a just appre-[6]ciation of their comparative dignity and importance. In the acceptance of your professional offices, in this infirmary, it is presumed that you have been governed by the *love of reputation*; by the *desire of acquiring knowledge and experience*; and by that *spirit of philanthropy*, which delights in, and is never weary of well doing. Let us briefly consider each of these principles of action, and how they ought to be regulated.

If we analyze the *love of reputation*, as it exists in liberal and well-informed minds, it will be found to spring from the love of moral and intellectual excellence. For of what value is praise, when not founded on desert? But the consciousness of desert, by the constitution of our nature, is ever attended with self-approbation: And this delightful emotion, which is at once the concomitant and the reward of virtue, widely expands its operation, and by a social sympathy, encircles all who are the witness or judges of our generous deeds. From the same principle, piety itself derives its origin. For how shall he who loveth not, or is regardless of the approbation of his brother, whom he hath seen, love or regard the favour of God, whom he hath not seen! [7]

But let us remember, not to substitute for the legitimate and magnanimous love of fame, that spurious and sordid passion, which seeks applause by gratifying the caprices, by indulging the prejudices, and by imposing on the follies of mankind. To court the public favour by adulation, or empirical arts, is meanness and hypocrisy; to claim it by high and assumed pretensions, is arrogance and pride; and to exalt our own character, by the deprecation of that of our competitor, is to convert honourable emulation into professional enmity and injustice.

You have been elevated by the suffrages of your fellow-citizens: You have been honoured by their favour and confidence: Rejoice in the distinction conferred upon you; fulfil with assiduity and zeal the trust reposed in you; and by being unwearied in well doing, rise to higher and higher degrees of public favour and celebrity!

The *acquisition of knowledge and experience* is a farther incentive to your generous exertions, in this receptacle of disease and misery. It is one important design of the institution itself; which affords peculiar advantages for ascertaining the operation of remedies, and the comparative merit of different modes of medical and chirurgical treatment. For the strict rules which are en-[8]joined; the steadiness with which their observance is enforced; and the unremitting attendance of those who are qualified to make accurate observations, and to note every symptom, whether regular or anomalous, in the diseases under cure, are circumstances incompatible with the ordinary domestic care of the sick. To avail yourselves of them, therefore, is agreeable to sound policy and consonant to the purest justice and humanity. For every improvement in the healing art is a public good, beneficial to the poor as well as to the rich, and to the former in a proportionably greater degree, as they are more numerous, and consequently more frequently the objects of it. On this point, however, peculiar delicacy is required; and as the discretionary power, with which you are entrusted, is almost without controul, it should be exercised what the nicest honour and probity. When novelties in practice are introduced, be careful that they are conformable to reason and analogy; that no sacrifice be made to fanciful hypothesis, or experimental curiosity; that the infliction of pain or suffering be, as much as possible, avoided; and that the end in view fully warrant the means for its attainment.

But your noblest call to duty and exertion arises from the exalted *spirit of philanthropy*: And [9] on this occasion I may address you individually, in the language of the first of orators to the sovereign of imperial Rome: *Nihil habet fortuna tua majus quam ut possis, nec natura melius quam ut velis, servare quam-plurimos*. It is your honour and felicity to be engaged in an occupation which leads you, like our blessed Lord during his abode on earth, to go about doing good, healing the sick, and curing all manner of diseases. To you learning has opened her stores, that they may be applied to the sublimest purposes; to alleviate pain; to raise the drooping head; to renew the roses of the cheek, and the sparkling of the eye; and thus to gladden, whilst you lengthen life. Let this hospital be the theatre on which you display, with assiduous and persevering care, your science, skill, and humanity: And let the manner correspond with, and even heighten, the measure of your benevolence. With patience hear the tale of symptoms; silence not harshly the murmurs of a troubled mind; and by the kindness of your looks and words, evince that christian condescension may be compatible with professional steadiness and dignity.

It is, I trust, an ill-founded opinion, that compassion is not the virtue of a surgeon. This branch of the profession has been charged [10] with hardness of heart: And some of its members have formerly justified the stigma, by ridiculing all softness of manners by assuming the contrary deportment; and by studiously banishing from their minds that sympathy, which they falsely supposed would be unsuitable to their character, and unfavourable to the practical exercise of their art. But different sentiments now prevail. And a distinction should ever be made between true compassion, and that unmanly pity which enfeebles the mind; which shrinks from the sight of woe; which inspires timidity; and deprives him, who is under its influence, of all capacity to give relief. Genuine compassion rouses the attention of the soul; gives energy to all its powers; suggests expedients in danger; incites to vigorous action in difficulty; and strengthens the hand to execute, with promptitude, the purposes of the head. The pity which you should repress is a turbulent emotion. The commiseration which you should cultivate, is a calm principle. It is benevolence itself directed forcibly to a specific object. And the frequency of such objects diminishes not, but augments its energy: For it produces a tone or constitution of mind, constantly in unison with suffering; and prepared, on every call, to afford the full measure of relief. Appear, therefore, to your patients to be actuated by that fellow feeling, which na-[11]ture, education, and christianity require. Make their cases, in a reasonable degree, your own; *and whatsoever ye would that men should do unto you, do ye even so unto them.*

II. To you, the OFFICERS and SUPERINTENDANTS of this hospital, we may justly ascribe views the most pure and public-spirited. But zeal in the cause of charity, however sincere, can only be rendered usefully efficient by due attention to, and steady perseverance in, the wisest means for its accomplishment. On the mistaken humanity of crowding your wards with numerous patients, by which disease is generated, and death multiplied in all its horrors; on the fatal calculations of savings in medicines, diet, or clothing; and on a strict attention to ventilation, cleanliness, and all the domestic arrangements, which have order, utility, or comfort for their objects; I trust it is needless to enlarge. But you will suffer me, I hope, to offer a few hints on the *moral* and *religious* application of the institution which you govern; a topic hitherto little noticed, though of high importance.

The visitation of sickness is a wise and kind dispensation of Providence, intended to humble, to refine, and to meliorate the heart. And its salutary influence extends beyond the sufferer, to [12] those relatives and friends, whose office it is to minister unto him; exciting tenderness and commiseration; drawing closer the bonds of affection; and rousing to exertions, virtuous in their nature, profitable to man, and well-pleasing to God. A parent, soothed and supported under the anguish of pain, by the loving kindness of his children; a husband nursed with unwearied assiduity by the partner of his bed; a child experiencing all the tenderness of paternal and maternal love, are situations which form the ground-work of domestic virtue, and domestic felicity. They leave indelible impressions on the mind, impressions which exalt the moral character, and render us better men, better citizens, and better christians. It is wisdom, therefore, and duty, not to frustrate the benevolent constitutions of Heaven, by dissolving the salutary connections of sickness, and transporting into a public asylum those who may, with a little aid, enjoy in their own homes, benefits and consolations which, elsewhere, it is in the power of no one to confer.

But numerous are the sufferers under sickness and poverty, to whom your hospitable doors may be opened, with the highest moral benefit to themselves and to the community. When admitted within these walls, they form one great family, of which you are the heads, and conse-[13]quently responsible for all due attention to their present behavior, and to the means of their future improvement. Withdrawn from the habitations of penury, sloth, and dirtiness; from the conversation of the loose and the profligate; and from all their associates in vice, they may here form a taste for the sweets of cleanliness; learn the power of bridling their tongues; and be induced, by this temporary absence, to free themselves from all farther connection with their idle and debauched companions. Let it be your sedulous care to foster these excellent tendencies: Encourage in the patients every attention to neatness: Tolerate no filth or slovenliness, either in their persons or attire: Keep a strict guard on the decency of their behaviour: Urge them to active offices of kindness and compassion to each other: Furnish the convalescents with bibles, and with books of plain morality, and practical piety, suited to their capacities and circumstances; and which will neither delude the imagination, nor perplex the understanding: Oblige them to a regular attendance on the public worship of the hospital, or of their respective churches: And, agreeably to your laws, neglect not to make provision for the stated and frequent in administration of the holy sacrament. There is something in this office peculiarly adapted to comfort and fortify the mind, under the pressure [14] of poverty, pain, and sickness. In the contemplation of that love, which Christ manifested for us by his sufferings and death, all the consolation is experienced which divine sympathy can afford. *We have a high priest touched with the feeling of our infirmities*, and who holds forth to us this soothing invitation; *Come unto me, all Ye that are weary and heavy laden, and I will give you rest*. Promote the celebration of an ordinance, adapted thus to fill the mind with gratitude, and to alleviate every woe. And let the example of our Saviour's resignation to the appointments of God be enforced by it, who in his agony exclaimed, *Father, if it be thy will, let this cup pass from me, nevertheless not my will, but thine be done*.

III. I doubt not the cordial an entire concurrence of you, my REV. BRETHREN, the CLERGY who officiate in this hospital, in the recommendation of the holy sacrament, not only as a stated, but as a frequent ordinance of the institution. With you it will rest to obviate every objection to the rite, and to give it the full measure of spiritual efficacy. Enthusiasm and superstition cannot be dreaded in the offices of rational piety, conducted by those who are rational and pious. And you will neither betray men into false confidence, nor alarm them, when [15] languishing under sickness and pain, with unseasonable terrors. *The spirit of a man may sustain his infirmities, but a wounded spirit who can bear*? Under such circumstances, vain will be the aid of skill or medicine, without the supports and comforts, which it is your sacred function to afford. You can

------ "minister to a mind diseased; Pluck from the memory a rooted sorrow, Raze out the written troubles of the brain, And, with some sweet oblivious antidote, Cleanse the full bosom of that perilous stuff Which weighs upon the heart." (SHAKESPEARE)

Being thus the *Physicians* of the soul, you are essential constituents of this enlarged system of philanthropy. Apply, therefore, with diligence and zeal, the spiritual *medicines* which it is your office to dispense. Here you have a wide field *for exhortation , for correction, and for instruction in righteousness*. Convalescence peculiarly furnishes the *mollia tempora fandi*, the soft seasons of impressive counsel. The mind is then open to serious conviction; disposed to review past offences with contrition; and to look forward with sincere resolutions of amendment. Many diseases are the immediate consequences of vice: And he who has recently experienced the suffer-[16]ings of guilt, will deeply feel its enormity; and cherish those precepts, which will secure him from relapse, and convert his past misery into future blessings.

Lastly. But this large aggregate of good, which it is the design of the present anniversary to commemorate, depends, for its support and extension, on the GENERAL BODY OF CONTRIBUTORS TO THE CHARITY. How deeply interesting, then, are the claims, which your fellow-citizens have to make on your philanthropy! How important is it to the health of thousands, in rapid succession, that you should persevere in beneficence, and continue unwearied in well doing! Ordinary bounty terminates almost in the moment when it is bestowed. The object of it being withdrawn, solicitude and responsibility are no more. But in this noble institution, charity exerts itself in the steady and unceasing operations. It is a stream ever full, yet ever flowing; and through the grace of God, I trust, will be inexhaustible. From your zeal, your concord, and liberality, these SACRED *waters of life* proceed. Be watchful that they are not poisoned in their source, nor contaminated in their progress. Let your *zeal* be employed in searching out, and recommending proper objects of relief. *Call to you*, according to the injunction of our [17] Saviour, *the halt, and the maimed, the lame, and the blind; for they cannot recompense you: Ye shall be recompensed at the resurrection of just.* Suffer no prejudices, either political or religious, to contract the bounds of your charity. *Pass not by, on the other side, from a fellow-creature who has fallen amongst thieves*, because he is not of your party, of your sect, or even of your nation. But, like the good Samaritan, *have compassion on him, and let oil and wine be poured upon his wounds*, in this hospitable *Bethesda*. Guard, most sedulously guard, against the spirits of dissension. You are united in the labours of christian love; and having one common and glorious cause, the contest should be for pre-eminence in doing good, not for the gratification of pride, the indulgence of resentment, or even the interests of friendship.

To your liberality in contribution no appeal can be required, no new incitement can be urged. What your judgment approves; what experience has sanctioned; and what touches the tenderest feelings of your hearts, must have pleas that are irresistible.

It only remains, then, that we cordially unite in offering our devout supplications to the throne of grace, in behalf of all those *who are afflicted or distressed in mind, body, or estate; that* [18] *it may please the God of all consolation to relieve them, according to their several necessities; giving them patience under their sufferings, and they happy issue out of all their afflictions: And finally, that we will be delivered from all hardness of heart; from all covetous desires, and inordinate love of riches; and, having been taught that all our doings, without charity, profit nothing, that this most excellent gift, the bond of peace, and of all virtues, may be poured into us abundantly, through the merits and meditation of our blessed Lord and Saviour* [19].

[not paginated: 20]

ADVERTISEMENT

THE foregoing SERMON is inserted, by permission, as an APPENDIX to a work, which has long remained unfinished in the press, the prosecution of it having been suspended by the death of a beloved Son, for whose use it was peculiarly designed, who had nearly completed the course of his academical education, and whose talents, acquirements, and virtues, promised to render him an ornament to his profession. As it is uncertain when the author may resume his undertaking, he deems it necessary to apprize the friends, into whose hands this imperfect sketch may be delivered, that it was proposed, in a *fifth* SECTION, *to treat of the* POWERS, PRIVILEGES, HONOURS, *and* EMOLUMENTS *of the* FACULTY; *in a sixth* SECTION, *of the* MORAL, RELIGIOUS, *and* POLITICAL CHARACTER *of* PHYSICIANS, *and to subjoin to the whole*, NOTES *and* ILLUSTRATIONS.

MANCHESTER, *Feb.* 24, 1794

[not paginated: 21]

1803
Medical Ethics or, A Code of Institutes and Precepts, Adapted to the Professional Conduct of Physicians and Surgeons

Citation to Original Publication:

Percival, Thomas. 1803. *MEDICAL ETHICS OR, A CODE OF Institutes and Precepts,*

ADAPTED TO THE PROFESSIONAL CONDUCT OF PHYSICIANS AND SURGEONS: I: In Hospital Practice. II: In Private or General Practice. III: In relation to Apothecaries. IV: In Cases which may require a Knowledge of Law. To which is added, An Appendix; CONATAINING A DISCOURSE ON HOSPITAL DUTIES; ALSO, NOTES AND ILLUSTRATIONS. BY THOMAS PERCIVAL, M.D. F.R.S.AND A.S. LOND, F.R.S AND B.M.S. EDINB &c. &e. Manchester: Printed by S. Russell, for J. Johnson, St, Paul's Church Yard, and R. Bickerstaff, Strand, London.

Citation to Publication in this Volume:

Percival, Thomas. [1803] 2022. *MEDICAL ETHICS OR, A CODE OF Institutes and Precepts,*

ADAPTED TO THE PROFESSIONAL CONDUCT OF PHYSICIANS AND SURGEONS: I: In Hospital Practice. II: In Private or General Practice. III: In relation to Apothecaries. IV: In Cases which may require a Knowledge of Law. To which is added, An Appendix; CONATAINING A DISCOURSE ON HOSPITAL DUTIES; ALSO, NOTES AND ILLUSTRATIONS. BY THOMAS PERCIVAL, M.D. F.R.S.AND A.S. LOND, F.R.S AND B.M.S. EDINB &c. &e. Manchester: Printed by S. Russell, for J. Johnson, St, Paul's Church Yard, and R. Bickerstaff, Strand, London. In McCullough, Laurence B. 2022. Thomas Percival's *Medical Ethics* and the Invention of Medical Professionalism: With Three Key Percival Texts, Two Concordances, and a Chronology: 336–434. New York: Springer.

MEDICAL ETHICS

OR, A CODE OF

INSTITUTES AND PRECEPTS,

ADAPTED TO THE

PROFESSIONAL CONDUCT

OF

PHYSICIANS AND SURGEONS

[Not paginated: i]

NULLA ENIM VITÆ PARS, NEQUE PUBLICIS, NEQUE PRIVATIS, NEQUE FORENSIBUS, NEQUE DOMESTICIS IN REBUS, NEQUE SI TECUM AGAS QUID, NEQUE SI CUM ALTERO CONTRAHAS, VACARE OFFICIO POTEST: IN EOQUE COLENDO SITA VITÆ EST HONESTAS OMNIS, ET IN NEGLIGENDO TURPITUDO.

CIC. de Off. Lib. I. Cap. II

["For no phase of life, whether public or private, whether in business or in the home, whether one is working on what concerns oneself alone or dealing with another, can be without its moral duty; on the discharge of such duties depends all that is morally right, and in their neglect all that is morally wrong in life" (Cicero 1913, 7).]

[not paginated: ii]

MEDICAL ETHICS

OR, A CODE OF

Institutes and Precepts,

ADAPTED TO THE

PROFESSIONAL CONDUCT

OF

PHYSICIANS AND SURGEONS:

I: In Hospital Practice.

II: In Private or General Practice.

III: In relation to Apothecaries.

IV: In Cases which may require a Knowledge of Law.

To which is added,

An Appendix;

containing

A DISCOURSE ON HOSPITAL DUTIES;

ALSO,

NOTES AND ILLUSTRATIONS.

BY

THOMAS PERCIVAL, M.D.

F.R.S. AND A.S. LOND, F.R.S AND R.M.S. EDINB &c. &e.

Manchester:

PRINTED BY S. RUSSELL,

FOR J. JOHNSON, ST, PAUL'S CHURCH-YARD, AND

R. BICKERSTAFF, STRAND, LONDON,

1803

[not paginated; iii]

[not paginated: iv is blank]

TO

SIR GEORGE BAKER, BART.

PHYSICIAN TO THEIR MAJESTIES;

FELLOW OF THE ROYAL SOCIETY;

AND

LATE PRESIDENT OF THE COLLEGE OF PHYSICIANS;

&c. &c.

THIS CODE OF

PROFESSIONAL ETHICS;

WHICH HE HAS

HONOURED WITH HIS SANCTION,

AND IMPROVED BY HIS COMMUNICATIONS,

IS GRATEFULLY AND RESPECTFULLY

INSCRIBED,

BY HIS

OBLIGED AND AFFECTIONATE FRIEND,

THE AUTHOR.

[not paginated: v]

[not paginated: vi is blank]

TO

E.C. PERCIVAL.

PERMIT me, my dear son, to offer to your acceptance this little Manual of MEDICAL ETHICS. In the composition of it, my thoughts were directed towards your late excellent Brother, with the tenderest impulse of paternal love: And not a single moral rule was framed without a secret view to his designation; and an anxious wish that it might influence his future conduct.

To you, who possess, in no inferior degree, my esteem and attachment; who are prosecuting [vii] the same studies, and with the same object; my solicitudes are naturally transferred. And I am persuaded, these united considerations will powerfully and permanently operate upon your ingenuous mind.

It is the characteristic of a wise man to act on determinate principles; and of a good man to be assured that they are conformable to rectitude and virtue. The relations in which a physician stands to his patients, to his brethren, and to the public, are complicated, and multifarious; involving much knowledge of human nature, and extensive moral duties. The study of professional Ethics, therefore, cannot fail to invigorate and enlarge your understanding; whilst [viii] the observance of the duties which they enjoin, will soften your manners, expand your affections, and form you to that propriety and dignity of conduct, which are essential to the character of a GENTLEMAN. The academical advantages you have enjoyed at Cambridge, and those you now possess in Edinburgh, will qualify you, I trust, for an ample and honourable sphere of action. And I devoutly pray, that the blessing of God may attend all your pursuits; rendering them at once subservient to your own felicity, and the good of your fellow-creatures.

Sensible that I begin to experience that pressure of advancing years, I regard the present publi-[ix]cation as the conclusion, in this way, of my professional labours. I may, therefore, without impropriety, claim the privilege of consecrating them to you, as a paternal legacy. And I feel cordial satisfaction in the occasion, of thus testifying the esteem and tenderness with which, whilst life subsists, I shall remain.

Your affectionate friend,
THOMAS PERCIVAL.
Manchester, February 20, 1803.
[x]

CONTENTS

N.B. The Roman Numerals refer to the Sections, and the Figures to the Pages.
PREFACE-Origin of the work.-Suspension of it.-Farther progress of it. – Addition of supplementary notes and illustrations......................…................... 1–7
CHAP. I. *Of professional conduct relative to hospital or other medical charities.*

> Duties of hospital physicians and surgeons.-Tenderness.-Steadiness.-Condescension.-Authority. I.-Choice of their attendant physician or surgeon, how far allowable to hospital patients. II.-Feelings and emotions of patients, under critical circumstances, to be duly regarded. III.-No discussion concerning the nature of their case to be entered into before them. IV.-Delicacy in many cases particularly required; and secrecy sometimes to be strictly observed. V.-Moral and religious influence of sickness to be cherished and promoted. VI.-Propriety of suggesting to patients, under certain circumstances, the importance of making their last will and testament. VII.-Parsimony in prescribing wine and drugs of high price reprobated. VIII.-Hospital affairs and occurrences not to be incautiously revealed. IX.-Professional charges to be made only before meeting of the faculty. X.-Proper discrimination between

the medical and chirurgical cases to be strictly adhered to. XI.-What circumstances authorize new remedies and new methods of chirurgical treatment. XII.-Unreserved intercourse [xi] should subsist between the gentlemen of the faculty; and an account of every case or operation which is rare, curious, or instructive, should be regularly drawn up and preserved. XIII.-Scheme for hospital registers. XIV.-Advantages arising from the scheme. XV.-Close and crowded wards reprobated. XVI.-Establishment of a committee of the gentlemen of the faculty considered. XVII.-Importance of frequent consultations, and the mutual assistance of the physicians and surgeons. XVIII.-Rules to be observed in consultations. XIX.-Rules to be observed respecting operations. XX.-Hospital consultations ought not to be held on Sundays, except in cases urgent necessity. XXI.-Stated days for operations, often inconvenient and improper. XXII.-Dispensaries. XXIII.-Asylums for female patients labouring under syphilis. -Rules to be observed in lock hospitals. XXIV.-Asylums for insanity. XXV.-Mode of acquiring knowledge in the treatment of insanity recommended. XXVI.-Treatment of lunatics-tenderness-indulgence. XXVII.-Boldness of practice sometimes required in cases of mania. -Hospitals for small-pox – Inoculation, &c. &c. require no professional duties not already enumerated. XXVIII.

CHAP II. *Of professional conduct in private, or general practice.*

Moral rules of conduct, the same with those to be observed towards hospital-patients. I.-The strictest temperance required. II.-Proper conduct to be observed respecting prognostications, and the disclosure of circumstances, to the friends of the patients. III.-Proper conduct respecting interference in cases under the charge of another. IV.-Conduct to be observed towards a physician formerly employed by the patient, [xii] but not now consulted. V.-Distinction between the provinces of physic and surgery to be steadily maintained. VI.-Consultations to be promoted in difficult or protracted cases. VII.-Special consultation. -Conduct of the physician called in. VIII.-Theoretical discussions to be avoided in consultations. IX.-Rules for consultations the same with those prescribed to the faculty attending hospitals. -Seniority, how determined. X.-Education of medical men-what influence it ought to have in the confederation of their brethren. XI.-Punctuality of visits of consultation-further rules to be observed. XII.-Visits to the sick not to be unseasonably repeated. XIII.-Rules to be observed with regard to fees, when a physician officiates in the absence, or at the request, of another. XIV.-Importance of adopting some general rule respecting pecuniary acknowledgments. XV.-Medical men and their families, when to be attended gratuitously. XVI.-Peculiar delicacy and attention often required in attendance upon them. XVII.-Attendance on clergymen in narrow circumstances. XVIII.-Consultation by letter. XIX.-Rules to be observed in furnishing certificates. XX.-Use of quack medicines discouraged. XXI.-The dispensing of nostrums reprobated, XXII.-Duty incumbent on individuals to promote the general reputation of the faculty collectively. XXIII.-Rule to be observed in professional controversy and contention. XXIV.-Giving advice gratis. XXV.-Rule to be observed in visiting the patient of another physician. XXVI.-Another case of the same. XXVII.-Review of the treatment and progress of interesting cases recommended. XXVIII.-Moral and religious advice to patients. XXIX.-Observance of the Sabbath, by medical gentlemen, considered. XXX.-Cooperation of young [xiii] and aged practitioners. XXXI.-Period of senescence in physicians considered. XXXII.

CHAP III. *Of the conduct of physicians to apothecaries.*

Connection between the apothecary and physician. I.-Apothecary often precursor to the physician, and commonly acquainted with the diseases of the family. II.-Rule to be observed in the intercourse and co-operation of the physician and apothecary. III.- Duty and responsibility of the physician. IV.- Particular directions to be observed in visiting country patients with the apothecary. V.-Profits of apothecaries. VI.- Physicians visiting the patients of apothecaries, in their absence, not approved of. VII.-Duty of apothecaries in recommending physicians to families. VIII.- Establishment of funds for the benefit of the widows, and children of apothecaries. IX

CHAP IV. *Of professional duties in certain cases which require a knowledge of law.*

Medical gentlemen exempt from serving on inquests, juries, &c; but frequently called upon to exercise duties which require juridical knowledge. I.-Duty of physicians in cases of last will and testament-knowledge of law required. II.-Commissions of lunacy-appointment of a curator. III.-Treatment of lunatics as authorized by law. IV.-Asylums for lunatics subject to strict regulations of law. V.-Opinions given in cases of sudden death. VI.-Justifiable homicide. VII.-Excusable homicide. VIII.-Suicide. IX.-Manslaughter-Murder. X.-Murder of bastard children. XI.-Duelling. XII.-Duty of surgeons with respect to attending a duellist to the field of combat. XIII.-Private and personal duty of physicians with respect to duel-true honour considered. XIV.-Homicide by poison – cases adduced. XV.-Law in cases of rape. [xiv] XVI.- Nuisances defined and considered. XVII.-Duty of medical gentlemen, when summoned to attend coroners, magistrates, and judges. XVIII.-Importance to gentlemen of the faculty of settling their opinions concerning the right of magistrates to inflict capital punishment. -The limits prescribed to the exercise of the right; and the duty of giving full efficacy to law. XIX.-Cautions relative to professional testimony in cases of peculiar malignity. XX

A Discourse on Hospital Duties

Addresses.-I. To the faculty, p. 120. II.-To the officers and superintendants, p. 126. III.-To the clergy, p. 130. – IV. To the trustees of the Infirmary of Liverpool, p. 132.

Notes and Illustrations

I.	Hospital of Manchester...	133
II.	Distribution of printed copies of the Medical Ethics......................	139
III.	Situation, construction, and government of hospitals............	140
IV.	House of reception for patients ill of contagious fevers................	147
V.	Caution of temerity in practice.	152
VI.	Temperance of physicians...	154
VII.	A physician should be the minister of hope and comfort to the sick. -Enquiry, how far it is justifiable to violate truths or the supposed benefit of the patient.	156
VIII.	The practice of prior physicians should be treated with candour, and justified so far as truth and probity will permit.	168
IX.	Theoretical discussions should be generally avoided..................	169

[xv]

X.	Regular academical education...	170
XI.	Pecuniary acknowledgments..	174
XII.	Public worship; scepticism and infidelity................................	179
XIII.	Union and consultation of senior and junior physicians	200
XIV.	Retirement from practice-when-Letters from Dr. Heberden; and Sir G. Baker, Bart.	201
XV.	Partial insanity with general intelligence-Lucid interval...............	206
XVI.	Duelling-Letter from Dr. Franklin...	214
XVII.	Punishment of the crime of rape. -Disney's views of ancient laws against immorality, &c. Eden's principles of penal law.	228
XVIII.	Uncertainty in the external signs of rape-Communication from Mr. Ward.	231
XIX.	The smoke from large works, nuisance-Coalbrook-Dale...............	234
XX.	Discourse on Hospital Duties; by the Rev. T. B. Percival, LL B. -Brief memoirs of him.	238
XXI.	The salutary connections of sickness not to be rashly dissolved. -Cautions concerning the removal of patients into an hospital. -Extracts from the Memoirs of the Rev. Newcome Cappe................	239
XXII.	Duty of hospital trustees in electing the medical officers of the charity. -Advertisement of the governors of the Salisbury Infirmary. .-Memorial to the trustees of the Manchester Infirmary.	243

ERRATA

Reference to Note VII. wanting - Page	32
For *guilt* manslaughter – read *of* – line 10 - - - - - - - - - - - - - - - - - - -	78
For Note XVII – read Note XVI. -	93
For Note XVI – read Note XVII. -	99
For Note XVII – read XVIII. -	103

For *or* – read *for* – line 26 -   163
For *decripitude* – read *decrepitude* – line 4 - - - - - - - - - - - - - - - - -   197
[xvi]

PREFACE

THE first chapter of the following work was composed in the spring of 1792, at the request of the physicians and surgeons of the Manchester Infirmary: And the substance of it constitutes the code of laws, by which the practice of that comprehensive institution in now governed. (a)
[bottom page 1] (a) See Notes and Illustrations, No. I.
The author was afterwards induced, by an earnest desire to promote the honour and advancement of his profession, to enlarge the plan of his undertaking, and to frame a general system of MEDICAL ETHICS; that the official conduct, and mutual intercourse of the faculty, might be regulated by precise and acknowledged principles of urbanity and rectitude. Printed copies of the scheme were, therefore, distributed amongst his numerous correspon-[not paginated 1]dents; by most of whom it was warmly encouraged; and by many of them was honoured with valuable suggestions for its improvement. (b)
[bottom page 2] (b) See Notes and Illustrations, No. II.
Whilst the author was thus extending his views, and carrying on his work with ardour, he lost the strongest incentive to its prosecution, by death of a beloved son, who had nearly completed the course of his academical education; and whose talents, acquirements, and virtues, promised to render him an ornament to the healing art. This melancholy event was followed, not many years afterwards, by a second family loss, equally afflictive; and the design has ever since been wholly suspended. The author now resumes it, animated by the hope that it may prove beneficial to another son, who has lately exchanged the pursuits of general science at Cambridge, for the study of medicine at Edinburgh. He feels at the same time, impressed with the conviction, that the [2] languor of sorrow becomes culpable, when it obstructs the offices of an active vocation. "I hold every man," says Lord Bacon, in the preface to his Elements of the Common Laws of England, "a debtor to his profession; from the which as men of course do seek to receive countenance and profit, so ought they of duty to endeavor themselves, by way of amends, to be a help and ornament thereunto. This is preformed, in some degree, by the honest and liberal practice of a profession; when men shall carry a respect not to descend into any course that is corrupt and unworthy thereof; and preserve themselves free from the abuses wherewith the same profession is noted to be infected: But much more is this performed,

if a man be able to visit and strengthen the roots and foundation of the science itself; thereby not only gracing it in reputation and dignity, but also amplifying it in profession and substance." [3]

It was the author's original intention to have treated of the POWERS, PRIVILEGES, HONOURS, and EMOLUMENTS of the FACULTY. But he now conceives, that this would lead him into a field of investigation too wide and digressive; and therefore chooses to confine himself to what more strictly belongs to Medical Ethics.

To these institutes he has annexed an Anniversary Discourse, delivered by the late Rev. Thomas Bassnett Percival, LL. B. before the president, and governors of the Infirmary, at Liverpool. As it is and address to the gentlemen of the faculty, the officers, the clergy, and the trustees of the charity, on their respective hospital duties, by one competent to the subject from his early studies, it cannot but be deemed sufficiently appropriate to the present work, exclusively of a father's claim to privilege of its insertion.

The aphoristic form of this code of Medial Ethics, though adapted to such an undertaking, forbids in a great measure, all di-[4]gression; and even precludes the discussion of many interesting points, nearly connected with the subject. SUPPLEMENTARY NOTES AND ILLUSTRATIONS, therefore, are necessary to the completion of the author's plan: And he trusts the candid reader will grant him the liberty of thus stating his opinions more at large; of rectifying misconceptions, to which the brevity essential to the work may give rise; and of correcting whatever subsequent reflection, or the judicious observations of his friends, may discover to be erroneous.

A considerable portion of these sheets was communicated to the Rev. THOMAS GISBORNE, M. A. whilst engaged in the composition of his ENQUIRY into the DUTIES of MEN; a work that reflects the highest honour on the abilities and philanthropy of the author; and which may be justly regarded as the most complete system extant of PRACTICAL ETHICS. The chapter concerning physicians contains a reference to these institutes, ex-[5]pressed in the most gratifying terms of friendship: And it treats so largely of the duties of the faculty, as to seem, at first view, to supersede the use of the present manual. But the two publications differ not only in their plan, but in many of their leading objects; and it may be hoped they will rather illustrate than interfere with each other. The same remarks may be applied to the excellent lectures of Dr, Gregory. Even the STATUTA MORALIA of the college of physicians, whatever merit or authority they possess, are not sufficiently comprehensive for the existing sphere of medical and chirurgical duty: And by the few regulations which they establish, they tacitly sanction the recommendation of a fuller and more adequate code of professional offices.

Copies of the former unfinished impression of this work have been transmitted to the libraries of several Infirmaries, in different parts of the kingdom: And the author has reason to hope, that they have contributed to excite [6] attention to the subject of hospital police. Amongst other pleasing proofs of this truth, he refers with peculiar satisfaction to the late publications of his friends, Sir G. O. Paul, Bart. and Dr. Clark, of Newcastle-upon-Tyne.

This work was originally entitled, "MEDICAL JURISPRUDENCE"; but some friends having objected to the term JURISPRUDENCE, it has been changed to ETHICS. According to the definition of Justinian, however, Jurisprudence may be understood to include moral injunctions as well as positive ordinances. *Juris præcepta sunt hæc honeste vivere; alterum non lædere; suum cuique tribuere.-* INST. JUSTIN: Lib. I. p. 3.

Manchester, Feb. 15, 1803. [7]

-QUICQUID DIGNUM SAPIENTE BONO-QUE EST.

Hor. Lib. I. Ep. IV. [not paginated: 8]

MEDICAL ETHICS;

OR,

A CODE OF INSTITUTES AND PRECEPTS,

ADAPTED TO THE

PROFESSIONAL CONDUCT

OF

PHYSICIANS AND SURGEONS.

CHAPTER I.
OF PROFESSIONAL CONDUCT, RELATIVE TO HOSPITALS OR OTHER MEDICAL CHARITIES.

I. HOSPITAL PHYSICIANS and SURGEONS should minister to the sick, with due impressions of the importance of their office; reflecting that the ease, the health, and the lives of those committed to their charge depend on their skill, attention, and fidelity. They should study, also, in their deportment, so to unite *tenderness* with *steadiness*, and *condescension* with *authority*, as to inspire the minds of their patients with gratitude, respect, and confidence. [not paginated: 9]

II. The *choice* of a *physician*, or *surgeon*, cannot be allowed to hospital patients, consistently with the regular and established succession of medical attendance. Yet personal confidence is not less important to the comfort and relief of the sick-poor, than of the rich under similar circumstances: And it would be equally just and humane, to enquire into and to indulge their partialities, by occasionally calling into consultation the favourite practitioner. The rectitude and wisdom of this conduct will be still more apparent, when it is recollected that patients in hospitals not unfrequently request their discharge, on a deceitful plea of having received relief; and afterwards procure another recommendation, that they may be admitted under the physician or surgeon of their choice. Such practices involve in them a degree of falshood; produce unnecessary trouble; and may be the occasion of irreparable loss of time in the treatment of diseases.

III. The *feelings* and *emotions* of the patients, under critical circumstances, require to be known and to be attended to, no less than the symptoms of their diseases. Thus, extreme *timidity* with respect to venæsection, contraindicates its use in certain cases and [10] constitutions. Even the *prejudices* of the sick are not to be contemned, or opposed with harshness: For though silenced by authority, they will operate secretly and forcibly on the mind, creating fear, anxiety, and watchfulness.

IV. As misapprehension may magnify real evils, or create imaginary ones, no *discussion* concerning the nature of the case should be entered into before the patients, either with the house surgeon, the pupils of the hospitals, or any medical visitor.

V. In the large wards of an Infirmary, the patients should be interrogated concerning their complaints in a *tone* of *voice* which cannot be *overheard*. *Secrecy*, also, when required by peculiar circumstances, should be strictly observed. And females should always be treated with the most scrupulous *delicacy*. To neglect or to sport with their feelings is cruelty; and every wound thus inflicted tends to produce a callousness of mind, a contempt of decorum, and an insensibility to modesty and virtue. Let these considerations be forcibly and repeatedly urged on the hospital pupils.

VI. The *moral* and *religious influence* of sickness is so favourable to the best interests [11] of men and of society, that is justly regarded as an important object in the establishment of every hospital. The *institutions* for promoting it should, therefore, be encouraged by the physicians and surgeons, whenever seasonable opportunities occur. And by pointing out these to the officiating clergymen, the sacred offices will be performed with propriety, discrimination, and greater certainty of success. The character of a physician is usually remote either from superstition or enthusiasm: And the aid, which he is now exhorted to give, will tend to their exclusion from the sick wards of the hospital, where their effects have often been known to be not only baneful, but even fatal.

VII. It is one of the circumstances which softens the lot of the poor, that they are exempt from the solicitudes attendant on the disposal of property. Yet there are exceptions to this observation: And it may be necessary that an hospital patient, on the bed of sickness and death, should be reminded, by some friendly monitor, of the importance of a *last will* and *testament* to his wife, children, or relatives, who, otherwise, might be deprived of his effects, of his expected prize money, or of some future residuary legacy. This kind [12] office will be best performed by the house-surgeon, whose frequent attendance on the sick diminishes their reserve, and entitles him to their familiar confidence. And he will doubtless regard the performance of it as a duty. For whatever is right to be done, and cannot by another be so well done, has the full source of moral and personal obligation.

VIII. The physicians and surgeons should not suffer themselves to be restrained, by parsimonious considerations, from prescribing *wine*, and *drugs* even at *high price*, when required in diseases of extraordinary malignity and danger. The efficacy up every medicine is proportionate to his purity and goodness; and on the degree of these properties, *cæteris paribus* [other things being equal], both the cure of the sick, and the speediness of its accomplishment must depend. But when drugs of inferior quality are employed, it is requisite to administer them in large doses, and to continue the use of them a longer period of time; circumstances which, probably, more than counterbalance any savings in their original price. If the case, however, were far from otherwise, no œconomy, of a fatal tendency, ought to be admitted into institutions, founded on principles of the purest beneficence, and which, in this age and country, [13] when well conducted, can never want contributions adequate to their liberal support.

IX. The medical gentlemen of every charitable institution are, in some degree, responsible for, and the guardians of, the honour of each other. No physician or surgeon, therefore, should *reveal* occurrences in the hospital, which may injure the reputation of any one of his colleagues; except under the restriction contained in the succeeding article.

X. No *professional charge* should be made by a physician or surgeon, either publicly or privately, against any associate, without previously laying the complaint before the gentlemen of the faculty belonging to the institution, that they may judge concerning the reasonableness of its grounds, and the measures to be adopted.

XI. A proper *discrimination* being established in all hospitals between the *medical* and *chirurgical* cases, it should be faithfully adhered to, by the physicians and surgeons, on the admission of patients.

XII. Whenever cases occur, attended with circumstances not heretofore observed, or in which the ordinary modes of practice have been attempted without success, it is for the public good, and in an especial degree ad-[14]vantageous to the poor (who, being the most numerous class of society, are the greatest beneficiaries up the healing art) that new *remedies* and *new methods* of *chirurgical treatment* should be devised. But in the accomplishment of this salutary purpose, the gentlemen of the faculty should be scrupulously and conscientiously governed by sound reason, just analogy, or well-authenticated facts. And no such trials should be instituted, without a previous consultation of the physicians or surgeons, according to the nature of the case.

XIII. To advance professional improvement, a family and unreserved *intercourse* should subsist between the gentlemen of the faculty, with a free communication of whatever is extraordinary or interesting in the course of their hospital practice. And an *account* of every *case* or *operation*, which is rare, curious, or instructive, should be drawn up by the physician or surgeon, to whose charge it devolves, and entered in a register kept for the purpose, but open only to the physicians and surgeons of the charity.

XIV. *Hospital registers* usually contain only a simple report of the number of patients admitted and discharged. By adopting a more comprehensive plan, they might be rendered [15] subservient to medical science, and beneficial to mankind. The following sketch is offered, with deference, to the gentlemen of the faculty. Let the register consist up three tables; the first specifying the number of patients admitted, cured, relieved, discharged, or dead; the second, the several diseases of the patients, with their events; the third, the sexes, ages, and occupations of the patients. The ages should be reduced into classes; and the tables adapted to the four divisions of the year. By such an institution, the increase or decrease of sickness; the attack, progress, and cessation of epidemics; the comparative healthiness of different situations, climates, and seasons; the influence of particular trades and manufactures on health and life; with many other curious circumstances, not more interesting to physicians than to the community; would be ascertained with sufficient precision.

XV. By the adoption of the *register*, recommended in the foregoing article, physicians and surgeons would obtain a clearer insight into the comparative success of their hospital and private practice; and would be incited to a diligent investigation of the causes of such difference. In particular diseases is it will be found to subsist in a very remarkable [16] degree. And the discretionary power of the physician or surgeon, in the admission of patients, could not be exerted with more justice or humanity, than in refusing to consign to lingering suffering, and almost certain death, a numerous class of patients, inadvertently recommended as objects of these charitable institutions. "In judging of diseases with regard to the propriety of their reception into hospitals," says an excellent writer, " the following general circumstances are to be considered:

"Whether they be capable of speedy relief; because, as it is the intention of charity to relieve as great a number as possible, a quick change of objects is to be wished; and also because the inbred disease of hospitals will almost inevitably creep, in some degree, upon one who continues a long time in them, but will rarely attack one, whose stay is short."

"Whether they require in a particular manner the superintendence of skilful persons, either on account of their acute and dangerous nature, or any singularity or intricacy attending them, or erroneous opinions prevailing among the common people concerning their treatment [17]."

"Whether they be contagious, or subject in a peculiar degree to taint the air, and generate pestilential diseases."

"Whether a fresh and pure air peculiarly requisite for their cure, and they be remarkably injured by any vitiation of it." *

[bottom page 18] * See Dr. Aikin's Thoughts on Hospitals, p. 21.

XVI. But no precautions relative to the reception of patients, who labour under maladies incapable of relief, contagious in their nature, or liable to be aggravated by confinement in an impure atmosphere, can obviate the evils arising from *close wards*, and the false œeconomy of crowding a number of persons into the least possible space. There are inbred diseases which it is the duty of the physician or surgeon to prevent, as far as lies in his power, by a strict and persevering attention to the whole medical polity of the hospital. This comprehends the discrimination of cases admissible, air, diet, cleanliness, and drugs; each of which articles should be subjected to a rigid scrutiny, at stated periods of time. (c)

[bottom page 18] (c) See Notes and Illustrations, No. III.

XVII. The establishment of a *committee* of the *gentlemen* of the *faculty*, to be held [18] monthly, would tend to facilitate this interesting investigation, and to accomplish the most important objects of it. By the free communication of remarks, various improvements would be suggested; by the regular discussion of them, they it would be reduced to a definite and consistent form; and by the authority of united suffrages, they would have full influence over the governors of the charity. The exertions of individuals, however benevolent or judicious, often give rise to jealousy; are opposed by those who have not been consulted; and prove inefficient, by wanting the collective energy of numbers.

XVIII. The harmonious intercourse which has been recommended to the gentlemen of the faculty, will naturally produce *frequent consultations*, viz. of the physicians on medical cases, of the surgeons on chirurgical cases, and of both united in cases of a compound nature, which falling under the department of each, may admit all elucidation by the reciprocal aid of the two professions.

XIX. In consultations on medical cases, the junior physician present should *deliver* his *opinion* first, and the others in the progressive order of their seniority. The same order should be observed in chirurgical cases; and a majo-[19]rity should be decisive in both: But if the numbers be equal, the decision should rest with the physicians or surgeon, under whose care the patient is placed. No decision, however, should restrain the acting practitioner from making such variations in the mode of treatment, as future contingences may require, or a further insight into the nature of the disorder may shew to be expedient.

XX. In consultations on mixed cases, the junior surgeon should *deliver* his *opinion* first, and his brethren afterwards in succession, according to progressive seniority. The junior physician present should deliver his opinion after the senior surgeon; and the other physicians in the order above prescribed.

XXI. In every consultation, the case to be considered should be *concisely stated* by the physician or surgeon, who requests the aid of his brethren. The opinions relative to it should be delivered with brevity, agreeably to the preceding arrangement, and the decisions collected in the same order. The order of seniority, among the physicians and surgeons, maybe regulated by the dates of their respective appointments in the hospital.

XXII. Due *notice* should be given of a consultation, and no person admitted to it, [20] except the physicians and surgeons of the hospital, and the house-surgeon, without the unanimous consent of the gentlemen present. If an examination of the patient be previously necessary, the particular circumstances of danger or difficulty should be carefully concealed from him, and every just precaution used to guard him from anxiety or alarm.

XXIII. No important *operation* should be determined upon, without a consultation of the physicians and surgeons, and the acquiescence of a majority of them. Twenty-four hours notice should be given of the proposed operation, except in dangerous accidents, or when peculiar circumstances occur, which may render delay hazardous. The presence of a *spectator* should not be allowed during an operation, without the express permission of the operator. All extra-official interference in the management of it should be forbidden. A decorous *silence* ought to be observed. It may be humane and salutary, however, for one of the attending physicians or surgeons to speak occasionally to the patient; to comfort him under his sufferings; and to give him assurance, if consistent with truth, that the [21] operation goes on well, and promises a speedy and successful termination.*

[bottom page 22] * The substance of the five preceding articles (XIX. XX. XXI. XXII. XXIII.) was suggested by Dr. Ferriar and Mr Simmons, at the time when I was desired, by them and my other colleagues, to frame a code of rules for the Manchester Infirmary. The additions, now made, are intended to adapt them to general use.

As a hospital is the best school for practical surgery, it would be liberal and beneficial to invite, in rotation, two surgeons of the town, who do not belong to the institution, to be present at each operation.

XXIV. Hospital consultations ought not to be held on Sundays, except in cases of urgent necessity; and on such occasions an hour should be appointed, which does not interfere with attendance on public worship.

XXV. It is an established usage, in some hospitals, to have a *stated day* in the week for the performance of operations. But this may occasion improper delay, or equally unjustifiable anticipation. When several operations are to take place in succession, one patient should not have his mind agitated by the knowledge of the sufferings of another. The surgeon should change his apron, when besmeared; and the table or instruments should [22] be freed from all marks of blood, and every thing that may excite terror.

XXVI. DISPENSARIES afford the widest sphere for the treatment of diseases, comprehending, not only such as ordinarily occur, but those which are so infectious, malignant, and fatal, as to be excluded from admissions into Infirmaries. Happily, also, they neither tend to counteract that spirit of independence, which should be sedulously fostered in the poor, nor to preclude the practical exercise of those relative duties, "the charities of father, son, and brother," which constitute the strongest moral bonds of society. Being institutions less splendid and expensive than hospitals, they are well adapted to towns of moderate size; and might even be established, without difficulty, in populous country districts. Physicians and surgeons, in such situations, have generally great influence. And it would be truly honourable to exert it in a cause subservient to the interests of medical science, of commerce, and of philanthropy. (d) [bottom page 23] (d) See Notes and Illustrations, No. IV.

The duties which devolve on gentlemen of the faculty, engaged in the conduct of Dispensaries, are so nearly familiar to those of hospital physicians and surgeons, as to be com-[23]prehended under the same professional and moral rules. But greater *authority* and greater *condescension* will be found requisite in domestic attendance on the poor. And human nature must be intimately studied, to acquire that full ascendancy over the prejudices, the caprices, and the passions of the sick, and of their relatives, which is essential to medical success.

XXVII. Hospitals, appropriated to particular maladies, are established in different places, and claim both the patronage and the aid of the gentlemen of the faculty. To an ASYLUM for FEMALE PATIENTS, labouring under SYPHILIS, it is to be lamented that discouragements have been too often and successfully opposed. Yet whoever reflects on the variety of diseases to which the human body is incident, will find, that a considerable part of them are derived from immoderate passions, and vicious indulgences. Sloth, intemperance, and irregular desires are the great sources of those evils, which contract the duration, and imbitter the enjoyment of life. But humanity, whilst she bewails the vices of mankind, incites us to alleviate the miseries which flow from them. And it may be proved that a LOCK HOSPITAL is an institution founded on the most benevo-[24]lent principles, consonant to sound policy, and favourable to reformation and to virtue. It provides relief for a painful and loathsome distemper, which contaminates, in its progress, the innocent as well as the guilty, and extends its baneful influence to future generations. It restores to virtue and to religion those votaries whom pleasure has seduced, or villainy betrayed; and who now feel, by sad experience, that ruin, misery, and disgrace *are the wages of sin*. Over such objects pity sheds the generous tear; austerity softens into forgiveness; and benevolence expands at the united pleas of frailty, penitence, and wretchedness.*

[bottom page 23] * See two Reports, intended to promote the establishment of a Lock Hospital at Manchester, in the year 1774, inserted in the author's Essays Medical, Philosophical, and Experimental. Vol. II. p. 263, 4th edit.

No *peculiar rules* of conduct are requisite in the medical attendance on LOCK HOSPITALS. But as these institutions must, from the nature of their object, be in a great measure shut from the inspection of the public, it will behove the faculty to consider themselves as responsible, in an extraordinary degree, for their right government; that the moral, no less than the medical, purposes of such esta-[25]blishments may be fully answered. The strictest decorum should be observed in the conduct towards the female patients; no young pupils should be admitted into the house; every ministering office should be performed by nurses properly instructed; and books adapted to the moral improvement of the patients should be put into their hands, and given them on their discharge. To provide against the danger of urgent want, a small sum of money, and decent clothes should at this time be dispensed to them; and, when practicable, some mode should be pointed out of obtaining a reputable livelihood.

XXVIII. ASYLUMS for INSANITY possess accommodations and advantages, of which the poor must, in all circumstances, be destitute; and which no private family, however opulent, can provide. Of these schemes of benevolence all classes of men may have equal occasion to participate the benefits; for human nature itself becomes the mournful object of such institutions. Other diseases leave man a rational and moral agent, and sometimes improve both the faculties of the head, in the affections of the heart. But lunacy subverts the whole rational and moral character; extinguishes every tender charity; an excludes the degraded sufferer from all the enjoyments and advan-[26]tages of social intercourse. Painful is the office of a physician, when he is called upon to minister to such humiliating objects of distress: Yet great must be his felicity, when he can render himself instrumental, under providence, in the restoration of reason, and in the renewal of the lost image of God. Let no one, however, promise himself this divine privilege, if he be not deeply skilled in the philosophy of human nature. For though casual success may sometimes be the result of empirical practice, the *medicina mentis* can only be administered with steady efficacy by him, who, to a knowledge of the animal œconomy, and of the physical causes which regulate or disturb its movements, unites an intimate acquaintance with the laws of association; the controul of fancy over judgment; the force of habit; the direction and comparative strength of opposite passions; and the reciprocal dependences and relations of the moral and intellectual powers of man.

XXIX. Even thus qualified with the pre-requisite attainments, the physician will find that he has a new region of medical science to explore. For it is a circumstance to be regretted, both by the faculty and the public, that the various diseases which are classed [27] under the title of insanity, remain less understood than any others with which mankind are visited. Hospital institutions furnish the best means of acquiring more accurate knowledge of their causes, nature, and cure. But this information cannot be attained, to any satisfactory extent, by the ordinary attention to single and unconnected cases. The synthetic plan should be adopted; and a regular *journal* should be kept of every species of the malady which occurs, arranged under proper heads, with a full detail of its rise, progress, and termination; of the remedies administered, and of their effects in its several stages. The age, sex, occupation, mode of life, and if possible hereditary constitution of each patient should be noted: And, when the event proves fatal, the brain, and other organs affected should be carefully exa-mined, and the appearances on dissection minutely inserted in the journal. A register like this, in the course of a few years, would afford the most interesting and authentic documents, the want of which, on a late melancholy occasion, was felt and regretted by the whole kingdom.

XXX. Lunatics are, in great measure, secluded from the observation of those who [28] are interested in their good treatment; and their complaints of ill-usage are so often false or fanciful, as to obtain little credit or attention, even when well founded. The physician, therefore, must feel himself under the strictest obligation of honour, as well as of humanity, to secure to these unhappy sufferers all the *tenderness* and *indulgence*, compatible with steady and effectual government.

XXXI. Certain cases of *mania* seem to require a *boldness of practice*, which a young physician of sensibility may feel a reluctance to adopt. On such occasions he must not yield to timidity, but fortify his mind by the councils of his more experienced brethren of the faculty. Yet, with this aid, it is more consonant to probity to err on the side of caution than of temerity. (e)

[bottom page 29] (e) See Notes and Illustrations, No. V.

Hospitals for the small-pox, for inoculation, for cancers, &c. &c. are established in different places; but require no professional duties, which are not included under, or deducible from, the precepts already delivered [29].

CHAPTER II.
OF PROFESSIONAL CONDUCT IN PRIVATE, OR GENERAL PRACTICE.

I. THE *moral rules of conduct*, prescribed towards hospital patients, should be fully adopted in private or general practice. Every case, committed to the charge of a physician or surgeon, should be treated with attention, steadiness, and humanity: Reasonable indulgence should be granted to the mental imbecility and caprices of the sick: Secrecy, and delicacy when required by peculiar circumstances, should by strictly observed. And the familiar and confidential intercourse, to which the faculty are admitted in their professional visits, should be used with discretion, and with the most scrupulous regard to fidelity and honour.

II. The strictest *temperance* should be deemed incumbent on the faculty; as the practice both of physic and surgery at all times requires the exercise of a clear and vigorous understanding: And on emergencies, for which no professional man should be unpre-[30]pared, a steady hand, an acute eye, and an unclouded head, may be essential to the well being, and even to the life, of a fellow-creature. Phillip of Macedon reposed with entire security on the vigilance and attention of his General Parmenio. In his hours of mirth and conviviality he was wont to say, "Let us drink, my friends; we may do it with safety, for Parmenio never drinks!" The moral of this story is sufficiently obvious when applied to the faculty; but it should certainly be construed with great limitation by their patients.(f)

[Bottom page 31] (f) See Notes and Illustrations, No. VI.

III. A physician should not be forward to make gloomy prognostications; because they savour of empiricism, by magnifying the importance of his services in the treatment or cure of the disease. But he should not fail, on proper occasions, to give to the friends of the patient, timely notice of danger, when it really occurs, and even to the patient himself, if absolutely necessary. This office, however, is so peculiarly alarming, when executed by him, that it ought to be declined, whenever it can be assigned to any other person of sufficient judgment and delicacy. For the phy-[31]sician should be the minister of hope and comfort to the sick; that by such cordials to the drooping spirit, he may smooth the bed of death; revive expiring life;

and counteract the depressing influence of those maladies, which rob the philosopher of fortitude, and the Christian of consolation.

[in ERRATA Percival notes that reference (g) to Note VII is "wonting"]

IV. *Officious interference*, in a case under the charge of another, should be carefully avoided. No meddling inquiries should be made concerning the patient; no unnecessary hints given, relative to the nature or treatment of his disorder; nor any selfish conduct pursued, that may directly or indirectly tend to diminish the trust reposed in the physician or surgeon employed. Yet though the character of the professional busy-body, whether from thoughtlessness or craft, is highly reprehensible, there are occasions which not only justify but require a spirited interposition. When artful ignorance grossly imposes on credulity; when neglect puts to hazard an important life; or rashness threatens it with still more imminent danger; a medical neighbour, friend, or relative, apprized of such facts, will justly regard his interference as a duty. But he ought to be careful that the information, on which he acts, is well founded; that his motives are pure and ho-[32]nourable; and that his judgment of the measures pursued is built on experience and practical knowledge, not on speculative or theoretical differences of opinion. The particular circumstances of the case will suggest the most proper mode of conduct. In general, however, a personal and confidential application to the gentlemen of the faculty concerned, should be the first step taken, and afterwards, if necessary, the transaction may be communicated to the patient or to his family.

V. When a physician or surgeon is called to a patient, who has been before under the care of another gentleman of the faculty, a consultation with him should be even proposed, though he may have discontinued his visits: His practice, also, should be treated with candor, and justified, so far as probity and truth will permit. For the want of success in the primary treatment of a case, is no impeachment of professional skill or knowledge; and it often serves to throw light on the nature of a disease, and to suggest to the subsequent practitioner more appropriate means of relief (g).

[Bottom page 33] (g) See Notes and Illustrations, No. VIII.

VI. In large and opulent towns, the *distinction* between the *provinces* of *physic* and [33] *surgery* should be steadily maintained. This distinction is sanctioned both by reason and experience. It is founded on the nature and objects of the two professions; on the education and acquirements requisite for their most beneficial and honourable exercise; and tends to promote the complete cultivation and advancement of each. For the division of skill and labour is no less advantageous in the liberal than in the mechanic arts: And both physic and surgery are so comprehensive, and yet so far from perfection, as separately to give full scope to the industry and genius of their respective professors. Experience has fully evinced the benefits of the discrimination recommended, which is established in every well regulated hospital, and is thus expressly authorized by the faculty themselves, and by those who have the best opportunities of judging of the proper application of the healing heart. No physician or surgeon, therefore, should adopt more than one denomination, or assume any rank or privilege is different from those of his order.

VII. *Consultations* should be *promoted*, in difficult or protracted cases, as they give rise to confidence, energy, and more enlarged views [34] in practice. On such occasions no rivalship or jealousy should be indulged: Candour, probity, and all due respect should be exercised towards the physician or surgeon first engaged: And as he may be presumed to be best acquainted with the patient and with his family, he should deliver all the medical directions agreed upon, though he may not have precedency in seniority or rank. It should be the province, however, of the senior physician, first to propose the necessary questions to the sick, but without excluding his associate from the privilege of making farther inquiries, to satisfy himself, or to elucidate the case.

VIII. As circumstances sometimes occur to render a *special consultation* desirable, when the continued attendance of another physician or surgeon might be objectionable to the patient, the gentleman of the faculty, whose assistance is required, in such cases, should pay only two or three visits; and sedulously guard against all future unsolicited interference. For this consultation a double gratuity may reasonably be expected from the patient, as it will be found to require an extraordinary portion both of time and attention.

In medical practice, it is not an unfrequent occurrence, that a physician is hastily [35] summoned, through the anxiety of the family, or the solicitation of friends, to visit a patient, who is under the regular direction of another physician, to whom notice of this call has not been given. Under such circumstances, no change in the treatment of the sick person should be made, till a previous consultation with the stated physician has taken place, unless the lateness of the hour precludes meeting, or the symptoms of the case are too pressing to admit of delay.

IX. *Theoretical discussions* should be avoided in consultations, as occasioning perplexity and loss of time. For there may be much diversity of opinion, concerning speculative points, with perfect agreement in those modes of practice, which are founded not on hypothesis, but on experience and observation. (h)

[Bottom page 36] (h) See Notes and Illustrations, No. IX.

X. The rules prescribed for hospital consultations may be adopted in private or general practice.*

[Bottom page 36] * See Articles XIX. XX. XXX. Chap. I.

And the *seniority* of a physician may be determined by the period of his public and acknowledged practice as a physician, and that of a surgeon by the period of his practice as a surgeon, in the place where [36] each resides. This arrangement, being clear and obvious, is adapted to remove all grounds of dispute amongst medical gentlemen: And it secures the regular continuance of the order of precedency, established in every town, which might otherwise be liable to troublesome interruptions by new settlers, perhaps not long stationary.

XI. A regular *academical education* furnishes the only presumptive evidence of professional ability, and is so honourable and beneficial, that it gives a just claim to pre-eminence among physicians, in proportion to the degree in which it has been enjoyed and improved: Yet as it is not indispensably necessary to the attainment of knowledge, skill, and experience, they who have really acquired, in a competent measure, such qualifications, without its advantages, should not be fastidiously excluded from the privileges of fellowship. In consultations, especially, as the good of the patient is the sole object in view, and is often dependent on the personal confidence, the aid of an intelligent practitioner ought to be received with candour and politeness, and his [37] advice adopted, if agreeable to sound judgment and truth. (i)

[Bottom page 38] (i) See Notes and Illustrations, No. X

XII. *Punctuality* should be observed in the visits of the faculty, when they are to hold consultation together. But as this may not always be practicable, the physician or surgeon, who first arrives at the place of appointment, should wait five minutes for his associate, before his introduction to the patient, that the unnecessary repetition of questions may be avoided: No visits should be made but in concert, or by mutual agreement: No statement or discussion of the case should take place before the patient or his friends, except in the presence of each of the attending gentlemen of the faculty, and by common consent: And no *prognostications* should be delivered, which are not the result of previous deliberation and concurrence.

XIII. *Visits* to the sick should not be *unseasonably repeated*; because, when too frequent, they tend to diminish the authority of the physician, to produce instability in his practice, and to give rise to such occasional indulgences, as are subversive of all medical regimen.

Sir William Temple has asserted, that "an honest physician is excused for leaving his [38] patient, when he finds the disease growing desperate, and can, by his attendance, expect only to receive his fees, without any hopes or appearance of deserving them." But this allegation is not well founded: For the offices of a physician may continue to be highly useful to the patient, and comforting to the relatives around him, even in the last period of a fatal malady; by obviating despair, by alleviating pain, and by soothing mental anguish. To decline attendance, under such circumstances, would be sacrificing, to fanciful delicacy and mistaken liberality, that moral duty which is independent of, and far superior to, all pecuniary appreciation.

XIV. Whenever a physician or surgeon *officiates* for another, who is sick or absent, during any considerable length of time, he should receive the fees accruing from such additional practice: But if this fraternal act be of short duration, it should be gratuitiously performed; with an observance always of the utmost delicacy towards the interest and character of the professional gentleman, previously connected with the family.

XV. Some general rules should be adopted, by the faculty, in every town, relative to the *pecuniary acknowledgments* of their patients; [39] and it should be deemed a point of honour to adhere to this rule, with as much steadiness as varying circumstances will admit. For it is obvious that an average fee, as suited to the general rank of patients, must be an inadequate gratuity from the rich, who often require attendance not absolutely necessary; and yet too large to be expected from that class of citizens, who would feel a reluctance in calling for assistance, without making some decent and satisfactory retribution.

But in the consideration of fees, let it ever be remembered, that though mean ones from the affluent are both unjust and degrading, yet characteristical beneficence of the profession is inconsistent with sordid views, and avaricious rapacity. To a young physician, it is of great importance to have clear and definite ideas of the primary ends of his profession; of the means for their attainment; and of the comparative value and dignity of each. Wealth, rank, and independence, with all the benefits resulting from them, are the ends which he holds in view; and they are intersecting, wise, and laudable. But knowledge, benevolence, and active virtue, the means to be adopted in their acquisition, are of still higher estimation. And he has the privilege and fe-[40]licity of practicing an art, even more intrinsically excellent in its mediate than in its ultimate objects. The former, therefore, have a claim to uniform pre-eminence (k).

[Bottom page 41] (k) See Notes and Illustrations, No. XI.

XVI. All members of the profession, including apothecaries as well as physicians and surgeons, together with their wives and children, should be attended *gratuitously* by any one or more of the faculty, residing near them, whose assistance may be required. For as solicitude obscures the judgment, and is accompanied with timidity and irresolution, medical men, under the pressure of sickness, either as affecting themselves or their families, are peculiarly dependent upon each other. But visits should not be obtruded officiously; as such unasked civility may give rise to embarrassment, or interfere with that choice, on which confidence depends. Distant members of the faculty, when they request attendance, should be expected to defray the charges of traveling. And if their circumstances be affluent, a pecuniary acknowledgement should not be declined: For no obligation ought to be imposed, which the party would rather compensate than contract [41].

XVII. When a physician attends the wife or child of a member of the faculty, or any person very nearly connected with him, he should manifest peculiar attention to his opinions, and tenderness even to his prejudices. For the dear and important interests which the one has at stake, supersede every consideration of rank or seniority in the other; since the mind of a husband, a father, or a friend, may receive a deep and lasting wound, if the disease terminate fatally, from the adoption of means he could not approve, or the rejection of those he wished to be tried. Under such delicate circumstances, however, a conscientious physician will not lightly sacrifice his judgment; but will urge, with proper confidence, the measures he deems to be expedient, before he leaves the final decision concerning them to his more responsible coadjutor.

XVIII. Clergymen who experience the *res angusta domi*, should be visited gratuitously by the faculty. And this exemption should be an acknowledged general rule, that the feeling of individual obligation may be rendered less oppressive. But such of the clergy as are qualified, either from there stipends or fortunes, to make a reasonable remuneration for medical [42] attendance, are not more privileged than any other order of patients. Military or naval subaltern officers, in narrow circumstances, are also proper objects of professional liberality.

XIX. As the first *consultation* by *letter* imposes much more trouble and attention than a personal visit, it is reasonable, on such an occasion, to expect a gratuity of double the usual amount. And this has long been the established practice of many respectable physicians. But a subsequent epistolary correspondence, on the further treatment of the same disorder, may justly be regarded in the light of ordinary attendance, and may be compensated, as such, according to the circumstances of the case, or of the patient.

XX. Physicians and surgeons are occasionally requested to furnish certificates, justifying the absence of persons who hold situations of honour and trust in the army, the navy, or the civil departments of government. These testimonials, unless under particular circumstances, should be considered as acts due to the public, and therefore not compensated by any gratuity. But they should never be given without an accurate and faithful scrutiny into the café; that truth and probity may not be violated, nor the good of the commu-[43]nity injured, by the unjust pretences of its servants. The same conduct is to be observed by medical practitioners, when they are solicited to furnish apologies for non-attendance on juries; or to state the valetudinary incapacity of persons appointed to execute the business of constables, church-wardens, or overseers of the poor. No fear of giving umbrage, no view to present or future emolument, nor any motives of friendship, should incite to a false , or even dubious declaration. For the general weal requires that every individual, who is properly qualified, should deem himself obliged to execute, when legally called upon, the juridical and municipal employments of the body politic. And to be accessory, by untruths or prevarication, to the evasion of this duty, is at once a high misdemeanour against social order, and a breach of moral and professional honour.

XXI. The use of *quack medicines* should be discouraged by the faculty, as disgraceful to the profession, injurious to health, and often destructive even of life. Patients, however, under lingering disorders, are sometimes obstinately bent on having recourse to such as they see advertised, or hear recommended, with a boldness and confidence, which no intelligent [44] physician dares to adopt with respect to the means that he prescribes. In these cases, some indulgence seems to be required to a credulity that in insurmountable: And the patient should neither incur the displeasure of the physician, nor be entirely deserted by him. He may be apprized of the fallacy of his expectations, whilst assured, at the same time, that diligent attention should be paid to the process of the experiment he is so unadvisedly making on himself, and the consequent mischiefs, if any, obviated as timely as possible. Certain active preparations, the nature, composition, and effects of which are well known, ought not to be prescribed as quack medicines.

XXII. No physician or surgeon should dispense a secret *nostrum*, whether it be his invention, or exclusive property. For if it be of real efficacy, the concealment of it is inconsistent with beneficence and professional liberality. And if mystery alone give it value and importance, such craft implies either disgraceful ignorance, or fraudulent avarice.

XXIII. The *Esprit du Corps* is a principle of action founded in human nature, and when duly regulated, is both rational and laudable. Every man who enters into a fraternity engages, by a tacit compact, not only to submit [45] to the laws, but to promote the honour and interest of the association, so far as they are consistent with morality, and the general good of mankind. A physician, therefore, should cautiously guard against whatever may injure the general respectability of his profession; and should avoid all contumelious representations of the faculty at large; all general charges against their selfishness or improbity; and the indulgence of an affected or jocular scepticism, concerning the efficacy and utility of the healing art.

XXIV. As diversity of opinion and opposition of interest may, in the medical, as in other professions, sometimes occasion *controversy*, and even *contention*; whenever such cases unfortunately occur, and cannot be immediately terminated, they should be referred to the arbitration of a sufficient number of physicians or of surgeons, according to the nature of the dispute; or to the two orders collectively, if belonging both to medicine an surgery. But neither the subject matter of such references, nor the adjudication, should be communicated to the public; as they may be personally injurious to the individuals concerned, and can hardly fail to hurt the general credit of the faculty [46].

XXV. A wealthy physician should not give advice *gratis* to the affluent; because it is an injury to his professional brethren. The office of physician can never be supported but as a lucrative one; and it is defrauding, in some degree, the common funds for its support, when fees are dispensed with, which might justly be claimed.

XXVI. It frequently happens that a physician, in his incidental communications with the patients of other physicians, or with their friends, may have their cases stated to him in so direct a manner, as not to admit of his declining to pay attention to them. Under such circumstances, his observations should be delivered with the most delicate propriety and reserve. He should not interfere in the curative plans pursued; and should even recommend a steady adherence to them, if they appear to merit approbation.

XXVII. A physician, when visiting a sick person in the country, may be desired to see a neighbouring patient, who is under the regular direction of another physician, in consequence of some sudden change or aggravation of symptoms. The conduct to be pursued, on such an occasion, is to give advice adapted to present circumstances; to interfere no farther than is [47] absolutely necessary with the general plan of treatment; to assume no future direction, unless it be expressly desired; and, in this case, to request an immediate consultation with the practitioner antecedently employed.

XXVIII. At the close of every interesting and important case, especially when it hath terminated fatally, a physician should trace back, in calm reflection, all the steps which he had taken in the treatment of it. This review of the origin, progress, and conclusion of the malady; of the whole curative plan pursued; and of the particular operation of the several remedies employed, as well as of the doses and periods of time in which they were administered, will furnish the most authentic documents, on which individual experience can be formed. But it is in a moral view that the practice is here recommended; and it should be performed with the most scrupulous impartiality. Let no self-deception be permitted in the retrospect; and if errors, either of omission or commission, are discovered, it behoves that they should be brought fairly and fully to the mental view. Regrets may follow, but criminality will thus be obviated. For good intentions, and the imperfection of human skill, which cannot anticipate [48] the knowledge that events alone disclose, will sufficiently justify what is past, provided the failure be made conscientiously subservient to future wisdom and rectitude and professional conduct.

XXIX. The opportunities, which a physician not unfrequently enjoys, of promoting and strengthening the good resolutions of his patients, suffering under the consequences of vicious conduct, ought never to be neglected. And his councils, or even remonstrances, will give satisfaction, not disgust, if they be conducted with politeness; and evince a genuine love of virtue, accompanied by a sincere interest in the welfare of the person to whom they are addressed.

XXX. The observance of the sabbath is a duty to which medical men are bound, so far as is compatible with the urgency of the cases under their charge. Visits may often be made with sufficient convenience and benefit, either before the hours of going to church, or during the intervals of public worship. And in many chronic ailments, the sick, together with their attendants, are qualified to participate in the social offices of religion; and should not be induced to forgo this important privilege, by [49] the expectation of a call from their physician or surgeon. (l)

[Bottom page 50] (l) See Notes and Illustrations, No. XII.

XXXI. A physician who is advancing in years, yet unconscious of any decay in his faculties, may occasionally experience some change in the wonted confidence of his friends. Patients, who before trusted solely to his care and skill, may now request that he will join in consultation, perhaps with a younger coadjutor. It behoves him to admit this change without dissatisfaction or fastidiousness, regarding it as no mark of disrespect; but as the exercise of a just and reasonable privilege in those by whom he is employed. The junior practitioner may well be supposed to have more ardour, than he possesses, in the treatment of diseases; to be bolder in the exhibition of new medicines; and disposed to administer old ones and doses of greater efficacy. And this union of enterprize with caution, and of fervour with coolness, may promote the successful management of a difficult and protracted case. Let the medical parties, therefore, be studious to conduct themselves towards each other with candour an impartiality; co-operating, by [50] mutual concessions, in the benevolent discharge of professional duty. (m)

[Bottom page 51] (m) See Notes and Illustrations, No. XIII.

XXXII. The commencement of that period senescence, when it becomes incumbent on a physician to decline the offices of his profession, it is not easy to ascertain; And the decision on so nice a point must be left to the moral direction of the individual. For, one grown old in the useful and honourable exercise of the healing art, may continue to enjoy, and justly to enjoy, the unabated confidence of the public. And whilst exempt, in a considerable degree, from the privations and infirmities of age, he is under indispensable obligations to apply his knowledge and experience, in the most efficient way, to the benefit of mankind. For the possession of powers is a clear indication of the will of our Creator, concerning their practical direction. But in the ordinary course of nature, the bodily and mental vigour must be expected to decay progressively, though perhaps slowly, after the meridian of life is past. As age advances, therefore, a physician should, from time to time, scrutinize impartially the state of his faculties; that he may determine, *bona fide*, the precise degree in [51] which he is qualified to execute the active and multifarious offices of his profession. And whenever he becomes conscious that his memory presents to him, with faintness, those analogies, on which medical reasoning and the treatment of diseases are founded; that diffidence of the measures to be pursued perplexes his judgment; that, from a deficiency in the acuteness of his senses, he finds himself less able to distinguish signs, or to prognosticate events; he should at once resolve, though others perceive not the changes which have taken place, to sacrifice every consideration of fame or fortune, and to retire from the engagements of business. To the surgeon under similar circumstances, this rule of conduct is still more necessary. For the energy of the understanding often subsists much longer than the quickness of eyesight, delicacy of touch, and steadiness of hand, which are essential to the skilful performance of operations. Let both the physician and surgeon never forget, that their professions are public trusts, properly rendered lucrative whilst they fulfil them; but which they are bound, by honour and probity, to relinquish, as soon as they find themselves unequal to their adequate and faithful execution. (n) [52]

[Bottom page 52] (n) See Notes and Illustrations, No. XIV.

CHAPTER III.
OF THE CONDUCT OF PHYSICIANS TOWARDS APOTHECARIES.

I. IN the present state of physic, in this country, where their profession is properly divided into three distinct branches, a connection peculiarly intimate subsists between the physician and the apothecary; and various obligations necessarily result from it. On the knowledge, skill, and fidelity of the apothecary depend, in a very considerable degree, the reputation, the success, and the usefulness of the physician. As these qualities, therefore, justly claim his attention and encouragement, the possessor of them merits his respect and patronage.

II. The apothecary is, and almost every instance, the præcursor of the physician; and being acquainted with the rise and progress of the disease, with the hereditary constitution, habits, and disposition of the patient, he may furnish very important information. It is in general, therefore, expedient, and when health or life are at stake, expediency becomes a moral [53] duty, to confer with the apothecary, before any decisive plan of treatment is adopted; to hear his account of the malady, of the remedies which have been administered, of the effects produced by them, and of his whole experience considering the *juvantia* and *lædentia* in the case. Nor should the future attendance of the apothecary be superseded by the physician: For if he be a man of honour, judgment, and propriety of behaviour, he will be a most valuable auxiliary through the whole course of the disorder, by his attention to varying symptoms; by the enforcement of medical directions; by obviating misapprehensions in the patient, or his family; by strengthening the authority of the physician; and by being at all times an easy and friendly medium of communication. To subserve these important purposes, the physician should occasionally make his visits in conjunction with the apothecary, and regulate by circumstances the frequency of such interviews: For if they be often repeated, little substantial aid can be expected from the apothecary, because he will have no intelligence to offer which does not fall under the observation of the physician himself; nor any opportunity of executing his *peculiar* trust, with-[52]out becoming burthensome to the patient by multiplied calls, and unseasonable assiduity.

III. This amicable *intercourse* and *co-operation* of the physician and apothecary, if conducted with the *decorum* and attention to *etiquette*, which should always be steadily observed by professional men, will add to the authority of the one, to the respectability of the other, and to the usefulness of both. The patient will find himself the object of watchful and unremitting care, and will experience that he is connected with his physician, not only personally, but by a sedulous representative and coadjutor. The apothecary will regard the free communication of the physician as a privilege and mean of improvement; he will have a deeper interest in the success of the curative plans pursued; and his honour and reputation will be directly involved in the purity and excellence of the medicines dispensed, and in the skill and care with which they are compounded.

IV. The duty and responsibility of the physician, however, are so intimately connected with these points, that no dependence on the probity of the apothecary should prevent the occasional inspection of the drugs, which he prescribes. In London, the law not only [53] authorizes, but enjoins a stated examination of the simple and compound medicines kept in the shops. And the policy that is just an reasonable in the metropolis, must be proportionally so in every provincial town, throughout the kingdom. Nor will any respectable apothecary object to this necessary office, when performed with delicacy, and at seasonable times; since his reputation and emolument will be increased by it, probably in the exact *ratio*, thus ascertained, of professional merit and integrity.

V. A physician called to visit a patient and the country, should not only be *minute* in his *directions*, but should *communicate* to the apothecary the *particular view* which he takes of the *case*; that the indications of cure maybe afterwards pursued with precision and steadiness; and that the apothecary may use the discretionary power committed to him, with as little deviation as possible from the general plan prescribed. To so valuable a class of men as the country apothecaries, great attention and respect is due. And as they are the guardians of health through large districts, no opportunities should be neglected of promoting their improvement, or contributing to their stock of knowledge, either by the loan of books, the [56] direction of their studies, or by unreserved information on medical subjects. When such occasions present themselves, the maxim of art judicious poet is strictly true, "the worst avarice is that of sense." For practical improvements usually originate in towns, and often remain unknown or disregarded in situations, where gentlemen of the faculty have little intercourse, and where sufficient authority is wanting to sanction innovation.

VI. It has been observed, by a political and moral writer of great authority that "apothecaries' profit is become a bye-word, denoting something uncommonly extravagant. This great apparent profit, however, is frequently no more than the reasonable wages of labour. The skill of an apothecary is a much nicer and more delicate matter then that of any artificer whatever; and the trust which is reposed in him is of much greater importance. He is the physician of the poor in all cases, and of the rich when the distress or danger is not very great. His reward, therefore, ought to be suitable to his skill and his trust, and it arises generally from the price at which he sells his drugs. But the whole drugs which the best employed apothecary in a large market town, will sell any year, may not [57] perhaps cost him above thirty or forty pounds. Though he should sell them, therefore, for three or four hundred, or a thousand per cent. profit, this may frequently be no more than the reasonable wages of his labour charged, and the only way in which he can charge them, upon the price of his drugs."*

[Bottom page 58] * See Smith's Wealth of Nations, book I. chap. x.

The statement here given exceeds the emoluments of the generality of apothecaries, in country districts. And a physician, who knows the education, skill, and persevering attention, as well as the sacrifice of ease, health, and sometimes even of life, which this profession requires, should regard it as a duty not to withdraw, from those who exercise it, any sources of reasonable profit, or the honourable means of advancement in fortune. Two practices prevail in some places injurious to the interest of this branch of the faculty, and which ought to be discouraged. One consists in suffering prescriptions to be sent to the druggist, for the sake of a small saving an expence: The other an receiving an annual stipend, usually degrading in its amount, and in the services it imposes, for being consulted on the slighter indispositions to which all fami-[58]lies are incident, and which properly fall within the province of the apothecary.

VII. Physicians are sometimes requested to visit the patients of the apothecary, in his absence. Compliance, in such cases, should always be refused, when it is likely to interfere with the consultation of the medical gentleman ordinarily employed by the sick person, or his family. Indeed this practice is so liable to abuse, and requires, in its exercise, so much caution and delicacy, that it would be for the interest and honour of the faculty to have it all together interdicted. Physicians are the only proper substitutes for physicians; surgeons for surgeons; and apothecaries for apothecaries.

VIII. When the aid of a physician is required, the apothecary to the family is frequently called upon to recommend one. It will then behove him to learn fully whether the patient or his friends have any preference or partiality; and this he ought to consult, if it lead not to an improper choice. For the maxim of Celsus is strictly applicable on such an occasion: *ubi par scienta, melior est amicus medicus quam extraneus* ["Where the two are equal in knowledge and skill, the physician who is a friend is better than a physician who is a stranger."] But if the parties concerned be entirely indifferent, the apothecary is bound to decide according to his best judgment, with a conscientious an exclusive [59] regard to the good of the person for whom he is commissioned to act. It is not even sufficient that he selects the person on whom, in sickness, he reposes his own trust; for in this case friendship justly gives preponderancy; because it may be supposed to excite a degree of zeal and attention, which might overbalance superior science or abilities. Without favour or regard to any personal, family, or professional connections, he should recommend the physician whom he conscientiously believes, all circumstances considered, to be best qualified to accomplish the recovery of the patient.

IX. In the County of Norfolk, and in the city of London, benevolence institutions have been lately formed, for providing funds to relieve the widows and children of apothecaries, and occasionally also members of the profession who become indigent. Such schemes merit the sanction and encouragement of every liberal physician and surgeon. And were they thus extended, their usefulness would be greatly increased, and their permanency almost with certainty secured. Medical subscribers, from every part of Great-Britain, should be admitted, if they offer satisfactory testimonials of their qualifications. One comprehensive establish-[60]ment seems to be more eligible than many on a smaller scale. For it would be conducted with superior dignity, regularity, and efficiency; with fewer obstacles from interest, prejudice, or rivalship; with considerable saving in the aggregate of time, trouble, and expence; with more accuracy in the calculations relative to its funds, and consequently with the utmost practicable extension of its dividends.

CHAPTER IV.
OF PROFESSIONAL DUTIES, IN CERTAIN CASES WHICH REQUIRE A KNOWLEDGE OF LAW.

I. Gentlemen of the faculty of physic, by the authority of different parliamentary statutes, enjoy an exemption from serving on inquests or juries; from bearing armour; from being constables or church-wardens; and from all burdensome offices, whether leet or parochial. These privileges are founded on reasons highly honourable to medical men; and should operate as incentives to that diligent and assiduous discharge of professional duty, which the legislature has generously presumed to occupy the time, and to employ the talents, of physi[61]cians and surgeons, in some of the most important interests of their fellow-citizens. It is perhaps on account of their being thus excused from many civil functions, that Sir William Blackstone, in his learned commentaries, judges the study of the law to be less essential to them, than to any other class of men. He observes, that "there is no special reason why gentlemen of the faculty of physic should apply themselves to the study of the law, unless in common with other gentleman, and to complete the character of general and extensive knowledge, which this profession, beyond others, has remarkably deserved."*

[Bottom page 62] * Vol. I. sect. I. introduction.

But I apprehend it will be found that physicians and surgeons are often called upon to exercise appropriate duties, which require not only a knowledge of the principles of jurisprudence, but of the forms of regulations adopted in our courts of judicature. The truth of this observation will sufficiently appear from the following *brief detail* of some of the principal cases, in which the science of law is of importance to medical practitioners. To enter at large on so comprehensive a subject, would far exceed the bounds of the present undertaking [62].

II. When a physician attends upon a patient, under circumstances of imminent danger, his counsel may be required about the expediency of a *last will* and *testament*. It behoves him, therefore, to know whether, in cases of intestacy, the daughters, or younger children of the sick person would be legally entitled to any share of his fortune: Whether the fortune would be equally divided, when such equality would be improper or unjust: Whether diversity of claims and expensive litigations would ensue, without a will, from the nature of the property in question: And whether the creditors of the defunct would, by his neglect, be defrauded of their equitable claims. For it is a culpable deficiency in our laws, that real estates are not subject to the payment of debts by simple contract, unless expressly charged with them by the last will and testament of the proprietor; although credit is often founded, as Dr. Paley well observes, on the possession of such estates. This acute moralist adds, "He, therefore, who neglects to make the necessary appointments for the payment of his debts, as far as his effects extend, sins in his grave; and if he omits this on purpose to defeat the demands of his [63] creditors, he dies with a deliberate fraud in his heart."*

[Bottom page 64] * See Paley's Principles of Moral and Political Philosophy, book III. part I. chap. xxiii

Property is divided by the law into two species, *personal* and *real*; each requiring appropriate modes of transfer or alienation, with which a physician should be well acquainted. It may also be required of him to deliver an opinion, and even a solemn judicial evidence, concerning the *capacity* of his patient to make a *will*, a point sometimes of difficult and nice decision. For various disorders obscure, without perverting, the intellectual faculties. And even in delirium itself there are lucid intervals, when the memory and judgment become sufficiently clear, accurate, and vigorous, for the valid execution of a testament. In such cases the will should commence with the signature of the testator, concluding with it also, if his hand be not, after continued mental exertions, too tremulous for subscription; and it should be made with all possible consciousness, and expedition."†

[Bottom page 64, continuing to bottom page 65] † "In the construction of the statue, 29, Car. II. c. Iii. it has been adjudged, that the testator's name, written [65] with his own hand, at the beginning of the will, as I John Mills do you make this my last will and testament; is a sufficient signing, without any name at the bottom; though the other is the safer way." See Blackstone's Comment. Book II. chap. xxiii [65].

If the patient be surprized by sudden and violent sickness, the law authorizes a *nuncupative will* in the disposal of personalty. But to guard against fraud, the testamentary words must be delivered with an explicit intention to bequeath; the will must be made at home, or among the testator's family and friends, unless by unavoidable accident; and also in his last sickness: For if he recover, it is evident that time is given for a written will.*

[Bottom page 65] * Id. Book II. c. 32.

The law excludes from the privilege of making a will *madmen*, *ideots*, persons in their *dotage*, or those who have stupefied their understandings by drunkenness. But there is a high degree of hypochondriacism, which not unfrequently falls under the cognizance of a physician, and on which he may be required to decide whether it amounts to mental incapacity for the execution of a last will and testament. To define the precise boundaries of rationality is perhaps impossible; if it be true, according to Shakespeare, that "the lunatic, the lover, and the [65] poet are of imagination all compact." But a partially distempered fancy is known to subsist with general intelligence: And a man, like Mr. Simon Browne, believing the extinction of his rational soul by the judgment of God, may uniformly evince, in every other instance, very distinguished intellectual powers; and be capable of directing his concerns, and disposing of his property, with sufficient discretion. To preclude one, so affected, from being a testator, seems inconsistent either with wisdom or justice; especially if the will, which has been made, discover, in its essential parts, no traces of a disturbed imagination or unsound judgment. But whenever false ideas of a *practical kind* are so firmly united as to be constantly and invariably mistaken for truth, we properly denominate this unnatural alliance INSANITY. And if it give rise to a train of subordinate wrong associations, producing incongruity a behaviour, incapacity for the common duties of life, or unconscious deviations from morality and religion, MADNESS has then its commencement (o) [66].

[Bottom page 66] (o) See the Author's Moral and Literary Dissertations, p. 127, second edit; –also Notes and Illustrations, no. XV.

III. A lunatic, or *non compos mentis*, in the eye of the law, is one who has had understanding, but has lost it by disease, grief, or other accident. The king is the trustee for such unfortunate persons, appointed to protect their property, and to account to them, if they recover, for their revenues; or, after their decease, to their representatives. The Lord Chancellor , therefore, grants a commission to inquire into the state of mind of the insane person; and if he be found *non compos*, he usually commits the care of his person, with a suitable allowance for his maintenance, to some friend, who was then called his committee." *

[Bottom page 76] * Blackstone's Comment, book. I. chap. viii.

The physician, who has been consulted about the case, will doubtless be called upon to deliver an opinion concerning his patient. And before he becomes accessary to his deprivation, as it were, of all legal existence, he will weigh attentively the whole circumstances of the disorder, the original cause of it; the degree in which it subsists; its duration, and probable continuance. For if the malady be not fixed, great, and permanent, this solemn act of law must be deemed inexpedient, because it cannot be reversed without difficulty: and when insanity [67] has been once formally declared, there may be grounds of apprehension, that the party will be consigned to neglect and oblivion. With regard to the waste or alienation of property by the person thus afflicted, little risque is incurred, if he be put under the ordinary restraint of a judicious *curator*. For whilst his mind remains in the state of alienation, he is incapable of executing any act of validity; and the next heir, or other person interested may set it aside, on the plea of his incapacity. But the use of a guardian or committee of a lunatic is chiefly renew, in his right, under the direction of the court of chancery, any lease for lives or years, and to apply the profits for the benefit of the insane person, of his heirs, or executors.

IV. The law justifies the *beating of a lunatic, in such manner as the circumstances may require.**

[Bottom page 68] * I. Hawkins 130. Burn's Justice, vol. III. pag. 117.

But it has been before remarked that a physician, who attends an asylum for insanity, is under an obligation of honour as well of as humanity, to secure to the unhappy sufferers, committed to his charge, all the tenderness and indulgence compatible with steady and the effectual [68]

[Bottom page 69] * Chap. II. sect. XXX.

government.* And the strait waistcoat, with other improvements in modern practice, now preclude the necessity of coercion by corporal punishment.

V. Houses for the reception of lunatics are subject to strict regulations of law. These regulations refer to the persons keeping such houses, to the admission of patients into them, and to their inspection by visitors, duly authorized and qualified. If any one conceal more than a single lunatic without a license, he becomes liable to a penalty of five hundred pounds. The licenses in the cities of London and Westminster, or within seven miles of the metropolis, are granted by the college of physicians; who are empowered to elect five of their fellows to act as commissioners for inspecting the lunatic asylums, within their jurisdiction. Houses for the reception of lunatics in the country, are to be licensed by the justices of the peace, during their quarter sessions: And at the time when the license is granted, the magistrates are directed to nominate two of their own body, and also one physician, to visit and inspect such licensed houses. This inspection they are empowered to make as often [69] as they judge is to be expedient; and an allowance is to be granted for the expences incurred. The keeper of every licensed house is bound, under the penalty of one hundred pounds, not to admit or confine any person as a lunatic, without having a certificate in writing, under the hand and seal of some physician, surgeon, or apothecary, that such person is proper to be received into the house, as being *non compos mentis*. And he is further required, under the same penalty, to give notice of this certificate to the secretary of the commissioners, appointed either by the college of physicians, or the magistrates at their quarter-sessions. The act of parliament, which establishes these regulations, states this important proviso: "That in all proceedings which shall be had under his Majesty's writ of *Habeas Corpus*, and in all indictments, informations, and actions, that shall be preferred or brought against any person or persons for confining or ill treating any of his Majesty's subjects, in any of the said houses, the parties complained of shall be obliged to justify their proceedings according to the course of the common law, in the same manner as if this act had not been made." * [70]

[Bottom page 70] * See Statutes at Large, Vol. VIII. 14 Geo. III. C. 49.

The legal allowance to a medical commissioner, for the visitation an inspection of a lunatic asylum, is fixed, by the statute, at one guinea. This gratuity, which cannot be regarded as a just compensation for the time and trouble bestowed, it may often be proper to decline. For to a physician, of a liberal mind, an inadequate pecuniary acknowledgement is felt as a degradation; but he will be amply remunerated by the consciousness of having performed an office, enjoined at once by the laws of humanity, and of his country.

VI. In the case of *sudden death*, the law has made provision for examining into the cause of it by the *Coroner*, an officer appointed for the purpose, who is empowered to summon such evidence as is necessary, for the discharge of his inquisitorial and judicial functions. On these occasions, the attendance of a physician or surgeon may often be required, who should be qualified to give testimony consonant to legal, as well as to medical knowledge. To this end, he must not only be acquainted with the signs of natural death, but also of those which occur, when it is produced by accident or violence. And he should not be a stranger to the several distinctions of homicide, established in our courts of judicature. For the division of [71] this act into *justifiable*, *excusable*, and *felonious*, will aid his investigation, and give precision to the opinion which he delivers.

VII. When a crime, which the law has adjudged to be capital, is attempted to be committed by force, the resistance of such force, even so as to occasion the death of the offender, it deemed *justifiable homicide*. Mr. Locke, in his Essay on Government, carries this doctrine to a much greater extent; asserting, that "all manner of force, without a right, up on a man's person puts him in a state of war with the aggressor, and of consequences, being in such a state of war, he may lawfully kill him that puts him under this unnatural restraint." *

[Bottom page 72] * Essay on Government, Part II. ch. iii.

But Judge Blackstone considers this conclusion as applicable only to a state of uncivilized nature; and observes, that the law of England is too tender of the public peace, too careful of the life of the subject, to adopt so contentious a system; nor will suffer, with impunity, any crime to be *prevented* by death, unless the same, if committed, would also be punished by death. † [72]

[Bottom page 72] † Blackstone's Comment. Book IV. ch. xiv.

VIII. With cases of justifiable homicide, however, gentlemen of the faculty are seldom likely to be professionally concerned. But *excusable homicide* may frequently fall under their cognizance, and require their deliberate attention, and accurate investigations. It is of two sorts; either *per infortunium*, by misadventure; or *se defendendo*, upon a principle of self-preservation. Death may be the consequence of a lawful act, done without any intention of hurt. Thus if an officer, in the correction of a soldier, by the sentence of a court martial, happen to occasion his death, it is only misadventure; the punishment being lawful. But if the correction be unwarrantably severe, either in the manner, the instrument, or the duration of punishment, and death ensue, the offender is at least guilty of manslaughter, and in some circumstances, of murder. A surgeon, therefore, is usually present, when soldiers are chastized with the lash; and on his testimony must depend the justification of the mode and degree of punishment inflicted. –When medicines administered to a sick patient, with an honest design, to produce the alleviation of his pain, or cure of his disease, occasion death, this is misadventure, in the view of the law; and the physician or surgeon who di-[73]rected them, is not liable to punishment criminally, though a civil action might formerly lie for neglect or ignorance. But it hath been holden that such immunity is confined to *regular* physicians and surgeons. Sir Matthew Hale , however, justly questions the legality of this determination; since physic and salves were in use before licensed physicians and surgeons. "Wherefore he treats the doctrine as apocryphal, and fitted only to qualify and flatter licenciates and doctors in physic; though it may be of use to make people cautious how they meddle too much and so dangerous an employment." The college of physicians, however, within their jurisdiction, which extends seven miles round London, are vested by charter with the power of fine and imprisonment *pro mala praxi*. Yet doctor Groenevelt, who was cited, in the year 1693, before the Censors of the College, and committed to Newgate, by a warrant from the president, for prescribing *cantharides* in substance, was acquitted on the plea that bad practice must be accompanied with a bad intention, to render it criminal. This prosecution, whilst it ruined the doctor's reputation, and injured his fortune, so that he is said to have died in want, excited general attention to the remedy, and afterwards [74] established the use of it: though it must be acknowledged that his doses were too bold and hazardous. But whatever be the indulgence of the law towards medical practitioners, they are bound by a higher authority than that of the most solemn statute, not to exercise the healing art without due knowledge, tenderness, and discretion: And every rash experiment, every mistake originating from gross inattention, or from that ignorance which necessarily results from defective education, is, in the eye of conscience, a crime both against God and man.

It must frequently devolve on the faculty to decide concerning the nature and effects of blows, strokes, or wounds inflicted, and how far the death of the sufferer is to be ascribed to them, or to some antecedent or subsequent disease. In homicide, also, *se defendendo*, the manner and time of the defence are to be considered. For if the person assaulted fall upon the aggressor, when the fray is over and he is running away, this is revenge and not defence. And though no witness were present, the situation of the wound or of the blow would afford, if in the back of the assailant, presumptive evidence of *felonious homicide*.

IX.   This crime, which in atrocity exceeds every other, is considered by the law under the [75] three heads of *suicide*, *manslaughter*, and *murder*, concerning each of which the faculty are occasionally obliged to give professional evidence. A *felo de se* is one who has deliberately put an end to his existence, or committed any unlawful malicious act, the immediate consequences of which proved death to himself. To constitute this act a crime, the party must have been of years of discretion, and in the possession of reason. A physician, therefore, may be called upon, by the coroner, to state his opinion of the mental capacity of defunct. And the law will not authorize the plea, that every melancholic or hypochrondriac fit deprives a man of the power of discerning right from wrong. Even if a lunatic kill himself in a lucid interval, Sir M. Hale affirms that he is a *felo de se*: –And the physician, who has attended him, is best qualified to judge of the degree, the duration, or periodical seasons of such returns of sanity. But there are cases of temporary distraction, when death maybe rushed upon apparently with design, but really from the influence of terror, or the want of that presence of mind, which is necessary to the exercise of judgment, and the discrimination of actual from imaginary evil. Of this kind the reader will find an affecting influence, related [76] by Dr. Hunter, in the medical observations and inquiries published by a Society of Physicians, in London." *

[Bottom page 77] * Vol. VI. p. 279.

X. *Manslaughter* is defined "the unlawful killing of another, without malice, express or implied; which may be either *voluntary*, upon a sudden heat; or *involuntarily*, but in the commission of some unlawful act." Yet though this definition is delivered from Sir Matthew Hale, by the excellent commentator on the laws of England so often quoted, it is not sufficiently precise and comprehensive. For when a person does an act lawful in itself, but which proves fatal to a fellow-citizen, because done without due circumspection, it may, according to circumstances, be either misadventure, manslaughter, or murder. Thus when a workman kills any one, by flinging down a stone or piece of timber into the street, if the accident be in a country village, where there are few passengers, and if he give warning by calling out to them, it is only misadventure. But if it be in London, or any other populous town, where persons are continually passing, it is manslaughter, though warning be loudly given: And it is murder, if he know of their [77] passing, and yet gives no warning; for this is malice against all mankind.*

[Bottom page 78] * Blackstone's Comment. Book. IV. ch. xiv.

On the like grounds we may reason concerning the cases of death, occasioned by drugs designed to produce abortion. This purpose is not always unlawful: For the configuration of the *pelvis*, in some females, is such as to render the birth of a full grown child impossible, or inevitably fatal. But even in such instances the guilt of manslaughter may be incurred by ignorance of the drastic quality of the medicine prescribed, or want of due caution in the dose administered. And when no moral or salutary end as in view, the simple act itself, if fatal in the issue, falls under the denomination of murder. †

[Bottom page 78] See Burn's Justice of Peace, vol. I. p. 216.

"If a woman be quick with child, and, by a potion or otherwise, killeth it in her womb, this is a great misprision, yet no murder: But if the child be born alive, and dieth of the potion or other cause, this is murder." ‡

[Bottom page 78] ‡ Id. vol. II. p. 110.

The procuring of abortions was common amongst the Romans; and, it is said, was liable to no penalty, before the reigns of Severus and Antoninus. Even those princes made it criminal only in the case of a married woman, practicing it to [78] defraud her husband of the comforts of children, from motives and resentment. For the *fœtus* being regarded as a portion of the womb of the mother, she was supposed to have an equal and full right over both. This false opinion may have its influence in modern, as well as in ancient times; and false it must be deemed, since no female can be privileged to injure her own bowels, much less the *fœtus*, which is now well known to constitute no part of them. To extinguish the first spark of life is a crime of the same nature, both against our Maker and society, as to destroy an infant, a child, or a man; these regular and successive stages of existence being the ordinances of God, subject alone to his divine will, and appointed by sovereign wisdom and goodness as the exclusive means of preserving the race, and multiplying the enjoyments of mankind. Hence the father of physic, in the oath enjoined on his pupils, which some universities now impose on the candidates for medical degrees, obliged them solemnly to abjure the practice of administering the πεσσος φθοριος. But in weighing the charge, against any person, of having procured abortion, the methods employed should be attentively considered by the faculty; as this effect has often been ascribed to causes inadequate to its [79] production. Even the pessary, so sanctimoniously forbidden by Hippocrates, has little of that activity and power, which superstition assigned to it.

XI. The law of England guards, with assiduous care, the lives of infants, when endangered by motives which counteract, and too often overbalance, the strong operations of maternal love. In cases of *bastardy*, therefore, it is declared, by a statute passed in the reign of James the first, that "If any woman be delivered of any issue of her body, male or female, which being born alive, should by the laws of this realm be a bastard, and she endeavour privately, either by drowning, or secret burying thereof, or any other way, either by herself, or the procuring of others, so to conceal the death thereof, as that it may not come to light whether it was born alive or not, but be concealed, she shall suffer death, as in cases of murder; except she can prove, by one witness at least, that the child was born dead." *

[Bottom page 80] * Burn's Justice, vol. I. p. 216.

This law, though humane in its principle, is much too severe and its construction. To give certainty to punishment, by facilitating conviction, is doubtless an essential [80] object of jurisprudence. And it has been well observed, that the statute, which made the possession of the implements of coining a capital offense, by constituting such possession complete evidence of guilt, has proved the most effectual mean of enforcing the denunciation of law against this dangerous and tempting crime.*

[Bottom page 81] * See Paley's Moral and Political Philosophy, 4to. p. 350.

But the analogy, which the able moralist has drawn between this ordinance and that relating to bastardy, is not fully conclusive. For possession, in the former case, clearly implies a specific purpose, for which the legislature, with sufficient wisdom and justice, has provided a specific punishment: Whereas secrecy in the mother, concerning the death of her illegitimate offspring, hardly amounts to the lowest degree of presumptive evidence of a felonious homicide. Gentlemen of the faculty have often melancholy experience of the distraction and misery, which females suffer under these unhappy circumstances. And when it becomes their painful office to deliver evidence, on such occasions, justice and humanity require, that they should scrutinize the whole truth, and *nothing extenuate, nor set down aught* [81] *in malice.* "What is commonly understood to be the murder of a bastard child by the mother," says Dr. Hunter, "if the real circumstances were fully known, would be allowed to be a very different crime in different circumstances. In some (it is to be hoped *rare*) instances, it is a crime of very deepest dye.... But, as well as I can judge, the greatest number of what are called murders of bastard children, are of a very different kind. The mother has an unconquerable sense of shame, and pants after the preservation of character: So far she is virtuous and amiable. She has not the resolution to meet and avow infamy. In proportion as she loses the hope either of having been mistaken with regard to pregnancy, or of being relieved from her terrors by a fortunate miscarriage, she every day sees her danger greater and nearer, and her mind overwhelmed with terror and despair. In this situation many of these women, who are afterwards accused of murder, would destroy themselves, if they did not know that such an action would infallibly lead to an inquiry, which would proclaim what they are so anxious to conceal. In this perplexity, and meaning nothing less than the murder of the infant, they are me-[82]ditating different schemes for concealing the death of the child; but are wavering between difficulties on all sides, putting the evil hour off, and trusting too much to chance and fortune. In that state often they are overtaken before they expected; their schemes are frustrated; their distress of body and mind deprives them of all judgment and rational conduct; they are delivered by themselves wherever they happen to retire in their fright or confusion; sometimes dying in the agonies of childbirth; and sometimes being quite exhausted, they faint away, and become insensible of what is passing; and when they recover a little strength, find that the child, whether still-born or not, is completely lifeless. In such a case, is it to be expected, when it would answer no purpose, that a woman should divulge the secret? Will not the best dispositions of mind urge her to preserve her character? She will therefore hide every appearance of what has happened as well as she can, though if the discovery be made, that conduct will be set down as a proof of her guilt...... Here let us suppose a case, which every body will allow to be very possible. An unmarried woman, becoming pregnant, is striving to conceal [83] her shame, and laying the best scheme that she can devise, for saving her own life and that of the child, and at the same time concealing the secret; but her plan is at once disconcerted by her being taken ill by herself, and delivered of a dead child. If the law punishes such a woman with death for concealing her shame, does it not require more from human nature, than weak human nature can bear? In a case so circumstanced, surely the only crime is the having been pregnant, which the law does not mean to punish with death; and the attempt to conceal it by fair means should not be punishable with death, as that attempt seems to arise from a principle of virtuous shame." *

[Bottom page 84] * Med. Obs. and Inq. vol. VI. p. 271. et seq.

The observations, here quoted, have a just claim to attention, from the extensive experience which the author possessed, and still more from his intimate knowledge of the female character. Yet to the moral and political philosopher, Dr. Hunter may appear to have exalted the sense of shame into the principle of virtue; and to have mistaken the great end of penal law, which is not vengeance, but the prevention of crimes. The statute, indeed, [84] which makes the concealment of the birth of a bastard child full proof of murder, confounds all distinctions of innocence and guilt, as such concealment, whenever practicable, would be the wish and act of all mothers, virtuous or vicious, under the same unhappy predicament. Law, however, which is the guardian and bulwark of the public weal, must maintain a steady, and even rigid watch, over the general tendencies of human actions: And when these are not only clearly understood, but interpreted according to the rules of wisdom and rectitude, that may justly be constituted a civil crime, which, if permitted, might give occasion to atrocious guilt, though in its own nature innocent. The measure of punishment, however, should be proportionate, as nearly as possible, to the temptations to offend, and to the kind and degree of evil produced by the offence. If inadequate to the former, it will be nugatory; and if too severe for the latter, it will defeat itself, by furnishing a just plea for superseding its execution.*

[Bottom page 85] * "L' atrocité des lois en empêche l'exécution. Lorsque la peine est sans mesure, on est souvent obligé de lui préférer l'inpunité." – MONTESQUIEU.

A revision of our sanguinary statutes is much wanted; and it would be [85] happy if means could be devised of suppressing the punishment, by obviating the crime, when it is merely positive or municipal. This we have seen accomplished with respect to the coinage of money, by the simple introduction of a standard weight in the payment of gold. And a sagacious legislator might doubtless discover and adopt similar improvements, in other branches of penal jurisprudence.

Much observation is required to discriminate between a child stillborn, and one that has lived after birth only a short space of time. Various appearances, also, both internal and external, may be mistaken for marks of violent death. Even the swimming of the lungs in ter, a test on which so much reliance is placed, will, on many occasions, be found fallacious. But these are points of professional science, which do not strictly fall under the subject of this section; and the reader is particularly referred to the paper already quoted, and also to the *Elementa Medicina Forensis Job. Fred. Faselii*; or to a valuable epitome of the same work in English by Dr. Farr.* [86]

[Bottom page 86, continuing to bottom page 87] Elements of Medical Jurisprudence; or a succinct and compendious Description of such Tokens in the Human Body, as are requisite to determine the Judgment of [86] a Coroner, and of Courts of Law, in Cases of Divorce, Rape, Murder, &c. London, Becket, 1788.

XII. *Duelling* is another species of felony, even though the consequences of it should not prove fatal: And gentlemen of the faculty are peculiarly interested in the knowledge are the laws relating to it; because they are not only liable to be summoned on the trial of the parties, if either or both of them be wounded, but are frequently professional attendants on them in the field of combat. It is astonishing that a practice, which originated in ages of Gothic ignorance, superstition, and barbarism should be continued in the present enlightened period, though condemned by the ordinances of every state, and repugnant to the spirit and percepts of Christianity. Sir Francis Bacon, when attorney-general, in the reign of James I. delivered a charge, before the court of star-chamber, touching duels, which gives a clear and animated view of the light in which they were then regarded. "The first motive," he says, "is a false and erroneous imagination of honour and credit; and therefore the king, in his proclamation, doth mostly aptly call them *bewitching duels*. For if one judge of it truly, it is no better than a sorcery, [87] that enchanteth the spirits of young men; and a kind of satanical illusion and apparition of honour against religion, against law, and against moral virtue. Hereunto maybe added that men have almost lost the true notion and understanding of fortitude and valor. For fortitude distinguisheth of the grounds of quarrels whether they be just; and not only so, but whether they be worthy; and setteth a better price upon men's lives than to bestow them idly. Nay, it is weakness and disesteem of a man's self, to put a man's life upon such liedger performances: A man's life is not to be trifled away; it is to be offered up and sacrificed to honourable services, public merits, good causes, and noble adventurers. It is in expence of blood as it is in expence of money; it is no liberality to make a profusion of money upon every vain occasion; nor no more is it fortitude to make effusion of blood, except the cause be of worth." *

[Bottom page 88] Bacon's Works, 4to. Birch's edit. vol. II, p. 565.

The decree of the Star Chamber against Priest and Wright, the objects of Sir Francis Bacon's charge, was, that they should both be committed to prison; that the former should be fined £500. and the latter 500 marks; and [88] that at the next assizes they should publicly acknowledge their high contempt of, and offence against God, the king's majesty, and his laws, shewing themselves penitent for the same. –Though this judgment appears to have been founded in wisdom and equity, yet, happily for our country, the court, which passed the sentence, has been long suppressed; and we are now governed not by arbitrary will, but by known and fixed laws. Those which subsist against duelling, I shall quote on the authorities of Foster, Blackstone, Hawkins, and Burn. "Deliberate duelling, if death ensueth, is, in the eye of the law, murder; for duels are generally founded in deep revenge; and though a person should be drawn into a duel, not upon a motive so criminal, but merely upon the punctilio of what the swordsmen falsely call honour, that will not excuse; for he that deliberately seeketh the blood of another upon a private quarrel, acteth in defiance of all laws human and divine."*

[Bottom page 89] * Sir Michael Fosters Reports, 8vo. p. 297.

"Express malice is when one, with a sedate deliberate mind formed design, doth kill another. This takes in the case of deliberate duelling, where both parties meet, avowedly, with any [89] intent to murder; thinking it their duty as gentlemen, and claiming it as their right, to wanton with their own lives, and those of their fellow-creatures, without any warrant or authority from any power either human or divine, but in direct contradiction to the laws both of God and man. And therefore, the law has justly fixed the crime and punishment of murder on them, and on their seconds also." *

[Bottom page 90] * Blackstone's Comment. Book IV. ch. xiv.

"The law so abhors all duelling in cold blood, that not only the principal who actually kills the other, but also his seconds, are guilty of murder, whether they fought or not: and it is holden that the seconds of the party slain are also guilty as accessaries." †

[Bottom page 90] † I. Hawkins, 82; and Burn's Justice, vol. II. p. 509.

– From variations in the moral and intellectual character of man, it is impossible to ascertain the precise period, when the passions maybe supposed to become cool, after having been violently agitated. Judgment, therefore, must be founded on the circumstances of deliberation, which are delivered in the course of evidence. In many cases, it has been determined that death, in consequence of an appointment and [90] meeting, a few hours subsequent the provocation, is murder.*

[Bottom page 91] * See Legg's ca. Kelyng 27; Eden's Principles of Penal Law, p. 224.

XIII. Before a surgeon engage professionally to *attend a duellist* to the *field of combat*, it behoves him to consider well, not only how far he is about to countenance a deliberate violation of the duties of morality and religion; but whether, in the construction of law, he may not be deemed an aider and abettor of a crime, which involves in it such turpitude, that death is alike denounced against the principal and the accessary. Does he not voluntarily put himself into a predicament, similar in many essential points, to that of the *second*, who is expressly condemned by the legislature of this country? Both are apprized of the purpose to commit an act of felony: Both take an interest in the circumstances attendant upon it: And both are present during the execution; the one to regulate its antecedents, the other to alleviate its consequences. But I suggest these considerations with much diffidence: And though I observe some passages, in Sir Michael Foster's Discourse concerning Accomplices, which seem to confirm them; yet it may be proper to quote the following, apparently adverse, opinion of [91] this excellent judge. "In order to render a person an accomplice and a principal in felony, he must be aiding and abetting at the fact, or ready to afford assistance, if necessary. And therefore, if A happeneth to be present at a murder, for instance, and taketh no part in it, nor endeavoureth to prevent it, nor apprehendeth the murderer, nor levieth hue and cry after him, this strange behaviour of his, though highly criminal, will not of itself render him either principal or accessary."*

[Bottom page 92] * Foster's Crown Law, 8vo. p. 350.

But whatever be the objections against the attendance of a surgeon in the field of combat, they cannot be construed to extend to the affording of all possible assistance, to any unfortunate sufferer in an affair of honour; provided such assistance be not preconcerted, but required as in ordinary accidents or emergencies. For in the offices of the healing art, no discrimination can be made, either of occasions or of characters. And it must be acknowledged, that many of the victims of duelling have been men, from their talents and virtues, possessing the justest claim to assiduous and tender attention. That lives of such inestimable va-[93]lue to their friends, to their families, and to the public, should be at the mercy of any profligate rake, who wantonly gives affronts, or idly fancies he receives them, is a great aggravation of the folly, as well as of the guilt of duelling. This reflection seems to shew the propriety of a change in the penal code, respecting it; and that the punishment inflicted should be confined to the aggressor; strict inquisition into the circumstances of the case being previously made, by the coroner, or some magistrate authorized and bound to exercise this important trust. And he may, with reason, be regarded as the aggressor, who either violates the rules of decorum, by any unprovoked rudeness or insult; or who converts into an offence, what was intended only as convivial pleasantry. (p)

[Bottom page 93] (p) * See Notes and Illustrations, No. XVII. [Should be XVI, per erratum page xvi]

XIV. A physician has no special interest in an acquaintance with the statutes relative to duelling. But as he possesses the rank of a gentleman, both by his liberal education and profession, the *law of honour*, if that may be termed a law which is indefinite and arbitrary, has a claim to his serious study and attention. As a philosopher, also, it becomes him to trace [93] its origin, and to investigate the principles on which it is founded: and as a moralist, duty calls upon him to counteract its baneful influence and ascendancy. For, in principle, it is distinct from virtue; and, as a practical rule, it extends only to certain formalities and decorums, of little importance in the transactions of life, and which are spontaneously observed by those, who are actuated with the true sense of propriety and rectitude. Genuine honour, in its full extent, may be defined a quick perception and strong feeling of moral obligation, in conjunction with an acute sensibility to shame, reproach, or infamy. In different characters, these constituent parts of the principle are found to exist in proportions to diversified, as sometimes to appear almost single and detached. The former always *aids and strengthens virtue*; the latter may *occasionally imitate her actions*,*

[Bottom page 94] * Addison's Cato

when fashion happily countenances, or high example prompts to rectitude. But being connected, for the most part, with a jealous pride and capricious irritability, it will be more shocked with the *imputation*, then with the *commission* of what is wrong. And thus it will constitute that spurious honour, [94] which, by a perversion ff the laws of association, *puts evil for good, and good for evil*; and, under the sanction of a name, perpetrates crimes without remorse, and even without ignominy.*

[Bottom page 95] * See the Author's Mor. And Lit. Diss. p. 295. 2d. Edit.

XV. *Homicide* by *poison* is another very important object of medical jurisprudence. When it is the effect of inadvertency, or the want of adequate caution, in the use of substances dangerous to health and life, the law regards it as a misdemeanor: When it is the consequences of rashness, of wanton experiment, or of motives unjust, though not malicious,†

[Bottom page 95] † "If an action unlawful itself be done deliberately, and *with intention of mischief*, or great bodily harm to particulars, or of mischief indiscriminately, fall it where it may, and death ensue against or beside the original and intention of the party, it will be murder. But if such *mischievous intention* doth not appear, which is matter of fact, and *to be collected from circumstances*, and the act was done heedlessly and incautiously, it will be manslaughter: not accidental death, because the act which ensued was unlawful." Foster, p. 261.

it becomes manslaughter: And when the express purpose is to kill, by means of some deleterious drug, it constitutes a most atrocious species of murder. In cases of this nature, [95] the faculty are called upon to give evidence concerning the nature of the poison, the symptoms produced by it, and the actual fatality of its operation. I know not whether the period of this fatal operation be extended, as in the infliction of blows and wounds, to a year and a day. But if it be, the most nice and accurate investigation of the progressive advances of disease and death will be incumbent on the physician or surgeon, who was consulted on the occasion. No subject has given rise to more misconception and superstition, than the action of poisons. Numberless substances had been classed as such, which, if not inert, are at least innoxious; and powers have been ascribed to others, far exceeding their real energy. –Even Lord Verulam, the great luminary of science, in his charge against the Earl of Somerset, for the murder of Sir Thomas Overbury, in the Tower of London, seems to give credit to the story of Livia, who was said to have poisoned the figs up on the tree, which her husband was won't to gather with his own hands. And he seriously states, that "Weston chased the poor prisoner with poison after poison; poisoning salts , poisoning meats, poisoning sweet-meats, poisoning medicines and vomits, until at last his body was almost [96] come, by the use of poisons, to the state that Mithridates's body was by the use of treacle and preservatives, that the force of the poisons was blunted upon him: Weston confessing, when he was tried for not dispatching him, that he had been given enough to poison twenty men." *

[Bottom page 97] * Bacon's Works, vol. II. p. 614.

In this criminal transaction the truth probably was, what has been judiciously suggested by Rapin, that the lieutenant of the tower, refusing to be concerned in the crime, yet not daring to discover it, from the fear of the Viscount Rochester's resentment, seized the victuals sent from time to time for the prisoner, and threw them into the house of office. Sir Thomas Overbury, however, fell a victim at last to empoisoned glyster.

When the particular drug, or other mean employed, can be accurately ascertained, its deleterious qualities should be fully investigated; and these should be cautiously compared with the effects ascribed to it, in the case under consideration. It may often be expedient, also, to examine the body of the sufferer by dissection; and this should be accomplished as expeditiously as possible; that the changes [97] imputed to death may not be confounded with those which are imputed to poison. But on such points reference can alone be made to the knowledge and experience of the practitioner, and to the lights which he may acquire by consulting Faselius, and other works of a similar nature. I shall, therefore, close this article with a few passages of the charge of Mr. Justice Buller to the grand jury, relative to the trial of Captain Donellan, for the murders of Sir Theodosius Boughton, at the Warwick assizes, in March 1781. "In this case, gentlemen," he says, "you will have two objects to consider, first, whether the deceased did die of *poison*? secondly, whether the person suspected did assist in *administering* the poison? With respect to the first of these considerations, you will, no doubt, *hear the sentiments of those who are skilled in the nature and effects of poison*, which is of various sorts, and most subtile in its operation. –From the *information* of such persons you will be able to form an opinion of the effects which *different poisons* have on *different* persons; and also the effects the *same poisons* have on persons of *different habits and constitutions*. If you find he did get his death by poison, the next case is, to consider, [98] who gave him that poison. Where poison is knowingly given, and death ensues, it is wilful murder; and if one is present, when poison is given by another, he is not an accessary, but a principal."*

[Bottom page 99] * Hist. Sketches of Civil Liberty, p. 209.

XVI. In all civilized countries, the honour and chastity of the female sex are guarded from violence, by the severest sanctions of law. And this protection is at once humane, just, and necessary to social morality. It is consonant to humanity that weakness should be secure against the attacks of brutal strength: It is just that the most sacred of all personal property should be preserved from invasion: –And it is essential to morality that licentious passion should be restrained; that modesty should not be wounded; nor the mind contaminated, in some instances, before it is capable of forming adequate conceptions of right and wrong. The crime of *rape*, therefore, subjects the perpetrator to condign punishment by every code of jurisprudence, ancient or modern. (q)

[Bottom page 99] (q) See Notes and Illustrations, No. XV. [Should be XVII per erratum page xvi]

Amongst the Jews death was inflicted, if the damsel were betrothed to another man: and if not betrothed, a fine, amounting to fifty she[99]kels of silver, was to be paid to her father by him who had *laid hold of the virgin*, and she was to become his wife: And because *he had humbled her, he might not put her away all his days*: *

[Bottom page 100] * Deuteronomy xxii. 28, 29.

For the privilege of divorce was authorized by the Jewish institutions. The Romans made this offence capital, superadding the confiscation of goods. Even the carrying-off a woman from her parents or guardians, and cohabiting with her, whether accomplished by force, or with her full consent, were made equally penal with a rape, by an imperial edict. For the Roman law seems to have supposed, that women never deviate from virtue, without being seduced by the arts of the other sex. –And, therefore, by imposing a powerful restraint on the solicitations of men, they aimed at a more effectual security of the chastity of women. *Nisi etenim eam solicitaverit, nisi, odiosis artibus circumvenerit, non faciet eam velle in tantum dedecus sese prodere*. But the English law, as Judge Blackstone has observed, does not entertain such sublime ideas of the honour of either sex, as to lay the blame of a mutual fault on one only of the transgressors. And it is, therefore, essential to the crime of [100] rape, that the woman's will is violated by the execution. But, by a statute of Queen Elizabeth, if the crime be perpetrated on a female child under the age of *ten* years, the consent or non-consent is immaterial, as she is supposed to be of insufficient judgment. Sir Matthew Hale is even of opinion, that such profligacy committed on an infant under *twelve* years, the age of female discretion by common law, either with or without consent, amounts to a rape and felony. But the decisions of the courts have, generally, been founded on the statute above-mentioned.

A male infant, under the age of fourteen years, is deemed, by law, incapable of committing, and therefore cannot be found guilty of a rape, from a presumed imbecility both of body and mind. This detestable crime, being executed in secrecy, and the knowledge of it being confined to the party injured, it is just that her single testimony should be adducible in proof of the fact. Yet the excellent observation of Sir Matthew Hale merits peculiar attention: "It is an accusation," he says, "easy to be made, and harder to be proved; but harder to be defended by the party accused, though innocent." He then relates two extraordinary cases of malicious prosecution for [101] this crime, which had fallen under his own cognizance; and concludes, "I mention these instances, that we may be more cautious upon trials of offences of this nature, wherein the court and jury may, with so much ease, be imposed upon, without great care and vigilance; the heinousness of the offense many times transporting the judge and jury with so much indignation, that they are over-hastily carried to the conviction of the person accused thereof, by the confident testimony of sometimes false and malicious witnesses." Collateral and concurrent circumstances of time and place;*

[Bottom page 102] * These circumstances are particularly adverted to in the Mosaic Law. See Deut. xxii. 25, 26, 27.

appearances of violence on examination &c. are, therefore, necessary to be added to the mere affirmative evidence of the prosecutor. And the inspection of a surgeon is often required, to ascertain the reality of the alledged violence. On such occasions, his testimony should be given with all possible delicacy, as well as with the utmost caution. Even external signs of injury may originate from disease, of which the following examples, which have occurred in Manchester, are adduced on very respectable authorities [102].

A girl, about four years of age, was admitted into the Manchester Infirmary, on account of a mortification in the female organs, attended with great soreness and general depression of strength. She had been in a bed with a boy, fourteen years old; and there was reason to suspect, that he had taken criminal liberties with her. The mortification increased, and the child died. The boy, therefore, was apprehended, and tried at the Lancaster assizes; but was acquitted on sufficient evidence, that several instances of a familiar disease had appeared, near the same period of time, in which there was no possibility of injury or guilt. In one of these cases the body was opened after death. The disorder had been a *typhus* fever, accompanied with the mortification of *pudenda*. There was no evident cause of this extraordinary symptom discoverable on inspection. The lumbar glands were of a dark colour; but all the *viscera* were sound. (r)

[Bottom page 103] (r) See Notes and Illustrations, No. XVII. [Should be XVIII per erratum page xvi]

XVII. Concerning *nuisances* , the investigation and testimony of the faculty may be required, whenever they are of a nature offensive by the vapours which they emit, and injurious to the health of individuals, or of the commu-[103]nity. The law defines any thing that worketh hurt, inconvenience, or damage, to be a nuisance.*

[Bottom page 104] * Blackstone's Comment. Book III. ch. xiii.; and Book IV. ch. xiii.

Thus if a person keep hogs, or other noisome animals, so near the house of another, that the stench incommodes him, and renders the air unwholesome, this is a nuisance; because it deprives him of the enjoyments and benefits of his habitation. A smelting house for lead, the smoke of which kills the grass and corn, and injures the cattle of a neighbouring proprietor of land, is deemed a nuisance. Dye-houses, tanning-yards &c. are nuisances, if erected so near a water-course, as to corrupt the stream. But a chandler's factory, even when situated in a crowded town, is said to be privileged from action or indictment, because candles are regarded as necessaries of life. Hawkins, however, questions the authority of this opinion, since the making of candles may be carried on in the country without annoyance. †

[Bottom page 104] † 1 Hawk. 199. Burn's Justice, vol. III. p. 239.

But this is scarcely practicable in a populous neighbourhood: And as Lord Mansfield has adjudged, that, in such cases, what makes the enjoyment of being and property [104] uncomfortable is, in the view of the law, a nuisance;*

[Bottom page 105] * Burron Mansfield, 333. Burn U. S.

various works and trades, essential to the happiness and interest of the community, may fall under this construction. But chemistry, mechanics, and other arts and sciences, furnish methods of diminishing, or obviating almost every species of noisome vapour. And there can be no doubt that vitriol works, aqua-fortis works, marine acid-bleaching works, the singeing of velvets &c. may be carried on with very little inconvenience to a neighbourhood, by means neither difficult nor expensive. The same observation may be applied to the business of the dyer, the fellmonger, the tanner, the butcher, and the chandler. And as these with many other disgustful trades are, in some degree, necessary in large towns, justice and policy require, that they should only be prosecuted as nuisances, when not conducted in the least offensive mode possible. To guard against arbitrary powers in municipal government, and to render the decision and investigation of such points perfectly consistent with the liberty of the subject, the reference should be made to a jury; or at least, any individual should be allowed an appeal to one, if he think himself aggrieved [105].

The frequency of fires, in large manufacturing towns, makes it expedient that magistrates, or commissioners, should be authorized to scrutinize rigidly into the causes of them, when they occur; to punish neglect or carelessness, as well as malicious intention; and to enforce suitable measures of prevention. The plans, proposed for this last very important purpose, by Mr. Hartley and Lord Stanhope, have been proved to be effectual, and are not expensive. The adoption of them, therefore, or of other means which may hereafter be discovered, should be required, under a heavy penalty, in cases deemed by insurers *doubly hazardo*us.

XVIII. It is a complaint made by coroners, magistrates, and judges, that medical gentlemen are often reluctant in the performance of the offices, required from them as citizens qualified, by professional knowledge, to aid the execution of public justice. These offices, it must be confessed, are generally painful, always inconvenient, and occasion an interruption to business, of a nature not to be easily appreciated or compensated. But as they admit of no substitution, they are to be regarded as appropriate debts to the community, which [106] neither equity nor patriotism will allow to be cancelled.

When a physician or surgeon is called to give evidence, he should avoid, as much as possible, all obscure and technical terms, and the unnecessary display of medical erudition. He should deliver, also, what he advances, in the purest and most delicate language, consistent with the nature of the subject in question. –When two or more gentlemen of the faculty are to offer their opinions or testimony, it would sometimes tend to obviate contrariety, if they were to confer freely with each other before their public examination. Intelligent and honest men, fully acquainted with their respective means of information, are much less likely to differ, than when no communication has previously taken place. Several years ago, a trial of considerable consequence occurred, relative to a large copper work; and two physicians of eminence were summoned to the assizes, to bear testimony concerning the salubrity or insalubrity of the smoke issuing from the furnaces. The evidence they offered was entirely contradictory. One grounded his testimony on the general presumption that the ores of copper contain arsenic; and consequently that the effluvia, proceeding from the roasting [107] of them, must be poisonous because arsenical. The other had made actual experiments on the ore, employed in the works under prosecution, and on the vapours which it yielded: He was thus furnished with full proof that no arsenic was discoverable in either. But the affirmative prevailed over the negative testimony, from the authority of the physician who delivered it; an authority which he probably would not have misapplied, if he had been antecedently acquainted with the decisive trials made by his opponent. (s)

[Bottom page 108] (s) See Notes and Illustrations, No. XIX.

XIX. It is the injunction of the law, sanctioned by the solemnity of an oath, that in judicial testimony, *the truth, the whole truth,* and *nothing but the truth* shall be delivered. A witness, therefore, is under a sacred obligation to use his best endeavours that his mind be clear and collected, unawed by fear, and uninfluenced by favour or enmity. But in criminal prosecutions, which affect the life of the person accused, scruples will be apt to arise in one who, by the advantages of a liberal education, has been accustomed to serious reflection, yet has paid no particular attention to the principles of political ethics. It is incumbent, [108] therefore, on gentlemen of the faculty, to settle their opinions concerning the right of the civil magistrate to inflict capital punishment; the moral and social ends of such punishment; the limits prescribed to the exercise of the right; and the duty of a citizen to give full efficiency to the laws.

The magistrate's *right* to inflict punishment, and the ends of such punishment, though intimately connected, are in their nature distinct. The right is clearly substitution or transfer of that which belongs to every individual, by the law of nature, viz. instant self-defence, and security from future violence or wrong. The ends are more comprehensive, extending not only to complete security against offence, but to the correction and improvement of the offender himself, and to counteract in others the disposition to offend. Penal laws are to be regulated by this standard; and the lenity or severity, with which they are executed, should, if possible, be exactly proportionate to it. In different circumstances, either personal or public considerations may preponderate: And in cases of great moral atrocity, or when the common weal is essentially injured, all regard to the reformation of a criminal is superseded; and his life is justly forfeited to [109] the good of society. In the participation of the benefits of the social union, he has virtually acceded to its conditions; and the violation of its fundamental articles renders him a rebel and an enemy, to be expelled or destroyed, both for the sake of security, and as an awful warning to others. When capital punishments are viewed in this light, the most humane and scrupulous witness may consider himself as sacrificing private emotions to public justice and social order; and that he is performing an act at once beneficial to his country and to mankind. For political and moral œconomy can subsist in no community, without the steady execution of wise and salutary laws: And every atrocious act, perpetrated with impunity, operates as a terror to the innocent, a snare to the unwary, and an incentive to the flagitious. The criminal, also, who evades the sentence of justice, like one infected with the pestilence, contaminates all whom he approaches. He, therefore, who, from false tenderness, or misguided conscience, has prevented conviction, by withholding the necessary proofs,*

[Bottom page 110, continuing to bottom page 111] * "The oath administered to the witness, is not only that what he deposes shall be true, but that he shall also depose the whole truth: *So that he is not to conceal any [110] part of what he knows, whether interrogated particularly to that point or not*." – Blackstone, B III. ch. xxiii. is on accessary to [110] all the evils which ensue. The maxim, that *it is better ten villains should be discharged than a single person suffer by a wrong adjudication*, is one of those partial truths which are generally misapplied, because not accurately understood. It is certainly eligible that the rules and the forms of law should be so precise and immutable, as not to involve the innocent in any decision obtained by corruption, or dictated by passion and prejudice; though this should sometimes furnish an outlet for the escape of actual offenders. The plea, also, may have some validity, in crimes of a nature chiefly political, (with which, however, the faculty can professionally have no concern,) such as coining and forgery, or in cases wherein the punishment much exceeds the evil or turpitude of the offense. For Lord Bacon has well observed, that "over-great penalties, besides their acerbity, deaden the execution of the law." *

[Bottom page 111] * See proposal for amending the Laws of England. – Bacon's Works, 4to. vol. II. p. 542.
And when they are discovered to be unjustly inflicted, its authority is impaired, its sanctity dishonored, and veneration gives place to disgust and abhorrence [111].

But the dread of *innocent blood being brought upon us*, by explicit and honest testimony, is one of those superstitions which the nurse has taught, and which a liberal education ought to purge from the mind. And if, in the performance of our duty, innocence should unfortunately be involved in the punishment of guilt, we shall assuredly stand acquitted before God and our own consciousness. The convict himself, lamentable as his fate must be regarded, may derive consolation from the reflection, that, though his sentence be unjust, "he falls for his country, whilst he suffers under the operation of those rules, by the general effect and tendency of which the welfare of the community is maintained and upheld."*

[Bottom page 112] * Paley's Moral and Political Phil. B. VI. ch. ix. p. 553. 4to.

XX. When professional testimony is required, in cases of such peculiar malignity as to excite general horror and indignation, a virtuous mind, even though scrupulous and timid, is liable to be influenced by too violent impressions; and to transfer to the accused that dread and aversion, which, before conviction, should be confined to the crime, and as much as possible withheld from the supposed offender. If the charge, for instance, be that of a parricide, [112] accomplished by poison, and accompanied with deliberate malice, ingratitude, and cruelty; the investigation should be made with calm and unbiased precision, and the testimony delivered with no colouring of passion, nor with any deviation from the *simplicity of truth*. When *circumstantial proofs* are adduced, they should be arranged in the most lucid order, that they may be contrasted and compared, in all their various relations, with facility and accuracy; and that their weight may be separately and collectively determined in the balance of justice. For, in such evidence, there subsists a regular graduation from the slightest presumption to complete moral certainty. And if the witness possesses sufficient information in this branch of philosophical and juridical science, he will always be competent to secure himself, and on many occasions the court also, from fallacy and error. The Marquis de Beccaria has laid down the following excellence theorems, concerning judicial evidence: "When the proofs of a crime are dependent on each other, that is, when the evidence of each witness, taken separately, proves nothing; or when all the proofs are dependent upon one, the number of proofs neither increases nor diminishes the probability of the fact; [113] for the force of the whole is no greater than the force of those on which they depend; and if this fails, they all fall to the ground. When the proofs are independent of each other, the probability of the fact increases in proportion to the number of proofs; for the falsehood of one does not diminish the veracity of another .... The proofs of a crime may be divided into two classes, perfect and imperfect. I call those perfect, which exclude the possibility of innocence; imperfect, those which do not exclude this possibility. Of the first, one only is sufficient for condemnation; of the second, as many are required as form a perfect proof; that is to say, each of these, separately taken, does not exclude the possibility of innocence; it is nevertheless excluded by their union." *

[Bottom page 114] * Beccaria's Essay on Crimes and Punishment, chap. xiv.

AN

APPENDIX

CONTAINING,

I. A DISCOURSE,

ADDRESSED TO

THE GENTLEMEN OF THE FACULTY;

THE OFFICERS;

THE CLERGY; AND THE TRUSTEES OF THE

INFIRMARY AT LIVERPOOL,

ON THEIR RESPECTIVE HOSPITAL DUTIES.

BY THE

Rev. THOMAS BASSNETT PERCIVAL, LL. B.

Of Saint John's College, Cambridge; Chaplain to the Marquis of Waterford; and to the Company

of British Merchants at Saint Petersburg.

II. NOTES AND ILLUSTRATIONS. [not paginated: 115]

....LO! A GOODLY HOSPITAL ASCENDS,

IN WHICH THEY BADE EACH LENIENT AID BE NIGH,

THAT COULD THE SICK-BED SMOOTH OF THAT SAD COMPANY.

IT WAS A WORTHY EDIFYING SIGHT,

AND GIVES TO HUMAN KIND PECULIAR GRACE,

TO SEE KIND HANDS ATTENDING DAY AND NIGHT,

WITH TENDER MINISTRY, FROM PLACE TO PLACE:

SOME PROP THE HEAD; SOME, FROM THE PALLID FACE,

WIPE OFF THE FAINT COLD DEWS WEAK NATURE SHEDS;

SOME REACH THE HEALING DRAUGHT; THE WHILST TO CHACE

THE FEAR SUPREME, AROUND THEIR SOFTENED BEDS,

SOME HOLY MAN BY PRAYER ALL OPENING HEAVEN DISPREDS."

THOMSONS'S Castle of Indolence; Canto II. [not paginated: 116]

A

DISCOURSE ON HOSPITAL DUTIES:

BEING AN

ANNIVERSARY SERMON,

Preached in May 1791;

FOR THE BENEFIT OF THE INFIRMARY AT LIVERPOOL. (s)

[Bottom page 117] (s) See Notes and Illustrations, No. XX.

"*Let us not be weary in well doing, for in due season we shall reap if we faint not.*" – Galations

vi. 9.

IF we consider the circumstances of man, as placed in this great theatre of action; as connected with his fellow-creatures by various ties and relations; and with God himself, his creator and judge: If we consider the powers and faculties with which he is endowed, and that these are talents committed to his trust, capable of indefinite degrees of improvement, and which the Lord, at his coming, will demand with usury; we shall see the fullest reason for the apostolical injunction, *be not weary in well doing*, and rejoice in the assurance, that *in due season we shall reap, if we faint not.* The sphere of human duty has no limits [117] to its extent. Every advance in knowledge widens its boundaries; every increase of power and wealth multiplies and diversifies the objects of it; and length of years evinces their unceasing succession. Therefore, *whatsoever thy hand findeth to do, do it with all thy might.* Vigour and perseverance are essential to every noble pursuit; and no virtuous effort is in vain. To be discouraged by opposition; to be alarmed by danger; or overcome by difficulty, is a state of mind unfitted for the Christian warfare.

But the present interesting occasion calls for a specific application of the precept, contained in our text. What is just and true, concerning the whole duty of man, must be equally just and true of every individual branch of moral and religious obligation. And it can require no deep research, no abstruse investigation , to work conviction on our minds, that the higher is the object we have in view, the more active and incessant should be our exertions in the attainment of it. The institution, which now claims your most serious attention, is founded on the; *wisest policy*; adapted to the noblest purposes of *humanity*; and capable of being rendered subservient to the *everlasting welfare* of mankind [118].

The wisdom of such charitable foundations can admit of no dispute. On the lower classes of our fellow-citizens alone, we depend for food, for raiment, for the habitations in which we dwell, and for all the conveniences and comforts of life. But health is essential to their capacity for labour; and in this labour, I fear, it is too often sacrificed. An additional obligation, therefore, to afford relief, springs from so affecting a consideration. He, who at once toils and suffers for our benefit, has a multiplied claim to our support; and to withhold it, would be equally chargeable with folly, ingratitude, and injustice.

But *humanity* prompts, when the still voice of wisdom is not heard. Sickness, complicated with poverty, has pleas, that, to a feeling mind are irresistible. *To weep with those that weep*, was the character of our divine master; and, to the honour of our nature, we are capable of the same generous sympathy. Vain and idle, however, are the softest emotions of the mind, when they lead not to correspondent actions. And he who views the naked, without cloathing them, and those who are sick, without ministering unto them, incurs the dreadful denunciation, *Depart from me, ye* [119] *cursed, into everlasting fire, prepared for the devil and his angels. For in as much as ye did it not to one of the least of these my brethren, ye did it not unto me.*

It were an easy and pleasing task to enlarge on these general topics. But they come not sufficiently "home to men's business and bosoms." And honoured as I am, by being thus called to the privilege of addressing you, I feel it incumbent on me to be more appropriate, by suggesting to your candid attention, the distinct and relative duties attached to the several orders, which compose this most excellent community. Permit me, therefore, to claim your indulgence, whilst I offer, with all deference and respect, but with the plainness and freedom of gospel sincerity, a few words of exhortation:

  I. TO THE FACULTY;
 II. TO THE OFFICERS AND SUPERINTENDANTS;
III. TO THE CLERGY;

And lastly, TO THE GENERAL BODY OF TRUSTEES AND CONTRIBUTORS.

I. TO THE FACULTY. As man is placed by Divine Providence in a situation which involves a variety of interests and duties, often compli-[120]cated in mixed together, the motives which influence human actions must necessarily be mixed and complicated. Wisdom and virtue consist in the selection of those which are fit and good, and in the arrangement of all, by a just appreciation of their comparative dignity and importance. In the acceptance of your professional offices, in this Infirmary, it is presumed that you have been governed by the *love of reputation*; by the *desire of acquiring knowledge and experience*; and by that *spirit of philanthropy*, which delights in, and is never weary of well-doing. Let us briefly consider each of these principles of action, and how they ought to be regulated.

If we analyze the *love of reputation*, as it exists in liberal and well-informed minds, it will be found to spring from the love of moral and intellectual excellence. For of what value is praise, when not founded on desert? But the consciousness of desert, by the constitution of our nature, is ever attended with self-approbation: And this delightful emotion, which is at once the concomitant, and the reward of virtue, widely expands its operation, and by a social sympathy, encircles all who are the witness or judges of our generous [121] deeds. From the same principle, piety itself derives its origin. For how shall he who loveth not, or is regardless of the approbation of his brother, whom he hath seen, love or regard the favour of God, whom he hath not seen!

But let us remember, not to substitute, for the legitimate and magnanimous love of same, that spurious and sordid passion which seeks applause by gratifying the caprices, by indulging the prejudices, and by imposing on the follies of mankind. To quote the public favour by adulation, or empirical arts, is meanness and hypocrisy; to claim it, by high and assumed pretensions, is arrogance and pride; and to exalt our own character, by the deprecation of that of our competitor, is to convert honourable emulation into professional enmity and injustice.

You have been elevated by the suffrages of your fellow-citizens: You have been honoured by their favour and confidence: Rejoice in the distinction conferred upon you; fulfil with assiduity and zeal the trust reposed in you; and by being unwearied in well doing, rise to higher and higher degrees of public favour and celebrity!

The *acquisition of knowledge and experience* is a farther incentive to your generous exertions, [122] in this receptacle of disease and misery. It is one important design of the institution itself; which affords peculiar advantages for ascertaining the operation of remedies, and the comparative merit of different modes of medical and chirurgical treatment. For the strict rules which are enjoined; the steadiness with which their observance is enforced; and the unremitting attendance of those who are qualified to make accurate observations, and to note every symptom, whether regular or anomalous, in the diseases under cure, are circumstances incompatible with the ordinary domestic care of the sick. To avail yourselves of them, therefore, is agreeable to sound policy, and consonant to the purest justice and humanity. For every improvement in the healing art is a public good, beneficial to the poor as well as to the rich, and to the former in a proportionably greater degree, as they are more numerous, and consequently more frequently the objects of it. On this point, however, peculiar delicacy is required; and as the discretionary power, with which you are entrusted, is almost without controul, it should be exercised what the nicest honour and probity. When novelties in practice are introduced, be careful that [123] they are conformable to reason and analogy; that no sacrifice be made to fanciful hypothesis, or experimental curiosity; that the infliction of pain or suffering be, as much as possible, avoided; and that the end in view fully warrant the means for its attainment.

But your noblest call to duty and exertion arises from the exalted *spirit of philanthropy*. And on this occasion I may address you individually, in the language of the first of orators to the sovereign of imperial Rome: *Nihil habet fortuna tua majus quam ut possis, nec natura melius qua ut velis, servare quam plurimos.* It is your honour and felicity to be engaged in an occupation which leads you, like our blessed Lord during his abode on earth, to go about doing good, healing the sick, and curing all manner of diseases. To you learning has opened her stores, that they may be applied to the sublimest purposes; to alleviate pain; to raise the drooping head; to renew the roses of the cheek, and the sparkling of the eye; and thus to gladden, whilst you lengthen life. Let this hospital be the theatre on which you display, with assiduous and persevering care, your science, skill, and humanity. And let the manner correspond with, and even heigh-[124]ten, the measure of your benevolence. With patience hear the tale of symptoms; silence not harshly the murmurs of a troubled mind; and by the kindness of your looks and words, evince that Christian condescension may be compatible with professional steadiness and dignity.

It is, I trust, an ill-founded opinion, that compassion is not the virtue of a surgeon. This branch of the profession has been charged with hardness of heart: And some of its members have formerly justified the stigma, by ridiculing all softness of manners; by assuming the contrary deportment; and by studiously banishing from their minds that sympathy, which they falsely supposed would be unsuitable to their character, and unfavourable to the practical exercise of their art. But different sentiments now prevail. And a distinction should ever be made between true compassion, and that unmanly pity which enfeebles the mind; which shrinks from the sight of woe; which inspires timidity; and deprives him, who is under its influence, of all capacity to give relief. Genuine compassion rouses the attention of the soul; gives energy to all its powers; suggests expedients in dan-[125]ger; incites to vigorous action in difficulty; and strengthens the hand to execute, with promptitude, the purposes of the head. The pity which you should repress, is a turbulent emotion. The commiseration which you should cultivate is a calm principle. It is benevolence itself directed forcibly to a specific object. And the frequency of such objects diminishes not, but augments its energy: For it produces a tone or constitution of mind, constantly in unison with suffering; and prepared, on every call, to afford the full measure of relief. Appear, therefore, to your patients to be actuated by that fellow-feeling, which nature, education, and Christianity require. Make your cases, in a reasonable degree, your own; *and whatsoever ye would that men should do unto you, do ye even so unto them.*

II. To you, the OFFICERS and SUPERINTENDANTS of this hospital, we may justly ascribe views the most pure and public-spirited. But zeal in the cause of charity, however sincere, can only be rendered usefully efficient by due attention to, and steady perseverance in, the wisest means for its accomplishment. On the mistaken humanity of crowding your wards with numerous patients, by which disease is [126] generated, and death multiplied in all its horrors; on the fatal calculations of savings in medicines, diet, or clothing; and on a strict attention to ventilation, cleanliness, and all the domestic arrangements, which have order, utility, or comfort for their objects; I trust it is needless to enlarge. But you will suffer me, I hope, to offer a few hints on the *moral* and *religious* application of the institution which you govern; a topic hitherto little noticed, though of high importance.

The visitation of sickness is a wise and kind dispensation of Providence, intended to humble, to refine, and to meliorate the heart. And its salutary influence extends beyond the sufferer, to those relatives and friends, whose office it is to minister unto him; exciting tenderness and commiseration; drawing closer the bonds of affection; and rousing to exertions, virtuous in their nature, profitable to man, and well-pleasing to God. A parent, soothed and supported under the anguish of pain, by the loving kindness of his children; a husband nursed with unwearied assiduity by the partner of his bed; a child experiencing all the tenderness of paternal and maternal love, are situations which form the ground-work of domestic virtue, and [127] domestic felicity. They leave indelible impressions on the mind, impressions which exalt the moral character, and render us better men, better citizens, and better

Christians. It is wisdom, therefore, and duty, not to frustrate the benevolent constitutions of Heaven, by dissolving the salutary connections of sickness, and transporting into a public asylum those who may, with a little aid, enjoy in their own homes, benefits and consolations which, elsewhere, it is in the power of no one to confer. (t)

[Bottom page 128] (t) See Notes and Illustrations, No. XXI.

But numerous are the sufferers under sickness and poverty, to whom your hospitable doors may be opened, with the highest moral benefit to themselves and to the community. When admitted within these walls, they form one great family, of which you are the heads, and consequently responsible for all due attention to their present behavior, and to the means of their future improvement. Withdrawn from the habitations of penury, sloth, and dirtiness; from the conversation of the loose and the profligate; and from all their associates in vice, they may here form a taste for the sweets of cleanliness; learn the power of bridling [128] their tongues; and be induced, by this temporary absence, to free themselves from all farther connection with their idle and debauched companions. Let it be your sedulous care to foster these excellent tendencies: Encourage in the patients every attention to neatness: Tolerate no filth or slovenliness, either in their persons or attire: Keep a strict guard on the decency of their behaviour: Urge them to active offices of kindness and compassion to each other: Furnish the convalescents with bibles, and with books of plain morality, and practical piety, suited to their capacities and circumstances; and which will neither delude the imagination, nor perplex the understanding: Oblige them to a regular attendance on the public worship of the hospital, or of their respective churches: And, agreeably to your laws, neglect not to make provision for the stated and frequent in administration of the holy sacrament. There is something in this office peculiarly adapted to comfort and fortify the mind, under the pressure of poverty, pain, and sickness. In the contemplation of that love which Christ manifested for us by his sufferings and death, all the consolation is experienced which divine sym[129]pathy can afford. *We have a high priest touched with the feeling of our infirmities*, and who holds forth to us this soothing invitation; *Come unto me all ye that are weary and heavy laden, and I will give you rest*. Promote the celebration of an ordinance, adapted thus to fill the mind with gratitude, and to alleviate every woe. And let the example of our Saviour's resignation to the appointments of God be enforced by it, who in his agony exclaimed, *Father, if it be thy will, let this cup pass from me, nevertheless, not my will, but thine be done*.

III. I doubt not the cordial an entire concurrence of you, my REV. BRETHREN, the CLERGY who officiate in this hospital, in the recommendation of the holy sacrament, not only as a stated, but as a frequent ordinance of the institution. With you it will rest to obviate every objection to the rite, and to give it the full measure of spiritual efficacy. Enthusiasm and superstition cannot be dreaded in the offices of rational piety, conducted by those who are rational and pious. And you will neither betray men into false confidence, nor alarm them, when languishing under sickness and pain, with unseasonable terrors. *The* [130] *spirit of a man will sustain his infirmity, but a wounded spirit who can bear*? Under such circumstances, vain will be the aid of skill or medicine, without the supports and comforts, which it is your sacred function to afford. You can

------ "minister to a mind diseased; Pluck from the memory a rooted sorrow, Raze out the written troubles of the brain, And, with some sweet oblivious antidote, Cleanse the full bosom of that perilous stuff Which weighs upon the heart." (SHAKESPEARE)

Being thus the *Physicians* of the soul, you are essential constituents of this enlarged system of philanthropy. Apply, therefore, with diligence and zeal, the spiritual *medicines* which it is your office to dispense. Here you have a wide field *for exhortation, for correction, and for instruction in righteousness.* Convalescence peculiarly furnishes the *mollia tempora fandi,* the soft seasons of impressive counsel. The mind is then open to serious conviction; disposed to review past offences with contrition; and to look forward with sincere resolutions of amendment. Many diseases are the immediate consequences of vice: And he who has recently experienced [131] the sufferings of guilt, will deeply feel its enormity; and cherish those precepts, which will secure him from relapse, and convert his past misery into future blessings.

IV. But this large aggregate of good, which it is the design of the present anniversary to commemorate, depends, for its support and extension, on the GENERAL BODY OF CONTRIBUTORS to the charity. How deeply interesting, then, are the claims which your fellow-citizens have to make on your philanthropy! How important is it to the health of thousands, in rapid succession, that you should persevere in beneficence, and continue unwearied in well doing! Ordinary bounty terminates almost in the moment when it is bestowed. The object of it being withdrawn, solicitude and responsibility are no more. But in this noble Institution, charity exerts itself in the steady and unceasing operations. It is a stream ever full, yet ever flowing; and through the grace of God, I trust, will be inexhaustible. From your zeal, your concord, and liberality, these SACRED *waters of life* proceed. Be watchful that they are not poisoned in their source, nor contaminated in their progress. Let your *zeal* [132] be employed in searching out, and recommending proper objects of relief. *Call to you,* according to the injunction of our Saviour, *the halt, and the maimed, the lame, and the blind; for they cannot recompense you: Ye shall be recompensed at the resurrection of just.* Suffer no prejudices, either political or religious, to contract the bounds of your charity. *Pass not by, on the other side, from a fellow-creature who has fallen amongst thieves,* because he is not of your party, of your sect, or even of your nation. But, like the good Samaritan, *have compassion on him, and let oil and wine be poured upon his wounds* in this hospitable *Bethesda.* Guard, most sedulously guard, against the spirits of dissension. You are united in the labours of Christian love; and having one common and glorious cause, the contest should be for pre-eminence in doing good, not for the gratification of pride, the indulgence of resentment, or even the interests of friendship. (u)

[Bottom page 133] (u) See Notes and Illustrations, No. XXII.

To your liberality in contribution no appeal can be required, no new incitement can be urged. What your judgment approves, what experience has sanc-[133]tioned, and what touches the tenderest feelings of your hearts, must have pleas that are irresistible.

It only remains, then, that we cordially unite in offering our devout supplications to the throne of grace, in behalf of all those *who are afflicted or distressed in mind, body, or estate; that it may please the God of all consolation to relieve them, according to their several necessities; giving them patience under their sufferings, and a happy issue out of all their afflictions: And finally, that we will be delivered from all hardness of heart; from all covetous desires, and inordinate love of riches; and, having been taught that all our doings, without charity, profit nothing, that this most excellent gift, the bond of peace, and of all virtues, may be poured into us abundantly, through the merits and meditation of our blessed Lord and Saviour* [134].

NOTES

AND

ILLUSTRATIONS

I. Note. Preface. Page 1.

HOSPITAL AT MANCHESTER

THIS Institution comprehends an Infirmary, Lunatic Hospital, and Dispensary; and has now connected with it a House of Recovery, for the reception of patients ill of contagious fevers. It provides, also, for inoculation both variolous and vaccine; and for the delivery of pregnant women at their own habitations. From the 24th of June 1792, to the 24th of June 1802, the in-patients, admitted during the space of 10 years, amounted to 8769 [In ink by hand, this is struck out and replaced with 8083. This is the number reported in *Works* (Percival 1807, Vol. II, 479)]; of which number 360 one died: The out-patients amounted to 31,890; of which number 676 died. The home-patients amounted to 24,439; of which number 1970 died. The Lunatic Hospital was established in the year 1766; from which time to June 24th, 1802, the patients admitted have amounted to 1575. Of this number 627 have been cured; 212 have been [not paginated 135] relieved; 488 have been discharged at the request of their friends; 171 have died; 8 have been deemed incurable; and 69 remained in the house on the 24th of June 1802. The House of Recovery, for the admission of patients ill of contagious fever, is appropriated to those, who, from extreme penury, are incapable of receiving proper aid in their own close and noisome habitations, or who are liable to communicate contagion to a numerous family, and, if in a crowded neighbourhood, even to perpetuate its virulence. It is attended by the physicians of the Infirmary; and is furnished with wine and medicines from the funds of that charity: But all other expences are defrayed by an establishment, entitled the BOARD OF HEALTH, which commenced in the spring of 1796.

The general objects of this benevolent charity are threefold. I. To obviate the generation of diseases. II. To prevent the spread of them by contagion. III. To shorten the duration of existing diseases; and to migrate their evils, by affording the necessary aids and comforts to those who labour under them. – I. Under the first head are comprehended – the inspection and improvement of the general accommodations of the poor; – the prohibition of such ha-[136]bitations, as are so close, noisome or damp, as to be incapable of being rendered tolerably salubrious: – the removal of privies placed in improper situations; – provision for white-washing and cleansing the houses of the poor twice every year: – attention to their ventilation, by windows with open casements, &c.: – the inspection of cotton-mills or other factories, at stated seasons; with regular returns of the condition as to health, clothing, appearance, and behaviour of the persons employed in them; of the time allowed for their refreshment, at breakfast and dinner; and of the accommodations of those who are parochial apprentices, or who are not under the immediate direction of their parents or friends: – the limitation and regulation of lodging-houses; on the establishment of *caravanseras* for passengers, are those who come to seek employment, unrecommended or unknown: – the establishment of public warm and cold baths: provision for particular attention to the cleaning of the streets, which are inhabited by the poor; and for the speedy removal of dunghills, and every other species of filth: – the diminution, as far as is practicable, of noxious effluvia from different sources, such as those which arise from the work-houses of the fell-[137]monger, the yards of the tanner, and the slaughter-houses of the butcher: – the superintendance of the several markets; with a view to prevent the sale of putrid flesh or fish, and of unsound flour, or other vegetable productions.

Under the second general head are included – the speedy removal of those who are attacked with symptoms of fever, from the cotton-mills, or factories, to the habitations of their parents or friends, or to commodious houses which may be set apart for the reception of the sick, and the different districts of Manchester: – the requisite attentions to preclude unnecessary communications with the sick, in the houses wherein they are confined; and to the subsequent changing and ventilation of their chambers, bedding, and apparel: – and the allowance of a sufficient time for perfect recovery, and complete purification of their clothes, before they return again to their works, or mix with their companions in labour. III. Under the third head are comprehended – medical attendance: – the care of nurses: – and supplies of medicine, wine, appropriate diet, fuel, and clothing.

From the opening of the House of Recovery on the 31st of May 1796, to the 31st of May 1802, 3210 patients have been admitted; [138] of whom 2939 have been cured; and 271 have died.

Note II. Preface. Page 2.

DISTRIBUTION OF PRINTED COPIES OF THE MEDICAL ETHICS

When it was first recommended to me to enlarge and publish this code of professional Ethics, I felt extremely diffident in the adoption of an undertaking so liable to the charge of presumption, in an individual conscious of inadequate powers, and possessing no claim or authority to dictate rules to his medical brethren. With much solicitude, therefore, I availed myself of the aid and support of various judicious and learned friends, in different stations of life, by communicating to them printed copies of the general scheme. And I record not only with *gratitude*, but as the *necessary sanction* of my work, the names of those who have honoured it what their approbation or assistance. John Aikin, M.D.; Sir George Baker, Bart.; S.A. Bardsley, M.D.; Thomas Butterworth Bayley, esq,; Foster Bower, esq. Barrister; John Cross, esq. Barrister, James Currie, M.D.; Erasmus Darwin, M.D.; William Falconer, M.D.; John [139] Ferriar, M.D.; Rev. Thomas Gisborne, M.A.; John Haygarth, M.D.; William Heberden, M.D.; Mr. Thomas Henry; Samuel Heywood, esq. Sergeant at law; Edward Holme, M.D.; George Lloyd, esq. Barrister; Rev. Archdeacon Paley; Sir G. O. Paul, Bart.; Robert Percival, of Dublin, M.D.; Mr. Simmons; Richard Warren, M.D.; Right Rev. Richard Watson, D.D. Bishop of Landaff; Charles White, esq.; and William Withering, M.D.

If it were not from the apprehension of swelling this long list of names, I should not omit friends, to whom copies of the Medical Ethics were transmitted, subsequently to the first circulation of the scheme.

Note III. Chap. I. Sect. XVII.

SITUATION, CONSTRUCTION, AND GOVERNMENT OF HOSPITALS

"In the cry in particular drew our attention, as a model which might be adopted in other countries with great advan-[140]tage. It consists of a long room, on one side of which are the windows, and an altar for the convenience of administering the sacrament to the sick. The other side is divided into wards, each of which is just big enough to contain a bed, and neatly lined with gally-tiles. Behind these wards, and parallel to the room in which they stand, there runs a long gallery, with which each ward communicates by a door; so that the sick may be separately supplied with whatever they want, without disturbing their neighbours." – See *Voyages round the World,* published by Dr. Hawkesworth, vol. II. p. 8.

In the year 1790, I was consulted concerning the situation, structure, and government of a large county-hospital, about to be erected; and I shall hear insert the hints, which I then suggested.

The SITUATION must, and some measure, be dependent on local circumstances: But, as far as is compatible with these, it should be dry, airy, moderately elevated, at a commodious distance from the town, and well supplied with salubrious water. If swampy grounds happen to be in the neighbourhood, particular attention should be paid to the winds which most frequently prevail, that it may be as little as pos-[141]sible influenced by the vapours those winds are likely to convey. The same precaution is applicable to the smoke of the town. The hospital at Manchester is three-fourths of the year involved in smoke, by being erected on the eastern side of the town; an evil which might easily have been avoided, by the choice of an opposite site.

The STRUCTURE includes accommodation and ventilation: and the form best adapted (*mutatis mutandis*) to these essential purposes, appears to be that of the new prison at Manchester, which is constructed on the well-known plan of MR. HOWARD. The building, which forms the gate-way, will afford a large and commodious room above, for the governors of the charity; and below, a shop for the apothecary, and a hall for the reception of out-patients, who would thus have no communication with the Infirmary; and consequently incur no risque, either of bringing or carrying back with them febrile or other contagion. The central part of the building is well adapted for kitchens, and other offices, over which the chapel might be constructed. The four *radii*, or buildings which project from the centre, might each contain six wards, fifteen feet square by thirteen high, in each story, [142] with a gallery interposed. No ward should have more than two beds in it. For the contamination of the air arises chiefly from the crowding too many sick persons in one chamber. And contagion not only spreads by this means, but the patients sustain great injury from the multiplied spectacles of suffering, to which they are witnesses in the large apartments of an hospital. Small chambers, also, have the advantage of being quickly ventilated. The three stories should be of the same height; and if the roof be lined with boards under the slates, the temperature of the highest story will be much less than usually affected by the heat of summer or cold of winter. In each gallery a room should be set apart for the convalescents, and for those patients who are able to quit their bed-chambers occasionally in the day time.

In the provision for ventilating the wards, it should be remembered, that though adequate supplies of FRESH AIR are essential to its purity, the *temperature* of it, also, must be regarded with a view of salubrity. For cold is not only ungrateful to the feelings of the sick, commonly very acute, but in many diseases injurious by its sedative action: And it has often been suspected of giving energy to infection. The ventilation, too, should be accomplished with-[143]out any current of wind perceptible by the patients; who, being ignorant of the nature and effects of contagion, have no apprehension of danger from it, but entertain strong prejudices against a flow of cool air; especially when in bed, or asleep. These prejudices, if they are to be deemed such, claim not only tenderness, but indulgence. For though silenced by authority, as I have before observed, they will operate secretly and forcibly on the mind, creating fear, anxiety, and watchfulness.

The GOVERNMENT of the hospital is an object of great importance, and will demand very mature consideration. The system adopted in most of our charitable institutions, appears to me neither sufficiently comprehensive nor efficient; and some unhappy disputes in the Manchester Infirmary, induced me to draw up the following propositions, for the consideration of the trustees:

I. A committee, for the purpose of mediation, superintendance, and improvement, should be chosen, by ballot, from among the trustees: It should consist of nine gentlemen of talents, respectability, and independence, to give dignity and authority to their proceedings: it should be stiled the COUNCIL of the Infirmary; [144] or be distinguished by some other honourable and expressive appellation: And, when regularly convened, five members should be competent to transact business.

II. No officer of the Infirmary, nor any physician or surgeon belonging to it, should be eligible into the council.

III. No member of the council should continue in office more than three years: Three members should annually go out of office, and three others be chosen and their room: And the same gentleman may be re-elected after the expiration of one or more years.

IV. The council should be a board of arbitration, for adjudicating whatever differences or disputes may arise between the several members of the Infirmary. It should take cognizance of every thing relative to the polity of this institution, and of its appendages, the Lunatic Hospital and Dispensary: It should enquire into the progress and present state of the charity: It should suggest to the annual board of trustees, such improvements as may be deemed expedient: And it should receive, methodize, and deliberate upon the several laws and regulations, which may be proposed by the weekly board, or by any individual trustee, [145], according to the prescribed form of notice, previous to a final decision.

V. The council should be convened fourteen days before each Quarterly Board, or oftener, if necessary: They should then communicate to the physicians and surgeons of the Infirmary, whatever laws or regulations, relative to medical or chirurgical departments, fall under their discussion: And they should attend, either personally or by their chairman, the succeeding Quarterly or Annual Board, to state the result of their investigations, and to assist the deliberations or decisions of the general body of trustees.

VI. The physicians and surgeons of the Infirmary should be requested to form themselves into a committee, to aid the council with their experience, knowledge, and advice; and to take into consideration whatever laws or regulations may be proposed, relative to their peculiar departments, before they be referred to the decision of the general body of trustees.

VII. The meetings of the committee of physicians and surgeons, should be held the day after the assembly of the council: And they should deliver, in writing, by the senior physician or surgeon, the result of their deliberations, in due time before the succeeding [146] Annual or Quarterly Board, to an adjourned meeting of the council.

N. B. The council may be either a permanent or a temporary institution, and subsist only during the space of two or three years, being renewable at stated periods of time, or whenever emergencies shall require such an establishment.

Note IV. Chap. I. Sect. XXVI.

HOUSE OF RECEPTION FOR PATIENTS ILL OF CONTAGIOUS FEVERS

In note, No. I. it has been stated that a house of reception for patients ill of infectious fevers now forms part of the system of the Manchester Dispensary. To aid the establishment of similar institutions in other places, I shall insert the regulations which form the polity of the house.

REGULATIONS FOR THE ADMISSION OF PATIENTS INTO THE HOUSE OF RECOVERY

I. The physicians of the Infirmary shall be authorized, to give one or two shillings, from the funds of the institution, (by a ticket to the secretary of the Board of Health,) to the person [147] who shall furnish the earliest information of the appearance of Fever in any poor family, within the limits of their respective districts.

II. As soon as the secretary has received this ticket, he shall apply, or take care that application be made, to some trustee of the Board of Health, living within the district, and who is a subscriber to the Infirmary, for an immediate recommendation of the sick person as an home patient.

III. Such patients, as the physicians shall deem peculiar objects of recommendation, either on account of their extreme poverty, or of the close and crowded state of their habitations, shall be conveyed in a sedan-chair (provided with a moveable washing lining, kept for this sole purpose, and distinguished by proper marks) to the House of Recovery.

IV. The physicians shall be requested to form the necessary regulations, for the domestic government of the families of the home patients, afflicted with fever.

V. A reward, to the amount of _____ [space intentionally left blank] shall be given to the heads of the family, after the cessation of the fever, on condition that they have faithfully observed the rules prescribed for cleanliness, ventilation, and the prevention of infection, amongst their neighbours. This [148] reward shall be doubled, in cases of extraordinary danger, and when the attentions have been adequate and successful.

VI. After the visitation of fever has seized and any poor dwelling-house, the sum of _____ [space intentionally left blank], or a sufficient sum, shall be allowed (to be expended under the direction of an inspector) for white-washing and cleansing the premises, and for the purchase of new bed-clothes, or apparel, in lieu of such as it may be deemed necessary to destroy, to obviate the continuance of propagation of fever.

VII. An inspector shall be appointed, in each district of the Infirmary, to aid the execution, and to enforce the observance of the foregoing regulations. And the gentlemen of the Strangers' Friend Society shall be required to undertake this office.

INTERNAL REGULATIONS FOR THE HOUSE OF RECOVERY

I. Every patient, on admission, shall change his infectious, for clean, linen; the face and hands are to be washed clean with lukewarm water, and the lower extremities fomented.

II. The clothes brought into the house by patients shall be properly purified and aired [149].

III. All linen and bed-clothes, immediately on being removed from the bodies of the patients, shall be immersed in cold water, before they are carried down stairs.

IV. All discharges from the patients shall be removed from the wards without delay.

V. The floors of the wards shall be carefully washed twice a week, and near the beds every day.

VI. Quick-lime shall be slaked in large open vessels, in every ward, and renewed whenever it seizes to bubble on the affusion of water. The walls and roofs shall be frequently washed with this mixture.

VII. No relation or acquaintance shall be permitted to visit the wards, without particular orders from one of the physicians.

VIII. No strangers shall be admitted into the wards; and the nurses shall be strictly enjoined not to receive unnecessary visits.

IX. No linen or clothes shall be removed from the House of Recovery till they have been washed, aired, and freed from infection.

X. No convalescents shall be discharged from the house, without a consultation of the physicians.

XI. The nurses and servants of the house shall have no direct communication with the [150] Infirmary; but shall receive the medicines in the room already appropriated to messengers from the home patients.

XII. The committee of the Strangers' Friend Society, shall be requested to undertake the office of inspecting the House of Recovery.

XIII. A weekly report of the patients admitted and discharged, shall be published in the Manchester newspapers.

XIV. When a patient dies in the wards, the body shall be removed as soon as possible, into a room appropriated to that use; it shall then be wrapt in a pitched cloth, and the friends shall be desired to proceed to the interment as early as is consistent with propriety.

XV. All provisions and attendance for the patients in this House of Recovery, shall be provided from the funds of this institution, without any communication with the Infirmary.

The establishment of fever-wards was proposed in 1774, and a few years afterward carried into complete execution by my excellent, and truly philanthropic friend Dr. Haygarth; whose life has been actively devoted to the promotion of science, the improvement of his profession, and the general good of mankind. The reader will find in his writings [151] views concerning the nature, causes, and prevention of contagion, derived from philosophic principles and confirmed by extensive and accurate observation.*

[Bottom page 152] * See Haygarth's Enquiry how to prevent the Small-ox. – Sketch of a Plan to exterminate the casual Small-pox. –Letter to Dr. Percival on the Prevention of Infectious Fevers.

These interesting subjects have lately, in a peculiar degree, engaged the attention, and employed the pens, of various other distinguished writers, as appears by the works of Dr. Wall, Dr. Currie, Dr. Ferriar, and Dr. Clark.†

[Bottom page 152] † See the Reports of the Society for bettering the condition and increasing the comforts of the Poor. –Dr. Stranger's Remarks on the necessity and means of suppressing contagious Fever. –Also Thoughts on the Means of preserving the Health of the Poor, by the Revd. Sir W. Clarke, Bart. and several other valuable modern works.

Note V. Chap. I. Sect. XXXI.

CAUTION OR TEMERITY IN PRACTICE

It is the observation of an elegant writer on the subject of morals, and applicable to medical practice, that "the best character is that which is not swayed by temper of any kind; but alternately employees enterprise and caution, as each is useful to the particular purpose in-[152]tended. Such is the excellence which St. Evremond ascribes to Mareschal TURENNE; who displayed every campaign, as he grew older, more temerity in his military enterprises; and being now, from long experience, perfectly acquainted with every incident in war, he advanced with greater firmness and security, in a road so well known to him."*

[Bottom page 153] * * Hume's Essays, vol. II. p. 284.

Yet it is said of the great Duke of Marlborough, that ten years of such uninterrupted and splendid success as no other general could boast of, never betrayed him into a single rash action.†

[Bottom page 153] † See Smith's Theory of Moral Sentiments, vol. II. p. 158.

That boldness in medical practice is more frequently the antecedent than the consequence of experience, is a melancholy truth; for it is generally founded either on theoretical dogmas, or on pride, which disclaims authority. To the consideration of physicians, who are thus prematurely confident in their own powers, the remark of Lord Verulam may be recommended. "This is well to be weighed, that boldness is ever blind; for it seeth not dangerous and inconveniences; therefore it is ill in counsel, good in execution: so that the right use of [153] bold persons is, that they never command in chief, but be seconds, and under the direction of others. For in counsel it is good to see dangers; and in execution not to see them, except they be very great."

Note VI. Chap. II. Sect. II.

TEMPERANCE OF PHYSICIANS

"Though much has been said, and with some truth, of the good effects of wine in producing rapidity and vivacity of thought, it has scarcely ever been pretended that it favoured the exercise of discrimination and judgment. The only persons in whom it has ever been supposed not to have the opposite effects, are some gentlemen of the faculty. The ignorant vulgar would think, *a priori*, that, *cæteris paribus*, a physician who was sober, would attend more accurately to the case of his patient, and compare and distinguish all circumstances better, and judge more soundly, and prescribe more rationally, than he could do when he was drunk. But some physicians, who should be supposed to know themselves best, and who certainly must have known how they acquitted themselves and those different situations, have boasted [154] that they prescribed as well drunk as sober. In this they could not be mistaken; for, whether we consider the matter physically or logically, their boast amounts precisely to this, that they prescribed no better when they were sober than they did when they were drunk; which is undoubtedly a noble accomplishment; but it is not surely either wonderful or rare."*

[Bottom page 155] * See the Introduction to Philosophical and Literary Essays, by Dr. Gregory, of Edinburgh, p. 187.

Tacitus, in his admirable treatise *De Moribus Germanorum*, has stated, that those nations – *de reconciliandis invicem inimicis, et jungendis affinitatibus, et adsciscendis principibus, de pace denique ac bello, plerumque in conviviis consultant: tamquam nullo magis tempore aut ad simplices cogitationes pateat animus, aut ad magnas incalescat. Gens non astuta nec callida aperit adhuc secreta pectoris licentia loci. Ergo detecta at nuda omnium mens postera die retractatur; et salva utriusque temporis ratio est. Deliberant dum fingere nesciunt: constituunt dum err are non possunt.* †

[Bottom page 155] † Taciti Opera á Lipsio. fol. 1627, p. 444. – The learned editor observes, in his note on this passage, *Persarum similis mos, et Cretensium, et Græcorum omnium veterum.*

In deliberation, it may, on some peculiar occasions, be of importance to break off all [155] former strong associations. A fit of drunkenness accomplishes this fully: Sleep has the same tendency; and hence the proverb, *I will sleep upon it*. But such deliberation bears no analogy to what is required from a physician, when he is to consider the case of a patient.

"Universal temperance," says Mr. Gisborne, "both in eating and drinking, is particularly incumbent on a physician an every period of his practice. not merely as being essentially requisite to preserve his faculties in that alert an unclouded state, which may render him equally able at all times to pronounce on the cases which he is called to inspect, but because it is a virtue which he will very frequently find himself obliged to inculcate on his patients; and will inculcate on them with little effect, if it not be regularly exemplified in his own conduct."*

[Bottom page 156] * Duties of Men, vol. ii. p. 139. Note.

Note VII. Chap II. Sect. III.

"A PHYSICIAN SHOULD BE THE MINISTER OF HOPE AND COMFORT TO THE SICK"

Mr. Gisborne, in one of his interesting letters to me on the subject of Medical Ethics, [156] suggests, that it would be advisable to add, *as far as truth and sincerity will admit*. "I know very well," says he, "that the sentence, as it now stands, conveys to you, and was meant by you to convey to others, the same sentiment which it would express after the proposed addition. But if I am not mistaken in my idea, that there are few professional temptations to which medical men are more liable, and frequently from the very best principles, then that of unintentionally using language to the patient and his friends more encouraging than sincerity would vindicate, on cool reflection; it may be right scrupulously to guard the avenues against such an error."

In the *Enquiry into the Duties of Men*, the same excellent moralist thus deliverers his sentiments more at large. "A professional writer, speaking, in a work already quoted,*

[Bottom page 157] * Percival's Medical Ethics, chap. I.

respecting the performances of surgical operations in hospitals, remarks, that it may be a salutary as well as an humane act, in the attending physician, occasionally to assure the patient that everything goes on well, *if that declaration can be made with truth*. This [157] restriction, so properly applied to the case and question, may with equal propriety be extended universally to the conduct of a physician, when superintending operations performed, not by the hand of a surgeon, but by nature and medicine. Humanity, we admit, and the welfare of the sick man commonly require, that his drooping spirits should be revived by every encouragement and hope, which can honestly be suggested to him. But truth and conscience forbid the physician to cheer him by giving promises, or raising expectations, which are known, or intended, to be delusive. The physician may not be bound, unless expressly called upon, invariably to divulge, at any specific time, his opinion concerning the uncertainty or danger of the case: but he is invariably bound never to represent the uncertainty or danger as less than he actually believes it to be; and whenever he conveys, directly or indirectly, to the patient or to his family, any impression to that effect, though he may be misled by mistaken tenderness, he is guilty of positive falsehood. He is at liberty to say little; but let that little be true. St. Paul's [158] direction, *not to do evil, that good may come*, is clear, positive, and universal."*

[Bottom page 159] * Duties of Men, vol. II. p. 148.

Whether this subject be viewed as regarding general morality, or professional duty, it is of high importance; and we may justly presume, that it involves considerable difficulty and intricacy, because opposite opinions have been advanced upon it by very little distinguished writers. The ANCIENTS, though sublime and the abstract representations of virtue, are seldom precise and definite in the detail of rules for its observance. Yet in some instances they extend their precepts to particular cases: and Cicero, in the Third Book of his Offices, expressly admits of limitations to the absolute and immutable obligation of fidelity and truth.

The maxim of the poet, also, maybe adduced as intended to be comprehensive of the moral laws by which humans conduct is to be governed:

–"Sunt certi denique fine,
"Quos ultrá citráque nequit consistere rectum."†

[Bottom page 159] † Horat, Sat. lib. I. Sat. I. 106.

The early FATHERS of the Christian Church, Origen, Clement, Tertullian, Lactantius, Chrysostom, and various others, till the period of [159] St. Augustine, were latitudinarians on this point. But the holy father last mentioned, if I mistake not, in the warmth of his zeal, declared that he would not utter a lie, though he were assured of gaining Heaven by it. In this declaration there is a fallacy, by which Augustine probably imposed upon himself. For a lie is always understood to consist in a *criminal* breach of truth, and therefore under no circumstances can be justified. It is alledged, however, that falsehood may lose the essence of lying, and become even praise-worthy, when the adherence to truth is incompatible with the practice of some other virtue of still higher obligation. This opinion almost the whole body of CIVILIANS adopt, with full confidence of its rectitude. The sentiments of' Grotius may be seen at large in the satisfactory detail which he has given of the controversy relating to it.*

[Bottom page 160] * See the second, third, and fourth paragraphs of the 10th Sect. Cap. I, Lib. III, of Grotius de Jure Bell. ac Pac. – Also, the 14th, 15th, and 16 Sections of the same Chapter.

Puffendorff, who may be regarded as next to this great man in succession as well as authority, delivers the following observations in his *Law of Nature and Nations*, which are point-[160]edly applicable to the present subjects, yet carried assuredly to a very reprehensible extent: "Since those we talk to may often be in such circumstances, that if we should tell them the downright truth of the matter, it would prejudice them, and would incapacitate us for procuring that lawful end we propose to ourselves for their good; we may in these cases use a fictitious or figurative way of speech, which shall not directly represent to our hearers our real thoughts and intentions: For when a man is desirous, and it is his duty, to do a piece of service, he is not bound to take measures that will certainly render his attempts unsuccessful." *

[Bottom page 161] * Puffendorff, vol. II. Chap. I. p. 6.

–"Those are by no means guilty of lying, who, for the better information of children, or other persons not capable of relishing the naked truth, entertain them with fictions and stories: Nor those who invent something that is false, for the sake of a good end, which by the plain truth they could not have compassed; as, suppose, for protecting an innocent, for appeasing a man in his passion, for *comforting the afflicted*, for *animating the timorous*, for *persuading a nauseating patient to take his physic*, for overcoming an obstinate humour, for making an ill design miscarry."† [161]

[Bottom page 16] † Ibid. p. 9.

Several modern ETHICAL WRITERS, of considerable celebrity, have been no less explicit and indulgent on this question. Amongst these, it may suffice to cite the testimony of the late Dr. Francis Hutcheson, of Glasgow; of whom it is said by his excellent biographer, that "he abhorred the least appearance of deceit, either in words or action." *

[Bottom page 162] * Dr. Leechman's Biographical Preface to Hutcheson's System of Moral Philosophy, p. 26.

"When in certain affairs," says he, "it is known that men do not conceive it an injury to be deceived, there is no crime and false speech about such matters. – No man censures a physician for deceiving a patient too much dejected, by expressing good hopes of him; or by denying that he gives him a proper medicine which he is foolishly prejudiced against: the patient afterwards will not reproach him for it. – Wise men allow this liberty to the physician, in whose skill and fidelity they trust: Or if they do not, there may be a just plea from necessity." †

[Bottom page 162] † | Hutcheson's System of Moral Philosophy, vol. I. p. 32, 33.

"These pleas of necessity some would exclude by a maxim of late received, *We must not do evil that good may come of it*. The author of this [162] maxim is not well known. It seems by a passage in St. Paul, that Christians were reviled as teaching that since the mercy and veracity of God were displayed by the obstinate wickedness of the Jews, they should continue in sin, that this good might ensue from it. He rejects the imputation upon his doctrine; and hence some take up the contradictory proposition, as a general maxim of great importance in morality. Perhaps it has been a maxim among St. Paul's enemies, as they upbraid him with counteracting it. Be the author who they please, it is of no use in morals, as it is quite vague and undetermined. Must one do nothing for a good purpose, which would have been evil without this reference? It is evil to hazard life without a view to some good; but when it is necessary for a public interest, it is very lovely and honourable. It is criminal to expose a good man to danger for nothing; but it is just even to force him into the greatest dangers for his country. It is criminal to occasion any pains to innocent persons, without a view to some good; but for restoring of health we reward chirurgeons for scarifyings, burnings, and amputations. *But*, say they, *such actions, done for* [163] *these ends, are not evil. The maxim only determines that we must not do, for a good end, such actions as our evil when done for a good end.* But this proposition is identic and useless; for who will tell us next, what these actions, sometimes evil, are, which may be done for a good end? and what actions are so evil that they must not be done even for a good end? The maxim will not answer this question; and truly it amounts only to this trifle; *you ought not for any good to do what is evil, or what you ought not to do even for a good end*."*

[Bottom page 164] * Hutchinson's System of Mor. Phil. vol. II. p. 132

Dr. Johnson, who admits of some exception to the Law of Truth, strenuously denies the right of telling a lie to a sick man for fear of alarming him. "You have no business with consequences," says he, "you are to tell the truth. Besides, you are not sure what effect your telling him that he is in danger may have. It may bring his distemper to a crisis, and that may cure him. Of all lying I have the greatest abhorrence of this, because I believe it has been frequently practiced on myself." † [164]

[Bottom page 164] † See Boswell's life of Johnson, p. 570.

If the medical reader wishes to investigate this nice and important subject of casuistry, he may consult *Grotius de sure Bell. ac Pacis*; Puffendorff; Grove's

Ethics; Balguy's Law of Truth, Cambray's Telemachus: Butler; Hutcheson; Paley; and Gisborne. Every practitioner must find himself occasionally in circumstances of very delicate embarrassment, with respect to the contending obligations of veracity and professional duty: And when such trials occur, it will behove him to act on fixed principles of rectitude, derived from previous information, and serious reflection. Perhaps the following brief considerations, by which I have conscientiously endeavored to govern my own conduct, may afford some aid to his decision.

Moral truth, in a professional view, has two references; one to the party to whom it is delivered, and another to the individual by whom it is uttered. In the first, it is a *relative duty*, constituting a branch of justice; and maybe properly regulated by the divine rule of equity prescribed by our Saviour, to *do unto others as we would*, all circumstances duly weighed, *they should do unto us*. In the second, it is a *personal duty*, regarding solely the sincerity, the purity, and the probity of the physician [165] himself. To a patient, therefore, perhaps the father of a numerous family, or one whose life is of the highest importance to the community, who makes inquiries which, if faithfully answered, might prove fatal to him, it would be a gross and unfeeling wrong to reveal the truth. His right to it is suspended, and even annihilated; because its beneficial nature being reversed, it would be deeply injurious to himself, to his family, and to the public: And he has the strongest claim, from the trust reposed in his physician, as well as from the common principles of humanity, to be guarded against whatever would be detrimental to him. In such a situation, therefore, the only point at issue is, whether the practitioner shall sacrifice that delicate sense of veracity, which is so ornamental to, and indeed forms a characteristic excellence of the virtuous man, to this claim of professional justice and social duty. Under such a painful conflict of obligations, a wise and good man must be governed by those which are the most imperious; and will therefore generously relinquish every consideration, referable only to himself. Let him be careful, however, not to do this, but in cases of real emergency, which happily seldom occur; and to guard his mind sedulously against the injury it may sus-[166]tain by such violations of the native love of truth.

I shall conclude this long note with two following very interesting biographical facts. The husband of the celebrated Arria, Cæcinna, Pætus, was very dangerously ill. Her son was also sick at the same time, and died. He was a youth of uncommon accomplishments; and fondly beloved by his parents. Arria prepared and conducted his funeral in such a manner, that her husband remained entirely ignorant of the mournful event which occasioned that solemnity. Pætus often enquired with anxiety about his son; to whom the cheerfully replied, that he had slept well, and was better. But if her tears, too long restrained, were bursting forth, she instantly retired, to give vent to her grief; and when again composed, returned to Pætus, with dry eyes, and a placid countenance, quitting, as it were, all the tender feelings of the mother at the threshold of her husband's chamber.*

[Bottom page 167] * Plin. Epist. 16. Lib.. III.

Lady Russel's only son, Wriothesley, Duke of Bedford, died of the small-pox in May 1711, in the 31st year of his age. To this affliction succeeded, in Nov. 1711, the loss of her daugh-[167]ter, the Duchess of Rutland, who died in child-bed. Lady

Russell, after seeing her in the coffin, went to her other daughter, married to the Duke of Devonshire, from whom it was necessary to conceal her grief, she being at the time in child-bed likewise; therefore she assumed a chearful air, and with astonishing resolution, verbally agreeable to truth, answered her anxious daughters enquiries with these words,– "I have seen your sister out of bed to-day."*

[Bottom page 168] * Note to Letters of Lady Russel, 4 to. Letter 149, p. 204.

Note VIII. Chap. II. Sect. V.

THE PRACTICE OF A PRIOR PHYSICIAN SHOULD BE TREATED WITH CANDOUR, AND JUSTIFIED SO FAR AS TRUTH AND PROBITY WILL PERMIT

Montaigne, In one of his essays, treats, with great humour, of physic and physicians; and makes it a charge against them, that they perpetually direct variations in each other's prescriptions. "Whoever saw," says he, "one physician approve of the prescription of another, without taking something away, or adding something to it? By which they suffice-[168]ently betray their act, and make it manifest to us, that they therein more consider their own reputation, and consequently their profit, than their patient's interest."*

[Bottom page 169] * *Montaigne's Essays*, book II. Ch. XXXVII. p. 703. – Consult also the same chapter, page 719.

Note IX. Chap. II. Sect. IX.

THEORETICAL DISCUSSIONS SHOULD BE GENERALLY AVOIDED

THIS rule is not only applicable to consultations, but to any reasonings on the nature of the case, and of the remedies prescribed, either with the patient himself or his friends. It is said by my lamented friend Mr. Seward, in his entertaining anecdotes, that the late Lord Mansfield gave this advice to a military gentleman, who was appointed governor of one of our islands in the West-Indies, and who expressed his apprehensions of not being able to discharge his duty as chancellor of his province: "When you decide, never give reasons for your decision. You will in general decide well; yet may give very bad reasons for your judgment." † [169]

[Bottom page 169] † Anecdotes of distinguished Persons, vol. II. p. 361.

Note X. Cap. II. Sect. XI.

REGULAR ACADEMICAL EDUCATION

"IT has been the general opinion," says doctor Johnson, "that Sydenham was made a physician by accident and necessity; and Sir R. Blackmore reports, in the preface to his Treatise on the Small-pox, that he engaged in practice without any preparatory study, or previous knowledge of the medicinal sciences; affirming, that when he was consulted by him what books he should read to qualify him for the said profession, he recommended Don Quixote. That he recommended Don Quixote to Blackmore (continues Dr. Johnson) we are not allowed to doubt; but the relator is hindered, by the self-love which dazzles all mankind, from discovering that he might intend a satire, very different from a general censure of all ancient and modern writers on medicine; since he might perhaps mean, either seriously, or in jest, to insinuate, that Blackmore was not adapted by nature to the study of physic; and that, whether he should read Cervantes or Hippocrates, he would be equally unqualified for practice, and equally unsuccessful in it. Whatsoever was his meaning, nothing is more evident [170] than that it was a transient sally of an imagination warmed with gaiety; or the negligent effusion of a mind intent upon some other employment, and in haste to dismiss a troublesome intruder." Sydenham himself has declared, that after he determined upon the profession of physic, he applied in earnest to it, and spent several years in the University of Oxford, before he began to practice in London. He traveled afterwards to Montpelier in quest of more information; so far was he from any contempt of academical institutions; and so far from thinking it reasonable to learn physic by experiments alone, which must necessarily be made at the hazard of life."*

[Bottom page 171] *See Johnson's Life of Sydenham

But it is highly injurious to the usefulness and honour of the profession, to suppose the education of a physician may be confined to the pursuit of medicine as an *art*. Sir W. Blackstone, in his Introduction to his Commentaries on the Laws of England, has reprobated the custom of placing the juridical student at the desk of some skilful attorney, in order to initiate him early in all the depths of practice, and to render him more dexterous in the mechanical part of business. This illiberal path to the bar [171] is not to be sanctioned, he observes, by a few particular instances of persons, who, through the force of transcendant genius, have been able to overcome every disadvantage. And he points out, in very forcible terms, and with sound argument, how essential it is to the lawyer to form his sentiments by the perusal of the purest classical authors; to learn to reason with precision, by the simple but clear rules of unsophisticated logic; to fix the attention, and steadily to pursue truth through the most intricate deductions, by an acquaintance with mathematical demonstration; and to acquire enlarged conceptions of nature and of art, by a view of the several branches of experimental philosophy. Now if this be the *vantage ground*, to adopt the language of Lord Bacon, from which the study of the law should commence; it ought to be deemed at least equally necessary to qualify for the prosecution of medicine – a science which has man, as a compound of matter and mind, for its subject, and an infinitude of substances derived from the animal, vegetable, and mineral kingdoms, for its instruments. This sentiment seems to have been early prevalent in this celebrated school of physic, established at Salerno in Italy. For it was enacted, A. D. 1237, by the heads of colleges there, that the [172] pupils should be bound to pass three years in the acquisition of philosophy, and five subsequent years in that of medicine.*

[Bottom page 173] * Vide Bulaei Hist. Univers. Paris, vol. p. 158. – Henry's History of Great-Britain, vol. VIII. p. 206.

Dr. Friend, in his *Hist. Medecinæ*, has given a somewhat different account of the celebrated School of Salernum. "*Sunt in eo decem Doctores, qui sibi invicem, juxta creationis ordinem, succedunt. Candidatortum examinatio severissima est, que sit aut in Galeni Therapeuticis, aut in primo primi Cantonis Avicennæ, aut in Aphorismis. Is qui Doctoratum ambit unum ac viginti annos habere debet (verum hic lapsum subesse autumo, cum scribendum sit viginti quinque vel septem) ac testimonia proferre, quæ per septem annos eum Medicinæ studuisse doceant. Quod si inter Chirurgos recipi cupiat, Anatomiam per anni spatium didicisse hunc oportet: jurandum ei est, fidelem se ac morigerum Societati futurum, præmia a pauperibus oblata recusaturum, neque Pharmacopolarum lucri participem fore. Tum liber in ejus manum traditur, annulus digito induitur, Caput laurea redimitur, atque ipse osculo dimittitur. Multá alia Statuta sunt ad Praxeos ordinationem pertinentia; Pharmacopolæ præsertim, ut juxta Medici præcepta componant Medicamenta, et ut ea certo pretio divendant, obligantur.*"

I. FRIEND OPERA MED. p. 537.

The like regulations were afterwards adopted in other universities; but in various countries have fallen into disuse.

On the first revival of learning in Europe, science was held in the highest estimation; and the three faculties of law, physic, and divinity, as-[173]sumed particular honours and privileges. Academical degrees were conferred on their members; and these titles, with the rank annexed to them, were admitted *ubique gentium*; being, like the order of knighthood, of universal validity. Doctors indeed contended sometimes with knights for precedence, and the disputes were not unfrequently terminated by advancing the former to the dignity of knighthood. It was even asserted that a doctor had a right to that title, without creation.*

[Bottom page 174] * Consult. *Seb. Bachmeisteri Autiqitates Rostoch; Crevier Hist. de l' Univers. de Paris*; and Dr. Robertson's Proofs and Illustrations, annexed to his View of the State of Europe. – Hist. Charles V. vol. I. p. 387, 8vo.

Note XI. Chap. II. Sect. XV

PECUNIARY ACKNOWLEDGEMENTS

THE following fact, related in Dr. Johnson's life of Addison, is applicable to the professional conduct of physicians towards their friends. "When Addison was in office, (under the Duke of Wharton, as Lord Lieutenant of Ireland,) he made a law to himself, as Swift as stated, never to remit his regular fees, in civility to his [174] friends. "For," said he, "I may have an hundred friends, and if my fee be two guineas, I shall, by relinquishing my right, lose two hundred guineas, and no friend gain more than two; there is therefore no proportion between the good imparted, and the evil suffered."*

[Bottom page 175] * See Johnson's Lives of the Poets

In recording Mr. Addison's *prudential* conduct, his probity, with respect to pecuniary acknowledgements, should not be unnoticed. In a letter, relative to the case of Major Dunbar, he says, "And now, Sir, believe me, when I assure you, I never did, nor ever will, on any pretence whatsoever, take more than the stated or customary fees of my office. I might keep the contrary practice concealed from the world, where I capable of it; but I could not from myself; and I hope I shall always fear the reproaches of my own heart, more than those of all mankind." †

[Bottom page 175] † Idem.

At a period when empirics and empiricism seem to have prevailed much in Rome, the exorbitant demands of medical practitioners, particularly for certain secret compositions which they dispensed, induced the Emperor Valentinian to ordain, that no individual of the faculty [175] should make an express charge for his attendance on a patient; nor even avail himself of any promise of remuneration during the period of sickness; but that he should rest satisfied with the donative voluntarily offered at the close of his ministration.*

[Bottom page 176] * *Vide. Cod. Theodos. Lib. XIII. Tit. III.*

By the same law however, the Emperor provided that one practitioner, at least, should be appointed for each of the fourteen sections into which the Roman metropolis was divided, with special privileges, and a competent salary for his services; thus indirectly, yet explicitly acknowledging that a physician has a full claim in equity to his professional emoluments. Is it not reasonable, therefore, to conclude, that what subsisted as a *moral right*, ought to have been demandable, under proper regulations, as a *legal right*? For it seems to be the office of law to recognize and enforce that which natural justice recognizes and sanctions.

The Roman advocates were subject to the like restrictions, and from a similar cause. For their rapacity occasioned the revival of the Cincian ordinance –"*qua cavetur antiquitus, ne quis ob causam orandam pecuniam donumve accipiat.*" But Tacitus relates, that [176] when the subject was brought into discussion before Claudius Caesar, amongst other arguments in favor of receiving fees, it was forcibly urged, *sublatis studiorum pretiis, etiam studia peritura*; and that, in consequence, the prince, "*capiendis pecuniis posuit modum, usque ad dena sestertia, quæ egressi repetundarum tenerentur.*" *

[Bottom page 177] * Annal. Lib. XI. p. 168. Edit. Lipsii.

A precise and invariable *modus*, however, would be injurious both to the barrister and the physician, because the fees of each ought to be measured by the value of his time, the eminence of his character, and by his general rule of practice. This rule, with its antecedents, being well known, a *tacit compact* is established, restrictive on the claims of the practitioner, and binding on the probity of the patient. Law cannot properly, by its ordinances, establish the custom, which will and ought to vary in different situations, and under different circumstances. But a court of judicature, when formally appealed to, seems to be competent to authorize it if just, and to correct it if unjust. Such decisions could not wholly change the honorary nature of fees;

because they would continue to be increased, at the direction of the affluent, according to [177] their liberality and grateful sense of kind attentions; and diminished, at the option of the physician, to those who may, from particular circumstances, require his beneficence.

From the Roman code, the established usage, in different countries in Europe, relative to medical fees, has probably originated. This usage, which constitutes common law, seems to require considerable modification to adapt it to the present state of the profession. For the general body of the faculty, especially in the united kingdoms of Great-Britain and Ireland, are held in very high estimation, on account of their liberality, learning, and integrity:*

[Bottom page 178 continued to bottom page 179] * Of this truth, it has been my duty and inclination to offer several proofs, of unquestionable authority, and different parts of the present work. Two additional ones now occur to my recollection, which I shall here insert. Mr. Pope, writing to Mr. Allen concerning his obligations to Dr. Mead and other physicians, about a month before his death, says, "There is no end of my kind treatment from the faculty. They are in general the most amiable companions and the best friends, as well as the most learned men I know." –The Rev. Dr. Samuel Parr, in a letter, with which he honoured me in September 1794, thus expresses himself: "I have long been in the habit of reading on medical subjects; and a great advantage I have derived from this circum-[178]stance is, that I have found opportunities for conversation and friendship with a class of men, whom after a long and attentive survey of literary characters, I hold to be the most enlightened professional persons in the whole circle of human arts and sciences."

and it would be difficult to assign [178] a satisfactory reason why they should be excluded from judicial protection, when the just remuneration of their services is wrongfully with-held. Indeed a medical practitioner, one especially who is settled in a provincial town, or in the country, may have accumulated claims from long-protracted and often expensive attendance; and his pecuniary acknowledgements may be refused from prejudice, from captiousness, from parsimony, or from dishonesty. Under such circumstances, considerations of benevolence, humanity, and gratitude, are wholly set aside: For when disputes arise, they must be suspended or extinguished; and the question at issue can alone be decided on the principles of *commutative justice*.

Note. XII. Chap. II. Sect. XXX.

PUBLIC WORSHIP, SCEPTICISM, AND INFIDELITY

THE neglect of social worship, with which physicians have been too justly charged, may be traced, and many instances, to the period of their [179] academical education, particularly in the universities where young men are permitted to live at large, and are subject to no collegiate discipline. Sunday, affording a recess for public lectures, is devoted, by those who are ardent in study, to a review of the labours of the past week; to preparations for medical or scientific discussions in the societies of which they are members; or to other pursuits, belonging to their profession, but unconnected with religion. The idle and the gay, in such situations, are eager to avail themselves of opportunities so favourable to their taste for recreation, or to their aversion to business and confinement. In each of these classes, though actuated by different principles, there is much danger that devotional impressions will be gradually impaired, for want of stated exercise and renewal: And a foundation will thus be laid for habitual and permanent indifference, in future life, to divine services, whenever medical avocations furnish a *salvo* to the mind, and a plausible excuse to the world, for non-attendance on them. This coldness of heart, this moral insensibility, should be sedulously counteracted before it has acquired an invincible ascendancy. No apology should be admitted for absence from the stated offices of [180] piety, but that of duties to be performed of immediate and pressing necessity. When the church is entered with just views, it will be found that there is a sympathy in religious homage, which at once inspires and heightens devotion: And that to hold communion with God in concert with our families, our friends, our neighbours, and our fellow-citizens, is the highest privilege of human nature. But with a full conviction of the obligation of public worship, as a social institution, founded on a common consent, and enjoined by legal authority; as a moral duty connecting us by the most endearing ties with our brethren of mankind, who are joint dependants with ourselves, on the pardon, the protection, and the bounty of God; and as a debt of general homage to our creator, benefactor, and judge; yet there may subsist in a devout and benevolent mind scruples, respecting doctrines and forms, sufficient to produce an alienation from the sacred offices of the temple. Such doubts, when they originate from serious enquiry, and are not the result of fastidiousness or arrogance, have a claim to tenderness and indulgence; because, to act in contradiction to them, whilst they subsist, would be a violation of sincerity, amounting in some cases [181] to the guilt of hypocrisy. But in a country where private judgment is happily under no restraint, and where so great diversity of sects prevails, it will be strange, if a candid and well-informed man can find no christian denomination, with which he might accord in spirit and in truth. Sir Thomas Brown, in the statement which he is given in his *Religio Medici*, seems to have allowed himself on these points very extensive latitude. – "We have reformed from them, viz. the Papists, not against them – therefore I am not scrupulous to converse and live with them, to enter their churches in defect of ours, and either pray with them or for them. I could never perceive that a resolved conscience may not adore her creator any where, especially in places devoted to his service; where if their devotions offend him, mine may please him; if theirs profane it, mine may hallow it. I could never hear the *Ave Maria* bell without an elevation, or think it a sufficient warrant, because they erred in one circumstance, for me to err in all – that is in silence and dumb contempt: Whilst therefore they direct their devotions to the virgin, I offer mine to God, and rectify the errors of their prayers by rightly ordering my own." [182]

But authority, much more respectable than that of Sir Thomas Brown, may be adduced in favour of the spirit of catholicism in christian communion. Mr. Locke, a short time before his death, received the sacrament according to the rites of the Church of England, though it is evident from his writings that he dissented for many of her doctrines. When the office was finished, he told the minister –"that he was in perfect charity with all men, and sincere communion with the church of Christ, by what name forever it might be distinguished.["] *

[Bottom page 183] * See Brit. Biog. vol. VII. page 13.

– Dr. David Hartley was originally intended for the clerical profession, but was prevented from going into holy orders by his scruples concerning subscription to the thirty-nine articles. He continued, however, to the end of his life, a well-affected member of the establishment, approving of its practical doctrines, and conforming to its public worship." He was a catholic christian, says his son and biographer, in the most extensive and literal sense of the term. On the subject of religious controversy, he has left the following testimony of his sentiments: – "The great differences of opinion and contentions, which [183] happen on religious matters, are plainly owing to the violence of men's passions more than to any other cause. When religion has had its due effect in restraining these, and begetting true candour, we may expect a unity of opinion in both and religious and other matters, as far as is necessary for useful and practical purposes."

These examples of the conduct of wise and conscientious christians evince that, in their estimation, forms, ceremonies, and doctrines, are of a moment subordinate to the benefits and obligations of social worship. But they are not adduced to sanction an *indifference*, either to religious rites, or religious truth. The mind will always be in the best frame for holy exercises, when the modes by which they are conducted are consonant to its sentiments of propriety and rectitude. And that church should be habitually resorted to, if practicable, the public services of which accord most satisfactorily with the views of the individual, concerning the attributes of God, and the revelation of his will and promises to man. No personal friendship, no party connection, no professional interest should be allowed to predominate in the choice. For genuine piety, which is the joint offspring of reason and of [184] sentiment, admits of no substitutions. It consists in a full conviction of the understanding, accompanied with correspondent affections of the heart; and in its exercises calls forth their united and noblest energies.

It will not be foreign to the subject of this note to investigate briefly, the imputation of scepticism and infidelity, which has been laid against the medical faculty. The Rev. Dr. Samuel Parr, whose candour is unquestionable, and who's learning and genius entitle him to the highest respect, has lately sanctioned it, as will appear by the following passage from his *Remarks on the Statement of Dr. Charles Combe*, pages 82, 83. – "While I allow," says he, "that peculiar and important advantages arise from the appropriate studies of the three liberal professions, I must confess, that in erudition, in science, and in habits of deep and comprehensive thinking, the pre-eminence, in some degree, must be assigned to physicians. The propensity which some of them have shewn to scepticism, upon religious topics, is indeed to be seriously lamented; and it may be satisfactorily explained, I think, upon metaphysical principles, which evince the strength rather than the weakness of the human mind, when contemplating, under certain circumstances, the [185] multiplicity and energy of physical causes. But I often console myself with reflecting on the sounder opinions of Sir Thomas Browne, Sydenham, Boerhaave, and Hartley, in the days that are past; and of our own times, posterity will remember that they were adorned by the virtues, as well as the talents, of a Gregory, a Heberden, a Falconer, &c."

Mr. Gisborne, in his *Enquiry into the Duties of Men, In the higher and middle Classes of Society*, a work to which I have already referred, as an admirable system of practical and appropriate ethics, has very explicitly and forcibly delivered his sentiments on this interesting subject. "The charge," he says, "may have been made on partial and insufficient grounds; but the existence of it should excite the efforts of every conscientious physician, to rescue himself from the general stigma. It should stimulate him, not to affect a sense of religion which he does not entertain, but openly to avow that which he actually feels. If the charge be in some measure true, it is of importance, to the physician, to ascertain the causes from which the fact has originated, that he may be the more on his guard against their influence. The following circumstances may not have been without their weight. They [186] who are accustomed to deep researches into any branch of philosophical science; and find themselves able to explain, to their own satisfaction, almost every phænomenon, and to account, as they apprehend, for almost every effect, by what are termed natural causes, or apt to acquire extravagant ideas of the sufficiency of human reason on all subjects; and thus learning to doubt the necessity, become prejudiced against the belief of divine revelation. In the next place, they who justly disclaim the empire of authority in medical theories, may carelessly proceed to regard religious doctrines as theories, resting on no other foundation, and deserving of no better fate. Thirdly, it is to be observed, that men may be divided into two distinct classes, with respect to the sort of testimony on which they receive truths of any kind. They who are chiefly addicted to investigations and reasonings, founded on analogy, look primarily and with extreme partiality to that species of evidence; and if the thing asserted appear contrary to the common course of nature, more especially if it militate against any theory of their own, (and such persons are much disposed to theorize,) they are above measure reluctant to admit the reality of it; and withhold their assent until such a number of particular proofs, incapable [187] of being resolved into fraud or misconception, is produced, as would have been far more than sufficient to convince an unbiased judgment. Whereas other men, little used to analogical enquiries, look not around for such testimony, either in support or in refutation of an extraordinary circumstance affirmed to them; but readily give credit to the fact on its own distinct proofs, or from confidence in the veracity and discernment of the relator. It is evident that physicians are to be ranked in the class first described, and are consequently liable to its prejudices: And it is equally evident, that those prejudices will render all, on whom they fasten, particularly averse to recognize the truth of miracles; and will probably prevent them from examining, with impartiality, the evidence of a religion founded on miracles, and perhaps from examining it at all. Fourthly; to the preceding circumstances must be added the neglect of divine worship, too customary among persons of the medical profession. This neglect seems to have contributed not only to excite and strengthen the opinion of their scepticism and infidelity; but sometimes to produce scepticism and infidelity itself. For it is a natural progress, that he who habitually disregards the public duties of religion, should [188] soon omit those which are private; should speedily begin to with that religion may not be true; should then proceed to doubt its truth; and at length should disbelieve it." Vol. II. p. 192, edit. 4.

The late Dr. Gregory, of Edinburgh, anxious to support the honour of a profession which he loved, and of which he was a distinguished ornament, very strenuously repels the charge against it of scepticism and infidelity. Though his excellent lectures are, doubtless, in the hands of most physicians, yet I am tempted to make a transcript from them, because I with the present important subject to be viewed in the several lights, in which it has been presented to the mind by different writers of acknowledged probity, information, and judgment. "I think the charge," he observes, "ill-founded, and well venture to say, that the most eminent of our faculty have been distinguished for real piety. I shall only mention as examples, Harvey, Sydenham, Arbuthnot, Boerhaave, Stahl, and Hoffmann. – It is easy, however, to see whence this calumny has arisen. Men whose minds have been enlarged by knowledge, who have been accustomed to think, and to reason upon all subjects with a generous freedom, are not apt to become [189] bigots to any particular sect or system. They can be steady to their own principles, without thinking ill of those who differ from them; but they are impatient of the authority and controul of men, who would lord it over their consciences, and dictate to them what they are to believe. This freedom of spirit, this moderation and charity for those of different sentiments, have frequently been ascribed, by narrow-minded people, to secret infidelity, scepticism, or, at least, to lukewarmness in religion; while some who were sincere Christians, exasperated by such reproaches, have sometimes expressed themselves unguardedly, and thereby afforded their enemies a handle to calumniate them. This, I imagine, has been the real source of that charge of infidelity, so often and so unjustly brought against physicians." _____ "The study of medicine, of all others, should be the least suspected of leading to impiety. An intimate acquaintance with the works of nature raises the mind to the most sublime conceptions of the Supreme Being, and at the same time dilates the heart with the most pleasing views of Providence. The difficulties that necessarily attend all deep enquiries into a subject two disproportionate to the human faculties, should not be suspected [190] to surprise a physician, who, in his practice, is often involved in perplexity, even in subjects exposed to the examination of his senses."

"There are, besides, some peculiar circumstances in the profession of a physician, which should naturally dispose him to look beyond the present scene of things, and engage his heart on the side of religion. He has many opportunities of seeing people, once the gay and the happy, sunk in deep distress; sometimes devoted to a painful and lingering death; and sometimes struggling with the tortures of a distracted mind. Such afflictive scenes, one should imagine, might soften any heart, not dead to every feeling of humanity; and make it reverence that religion which alone can support the soul in the most complicated distresses; that religion, which teaches to enjoy life with cheerfulness, and to resign it with dignity."

The judicious and animated considerations which are here delivered, could proceed only from a mind actuated by the principles of virtue and religion: And I trust, the great majority a physicians have their feelings in unison with those of the amiable writer I have quoted. But there may be some who have been hardened to moral apathy, by the very causes which should excite benevolence and [191] piety. It has been well remarked, by divines and metaphysicians, that *passive impressions* become progressively weaker by frequent recurrence; and that the heart is liable to grow callous to scenes of horror and distress, and even to the view of death itself. This law of nature is intended, by the wise and benignant author of our frame, to answer the most salutary purposes, by co-operating with another of equal, perhaps superior, force. For *active propensities* are formed, and gradually strengthened, by the like renewal of the circumstances which excite them. The love of goodness is thus rendered habitual; and rectitude of conduct is steadily and uniformly pursued, without struggle or perturbation.

The human character then attains the highest excellence, of which this probationary state is capable; and, perhaps, no profession is more favourable, than that of physic, to the formation of a mental constitution, that unites and it very high degrees of intellectual and moral vigour; because it calls forth the steady and unremitting exertions of benevolence, under the direction of cultivated reason; and, by opening a wider and wider sphere of duty, progressively augments their reciprocal energies. But the connection between the laws [192] of impression, and of habit, is not so determinate and necessary as to be wholly independent of the agent who is under their influence. By a perversion of the understanding and the will, they may be, and sometimes are, separated. The affections also, when the temperament is phlegmatic, subsist only in a languid state; and are too evanescent to produce a permanently correspondent frame of mind. If with this coldness of heart, a sceptical turn of thinking happen to be associated, either constitutionally or from the casualties of study and connections, virtuous principles will gradually decay; all the tender charities of life will soon be extinguished; a future state will be either disbelieved or regarded with indifference; and practical atheism will ensue, with the whole train of evils which result from a denial of the creative agency of God, or his divine administration. Allowing this to be an extreme, and barely possible case, a concession which I am solicitous to grant to my country-men, notwithstanding what has been fatally experienced in a neighbouring kingdom; yet different gradations towards it may subsist, and the first step should be avoided with sedulous care. The countervailing power of religion is here essentially necessary, because nothing be-[193]sides can furnish motives to rectitude, of adequate dignity, weight, and authority. To restore the impressions of piety which have been lost or impaired, without falling into the fervours of enthusiasm, or the gloom of superstition, may be an arduous task, a task that will require time and perseverance to accomplish. But the attainment will amply repay the labour, by the sweet satisfaction which a physician cannot fail to derive from the consciousness, that he exercises his profession under the inspection of a Being, who approves, and will reward every effort to acquire his favour by doing good to mankind. In his offices of humanity, he will feel an interest and elevation, of which those can have no conception who regard the human race, and consequently the sufferers under their care, not as the offspring of God, or as expectants of immortality, but as the creatures of a day, formed by the casual concourse, or the natural appetencies of atoms, and born only to perish. Such degrading and unhappy notions often spring from a love of paradox; a passion for novel hypothesis;

ambition to be victorious in subtle disputation; and a contempt for established authority, accompanied, for the most part, with an implicit submission to empirics in science, [194] who dogmatize most, when they assume the mask of scepticism. To the successful pursuit of truth, it is necessary to bring a well-disciplined mind, modest and sober in its views, uninfluenced not only by vulgar, but by philosophical prejudices, which are far more dangerous, because more plausible and fascinating. When subjects which relate to theology are investigated, reverence and humility should be associated with all our reasonings. No practice is more subversive of devotional sentiment, than that of carrying into religious discussions the licentiousness of thought and expression, which young physicians are too apt to indulge on medical topics. He who can suffer himself to treat his Maker with indifference and with levity, whether it be an utterance or in contemplation, will soon lose the religious impressions of reverence, gratitude, and love; and his mind will then be prepared for the systems of impiety and atheism, which of late have been so boldly promulgated under the imposing name of philosophy. Productions of this class should be shunned, even by those who are thoroughly grounded in rational faith; because familiarity with them can hardly fail to impair the moral sensibilities of the heart [195]. They are *evil communications*, which forcibly tend to *corrupt good manners*.

To the comprehensive view of a well-educated physician, the Divine Being will appear, with the fullest manifestation, in all without and all within him. Through the several kingdoms of nature, with which he is intimately acquainted, he traces every where design, intelligence, power, wisdom, and goodness. And in the frame of his own body, as well as in the constitution of his mental faculties, he finds especial reason to conclude, that above all other works of the creation, *he is fearfully and wonderfully made*. The daily offices of his profession disclose to him irrefragable proofs of the providence and moral government of God. – Health, as consisting in the soundness and vigour of the bodily organs, and in their complete aptitude for exertion and enjoyment, is doubtless of inestimable consideration. But the occasional suspension of this blessing may be necessary to obviate the abuses to which it is liable; to evince its high value; to remedy the injuries it may have sustained; and to ensure its future more permanent duration. A strong constitution is too often made subservient to sensuality, ebriety, and other licentious indulgences; [196] which, if not seasonably interrupted by the experience of *consequential suffering*, would prove destructive to the animal œconomy, and bring on premature decripitude [corrected to 'decrepitude' in errata, page xvi] or death. Diseases, under these circumstances, furnish a beneficial restraint, and preserve the mind from contamination; whilst they are often the remedies, which nature has kindly provided, for the restoration of the vital functions. A good, which has been lost and beneficently restored, will be prized according to its high desert; and being cherished with assiduous care, will be prolonged and applied to its proper uses, in the great business of life. But sickness, it must be acknowledged, is not always remedial in its tendency; and frequently produces degrees of protracted languishment and pain, grievous to endure, an obstructive to those *active offices*, which, in this present sphere, man is called upon to perform. There are duties, however, of another class, not less essential to the improvement and excellence of his *moral* and *religious character*: And where is a school to be found, like the chamber of sickness for meekness, patience, resignation, gratitude, and devout trust and God? There pride is humbled; the angry passions subside; animosities cease; and the vanities of the [197] world lose their bewitching attractions. False associations are there corrected; true estimates are formed; and whilst the *passive virtues* are cultivated in the suffering individual, all who minister to him have their best dispositions exercised, and improved. Tenderness, humanity, sympathy, friendship, and domestic love, on such occasions, find that sphere which is peculiarly adapted to their exertion; and all the softer charities derive from these sources their highest refinements. (a)

[Bottom page 198] (a) See a Father's Instructions, part III. p. 312, 9th edition.

Rational theism leads the mind, by fair and necessary induction, to extend its views to revelation. He who has discovered the divine wisdom, power, and goodness, through the various works of creation, will feel a solicitude to make farther advances in sacred knowledge; and the more profoundly he venerates the author of his being, the more earnest will he be to become acquainted with his will; with the means of conciliating his favour; with the duration of his own existence; and with his future destination. Several distinguished characters in the heathen world have, in a very explicit manner, testified the truth of his observation. Suffice it to state only the following remarkable passages from Plato: "A divine revelation is [198] necessary to explain the true worship of God – to add authority to moral precepts – to assist our best endeavours in a virtuous course – to fix the future rewards and punishments of virtuous and vicious conduct – and to point out some acceptable expiation for sin." He introduces Socrates, assuring Alcibiades, "that in a future time a divine person will appear, who, in pure love to man, shall remove all darkness from his mind, and instruct him how to offer his prayers and praises in the most acceptable way to the Divine Being." The privileges which this intelligent and amiable philosopher ardently looked for, we happily enjoy. Christianity has brought life and immortality to light: And the gospel is the sacred charter of our expected inheritance of felicity. To regard with indifference what is so momentous, is the grossest folly; to be dissatisfied with its evidence argues the want of discernment and of candour; and to reject it, without deliberate and conscientious investigation, is a high degree of impiety: The appeal, however, must finally be made to the judgment of every individual: And we may humbly hope, that he who *knoweth our frame*, will pity intellectual infirmary, and pardon involuntary error [199].

Note XIII. Chap. II. Sect. XXXI.

UNION IN CONSULTATION OF SENIOR AND JUNIOR PHYSICIANS

"Heat and vivacity in age," says Bacon, "is an excellent composition for business. Young men are fitter to invent than to judge, fitter for execution than for counsel, and fitter for new projects than for settled business; for the experience of age in things that fall within the compass of it, directeth them, but in new things abuseth them. The errors of young men are the ruin of business; but the errors of aged men amount but to this, that more might have been done, or sooner. Young men, in the conduct and manage of actions, embrace more than they can hold; stir more than they can quiet, fly to the end without consideration of the means and degrees, pursue some sew principles which they have chanced upon absurdly, care not to innovate, which draws unknown inconveniences; use extreme remedies at first, and that which doubleth all errors, will not acknowledge or retract them, like an unruly horse that will neither stop nor turn. Men of age object too much, consult too long, adventure too little, repent too soon, and sel-[200]dom drive business home to the full period, but content themselves with a mediocrity of success. Certainly it is good to compound employments of both; for that will be good for the present, because the virtues of either age may correct the defects of both; and good for succession, that young men may be learners, while men in age are actors. And lastly, good for extern accidents, because authority followeth old men, and favour and popularity youth: But for the moral part, perhaps youth will have the pre-eminence, as age hath for the politick." – Bacon's Essay of Youth and Age.

Note XIV. Chap. II. Sect. XXXII.

RETIREMENT FROM PRACTICE

THE following letters afford so admirable a comment on the rule to which this note refers, that it would be a false and unjustifiable delicacy not to lay them before the reader. I shall copy them without abridgement, because they present at once a striking display of Dr. Heberden's nice sense of honour and probity; of the peculiar urbanity of his manners; and of the vigour of his intellect at a very advanced period of life. His commendations of [201] this little work, I may be allowed to confess, are gratifying to my feelings; though I am sensible of the partiality from which they flow. But the partiality of a character, dignified by science and virtue, is itself an honour.

Copy of a letter from William Heberden,

M. D. F. R. S. &c. &c.

DEAR SIR,   Windsor, 28 August, 1794

IT is owing to my distance from London, that I have not sooner made my acknowledgments, and returned my thanks for your very obliging letter. Your being able to resume the work you had in hand, makes me hope that your good principles, with the aid of time, have greatly recovered your mind from what you must have suffered on occasion of the great loss in your family; and your attention in the further prosecution of it, will powerfully assist in perfectly restoring your tranquility. What you have already communicated to the public, with so much just applause, shews you to be peculiarly well qualified for drawing up a Code of Medical Ethics, by the just sense you have of your duties as a man, and by the masterly knowledge of your profession as a physician. I [202] hope it will not be long before the sheets already printed come to my hands; and I return you many thanks for intending to favour me with a sight of them.

The pleasure of a visit from one of Dr. Haygarth's merit, whom I have long known and esteemed, would probably give me spirits, and make him think me less broken than I am. I have entered my 85th year; and when I retired, a few years ago, from the practice of physic, I trust it was not from a wish to be idle, which no man capable of being usefully employed has a right to be, but because I was willing to give over, before my presence of thought, judgment, and recollection were so impaired, that I could not do justice to my patients. It is more desirable for a man to do this a little too soon, than a little too late; for the chief danger is on the side of not doing it soon enough.   I am, my dear sir

With great esteem and regard,

Your affectionate, humble servant,

W. HEBERDEN.

From the Same

DEAR SIR,   Pall-Mall, 15th October 1794.

BY The mistake or neglect of the person left in my house in London (to which [203] I am just returned) your Code of Medical Ethics had been sent thither some time before I was made acquainted with it. I have read it, and do not wonder, that nothing could be found by me, or by any one to add or alter, after a work of this kind had passed through the hands of one so much master of the subject; and who had taken no little time to consider it, and to make the proper improvements. I am confident that the same might be said of them, where I to read the two chapters which remain to be finished. If your judicious advice and rules were duly observed, they would greatly contribute to support the dignity of the profession, and the peace and comfort of the professors. There has lately been established, in several of the London hospitals, a plan of courses of lectures in all the branches of knowledge useful to a student in physic. Such plans, if rightly executed, as I have no reason to doubt they will be, must make London a school of physic superior to most in Europe. The experience afforded in an hospital, will keep down the luxuriance of plausible theories. Many such have been delivered in lectures, by celebrated teachers, with great applause; but the students, though perfectly masters of them, not having corrected them with what nature [204] exhibits in an hospital, have found themselves more at a loss in the cure of a patient, than an elder apprentice of an apothecary. I please myself with thinking, that the method of teaching the art of healing is becoming everyday more conformable to what reason and nature require; that the errors introduced by superstition an false philosophy are gradually retreating; and that medical knowledge, as well as all other dependent upon observation and experience, is continually increasing in the world. The present race of physicians are possessed of several most important rules of practice, utterly unknown to the ablest in former ages, not expecting Hippocrates himself, or even Æsculapius.

I am, dear Sir,

Your affectionate, humble servant,

W. HEBERDEN.

It is an observation of Bacon, that letters written by wise men, are the best of all human works. To these admirable communications, I shall, therefore, take the liberty of subjoining the extract of one, equally interesting and of similar import, from another Nestor in medicine; who has long and justly held the first rank amongst his brethren, for classical taste, [205] elegance of style, and professional erudition. "I have lately," says Sir George Baker, in a letter, dated Richmond, August 11th, 1802, "been in habit of spending much of my time in this place; avoiding, when possible, all medical employment. Many months have passed, since Dr. Haygarth took so favourable a measure of me: I will not, however, trouble you with an account of the infirmities and privations incident to my time of life. Be it sufficient to say, then I am contented with the fare that I have met with; and hope to retire from the feast of life, *uti conviva satur.*"

Note XV. Chap. IV. Sect. II.

PARTIAL INSANITY, WITH GENERAL INTELLIGENCE. LUCID INTERVAL

SIR Matthew Hale, in his *Historia Placitorum Coronae*, C. iv. has stated, that "There is a partial insanity of mind; and a total insanity. The former is either in respect to things, *quod hoc vel illud insanire*; some persons that have a competent use of reason in respect to some subjects, are yet under a particular *dementia* in respect to some par-[206]ticular discourses, subjects, or applications; or else it is particular in respect of degrees; and this is the condition of very many, especially melancholy persons, who, for the most part, discover their defect in excessive fears and griefs, and yet are not wholly destitute of the use of reason; and this partial insanity seems not to excuse them in the committing of any offence for its matter capital, for doubtless most persons that are felons of themselves, and others, are under a degree of partial insanity, when they commit these offences." – "The person that is absolutely mad for a day, killing a man in that distemper, is equally not guilty, as if he were mad without intermission. But such persons as have their lucid intervals, (which ordinarily happen between the full and change of the moon) in such intervals have usually at least a competent use of reason, and crimes committed buy them in these intervals are of the same nature, and subject to the same punishment, as if they had no such deficiency, nay, the alienations and contracts made by them in such intervals, are obliging to their heirs and executors."

Partial insanity and general intelligence may subsist, in various degrees and proportions to each other, and different persons; and even [207] in the same person at different times. If Socrates had lived at this period, and had not only professed himself to be governed by the influences of a familiar spirit, or dæmon, but had, also, uniformly regulated his conversation and actions by this persuasion, he would have been justly chargeable with derangement of mind, notwithstanding the profound wisdom which he displayed in his instructions concerning morals, and the conduct of life. Lord Herbert, of Cherbury, was highly distinguished both for talents and erudition: But having unfortunately adopted prejudices against Christianity, he wrote an elaborate work entitled, *De Veritate, prout distinguitur a Revelatione*; and knowing it would meet with much opposition, he remained sometime in anxious suspense about the publication of it. Providence, however, as he informs us in his own biographical memoirs, kindly interposed, and determined his wavering resolutions. "Being thus doubtful in my chamber, one fair day in the summer, my casement being open towards the south, and no wind stirring, I took my book *De Veritate* in my hand, and kneeling on my knees, devoutly said, *O thou eternal God, I am not satisfied enough whether I shall publish this book; if it be to thy* [208] *glory, I beseech thee give me some sign from heaven; if not, I shall suppress it.* I had no sooner spoken these words, but a loud, though yet gentle, noise came from the heavens; which did so comfort and chear me, that I took my petition as granted, and that I had the sign I demanded; whereupon also I resolved to print my book." This was not a temporary delusion of the imagination, but continued a permanent object of belief through life. And the impression was more extraordinary, and more indicative of an unsound mind, because Lord Herbert's chief argument against Christianity is, the improbability that Heaven shall reveal its laws only to a *portion of the earth*. For how could he, who doubted of a *partial*, confide in an *individual* revelation? Or is it possible that he could rationally think his book of sufficient importance to extort a declaration of the divine will, when the interest and happiness of a fourth part of mankind were deemed, by him, objects inadequate to the like display of goodness.*

[Bottom page 209] * See Walpole's Catalogues of royal and noble Authors; also Percival's Mor. and Lit. Diss. p. 82.

The history of the Rev. Simon Browne still more remarkably exemplifies the union of vi-[209]gour and imbecility, of rectitude and perversion, in the same understanding. The loss of his wife, and of his only son, so powerfully affected him, that he desisted from the duties of his clerical function, and could not be persuaded to join in any act of worship to the Deity, either public or private. He "conceived that Almighty God, by a singular instance of divine power, had, in a gradual manner, annihilated in him the thinking substance, and utterly divested him of consciousness: That though he retained the human shape, and the faculty of speaking, in a manner that appeared to others rational, he had all the while no more notion of what he said than a parrot. And, very consistently with this, he looked upon himself as no longer a moral agent, a subject of reward or punishment." In this conviction he continued, with very little variation, to the close of life. Yet, whilst under the influence of this strange phrensy, his faculties, in all other respects, appeared to be in full vigour. He applied himself with ardour to his studies; and was so acute a disputant, that his friends were wont to say, *he could reason as if possessed of two souls.* Indeed, both his imagination and his judgment were so improved, [210] as to surpass the state in which they subsisted during his perfect sanity.*

[Bottom page 211] * See Biog. Britan. Art. Simon Browne.

In J. J. Rousseau, we have a most interesting example of morbid sensibility and depraved imagination, combined with extensive knowledge and pre-eminent genius. It is said by Madame de Stael, in her Reflections on his Character and Writings, that "sometimes he would part with you, with all his former affection: but if an expression had escaped you, which might bear an unfavourable construction; he would recollect it, examine it, exaggerate it, perhaps dwell upon it for a month, and conclude by a total breach with you. Hence it was, that there was scarce a possibility of undeceiving him; for the light which broke in upon him at once, was not sufficient to efface the wrong impressions which had taken place so gradually in his mind. It was extremely difficult too to continue long on an intimate footing with him. A word, a gesture, furnished him with matter of profound meditation; he connected the most trifling circumstances, like so many mathematical pro-[211]positions, and conceived his conclusion to be supported by the evidence of demonstration."*

[Bottom page 212] * The reader is referred to the Elements of the Philosophy of the Human Mind, Sect V. by professor Dugald Stewart, for some admirable remarks on the evils which result from an ill-regulated imagination

I have hazarded an opinion in the text, contrary to what, I believe, is usually adopted by lawyers, that there may be cases of partial insanity with a high degree of general intelligence, in which the individual ought not to be precluded from the privilege of making a last will and testament. To deny the testamentary qualification to one, who, notwithstanding some false predominant conception, has been held capable of managing his concerns with discretion, and whose bequests discover no traces of a disturbed imagination, or unsound judgment, seems to be inconsistent both with wisdom and with natural justice. Such a person, I presume, is capable of acquiring property by legacy, by bargain, by transfer, by industry, or by office: and he is not prohibited, during life, from giving or expending possessions thus obtained. Why then does the law deprive him of the right of bequeathing after death, that which he might have dispensed, when alive, without controul? Whatever be the opinion which a medical prac-[212]titioner may have entertained, concerning the capacity or incapacity for making a will of one under these circumstances, it can hardly be necessary to observe, that his evidence, when called for in a course of legal enquiry, should be delivered explicitly, and without any bias from his preconceptions. On the point litigated, it is the exclusive province of the judge and jury to decide, after a full investigation of the case.

To determine the existence of a LUCID INTERVAL in the *delirium of fever,* or in the more permanent alienation of mind which constitutes *insanity,* the testimony of a physician is sometimes required, in courts of law. It will be incumbent on him, therefore, to possess a clear and definite opinion on the subject, founded both on the nature of the malady, and the state of the patient. The cessation of febrile delirium is not difficult to ascertain; because the rational faculties being unimpaired by a short suspension, at once manifest their renewal by signs which cannot be misunderstood. But the complete remission of madness, is only to be decided by reiterated and attentive observation. Every action, and even gesture of the patient should be sedulously watched; and he should be [213] drawn into conversations at different times, that may insensibly lead him to developed the false impressions under which he labours. He should also be employed, occasionally, in business, or offices connected with, and likely to renew his wrong associations. If these trials produce no recurrence of insanity, he may, with full assurance, be regarded as legally *compos mentis* during such period; even though he should relapse, a short time afterward, into his former malady.

Note XVI. Chap. IV. Sect. XIII.

DUELLING

IN the usages of the ancient Germans, evident traces of DUELLING may be discovered: But it was employed by them either as an appeal to the justice, or to the prescience of the gods. Velleius Paterculus informs us, that questions, decided amongst the Romans by legal trial, were terminated amongst the Germans by arms or judicial combat.*

[Bottom page 214] * Vellei Patercul. lib. II. cap. cxviii.

Tacitus describes it as a species of divination, by which the future events of important wars were explored. A captive from the enemy was com-[214]pelled to fight with a man selected from their own nation. Each was accoutred with his proper weapons; and the presage of success was determined by the issue of the battle.*

[Bottom page 215] * Vide Tacit. de Situ, Morib. et Populis Germaniæ, Sect. X.

A law is quoted by Stiernhook, which shews, that judicial combat was, at first, appropriated to points respecting personal character, and that it was only subsequently extended to criminal cases, and to questions relative to property. The terms of the law are, "If any man shall say to another these reproachful words, 'you are not a man equal to other men;' or, 'you have not the heart of a man;' and the other shall reply, 'I am a man as good as you;' let them meet on the highway. If he who first gave offence appear, and the person absent himself, let the latter be deemed worse than he was called; let him not be admitted to give evidence in judgment either for a man or woman, and let him not have the privilege of making a testament. If the person offended appear, and he who gave the offence be absent, let him call upon the other thrice with a loud voice, and make a mark upon the earth, and then let him who absented himself [215] be deemed infamous, because he uttered words which he durst not support. If both shall appear properly armed, and the person offended shall fall in the combat, let a half compensation be paid for his death. But if the person who gave the offence shall fall, let it be imputed to his own rashness. The petulance of his tongue hath been fatal to him. Let him lie in the field without any compensation being made for his death.*

[Bottom page 216] * Lex Uplandica apud Stiern. – Robertson's History of Charles V. Vol. I. Note 22.

Montesquieu, on the authority of Beaumanoir, whom he quotes with great respect, deduces the rise and formation of the articles, relative to the point of honour, from the following particular judicial usages. The accuser declared, in the presence of the judge, that such a person had committed such an action: The accused made answer that *he lied*; upon which the judge gave orders for the duel. Thus it became an established rule, that whenever the lie was given to a person, it was incumbent on him to fight. *Gentlemen* combated on horseback, completely armed. *Villeins* fought on foot and with bastons. The baston, therefore, was regarded as an instrument of affront, because to strike a man with it was to treat him as a [216] villein. For the like reason, a box on the ear, or blow on the face, was deemed a contumely, to be expiated with blood; since villeins alone were liable to receive such disgraceful blows, as it was peculiar to them to fight with their heads uncovered.*

[Bottom page 217] * See Montesquieu, Liv. XXVIII. C. XX.

Practices like these were so congenial to the proud and martial spirit of the times, as well as to the superstition which prevailed, but they became universal throughout Europe. That it is evident that they could not fail to subvert the regular course of justice, diminish the authority of government, and violate the sacred ordinances of the church. For the clergy uniformly remonstrated against, and even anathematized them, as adverse to christianity; and the civil power frequently interposed, to set bounds to usages, which its authority was too feeble to suppress. Henry I. of England, in the twelfth century, prohibited trial by combat, in all questions concerning property of small value. Louis VII. of France, issued an edict to the same effect. St. Louis, who was a distinguished legislator, considering the rude age in which he reigned, attempted a more perfect jurisprudence, by substituting trial by evidence, in place of that by [217] combat. And afterwards it became the policy of every monarch, who possessed power or talents, to explode these relics of Gothic barbarism. By degrees the practice became less and less frequent; courts of judicature, acquired an ascendancy; law was studied as a science, and administered with great regularity; and the ferocious manners of the inhabitants of Europe yielded to the arts of peace, and to the benefits of social and civilized life. But an event occurred, in the year 1528, which both revived the practice of single combat, and gave a new form to it, more absurd and fatal. The political and personal enmity, which subsisted between the Emperor Charles V. and Francis I., led the former to commission the French herald, sent to him with a denunciation of war, to acquaint his sovereign, that he should from that time consider him not only as a base violator of public faith, but as a stranger to the honour and probity of a gentleman. Francis instantly sent back the herald, with a *cartel* of defiance, giving the Emperor *the lie*, and challenging him to single combat. Charles accepted the challenge; but it being impracticable to settle the preliminaries, this romantic and ridiculous enterprize of course was never accomplished. The trans-[218]action, however, excited such universal attention, and reflected so much splendour and dignity on this novel mode of single combat, that every gentleman thought himself entitled, and even bound in honour to draw his sword, and to demand satisfaction of his adversary, for affronts trivial and even imaginary.*

[Bottom page 219] * See Robertson's History of Charles V. Book V.

The best blood in Christendom was shed; personages of the first distinction were devoted to death; the ease, the familiarity, and the confidence of private intercourse were interrupted; and war itself was hardly more destructive to life, and to its dearest enjoyments, then this fatal and seductive frenzy. † [219]

[Bottom page 219 continued to bottom page 220] † The History of Lord Herbert of Cherbury, who lived in the reigns of Queen Elizabeth and James I., fully exemplifies the folly and danger of adopting false principles of honour. During the abode of this romantic nobleman, at the Duke of Montmorenci's, about twenty-four miles from Paris, it happened, one evening, that a daughter of the Duchess de Ventadour, of about ten or eleven years of age, went to walk in the meadows, with his lordship, and several other gentlemen and ladies. The young lady wore a knot of ribband on her head, which a French chevalier snatched away, and fastened to his hatband. He was desired to return it, but refused. The lady then requested Lord Herbert to recover it for her. A race ensued; and the chevalier, [219] finding himself likely to be overtaken, made a sudden turn, and was about to deliver his prize to the young lady, when Lord Herbert seized his arm, and cried out, "I give it to you." "Pardon me," said the lady, "it is he who gives it me." "Madam," replied Lord Herbert, "I will not contradict you, but if the chevalier do not acknowledge that I constrain him to give the ribband, I will fight with him." And the next day he sent him a challenge, "being bound thereto," says he, "by the oath taken when I was made knight of the bath." See the Life of Lord Herbert of Cherbury; also Percival's Moral and Lit. Dissert. p. 299, second edit.

Evils of such magnitude required adequate remedies; and all the terrors of law were every where exerted to repress them. But they have hitherto been employed in vain. Nor is it likely that sanguinary punishments will prevail, because the dread of such punishment would be deemed equally dishonorable with the fear of death, in the chances of combat. A heavy fine, strictly levied, would operate with greater force, on some of the most active principles of the human mind: And if it amounted to half or one third of the convicted person's fortune, such portion being placed in chancery, for the benefit of his heirs or children, this privation would not only extend to his comforts and accommodations, but would be felt as a species of infamy, [220] by depriving him of the means of maintaining his rank and station in life. Lord Verulam has proposed the following remedy for duelling; which, if effectual with men of quality, would soon disgrace the practice amongst those inferior degree: "The fountain of honour is the king; and his aspect, and the access to his person, continueth honour in life; and to be banished from his presence is one of the greatest eclipses of honour that can be; if his Majesty shall be pleased, that when this court shall censure any of these offences, in persons of eminent quality, to add this out of his own power and discipline, that those persons shall be banished and excluded from his court for certain years, and the courts of his Queen and Prince, I think there is no man that hath any good blood in him, will commit an act that shall cast him into that darkness, that he may not behold his sovereign's face." *

[Bottom page 221] * Bacon's Works, Vol. II. page 516.

This proposal of Lord Verulam seems to receive some confirmation from a story related by Lord Shaftsbury in his Characteristicks. †

[Bottom page 221] † Vol. I. Sect. III. page 273.
"A certain gallant of our court, being asked by his friends, why one of his established character for cou-[221]rage and good-sense would answer the challenge of a coxcomb, replied, "that for his *own* sex he could safely trust their judgment. But how could he appear at night before the *maids of honour?*"

Thus the principle, on which duelling is founded, is now neither an appeal to the justice of heaven, nor an expression of resentment for wrong sustained; but generally a mere punctilio of honour, which would affix a *stigma* on the character for courage of him, who omits the offer, and on the opponent who declines the acceptance of a challenge. Hence forgiveness of injury, and reparation from the consciousness of having committed it, those noble sentiments of just and generous minds, are wholly precluded in the intercourse of fashionable life.

A very able moralist, whom I have often quoted with peculiar satisfaction, has reduced the question concerning duelling, as now practiced, to this single point: Whether a regard for our own reputation is, or is not, sufficient to justify the taking away the life of another. "A sense of shame," says he, "is so much torture; and no relief presents itself, otherwise than by an attempt upon the life of our adversary. What then? The distress which [222] men suffer by the want of money is often times extreme, and no resource can be discovered but that of removing a life, which stands between the distressed person and his inheritance. The motive in this case is as urgent, and the means much the same, as in the former; yet this case finds no advocates."

"For the army, where the point of honour is cultivated with exquisite attention and refinement," continues the same excellent writer, "I would establish a court of honour, with a power awarding those submissions and acknowledgements, which it is generally the object of a challenge to obtain; and it might grow into a fashion with persons of rank of all professions to refer their quarrels to the same tribunal."*

[Bottom page 223] * Dr. Paley's Principles of Moral Philosophy, Chap. IX.
An institution, like the one thus forcibly recommended by Dr. Paley, might probably have prevented the late fatal duel between Colonel Montgomery and Captain M'Namara. The address of the latter to the gentlemen of the jury gives just grounds for this opinion, and claims on that account the attention of the legislator. "Gentlemen," said he, "I am a cap-[223]tain of the British navy. My character you can only hear from others; but to maintain any character, in that station, I must be respected. When called upon to lead others into honourable dangers, I must not be supposed to be a man who had sought safety, by submitting to what custom has taught others to consider as a disgrace. I am not presuming to urge anything against the laws of God, or of this land. I know that, in the eye of religion and reason, obedience to the law, though against the general feelings of the world, is the first duty, and ought to be the rule of action: but in putting a construction upon my motives, so as to ascertain the quality of my actions, you will make allowances for my situation."*

[Bottom page 224] * Courier, April 23, 1803.

In referring to the foregoing disastrous case, it is proper to notice, that a surgeon of considerable eminence, who attended on the field of combat in his *professional capacity*, was on this account arrested, and sent to Newgate, by a warrant from the civil magistrate, as a *principal* in the alleged murder, having been present at the deal, and antecedently privy to it. Nor was he liberated [224] from prison till the grand jury had rejected the indictment.

It has recently been stated, in one of the periodical prints, that a law to prevent duelling was passed in the general assembly of North Carolina during their last session, by which it was enacted, "That no person sending, accepting, or being the bearer of a challenge, for the purpose of a fighting or duel, even though no death should ensue, shall ever after be eligible to any office of trust, power, or profit in the state, any pardon or reprieve notwithstanding: And that the said person shall further be liable to be indicted, and on conviction shall forfeit and pay the sum of one hundred pounds to the use of the state. And if anyone who fight a duel, by which either of the parties shall be killed, then the survivor, on conviction thereof, shall suffer death without benefit or clergy; and the seconds shall, be considered as accessaries before the fact, and likewise suffer death."*

[Bottom page 225] * Courier, March 9th, 1803.

I shall insert the following communication from my late venerable friend Dr. Benjamin Franklin, on the subject of duelling, be-[225]cause the deliberate opinion of a man, peculiarly distinguished by perspicacity, soundness of judgment, and extensive knowledge of the world, cannot fail to be interesting to the reader. The letter was written in the 79th year of his age, and evinces the same vein of humour which characterized him through life. A few passages are omitted, being merely complementary and personal.

Passy, near Paris, July 17, 1784

DEAR SIR,

I Received, yesterday, by Mr. White, your kind letter of May 11th, with the most agreeable present of your new book. I read it all before I slept. * It is astonishing that the murderous practice of duelling, which you so justly condemn, should continue so long in vogue. Formerly, when duels were used to determine law-suits, from an opinion that Providence would, in every instance, favour truth and right with victory, they were more excusable. At present they decide nothing. A man says something, which another tells him is a lie. They fight; but whichever is killed, the point [226] in dispute remains unsettled. To this purpose they have a pleasant little story here: A gentleman, in a coffee-house, desired another to sit farther from him. – Why so? – Because, Sir, you smell offensively. – That is an affront, and you must fight me. I will fight you, if you insist upon it: But I do not see how that will mend the matter. For if you kill me I shall smell too; and if I kill you, you will smell, if possible, worse than you do at present. – How can such miserable sinners as we are, entertain so much pride asked you conceive that every offense against our imagined honour merits death? These petty princes, in their own opinion, would call that sovereign a tyrant, who should put one of them to death for a little uncivil language, though pointed at his sacred person. Yet every one of them makes himself judge in his own cause; condemns the offender without a jury, and undertakes himself to be the executioner.

Our friend Mr. Vaughan May, perhaps, communicate to you some conjectures of mine, relating to the cold of last winter, which I sent in return for the observations on cold of Professor Wilson. If he should, and you think them worthy so much notice, you may shew then to your philosophical society, to which I [227] wish all imaginable success. Their rules seem to me excellent.

With sincere and great esteem, I have the honour to be, your most obedient, and most humble servant, (B. FRANKLIN).

Note. XVII. Chap. IV. Sect. XVI.

PUNISHMENT OF THE CRIME OF RAPE

THE atrocity of this crime appears to have been variously estimated at different periods, and in different countries; if we may judge from the diversity of punishments inflicted on the perpetrators of it. The reader will find a copious and interesting enumeration of them, in a folio volume, entitled, *A View of Ancient Laws against Immorality and Profaneness, by John Disney, M. A. Cambridge printed, 1729.* I would refer him also to the *Principles of Penal Law*, by Mr. Eden, now Lord Auckland. As both these valuable works are out of print, a few extracts from each may form an acceptable addition to the present note.

The Burgundian laws provided, that if the young woman carried off returned to her pa-[228]rents actually corrupted, the offender should pay six times her price, or legal valuation; and also a mulct of twelve shillings. If he had not wherewithal to pay these sums, he should be given up to her parents, or near relations, to take their revenge of him in what way they pleased.

By the law of Æthelbert, the first Christian king of Kent, it was enacted, that if any person take a young woman by force, he shall pay her parent, or guardian, fifty shillings; and shall make a farther composition for her ransom. If she were espoused, he shall compensate the husband by an additional payment of twenty shillings. But if she were with child, the augmented fine shall be five and thirty shillings, and fifteen more to the king.

There is an ordinance of king Alfred, for the punishment of Rapes, committed upon country wenches who were servants, an offence which may be supposed to have been prevalent at that time. It is delivered in the following terms: "*Si quis Coloni mancipium ad stuprum comminetur 5 Sol. Colono emendet, et 60 Sol. Mulctæ loco. Si Servus Servam ad stuprum coegerit, compenset hoc Virgâ suâ virili. Si quis puellam teneræ aetatis ad illicitum concubitum comminetur, eodem modo* [229] *puniatur quo ille qui adultæ servæ hoc secerit.*"

By the Welsh laws of Prince Höel Dha, if two women were walking together without other company, and violence was offered to either or both of them, it was not punishable as a rape; but if they had a third person with them, they might claim their full legal redress. If the perpetrator of a rape, being accused, confessed the fact, besides full satisfaction to the woman, he was to answer for the crime to his sovereign, by the present of a silver stand as high as the king's mouth, and as thick as his middle finger, with a gold cup upon it, so large as to contain what he could take off at one draught, and as thick as the nail of a country fellow who had worked at the plough seven years. If the offender was not able to make such a present, *virilia membra amittat.*

Sir Edward Coke states this offense as a felony at the common law, which had a punishment, "under such a condition as no other felony had the like." The criminal was adjudged *amittere oculos, quibus virginem concupivit; amittere etiam testiculos, qui calorem stupri induxerunt.*

In the ancient law of England, exclusive of the punishment inflicted on the criminal, [230] his horse, greyhound, and hawk, were also subjected to great corporal infamy: But the woman who was the sufferer, might prevent all the penalties, if, before judgment, she demanded the offender for her husband. The Roman law was in the same spirit. "*Rapta raptoris, aut mortem, aut indotatas nuptias opiet*;" upon which there arose what was thought a doubtful case, "*Una nocte quidam duas rapuit, altera mortem optat, altera nuptias.*"

Note XVIII. Chap. IV. Sect. XVII.

UNCERTAINTY IN THE EXTERNAL SIGNS OF RAPE

I Have been favoured by Mr. Ward, one of the surgeons to the Manchester Infirmary, with the following particulars of the case, to which this note refers.

"Jane Hampson, aged four, was admitted an out-patient of the Infirmary, February 11th, 1791. The female organs were highly inflamed, sore, and painful; and it was stated by the mother, that the child was as well as usual till the preceding day, when she complained of pain in making water. This in-[231]duced the mother to examine the parts affected, when she was surprised to find the appearances above described. The child had slept, two or three nights, in the same bed with a boy, fourteen years old; and had complained that morning of having been hurt by him very much in the night."

"Leeches, and other external applications, together with appropriate internal remedies, were prescribed: But the debility increased, and on the 20th of February the child died. The coroner's inquest was taken, previously to which the body was inspected, and the abdominal and thoracic *viscera* were found to have been free from disease. The circumstances above related having been proved to the satisfaction of the jury, and being corroborated by the opinion I gave, that the child's death was occasioned by external violence, a verdict of murder was returned against the boy with whom she had slept. A warrant was, therefore, issued to apprehend him; but he had absconded, a circumstance which was considered as a confirmation of his guilt, when added to the circumstantial evidence alledged against him."

"Not many weeks had elapsed, however, before several similar cases occurred, in which [232] there was no reason to suspect that external violence had been offered; and some in which it was absolutely certain that no such injury could have taken place. A few of the patients died; though from the novelty and fatal tendency of the disease, more than common attention was paid to them. I was then convinced that I had been mistaken, in attributing Jane Hampson's death to external violence; and I informed the coroner of the reasons which produced this change of opinion. The testimony I gave was designedly made public; and the friends of the boy hearing of it, prevailed upon him to surrender himself."

"When he was called to the bar at Lancaster, the judge informed the jury, that the evidence adduced was not sufficient to convict him; that it would give rise to much indelicate discussion, if they proceeded on the trial; and that he hoped, therefore, they would acquit him without calling any witnesses. With this request the jury immediately complied."

"The preceding narrative may teach the young surgeon to act with great circumspection, when called upon to give an opinion in cases which are involved in any degree of obscurity. It behoves him to consider well the important duty he has to discharge both to an individual, [233] and to the community: and that he makes himself responsible for the consequences which may result from the influence of his judgment on the minds of the jury."

Note XIX. Cap. IV. Sect. XVIII.

THE SMOKE FROM LARGE WORKS, A NUISANCE

THE smoke issuing from large works, without any arsenical or other poisonous impregnation, may prove a great annoyance to the neighbourhood in which they are situated: And the proprietors should be compelled, by law, to diminish this evil, as much as possible, by the adoption of the improved methods of burning fuel, which have been lately invented. But it may be doubted whether the sooty matter, sublimed by the combustion of pit-coal, be so injurious, as is commonly supposed, to the animal œconomy, unless it should subsist in the atmosphere in a very extraordinary degree of accumulation. The inhabitants Coalbrook-Dale, who live in a narrow valley, where the air is almost constantly loaded with vapours from numerous furnaces, employed in the smelting of iron, are not, is I have been informed, peculiarly subject to pulmonary af-[234]fections. And the people of Birmingham, Sheffield, Newcastle, and Manchester, towns which are often enveloped in smoke, from the nature of their respective manufactures, seem to suffer no abridgement in the general duration of life, as it subsists in crowded places, which can be ascribed exclusively to this cause. Hoffmann maintains, that the fumes of pit-coal are not injurious to health, in the ordinary modes of exposure to them: and Caspar Neumann confirms this testimony, by his experience and observation during a long residence in London.*

[Bottom page 235] * See Neumann's Chemical Works, by Lewis, page 246, 4to.

In mentioning Coalbrook-Dale, I might have stated the following fact, as corroborating the observation above advanced. A few years ago, a lady, accompanied by her husband, undertook a journey for the recovery of health, after a severe attack of asthma, to which she was often incident. The root lay through Coalbrook-Dale; and they arrived there on Sunday evening, about eight o'clock; when all the fires fresh lighted for working the furnaces. A thick smoke pervaded the whole valley; and the gentleman was [235] alarmed with the danger, which his wife incurred, of suffocation. But, to his surprize and satisfaction, she experienced no difficulty of breathing; and passed the night, inhaling the gross vapours with which she was surrounded, without present inconvenience or subsequent inquiry. May it be supposed that the sooty matter undergoes a decomposition in the lungs, by which it becomes capable of absorption, and innoxious to the animal œconomy? For the accumulation of it, as a solid substance, in the bronchial vesicles, could hardly fail to occasion immediate and permanent evils. It will, however, be alledged, that travelers breathe whole days in dusty roads, and yet experience no lasting bad effects. The case of masons, who are sometimes incident to hæmoptoe and pulmonary consumption, is widely different, as the particles, which they draw in by respiration, are large and angular.

Conceiving it to be of importance to obtain full and precise information relative to the effects of smoke in Coalbrook-Dale, I wrote on this subject to Mr. Edwards, an eminent [236] surgeon who is settled there, from whom I have been favoured with the following judicious answer:

"I have never observed that asthmas, and other pulmonic affections, are more frequent in the Dale than elsewhere, but rather the contrary; as I have been told, that the smoke in London agrees better with some asthmatic persons, than the keen country air. Old colliers, indeed, and such work in iron, stone-mines, and lime-rocks, are very subject, in the decline of life, to coughs and shortness of breath, especially hard drinkers; but in other respects the inhabitants are remarkably healthy, and the principal part of the practice is surgery, the smoke arising from the coal and iron not being so prejudicial as from the copper-works, in Cornwal and other parts. Such colliers and miners as are troubled with coughs, &c. always ascribe it to the dust arising in getting the coal or mineral, and from the smoke in the burning of lime, for which they take frequent emetics and purges." [237]

Note XX. Page 117.

DISCOURSE ON HOSPITAL DUTIES; BY THE REV. THO. B. PERCIVAL, LL. B.

THIS Anniversary Discourse was addressed to the gentlemen of the faculty; the officers; the clergy; and the trustees of the Infirmary, at Liverpool, for the benefit of the charity; and I believe was highly approved by the judicious audience, before whom it was delivered. As the preacher assumed topics of exhortation, not before adopted by divines on such occasions, it may be proper to state, that he was peculiarly qualified, from his knowledge of the polity of hospitals, to execute with ability so delicate and so arduous a task. After passing several years at St. John's College, in Cambridge, in the pursuits of general science, he removed to Edinburgh to engage in the study of physic. But notwithstanding his acquisitions in the HEALING ART, to which he applied himself with great assiduity, he uniformly discovered a predilection for THEOLOGY. It became expedient, therefore, not to oppose the strong direction of his mind. He returned to Cambridge; and when he had taken the degree of LL. B. was [238] admitted into holy orders. Being appointed to the chaplaincy of the British company of merchants at St. Petersburgh, he removed thither; and executed the duties of that honourable and important station with exemplary fidelity, and with the general approbation of the factory. In this office he died, after a lingering and painful illness, on the 27th of May, 1798, in the thirty-second year of his age.

Note XXI. Page 128.

THE SALUTARY CONNECTIONS OF SICKNESS ARE NOT TO BE RASHLY DISOLVED, BY REMOVING INTO AN HOSPITAL THOSE WHO MAY, WITH A LITTLE AID, ENJOY IN THEIR OWN HOMES, BENEFITS AND CONSOLATIONS, WHICH ELSEWHERE IT IS EMPTY POWER OF NO ONE TO CONFER

THE domestic benefits of sickness to the sufferer, and to his family, in fostering the tender attachment of affinity; – "the charities of father, son, and brother," are thus eloquently displayed by a late excellent divine.

"CHRISTIAN, when, in the season of *sickness*, you saw the solitude of your friends: the assiduity, perhaps, of a pious offspring [238] to repay your care of them in doing for you what now you could do no longer for yourself; when you observed their anxiety, if any human care or intercession could avail to snatch you from the impending danger; when you saw them sacrificing ease, and rest, and health, to administer to your deliverance and comfort, holding nothing dear to them, that if the will of God were such, they might by any means restore you and retain you; when you saw their zealous care to do *all* to which their power extended; and their heartfelt anguish as to that which their power could not reach: when in their countenances you perceived the alternate marks of hope and apprehension, of comfort and distress: while you saw *all* this, while you experienced the benefits and the consolations of their friendship, were your hearts *so hard*, that such powerful attachment, and such zealous service, could draw forth from you no more than the *ordinary* current of affection? No, Christian, surely that could not be. In such a situation, the lightest expression of sincere friendship, come *full* upon the heart to a warmer welcome, and with more than ordinary weight. When we are about to lose our blessings, [240] it is then, perhaps, that we first see them in their true importance. It is the same when it seems to us that we are about to *leave* them. The last conversation, the last kind offices, the last mutual interchange of tender words, and silent looks; that last scene, my friends, will agitate the inmost heart, and set open all the springs of sympathy and benevolence. While that last scene is drawing nigh, and as long, also, as the impression of it remains in memory, every thing partakes of its tender influences. While the heart is thus mollified, by the united power of sharp affliction and solemn expectation, every kindness, every condolence, every good wish, every even the lightest token of benevolent attention, sinks deep into it. The merit of friends puts on an unusual amiableness, and every thing we love is inexpressibly endeared to us. Christians, have you ever felt these sentiments? If you have, you cannot willingly abandon them; for as surely as you have felt them, you approve them. You would have loved yourselves the better, if in all time past, *these* had on all occasions been the abiding sentiments of your hearts. The man who is as sensible as [241] he ought to be, and by a very little measure of reflection might be, of what mighty use may be made of such circumstances, and their influences, to give pleasantness, acceptableness, and accuracy to his social duties, not only within the more contracted circle of his family and friends, but also in the wider range of his benevolent affections, will often be retracing these circumstances, and their influences in his mind and heart, that he may avail himself of them in the services that he owes to the universal family of God, and in the improvement of his own soul, to a resemblance of the universal parent. In such cases he will be more assiduous, if he will permit himself to think, that the heart which has once been exposed to such powerfully humanizing and attendering influences, if it is not much the better, must of necessity become much the worse for them."* [242]

[Bottom page 242] * See Life of Rev. Newcome Cappe, prefixed to his posthumous works, published by Mrs. C. Cappe, in 2 vol. 8vo. page 48.

Note XXII. Page 133.

DUTY OF HOSPITAL TRUSTEES IN ELECTING THE MEDICAL OFFICERS OF THE CHARITY

ON the 17th of March, 1798, the governors of the Salisbury Infirmary published the following judicious advertisement, concerning the nomination of a physician to the charity:

"Whereas it is the common practice to solicit votes on a vacancy of the offices of physician, surgeon, apothecary, secretary, &c. and as many and great inconveniencies have frequently arisen from a too hasty compliance with such solicitations, to the exclusion of the most worthy candidates, and the permanent detriment of the charity; and as such inconsiderate promises may render even the most judicious statutes and prudential rules of any society intellectual; it is hoped that every governor of this charitable institution will, on all such occasions, keep himself entirely disengaged till the day of election; and then, after a due examination into the real merits of the candidates, give his vote according to what he apprehends most beneficial to that charity, of which he is the guardian as well as the benefactor. The [243] reasonableness of not promising votes will be further evident, when it is considered that such promises, previous to the day of election, prevent perhaps him who is the best qualified from appearing as a candidate, well knowing it would be impossible for him to succeed."

The following Memorial was presented, several years ago, to the trustees of the Manchester Infirmary; and the rule, recommended in it, has been ever since adopted.

"The medical committee, having been invited to lay before you their opinion concerning the qualifications requisite in your apothecary and house-surgeon, are naturally induced to extend their attention to the more important office, with which the physicians to these charities are invested. And they are persuaded you will feel, with them, an earnest solicitude that the vacancies, which now subsist, may hereafter be filled by men of approved respectability, and liberal education.

"By the established usage of the hospital, it is required, that every candidate for the office of physician shall produce his DIPLOMA, for the inspection of the trustees; together with satisfactory attestations of his moral character, and professional endowments. In addition to [244] these credentials, they conceive it to be highly expedient that he should deliver an extract from the register of the university of which he was a member; specifying the several branches of science which he has cultivated, and the period of his collegiate residence. Such a testimonial may always be claimed, and is generally in the possession of physicians who have been regularly educated: No candidate, therefore, who does not produce it, should be deemed eligible: For he thus tacitly acknowledges, that he has not enjoyed the requisite advantages of academical instruction; nor received his degree as the reward of legitimate examination, either during the course, or after the completion of his academical studies.

"No candidate having yet offered, nor anyone being known to have the design of offering himself for either of the present medical vacancies in the hospital, the considerations they now take the liberty of suggesting to your serious attention, cannot even be suspected of personal reference, or invidious allusion. And they are conscious, on this occasion, of being actuated by a sincere desire to promote the best and most permanent interests of the in-[245]stitutions, with which, by your suffrages, they have the honour to be connected."

This memorial, under the form of a letter, having been presented to the trustees of the Manchester Infirmary, produced the two following resolutions:

1. The trustees are fully sensible of the importance of the considerations, which the physicians have stated to them in the above letter; and feel an earnest solicitude that the present and all future vacancies in the medical department of the hospital, should be filled by men of liberal education, good moral character, and respectable professional endowments.

2. It was moved, seconded, and resolved unanimously, that it be recommended to every succeeding board, to send a copy of the preceding letter to every gentleman, who may offer himself a candidate for the office of physician to these charities.

Manchester: Printed by S. Russell, No. 125, Deansgate [246]

1823
Extracts from the Medical Ethics of Dr. Percival

Citations to Original Publication:

Kappa Lambda Society. 1823. *Extracts from the Medical Ethics of Dr. Percival*. Philadelphia: Published privately for the Kappa Lambda Secret Society of Hippocrates by Clark & Fraser, Printers, 33 Carter's Alley.

Percival, Thomas. 1823. *Extracts from the Medical Ethics of Dr. Percival*. Philadelphia [Clark & Raser, printers].

Citations to Publication in this Volume:

Percival, Thomas. [1823] 2022. *Extracts from the Medical Ethics of Dr. Percival*. Philadelphia [Clark & Raser, printers]. In McCullough, Laurence B. 2022. Thomas Percival's *Medical Ethics* and the Invention of Medical Professionalism: With Three Key Percival Texts, Two Concordances, and a Chronology: 435–443. New York: Springer.

Kappa Lambda Society. [1823] 2022. *Extracts from the Medical Ethics of Dr. Percival*. Philadelphia: Published privately for the Kappa Lambda Secret Society of Hippocrates. In McCullough, Laurence B. 2022. Thomas Percival's *Medical Ethics* and the Invention of Medical Professionalism: With Three Key Percival Texts, Two Concordances, and a Chronology: 435–443. New York: Springer.

EXTRACTS

FROM THE

MEDICAL ETHICS

OF

DR. PERCIVAL

PHILADELPHIA.

1823 [not paginated 1]

[not paginated: 2 blank]

I. PHYSICIANS and SURGEONS should minister to the sick, with due impressions of the importance of their office; reflecting that the ease, the health, and the lives of those committed to their charge depend on their skill, attention, and fidelity. They should study, also, in their deportment, so to unite *tenderness* with *steadiness*, and *condescension* with *authority*, as to inspire the minds of their patients with gratitude, respect, and confidence.

[Editor's Note: 'Hospital' deleted from beginning of first sentence of Chapter I, Section I of *Medical Ethics*. The rest of *Medical Ethics* Chapter I is deleted.]

II. Every case, committed to the charge of a physician or surgeon, should be treated with attention, steadiness, and humanity: reasonable indulgence should be granted to the mental imbecility and caprices of the sick. Secrecy and delicacy, when required by peculiar circumstances, should be strictly observed: and the familiar and [3] confidential intercourse, to which the faculty are admitted in their professional visits, should be used with discretion, and with the most scrupulous regard to fidelity and honour.

[Editor's Note: This is *Medical Ethics* Chapter II, Section I, less first sentence: "THE *moral rules of conduct*, prescribed towards hospital patients, should be fully adopted in private or general practice." Sections II-IV are from *Medical Ethics* Chapter II, with each original section number increased by 1. Chapter II, Section VI is omitted. This results in return to original section numbering in *Medical Ethics* Chapter II. Section X combines text from *Medical Ethics* Chapter I, Section XIX and from Chapter II, Section X. Further explanation is provided in Section X, below.]

III. The strictest *temperance* should be deemed incumbent on the faculty; as the practice both of physic and surgery at all times requires the exercise of a clear and vigorous understanding: and on emergencies, for which no professional man should be unprepared, a steady hand, an acute eye, and an unclouded head, may be essential to the well-being, and even to the life, of a fellow creature. Phillip of Macedon reposed with entire security on the vigilance and attention of his General Parmenio. In his hours of mirth and conviviality, he was wont to say, "Let us drink, my friends; we may do it with safety, for Parmenio never drinks!" The moral of this story is sufficiently obvious, when applied to the faculty; but it should certainly be construed with great limitation by their patients.

IV. A physician should not be forward to make gloomy prognostications; because they savour of empiricism, by magnifying the importance of his services in the treatment or cure of the disease. But he should not fail, on proper occasions, to [4] give to the friends of the patient timely notice of danger, when it really occurs, and even to the patient himself, if absolutely necessary. This office, however, is so peculiarly alarming, when executed by him, that it ought to be declined, whenever it can be assigned to any other person of sufficient judgment and delicacy. For the physician should be the minister of hope and comfort to the sick; that, by such cordials to the drooping spirit, he may smooth the bed of death, revive expiring life, and counteract the depressing influence of those maladies, which rob the philosopher of fortitude, and the Christian of consolation.

V. *Officious interference*, in a case under the charge of another, should be carefully avoided. No meddling inquiries should be made concerning the patient; no unnecessary hints given, relative to the nature or treatment of his disorder; nor any selfish conduct pursued, that may directly or indirectly tend to diminish the trust reposed in the physician or surgeon employed. Yet, though the character of the professional busy-body, whether from thoughtlessness or craft, is highly reprehensible, there are occasions which not only justify, but require a spirited interposition. When artful ignorance grossly imposes on credulity; when ne-[5]glect puts to hazard an important life; or rashness threatens it with still more imminent danger; a medical neighbour, friend, or relative, apprized of such facts, will justly regard his interference as a duty. But he ought to be careful, that the information, on which he acts, is well founded; that his motives are pure and honourable; and that his judgment of the measures pursued is built on experience and practical knowledge, not on speculative or theoretical differences of opinion. The particular circumstances of the case will suggest the most proper mode of conduct. In general, however, a personal and confidential application, to the gentlemen of the faculty concerned, should be the first step taken; and afterwards, if necessary, the transaction may be communicated to the patient or to his family.

VI. When a physician or surgeon is called to a patient, who has been before under the care of another gentleman of the faculty, a consultation with him should be proposed, even though he may have discontinued his visits: his practice, also, should be treated with candour, and justified, so far as probity and truth will permit. For, the want of success in the primary treatment of a case, is no impeachment of professional skill or knowledge; [6] and it often serves to throw light on the nature of a disease, and to suggest to the subsequent practitioner more appropriate means of relief.

VII. *Consultations* should be *promoted*, in difficult or protracted cases, as they give rise to confidence, energy, and more enlarged views in practice. On such occasions, no rivalship or jealousy should be indulged: candour, probity, and all due respect should be exercised towards the physician or surgeon first engaged: and as he may be presumed to be best acquainted with the patient and with his family, he should deliver all the medical directions agreed upon, though he may not have precedency in seniority or rank. It should be the province, however, of the senior physician first to propose the necessary questions to the sick, but without excluding his associate from the privilege of making farther inquiries, to satisfy himself, or to elucidate the case.

VIII. As circumstances sometimes occur to render a *special consultation* desirable, when the continued attendance of another physician or surgeon might be objectionable to the patient, the gentleman of the faculty, whose assistance is required, in such cases, should pay only two or three visits; and sedulously guard against all future un-[7]solicited interference. For this consultation a double gratuity may reasonably be expected from the patient; as it will be found to require an extraordinary portion both of time and attention.

In medical practice, it is not an unfrequent occurrence, that a physician is hastily summoned, through the anxiety of the family, or the solicitation of friends, to visit a patient, who is under the regular direction of another physician, to whom notice of this call has not been given. Under such circumstances, no change in the treatment of the sick person should be made, till a previous consultation with the stated physician has taken place; unless the lateness of the hour precludes meeting, or the symptoms of the case are too pressing to admit of delay.

IX. *Theoretical discussions* should be avoided in consultations, as occasioning perplexity and loss of time. For there may be much diversity of opinion, concerning speculative points, with perfect agreement in those modes of practice, which are founded not on hypothesis, but on experience and observation.

X. [The first three sentences are taken from *Medical Ethics* Chapter I, Section XIX.] In consultations, the junior physician present should *deliver* his opinion first, and the others in the progressive order of their seniority; and a [8] majority should be decisive. But, if the numbers be equal, the decision should rest with the physician, under whose care the patient is placed. No decision, however, should restrain the acting practitioner from making such variations in the mode of treatment, as future contingences may require, or a further insight into the nature of the disorder may shew to be expedient.

[Editor's Note: These two sentences are taken from *Medical Ethics* Chapter II, Section X] The *seniority* of a physician may be determined by the period of his public and acknowledged practice as a physician, and that of a surgeon, by the period of his practice as a surgeon, in the place where each resides. This arrangement, being clear and obvious, is adapted to remove all grounds of dispute amongst medical gentlemen; and it secures the regular continuance of the order of precedency, established in every town, which might otherwise be liable to troublesome interruptions by new settlers, perhaps not long stationary.

XI. A regular *academical education* furnishes the only presumptive evidence of professional ability, and is so honourable and beneficial, that it gives a just claim to pre-eminence among physicians, in proportion to the degree, in which it has been enjoyed and improved: yet as it is not indispensably necessary to the attainment of know-[9]ledge, skill, and experience, they, who have really acquired, in a competent measure, such qualifications, without its advantages, should not be fastidiously excluded from the privileges of fellowship. In consultations especially, as the good of the patient is the sole object in view, and is often dependent on the personal confidence, the aid of an intelligent practitioner ought to be received with candour and politeness, and his advice adopted, if agreeable to sound judgement and truth.

XII. *Punctuality* should be observed in the visits of the faculty, when they are to hold consultation together. But as this may not always be practicable, the physician or surgeon, who first arrives at the place of appointment, should wait five minutes for his associate, before his introduction to the patient, that the unnecessary repetition of questions may be avoided: No visits should be made, but in concert, or by mutual agreement: no statement or discussion of the case should take place before the patient or his friends, except in the presence of each of the attending gentlemen of the faculty, and by common consent: and no *prognostications* should be delivered, which are not the result of previous deliberation and concurrence.

XIII. *Visits* to the sick should not be *unseason-[10]ably repeated*; because, when too frequent, they tend to diminish the authority of the physician, to produce instability in his practice, and to give rise to such occasional indulgences, as are subversive of all medical regimen.

Sir William Temple has asserted, that "an honest physician is excused for leaving his patient, when he finds the disease growing desperate, and can, by his attendance, expect only to receive his fees, without any hopes or appearance of deserving them."

But this allegation is not well founded: for, the offices of a physician may continue to be highly useful to the patient, and comforting to the relatives around him, even in the last period of a fatal malady, by obviating despair, by alleviating pain, and by soothing mental anguish. To decline attendance, under such circumstances, would be sacrificing, to fanciful delicacy and mistaken liberality, that moral duty, which is independent of, and far superior to, all pecuniary appreciation.

XIV. Whenever a physician or surgeon *officiates* for another, who is sick or absent, during any considerable length of time, he should receive the fees accruing from such additional practice: but, if this fraternal act be of short duration, it [11] should be graciously performed; with an observance always of the utmost delicacy towards the interest and character of the professional gentleman previously connected with the family.

XV. Some general rules should be adopted, by the faculty, in every town, relative to the *pecuniary acknowledgments* of their patients; and it should be deemed a point of honour to adhere to this rule, with as much steadiness as varying circumstances will admit. For it is obvious, that an average fee, as suited to the general rank of patients, must be an inadequate gratuity from the rich, who often require attendance not absolutely necessary; and yet too large to be expected from that class of citizens, who would feel a reluctance in calling for assistance, without making some decent and satisfactory retribution.

But, in the consideration of fees, let it ever be remembered, that though mean ones from the affluent are both unjust and degrading, yet characteristical beneficence of the profession is inconsistent with sordid views, and avaricious rapacity. To a young physician, it is of great importance to have clear and definite ideas of the ends of his profession; of the means for their attainment; and of the comparative value and dignity of each [12]. Wealth, rank, and independence, with all the benefits resulting from them, are the ends, which he holds in view; and they are interesting, wise, and laudable. But knowledge, benevolence, and active virtue, the means to be adopted in their acquisition, are of still higher estimation. And he has the privilege and felicity of practising an art, even more intrinsically excellent in its mediate than in its ultimate objects. The former, therefore, have a claim to uniform pre-eminence.

XVI. All members of the profession, together with their wives and children, should be attended *gratuitously* by any one or more of the faculty, residing near them, whose assistance may be required. For, as solicitude obscures the judgement, and is accompanied with timidity and irresolution, medical men, under the pressure of sickness, either as affecting themselves or their families, are peculiarly dependent upon each other. But visits should not be obtruded officiously; as such unasked civility may give rise to embarrassment, or interfere with that choice, on which confidence depends. Distant members of the faculty, when they request attendance, should be expected to defray the charges of traveling. And if their circumstances be affluent, a pecuniary acknowledge-[13]ment should not be declined: for, no obligation ought to be imposed, which the party would rather compensate than contract.

XVII. When a physician attends the wife or child of a member of the faculty, or any person very nearly connected with him, he should manifest peculiar attention to his opinions, and tenderness even to his prejudices. For the dear and important interests, which the one has at stake, supersede every consideration of rank or seniority in the other; since the mind of a husband, a father, or a friend, may receive a deep and lasting wound, if the disease terminate fatally, from the adoption of means he could not approve, or the rejection of those he wished to be tried. Under such delicate circumstances, however, a conscientious physician will not lightly sacrifice his judgment; but will urge, with proper confidence, the measures he deems to be expedient, before he leaves the final decision concerning them to his more responsible coadjutor.

XVIII. Clergymen who experience the *res angusta domi*, should be visited gratuitously by the faculty: and this exemption should be an acknowledged general rule, that the feeling of individual obligation may be rendered less oppressive. But [14] such of the clergy, as are qualified, either from there stipends or fortunes, to make a reasonable remuneration for medical attendance, are not more privileged than any other order of patients. Military or naval subaltern officers, in narrow circumstances, are also proper objects of professional liberality.

XIX. As the first *consultation* by *letter* imposes much more trouble and attention than a personal visit, it is reasonable, on such an occasion, to expect a gratuity of double the usual amount: and this has long been the established practice of many respectable physicians. But a subsequent epistolary correspondence, on the further treatment of the same disorder, may justly be regarded in the light of ordinary attendance, and may be compensated as such, according to the circumstances of the case, or of the patient.

XX. Physicians and surgeons are occasionally requested to furnish certificates, justifying the absence of persons, who hold situations of honour and trust in the army, the navy, or the civil departments of government. These testimonials, unless under particular circumstances, should be considered as acts due to the public, and therefore, not to be compensated by any gratuity. But they should [15] never be given without an accurate and faithful scrutiny into the case; that truth and probity may not be violated, nor the good of the community injured, by the unjust pretences of its servants. The same conduct is to be observed by medical practitioners, when they are solicited to furnish apologies for non-attendance on juries; or to state the valetudinary incapacity of persons appointed to execute the business of constables, churchwardens, or overseers of the poor. No fear of giving umbrage, no view to present or future emolument, nor any motives of friendship, should incite to a false, or even dubious declaration. For the general weal requires, that every individual, who is properly qualified, should deem himself obliged to execute, when legally called upon, the juridical and municipal employments of the body politic. And to be accessary, by untruths or prevarication, to the evasion of this duty, is at once a high misdemeanour against social order, and a breach of moral and professional honour.

XXI. The use of *quack med*icines should be discouraged by the faculty, as disgraceful to the profession, injurious to health, and often destructive even of life. Patients, however, under lingering disorders, are sometimes obstinately bent [16] on having recourse to such as they see advertised, or hear recommended, with a boldness and confidence, which no intelligent physician dares to adopt with respect to the means that he prescribes. In these cases, some indulgence seems to be required to a credulity that in insurmountable: and the patient should neither incur the displeasure of the physician, nor be entirely deserted by him. He may be apprized of the fallacy of his expectations, whilst assured, at the same time, that diligent attention should be paid to the process of the experiment, he is so unadvisedly making on himself, and the consequent mischiefs, if any, obviated as timely as possible. Certain active preparations, the nature, composition, and effects of which are well known, ought not to be prescribed as quack medicines.

XXII. No physician or surgeon should dispense a secret *nostrum*, whether it be his invention, or exclusive property. For if it be of real efficacy, the concealment of it is inconsistent with beneficence and professional liberality: and, if mystery alone give it value and importance, such craft implies either disgraceful ignorance, or fraudulent avarice [17].

XXIII. The *Esprit du Corps* is a principle of action founded in human nature, and, when duly regulated, is both rational and laudable. Every man, who enters into a fraternity, engages, by a tacit compact, not only to submit to the laws, but to promote the honour and interest of the association, so far as they are consistent with morality, and the general good of mankind. A physician, therefore, should cautiously guard against whatever may injure the general respectability of his profession; and should avoid all contumelious representations of the faculty at large; all general charges against their selfishness or improbity; and the indulgence of an affected or jocular scepticism, concerning the efficacy and utility of the healing art.

XXIV. As diversity of opinion and opposition of interest may, in the medical, as in other professions, sometimes occasion *controversy*, and even *contention*; whenever such cases unfortunately occur, and cannot be immediately terminated, they should be referred to the arbitration of a sufficient number of physicians or of surgeons, according to the nature of the dispute; or to the two orders collectively, if belonging both to medicine and surgery. But neither the subject matter of such [18] references, nor the adjudication, should be communicated to the public; as they may be personally injurious to the individuals concerned, and can hardly fail to hurt the general credit of the faculty.

XXV. A wealthy physician should not give advice *gratis* to the affluent; because it is an injury to his professional brethren. The office of physician can never be supported but as a lucrative one; and it is defrauding, in some degree, the common funds for its support, when fees are dispensed with, which might justly be claimed.

XXVI. It frequently happens, that a physician, in his incidental communications with the patients of other physicians, or with their friends, may have their cases stated to him in so direct a manner, as not to admit of his declining to pay attention to them. Under such circumstances, his observations should be delivered with the most delicate propriety and reserve. He should not interfere in the curative plans pursued; and should even recommend a steady adherence to them, if they appear to merit approbation.

XXVII. A physician, when visiting a sick person in the country, may be desired to see a neighbouring patient, who is under the regular direc-[19]tion of another physician, in consequence of some sudden change or aggravation of symptoms. The conduct to be pursued on such an occasion is to give advice adapted to present circumstances; to interfere no farther than is absolutely necessary with the general plan of treatment; to assume no future direction, unless it be expressly desired; and, in this case, to request an immediate consultation with the practitioner antecedently employed.

XXVIII. At the close of every interesting and important case, especially when it hath terminated fatally, a physician should trace back, in calm reflection, all the steps which he had taken in the treatment of it. This review of the origin, progress, and conclusion of the malady; of the whole curative plan pursued; and of the particular operation of the several remedies employed, as well as of the doses and periods of time in which they were administered; –will furnish the most authentic documents, on which individual experience can be formed. But it is in a moral view, that the practice is here recommended; and it should be performed with the most scrupulous impartiality. Let no self-deception be permitted in the retrospect; and, if errors, either of omission or com-[20]mission, are discovered, it behoves, that they should be brought fairly and fully to the mental view. Regrets may follow, but criminality will thus be obviated. For, good intentions and the imperfection of human skill, which cannot anticipate the knowledge that events alone disclose, will sufficiently justify what is past, provided the failure be made conscientiously subservient to future wisdom and rectitude and professional conduct.

XXIX. The opportunities which a physician not unfrequently enjoys, of promoting and strengthening the good resolutions of his patients, suffering under the consequences of vicious conduct, ought never to be neglected. And his councils, or even remonstrances, will give satisfaction, not disgust, if they be conducted with politeness, and evince a genuine love of virtue, accompanied by a sincere interest in the welfare of the person to whom they are addressed.

XXX. The observance of the Sabbath is a duty, to which medical men are bound, so far as is compatible with the urgency of the cases under their charge. Visits may often be made with sufficient convenience and benefit, either before the hours of going to church, or during the intervals of public worship. And in many chronic ail-[21]ments, the sick, together with their attendants, are qualified to participate in the social offices of religion; and should not be induced to forgo this important privilege, by the expectation of a call from their physician or surgeon.

XXXI. A physician who is advancing in years, yet unconscious of any decay in his faculties, may occasionally experience some change in the wonted confidence of his friends. Patients, who before trusted solely to his care and skill, may now request that he will join in consultation, perhaps with a younger coadjutor. It behoves him to admit this change without dissatisfaction or fastidiousness; regarding it as no mark of disrespect, but has the exercise of a just and reasonable privilege in those by whom he is employed. The junior practitioner may well be supposed to have more ardour, than he possesses, in the treatment of diseases; to be bolder in the exhibition of new medicines; and disposed to administer old ones in doses of greater efficacy. And this union of enterprise with caution, and of fervour with coolness, may promote the successful management of a difficult and protracted case. Let the medical parties, therefore, be studious to conduct themselves towards each other with candour an impartiality; [22] co-operating, by mutual concessions, in the benevolent discharge of professional duty.

XXXII. The commencement of that period senescence, when it becomes incumbent on a physician to decline the offices of his profession, it is not easy to ascertain; and the decision on so nice a point must be left to the moral direction of the individual. Because, one grown old in the useful an honourable exercise of the healing art may continue to enjoy, and justly to enjoy, the unabated confidence of the public. And whilst exempt, in a considerable degree, from the privations and infirmities of age, he is under indispensable obligations to apply his knowledge and experience, in the most efficient way, to the benefit of mankind; for, the possession of powers is a clear indication of the will of our Creator, concerning their practical direction. But, in the ordinary course of nature, the bodily and mental vigour must be expected to decay progressively, though perhaps slowly, after the meridian of life is past. As age advances, therefore, a physician should, from time to time, scrutinize impartially the state of his faculties; that he may determine, *bona fide*, the precise degree in which he is qualified to execute the active and multifarious offices [23] of his profession. And whenever he becomes conscious, that his memory presents to him with faintness those analogies, on which medical reasoning and the treatment of diseases are founded; that diffidence of the measures to be pursued perplexes his judgment; that, from a deficiency in the acuteness of his senses, he finds himself less able to distinguish signs, or to prognosticate events; –he should at once resolve, though others perceive not the changes which have taken place, to sacrifice every consideration of fame or fortune, and to retire from the engagements of business. To the surgeon under similar circumstances, this rule of conduct is still more necessary; for the energy of the understanding often subsists much longer than the quickness of eye-sight, delicacy of touch, and steadiness of hand, which are essential to the skilful performance of operations. Let both the physician and surgeon never forget, that their professions are public trusts, properly rendered lucrative whilst they fulfil them; but which they are bound, by honour and probity, to relinquish, as soon as they find themselves unequal to their adequate and faithful execution [24].

Clark & Fraser, Printers, 33 Carter's Alley,
Philadelphia

Chapter 6
Two Concordances

Concordance of *Medical Jurisprudence* with *Medical Ethics*

Abbreviations: MJ=*Medical Jurisprudence*; ME=*Medical Ethics*

TITLE PAGE

> MJ: *MEDICAL JURISPRUDENCE* OR A CODE OF *ETHICS AND INSTITUTES*, ADAPTED TO THE PROFESSIONS OF PHYSIC AND SURGERY
> ME: MEDICAL ETHICS OR, A CODE OF INSTITUTES AND PRECEPTS, ADAPTED TO THE PROFESSIONAL CONDUCT OF *PHYSICIANS AND SURGEONS*

LATIN INSCRIPTION

> MJ: QUICQUID DIGNUM SAPIENTE BONO-QUE EST Hor. Lib I. Ep IV.
> MJ and ME: *Nulla enim vitae pars, neque publicis, neque privatis, neque forensibus, neque domesticis in rebus, neque si tecum agas quid, neque si cum altero contrabas, vacare officio potest: In toque colendo sita vitae est bonestas omnis, et in negligendo turpitudo.* Cic. De Off. Lib I, Cap ii.

DEDICATION

> MJ: None
> ME: To Sir George Baker, Bart.
> PREFACE-Origin of the work.-Suspension of it.-Farther progress of it. – Addition of supplementary notes and illustrations. MJ None; ME pages 1–7

CHAP. I. *Of professional conduct relative to hospital or other medical charities.*

Institute on Baconian professional ethics in medicine. MJ I.I; ME I.I.
Choice of their attendant physician or surgeon. MJ I.II; ME I.II.
Feelings and emotions of patients. MJ I.III; ME I.III.
No discussion before patients. MJ I.IVME. I.IV.
Confidentiality. MJ I.V; ME I.V.
Moral and religious influence of sickness. MJ I.VI; ME I.VI.
Propriety of suggesting to patients making their last will and testament. MJ I.VII; ME I.VII.
Parsimony in prescribing wine and drugs of high price. MJ I.VIII; ME I.VIII.
Hospital affairs and occurrences not to be incautiously revealed. MJ I.IX; ME I.IX.
Professional charges to be made only before meeting of the faculty. MJ I. X; ME I.X.
Proper discrimination between the medical and chirurgical cases. MJ I.XI; ME I.XI.
New remedies and new methods of chirurgical treatment. MJ I.XII; ME I.XII.
Unreserved intercourse between the gentlemen of the faculty and accounts of cases. MJ I.XIII; ME I.XIII.
Scheme for hospital registers. MJ I.XIV; ME I.XIV.
Advantages arising from registers . MJ I.XV; ME I.XV.
Close and crowded wards. MJ I.XVI; ME I.XVI.
Establishment of a committee of the gentlemen of the faculty. MJ I.XVII; ME I.XVII.
Importance of frequent consultations. MJ I.XVIII; ME I.XVIII.
Rules to be observed in consultations. MJ I.XIX; ME I.XIX.
Rules to be observed in consultations continued. MJ I.XX; ME I.XX.
Rules to be observed in consultations continued MJ I.XXI; ME I.XXI.
Due notice for consultations. MJ I.XXII; ME I.XXII.
Consultation about and notice for operations. MJ I.XXIII; ME I.XXIII.
Consultations on Sundays. MJ not addressed; ME I.XXIV.
Stated day for operations. MJ I.XXIV; ME I.XXV
Dispensaries. MJ I.XXV; MJ I.XXVI.
Asylums for female patients labouring under syphilis. MJ I.XXVI; ME I.XXVII.
Asylums for insanity. MJ I.XXVII; ME I.XXVIII.
Treatment of insanity. MJ I.XXVII; ME I.XXIX.
Treatment of lunatics. MJ I.XIX; ME I.XXX
Boldness of practice in cases of mania. –Hospitals for small-pox – Inoculation MJ I.XXX; ME I.XXXI.

Concordance of *Medical Jurisprudence* with *Medical Ethics* 447

CHAP II. *Of professional conduct in private, or general practice.*

Institute on private practice. MJ II.I; ME II.I.
The strictest temperance. MJ II.II; ME II.II.
Gloomy prognostications. MJ II.III; ME II.III.
Officious interference in cases under the charge of another. MJ II.IV; ME II.IV.
Request to see a patient under the care of another physician or surgeon. MJ II.V; ME II.V.
Distinction between physic and surgery. MJ II.VI; ME II.VI.
Consultations to be promoted in difficult or protracted cases. MJ II.VII; ME II.VII.
Special consultation when patient objects to current physician or surgeon. MJ II.VIII; ME II.VIII.
Theoretical discussions to be avoided in consultations. MJ II.IX; ME II.IX.
Rules for consultations the same as hospital consultations. MJ II.X; ME II.X.
Education of medical men. MJ II.XI; ME II.XI.
Punctuality of visits of consultation. MJ II.XII; ME II.XII.
Visits to the sick not to be unreasonably repeated. MJ II.XIII; ME II.XIII.
Fees, when a physician officiates in the absence, or at the request, of another. MJ II.XIV; ME II.XIV.
General rule respecting pecuniary acknowledgments. MJ II.XV; ME II.XV.
Medical men and their families, when to be attended gratuitously. MJ II.XVI; ME II.XVI.
Peculiar delicacy and attention often required in attendance upon them. MJ: Not addressed; ME II.XVII.
Attendance on clergymen in narrow circumstances. MJ: Addressed in last sentence of II.XVI; ME II.XVIII.
Consultation by letter. MJ II.XVII; ME II.XIX.
Furnishing certificates justifying absence. MJ: Not addressed; ME II.XX
Quack medicines. MJ II.XVIII; ME II.XXI.
The dispensing of nostrums. MJ II.XIX; ME II.XXII.
Esprit du Corps MJ: Not addressed; ME II.XXIII.
Rule to be observed in professional controversy and contention. MJ II.XX; ME II.XXIV.
Giving advice gratis. MJ: Not addressed; ME II.XXV.
Rule to be observed in visiting the patient of another physician. MJ: Not addressed; ME II.XXVI.
Another case of the same. MJ: Not addressed; ME II.XXVII.
Review of the treatment and progress of interesting cases recommended. MJ: Not addressed; ME II.XXVIII.
Moral and religious advice to patients. MJ: Not addressed; ME II.XXIX.
Observance of the Sabbath. MJ: Not addressed; ME II.XXX.
The aging physician and cooperation with young practitioners. MJ: Not addressed; ME II.XXXI.
Period of senescence in physicians considered. MJ: Not addressed; ME II.XXXII.

CHAP III. *Of the conduct of physicians to apothecaries.*

> Institute on relationship of apothecary and physician. MJ III.I; ME III.I.
> Apothecary often precursor to the physician. MJ III.II; ME III.II.
> Co-operation of the physician and apothecary. MJ III.III; ME III.III.
> Physician's inspection of apothecary shop. MJ III.III; ME III.IV.
> Visiting country patients with the apothecary. MJ III.IV; ME III.V.
> Profits of apothecaries. MJ III.V; ME III.VI.
> Benevolent institutions for apothecaries and their families. MJ III.V; ME: III.IX.
> Physicians visiting the patients of apothecaries in their absence. MJ: Not addressed; ME III.VII.
> Duty of apothecaries in recommending physicians to families. MJ: Not addressed; ME III.VIII.

CHAP IV. *Of professional duties in certain cases which require a knowledge of law.*

> Institute on relationship of profession of medicine and law. MJ IV.I; ME IV.I.
> Duty of physicians in cases of last will and testament. MJ IV.II; ME IV.II.
> Lunacy. MJ IV.III; ME IV.III.
> Treatment of lunatics as authorized by law. MJ: Not addressed; ME IV.IV.
> Asylums for lunatics subject to strict regulations of law. MJ: Not addressed; ME IV.V.
> Opinions given in cases of sudden death. MJ: IV.IV; ME IV.VI.
> Justifiable homicide. MJ IV.V; ME IV.VII.
> Excusable homicide. MJ IV.VI; ME IV.VIII.
> Suicide. MJ IV.VII; ME IV.IX.
> Manslaughter-Murder. MJ: IV.VIII; ME IV.X.
> Murder of bastard children. MJ IV.IX; ME IV.XI.
> Duelling. MJ IV.X; ME IV.XII.
> Surgeons attending a duellist to the field of combat. MJ IV.XI; ME IV.XIII.
> Private and personal duty of physicians with respect to duel; true honour considered. MJ IV.XII; ME IV.XIV.
> Homicide by poison. MJ IV.XIII; ME IV.XV.
> Law in cases of rape. MJ IV.XIV; ME IV.XVI.
> Nuisances defined and considered. MJ IV.XV; ME IV.XVII.
> Judicial testimony. MJ IV.XVI; ME IV.XVIII.
> Cases of capital punishment. MJ IV.XVII; ME IV.XIX.
> Cautions relative to professional testimony in cases of peculiar malignity. MJ IV.XVIII; ME IV.XX

A Discourse on Hospital Duties.

> Addresses.-I. To the faculty, MJ 6; ME 120. II.-To the officers and superintendants, MJ 12; ME 126. III.-To the clergy, MJ 15; ME 130. - IV. To the trustees of the Infirmary of Liverpool, MJ 17; ME 132.

Notes and Illustrations.

> ME Only

Concordance of *Medical Ethics* with *Extracts*

Abbreviations: ME=*Medical Ethics*; E=*Extracts*

TITLE PAGE

> ME: MEDICAL ETHICS OR, A CODE OF INSTITUTES AND PRECEPTS, ADAPTED TO THE PROFESSIONAL CONDUCT OF *PHYSICIANS AND SURGEONS*
> E: EXTRACTS FROM THE MEDICAL ETHICS OF DR. PERCIVAL.

LATIN INSCRIPTION

> MJ and ME: *Nulla enim vitae pars, neque publicis, neque privatis, neque forensibus, neque domesticis in rebus, neque si tecum agas quid, neque si cum altero contrabas, vacare officio potest: In toque colendo sita vitae est bonestas omnis, et in negligendo turpitudo.* Cic. De Off. Lib I, Cap ii.
> E: None

DEDICATION

> ME: To Sir George Baker, Bart.
> E: None
> PREFACE-Origin of the work.-Suspension of it.-Farther progress of it. – Addition of supplementary notes and illustrations. ME 1–7; E None

CHAP. I. *Of professional conduct relative to hospital or other medical charities.*

> Institute on Baconian professional ethics in medicine. ME I.I; E I with first word, 'Hospital' deleted.
> Rules to be observed in consultations. ME I.XIX; E X includes first three sentences.

CHAP II. *Of professional conduct in private, or general practice.*

> Institute on private practice. ME II.I; E II with first sentence omitted.
> The strictest temperance.; ME II.II; E III.
> Gloomy prognostications. ME II.III; E IV.
> Officious interference in cases under the charge of another. ME II.IV; E V.
> Request to see a patient under the care of another physician or surgeon. ME II.V; E VI.
> Distinction between physic and surgery. ME II.VI; E omitted.
> Consultations to be promoted in difficult or protracted cases. ME II.VII; E VII.
> Special consultation when patient objects to current physician or surgeon. ME II.VIII; E VIII.
> Theoretical discussions to be avoided in consultations. ME II.IX; E IX.
> Rules for consultations the same as hospital consultations. ME II.X; E three sentences from ME I.XIX and two sentences from ME II.X.
> Education of medical men. ME II.XI; E XI.

Punctuality of visits of consultation. ME II.XII; E XII.
Visits to the sick not to be unreasonably repeated. ME II.XIII; E XIII.
Fees, when a physician officiates in the absence, or at the request, of another. ME II.XIV; E XIV.
General rule respecting pecuniary acknowledgments. ME II.XV; E XV.
Medical men and their families, when to be attended gratuitously. ME II.XVI; E XVI.
Peculiar delicacy and attention often required in attendance upon them. ME II.XVII; E XVII.
Attendance on clergymen in narrow circumstances. ME II.XVIII; E XVIII.
Consultation by letter. ME II.XIX; E XIX.
Furnishing certificates justifying absence. ME II.XX; E XX.
Quack medicines. ME II.XXI; E XXI.
The dispensing of nostrums. ME II.XXII; XXII.
Esprit du Corps. ME II.XXIII; E XXII.
Rule to be observed in professional controversy and contention. ME II.XXIV; E XXIV.
Giving advice gratis. ME II.XXV; E XXV.
Rule to be observed in visiting the patient of another physician. ME II.XXVI; E XXVI.
Another case of the same. ME II.XXVII; E XXVII.
Review of the treatment and progress of interesting cases recommended. ME II.XXVIII; E XXVIII.
Moral and religious advice to patients. ME II.XXIX; XXIX.
Observance of the Sabbath. ME II.XXX; E XXX.
The aging physician and cooperation with young practitioners. ME II.XXXI; E XXXI.
Period of senescence in physicians considered. ME II.XXXII; E XXXII.
Extracts omits Chapter III, Chapter IV, "Discourse on Hospital Duties," Notes and Illustrations.

Chapter 7
Chronology

Chronology of Thomas Percival's Life and Works

Note: I prepared the cal scholarship reported in Chaps. 2 and 3 of Part I. Names of works by Percival and others are in italics.

Late 17th century	Peter Percival (d. 1701), Percival's grandfather, settles in Warrington
1691–1750	Thomas Percival, Percival's uncle
1740, September 29	Thomas Percival born, in Warrington to Joseph and Margaret (Orred) Percival
1743	Percival's parents die; he is raised by his only other surviving sibling, Elizabeth Percival, and his uncle, Peter Percival
1750	Percival comes into a "patrimonial fortune" of a "valuable library and moderate competency," a legacy from his Uncle Thomas
1750	Student at Warrington Grammar School
	Student at Manchester Grammar School
1752	Manchester Infirmary founded by the surgeon Charles White and Joseph Bancroft, a Manchester mercantilist
1754	Committee formed to plan Warrington Academy, including rules for "answering the Ends of a Liberal Education"
1757	Warrington Academy opens; Percival is its first student, took a special interest in ethics
1761, June 30	Percival departs for University of Edinburgh, to study medicine; makes acquaintance of David Hume and William Robertson, Principal of the University of Edinburgh
1763	Presents *An Inquiry into the Resemblance between Chyle and Milk* to Royal Medical Society of Edinburgh. Later published in *Essays Medical and Experimental* (1767)
1765, March 7	Elected to Royal Society, upon recommendation of Lord Willoughby, who died before Percival was elected
1765, April	Percival departs for University of Leyden, to continue his medical studies

© The Author(s), under exclusive license to Springer Nature Switzerland AG 2022
L. B. McCullough, *Thomas Percival's Medical Ethics and the Invention of Medical Professionalism*, Philosophy and Medicine 142,
https://doi.org/10.1007/978-3-030-86036-3_7

1765, July 6	Presents and defends his "inaugural dissertation," *Dissertatio Medica Inauguralis De Frigore*
1765	*Dissertatio Medica Inauguralis De Frigore*
	Brief tour of France and Holland
	John Gregory. *A Comparative View of the State and Faculties of Man with Those of the Animal World.*
1765, fall	Returns to Warrington, a time of "studious leisure"
1766, March 24	Warrington: Marries Elizabeth Bassnett (1747–1822), "the daughter and only surviving child of Nathanial Bassnett, esq; merchant, of London"
1767	Birth of Thomas Bassnett Percival (1767–1798)
	Percival and his family move to Manchester, where he resides until his death in 1804
	Essays Medical and Experimental : on the Following Subjects, viz. I. The Empiric. II. The Dogmatic. Or, Arguments for and against the Use of Theory and Reasoning in Physick. III. Experiments and Observations on Astringents and Bitters IV. On the Uses and Operation of Blisters. V. On the Resemblance between Chyle and Milk
	Experiments on the Peruvian bark by Thomas Percival M.D. F.R.S.
	Experiments and Observations on Astringents and Bitters
	On the uses and Operation of Blisters
1768	Birth of Anne Percival (1768–1847)
	Percival becomes a life-time subscriber to Manchester Infirmary
	Extract from the essays medical and experimental
	On the Disadvantages which Attend the Inoculation of Children in Early Infancy
1769	Birth of James Percival (1769–1793)
1769	*Experiments and Observations on Water; particularly on the hard pump water of Manchester*
1770	*Miscellaneous Observations Concerning the Action of Different Manures*
	On the Efficacy of External Applications in the Angina Maligna, or Ulcerous Sore Throat
	John Gregory. *Observations on the Duties and Offices of a Physician, and on the Method of Prosecuting Enquiries in Philosophy*
1771	Begins years-long service as trustee of Warrington Academy
	An Attempt to Account for the Different Quantities of Rain, which Fall at Different Heights over the Same Spot of Ground
	Letter from Thomas Percival, of Manchester, M.D., F.R.S. On the Efficacy of External Applications in the Angina Maligna
	On the Internal Regulation of Hospitals, Addressed to Mr. Aikin
1772	*Essays Medical and Experimental. The second edition, revised and considerably enlarged, to which is added an appendix*
	Experiments and Observations of the Waters of Buxton and Matlock in Derbyshire, by Thomas Percival, M.D. and F.R.S.
	The history and cure of a difficulty in deglutition, of long continuance, arising from a spasmotic affection of the œsophagus
	Observations and Experiments on the Colombo Root

Chronology of Thomas Percival's Life and Works   453

	Observations on the Medicinal Uses of Fixed Air
	On the Antiseptic and Sweetening
	Powers, and on the Varieties of Factitious Air
	On the Atrabilis
	On Coffee
	On the Noxious Vapors of Charcoal
	On the Septic Quality of Sea Salt
	On the Uses and Operation of Blisters
	Select Histories of Diseases with Remarks
	John Gregory. *Lectures on the Duties and Qualifications of a Physician*
1773	Made an Honorary Fellow of the Medical Society of London
	Observations on the State of Population in
	Manchester and other Adjacent Places
	Proposal for Establishing More Accurate, and
	Comprehensive Bills of Mortality, in Manchester
1774	*Further Observations on the State of*
	Population in Manchester and other Adjacent Places
	Observations and Experiments on the Poison of Lead
	John Gregory. *A Father's Legacy to his Daughters*
1775	Purchases Hart-Hill, a residence in the countryside
	outside Manchester, for reasons of health and as a retreat
	Experiments and Observations on the
	Effects of Fixed Air on the Colours and Vegetation of Plants
	Experiments and Observations on the Nature
	and Composition of Urinary Calculi
	On the Small-Pox and Measles
1776	*Philosophical, Medical, and Experimental Essays*
	Published anonymously. *A Father's Instructions: to his Children:*
	Consisting of Tales, Fables, and Reflections; Designed
	to Promote the Love of Virtue, a Taste for Knowledge,
	and an Early Acquaintance with the Works of Nature
	On the Solution of Human Calculi by Fixed Air
	Remarks on Different Absorbents
1777	Elected "Foreign Fellow" of Royal Society of Paris
	Birth of Maria Percival (1777?-1780)
	An Account of an Earthquake in September 1777
	A Father's Instructions to his Children,
	Consisting of Tales, Fables and Reflections, etc.
	Elected Fellow of the Royal Society of Edinburgh
1778	Birth of Edward Bayley Percival (1778?-1780)
1779	Percival appointed to honorary position at Manchester Infirmary
1780	Percival resigns this position, citing reasons of health
1780, May 15	Maria Percival dies "in the third year of her age"
1780, May 25	Edward Bayley Percival dies "in the second year of his age"
1780	*On a New and Cheap Method of Preparing Pot-Ash, with Remarks*
1781	Co-founds Literary and Philosophical Society of
	Manchester, of which he served as President for many years
	A Socratic discourse on Truth and Faithfulness;
	in which the nature, extent, and obligation, ... of these moral duties
	are explained ...: being the sequel to "A Father's Instructions."
1782	*Observations on the Medicinal Uses of the*
	OLEUM JECORIS ASELLI *or Cod Liver Oil in the Chronic*
	Rheumatism, and other Painful Disorders
	A Tribute to the Memory of C. de Polier,
	addressed to the Literary and Philosophical Society of Manchester

1783	Birth of Edward Cropper Percival (1783–1819), the author of *Memoirs* in *Works* *Miscellaneous Facts and Observations Addressed to Doctor Simmons On the Fatal Effects of Pickles Inpregnated with Copper*
1784	*Moral and literary dissertations, on the following subjects: 1. On truth and faithfulness. 2. On habit and association. 3. On inconsistency of expectation in literary pursuits. 4. On a taste for the general beauties of nature. 5. On a taste for the fine arts. 6. On the alliance of natural history, and philosophy, with poetry. To which are added a tribute to the memory of Charles de Polier, Esq. and an appendix* *A Narrative of the Sufferings of a Collier, Who was confined more than seven Days without SUSTENANCE, and exposed to the CHOKE-DAMP, in a COAL PIT, not far from Manchester, with Observations on the Effects of Famine; on the MEANS of ALLEVIATING them; and on the ACTION of FOUL AIR on the HUMAN BODY*
1785	Joins other Dissenters to plan an academy in Manchester *A history of the fatal effects of pickles impregnated with copper, together with observations on that mineral poison* *Speculations on the Perceptive Power of Vegetables: addressed to the Literary and Philosophical Society of Manchester*
1786	Warrington Academy moves to Manchester and becomes Manchester Academy, later Manchester College on London. Its descendant is a member college by royal charter of the University of Oxford, Harris Manchester College (1996) Elected to American Philosophical Society of Philadelphia, with sponsorship by Benjamin Franklin, which is founded in 1743 and which still exists
1787	*Experiments with the Solvent Powers of Camphor, and other Miscellaneous Communications*
1788	Newly arrived in Manchester, physician John Ferriar and others called for repeal of Rule 13 of the Manchester Infirmary that limited number of honorary physicians *Moral and Literary Dissertations; Chiefly Intended as a Sequel to A Father's Instructions*
1788, December	A group of Manchester Infirmary trustees support Ferriar's proposal
1788–1789	*Essays Medical, Philosophical, and Experimental. Fourth Edition*
1789	The honorary surgeons and physicians, whose decades-long monopoly control of Manchester Infirmary was threatened, publicly oppose the trustees in *Manchester Mercury* An outbreak of typhus disrupts this public dispute about the control of Manchester Infirmary Birth of Stanley Orred Percival (1789–1877) *Facts and Queries Related to Attraction and Repulsion* *Hints towards the investigation of the nature, cause and cure of the Rabies Canina; addressed to Dr. Haygarth*

Index

A
Aberdeen Grammar School, 23
Aberdeen Philosophical Society, 24, 36, 63
Abortion, 7, 105, 136, 157, 180, 220, 224–226, 312, 313, 372, 373
Act of Supremacy, 69
Act of Toleration, 70
Act of Union of 1707, 14, 39
Aegrotus, 7, 13, 20, 60, 146
    See also Patient
Aikin, John, 59, 70–71, 395
    on hospital improvement, 106–109
American Association for Physician Leadership, xi
American College of Physician Executives, xi
American Medical Association (AMA)
    1847 *Code of Medical Ethics*, 10, 246
Angelelli, Ignazio, xii
Anti-paternalism, 175
Apothecaries, viii, 33, 40, 76, 92, 101, 144, 146, 147, 153–156, 162, 165, 180, 197, 200, 213–219, 233, 234, 236, 237, 242, 243, 245, 252, 255, 262, 304–307, 336, 338, 343, 359, 363–366, 369, 396, 419, 433, 434, 448
Aristotle, 10, 16, 17, 261
Articles of Faith of the Church of England, 41, 235
Art, The, 10
Audi, Robert, 6
Austen, Jane, 56
Autonomy
    ethical principle of, 5–6, 31, 260–261
    of medicine from the state, viii, 145, 229
    professional, viii, 145, 180
Avicenna, 16

B
Bacon, Francis
    on Cartesian method, 25
    on "experience," viii, 23, 25, 27, 68, 84, 94, 172, 226, 240
    on the "Four Capitall Enquirys" of medicine, 28
    on idols, 25, 27
    on levels of certainty, 26
    and quest for certainty, 25, 26, 86
    and quest for reliability, 25, 26, 86, 263
    on scientific method, 24, 25, 29, 34, 36, 84, 93, 95, 110, 226, 228, 240
Baconian deism, vii, 75, 114, 174, 210, 232, 234, 236, 259, 260, 267
Baconian Dissent, vii, 72, 73, 75, 76, 78, 174, 228, 229, 232, 234, 236, 255, 259, 260, 267
Baconian moral science, 3, 36–46, 58, 68, 73, 77, 81, 86, 92, 100, 102, 104, 109, 112, 115, 118, 120, 135, 136, 141, 146, 152–154, 160, 162, 164, 167, 168, 170, 171, 173, 174, 177, 178, 180, 206, 207, 222–224, 229–231, 233, 236, 240, 252, 255, 257, 258, 260, 261, 263
    See also Moral science
Baconian project, 28, 29
Baconian scientific medicine, 3, 258

Baker, Robert, vii, ix, x, 4, 7, 9, 10, 20, 22, 33, 49, 53, 97, 135, 146, 181, 185, 249–253, 255, 256, 260
Baker, Sir George, 395
    on *Medical Jurisprudence*, 165, 166, 186
Bancroft, Joseph, 150, 451
Barbauld, Anne Laetitia, 71
Barber-Surgeons of Edinburgh, 14
Bardsley, S.A., 395
Bastardy, 44, 157, 313, 314, 373
Bayley, Thomas Butterworth, 117, 118, 395
Baylor College of Medicine, x, xiii
Beauchamp, Tom L., 6, 7, 196, 197
Beck, Theodoric, 158
Bell, John, 249, 251, 257, 258
Beneficence
    ethical principle of, 179, 260
    purest, 179, 180, 184, 244, 294, 349
Berlant, Jeffrey, 252
Berlin, Isaiah, 67
Bioethics Program, The, xi, 5
Blackmail, 21, 194, 198
Blackstone, William, 156, 222, 254, 308–312, 319, 323, 324, 326, 366–368, 370, 372, 376, 380, 382, 384, 407
Bluestocking Circle, 24
Boerhaave, Herman, 23, 24, 26, 46, 60, 62, 85, 94, 158, 234, 240, 412, 414
"Boerhaave's men," 23, 60
Boundary between medicine and surgery, 45, 46, 155, 181–182, 199
Bower, Foster, 395
Bright, Henry Arthur, 69–71, 77
Brody, Baruch A., xiii
Brody, Howard, 239, 251
Browne, Simon, 309, 368, 421, 422
Brown, Samuel, 250, 257
Buchan, William, 30, 206
Burton, Richard, 264, 265
Butler, Bishop Joseph, 119

C
Candor, 23, 30–34, 44, 47, 71, 104, 112, 113, 115, 128, 144, 198, 199, 204, 233, 240–243, 356
Castro, Rodrigo de, 16–18, 20
Cautious entrepreneurialism, 11, 15, 20
Chapone, Hester, 24
Character, 4, 5, 9, 13, 17, 21, 22, 39, 40, 42, 43, 46, 49, 57, 64, 65, 73, 74, 89, 117, 118, 122–124, 132, 134–136, 140, 143, 147, 152, 157, 159, 167, 173, 175, 177, 190, 191, 194, 200, 208, 209, 223, 224, 233, 247, 294, 299, 301, 308, 314–316,

319, 320, 330–333, 336, 341, 348, 354, 356, 358, 366, 374, 377, 378, 388–390, 400, 409, 410, 415, 417, 418, 422, 423, 426, 434, 436, 439
    See also Moral formation
Childress, James F., 6, 7, 196, 197
Church of England, vii, 41, 58, 69, 72–75, 118, 120, 143, 174, 235, 243, 244, 255, 411
Cicero, x, 130, 222, 253, 292, 337, 402
    on offices, 402
Cimabue, 264–265
Clinical judgment, deliberative, 20, 32, 34, 179
Clinical research, ethics of, 50–52, 123, 182, 192
Coan School, 11, 12, 129
Code, meaning of, 154
Code of Medical Ethics, 10, 246
Company of Barber-Surgeons, 14
Company of Surgeons, 14
Compassion, 5, 42, 106, 124, 230, 332, 334, 335, 390–392
Concepts
    discovered, 5, 6, 8
    invented, xi, 5, 8, 9, 22–23, 26
    timeless, 5–9
Condescension, viii, 79–81, 118, 124–125, 131, 144, 155, 162, 169, 171, 173, 174, 189, 192–194, 223, 230, 233, 234, 240, 241, 253, 255–258, 293, 298, 332, 347, 353, 390, 435
Confidentiality, 21, 22, 44, 138, 155, 176–177
Conflict of commitment, 187, 203, 209–210, 219
Conflict of interest, 44, 187, 242
Conscience, tribunal of, 258
Consultations, 155, 156, 175, 182, 186–187, 199–202, 204, 208, 211, 293, 295–297, 301–304, 342, 344, 348, 349, 351, 352, 356–359, 361, 362, 365, 406, 417–418, 437, 438, 440, 442, 446, 447, 449, 450
Controversy, among physicians, 441
Cook, Captain James, 97, 98, 137
Corporation spirit, 15, 22, 47–48, 52, 129, 242
    John Gregory on, 15, 22, 47, 48, 129
Covenant
    Hippocratic Oath as, 11
Cowling, John, 150
Crawford, Catherine
    on law and medicine in eighteenth-century England, 219
Crawford, James, 36
Crepe hanging, 156, 195
Cross, John, 395

Index

Cullen, William, 45, 60, 62, 154, 155, 158, 234
Currie, John, 395

D
Dangerous remedies, 192
Darwin, Charles, 38, 261
Darwin, Erasmus, 395
De Augmentis Scientiarum, 29
De Cautelis, 15, 16, 20, 29, 60, 112, 193
De Frigore, 61, 83–86, 93, 218, 226, 232, 240
Deism, vii, 27, 28, 45, 46, 72, 74, 75, 114, 115, 119, 143, 168, 174, 210, 223, 232, 234–236, 244, 259, 260, 267
Descartes, René, 25, 26, 89
Discourse ... on ... Hospital Duties, 431–432
    on acquisition of knowledge and experience, 389
    on charitable institutions, 396
    on compassion, 392
    on decency of the physician's and surgeon's behavior, 391
    on the Golden Rule, 182
    on humanity, 387, 388
    its inclusion in *Medical Ethics*, ix
    its inclusion in *Medical Jurisprudence*, ix
    on love of reputation, 331, 388
    on physicians of the soul, 334, 392
Dispensary, 149, 155, 180, 188, 189, 246, 298, 342, 352, 353, 398, 446
Disputes among physicians, 180
Dissent, vii, 58, 65
    Baconian dissent, vii, 72, 73, 75, 76, 78, 174, 228, 229, 232, 234, 236, 255, 259, 260, 267
    rational dissent, 3
    and Warrington Academy, 64, 65, 69–71, 76–78, 118, 210, 229, 235, 244, 267
Dissenters, *see* Dissent
Dissenting Unitarian, 3, 119, 235
Distrust of physicians, 20–22
    John Gregory's response to, 31, 33–34, 40–43
Domestic Medicine, 30, 206
Dr. Williams Library, xi, xii
Dueling, 134, 147, 157
Duncan, Andrew, 113

E
Eason, Alexander, 150
Elements of Medical Jurisprudence, 154, 157, 220
Elizabeth I, Queen, 69, 323, 380

Emanuel, Ezekiel, 31
Emanuel, Linda, 31
Enfield, William, 82, 124
Engelhardt, H. Tristram, Jr., xiii, 6, 39, 172, 233, 260
Enlightenment, English, ix, 64–67
    and improvement, 64–67, 100, 117, 145, 216, 245
Enlightenment, national, 37, 67–69
Enlightenment, Scottish, 68
    and improvement, 81
Enquiry into the Duties of Men, 168, 169, 173, 196, 402, 413
Enslavement of persons, 5, 115, 118, 123, 126–128, 131, 147
Enthusiasm, 27, 29, 72, 88, 94, 106, 115, 118, 144, 177, 178, 294, 334, 348, 391, 414
Entrepreneurialism, 4, 10–20, 53, 197, 234, 235, 264, 265
Epidemics, 10
Esprit du Corps, 206–207, 360, 441
Essays Medical and Experimental, 61, 64, 83, 86, 97, 98, 247
Essays Medical, Philosophical and Experimental, 65, 86–114, 190, 299, 353
Essentialism, 7–10, 13, 26, 31, 53
Ethical concept of medicine as profession
    as secular, 232
    three commitments of, 51, 52, 146, 187, 212, 232, 234, 242, 245, 255, 260, 264
    as transcultural, 7, 8, 260, 263
    as transnational, 8, 260, 263
    as transreligious, 8, 260, 263
Ethical reasoning
    principled, 263
Etiquette, 44, 215, 252, 253, 305, 364
Euthyphro, 5
Extracts from the Medical Ethics of Dr. Percival
    as bridge from *Medical Ethics* to American Medical Association 1847 Code of Medical Ethics, ix
    on consultations, 437
    on contention among physicians, 441
    on controversies among physicians, 441
    on *Esprit du Corps*, 441
    on fees, 438, 439, 441
    on gloomy prognostications, 436
    on gratuitous care of clergy, 204, 359, 440
    on gratuitous care of colleagues, 156, 203, 304, 359, 439
    on gratuitous care of colleagues' family members, 156, 203, 304, 359, 439
    on the importance of medicine, 436

Extracts from the Medical Ethics of Dr. Percival (cont.)
  on the observance of the Sabbath, 442
  on officious interference, 436–437
  on punctuality, 438
  on quack medicines, 440–441
  on a regular academic education, 438
  on retirement of a physician, 443
  on secrecy, 436
  on secret nostrums, 441
  on senescence of a physician, 443
  on seniority, 438, 440
  on strengthening the good resolutions of patients, 442
  on temperance, 436
  on theoretical discussions, 437
  on virtues of a physician, 442
Eyres, William, 71, 267

F
Faison, Lane, 265
Falconer, William, 395, 413
Farr, Samuel, 154, 157, 158, 220, 315, 375
Father's Instructions, A, 3, 61, 63, 65, 66, 89, 110, 119–120, 133–143, 148, 152, 154, 160, 223, 230, 236, 237, 246
Feelings, of patients, 175
Fees, 7, 11, 15, 20, 150, 193, 198, 199, 201–205, 214, 218, 303, 342, 358, 361, 408–410, 438, 439, 441, 447, 450
Female patients, 20, 21, 43, 44, 108, 169, 176, 177, 188, 190, 191, 194, 262, 298, 299, 342, 353, 446
Feminine ethics, 44
Feminist ethics, 44
Ferriar, John, 150, 151, 180, 257, 297, 352, 395, 400, 454, 455
Florence: Days of Destruction, 264
Flyting, 22, 181
Franklin, Benjamin, 65, 66, 94, 101, 103, 221, 427, 428

G
Galen, 13, 27, 98
Gelfand, Toby, 213
Gentleman
  character of, 167, 200, 341, 439
  Thomas Gisborne on, 135, 146
  Thomas Percival on, 117, 135, 167, 200
  virtues of, 117, 135, 146, 167, 200
George III, King, 14, 21, 74, 165, 191, 223
Georgetown University, x

Gevitz, Norman, 27
Gisborne, Thomas, 135, 395
  on infidelity, 210
  on lying, 196
  as moral realist, 135, 169
  on practical ethics, 135, 168, 170, 346
Giving evidence, 226, 316, 321, 325, 379, 383, 423
Gloomy prognostications, 156, 195–197, 301, 355, 436, 447, 449
Golden Rule, 182
Government, 52, 58
  of a hospital, 184, 185, 245, 395–497
  just, 114, 116, 224
  of patients, 44, 144, 172, 174–175, 190, 194, 233, 241, 398
Gracia, Diego
  on quest for certainty, 9
  on quest for reliability, 9
Gratuitous care, 156
  of clergy, 204, 359, 440
  of colleagues, 156, 203, 303, 358, 439
  of colleagues' family members, 156, 203, 303, 359, 436
Greenwald, Kimberly, 239
Gregorie, James, 23
Gregorie, Janet, 23
Gregory, Elisabeth, *nee* Forbes, 24
Gregory, James, 23, 159, 180, 455
Gregory, John
  on candor, 23, 30–34, 44, 47, 71, 104, 113, 115, 128, 198, 241–243
  on the concept of being a patient, 60, 146
  as conservative revolutionary, 53
  on ethics of cooperation, viii, 48, 197, 237, 262
  on genius, 41, 48
  on humanity, 32, 41, 50, 166, 178, 195
  on infidelity, 45, 142
  invention of ethical concept of medicine as a profession by, 7
  on laying medicine open, 32–34, 47, 172, 207, 242
  on the meaning of 'gentleman,' 52, 147
  on men of "interest," 35, 242
  on the "milk of human kindness," 42
  moral revolution against entrepreneurial medicine, 52–53, 240
  on nervous ailments, 44, 176
  on nostrums, 31, 45, 206, 240
  on openness to conviction, 30
  on professional ethics in medicine, vii, viii, xi, 3–4, 7, 8, 10, 13, 15, 21–52, 60,

107, 124, 146, 163, 197, 210, 232–234, 237, 239, 240, 243, 245, 254, 259–265
on professional ethics in research, 50–52, 182, 241
on religion and medicine, 45–46
on revolutionary meaning of 'physician,' 49
on the role of clergy, 177
on self-interest, 15, 31, 35, 40, 43, 45–49, 124, 128, 134, 135, 138, 164, 171, 177, 240–242, 255
on separation of medicine from surgery, 47, 243
on smoothing the avenues of death, 137
on steadiness, viii, xi, 3, 40–46, 48, 52, 112, 121, 122, 124, 142, 144, 162, 169–172, 192, 194, 241
on sympathy, 3, 23, 35, 36, 38–48, 50, 52, 53, 72, 107, 112, 120–122, 128, 138, 140, 141, 144, 147, 162, 169–171, 174, 175, 177, 188, 192, 210, 233, 241, 254
on tenderness, viii, 3, 23, 40–46, 48, 52, 121, 122, 124, 125, 129, 138, 141, 144, 162, 170–172, 177, 192, 194, 241
on truthtelling, 44
Grove, Henry, 79–81, 173, 189, 241, 404
Guild entrepreneurialism, 11, 14–15, 20

H

Haakonssen, Lisbeth, 41, 254, 255
Hall, Edward, 151
Hall, Richard, 151
Hartley, David, 325, 382, 412
Harwood, Edward, 74
Hawkesworth, John, 136, 137, 395
Haygarth, John, 395, 399, 400, 419, 420
Hays, Isaac, 249, 251, 257
Hayward, Thomas, 58
Heberden, William, 212, 395, 413, 418–419
Hegel, Georg Wilhelm Friedrich, 6
Henry VIII, King, 14, 69
Henry, Thomas, 395
Heywood, Samuel, 395
Hippocrates
  invoked as revered figure, 13
Hippocratic Corpus, 7, 10, 12–14, 22, 93
Hippocratic footnote, 10, 13
Hippocratic Oath, 11–14
  as guild oath, 14
  on reputation, 8, 12, 14, 16, 27, 46, 179
  on *techné*, 13, 93
History of England, The, 60
Hoffmann, Friedrich, 17

on enlightened self-interest, 17–20, 31, 137
on the politic physician, 21, 179
on prudence, 17–20, 31
Holme, Edward, 395
Holt, John, 70
Homicide, felonious, 220, 312, 314, 371, 373
Honor, 61, 65, 82, 117, 134, 135, 147, 215, 248, 259
Hospital, 21
  governance of, 114, 150, 153
  improvement of, 64, 68, 69, 100, 106, 113, 145
  polity of, 108, 116, 144–147, 153, 164, 174, 182, 184, 186, 230, 236, 237, 240, 242, 245, 250, 296, 351, 432
  register, 100, 183, 192, 207, 295, 342, 350, 446
  regulation of, 100, 106, 174, 452
  trustees of, 108, 144, 145, 147, 151, 153, 179, 183–185, 193, 229, 236, 244, 344, 346, 433–434
Humanity, xiii, 7, 32, 39, 41–43, 50, 51, 102, 106, 107, 109, 118, 123–125, 137, 138, 156, 166, 178, 190, 192, 195, 196, 203, 210, 251, 296, 298, 300, 314, 322, 330, 332, 333, 350, 353–355, 369, 370, 373, 380, 387–390, 402, 405, 410, 414, 415, 417, 436
  See also Sympathy
Hume, David
  on the concept of a principle, 23, 26, 27, 36–41, 84, 106, 141, 192, 261
  on the double relation of impressions and ideas, 38, 41, 43, 84
  on ideas, 37–39, 41, 43, 84, 139
  on impressions, 37–39, 41, 43, 84, 106, 139
  influence of, on John Gregory, viii, 23, 24, 26, 27, 34, 36, 38, 41–43, 72, 141, 192, 260, 261, 263
  influence of, on Thomas Percival, viii, 3, 24, 60, 61, 68, 139, 188, 192, 261, 263, 451
  on reason, 24, 26, 37, 38, 68, 72, 90, 261
  relationship of, with Thomas Percival, viii, 3, 24, 60, 61, 68, 139, 188, 192, 261, 263, 451
  on sympathy, 3, 23, 36–43, 68, 72, 84, 121, 141, 192, 261
  on the "terrible operations of surgery," 39, 41
Hunter, John, 164, 243, 312, 314, 315, 372, 374
Hutcheson, Francis, 72, 77, 196, 403–405

I

Infanticide, 21, 157, 220, 224–226
Infidelity, 45, 142, 209, 210, 344, 410–417
Infirmary, *see* Hospital, Manchester Infirmary
Ingelfinger, Franz, 52
Insanity
  partial, 344, 420–423
Institutes of Justinian, 154
Institutes of medicine, 60, 62, 158
Institutions of Medicine, 154, 155, 234
Interest, party, 23, 77, 78, 99, 128, 129, 145, 147, 152–155, 163, 164, 170, 171, 173, 180, 183, 185, 193, 198, 200, 206, 207, 212, 213, 233, 235, 237, 242, 243, 245, 252
International Academy of Perinatal Medicine, 263
International Federation of Gynecology and Obstetrics, 263
Intuition, 6, 26
Invention of Autonomy, The, 75

J

Jackson, Samuel, 250, 257
James, William, 263, 264
Johnson, Joseph, 267, 336, 339, 404, 406–409
Johnson, Samuel, 24, 124, 154, 158, 166, 171–173, 201, 205
Jones, James Earl, 265
Jouanna, Jacques, 11
Judgment, moral, 5, 9, 38, 40, 42, 43, 100, 109, 154, 175, 243
Justinian, 71, 154, 157, 158, 170, 178, 347

K

Kant, Immanuel
  on Reason, 6, 26, 67, 68, 90
Kendrick, James, 70, 248, 267
Killoran, Susan, xii
King, Lester, 62
King's College, Aberdeen, 23, 24, 63
Klee, Paul, 265
Kline, Franz, 264
Kuhn, Thomas, 4

L

Last will and testament, 155, 157, 178, 221, 294, 308, 309, 341, 343, 348, 367, 368, 422, 446, 448
Law
  just, 224, 225, 319, 376
  relation of, to medicine, 99, 116, 156, 216, 219, 221, 224, 226, 228, 229, 244, 253, 448
Leake, Chauncey, 44, 251, 252, 456
Lectures on the Duties and Qualifications of a Physician, 10, 29, 159, 249, 453
Lehrnfreiheit, 41, 59, 260
Lieb, Irwin C., xii
Lloyd, George, 395
Lock Hospital, 108, 149, 180, 188, 190, 191, 241, 298, 299, 342, 353
Lord Bacon, *see* Bacon, Francis
Lord Veralum, *see* Bacon, Francis
Lunatic asylum, 369, 370
Lunatics, 149, 150, 157, 188, 221, 244, 300, 309, 310, 312, 342, 343, 354, 368–371, 446, 448

M

Macbeth, Lady, 38
Magee, The Rev. William Conner, 248
Manchester Board of Health, 66, 254, 455
Manchester, city of, vii, 55–66, 149–152, 241, 291, 451
Manchester Infirmary, 393
  aims of, 100
  components of, 167, 194
  control of, by families of doctors, 149–153
  controversies at, 150, 237
  founding of, 150, 243
  medical staff of, 153, 251
  Percival as trustee of, 64, 108, 197, 237, 243
  role of trustees of, 76, 108, 153, 179, 188, 193, 197, 236, 243, 434, 452, 454, 455
Martineau, James, xii
McLachlan, H., 69–71
Medical ethics
  and entrepreneurialism, 4, 10, 234, 265
Medical Ethics
  on abortion, 136, 180, 372–373
  on accountability of law to professional ethics in medicine, 221
  aphoristic form of, 62, 165
  on apothecaries, ix, 76, 146, 162, 165, 213–219, 237, 243, 245, 252, 255, 262, 336, 456, 457
  on attending a duelist, 220–221, 319, 377, 378
  on the authority of the state, 16, 119, 136, 221, 228–229
  on the autonomy of professional ethics in medicine, 221

Index

as Baconian moral science, 92, 104, 112, 164, 170, 173, 180, 222, 233, 252, 254, 255, 257
on bastardy, 157, 194, 220, 224
begun in 1792, 243
on the boundary between medicine and surgery, 181, 199
on candor, 104, 240
on caution, 104, 241
on the character of a gentleman, 167, 341
on choice of physician or surgeon, 174
on circulation of *Medical Jurisprudence*, vii, 159
on clinical consultation, 186
on clinical trials, 87
as a code of medical ethics, ix, 165, 239, 246, 247
on a committee of gentlemen of the faculty, 185–186, 194, 207, 232, 296, 351, 397
completed in 1803, ix
concept of office in, 28, 29, 35, 171, 254–255
on condescension, 80, 118, 131, 162, 234, 255, 435
on confidentiality, 138
on conflicts of commitment, 219
on consultations, 138, 437
on controversy among clinicians, 159, 202, 207, 214, 361
on the council of a hospital, 185, 397
on dangerous remedies, 192
on death of his son, 66
discussions in front of patients, 176, 188, 294, 348
on dispensaries, 149, 155, 298, 352–353
on disputes among clinicians, 91, 150–153, 180, 185, 186, 200, 207–208, 302, 304–305, 361
and Dissent, 76, 136, 170, 232, 234, 244, 253, 267
on dueling, 134, 147
on duty of hospital trustees, 108, 144, 146, 180–183, 207, 229–232, 294, 349, 433–434
on *Esprit du Corps*, 206–207
on the ethics of clinical research, 50–52
on the ethics of cooperation, 76, 92, 101, 103, 118, 146, 166, 214, 219, 262
as etiquette, 251–253
on the execution of public justice, 325, 382
and *Extracts*, vii, ix, x, 251, 256–259, 291–443, 445, 449, 456, 457
on the feelings of patients, 175

on fees, 20, 198, 199, 202, 204, 358
on felonious homicide, 220, 310, 312, 370, 371
on female character, 315, 374
on female patients, 108
first book entitled "Medical Ethics," vii, 9, 232
first book with this title, vii, 9, 232
on the first commitment of the ethical concept of medicine as a profession, 171, 173–176, 181, 193, 195, 201, 217, 226, 236, 240
format of, 62, 165, 250, 258
on friendly and unreserved discourse, 185, 295, 349–350
on giving evidence, 379, 383, 423
on gloomy prognostications, 195–197, 301, 355, 436, 447, 449
on the government of a hospital, 185, 396–397
on the government of patients, 241
on gratuitous care of clergy, 204
on gratuitous care of colleagues' families, 203, 205
on gratuitous care of professional colleagues, 237, 243
on homicide by poison, 157, 227, 321, 343, 378
on honor, 134, 153, 160, 236, 248, 259
on hospital improvement, 69, 100, 106, 145, 296, 397
on hospital polity, 108, 145–147, 153, 164, 245, 250
on hospital registers, 100, 207, 342, 350
on hospital regulations, 185
on improvement of patient care, 243
on individual self-interest, 147, 183, 185, 193, 205, 211–213, 219, 241, 242
on indulgence of patients, 31, 300, 304, 355, 360
on infanticide, 157
on infidelity, 344, 410–417
influence of on American Medical Association 1947 Code of Medical Ethics, vii, ix, 10, 246, 249, 250, 256, 258, 259
as "Institutes", vii, ix, xiii, 62, 101, 111, 158, 162–164, 167, 173, 192, 214, 220, 222, 234, 235, 251, 254, 255, 257, 258, 291, 336–339, 344, 347, 445, 449, 455–457
on just government, 114, 136, 224

Medical Ethics (cont.)
  on last will and testament, 157, 294, 309, 341, 343, 348, 367, 368, 422
  on Lock Hospitals, 108, 149
  on lunatic asylums, 369, 370
  on lunatics, 149, 244, 300, 309, 343, 354, 368–371
  on lying, 196, 300–301, 356
  on Manchester Infirmary, x, 76, 78, 98, 100, 107–109, 129, 138, 145, 146, 149–153, 164, 167, 170, 171, 179, 185, 193, 213, 236, 241, 243, 245, 251, 344, 345, 352, 381, 396, 429, 434
  on medical jurisprudence, vii, viii, ix, x, 53, 62, 64, 65, 71, 76, 78, 83, 87, 92, 98, 100–104, 107, 111, 112, 117, 118, 129, 131, 134, 138, 140, 145–153, 158–162, 165–167, 170, 171, 181, 212, 214, 220, 221, 229, 230, 232–234, 239–266, 291–443, 445, 455, 456
  on medical testimony, 219
  and medicine as a monopoly, 252
  on medicine as a public trust, 100, 210, 246
  on men of interest, 99, 242
  on moral and religious influence of sickness, 177, 247, 294, 341, 348
  moral revolution of, 22, 53, 149–153, 160–228, 234, 235, 265
  on moral truth, 169, 197, 405
  on natural rights, 170
  on nostrums, 205, 206, 342, 360, 441, 447
  on nuisances, 157, 343, 381, 382, 430
  on observance of the Sabbath, 209, 343, 362, 442, 447
  on officious interference, 199, 356, 436, 447, 449
  on organizational culture of professionalism, viii, xi, 164, 183, 185, 186, 197, 218, 232, 246, 252, 256
  on partial insanity, 344, 420–423
  on party interest, 78, 129, 145, 164, 170, 171, 173, 183, 185, 193, 207, 213, 237, 242, 243, 245, 252
  on patients' moral formation, 215
  Percival's motivation for writing of, 78
  on the physician as minister of hope and comfort, 344, 355, 402, 436
  on political ethics, viii, 116, 157, 221–223, 234, 258
  as "Precepts," 107, 111
  on professional autonomy, 180, 185
  on professional charges against another physician, 349
  on professional ethics in medicine, viii, ix, 10, 101, 116, 119, 145, 153, 167, 214, 221, 233, 239, 243, 254
  on professional hierarchy, 213
  on the professional virtue of authority, 169, 174
  on the professional virtue of condescension, 173
  on the professional virtue of steadiness, 169, 228
  on the professional virtue of tenderness, 170, 171, 174, 184
  on public worship, 410–417
  on punctuality, 201–202, 342, 358
  on purest beneficence, 179, 180, 184, 244, 349
  on quack medicines, 205–206, 342, 360
  on rape, 380, 381, 428–430
  on rational and moral character of patients, 191
  on rational theism, 210, 253, 417
  on a regular academic education, 200
  on the relationship between medicine and surgery, 182
  on relationship of law and medicine, 219
  on religion, 166, 209–210, 253
  on resource management, 178–180
  on retirement of a physician, 210–213, 218–219, 362–363, 417–420
  on retirement of a surgeon, 210–213, 218–219, 362–363, 418–420
  role of Deism in, 232, 234, 244
  on sanguinary statutes, 225, 375
  on scepticism, 410–417
  on the science of clinical research, 91, 98, 183, 295, 349–350
  on the second commitment of the ethical concept of medicine as a profession, 202, 216, 217
  second edition of, 152, 232, 246, 247
  on secrecy, 138, 348
  on secret nostrums, 360
  as secular, 244
  on senescence of a physician, 211, 343
  on senescence of a surgeon, 211
  on sickness, 177–178, 247, 432–433
  on special consultations, 199, 342, 357
  on the structure of a hospital, 185, 193, 207
  on surgical operations, 187–188, 402
  on sympathy, 118, 254, 255
  on temerity, 191, 192
  on temperance, 131, 194–195, 342, 355, 401
  on theoretical discussions, 199–200, 342, 357, 406

Index

on the third commitment of the ethical concept of medicine as a profession, 129
third edition of, 246, 247, 249
on the tribunal of conscience, 258
on truthtelling, 178, 294, 348–357
Medical jurisprudence, 87, 153–160, 162, 165, 170, 180, 220, 221, 239, 321, 375, 378
Medical Jurisprudence
on abortion, 312, 313
on apothecaries, 76, 146, 154, 155, 165
on asylums for insanity, 299
on attending a duelist, 157
on bastardy, 157, 313
on choice of physician or surgeon, 293
as a code of ethics, 158
on a committee of gentlemen of the faculty, 296
composed in 1792, 167
on consultations, 155, 301
on controversy among clinicians, 304–305
on discussions in front of patients, 294
on dispensaries, 298
on the execution of public justice, 325
on fees, 198, 199, 202, 303
on felonious homicide, 220, 312, 314
on female character, 315
on female patients, 299
format of, 62, 165
on friendly and unreserved discourse, 295
on giving evidence, 312
on gloomy prognostications, 156, 301
on gratuitous care of clergy, 322
on gratuitous care of colleagues, 321–322
on gratuitous care of colleagues' families, 321–322
on homicide by poison, 157, 321
on honor, 147
on hospital registers, 100, 295
on infanticide, 157
on last will and testament, 155, 157, 294, 308, 309
on Lock Hospitals, 299
on lunatics, 157, 300, 309, 310, 312
on moral and religious influence of sickness, 294
on nuisances, 157, 324
on officious interference, 301
Percival's motivation for writing of, 78
on the physician as minister of hope and comfort, 301
plan of, 154
private publication of, viii, ix, 159, 160, 168

on professional charges against another physician, 295
on punctuality, 156, 303
on quack medicines, 304
on rape, 157
on the relationship between medicine and surgery, 162
on resource management, 155
on secrecy, 138
on secret nostrums, 156, 304
on temperance, 131
on theoretical discussions, 302
Medical paternalism, 8, 15, 20, 138, 196
Medical professionalism, 239–246, 260, 262, 264, 265
Medical testimony, 219
Medicine
Baconian, viii, 3, 23, 24, 26–30, 32–34, 41, 45, 46, 60, 82, 87, 88, 94, 104, 115, 144–145, 162–164, 169, 171, 173, 174, 180, 187, 189, 198, 201, 203, 206, 207, 210, 215, 221, 228, 229, 232–236, 240, 245, 254, 255, 258–260, 263, 446, 449
experience-based, 23, 25, 27, 32, 41, 51, 201, 240, 241, 258, 262
as a monopoly, 15
profession of, x, viii, 46, 100, 118, 145, 162, 163, 207, 210–213, 228, 229, 236, 237, 240, 244–246, 248, 251, 255, 261, 263, 264, 448
as a public trust, viii, 100, 210, 212, 213, 245, 246, 264, 363, 443
Medicus Politicus, 16–20, 60, 193, 244
Medicus politicus, 16–20, 60, 193, 244
Meditations on First Philosophy, 26
Meghani, Zahra, 239
Memoirs of the Life and Writings Thomas Percival, M.D., 55
Meno, 5
Men of interest, 35, 99, 242
Metaphysics, speculative, 25, 26, 37, 81
Miles, Steven, 10, 12, 13
Monro, Alexander, *primus*, 23
Montagu, Elizabeth, xii, 24, 44
Queen of the Bluestockings, 24
Montaigne, Michel de, 198, 406
Moral drift, 4
Moral formation, 67–82, 117–142, 146, 147, 154, 160, 167, 175, 177, 178, 203, 209, 215, 219, 231, 233, 236, 241
of patients, 147, 178, 203, 209, 215, 241
See also Character
Moral paradigm, 4, 22
Moral philosophy, xii, 8, 9, 36, 59, 70, 77, 80, 117, 154, 158, 170, 253, 254

Moral reform, 4, 209
Moral revolution, 3–53, 128, 146, 149–237, 240, 245, 255, 260, 265
Moral science
   of sympathy, 3, 23, 36–46, 118, 120, 138, 141, 143, 152, 154, 160, 162, 167, 173, 222, 230, 255 (*see also* Baconian moral science)
Moral truth, 133, 169, 197, 236, 405
Mount Sinai Medical School, xi
Museum of Modern Art, 265

N

National Library of Medicine, x
Natural religion, 70–75
Natural rights
   and god of Deism, 223
New York Hospital, 21
Noonan, John T., 7
Nostrums, 31, 45, 156, 205, 206, 240, 304, 342, 360, 441, 447, 450
Nuisances, 157, 220, 324, 343, 381, 382, 430, 448
Nutton, Vivian, 13

O

Oath, 8, 10–15, 26, 70, 93, 129, 226, 229, 313, 318, 325, 326, 373, 383, 384, 425
Oath of Supremacy, 70, 73
Observation of the Sabbath, 209, 343, 362, 442, 447, 450
Officious interference, 198, 199, 301, 356, 436–437, 447, 449
Organizational culture
   professional, 183
Owen, Charles, 69

P

Paley, William, 168, 169, 221, 308, 314, 327, 367, 373, 385, 395, 405, 426
Parr, Samuel, 410, 412
Parricide, 228, 327, 385
Partial insanity, *see* Insanity, partial
Paternalism
   concept of, 53
   good resolutions of, 362, 442
   rational and moral character, 191, 299, 354
   right to speak of, 31
   See also Aegrotus
Patient's Progress, 35

Paul, G.O., 347, 395
Pellegrino, Edmund, 6, 7, 10, 13, 253, 254
Pennsylvania Hospital, 21
Percival, Anne, 63
Percival, Edward Bayley, 63, 65, 121, 160, 161
Percival, Edward Cropper
   as biographer of Thomas percival, 55
   as role model for Thomas Percival, 57
   source of Thomas Percival's patrimony, 56
Percival, Elizabeth, *nee* Bassnett, ix, 63, 117, 121, 158, 161, 165, 166, 229–232, 242, 253, 346
Percival, Elizabeth, sister of Thomas Percival
   role in rearing Thomas Percival, 57
Percival, James, 63, 121
Percival, Joseph, 57
Percival, Margaret, *nee* Orred, 57
Percival, Maria, 63, 65, 121, 160, 161, 166
Percival, Martha, *nee* Wortley, 57
Percival, Peter, x, 56, 57, 191, 451
Percival, Robert, 395
Percival, Stanley Orred, 63
Percival, Thomas
   on affliction of death, 166
   on animal experimentation, 123–124, 146
   on appeal to experience, 84
   on authority, vii, viii, 114, 124–125, 131, 144, 184, 185, 189, 192, 194, 198, 201, 203, 216, 223, 224, 227, 228, 234–236, 240, 241, 247, 249, 253, 255–258
   on autonomy of morality, 136
   as Baconian dissenter, 3, 76, 78, 81, 82, 115, 117, 131, 143, 170, 177, 244, 253
   on Baconian experimentation, 86
   as Baconian moral scientist, vii, 76, 109, 115, 131, 148, 173, 180, 190, 203, 209, 232, 234, 240
   as Baconian scientist, 85, 92, 94, 101, 115, 118, 131, 139, 143, 148, 232, 240
   birth, 67, 68
   on condescension, 79–80
   on conflicts of interest, 187, 242
   on conscience, vii, 76, 118, 143, 227, 256, 258
   death of, 65, 125, 160, 166, 240
   deaths of his children, 160, 161
   as deist, vii, 115, 145, 177, 231, 232, 235
   on divine right of kings, 115
   on the dogmatic physician, 88
   on dueling, 134, 147, 157
   election to the Royal Society, 61
   on the empiric physician, 93

Index

on enslavement of persons, 5, 115, 118, 126–128, 131, 147, 247
on evil, 130, 131, 134, 140, 176, 184, 225
exemplar of English enlightenment, 64, 66, 117
on first commitment of the ethical concept of medicine as a profession, 86
Founder of Literary and Philosophical Society of Manchester, 65, 67, 116–117
Founder of Manchester Academy, 65
Founder of Manchester Board of Health, 66, 254
at home at Hart Hill, 64
on honor, 65
on hospital improvement, 106–109
on hospital polity, 108, 145, 153, 182, 186, 242, 245, 250
on infirmaries as agents of sympathy, 100, 179
on a just government, 114, 116, 224, 225
on lock hospitals, 108, 149, 180, 188, 190, 191
on lying, 122, 133, 136, 175, 197, 225
on the meaning of 'gentleman,' 135
on meaning of 'medical jurisprudence,' 170
on medicine as a public trust, 100, 210–213, 246, 264
membership in American Philosophical Society in Philadelphia, 65
membership in Congregation of Cross Street Unitarian Chapel, 66
membership in Medical Society of London, 65
membership in Royal Society, 61
membership in Royal Society of Paris, 65
on natural law, 115
on natural rights, 229
on the nature of things, 95, 104
on observance of the sabbath, 209
philosophy of medicine of, 87, 144–145, 240
philosophy of religion of, 82, 118, 128–129, 144–145
on polity, 114–116
on power, 57, 93, 99, 110, 112, 114, 116, 125, 126, 129, 130, 135, 136, 140, 141, 144, 153, 159, 162, 165, 168, 170, 172, 173, 178, 180, 185, 193, 198, 209, 213, 221, 223, 228, 229, 232–236, 240
on the prospect of his own death, 121
on rational theism, 210, 235, 236, 253, 417
on reason, 89
relationship of, with David Hume, 60–61

retirement from medical practice of, 161, 218, 219
on second commitment of the ethical concept of medicine as a profession, 124
on secrecy, 138, 156, 176, 177, 194
on self-love, 125, 134
on state power, 136, 221, 228, 229, 234, 240, 244
stoicism of, 119, 130–132, 148, 166
as a student at the University of Leiden, 23
as a student at University of Edinburgh, 91, 121
as a student at Warrington Academy, 58–59, 114
on sympathy, 123, 143, 173, 184
on sympathy for animals, 123–124
on sympathy for insects, 123
on taxation, 116
theodicy of, 129–130
on third commitment of the ethical concept of medicine as a profession, 129
On Truth, 80
on the truth of things, vii, 87, 101, 119, 126, 132, 135, 140, 141, 144, 187, 222–224, 226, 228, 229, 232, 234–236, 244, 253
on virtue, 16
Percival, Thomas Bassnett
deism of, vii, 45–46, 71, 114, 115, 119, 143, 210, 223, 232, 235, 236, 244, 259
Discourse on Hospital Duties, vii, ix, 431–432
influence of his *Discourse* on *Medical Ethics*, 108, 265
on sympathy, 124, 174, 184
Percival, Thomas, uncle of Thomas Percival
role in rearing Thomas Percival, 57
Philips, J.L., 152, 153
Physician
Baconian, 30, 34, 57, 86, 89, 173, 178, 206, 209, 234
cautious, 33
chaste, 19, 20
as Christian, 18
court, 17, 18
entrepreneurial, 17, 132
guild, 33
municipal, 16, 17, 33
politic, 16–18, 21, 33, 34, 179, 193
professional, 7, 20, 23, 30, 31, 34, 49, 51, 52, 132, 217, 245, 255, 260
prudent, 17, 20, 172, 194
virtues of, 16, 43

"Physician Charter," 10, 20
Pickstone, John, 55, 61, 64, 66, 119, 149–153, 159, 161, 181, 236, 237, 248
Pierson, William, Jr., 264
Plato, 5, 10, 17, 122, 133, 208, 223, 417
Plutarch, 17
Polier, Charles de, 117, 146
Political ethics, viii, 116, 157, 221–226, 228, 229, 234, 236, 258, 259, 326, 383
Politic entrepreneurialism, 11, 16–20
Politic physician, the, 16–18, 21, 33, 34, 179, 193
Porter, Dorothy, 21, 30–31
Porter, Roy, 21, 30–31, 64, 68, 81, 82, 261
Pragmatism, 263
Prayer, 59, 72, 77, 78, 411, 417
Precepts, ix, vii, 51, 57, 111, 134, 157, 158, 160, 162–229, 234–235, 250–252, 254, 255, 258, 300, 330, 334, 336–339, 347, 355, 387, 392, 402, 417
Presentism, 7–10, 28, 53, 102
Price, Richard
  on hospital improvement, 107
Priestley, Joseph, 59, 64, 77–79, 82, 97, 98, 103, 104, 224, 235, 267
Professional autonomy, *see* Autonomy, professional
Professional charges, against another physician, 181, 295, 349
Professional ethics in medicine
  as Baconian moral science, 3, 68–69, 92, 104, 167, 169, 171, 233–234, 240, 252, 254, 260
  co-invention of, by Thomas Percival, 4, 259–260, 265
  first commitment of, 23–34, 41, 86, 164, 171, 173–176, 181, 193, 195, 201, 217, 226, 236, 240
  invention of, by John Gregory, viii, 13, 21–50
  pragmatic nature of, 263
  second commitment of, 35–46, 48, 124, 129, 202, 216, 217, 241
  third commitment of, 46–49, 129, 171, 173, 193, 200
Professional hierarchy, 213
Professional organizational culture, *see* Organizational culture
Professional virtues
  authority, viii, 144, 169, 174, 184, 234
  candor, 23, 30–32, 34
  compassion, 230, 332
  condescension, viii, 144, 173, 174, 235
  steadiness, 40–46, 144, 169–171, 174, 191, 228
  tenderness, 40–46, 144, 170, 171, 174, 184
Prudence, 16–21, 31, 34, 80, 136–138, 178, 195, 219
Prudential entrepreneurialism
  public trust, 212
Public justice, 229, 325, 326, 384
Public worship, 209, 334, 352, 362, 391, 410–417, 442
Puffendorff, Samuel von, 403, 404
Punctuality, 156, 169, 201, 303, 342, 358, 438, 447, 450

Q

Quack medicine, 156, 205–206, 304, 342, 360, 440, 441, 447, 450
Quintanilla, Linda, xiii

R

Rachels, James, 6
Rape, 157, 220, 316, 322, 323, 343, 375, 380, 381, 428–429, 448
Rational theism, 210, 235, 236, 253, 417
Rawls, John
  on the original position, 6
Reason
  as calculating machine, 37, 68
  Pure, 6, 26, 90
  speculative, 125
Regular academic education, 200
Reid, Thomas, 24, 39, 41, 63
Religion of Nature Delineated, The, 74
Reputation, 7, 8, 12–16, 18, 20–22, 27, 31, 35, 40, 43, 46, 50, 69, 88, 99, 150, 155, 156, 177, 179, 181, 183, 184, 186, 191, 193, 194, 198, 206, 214–216, 237, 247, 295, 305, 306, 311, 331, 343, 346, 349, 363, 364, 371, 388, 406, 426
Resource management, 155
Retirement
  of a physician, 219, 419, 420
  of a surgeon, 218, 219
Rhodes, Rosamond, xi, 6
Risse, Gunther, 15, 40, 174, 179
Robertson, William, 60, 316, 317, 408, 423, 425, 451
Royal College of Physicians and Surgeons of Glasgow, 14, 49
Royal College of Physicians of Edinburgh, xi, 14, 49

Index 471

Royal College of Surgeons of London, 14
Royal College of Surgeons of the City of
  Edinburgh, 14
Royal Infirmary of Edinburgh, 24, 50,
  51, 60, 241
Royal Society of Scotland, 113
Rush, Benjamin, 41, 49, 249
Rutherford, John, 24, 60
Ryan, Michael
  reception of *Medical Ethics* by, 246

S

Sanguinary statutes, 225, 315, 375
Scepticism, 89, 141, 142, 207, 210, 361,
  410–417, 441
Schneewind, Jerome, 75, 76, 79
Secrecy, 21, 138, 156, 176, 177, 192, 194,
  294, 300, 314, 323, 341, 348, 355, 373,
  381, 436
Secret Kappa Lambda Society, vii, 250
Secret nostrums, 156, 206, 304, 360, 441
Secular, concept of, 232–233
Seddon, John (1725–1770), 58, 59, 71, 77, 78,
  173, 210, 235
Self-interest
  enlightened, 17–21, 31, 34, 43, 46,
    137, 193
  group, 13, 14, 40, 47, 48, 78, 129, 242
  guild, 15, 23, 47–48
  individual, 23, 35, 40, 46, 49, 147, 153,
    155, 171, 174, 180, 183, 185, 193, 200,
    204, 205, 208, 211–213, 219, 233, 237,
    241, 242
  at Manchester Infirmary, 185
  party, 78
  and professional ethics in medicine, 6,
    15, 23, 233
  shared, 78
Seneca, 17, 140
Senescence
  of a physician, 211, 343, 362, 443,
    447, 450
  of a surgeon, 211
Shaftsbury, Lord, 221, 425
Sidney, Sir Philip, 125
Simmons, Samuel Foart, 113, 395
Sketch of Moral Philosophy, 74
Smith, Robert Angus, 248
Socrates, 5, 223, 417, 421
Solomon R. Guggenheim Museum, 265
*Statuta Moralia Collegii Regalis Medicorum
  Londinensium*, 14, 186

Stoddard, Whitney, 264
Strawson, P.F., 6
Structure of Moral Revolutions, The, 4
Stubbs, Richard, xi
Sydenham, Thomas, 46, 90, 91, 94, 201, 407,
  412, 414
Sympathy
  feminine, 46, 48
  See also Humanity

T

Tacitus, 195, 316, 401, 409, 423
Taylor, John
  on Baconian dissent, 72, 73, 75, 76,
    81, 173–174
  on moral philosophy, 59, 70, 74, 77
  on natural religion, 70–75
  on prayer, 72, 77
Team care, 262
Techné, 11–13, 93
Teich, Mikláš, 36, 37, 68
Temerity, 191, 192, 300, 355, 400
Temperance, 44, 101, 131, 156, 194–195, 300,
  342, 353, 401, 436, 447, 449
Temple, Sir William, 201, 303, 358, 438
Terrence
  on *Homo sum & nihil humanum a me
    alienum puto*, 39
Texas A&M University, x, 96
Theism, 27, 72, 145, 166, 210, 231, 235, 236,
  253, 417
Theoretical discussions, 199–200, 302, 342,
  357, 406, 437, 447, 449
Therapeutic privilege, 196, 197
Thought experiment, 6
Thoughts on Hospitals, 100, 106, 183, 185,
  296, 350
Tong, Rosemary, 44, 172
Tractatus Logico-Philosophicus, 75
Treatise of Human Nature, A
  and Aberdeen Philosophical Society,
    24, 36, 63
  influence of, on John Gregory, 24
  influence of, on Thomas
    Percival, 24, 68
Treatise of Human Nature, A, 24, 68
Trolley example, 6

U

Union College, x
University of Aberdeen, 23

University of Cambridge, 59, 69, 70, 119, 165, 230, 328, 341, 345, 386, 428, 432
University of Edinburgh
  Baconian scientists at, 24, 27, 60, 240
  curriculum of, 61
  intellectual life of, 60
  spirit of *Lehrnfreiheit* at, 41, 59, 260
  teaching of medical ethics at, 60
University of Leiden, 23
University of Manchester, xi, 55
University of Oxford, xi, xii, 65, 407, 454

W

Waddington, Ivan, 252
Warren, Richard, 395
Warrington Academy
  campus of, 71
  commitment to Baconian science, 228–229
  curriculum, 69–71
  as dissenting academy, 69–71
  dissenting tutors of, 74, 82, 100, 106, 244
  faculty of, 59, 60, 64
  founding of, 69
  John Taylor's "charge" to the students of, 81
  Percival first student at, 58–59, 81
  planning for, 59
  rules of, 147
Warrington, city of
  free grammar school of, 57–58
Watson, Richard, 395

Weill Cornell Medical College, x
Wellcome Library and Museum, xii
West, Charles, 248–250
What is the Enlightenment?, 67
White, Charles, 150, 151, 395, 451
Whitehead, Alfred North, 10
White, Thomas, 151
Whytt, Robert, 27, 60, 85, 94
Williams Art History Mafia, 265
Williams College, xii, 264
Willoughby de Parham, Lord, 61
Withering, William, 395
Wittgenstein, Ludwig, 75
Wollaston, William, 74–76
Works, Literary, Moral, and Medical of Thomas Percival, The, 55, 456
World Association of Perinatal Medicine, 263
World Health Organization, 263
World Medical Association, 263
Wunderlich, Carl Reinhold August, 84, 85

Y

Young, Thomas, 60
Yuck factor, 39

Z

Zeffirelli, Franco, 264
Zerbi, Galbriel, 15, 20
Zucker School of Medicine at Hofstra/ Northwell, x